The Laws of the Internet

Second Edition

The Laws of the Internet

Second Edition

Clive Gringras
Partner, Olswang; LLB (Hons); M Juris (Oxon)

Competition
Daniel Beard
Barrister, Monckton Chambers

Tax
Raymond Hill
Barrister, Monckton Chambers

Ian Hutton
Barrister, Monckton Chambers

Butterworths™
LexisNexis™

Members of the LexisNexis Group worldwide

United Kingdom	LexisNexis Butterworths Tolley, a Division of Reed Elsevier (UK) Ltd, Halsbury House, 35 Chancery Lane, LONDON, WC2A 1EL, and 4 Hill Street, EDINBURGH EH2 3JZ
Argentina	LexisNexis Argentina, BUENOS AIRES
Australia	LexisNexis Butterworths, CHATSWOOD, New South Wales
Austria	LexisNexis Verlag ARD Orac GmbH & Co KG, VIENNA
Canada	LexisNexis Butterworths, MARKHAM, Ontario
Chile	LexisNexis Chile Ltda, SANTIAGO DE CHILE
Czech Republic	Nakladatelství Orac sro, PRAGUE
France	Editions du Juris-Classeur SA, PARIS
Hong Kong	LexisNexis Butterworths, HONG KONG
Hungary	HVG-Orac, BUDAPEST
India	LexisNexis Butterworths, NEW DELHI
Ireland	Butterworths (Ireland) Ltd, DUBLIN
Italy	Giuffrè Editore, MILAN
Malaysia	Malayan Law Journal Sdn Bhd, KUALA LUMPUR
New Zealand	LexisNexis Butterworths, WELLINGTON
Poland	Wydawnictwo Prawnicze LexisNexis, WARSAW
Singapore	LexisNexis Butterworths, SINGAPORE
South Africa	LexisNexis Butterworths, DURBAN
Switzerland	Stämpfli Verlag AG, BERNE
USA	LexisNexis, DAYTON, Ohio

A CIP Catalogue record for this book is available from the British Library.

First edition published in 1997

ISBN 0 406 908 087

ISBN 0-406-90808-7

Typeset by M Rules, London
Printed and bound in Great Britain by The Cromwell Press Limited, Trowbridge, Wiltshire

'. . . That is the Law. How could there be a mistake in that?'
'I don't know this Law,' said K.
'All the worse for you,' replied the warder.

The Trial, Franz Kafka

Preface to the Second Edition

This edition of 'The Laws of the Internet' describes a very different collection of laws to its predecessor. On the 15 March 1997, the final full stop fell on the first edition. The English courts had hardly been taxed with Internet questions; they had judged a handful of Internet cases. Our legislators had not yet set their draftsmen on regulating the Internet; there were a few statutes that had Internet mischief in mind. Now, the word 'Internet' crops up in many hundreds of English cases. Domain name disputes number in their thousands. Legislators both here and in Europe continue to blanket new legislation over the area.

Like the first edition, this book does not attempt to present a holistic view of a 'Law of the Internet'. Its pages simply examine the laws that have been, or may be, applied to the Internet. Unlike the first edition, this book no longer needs to conjure up so many hypothetical questions. As predicted, Internet legal issues are becoming more commonplace. There are now plenty of actual cases and statutes that merit attention in this work. Measurements of the Internet have also grown since the first edition. Lines on graphs stretch towards the top-right corner and numbers suffixed with 'millions' now end with 'billions'. What these statistics do not express is how pervasive the Internet has now become.

Many businesses and individuals cannot remember what it was like before the Internet and most could not now cope without it. And the Internet will not stop evolving and soaking into society and business. Watching and actually using the technology is therefore essential; this gives us clues as to where the law will need to follow. In this, I am fortunate. I am a partner at Olswang, a law firm with whose clients are the very companies which are responsible for guiding the Internet into these new areas. I also work with talented lawyers who are as concerned about the law as they are about the latest innovation.

To write this book, I have benefited from the help of these lawyers, in particular those in the Olswang ecommerce team; they know who they are. As with the previous edition, I have not written the Tax and Competition chapters. Thanks to Ian Hutton, Raymond Hill and Daniel Beard for their hard work and patience in seeing this through. As you may suspect, I am to blame for flaws in this book.

For believing that I would eventually finish this edition, and supporting me until I did, I must thank my publishers, Piera, friends, family, and Linzi.

Clive Gringras
Clive@Pobox.com
23 September 2002

Foreword to the First Edition

Judging by some of the stuff one reads – particularly from journalists – the Internet will throw laws, or many of them, into chaos. The suggestion seems to be the law cannot cope with the breakdown of national barriers, the cross-border implications of the interlinking of computers world-wide. The scenario painted is that the Internet will be a lawless dimension, with lawyers and clients having no idea what to do or how to control the activities of others. Clive Gringras is to be congratulated on not only debunking this myth but by doing so in a constructive (and readable) way. What he has done here is to consider, subject by subject, what rules the courts will develop and apply. As always what the law will do is develop appropriate rules by analogy. Contract, tort (including special variants of old torts, eg negligently allowing a virus to spread and new ways of defaming people), intellectual property (particularly trade marks and copyright), questions of jurisdiction, crime, data protection, and so on all have passed under his intelligent consideration. Of course there are, as yet, few actual cases on most points. So he has used his imagination to create problems and indicate how the law is likely to answer them. Because he understands the Internet and how it works well, his imaginary problems are realistic. Moreover he has up-to-date intelligence of case law from other countries (particularly the US) which supplement his fictional examples. Anyone with an Internet problem will find this book a first port of call – and in many cases may well find an answer, or a reasonable prediction of the answer. In one area where he obviously does not feel entirely at home, namely tax (who would blame him?), he has sought assistance from Conrad McDonnell of Gray's Inn Chambers.

There is something of a spate of books which carry the names of firms of solicitors. Many (but not all) are rather slight works, rushed out after some new piece of legislation and not telling you much that is not in the Act. This is far from such a work. Nabarro Nathanson are to be congratulated on allowing Mr Gringras to put in what must have been a vast amount of work.

Hon Sir Robin Jacob
January 1997

Preface to the First Edition

This book's title is carefully chosen. The book is a collection of the laws that apply to those who use the Internet. It does not attempt to present any overarching view of the Law of the Internet. It indulges in little of this prophecy. There is no single law that does or should apply to the Internet. The book is concerned only with the application of the *current* body of law to this new communications medium. Its pages present, in pragmatic form, the various laws that, directly or indirectly, impinge on the Internet; it provides reasoned answers to relevant questions. Often these answers are to questions not yet asked of English courts. For the moment, therefore, you, the reader, are the sole judge of their cogency.

Some say that, like a dog, one year for a human is like seven for the Internet. It has a substantial, and growing, presence in society. When I first used the Internet in August 1981 it consisted of only 213 computers connected together; conservative estimates suggest that there are now over sixteen million 'hosts', each acting like a single machine linked to the others. But the Internet is not merely growing. Every month it seems to pervade a new, unwired, area of culture and business. Legal issues and disputes involving the Internet will rapidly become more commonplace. For this reason this book does not apply the law to a 'snapshot' of the Internet but to the Internet as an evolving phenomenon. For similar reasons, those who rely on this book should not do so in isolation. Unlike any area of legal practice, it is not simply the laws of the Internet that are developing; its persona is too.

My five Internet-years writing this book have been greatly assisted by the solid support of Nabarro Nathanson. In particular, I wish to thank three of the firm's solicitors for their excellent contributions to the book: Chris Luck, Susan Knüfer and Peter Willis. I also wish to thank all members of the Intellectual Property department in London and Reading who provided their time and knowledge to review the book. In addition, thanks must go to Dan Levy for his painstaking library work, evident on each page.

I have also benefited from external help. Thanks to: Sir Robin Jacob for kindly writing the foreword; Conrad McDonnell of Gray's Inn Chambers for crafting the chapter on taxation; John Austen of New Scotland Yard; G C Borland of McGrigor Donald; Warren Burch of Microsoft, Seattle; John Browning of *Wired*; Rob Bradgate of the University of Sheffield; Adrian Briggs of St Edmund Hall College, Oxford; Simon Dawson of the Crown Prosecution Service, London; Stephen Dooley of Sidley & Austin, London; Richard Fentiman of Queen's College, Cambridge; Andrew Graham of Balliol College, Oxford; Rosemary Jay, of the Data Protection Registrar; Alistair Kelman of ILC/Telepathic, London; Mathew Mildenhall of Coopers & Lybrand, London; Paul Mitchell of Tory Tory Deslauriers & Binnington, Toronto; Yvonne Nobis, of the Bodleian Library, Oxford; Edwin Peel of Keble College, Oxford; David Rickard of Boult Wade Tennant, London; Peter Sommer of the London School of Economics; Colin Tapper of Magdalen College, Oxford; Sir Guenter Treitel of All Souls College, Oxford; and John Woolds, of the Data Protection Registrar. The flaws in the book are mine; any qualities I share with these generous people.

For sharing the pain, I want to thank my publishers, friends, family, and Linzi.

Clive Gringras
Clive@Pobox.com
Ides of March 1997

Contents

Table of Statutes

Page references in **bold** type indicate where the section is set out in part or in full. References in the Table to *Statutes* are to Halsbury's Statutes of England (Fourth Edition) including the volume and page number at which the annotated text of the Act may be found.

EC Regulations

Table of Statutory Instruments

Page references in **bold** indicate where the Statutory Instrument is set out in part or in full

Table of Cases

H

I

J

K

N

O

P

Q

R

S

T

Chapter One

Introduction

'The Lord came down to look at the city and tower that man had built, and the Lord said: "If, as one people with one language for all, this is how they have begun to act, then nothing that they propose to do will be out of their reach." . . . That is why it was called Babel, because there the Lord confounded the language of all the earth . . .'
Genesis 11:6–7

Most of us have heard of or used the Internet. Some may even wonder how they coped before it existed. To determine how laws may apply to the Internet one needs to have more than merely an observer's appreciation; a working knowledge is required. Fortunately, the Internet can be easily explained.

The Internet is a global network of computers all speaking the same language. To understand the Internet, therefore, it is useful first to appreciate computers. Computers are simple machines: they understand only the numbers zero and one. The reason that computers are able to show colours on a screen, play sounds and process data is that they are very accurate and quick translators. With incredible speed they are able to convert a full-length movie into a long stream of zeros and ones. And with the same speed they can convert a similar stream of zeros and ones into a sound, or a document, or a program. Everything passing into and out of a computer will, at some point, be reduced to binary: two numbers, zero and one.

It is not difficult to connect two computers, say by a wire, and send a stream of these binary numbers from one computer to the other. Each number one in the stream is represented by an 'on' electrical pulse; each zero by an 'off' pulse. These pulses last for a fraction of a second allowing the numbers describing a picture to be transmitted in minutes. A difficulty arises in ensuring that the computer receiving such a stream translates the zeros and ones correctly. As a simple example, the receiving computer may be ready to receive a binary description of a picture, but is instead sent a binary translation of a document. The receiving computer will attempt to translate the zeros and ones, actually a document, into a picture; there will be confusion. It is evidently crucial that to connect computers successfully they both must speak the same language. This 'digital Esperanto' is the key to the Internet.

LANGUAGE AND NETWORKS

The many variations of this digital Esperanto are called 'protocols'. As long as the sending and receiving computers are using the same protocols, they will be able to share information, in a raw binary form, with absolute accuracy.

A 'network' is a group of computers connected together using the same protocols; they are using the same phrase book. Information stored on one computer on the network can be readily sent, or accessed, by any other computer on the network. In a company this allows one individual to access a file that has been created on somebody else's machine across a network or 'intranet'. The connection between these computers on a network is not always a simple copper wire. A set of wireless radio devices can be used as a link; they convey information using pulses across the radio spectrum rather than electricity. Links between computers do not even have to be in the same building. Wide Area Networks, or WANs, can stretch across many hundreds of miles.

The key is to ensure that each of the computers connected to the network uses the same protocols. If they do, it will not matter greatly whether a stream of ones and zeros has come from across the corridor or from across the Atlantic Ocean. The receiving computer will be able to translate them appropriately, no matter the length of their journey. The Internet builds on this technology.

INTERNETWORKING

In 1969 America's Department of Defense commissioned the construction of a super-network called ARPANET: the Advanced Research Projects Agency Network. This military network was intended to connect computers across the American continent, with one special feature. If one part of this great network was destroyed, the communications system would remain operative. The information passing through the system was required to detour around the damaged part and arrive at its destination by another route.

In 1972 the ARPANET was demonstrated. The network consisted of forty computers connected by a web of links and lines. The detouring feature was accomplished by allowing a stream of binary information from one computer to pass through other computers on the network, rather than always having to flow directly from A to B.

One example will illustrate this: three computers, A, B and C, are connected in a triangle. A can communicate directly with both B and C. Similarly, B has a line of communication with A and C. If A has to send information to B it has a direct route. But if this route is damaged, or blocked, it can send the information to C with an instruction to pass it on to B: A to B through C. On a larger scale, this allows every computer connected to a network to send information to any other computer on the network. The information simply has to be passed from one computer to another, gradually nearing its destination.

One further advance was made to secure the information being sent from A to B. Instead of sending the information as one long stream, the sending computer splits the data into discrete packets. Each packet, like an envelope, contains the information being sent and has an address of where it must arrive. The packet also has a number that denotes its place in the whole data stream. If any packets are lost, or blocked, they can be re-sent. When all the packets have arrived, the receiver assembles the chunks of digital data into the continuous data stream. This so-called 'packet-switched' network allows many computers to use the same communication lines and allows one data stream to travel by different routes to speed delivery over congested lines.

The demonstration of packet-switched networks and routing in 1972 was such a success that the InterNetworking Working Group was created. The Internet was born. *The New York Times* wrote on 15 April 1972, '[the] experimental network . . . may help bring to realization a new era in scientific computation'.

THE INTERNET

The forty or so computers on the late seventies' ARPANET, each using the same protocols, were added to: by 1981, over 200 computers were connected, from all around the world. When the first edition of this book was published, in May 1997, this number of hosts had reached about 20 million. At the last count over *150 million* computers were permanently connected, each one able to speak the same language as the others. These computers now serve about 500 million individuals. This vast collection of computers is the Internet and it is the largest network of computers in the world.

The majority of the links and connections between computers are permanent and allow digital streams to be sent back and forth extremely quickly. In addition, each of these 150 million *host* computers connected to the Internet has a unique numeric address or Internet Protocol address. This means that a digital stream can be directed from any computer connected to the Internet to any other computer connected to the Internet, anywhere in the world. The impact of this is great when one appreciates that almost the whole of modern culture can now be reduced to a digital form. Digital information includes colour pictures, animations and movies, high-quality music and sound, text with typefaces and layout, even three-dimensional images.

The real power of today's Internet is that it is available to anyone with access to a computer and a telephone line. By connecting a piece of hardware called a modem to a personal computer any information can be converted into a digital stream of ones and zeros. The modem can then send this translation down a telephone or cable line to one of the computers already connected to the Internet. The two computers can then pass information between themselves, using a common protocol. Because the computer connected to the Internet can connect with any other computer on the Internet, a personal computer or even a pocket-sized device can now connect with any of the millions of computers on the Internet.

Like human languages, computer protocols work in both directions. They allow information to be easily sent from a home or office computer to any other computer on, or with access to, the Internet. What is more important is that they allow any computer to gain access to information from any other computer on the Internet: libraries are now literally at our fingertips; a shop simply needs to connect to the Internet to advertise to the world. One language allows the world of computers to share a world of information. The law, in contrast with this transnational system, operates within defined jurisdictional boundaries. The practical resolution of these opposites forms a common thread through each of the following chapters.

THE COST

Sharing a world of information sounds expensive, but it is not. To connect to the Internet, one needs only to connect to a computer already connected. The first cost is therefore the price of the connection, often a telephone call or subscription to allow connection to that connected computer. The user is not charged for the cost of sending or receiving information *beyond* that first computer unless a particularly quick or secure route is chosen. What is levied, however, is a price to connect to this computer.

The companies controlling these first-port-of-call computers are Internet Service Providers. Their computers are called 'servers', as is any computer permanently connected to the Internet. The computers that pay for the connection charges, the users' computers, are called 'clients'.

Some Internet Service Providers provide more than purely a connection to the Internet through their server: they provide materials and services on their own servers. This has the advantage of being quicker to view, safer to access and more focused on the needs of the users. Examples include AOL and Freeserve. These companies provide more than simply an email address and a ramp to the Internet: they commission, license and provide their own services tailored for their members. And they are paid for these value-added services either directly through a subscription, a share of the connection charges paid by their users or indirectly through selling advertising or 'space' on their pages.

These companies are often the targets for litigation. They are blamed for the copyright infringing material that other people leave on their computers; some say that they should be culpable for facilitating the transmission of obscene images and movies; there are even suggestions that they should be responsible for publishing others' defamatory statements. Each chapter raises the question of how the law treats these piggies-in-the-middle, as well as the individual primarily responsible.

INTERNET CONCEPTS

Using several different protocols, the Internet has been able to provide various services to its connected computers. In the similar way that the word 'chat' has a different meaning in French from its meaning in English, so can two protocols used across the Internet allow servers to pass different information to clients. Different uses of protocols give the Internet its utility. What follows is a tour of the different features of the Internet. To appreciate the tour it may help to remember that the information being shunted around the network is still that digital stream of ones and zeros. The various features are produced by simply applying a different protocol to this stream before and after it is sent between computers. The method of conversing is largely the same; what changes is the language being used.

Server addresses

Every server permanently connected to the Internet has a unique identification number, or Internet Protocol address. To make it easier for humans to remember, these numbers have a unique literary equivalent called a domain name that is allocated by one of the Internet Registries. The publisher of this book uses 'lexisnexis.co.uk'; the 'co.uk' suffix gives some indication that LexisNexis is a commercial organisation. Academic institutions use the suffix 'ac'. Often the suffix includes information relating to where the domain has been registered. For example, the University of Oxford has the domain, 'oxford.ac.uk'. Scuffles arise because there are a limited number of domain names and they are usually allocated on a first-come first-served basis. The chapter on intellectual property considers the legal implications of this.

Email

'Email' is short for electronic mail. The word 'mail' should be understood at its widest: the electronic mail system over the Internet can carry more than simple messages and letters. A picture, a sound, in fact anything that can be created and stored on a computer can be sent as electronic mail to any other computer connected to the Internet.

First, the item is digitally packed into an appropriate parcel. Like physical items sent by the post, items require suitable packaging. The equivalent of a vase sent through the conventional post is a picture, or a sound or a movie sent over the Internet. These require a digital 'padded envelope'; the common one is called Multipurpose Internet Mailing Extensions (MIME). MIME, and its more secure sister S/MIME have special ways of treating every eighth fragile one or zero that make up multimedia objects. Plain old text does not need each eighth one or zero so does not need to be parcelled up in any special way: the standard Internet protocols are adequate to cope with this simple text. Most email programs automatically choose the correct type of encoding to ensure that the object survives the electronic transmission to its recipient.

It is vital to realise that standard electronic mail copies the contents of the digital envelope; it does not actually send the material from the creator's machine. So, electronic mail, unlike its terrestrial equivalent, does not touch the original created by the sender; instead it provides an identical copy to each recipient. This has its advantages: copies are automatically retained of all outgoing mail. It also has some disadvantages: malicious code that piggybacks electronic messages may also be copied onto the recipient's computer. And, of course, in the eyes of copyright law, a copy is being made of a copyright work.

Once the text or multimedia object is appropriately encoded the sender simply needs to tack on an address for the email. 'clive@pobox.com' is an example of an email address. This may look complicated but this chapter has already introduced the back-half of the address: the domain name. All email addresses are in this format: username@domain. To receive electronic mail, one needs to have an agreement with the controller of the domain. Some domains, like lexisnexis.co.uk, are controlled by employers and they provide email addresses to their staff like direct telephone numbers. Members of staff will have their name, or other reference, before the '@'.

Controllers of other domains, like Internet Service Providers, rent out user names on their domains and also provide access to the Internet or other services.

Pseudo-anonymity

Sending a postcard anonymously is easy: simply do not sign it. Sending an email anonymously is more difficult: it is 'signed' by it being sent from you. The way that Internet users have attempted to remain anonymous is either to lie about who they are when they establish their own email address or to send their emails via an 'anonymous remailer'. This is a computer on the Internet which runs a special program. This program strips any incoming emails of their headers: this removes the identification of from where the email originated. The program then sends this stripped email to the intended recipient purporting to be from someone else. If the anonymous remailer keeps a log of who is the actual author of a message, they may be ordered by a court to reveal who is the actual sender of the message. If the remailer automatically deletes a log, or never even kept one, of course no court order can then restore the identification of the email sender.

A stronger method of remaining anonymous is to send an email via more than one anonymous remailer and to scramble or 'encrypt' all but the next email in the chain. In this way, even if a court were to order a remailer to reveal the sender's identity they would only have access to the details of the remailer who sent them the message and to the next in the chain. To reveal the identity, therefore, all the remailers would have to co-operate with the court order and then all the remailers would have had to maintain logs. This said, problems of identifying defendants over the Internet should not be exaggerated; it is far easier to send a truly anonymous postcard than a truly anonymous email.

Instant messaging

Instant messaging is just that. Email is a 'store and forward' system for exchanging information. When the email is sent from your computer its first destination is your Internet Service Provider or email provider. From there it is hurried across the Internet to an inbound mail server and finally into the recipient's mailbox. If the recipient is not connected to the Internet at the moment of receipt in their mailbox, they may not know it has arrived. Worse still, it is difficult for you to know that they weren't there.

Instant messaging addresses these two deficiencies of the email system: it is instant and you can tell whether someone is connected or not. Like email, messages can consist of more than mere text: pictures, documents and even, because of its instantaneous nature, video and audio can be sent using instant messaging.

Bulletin boards

Digital bulletin boards are similar to their physical counterparts. Anyone with access to the board can pin up a message or question and any other person can leave a reply on the board. Also like a physical bulletin board, someone is ultimately responsible for it. Someone must remove old messages; perhaps even remove rude or defamatory messages. On the Internet that person is often called a moderator or is simply the provider 'hosting' the bulletin board. This means that the provider stores the messages on equipment under their control; what is a moot point is whether the messages left by their users are also under their control. This will be considered throughout the book but particularly in relation to defamation and copyright.

When a message is posted onto a digital bulletin board what is technically occurring is that the person is sending an email to the board. This is reproduced in a readable format for any user of the board to see. If a reader wishes to reply to the message they have a choice. They may either send an email directly and privately to the person who left the message, or they can send a reply that will be stored on the bulletin board itself. It will be listed just below the first message for all to see. This process of replying to a message can occur many times, thus creating a 'conversation thread'.

As explained earlier, an email does not need to be a written note; it may be a digitised picture, a digitised sound recording or even a digital movie. These families of emails can also be left on bulletin boards not for people to reply to, but for people to download, to view or hear. Obscene and indecent pictures and copyright infringement are rife on bulletin boards. The issue of when the operator of the board becomes liable for such illegal postings is a vital point that is addressed throughout this book.

Forums

Many Service Providers run bulletin boards only for access by their members. These are called 'forums'. Each forum has a title that indicates the sorts of conversation threads and files that can be found on the board. An Internet Service Provider may host a legal forum. Within the forum there may be many different sections, some dealing with family law, others with recent cases. Occasionally these forums will be unmanned, or 'unmoderated'; anything posted on the board will remain for a certain time. It is more usual to find that forums have a moderator who vets and deletes offensive messages. This book tackles the vexed question of whether by doing this, the Internet Service Provider becomes legally responsible for the messages left on the system.

Usenet

Forums are accessible only by a Service Provider's members. 'Usenet', in contrast, is a collection of about 30,000 bulletin boards called newsgroups which can be accessed by any person with an Internet connection. Since 1981 there have been about 700 million postings to Usenet.

Instead of one particular Service Provider being responsible for maintaining and storing the newsgroups, like for a forum, all the subscribing Service Providers store the conversation threads. Each Provider is responsible for posting messages from its members onto the relevant newsgroups but is able to display the messages posted by all the other members. Newly posted messages are 'flooded' through the Usenet system until all the Providers are able to display the newly posted message. In this way, all the Providers who allow Usenet access are able only to regulate the content of the messages left by their members.

The majority, necessarily, of the messages displayed or files uploaded are out of the control of the majority of the Providers. There will therefore be times when a Provider has had no way of knowing the content of a file or of a message. But there are some good clues; most of the newsgroups have amply descriptive titles. For example, if a Provider were worried about allowing its members access to a pornographic newsgroup it would be wise not to provide access to 'alt.erotica.male'. Some Providers have seen this selective hosting of newsgroups as one of the easiest methods of avoiding the majority of complaints.

File Transfer Protocol

File Transfer Protocol, or 'ftp' for short, is what it purports to be: a language that allows files to be transferred from one computer to another. For ftp there are usually two significant computers: the ftp server and the client. The ftp server is simply a computer connected to the Internet that stores the files to be transferred. The client is the computer that receives the files stored, and transferred by, the server. To access an ftp site, unlike a website, one usually is required to enter a password. This should not indicate that an ftp site is particularly secure: the majority of ftp sites are termed 'anonymous ftp' meaning that anyone may gain access simply by using the word 'anonymous' or 'guest' as a password.

When a client has gained access to a site it is rather like seeing the contents of a computer's hard disk. There are directories or folders and within those directories there are files. Each of the files may be retrieved, usually by double-clicking on the file name or icon. In addition to retrieving files though, rather like a bulletin board, it is possible to upload a file from one's computer to the ftp server. This lack of control over the content of a site can cause legal problems for the owner of the ftp site. If copyright materials are uploaded by an anonymous depositor, the owner may be a secondary infringer of the copyright in the works. And because the primary defendant may be difficult to trace, the ftp site owner is an obvious alternative choice.

Telnet

Telnet is a way of allowing a user to gain full access to a remote computer via the Internet. Once a user has logged into such a computer they can easily run programs which are stored on the remote computer and view data also stored on that computer. It is as though the user is sitting at the keyboard of the remote computer rather than sitting thousands of miles away at the keyboard of another. For most users, Telnet has taken a back seat to the World Wide Web because it is text-based and requires the knowledge of some UNIX operating system commands. For hackers, in contrast, Telnet remains a useful tool. A hacker can cover his tracks by logging on to one computer and then, from that computer, logging on to another from that computer, and so on. This leapfrogging can make it very difficult for law enforcement officers to trace and find a hacker; it also makes it difficult to collect the necessary evidence to prove that the accused in court is the person who committed the crime.

World Wide Web

When most people refer to the 'Internet', they are really talking about a large aspect of it called the World Wide Web. In June 1993 there were only 130 websites; when the first edition of this book was published, five years ago, there were about one million websites. The World Wide Web is now roughly ten years old and sports over 38 million sites. One of the reasons for this staggering growth is that the World Wide Web, or 'the web', is the most user-friendly use for the Internet. But it is not the Internet and the Internet is not the World Wide Web.

The web, like all the technologies described so far, is merely a common language that allows one computer to understand another when they communicate across telecommunications lines.

Accessing a computer on the web allows a user, or viewer, to do many things. Viewers can see colourful images and graphics, hear sounds and music, see animations and short movies. They can also interact with the accessed computer, or server, in such a way as to allow the viewer to download any material in digital form to his own computer. They can share files across peer-to-peer networks. But these superficial aspects of the web do not explain where it got its name. This explanation reveals the most powerful aspect of the web and the source of the main legal issues involved in its use.

Links

Computers connected to the World Wide Web mainly store their information in a special form; it is called Hypertext Markup Language, or HTML. This common language is primarily a language of layout and design. It allows the owner of a computer to format some information, say a table, and store it on their website or 'home page'. Anyone who accesses that site will see the table as intended. The same goes for graphics, animations and so on. The web therefore offers, for the first time, an opportunity for the owner of a server computer to control exactly what is seen by a person accessing that computer. HTML also offers hypertext.

Hypertext is a way of designing a document with links to other documents. It is most easily understood with an example. Some of the footnotes in this book refer an interested reader to other materials, often a case. But if that interested reader wanted actually to read the referred case, they would have to go to their law library, pick the book from the shelf and turn to the appropriate page. A hypertext version of this book would work as follows. If a reader is interested in a footnote they would merely position an on-screen arrow over the footnote and depress a button on their mouse. The case would then appear on the screen replacing or neighbouring the page of the digitised book. So hypertext is a way of connecting one document to another by means of a link. Links on web pages are usually shown by the word denoting the link being underlined and coloured blue. Pictures, animations, in fact anything you can 'click' on, can also serve as links.

The real power of a link on a website can be understood when one appreciates that the link may be to a document held on any other computer anywhere else on the World Wide Web. So, an Internet version of this book could just as easily link a reader to an American case stored on a web server in the United States as to an English case stored on a web server at Butterworths in England. And having followed a link to another web page one can just as easily follow a link from that page to another page on the web. These vast numbers of links, criss-crossing between digital pages across the planet, warrant the title 'World Wide Web'.

Browsers

Like other aspects of the Internet, the web only works while all the computers that use it understand a common language. The web's main language is HTML. To allow a viewer's computer to interpret this language into a collection of text, pictures and sound, the computer must use a 'browser'. This is a program that not only shows the web page on the viewer's screen as was intended but also it helps the viewer navigate around the World Wide Web. All browsers have a core of common features. They all allow a user to visit a particular site on the web by typing in the site's address. All browsers also have a set of navigation buttons. These are vital if one is to get back to where one came from. In a sense, the browser lays down digital string through the maze of the web so allowing one to click the 'back' icon to the last turning. As a final aid to navigation, browsers will store a collection of the addresses of favourite pages or sites so that one can return to a favourite place without having to retrace one's steps.

Navigation aids

Of course, having millions of pages of information at one's fingertips is useful only if it is easy to find the information needed. However well-stocked a library, there will be few visitors if the books are in an uncatalogued random order. Portals and search engines bring order to the chaotic layout of the web.

Portals are, at their most basic, simply a collection of links under a particular topic. For example, a law firm may wish to advertise its clients. To do this it could have a page on its website that features a list of links to its clients' web pages. An academic may use a website to collect a series of links to useful websites for research purposes. Link lists bring to the Internet what the Dewey decimal system brings to our randomly stocked library.

Search engines are websites that find every site on the web that mentions a particular term. Google, a search engine, can trawl its record of two *billion* documents for one word in under a second. For example, in about a quarter of a second the Google search engine found over 26,000 instances of the phrase 'needle in a haystack' on the web.

SUNRISE FEATURES

The Internet is changing at a staggering rate. Companies spring up on a daily basis; many claim to have the new 'killer application'. Lawyers who seek to advise in this area should try to keep abreast of these changes. While some new technologies are legally superficial, others may have a profound impact on what constitutes good advice in relation to the Internet. Three examples are provided below of the features that are at the sunrise of the Internet industry and which are here to stay: executable code, bandwidth increases together with the peer-to-peer networks that they facilitate and device independence.

Executable code

At the beginning of 1996 most web pages were still and silent. Their graphics may have been colourful, but they were static; a short 'beep' indicated a page's presence at the most. This has now changed. The language used to construct web pages has been refined and it is now able to supply not only page layout details to viewer's computers, but also programs currently called applets or objects. These programs run automatically on a viewer's computer so long as the used browser understands the programming language.

The two most powerful and widespread program families are Java applets and ActiveX controls. They allow a website to show and perform almost all the same functions as an entire computer. This bears restating. Executable code allows a computer connected to the Internet to behave as though its user had loaded up the executable program from a CD-ROM. From a commercial perspective these applets and controls are big business; they are allow websites to do more than merely 'show' they allow them to 'perform'. Executable code allows websites to take orders, check pensions, plan a route; practically anything one can do with a computer and a CD-ROM.

From a legal perspective this executable code is also important. Executable code interacts directly with a viewer's computer, often without the user really knowing. This increases the risk that computer viruses, once thought to be rare on the World Wide Web, can be hosted, spread and contracted. But because executable code is usually run automatically, the first a viewer may know of a virus is its symptoms. For less malicious purposes, executable code allows viewers to instruct remote computers, over the World Wide Web, to perform certain tasks. One Java applet takes an order for a compact disc and then searches the web for the retailer selling it most cheaply. This code forms the backbone for any ecommerce business. To protect the code from being copied their creators must rely on strong intellectual property rights as technical copying of the program is far from difficult. And for each transaction with the code, a contract may have to be formed to secure the payment. But what happens when the code programmer or data inputter has made a mistake and the site sells the television or camera for less than the cost of postage?

Executable code has changed the face of the World Wide Web. This book refers to its implications, but advisers should periodically check the accuracy of their advice to ensure it has not been out-paced by technology.

Bandwidth increases

Bandwidth should be thought of as the digital width of the pipe that lies between a website or server and the client computer. At the moment, few people utilise a bandwidth of less than 56,000 baud; this means that every second the viewer's computer can receive a maximum of 56,000 on and off pulses. This is about as much data one can send down a normal telephone line in a second.

Bandwidth impacts on the amount of information that can be shown on the user's computer each second. For text-based websites, a 56k connection may be perfectly adequate; users may be happy to wait the few seconds it will take for the text to be delivered to their computers. If a website contains a video of a fabulous concert, the same users may not choose to wait for the entire file to download.

The telecommunication industry has made great advances to provide Internet users with greater bandwidth, so-called 'broadband'. Cable companies are now installing cable modems allowing a residential user, such as this author, to access up to a 1Mbyte line: *40* times faster to download and access material than the usual 56k modem! Digital Subscriber Lines, DSL for short, can be used to speed up standard copper telephone lines for data transmission. Telephone users can upgrade their telephone line in a matter of hours to allow them to receive Internet data up to ten times faster than their 56k modem neighbours.

This increase in user-bandwidth is influencing Internet users' activities. Broadband users are less reluctant to download very large files from the Internet. They are therefore tempted to download illegal copies of music, software and even full-length movies. This, in turn, has lead to a proliferation of sites serving up copies of this material. Some store the material on their own servers (making it easy for lawyers to shut them down); others, peer-to-peer networks, are more sophisticated. They allow their members to download material from *other* member's computers. Millions of illegal files are downloaded every day.

The legal implications should be obvious; intellectual property infringement actions have the same basic requirements for success as any legal action. Define the illegal activity, track down the defendant, win or settle the action and then be in a position to enforce the decision or settlement agreement. Peer-to-peer networks make it difficult to track down the infringers and then hold them to their word when you find them.

In addition, this increase in bandwidth is making it harder for users to distinguish Internet content from television content. Our grandchildren will probably be unable to spot the difference. But television and radio content is regulated in most countries. What are regulators to do when they spot what looks and sounds like a television programme but which is actually a video file being streamed over the Internet? The passage through Parliament of the Communications Bill will raise these challenging questions.

Device independence

Another sunrise concept is 'device independence'; one no longer needs a PC to access the Internet. One can use a pocket-sized Personal Digital Assistant (PDA) attached to a mobile phone by a small cable. Better still, one could use an infrared connection between the PDA and mobile phone, or even, if appropriate, utilise the wireless connectivity provided by a Bluetooth connection. Your mobile can sit in your briefcase while you merrily view websites on your PDA. But why have two devices when you can buy a combination of a phone and PDA? And when at home, don't be banished to the study while you wait for your PC to access the web; view websites on your wireless portable screen while in the living room or even the garden!

The main legal implications of this 'unteathered' and 'device independent' Internet access are twofold. First, lawyers and clients need to appreciate that they can't rely on their websites being viewed on PCs with hard drives and printers attached. A user may have no way of 'storing' a contract you provide to them. The second less formalistic implication is that definitions in draft contracts need to be kept under constant review. The definition of 'Internet' drafted two years ago may now be too wide or narrow for the client before you today.

THIS BOOK

This book tackles the legal issues arising from the Internet under the usual chapter headings for a law textbook. This does not mean that the book is for lawyers only. Where possible, the law is explained in plain English; it is hoped that someone in an ecommerce business or from the Internet industry will be able to use this book as a first port of call. To help both these clients and their advisers, the text is highlighted with hundreds of fictional scenarios and their legal effect. For some basic questions, a glance at one of these may be all that is needed to appreciate the law on a point. This said, readers should always seek specific legal advice rather than rely entirely on the text and scenarios in this book. It should be noted that these scenarios, and the names used, are fictitious and any resemblance to real persons or companies, alive or operating, now or in the past, is purely coincidental.

The author appreciates that even legal readers who use the Internet regularly will be unfamiliar with its use of technical Internet terms. For this reason three policies have been adopted. First, the book includes a glossary written by a leading journalist in the field. This is written in a non-technical style rather than in the form of a dictionary definition. The second policy is never to assume technical knowledge; whenever required, this book explains the technology either in the body of the text or in its glossary. The third policy adopted is never to use a technical term where a simplified one will suffice. It is more important that lawyers who advise about the Internet truly understand it rather than simply repeat the latest Internet jargon.

There are many excellent general texts on contract, tort, crime and the topics of the other chapters of this book. This book is not intended to replace these works; the intention is that it will supplement them. This book, therefore, only refers to laws when it is apparent that the Internet raises unique issues about the legal area that may not be covered in existing general literature. Even when this book does examine unique and new issues, it considers them conservatively. Despite the incoming tide of (mainly European) legislation, it remains this author's strong belief that most legal issues raised by the Internet can be resolved, at common law, from first principles. Of course, this belief, and others in this text, are not necessarily those of Olswang solicitors nor its clients.

Finally, a disclaimer. This book examines the English laws that apply to the Internet. The Internet is a transnational beast, however. It will therefore often be prudent to consult the laws from other jurisdictions to check what they have to say on the same issue. Similarly it is hoped that this book will serve those from abroad who wish to know English law's approach to an Internet issue.

Chapter Two

Contract

> *'The customer pays his money and gets a ticket. He cannot refuse it. He cannot get his money back. He may protest to the machine, even swear at it. But it will remain unmoved. He is committed beyond recall. He was committed at the very moment when he put his money into the machine.'*
>
> *Lord Denning, Thornton v Shoe Lane Parking*[1]

Electronic commerce, or ecommerce, is now part of our daily lives. Whatever financial reasons are given for this, whatever 'paradigm shifts' are held responsible, one fact is certain. If consumers and businesses did not believe that the commerce they were transacting was enforceable, they would not enter the digital marketplace provided by the Internet. The Internet, built for and used as a means of communication, provides a vast arena for agreements. This chapter will consider the English law of contract, so far as it relates to consumer contracts and business contracts entered into using the Internet.

The Internet gives businesses access to a vast number of consumers and gives businesses access to each other. The first large-scale consumer and business use that was made of the World Wide Web was the erection of websites for marketing and advertising purposes. These sites promoted companies and products. Initially, they did not offer the possibility of selling products and services. Sales took place in parallel through more traditional means of communication.

A majority of websites now offer international and cost-effective opportunities for selling goods and services to consumers. Businesses too are benefiting from transacting with other businesses over the Internet. A website is rapidly and easily accessible. It can include static or moving graphics, it can be interactive, it is easily updated and purchases can be made immediately. A website can operate like a shop window and a website can act as the cashier and till. Where appropriate, a website can send digital products directly to the consumer and transact services between businesses.

These commercial benefits create new issues for contract law. This chapter considers the following:

1. What are the requirements for a binding contract to be made over the Internet?
2. How do you decide when a contract formed over the Internet is made?

1 [1971] 2 QB 163 at 169.

3. What are, and why do we need, digital signatures?
4. How can digital forms of payment be used to bind agreements?
5. What type of contract should be used to provide digital information over the Internet?
6. Which country's courts will resolve the disputes arising out of an ecommerce contract?
7. Which country's law will apply to an ecommerce contract?
8. What are the special rules that apply to ecommerce contracts made with European consumers?

FORMATION OF CONTRACT

In the main this chapter does not consider the *terms* of a contract made over the Internet; the main concern is to analyse the validity of contracts made over the Internet. This is an important distinction. Under English common law, an agreement becomes legally binding when four elements of formation are in place: offer, acceptance, consideration and intention to create legal relations. For contracts entered into over the Internet, the Electronic Commerce Directive and the UK's Electronic Commerce (EC Directive) Regulations 2002 introduces new pre-contract formalities, in particular for consumers and businesses which do not agree otherwise[2]. Along with these formal requirements, law and statute limits the content of a contract. For example, an ecommerce contract may be validly formed, but one of its terms may be ineffective under other rules. This section focuses on the formation of a contract, examining each of the four factors in turn, highlighting those additional features special to the Internet about which businesses and their advisers should be aware.

Pre-offer information

The Electronic Commerce Directive and Regulations oblige almost every owner of a website established in the EU to provide certain information to its visitors, whether the website permits transactions or not. We examine these new requirements by first assessing where a website owner is 'established'. We then consider the manner of provision and nature of the information which EU-established entities must make available to all visitors to a website. Finally we analyse the contents of and way in which additional 'transactional' information may need to be provided prior to orders being taken.

ESTABLISHMENT OF PROVIDERS

The Electronic Commerce Directive and Regulations do not have extra-territorial reach; they bind only those established within the EU. With websites and servers,

2 Directive 2000/31/EC of the European Parliament and of the Council of 8 June 2000 on Certain Legal Aspects of Information Society Services, in particular electronic commerce, in the Internal Market, OJ L179/1 ('Electronic Commerce Directive'). This is implemented in the UK by the Electronic Commerce (EC Directive) Regulations 2002 ('Electronic Commerce Regulations').

the concept of establishment, however, is not so straightforward. Popular websites are hosted simultaneously on many so-called duplicating 'mirror servers'. These increase resilience. But they may be situated anywhere on the planet. Consequently, they may be many thousands of miles from the headquarters of those who control them.

Location of servers not conclusive

The Electronic Commerce Regulations take a pragmatic view of where a provider is established:

> '"established service provider" means a service provider who is a national of a Member State or a company or firm as mentioned in Article 48 of the Treaty and who effectively pursues an economic activity using a fixed establishment for an indefinite period, but the presence and use of the technical means and technologies required to provide the service do not, in themselves, constitute an establishment of the provider . . .'[3]

In effect, therefore, moving one's servers around the world does not change where one is established. To determine establishment one must look first to an economic activity being pursued from a fixed establishment. Having located this, one must determine whether or not that the use of the fixed establishment is for an indefinite period. Employees working in a leased building are the sort of situation envisaged here. One cannot conclude anything from the mere fact that servers are, or are not, inside the building.

Multiple establishments

Complications arise where more sophisticated companies have multiple locations providing support to a particular website. Imagine the following. A website company's headquarters is in Japan but a team based in California handles technical control of the website. Meanwhile, all the text on the website is written by a group of UK freelance journalists which posts finished articles to an editor in a small office in Oxford, and customer support is handled from Ireland. The site's credit card processing is conducted in Germany and all goods are shipped from local distribution centres around the world. Where is this company established?

The Regulations and Directive clearly envisage such a scenario. We are told, 'in cases where it cannot be determined from which of a number of places of establishment a given service is provided, that service is to be regarded as provided from the place of establishment where the provider has the centre of his activities relating to that service'[4].

There is a concern associated with this definition being used to interpret where a multiple-state-established service provider is established for the

3 Regulation 2(1), part definition.
4 Regulation 2(1). Recital 19 is similar.

purposes of the Directive and Regulations. The recital and definition would seem to suggest that different services may have different centres of activities relating to them. What follows from this is the possibility that the service of, say, ordering a product from a website is centred within the UK but the service of delivering it is centred in the US. In other words, one service is EU-centred; the other, from the same website, may not be. In such circumstances, the service provider may be unsure whether the legislation applies. As will be explained, however, the contractual sanctions for not complying with the Regulations are severe enough that such a service provider is advised to assume that they are established in the EU, for the purposes of the Regulations.

General information to all

If a service provider is established in the EU, they must make available certain general information about themselves. This information must be made available to the recipients of their service 'in a form and manner which is easily, directly and permanently accessible'. If a service provider fails to do this, they may be liable in damages by their visitors for breach of statutory duty[5].

Information to be made available

The scope of the information to be made available (discussed below) is straightforward. It is[6]:

1. the name of the service provider;
2. the geographic address at which the service provider is established;
3. the details of the service provider, including his electronic mail address, which make it possible to contact him rapidly and communicate with him in a direct and effective manner;
4. where the service provider is registered in a trade or similar register available to the public, the register in which the service provider is entered and his registration number, or equivalent means of identification in that register;
5. where the provision of the service is subject to an authorisation scheme, the particulars of the relevant supervisory authority;
6. where the service provider exercises a regulated profession:
   (i) the details of any professional body or similar institution with which the service provider is registered;
   (ii) his professional title and the Member State where that title has been granted;
   (iii) a reference to the professional rules applicable to the service provider in the Member State of establishment and the means to access them;
7. where the service provider undertakes an activity that is subject to value added tax, the VAT number; and

5 The Electronic Commerce (EC Directive) Regulations 2002, reg 13.
6 The Electronic Commerce (EC Directive) Regulations 2002, regs 6(1)(a)–(g) and 6(2).

8. where prices are referred to, these shall be indicated clearly and unambiguously and, in particular, shall indicate whether they are inclusive of tax and delivery costs.

Form and manner of information

The above information must be 'made available to the recipient of the service . . . in a form and manner which is easily, directly and permanently accessible'[7]. Unlike specific transactional information mentioned below, the above information may be made available *at any time* during the encounter with the website visitor. This said, one should note that this information must be 'easily' accessible. Burying the information after numerous other pages on a website is unlikely to satisfy this requirement. A link from the homepage to a list of this information is probably the most obvious way to make the information available. Some website operators may choose to include this information within their standard 'Terms and Conditions'. This too is likely to be acceptable but with one caveat. This information must be made available 'permanently'. Consequently, websites must not be designed so that the information is, say, only available while one is conducting a particular activity. The information must be able to accessed even *after* a visitor has enjoyed the site.

1. An online news service has a subscription service: individuals pay £15 each month to access the service's database of past news articles. The Electronic Commerce Regulations' 'General Information' is made available through a link to the right of the search area on the site. The link is called 'About Us' but the page on which it is housed is only accessible during the course of a paid month and not afterwards. It is therefore arguable that the information is not 'permanently' accessible and so is non-compliant.

Transactional information prior to order

If a service provider is established in the EU and is soliciting orders from visitors, it must provide specific information about its transactions to potential consumers and businesses who do not agree otherwise. This information must be provided to the recipients of their service 'in a clear, comprehensible and unambiguous manner'.

If a service provider fails to do this, they may be held liable by their visitors for damages in breach of statutory duty[8]. In addition, they must allow a consumer to identify and correct input errors prior to placing their order. If the service provider does not make this facility available, the consumer may rescind the contract.[9] Should the customer so cancel, the service provider may apply to the court to order that the consumer may not rescind the contract.'[10]

7 Regulation 6(1).
8 Regulation 13.
9 Regulation 15.
10 Regulation 15.

Website owners and their advisors are therefore strongly advised to pay particular attention to the following section. An owner of a website may well choose to ignore the requirement to make available the general information. If they do so, they are taking the low-cost risk of an action for damages for breach of statutory duty. Few website owners, in contrast, can afford to run the risk that any of their contracts could simply be rescinded by the customer at any time.

Provision of information in clear, comprehensible and unambiguous manner

The scope of the information to be provided in a 'clear, comprehensive and unambiguous manner' prior to the order being placed is simple to understand[11]. It nevertheless may be complex to implement and include on certain websites. The six headings below detail the information required and special concerns of each requirement.

Technical steps to conclude contract

The clearest and most comprehensive manner to provide the different technical steps to conclude a contract is to use a 'crumb trail' at the top of the ordering section of the site. What is meant by this is a line of text showing all the steps needed to enter the contract with the current step highlighted. Having, say, 'Choose – Provide Credit Card – Confirm' at the top of the screen certainly does go some way to be clear and comprehensive. What is needed in addition, however, is some explanation of the meaning of each of these steps. A link from each with a short description would ensure that the 'crumb trail' is not ambiguous as to, for example, when the order is complete.

Filing of concluded contract

This rather bizarre requirement obliges website owners to provide information before the order is placed whether or not the concluded contract will be filed and, if so, whether it will be accessible. Although it is obviously trivial to state this in such a way as to comply with the Regulations, it may be more difficult to comply with the actual statement itself.

Many well-built websites allow a user to access at any time in the future their previous fulfilled orders. This, of course, is only one aspect of the concluded contract. The other aspect is the text of the contract itself; usually, the Terms and Conditions from the website. The common difficulty with providing a link to the Terms and Conditions is that they are usually in constant flux. The Terms and Conditions used to sell an item in January may differ to those used to sell the same item in the following May. To comply with the filing requirement, therefore, one would need not only to provide customers with access to their completed orders but also to the potentially historical Terms and Conditions used to conclude each order.

11 Regulation 11.

The complexity of achieving this will tend to persuade most websites to take the easy and legal way out and not state that they file the contract!

How to identify and correct input errors

This aspect of the Directive and Regulations obliges websites to provide in a clear, comprehensible and unambiguous manner information about how customers may identify and correct input errors before they place an order. In addition, the website is obliged to make available 'appropriate, effective and accessible' technical means to identify and correct input errors.

Again, best practice would suggest that the easiest way to comply with this is to allow a user either to confirm an order, or adjust it. There is unlikely to be a problem so long as the customer is left in no doubt that the order details on the confirmation page of the ordering procedure may be rejected, and then altered, or accepted.

2. CD410.co.uk is a website which sells music CDs for no more than £10 each. Its designers cannot be bothered to alter their ordering pages to allow individuals to correct input errors. Instead, by the 'Confirm' button, they state: 'Don't worry if you've made a mistake and have ordered the wrong thing, simply pop it back unsealed in the post to us with 30 days and we'll credit the money back to you!' CD410.co.uk has not complied with the requirement to allow individuals to correct errors before they place their order; each customer will be able to rescind the contract *at any time* not only within their stipulated 30 days.

Languages offered for contract

Websites must provide details of the languages that are offered for conclusion of the contract. So that there is no misunderstanding: websites are not obliged to *offer* any particular language or languages; they are simply required to let visitors know what languages they do offer.

Relevant codes of conduct

Many website operators are members of voluntary or mandatory codes of conduct. Where this is the case, a list of these must be provided prior to the order being placed, together with information about how to consult the codes electronically[12].

Terms and conditions for storage and reproduction

It is sensible for most websites to allow each customer to see the site's Terms and Conditions before they can place an order. If they cannot see the Terms and Conditions, there is a risk that a court will deem that the Terms and Conditions

12 Regulation 9(2).

have not been 'incorporated' into the contract with the customer. This is discussed below.

Where Terms and Conditions are provided, the Directive and Regulations impose a further obligation on the website operator. The website operator must make the contract available to the recipient in such a way that allows him to 'store and reproduce' it[13]. The obvious way to comply with this requirement is to include a 'Print' button next to the Terms and Conditions.

Bearing in mind a court may require the service provider to comply, this author is of the opinion that websites should go further than merely permitting printing. They should allow the user to send the Terms and Conditions to themselves by email. This is recommended because websites are increasingly being accessed using devices other than computers. Interactive television allows websites to be viewed. Personal Digital Assistants connected to a mobile phone, and some mobile phones, allow websites to be visited. But these devices rarely are connected to a printer. Consequently, by allowing a user to send the contract to an email address, the website should be in a strong position to argue that they have complied with reg 9(3).

Offer

Having provided visitors with the requisite information described above, websites can (finally) get on with the formalities required to bind customers to contracts.

It is discussed below that an offer, met with suitable acceptance, consideration and an intention to create legal relations can form a contract binding both parties. An owner of a website may not want to contract with every party who gains access to their site. For example, the owner may want to contract with parties from the locale rather than from any country[14]. Owners of websites should therefore ensure that the advertising aspect of the site is construed as an 'invitation to treat', not as an offer.

WEBVERTISEMENTS

One fundamental of ecommerce is that suppliers use websites to conduct business. Like a billboard, a website advertises products and services, but unlike a billboard it can also assist the supplier to complete the sale. In doing so, a website can be designed to advertise the features of a product or services; it can even allow a viewer to examine the product in a restricted form[15]. After examining the product or the advertising, a viewer may then select the part of the website to enter a contract to acquire the product or services. The Internet in effect fuses the advertising and the shop. The law, in contrast, has distinguished between

13 Regulation 9(3).

14 This is happening increasingly where a supplier wishes to create geographical price differentials or where the supplier wishes to avoid the laws (often mandatory consumer protection in nature) of a particular jurisdiction.

15 Software can be downloaded from a website in a 'crippled' form. For example, a word processor may be downloaded but may be prevented from printing or saving: it provides a 'test drive'. If the user is content with the product he may then re-access the website to form a contract to receive the uncrippling key.

advertising and shop displays[16]. This unique commercial situation has legal ramifications.

Shops and adverts

Shop invitations

Old and much-considered authority explains that the display of goods and their prices in a shop window or on shop shelves are not offers to sell those goods; they are merely invitations to any customer to make an offer to make the purchase[17]. The mechanics are that a customer makes an offer to the retailer, which the retailer may choose to accept or reject. Website owners should desire the same legal mechanics, whether they are supplying to businesses or, in particular, to consumers. Indeed, by doing so, these website owners contracting with consumers will be more easily able to comply with the 'placing of the order' rules of the Electronic Commerce Directive[18].

Advertisement offers

For the purposes of offers, the law distinguishes shop displays from certain advertisements. It is therefore essential that those who wish to contract over the Internet understand this difference. The law assesses advertisements in two categories: those which promote unilateral contracts and those promoting bilateral contracts. A unilateral contract is one in which money, generally, is offered to another party to perform some act without that person promising anything in return. A person accepting the offer does not need to communicate this fact to the offeror or to complete the contract; he simply needs to do what is required of him.

This legal notion has been confirmed by the Court of Appeal[19]. A travel agent's physical premises displayed the standard ABTA scheme of protection notice. This included the statement: 'ABTA [a travel agent association] arranges for you to be reimbursed the money that you have paid for your holiday [if there are financial difficulties with the agent].' The travel agent became insolvent and the claimant sought to recover the cost of the holiday from ABTA. The Court of Appeal held that this published statement would constitute an offer and, as such, was accepted and formed a contract with the claimant and any customer doing business with the travel agent.

3. A website that offers advertising space to vendors runs a promotion. Its site advertises, 'If you visit our pages three times this month and don't buy anything from our advertisers, we'll credit £10 to your bank account!' This site risks creating a unilateral contract, which the entire Internet community may accept.

16 *Pharmaceutical Society of Great Britain v Boots Cash Chemists Ltd* [1952] 2 QB 795; cf *Carlill v Carbolic Smoke Ball Co* [1893] 1 QB 256.
17 See *Warlow v Harrison* (1859) 1 E & E 309 and its more modern equivalent, *Pharmaceutical Society of Great Britain v Boots Cash Chemists Ltd* [1952] 2 QB 795.
18 Article 11.
19 *Bowerman v Association of Travel Agents Ltd* [1995] NLJR 1815.

A bilateral contract, in contrast, has both parties making a promise. Each offer is usually accepted by a communication of the other's promise.

Web invitations

The owner of a website has little reason to prefer a unilateral contract to a bilateral contract, and where possible should seek to be viewed by the courts as a shopkeeper. The main point to make is that the law looks not simply at the words used for a contract, but the objective intention behind them. This means that if a website would induce a reasonable person into viewing statements on the pages as offers, so will a court. In *Bowerman*, Hobhouse, LJ states this succinctly:

> 'The document as reasonably read by a member of the public would be taken to be an offer of a legally enforceable promise . . . It suffices that ABTA intentionally published a document which had that effect. A contracting party cannot escape liability by saying that he had his fingers crossed behind his back.'

An owner of a website therefore must err on the side of caution in creating a web invitation.

One method is for the owner of the website to state that it will not be bound by any communication from a third party, but the site owner will inform that party if it accepts the communication. This creates three factors in favour of the site owner. First, it goes some way to preventing the reasonable person from thinking the owner has made an offer. The second point relates to the first: it provides evidence to a court that the site owner did not intend to make an offer. Simply using indicative words above a link such as 'make an offer' may not be enough[20]. Third, by explaining the stages to conclude the contract, the website will comply with art 10 of the Electronic Commerce Directive and reg 9 of the Electronic Commerce Regulations as discussed above. This legislation states that prior to an order being placed by *a consumer* or a business not having agreed otherwise, the service provider must 'clearly, comprehensively and unambiguously' provide[21]:

> '(a) the different technical steps to follow to conclude the contract;
> (b) whether or not the concluded contract will be filed by the service provider and whether it will be accessible;
> (c) the technical means for identifying and correcting input errors prior to the placing of the order;
> (d) the languages offered for the conclusion of the contract.'

In addition, the following information must also be made available:

> '[an indication of] any relevant codes of conduct to which [the website owner] subscribes and information on how these codes can be consulted electronically.'

20 Eg *Harvela Investments Ltd v Royal Trust Co of Canada (CI) Ltd* [1986] AC 207.
21 Article 9(1).

These pre-contractual consumer formalities may not be contracted out of by a supplier's contract. And, as described above, the sanctions for ignoring these requirements include not only damages but rescission of the contract[22].

4. A retailer advertises its products on a website. To process an order, the consumer must provide certain information and then click the button labelled 'Submit'. Before the consumer submits this information the website clearly states that their information is to allow the site owner to decide whether to accept their offer. This allows the site owner to check the product type and cost entered and reject, for example, any offer for a television less than £30 as a minimum price for any television. This application of 'backstop logic' reduces the cost of mistakes.

It is mentioned above that the courts view a shop's shelves as invitations to treat and not offers. A website owner may therefore attempt to argue that the site is more like a shop's shelves than anything else, and that it should be viewed accordingly. While this analogy appears reasonably accurate, it may not withstand the strain of a court's detailed scrutiny.

A justification for not holding shops as making offers is to ensure that, if the shop's stock is depleted, a willing consumer cannot sue the shopkeeper for damages[23]. Where a website is offering not physical but digital goods for 'sale'[24] it is difficult to assert that supplies can be exhausted. One of the features of digital products distributed over the Internet is that they are, in effect, in infinite supply. It may therefore be that the primary justification for the rule that shops do not offer but invite to treat is based in part on a commercial factor that is absent from a digitally distributing website[25]. Whatever the common law justification, the Electronic Commerce Directive is concerned with a consumer 'placing the order'. It follows, therefore, that to have known of the possibility of being able to place an order, the website displayed an invitation to treat[26].

Misrepresentations

The distinction between an invitation to treat and an offer is that an offer, met with acceptance, may form a contract. An invitation to treat does not serve as an offer: the courts construe that taking up the invitation is an offer (or possibly 'order' in the language of the Electronic Commerce Directive). The distinction does not entitle a website to induce a consumer to enter a contract by using misleading statements. If a factual statement prior to a contract being formed is classified as misleading, the induced party may be entitled to claim damages, rescind the contract, or even both. If an individual is concerned that an invitation to treat or statement on a website may constitute such a misrepresentation, he should take proper legal advice. It is worth noting that the established law and statute on misrepresentation are equally and fully applicable to a contract formed over the Internet as to one formed in other ways. Website owners who simply use their sites

22 See 'Transactional information prior to order' at p 18.
23 See *Esso Petroleum v Customs and Excise Comrs* [1976] 1 WLR 1 at 11.
24 See 'Type of contract', at p 45.
25 Of course, a limited licence may have been imposed on the supplier restricting the number of digital products he can supply.
26 Article 11(1).

as a 'billboard' for contracts that are formed in other ways must therefore consider that the content of their site may induce someone to enter a contract[27]. It makes no legal difference to the law of misrepresentation that the misrepresentation is on a website but that the contract is not formed over the Internet. They must also ensure that they provide the General Information as described above.

TIMING AND LOCATION OF OFFERS

That an offer was made provides two useful pieces of information: when the offer was made and where it was made. When a court deems an offer is made is often vital. At any moment up to acceptance, an offer can be retracted. Where an offer was made has some relevance to the applicable law for a contract, in the absence of choice, and the relevant section of this chapter will consider this in greater depth[28].

When an offer is made

It is often relevant for the purposes of a contract dispute to determine when an offer is made. Under the Electronic Commerce Directive (for consumers) or otherwise (not for consumers), any offer can be revoked before acceptance. Therefore the first question to answer is when was an offer made. The need for discussion arises because electronic communications are often delayed in transmission and a court will have to decide whether a revocation of the communication will be deemed to take effect before the conclusion of the contract. In short, the court has a choice: offers may be deemed to be made at the time of sending or at some time later.

Consumer's offers

The Electronic Commerce Directive appears, at first glance, to simplify greatly when a consumer's Internet offer is deemed received: 'the [offer] . . . [is] deemed to be received when the part[y] to whom [it is] addressed [is] able to receive [it]'[29].

This, however, leaves open the undergraduate law exam chestnut of a delayed or garbled offer.

Delayed offers

Adams v Lindsell[30] is old and approved authority as to when an offer is deemed to take effect. In the case wool was offered for sale by a letter sent to the claimants. Because of a mistake made by the offerors the letter arrived two days late at which time it was promptly accepted. The court held that the contract was formed on acceptance, despite the offer being delayed. The court indicated, more than once, that its decision was partially founded on the reason for

27 There may also be a misrepresentation by the viewer, say, as to the means of payment or the country of his residence.
28 See 'The Rome Convention', at p 61.
29 Article 11(1) and reg 11(2).
30 (1818) 1 B & Ald 681.

delay being the offeror's mistake. If the offeror had included a time limit on the efficacy of the offer, however, a late acceptance would not have bound them.

Despite the technology, email can suffer from the same delays and problems as experienced by the defendants in *Adams v Lindsell*. People wrongly consider email and even website offering to be a quick method of communication and compare it to a fax, or perhaps even a telephone.

Post, faxes and emails

An email is more like a posted letter being delivered to a pigeon-hole ready for collection. Emails are not instantaneous, unlike faxes and telephone calls. An email message is sent to an Internet Service Provider (ISP) who, like the Royal Mail, attempts to deliver it as quickly and accurately as possible. But as with the Royal Mail, mistakes can occur and emails can arrive garbled, late or even not arrive at all. The similarities with the Royal Mail go further: the Royal Mail does not usually deliver post abroad; that is left to the local postal system of the foreign country. The Royal Mail delivers the mail to only the 'first stop' outside England. The same applies to emails: they are passed between many different carriers to arrive at their final destination.

Unlike a telephone call and fax, some emails are delivered not to the recipient's desk, but to an electronic pigeon-hole for collection. This pigeon-hole is called an 'inbox'. Many users of email must dial their ISP to check on the arrival of an email; often users must collect their email, it is not 'delivered' to them. This technical framework serves as a useful backdrop for the discussion which now follows on when an offer is deemed to have been made. It will also be useful when acceptances are considered later[31].

Emails can be misaddressed, delayed by any server or router on the way, and worse than ordinary mail, they may not be 'collected' for some time after delivery. This is a situation comparable to sending an offer to a pigeon-hole abroad. Many parties are involved in the transmission of the message, and even on arrival the recipient must act to retrieve it.

Before dealing with the English and European legal resolutions to this situation, a technical point must be made. Certain email systems permit a 'read' and a 'receive' receipt to be automatically returned to a sender of an email. The 'receive' receipt usually informs the sender that the email has not been received by the individual, but by his ISP; if analogies are useful, the receipt informs senders when the mail arrives in the pigeon-hole. The 'read' receipt informs when the individual retrieves the email from the ISP. Even there, like a letter in an unopened envelope, the email may not be read for some time.

Consumers v business offers

Where the sender is a consumer, a sent and received email offer will be deemed received because it is able to be accessed; where the sender is not a consumer, the un-accessed offer is not deemed as being received[32].

31 See 'Timing of acceptances', at p 32.
32 The Electronic Commerce Directive, art 11 (1), second indent; Electronic Commerce (EC Directive) Regulations 2002, reg 11(2).

Consequently, if a consumer improperly addresses the email and it does not arrive, no order has been placed, no offer made. The same is true for a business offer.

If the consumer properly addresses the email, or properly uses the website, but the supplier is unable to access the order, the order is not deemed received. This will be the situation if it is the consumer's ISP that is at fault. It is even the conclusion if it is the supplier's website that is at fault. In short, a problem in transmission outside the consumer's control will affect the consumer's legal position in making an offer before a particular date.

Businessmen affected by delays outside their control are less certainly treated; they may want to argue that matters out of their control should not affect their ability to contract on time.

Practically, the best practice is to make any electronic offer subject to a date on which the offer will lapse. Specifying this date in relative terms, for instance, five days after receipt, poses problems unless the offeror provides a definition of exactly what is 'receipt'. A simpler and more certain method is to specify an objective date and time[33].

5. A businessman makes an email offer to another businessman which is delayed by two days owing to the recipient's Internet Service Provider having a computer fault. Unlike *Adams v Lindsell* the delay was out of the control of the offeror; a court is likely to assume the offer was made at the time it should have arrived.

Acceptance

There is little special about the terms of an acceptance made over the Internet, as opposed to one made in any other way. The acceptance must unequivocally express assent to all the terms of the offer. Much has been written about what constitutes such an acceptance. It is useful here to draw out the special methods of accepting over the Internet.

It has been mentioned that an email can have a 'read' and a 'receive' receipt[34]. Receiving one of these will not constitute an acceptance of an emailed offer. An automatically generated receipt of an offer (or order) is not an acceptance of the terms of an offer. Even an email sent in reply that states the recipient's intention to reply in due course will not be an acceptance[35].

An acceptance needs to assent to an offer. It does not, in general, need to be in writing, or by another means of communication. For this reason, where a website is established to make or complete contracts, its owner should be aware of what conduct may bind him. This is of paramount importance. Contracts made over the World Wide Web are rarely completed by two humans: a website operates automatically according to a set of instructions, often called a script. In

33 If no mention is made of the life-span of the offer the courts will imply a lapse after a reasonable time. See *Chemco Leasing SpA v Rediffusion Ltd* [1987] 1 FTLR 201. To assess what is reasonable the courts will take into account many factors including the subject matter of the contract and the method of communicating the offer. Clearly with an email offer, the expiration will be implied sooner than an offer made by post. See *Quenerduaine v Cole* (1883) 32 WR 185.

34 See 'Delayed offers', at p 25.

35 See *OTM Ltd v Hydranautics* [1981] 2 Lloyd's Rep 211.

this respect, it is crucial that the owner of a website understands how a contract can be completed because, generally, a website operates without supervision. This section examines two scenarios: one, where, as advised, a website accepts an offer and second, where it makes one.

Website acceptance and acknowledgement

Having discussed when and how offers can be made it is now relevant to determine how and when acceptances are made. The general rule is that an acceptance must be communicated to the person making the offer. The Electronic Commerce Directive also obliges offerees to acknowledge the receipt of an offer (order) 'without undue delay and by electronic means'[36]. An acknowledgement of receipt may well also be the acceptance of the offer. Fortunately the two may be dealt with separately. Otherwise this would then bind the supplier into accepting the offer 'without undue delay and by electronic means'. The supplier is entitled first to acknowledge receipt of the offer, and then (potentially later) to accept the offer. If a supplier does not acknowledge receipt of the order, they may be sued for damages for breach of statutory duty[37].

Suppliers should take care over the language used in any acknowledgement. They should ensure that it does not act as an acceptance and so, inadvertently, form a contract earlier than intended.

6. A young school child orders a birthday present from a website to arrive for her father the next day. The website, on receiving the order, immediately sends an email to the child stating: 'Thank you for your order. This is now being processed.' Such ambiguous language could be deemed as being an acceptance and not a mere acknowledgement. The website may now be unable to refute the order.

Any person making any *offer* may waive the general rule that acceptance must be communicated and can instead permit acceptance by conduct. This general rule is examined in the light of ecommerce transactions.

Communication of acceptance

The acknowledged rule is that acceptance of an offer must be communicated to the offeror[38]. This must not be confused with the Electronic Commerce Directive's rule that acknowledgement of a consumer's offer must also be communicated. In addition, as the Court of Appeal has stated[39]:

> 'We have all been brought up to believe it to be axiomatic that acceptance of an offer cannot be inferred from silence, save in the most exceptional circumstances . . .'

36 Electronic Commerce Directive, art 11(1), first indent; Electronic Commerce Regulations, reg 11(1)(a).
37 Regulation 13.
38 [1974] 1 WLR 155 at 157.
39 *Allied Marine Transport Ltd v Vale do Rio Doce Navegacao SA* [1985] 1 WLR 925 at 927.

The question is, what are the 'most exceptional circumstances' when it is appropriate for an acceptance to be silent? These exceptional circumstances stem from the reasons for the rule: to protect both offeror and offeree.

The rule protects the offeror from being bound by a contract without knowing that the offer is accepted. An exception to this may be, therefore, where the offeror expressly or impliedly waives the requirement of communication. For example, an offer to sell goods may be made by sending goods to an offeree who can accept the offer by using them[40]. Here there is not mere silence or inactivity; there is conduct indicating acceptance.

Conversely before the Electronic Commerce Directive, offerees were also protected by this rule. If they did not wish to accept an offer, it was not felt undesirable that offerors could put them to the trouble of communicating a refusal[41]. Indeed, authority from an established precedent, *Felthouse v Bindley*[42], indicates that the offeror can waive communication of acceptance, but not waive an unequivocal external manifestation of acceptance so as to bind the offeree. Communication of acceptance may also be deemed 'waived' by the 'custom and practice' of the area of commerce[43]. The Electronic Commerce Directive alters these common law rules for consumers and businesses who do not agree otherwise. Service providers must acknowledge offers/orders, whether they intend to accept them or not.

That the above is good law is not doubted; its bearing on standard practice for electronic commerce, is. For the most part it is suppliers who draft the offers being made over the Internet, particularly on the World Wide Web. In this situation it is difficult to see any unfairness in holding an acceptor, ie the supplier, bound despite making no contact to that effect: it would appear that the onus is on the owner of a website to state categorically what will constitute acceptance[44]. For consumer transactions, this is stipulated by art 10(1)(a), but for business transactions, it is surely best practice. Contracting over the Internet may therefore reverse the court's assumptions in *Felthouse v Bindley* because the offeree generally drafts the offer. If that party does not specify the method of acceptance, and also does not reply to a submitted offer it risks the serious possibility of being bound by numerous contracts without having made explicit approval. Even if a stipulation as to the method of acceptance is made in the email or on the website, if the offeree drafted these terms and accepts by another method, the offeree can be viewed as having waived that specified method. A court will look to whether the offeror has been prejudiced by the changed method of acceptance[45]. Of course, readers will recall that consumer-focused transactions are required to state the steps necessary to follow to conclude the contract[46].

40 *Weatherby v Banham* (1832) 5 C & P 228. Interestingly, the Electronic Commerce Directive, recital 34 and the Electronic Commerce Regulations, reg 11(2)(b), clearly envisage that acknowledgement of the order may only be by the provision of the *service* ordered.

41 *Chitty on Contracts* vol 1 at §2-063 (28th Edition) Sweet & Maxwell, 1999.

42 (1862) 11 CBNS 869.

43 *Minories Finance Ltd v Afribank Nigeria Ltd* [1995] 1 Lloyd's Rep 134 at 140.

44 See *Jonathan Wren & Co Ltd v Microdee plc* (5 July 1999, unreported) Technology and Construction Court.

45 See generally *Robophone Facilities v Blank* [1966] 1 WLR 1428.

46 Electronic Commerce Directive, art 10(1)(a).

Acceptance by conduct

The website can accept an offer, 'on behalf' of its owner, by certain conduct. For example, a viewer can click a button on a web page to send a request for some software and the software may then begin to download to the viewer's computer. This positive action can be viewed as an acceptance of the offer made by the viewer without the owner (or offeree) having expressly assented to the offer itself[47]. But, our courts commonly apply an 'objective' test to interpret the actions of the offeree. Conduct will therefore be regarded only as acceptance if the reasonable person would be induced into believing that the offeree has unequivocally accepted the offer.

Completing an order by downloading a file to the consumer is likely to be construed as acceptance by the reasonable person[48]. Owners must therefore carefully construct their websites. The owner must ensure that the website is able to validate the terms of the offer from the viewer. Generally this is achieved by the website having a contract page that the viewer is encouraged to submit, or offer, by clicking a link or button. On receiving this notification the website will automatically start the downloading of digital material to the viewer. But the automation of this acknowledgement of receipt and acceptance places a burden on the site owner: he must ensure that the terms of the offer submitted are the terms of the offer expected. It is essential that a viewer cannot submit an offer with an adjustment to the terms, say lowering the price. This would be a counter-offer which may, unwittingly, be accepted by downloading the requested material to the viewer.

There is a technical method to achieve this certainty. The web page should clearly state the terms of the order. Included within these terms should be a clause to the effect that an acceptance will only be valid where an offer is received through the website[49]. This, to some extent, prevents an adjusted offer being sent by email and automatically accepted.

If a website is not being used to receive orders, but orders are placed by email instead, the acceptor must have an automatic check as to the contents of that email. The use of a checksum is the most convenient method of checking this. Only if the checksum of the emailed order corresponds precisely with that of the expected order should the website accept the order. Controllers of sites should pay much attention to their automatic checking programs: an error may result in the owner being bound to a contract that would have been unacceptable.

7. A website provides the terms of an offer to download software from the site at a cost of £60. The site is structured so that the viewer must type the words, 'I Agree' in a box, at which point the website acknowledges and accepts the offer by downloading to the viewer the requested software. One viewer types 'I agree to pay £30'. Because the automatic checking program looks simply for the words 'I Agree', but not exclusively, the software is downloaded to the viewer in error. A contract may have been formed at the lower price.

47 See *Brogden v Metropolitan Rly* (1877) 2 App Cas 666.

48 See *Northern Foods plc v Focal Foods Ltd* [2001] EWCA Civ 1262, [2001] All ER (D) 306 (Jul), in which Focal supplied goods to Northern and later disputed that such supply deemed their acceptance of the loss-making price for the goods. The Court of Appeal held that a letter sent by Focal to Northern was accepted by the conduct of supplying the goods. See also Electronic Commerce Regulations, reg 11(2)(b) in relation to 'acknowledgement by providing services'.

49 See *Frank v Wright* (1937) OQPD 113 where acceptance was specified to be received in writing, but was not valid where made orally.

Consumer acceptance

This chapter advises against websites making offers. Nevertheless, for the sake of completeness, rather than recommendation, this section examines this method of contracting[50]. Many of the same legal considerations are applicable here as for when the website accepts an offer.

Acceptance by conduct

It has been explained that conduct can constitute acceptance[51]. In the scenario where a website makes an offer, it will be the conduct of the consumer, or viewer, which the courts will examine to check for acceptance. It is in the interests of the website to ensure that the conduct by the consumer is therefore as unequivocal and unambiguous as possible.

8. A web page has a scrollable window headed 'Licence'. Below this window is a button labelled, 'download software'. A viewer clicks on this button to download the software and is later accused of breaching the licence provisions. The viewer may have an arguable case that his conduct was not in relation to the terms of the licence, but in relation simply to gaining access to the software. A more thoughtful page design may have removed this problem.

Conduct is regarded as acceptance, and, for services, acknowledgement of receipt of the order, only if the reasonable person would be induced into believing the offeree has accepted. This 'objective' test can create difficulties for the operator and designer of a web page. Many digital consumers using the World Wide Web for commerce view it like a shop, only a 'virtual' one. They may therefore be surprised, and not aware, that to acquire a product they must not only provide payment but also then consent to a licence. Their more usual tangible purchases involve simply paying in exchange for receiving the product. On this basis it is difficult to fathom how a court could objectively construe as acceptance the clicking of a button that denotes downloading the product rather than accepting the licence. Under Scottish law, a case concerning 'shrink-wrapped' computer software showed the court's readiness to construct two contracts out of the supply of computer software transaction[52]. First, the retail sale of the physical box of software containing the product. This contract is between the retailer and consumer. The second is purported by the software publisher to be between them and the consumer; the so-called 'shrink-wrap licence'. In this case, the consumer did not break the 'shrink-wrapping' and so was decreed not to have a contract with the software publisher. Bearing in mind this case, owners of websites should not shy from explaining that clicking a button will bind that person to obligations regarding the material that they will acquire. This provides the background for the final issue pertaining to the acceptance by the conduct of a consumer – ignorance of offer.

50 See 'Shop invitations', at p 22
51 See 'Acceptance by conduct', at p 29
52 *Beta Computers (Europe) v Adobe Systems Europe* 1996 SLT 604.

IGNORANCE OF OFFER – LACK OF INTENTION

It can be appreciated that, even with provision of the information required by the Electronic Commerce Directive, consumers could click on a button labelled 'download' without envisaging that they may be entering an explicit, rather than implied, contract: consider the eagerness to acquire some new software or material and consider the typical ignorance that the acquisition is subject to an explicit licence. It is also possible to press the wrong button. In such a situation, Electronic Commerce Directive or not, the courts may be reluctant to bind unwitting offerees simply because they have performed an action[53] that purportedly indicates acceptance. A further reason that the courts may not hold consumers bound by their action is that, in not knowing of the offer, the consumers have no intention to be legally bound by their actions.

The solution to these possible problems is for any website that seeks to bind users to be explicit, avoid uncertainty and 'go further' than merely 'make available' the 'Terms and Conditions'. One method is to prevent the viewer being able to perform the conduct before they have scrolled, or paged, through the entire contract. True, an individual may simply click on a 'next page' link without actually reading the text of the contract; but, at least they then have a weaker argument that their conduct does not objectively indicate acceptance and that they were ignorant of the offer.

9. The home page of a website features only one line of legal text to avoid looking too ominous. It states, 'By proceeding you agree to be bound by our terms.' The word 'terms' is underlined on the site to indicate a link to the terms of the website. This may not bind the viewer, but if it does, there is a likelihood that onerous exclusions of liability will not operate against the viewer. The website owner should find other ways of ensuring that those onerous terms are definitely read by the viewer.

Timing of acceptances

Because an offer may normally be revoked at any point until acceptance, it is obviously vital to appreciate when acceptance is deemed to have taken place over the Internet. Unlike for offers, the Electronic Commerce Directive and Regulations do not specify when acceptance is deemed to be received.

10. onepotatotwo.com sells seeds to consumers through its website. During July, a consumer selects some seeds through the site and confirms his order by clicking an icon labelled 'I accept'. The moment he does this he receives an email from onepotatotwo.com thanking him for the order and confirming the seeds are on their way. Before reading the email, he sees the seeds being sold at seedyseedsmart.com at a reduced price. Even though he has not read the email, as he was able to, the contract was concluded.

53 For example, clicked on a link or icon. See *Specht v Netscape Communications Corpn and America Online Inc* US District Court of Southern District of New York, 3 July 2001.

One person may make an offer which is acknowledged as being received and is accepted immediately by the other person. But if that offer is withdrawn before the acceptance is received by them there may be a conflict. The possible legal outcomes are that the contract was made when the acceptance was sent; or when, and if, it arrives at the recipient. As no English law cases have covered this point in relation to email or website acceptances and the Electronic Commerce Directive is silent on the issue, it is necessary to extrapolate from the law relating to acceptance by post, telephone and telex.

When a viewer reads or views a website, packets of digital information pass between the site and the client. An acceptance by either party will, generally be immediately received by the other. The more difficult questions of timing of acceptances are therefore seldom pertinent for web communication or for 'instant' messages such as MSN Messenger. For emails the issues are more complex.

This discussion is therefore in halves: the first considers acceptance by email where it is reasoned that the 'postal rule' will usually apply; the second considers acceptance over a website where it is submitted the more general rule will apply that the contract is formed when the acceptance is received. Again, readers should note that the Electronic Commerce Directive addresses only timing of 'orders' and not acceptances.

Acceptance by post, telephone and telex

Where acceptances are sent by post there is a generally applicable rule that the English courts have used to determine the deemed time of acceptance[54]. Acceptance takes place when that letter is posted. Where acceptances are made by an instantaneous form of communication, such as telephone or telex, another rule has been generally applied[55]. Acceptance is deemed to take place when the acceptance is communicated to the offeror.

It is a moot point whether these rules should be mechanically applied, or whether they are, as is more likely, a starting point to assess what is fair between the parties. Certainly the courts have stated that the posting rules should not be applied where it would lead to 'manifest inconvenience or absurdity'[56]. And there are occasions where this is would be the case: it would be absurd for an acceptance to be deemed accepted at the time of posting if it is delayed in the post because the offeree wrongly addressed it. It is perhaps as much as can be hoped, therefore, that this chapter explains what would not be manifestly inconvenient or absurd for email acceptances. It is essential that those who would seek to rely on the following section for email acceptances are aware that it is simply guidance. Even after almost 200 years of examination of the postal rule, there is no universally applicable rule; there are merely pointers for the parties and the court[57].

54 See *Adams v Lindsell* (1818) 1 B & Ald 681.

55 See *Entores Ltd v Miles Far East Corpn* [1955] 2 QB 327, and *Brinkibon Ltd v Stahag Stahl und Stahlwarenhandelgesellschaft mbH* [1983] 2 AC 34.

56 *Holwell Securities Ltd v Hughes* [1974] 1 WLR 155 at 161.

57 This is not to say that organisations have not lobbied to clarify and harmonise the position: the UN Convention on Contracts for the International Sales of Goods (adopted in Vienna, 1980) contains provisions dealing with acceptance, offer and withdrawal of an offer (arts 14–24); see also, the EC Communication from the Commission to the Council and the European Parliament on European Contract Law, Com (2001) Final, 11 July 2001.

Acceptances by email

As mentioned earlier, email is not quite like the post and it is certainly not like instantaneous communication by the telephone[58]. It is sometimes slower than the post, and the arrival of the acceptance by email is far more reliant on the recipient than the sender. It is not like a fax or telephone for two reasons. First, there is no direct line of communication between sender and receiver. Instead, the email is broken into chunks and sent as a collection of packets, each with an 'address' for the recipient. The arrival of an email is therefore far more fragmented than a telephone call. The second, and central, difference between the two is that with a telephone call it is possible to check that the intended recipient has heard the acceptance. With email this is near to impossible but is often quite necessary. Emails are sent using protocols, precise languages, which allow one computer to pass on information accurately to another. But sometimes these protocols are used incorrectly and an email may arrive entirely garbled or missing a few important characters such as zeros and pound signs. This problem must be combined with the issue that an email requires its recipient to collect it, rather like collecting mail from a pigeon-hole. It is therefore difficult, unlike a phone call, to check that the offeror has received the acceptance and to check that it is unequivocal.

Reasonableness of email acceptance

Like the posting rules, the first issue to consider in relation to an acceptance is whether it is reasonable to use email to accept. A rule of thumb applied in postal cases has been that if an offer is made by post, it is reasonable to accept by post. This, at first blush, appears applicable to email; it may not be. Some email users are permanently connected to their Internet Service Provider: as soon as an email arrives for them, they are notified and can immediately view the message. What is more common, however, is that a user's email arrives to a server which the user must contact by modem to access any messages: the connection is not permanent. These users are rarely notified that an email awaits them. They must simply log-on on the off-chance that an email is ready for them. For these remote email users, a period of days may elapse before they check for any email. It may therefore be less reasonable that an important *acceptance* is emailed to one of these remote users, than for an offer to be sent from one of these users. That said, it is submitted that the senders have at least some responsibility to inform their recipients not to reply by email if they collect their email infrequently.

Priority over subsequent communications

Because an email is not instantaneous, if it is reasonable to use email to accept[59], it is not absurd to deem the time of making the contract as the time of sending

58 Readers should note that since the first edition of this text *Chitty* has now altered its view on this issue to confirm this point. See *Chitty on Contracts* (Sweet & Maxwell, 28th Edition, 1999) Volume 1 at §2-046; cf § 2-031 (27th Edition).

59 See 'Reasonableness of email acceptance', above.

the email where otherwise a later acceptance sent would act prejudicially. A later posting or email should not 'beat' the earlier acceptance sent by email. Of course, convenience and policy have a role to play in balancing the interests of the two competing offerees[60]. It would not be reasonable to prefer the earlier sent email if it was addressed incorrectly, or was sent in full knowledge that the offeror's email server had crashed[61].

Accepted but not received

Emails can be delayed in their transmission, sometimes through no fault of the offeree. On 13 April 1998, software flaws crippled an AT&T data network for about 24 hours. This affected millions of consumers who tried to send, and hoped to receive, emails during the period[62]. Less often an email will not be received at all. There are three possible reasons for this. First, the sender sends the acceptance to an incorrect email address: it is extremely unlikely that a court will grant such carelessness with the benefit of the doubt; the email will not be acceptance. A second reason that the email may not be received is owing to a fault at some point in the transmission process. As another example, on 17 July 1997 hundreds of thousands of email messages sent to known addresses simply 'bounced back' as though the addresses did not exist. The cause of this was an employee of Network Solutions Inc (who at the time maintained the 'master' address list) who was working the night shift and failed to react to an alarm[63]. Like a loss in the Royal Mail, a court must weigh the fairness to the offeree against the unfairness to the offeror, who may have already contracted with another party. Even so, it is still likely that the contract will have been formed at the time of sending the email[64]. The third, and most common, reason that an email acceptance will not be received is that its recipient does not retrieve it. This may be because the person no longer checks their email inbox, or because the person sees who the message is from and deletes it without reading it. In both of these situations, the email would constitute acceptance; an offeror's recklessness will not prevent the formation of a contract.

It follows from the above that an email acceptance sent, but not yet received, cannot be 'beaten' by a later sent revocation of the offer. This rule is well established under rules of postal acceptance and there seems little justification to adjust it for acceptances over the Internet[65].

Inaccurate transmission

It has been mentioned that an email may arrive missing, or including, certain characters and it may even be entirely illegible. The legal significance of a flawed email is that its sender may never know. In this way email differs to a large

60 *Brinkibon Ltd v Stahag Stahl und Stahlwarenhandelgesellschaft mbH* [1983] 2 AC 34 at 41.

61 See *Bal v Van Staden* [1902] TS 128 in which it was held unreasonable to insist that an acceptance be deemed accepted where the sender knew of postal delays.

62 *USA Today*, 23 April 1998.

63 *The Times*, 19 July 1997.

64 See *Household, Fire and Carriage Accident Insurance Co Ltd v Grant* (1879) 4 Ex D 216.

65 Offerors over the Internet must not forget that to revoke an offer the withdrawal must actually reach the offeree. A reversal of the postal rule will not apply. See *Re London* and *Northern Bank* [1900] 1 Ch 220.

extent from a telephone acceptance, and to a smaller extent to a fax acceptance. During a telephone call one can check that an acceptance has been heard; fax machines will report an error if a fax cannot be sent with sufficient quality, or there is no paper at the receiver's end. In contrast, if an email is garbled, it is impossible for the offeree to know before it is too late. For this reason, it would be both inconvenient and absurd for any other rule to apply other than making the offeror bound by a garbled email. The offeror, having not specified an alternative method of acceptance, is not at liberty to presume it is a counter-offer.

This rule is not purely based on technical realities and policy; it is also based on evidential matters. As with a fax, the sender retains a copy of that which is sent. On the other hand, it is often possible, using digital translators, to unscramble the received email to establish whether it was an unequivocal acceptance[66].

11. An insurance firm establishes a website and allows potential customers to submit details of their works of art for insurance. All valuations and contracts are formed over the Internet. The firm sends by email to a customer an offer of insurance for a painting; this customer types his acceptance by email but, unfortunately, this is not sent across the Internet as the customer has not paid his monthly fee to his Internet Service Provider. The painting is then stolen. The customer will not be able to benefit from the delay in the post, as the delay was attributable to his fault.

Acceptances over the World Wide Web

Unlike email communications, on the World Wide Web the client and server are in simultaneous communication for most purposes. The communication between the two has the quality of a telephone conversation between computers rather than humans. Either party will be immediately aware if the other party 'goes offline'. This is because when one party sends digital data to the other these data are sent together with a checksum which allows the receiving computer to check that the correct information has been received. A checksum is almost the equivalent of someone saying 'Okay?' after asking a question over the telephone; it is a way of checking that the silence is due to acquiescence rather than absence.

If the client loses contact with the server, the server will 'know' of this situation within seconds, as its checksums and 'received data' will not arrive; if the server loses contact from the client very often a message will appear to the effect of 'server not responding'. In law this 'knowledge' of non-transmission makes a crucial difference. In *Entores Ltd v Miles Far East Corpn* Lord Denning considered for the first time when an acceptance sent by telex should be considered as making a contract[67]. It is instructive to follow closely Denning LJ's reasoning in this case: this will demonstrate that a website acceptance greatly differs to an email acceptance and should be treated like a telephone, or telex, acceptance.

66 A binary document, say a word processing document, which is emailed as text, may be irreversibly scrambled. Other types of modification, however, such as a '£' becoming a '#', can be reversed to indicate to the court the true nature of the acceptance.

67 [1955] 2 QB 327. Applied by the House of Lords in *Brinkibon Ltd v Stahag Stahl GmbH* [1983] 2 AC 34.

First, Denning LJ considered the hypothetical case where one person, in the earshot of another, shouts an offer to the other person[68]. The person hears the offer and replies but his reply is drowned by noise from an aircraft flying overhead. Denning LJ was clear that there is no contract at the moment of the reply. The accepting person must wait until the noise has gone and repeat the acceptance so the other can hear it. Next, Lord Denning took the case of a contract attempted to be made over the telephone. An offer is made but in the middle of the reply of acceptance the line goes 'dead'. Denning LJ was again clear that there is no contract at this point because the acceptor will know that the conversation has abruptly been broken off. Finally, Lord Denning considered use of telex to form a contract. Again, if the line goes dead in the middle of the sentence of acceptance, the teleprinter motor will stop. If the line does not go dead, but, say, the ink dries up, the clerk at the receiving end will send back a message 'not receiving'. In all Denning's examples the person sending the acceptance knows that it has not been received or has reason to know it.

Parallels with acceptance over a website are now obvious: if a communication of acceptance is sent from or to a website, it will become immediately obvious if a problem has occurred which blocks the communication. Like a telephone acceptance, a server will always 'know' whether a message has been received by its intended recipient; it is waiting for received data to signify that the message has been received. And like a telex acceptance, if a client sends a message to the server but there is some problem preventing transmission, the client will receive, not unlike the telex clerk's message, a 'server not responding' message. It is therefore submitted that communications over the World Wide Web differ from those by email. The contract is complete when the acceptance is received by the offeror.

12. A company which sells ties establishes a website that allows viewers to select a pattern and length for a tie. After selecting the tie, the viewer is asked to click the 'I want to buy' icon. The company's web server then sends an automatic receipt of offer and acceptance of offer. The server is notified that this acceptance does not reach the viewer. No contract is formed because the non-delivery of the acceptance was known to the company before the viewer left its site. It should have retransmitted the acceptance, maybe by email.

Battle of the forms

The rapidity of email and automatic confirmations of receipt lend the Internet to contractual negotiations where previously faxes had been used. This may allow a 'battle of the forms' to commence. This is where two standard-form email contracts are exchanged, each differing slightly to the other but claiming to govern the legal relationship entirely. The situation may be resolved by no contract being formed; there is no agreement. What can be more problematic is that a contract is formed on one party's terms when that was not expected. Except for the issues of location and timing already mentioned, there is little that the Internet will add to established methods of judging the result of a battle of the forms[69].

68 [1955] 2 QB 327 at 332.
69 *British Road Services Ltd v Arthur V Crutchley Ltd* [1967] 2 All ER 785 and *Butler Machine Tool Co Ltd v Ex-Cell-O Corpn (England) Ltd* [1979] 1 WLR 401.

DIGITAL SIGNATURES

The signature is a familiar way of an individual making apparent on paper that he or she is who they say they are and that, often, they agree to be bound by whatever they are signing below. The signature, therefore, generally provides 'authentication' of the signatory. It is also an indication of 'acceptance' or 'consent' to a legally binding commitment. Sometimes, legislation and statute demands that a signature is provided, for example, in assignments of copyright[70]. Sometimes individuals decide that, for a particular contract, a signature will be their agreed sign of acceptance.

In both examples, the use of a computer, software and the Internet to provide, generate and deliver these signatures is an important issue. If legislation insists on ink and paper for certain commercial transactions, then ecommerce's benefits will not be felt in areas of commerce simply because of this bureaucracy. Similarly, if individuals do not feel comfortable in relying upon digital signatures, they too may not derive benefits from electronic commerce's speed and geographical reach. The European Union and the UK have implemented legislation to facilitate digital signatures being usable and relied upon in commerce.

The EC Directive on a Community Framework for Electronic Signatures[71] attempts, among other issues, to create a common understanding across Europe as to what constitutes an 'electronic signature'. Clearly, electronic commerce across Europe would be hampered if Member States differed on what an acceptable 'technical' standard is for an electronic signature. Further, the Directive requires that Member States ensure that an electronic signature is not denied legal effectiveness in legal proceedings merely because it is in an electronic form and has not been created by a secure electronic device or by a particular third party[72]. In short, basic electronic signatures, like paper ones, need not be generated in any particular way nor need they be created (read 'witnessed') by any particular person. As with paper signatures, it is open to a court to call into question the reliability, and possible forgery, of an electronic signature. Even so-called 'advanced signatures' are not beyond the rules applicable to proper signatures[73].

The UK's Electronic Communications Act 2000 and Electronic Signatures Regulations 2002 introduce the key element of the Electronic Signatures Directive being that merely because a signature is electronic does not prevent a court from relying upon its veracity in a dispute[74]. This said, two crucial aspects must be understood about the current state of this UK legislation. First, an electronic signature will only be deemed as such if a person makes a statement that[75]:

> '(a) the signature;
> (b) a means of producing, communicating or verifying the signature; or
> (c) a procedure applied to the signature;
> is (either alone or in combination with other factors) a valid means of

70 Copyright, Designs and Patents Act 1988, s 90.
71 OJ No L13, 19.1.00, p 12.
72 Article 5.
73 Articles 2 and 5 and recital 20.
74 Section 7(1).
75 Section 7(3).

> establishing the authenticity of the communication or data, the integrity of the communication or data, or both.'

What this means is that if one wishes to utilise a basic electronic signature to conclude a contract, one might also be required to produce a statement, technical in nature, which is a valid means of proving the signature and document are not forged and are reliable.

The second crucial issue about the Electronic Communications Act 2000 is that it does not 'fast-forward' existing legislation into the electronic world. It does not 'search and replace' the word 'signature' in legislation with the words 'signature, digital or otherwise'. If old legislation states currently that 'writing' and 'signatures' are required for a particular legal instrument, the grand-sounding Electronic Communications Act 2000 does nothing to change this requirement[76]. Article 5.1 of the Electronic Signatures Directive states:

> 'Member States shall ensure that advanced electronic signatures which are based on a qualified certificate and which are created by a secure-signature-creation device:
> (a) satisfy the legal requirements of a signature in relation to data in electronic form in the same manner as a handwritten signature satisfies these requirements in relation to paper-based data.'

As stated above, the concept of a 'signature' may not be relevant for the majority of private contracts. Consequently, this chapter does not examine this issue in great detail. In short only, therefore, this article of the Directive can be summarised as follows. The most secure type of electronic signatures, combined with a 'qualified certificate' do not need an accompanying statement to be admitted with the same weight as their paper counterparts[77]. Further still, these super-strength electronic signatures would satisfy any legal requirement for a signature in respect of the signed data. However, one must consider that UK legislation usually twins the word 'signature' with another, 'writing'. Every piece of legislation that refers to both these words remains impervious to digitalisation: the legislation itself will need amending to bring it into the binary age.

So, the Act introduces a way to allow the Government to quickly alter electronic-hindering legislation[78]. Advisors should therefore ensure that their clients, while eager to embrace electronic commerce, do not misread the European Directive and the Electronic Communications Act 2000 and Electronic Signatures Regulations 2002. Old legislation may still insist upon paper signatories. Existing contracts may too. Using digital signatures, however secure and certificated, may not comply with the necessary formalities.

76 Consultation on EC Directive 1999/93/EC of the European Parliament and Council on a Community Framework for Electronic Signatures, Department of Trade and Industry, March 2001.

77 Technically, these must meet the hurdles of Annexes I, II and III of the Directive.

78 Sections 8 and 9. As at 31 March 2002, 10 section 8 orders had been made with a further 13 slated for laying before 2004.

Consideration

As an oversimplification, perhaps, it can be stated that the English law of contract distinguishes breakable promises from enforceable contracts[79]. Consideration given in return for a promise is the main ingredient that turns promises into contracts. Consideration has been variously defined as 'something of value in the eye of the law'[80]; '[d]etriment to the promisee'[81]; 'the price for which the promise is bought'[82]; and there is much academic debate as to its exact ambit.

English law has always recognised that mutual promises may be adequate consideration for each other, thus forming a contract. If a builder promises to repair a roof and the unfortunate home owner promises to pay on completion of the repair, a binding contract is formed. No services have been provided yet and no money has been given[83]. Similarly, promises to pay over the Internet are enough to form the consideration to create a contract.

13. A video shop with a website offers DVDs for sale. A viewer selects a DVD for £15 from the website and types 'I Agree' in the requisite box together with a credit card number. The DVD is shipped immediately at which point the shop discovers that the credit card number is fictitious. That the agreement has been completed over the Internet is of no legal consequence: the viewer's promise to provide the £15 will be 'valuable' (ie of value) consideration for the shop to enforce the contract.

It is only important for this chapter to assess whether the factual reality of contracting using the Internet affects the doctrine of consideration. For general statements, readers are advised to look to specialist texts. One contractual situation is particular to the Internet: the consideration needed to cement a web-wrap contract[84]. These are agreements at the 'front' of a website which purport to bind their viewers to a contract should they proceed to view the rest of the site.

Web-wrap consideration

It is now common that to enter a website one must click a link labelled, 'I Agree to the terms above'. These terms are generally divided into two sections: the top section expresses the intellectual property rights that the site owner licenses to viewers; the bottom section attempts to exclude liability for any damage caused by the site. This section will not address the *terms* of these contracts, but merely whether there is consideration for the licence.

79 Although, a promise made in a deed may be enforceable. This is considered out of the scope of this chapter, but it may be noted that there appears little preventing a deed being made using electronic methods.

80 *Thomas v Thomas* (1842) 2 QB 851 at 859.

81 Holdsworth W, *History of English Law*, Vol 8, at p 11.

82 *Dunlop Pneumatic Tyre Co Ltd v Selfridge Ltd* [1915] AC 847 at 855.

83 If this was not the law, there could never be an action in contract for non-payment. The defendant would argue that, having not paid, no consideration has been provided, no contract therefore subsists.

84 The use of 'digital cash' in exchange for goods or services raises issues not of consideration but of performance of a contract. For this reason the legal issues involved with digital cash are examined under 'Performance: Payment' at p 42.

If a web-wrap contract is properly constructed it seems likely that there is consideration to form a binding contract with the viewer. What the developer of the website must attempt to create is a set of mutual promises that will form the consideration for the contract. One method of achieving this is to *actually prevent* a viewer who does not click the 'I Agree' link or icon from entering the site itself. Promising the viewer access to the site if the 'I Agree' link is selected then forms one of the promises to bind the contract. The other promise must come from the viewer. This, of course, is to promise to abide by the terms of licence. This prevention can then be classed as a promise to allow the viewer into the website if he agrees to the terms on the screen. Such a legally robust suggestion would have no commercial support unless the site was very worried about exposing itself to liability.

Website designers and legal advisers should work together to ensure that the contract is formed at the correct time. The contract will not work retroactively; if a website owner is concerned to exclude liability for material on his home page a contract should appear before the home page. From a designer's perspective, foisting a legal document on a new viewer may not be appropriate[85]. Ultimately the disciplines of law, design and IT must meet in the middle: the greater the risk of liability and infringement (outside an implied licence) the greater the need for a lawyer to ensure the site binds visitors to a contract. Many sites may well decide it is better to run the risk of there being no valid contract than to risk losing an annoyed visitor to a competing site.

Intention

The fourth and final ingredient to create a binding contract is an intention to create legal relations. The reason that this is a factor in resolving a contractual issue over the Internet is that often only one human is involved. When a person makes an agreement with a website, the site accepts or rejects the communication by the person according to a computer program being run at the time. A human does not sit on the server side of the website. This raises the issue of how the contract can be formed without this direct intention. It is not complicated, nor unique to the Internet, but is a factor which advisers should not overlook: bugs in these programs will not negative the owner's intention.

Programmed intention

In *Thornton v Shoe Lane Parking*[86] Mr Thornton accepted a contract by driving a car into a car park. In that case, Lord Denning stated that the automatic reaction of the car park turning a light from red to green and thrusting a ticket was enough to create a contract[87]. All the ingredients were present. It is of no legal consequence that the contract was physically completed by a machine. The court looks objectively to whether a contract can be said to have been made: has the user been induced reasonably to believe that a contract was being made or offered? In comparison, it is of no legal consequence that a computer program

85 A contract in a frame and a simple home page can be an acceptable compromise.
86 [1971] 2 QB 163.
87 [1971] 2 QB 163 at 169.

completes the contract over the Internet; many contracts are 'made' with machines. That a computer program is being relied upon, however, can be of commercial significance to its owner.

Usually web-wrap contracts and automated email contracts use an express agreement. If, as a result of a bug in the contracting program, the viewer's offer is accepted in error, the court will presume that there was the requisite intention. The offeror has the heavy burden to prove that there was no intention to have a legal consequence[88]. The subjective opinion of, say, the owner of the website is of little consequence to the court[89], unless the viewer knew of the lack of intention.

14. For the payment of £10 a website allows its viewers to download pictures of a certain quality. An additional payment of £2 allows viewers to download the pictures at a higher resolution, which are more appropriate for professional use in brochures and magazines. An error in the Java script permits viewers to download any of the pictures for £10. The website owner will be hard pressed to claim the extra £2: the viewers are unlikely to know of the private intention.

Owners of websites who seek to use them for forming contracts should be aware that an error in their automated program may be of great financial consequence. In December 2001, Kodak's website in error offered and accepted £100 credit card payments for a £329 camera. Such validation programs should be carefully checked and, where possible, the owner should seek to obtain an indemnity from the programmer against such loss or, if not, insurance.

PERFORMANCE: PAYMENT

Internet payment

It has been discussed that the Internet can be used to make an offer and accept that offer. What has not been explained is how the Internet can be used to pay for the goods or services that may be the subject of the offer.

The introduction to this book explains in detail that everything passing through the Internet consists of digital ones and zeros. What varies is the way that digital stream is translated into an item at the end of its journey. The same can be said for methods of payment: unless the payment is made outside the confines of the Internet, the payment must be converted into zeros and ones[90]. There are two problems with this that do not concern us, but which are mentioned for completeness. The first problem is associated with the way the Internet moves digital streams between computers: they do not move directly; they can pass through many different computers on their way to a destination. Passing money through unknown computers is clearly unsafe. The second problem is that if digital money consists of only ones and zeros in a long string, it

88 *Edwards v Skyways Ltd* [1964] 1 WLR 349 at 355.
89 See *Smith v Hughes* (1871) LR 6 QB 597.
90 A contract could be made over the Internet and a cheque sent by conventional mail.

may be easy to duplicate the money. Any computer could potentially become a forgery for digital bank notes.

The technical solutions to both these problems are being addressed by many companies across the world. There are many companies using sophisticated encryption methods to secure the payment technically. Internet browsers and website servers allow credit card details to be sent over the Internet securely; some companies issue what is, in effect, a digital travellers' cheque that can also be sent securely across the Internet. To the banking industry, the European Central Bank, the Bank of England and banking lawyers this issue of cash is obviously both interesting and important. Indeed, it has prompted the Electronic Money Directive and requisite UK legislation[91]. For the seller, buyer and their lawyers these new 'forms' of payment do not have any dramatic impact on contract law.

Credit card non-payment

That there is a contract must be distinguished from who should pay for the goods or services, and what happens if that payment does not arrive. With a charge or credit card, the customer, by presenting a valid card, or by issuing a valid set of numbers, honours his obligations under the contract. Of course, at this point, a further contract comes into existence between the card company and the user to pay to the card company the full sum under the vendor's contract. If the card company does not pay the vendor, *and the card was valid*, the vendor's right of action is against the card company, not the individual[92]. One justification for this is that if the vendor was entitled to pursue the customer for payment in cash, the customer would lose the benefit of the payment by credit and, often, the insurance over the goods[93]. This would therefore increase the burden on the customer.

The commercially safest way of trading over the Internet is for vendors to insist on receiving and then validating payment *before* providing their side of the bargain. Terms to this effect should be incorporated into any standard form electronic commerce contract.

Digital cash non-payment

Digital cash has two species. The first, more primitive, is like a charge card. The issuing bank provides the payment to the vendor on presentation of appropriate authority. The sum is then withdrawn from the user's account and transferred to the vendor's. Over the Internet this appropriate authority will be no more than the card number and, perhaps, its expiry date. This species can be called 'third party digital cash'. The second species of digital money is close to actual cash and will be called 'pure digital cash'. A customer has an agreement with a digital

91 Directive 2000/46/EC on the taking up, pursuit of and prudential supervision of the business of electronic money institutions (and to a lesser extent, Directive (2000/28/EC)); The Financial Services and Markets Act 2000 (Regulated Activities) (Amendment) Order 2002; The Electronic Money (Miscellaneous Amendments) Regulations 2002.

92 *Re Charge Card Services Ltd* [1989] Ch 497, generally approved by the Court of Appeal in *Re Bank of Credit and Commerce International SA (No 8)* [1996] 2 All ER 121 at 133.

93 See, for example, the Consumer Credit Act 1974, s 75 which makes the credit card company liable for the vendor's misrepresentations and breaches of contract.

cash provider[94] who allows the customer to send encrypted messages which represent sums of money. Once a customer sends one of these encrypted messages to a vendor, it can then be subsequently used by the vendor without having to go to the issuing bank for exchange into cash. The only time when the message will be exchanged into more regular currency is when someone seeks to deposit it in their bank. This new form of payment does not greatly strain existing contractual principles of payment.

Third party digital cash

As with a credit card, it is likely that a court will find that the issuing company is liable for the payment, rather than the user[95]. This view is carefully stated as being 'likely'. Both vendor and user should consider that the Court of Appeal has concluded that, merely because a third party has agreed to make payment to a vendor does not automatically mean that the risk of non-payment is removed from the user[96].

Pure digital cash

Paying by the second species of digital money can be thought of as sending cash for most legal purposes. If the encrypted sum is lost on the Internet, or perhaps intercepted, the intended receiver will, no doubt, claim that payment has not been made. To some extent this is the general rule: sending a banknote in the post, which is lost, will not constitute payment[97]. However, this appears inequitable where the intended receiver expressly permits payment to be made by such a method. Indeed, there is followed authority that if the intended receiver impliedly, or as will be the situation over the Internet, expressly, authorises transmission of payment in a particular way, the sender is discharged of liability if he follows the guidelines of transmission[98].

15. A website offers two methods for its viewers to pay to gain access to its materials: by credit card and by digital cash. A viewer sends by email the digital cash, accesses the materials, but the cash is never received. The viewer may not be liable to pay again. The site impliedly authorises its customers to pay using the Internet as the conduit: the owner may not be able to transfer this risk to its customers having so authorised them.

If a website seeks to allow payment to be made using digital cash, in either species, it must face the reality that the sum may not arrive. It should therefore incorporate into its contracts a term stipulating that its performance under the contract will be honoured only after receipt of the digital cash. Customers, in anticipation of this, should be wary of sending uninsured digital cash over the Internet. If the contract is suitably worded and held enforceable, the customer may lose the money and not benefit from the contract.

94 Or so-called 'ELMI', Electronic Money Institution, in the Electronic Money Directive.
95 See 'Credit card non-payment', at p 43.
96 See *Re Charge Card Services Ltd* [1988] 3 All ER 702 at 707.
97 See *Luttges v Sherwood* (1895) 11 TLR 233.
98 *Norman v Ricketts* (1886) 3 TLR 182.

TYPE OF CONTRACT

Many owners of websites do not only make contracts over the Internet, but also try to perform them over the Internet. Software companies distribute software from websites; information and picture libraries provide digital copies of their information. Movies and music are sent across the Internet for payment. The various intellectual property rights that may vest in these items are discussed in the chapter on intellectual property. What is important here is to examine what should be the nature of the contract with the receiver of the digital information. The answer is a licence, and certainly not a sale, but justification for this is provided below. The first justification is to attempt to side-step the principle of exhaustion of rights; the second, peculiar to digitised material, is to grant a licence to the user of the material.

Exhaustion of rights

If digitised copyright goods are *sold*, rather than licensed, within the EC there is a risk that the exhaustion of rights principle will apply. This principle is broadly that once goods protected by intellectual property rights are sold in any Member State with the consent of the owner, national intellectual property laws cannot be used to block the goods' entry into another Member State. The Copyright, Designs and Patents Act 1988 states this explicitly at s 27(5). Section 27(3A), for good measure, applies that principle to computer software: a copy of a computer program which has previously been sold in any Member State by or with consent of the copyright owner will not be classed as an infringing copying within s 27(3)[99].

Retention of title

Partially as an attempt to avoid the application of this principle, many producers of digital material do not sell it; they license it. To avoid being viewed as selling the material many manufacturers include a 'shrink-wrap' licence which explicitly retains title in the goods being passed to the consumer and states words to the effect, often in emboldened capitals, 'This software is not sold to you; we are licensing it to you'.

Using is copying

The material downloaded over the Internet is likely to be given legal recognition and protection as a copyright work under the Copyright, Designs and Patents Act 1988. It is this intellectual property right that forms the foundation for any transaction.

99 See also Directive 2001/29/EC of the European Parliament and of the Council of 22 May 2001 on the Harmonisation of Certain Aspects of Copyright and Related Rights in the Information Society, art 4(2).

For digital material to be used, it must first be transferred into a computer's memory[100]. This transfer exactly reproduces in the memory of the computer the words and characters of the material sent from the server. The material on the server remains unchanged and intact; two copies of the material now exist. An obvious comparison is that when one views a painting, the painting remains on the canvas and there is no need to copy the work. A digital version of the same painting can only be viewed by being copied.

The Copyright, Designs and Patents Act 1988 grants certain rights to the owner of a copyright work. In particular, s 16(1)(a) states that the owner has the exclusive right to copy the work. Thus, without a licence from the owner, under s 16(2), copying the work can constitute infringement of the copyright in the work. Copying any copyright work is defined widely as reproducing the work as a whole, or any substantial part, in any material form. This includes storing the work in a medium by electronic means[101].

The viewer of the actual painting, like the viewer of the digitised version, is able to enjoy viewing an artistic work which attracts copyright protection. However, the viewing of the canvas does not involve a reproduction of the work in a material form. It can be seen, therefore, that normal use of a painting does not copy the copyright work. Conversely, an accurate application of the Copyright, Designs and Patents Act 1988 suggests that normal usage of any downloaded material will be regarded as a copy of the copyright work. This is because the digitised material is necessarily reproduced by downloading it from the server into the computer's memory.

Implied licence

The above analysis may appear to indicate that if the owner of a website does not give an express licence to each viewer of the site, each viewer is an infringer. This is not the case: copying a copyright work is not infringement if there is a licence permitting that copying. In the situation of the Internet there is undoubtedly a licence for authorised viewers and downloaders of material to copy the work.

First, the law is likely to imply a licence into the actions of the website owner for reasons of business necessity. Second, a court could apply the so-called 'rule of non-derogation from grant' to prevent the publisher, having supplied the material, then alleging infringement[102]. Third, but specifically for computer programs, the Directive on the Legal Protection of Computer Programs at art 5.1 specifies that the 'lawful acquirer' of a computer program shall not require authorisation by the copyright owner to run a computer program in the absence of specific contractual provisions. Fourth, temporary copies of works other than new programs or databases will be permitted for lawful use of the work[103].

100 This transfer is called 'loading'. This should not be confused with 'running' a program when a computer carries out the instructions specified by a program that has already been loaded.

101 Copyright, Designs and Patents Act 1988, ss 16(3)(a) and 17(2).

102 See *British Leyland v Armstrong* [1986] RPC 279.

103 See the Copyright, Designs and Patents Act 1988, ss 50A, 50B, 50C, inserted by the Copyright (Computer Programs) Regulations 1992, SI 1992/3233, reg 8. Also, art 5.1 of the EC Copyright Directive 2001.

Express licence

For programs, therefore, the Copyright, Designs and Patents Act 1988 expressly provides that a user has a right to copy the program into memory for its use. Until the implementation of the Copyright Directive, art 5.1, viewers of graphics and sound, movies and music, must rely on implications by the common law to legitimise their activities. Even after the implementation of art 5.1, non-temporary use will rely on common law. And for programs, graphics and sound alike, the supplier of those materials may have to accept a court's wide understanding of what type of licence is implied. For example, a designer of a graphic image used as a backdrop for a website frame may not want its viewers to copy the image onto their own publications. To expressly prevent these unwanted uses, owners of copyright material used on the Internet are advised to use on-screen licences that leave no non-temporary uses of the material to doubt or disagreement.

In providing a licence over the copyright material some publishers go further to attempt to exclude liability for certain damage caused by the material. The efficacy of these exclusion clauses is examined in the chapter on tort, but one point is worth noting here. The English courts will not uphold every exclusion clause. This is particularly true where the clause excludes liability to a consumer.

The conclusion from this section is simple: publishers should include express licences over their digital work to avoid exhaustion of rights and disagreements over acceptable use of the work.

JURISDICTION

Every contract may form the basis of a dispute. Because the Internet allows an owner of a website to conduct transactions with consumers and businesses from anywhere on the planet it is convenient for that owner to know where he can rightfully sue and be sued. The question over where a contract should be litigated is a question of private international law, or the conflict of laws.

The Brussels Regulation on Jurisdiction and the Enforcement of Judgments in Civil and Commercial Matters is the appropriate starting place for any contract formed over the Internet with a European element[104]. First, one must assess whether the Regulation applies or whether it 'transfers' jurisdiction to the English common law.

Brussels Regulation Jurisdiction

Civil and commercial matter

Most contracts made over the Internet will fall within art 1, that is, the resulting dispute is a civil and commercial matter. Before deciding that the Regulation

104 This entered into force, replacing the Brussels Convention, on 1 March 2002 (2001 OJ L012, 16.01.2001).

applies, litigants are advised to consider specialist texts and cases from the European Court which highlight the broad scope of art 1 under the previous 1968 Brussels Convention.

Domicile of defendant

Subject to Articles outside the scope of this chapter, the fundamental issue is where the defendant is domiciled. Article 2 establishes that persons domiciled in a Member State[105] can be sued in the courts of that state, sometimes with the claimant having a choice of another forum. Articles 59 and 60 direct the English courts to consider the domicile of the defendant with reference to the UK's 'internal law'[106]. Even for ecommerce contracts, jurisdiction hinges on 'domicile', an essentially static concept which is mostly unrelated to the complex factors such as where a server is based[107].

For Regulation purposes, a defendant can be domiciled in one of two types of state: a Member State or a non-Member State. If the defendant is domiciled within a Member State, the Regulation rules apply; if outside, the common law rules will apply. These two outcomes are decided, currently, with reference to the Civil Jurisdiction and Judgments Act 1982, as amended.

Individual's domicile

UK domicile

An individual is domiciled within the UK only if he is resident in the UK and the nature and circumstances of his residence indicate that he has a substantial connection with the UK[108]. It is presumed, unless proved otherwise, that being resident for the last three months or more will constitute the requisite substantial connection[109]. The ownership, control or access to a website anywhere in the world is wholly irrelevant for the purposes of jurisdiction over an individual under the Regulation. If an individual is a UK resident nothing will be gained for jurisdiction purposes by locating a web server 'offshore'.

Member State domicile

If an individual is not domiciled in the UK for the purposes of the Regulation, one must decide whether the individual is domiciled within another member state. If he is not, the Regulation will not apply to the dispute; questions of jurisdiction will then be resolved at common law.

105 Ie any Member State with the exception of Denmark.

106 The Civil Jurisdiction and Judgments Act 1982 (as amended by both the Civil Jurisdiction and Judgments Act 1991 and the Civil Jurisdiction and Judgments Order 2001), ss 4 and 42.

107 Prescribed as being relevant tests by the Civil Procedure Rules 1998, rr 6.18(g) and 6.19(1).

108 Civil Jurisdiction and Judgments Act 1982 (as amended by both the Civil Jurisdiction and Judgments Act 1991 and the Civil Jurisdiction and Judgments Order 2001), s 41(2).

109 Civil Jurisdiction and Judgments Act 1982 (as amended by both the Civil Jurisdiction and Judgments Act 1991 and the Civil Jurisdiction and Judgments Order 2001), s 41(6).

An individual is domiciled in a state other than the UK if that other state would view him as domiciled in that state. Therefore, to determine whether a defendant in an Internet contract dispute is domiciled within a Member State that person's domicile must be assessed from that state's legal perspective[110]. Failing this, the Civil Jurisdiction and Judgments Act 1982 (as amended), s 41(7) establishes the test to determine whether a defendant is domiciled outside Member States.

Non-Member State domicile

An individual is domiciled outside all the Member States if none of those states would deem him to be domiciled within their jurisdiction and if a further two-part test is satisfied. First, the individual must be resident in the non-Member State, and second, the nature and circumstances of his residence indicate that he has a substantial connection with that state[111]. One is not required to consult the non-Member State's law on domicile.

16. An English programmer who lives in England allows downloads of his shareware programs to be made from an American web server. Another programmer, also from England, appropriately transfers his digital cash payment for the software but does not receive a working copy of the software and so litigates. Without a jurisdiction clause in the contract, the English courts will have jurisdiction over the dispute as the defendant is domiciled in England. The location of the server is of no relevance for jurisdiction over the programmer in the English courts.

If the result of the domicile tests is that an individual defendant is domiciled within a Member State, the Regulation will apply to any other questions of jurisdiction. If the result is that the defendant is domiciled outside the Member States, the English common law rules on jurisdiction will apply[112]. These are described after the Regulation regime[113].

Company's or other legal person's domicile

A company or other legal person has its domicile in the state where it has its statutory seat, or central administration, or principal place of business[114].

UK domicile

A company or other legal person is domiciled within the UK if it was incorporated or formed under a law of a part of the UK, and its registered office or

110 Brussels Regulation, art 59 (2).
111 Civil Jurisdiction and Judgments Act 1982 (as amended by both the Civil Jurisdiction and Judgments Act 1991 and the Civil Jurisdiction and Judgments Order 2001), s 41(7).
112 Article 4.
113 See 'Common law jurisdiction over contracts', at p 56.
114 Article 60(1).

other official address is in the UK; or if its central administration or principal place of business is in the UK[115]. Again, the ownership, control or access to a website anywhere in the world is mostly irrelevant for the purposes of jurisdiction under the Regulation. A corporation which is, in effect, based in the UK will not be able to avoid the jurisdiction of the English courts simply by using an offshore server.

Member State domicile

If a company or other legal person is not domiciled in the UK for the purposes of the Regulation, one must decide whether it is domiciled within another Member State. If it is not, the Regulation will not apply to the dispute; questions of jurisdiction are decided with recourse to the common law. A company or other legal person is domiciled in a state other than the UK if it satisfies two tests.

First, the English courts must be satisfied that the company or other legal person was incorporated or formed under the law of that other Member State, or, its central management and control is exercised in that State[116].

The second test that must also be affirmatively answered, is that the entity shall not have been incorporated or formed under the law of a part of the UK, or, shown not to be regarded by the courts of the other Member State to have its seat within that Member State[117]. If either test is not satisfied, the common law rules on jurisdiction will apply[118]; these are discussed after the Regulation rules.

17. A health-food company is incorporated and operates from England. It sells edible flowers across the world. Its server is physically based in New Zealand and the domain name has a suffix indicating a New Zealand firm. A French supplier of health food enters into a contract, over the Internet, for a large shipment of particular sweet edible flowers. The contract does not have a jurisdiction clause. The flowers do not arrive and the health-food company claims it is not at fault. The French supplier tries to sue the company in the English courts. The use of an offshore server will have no bearing on the court's jurisdiction over the company. The English courts will have jurisdiction over the company at least for the reason that it would consider the company as having its seat within England.

Non-Member State domicile

If both of the previous tests fail to establish the defendant as domiciled in the UK or another Member State, the common law rules on jurisdiction will apply.

115 Civil Jurisdiction and Judgments Act 1982 (as amended by both the Civil Jurisdiction and Judgments Act 1991 and the Civil Jurisdiction and Judgments Order 2001), s 42(2).
116 Civil Jurisdiction and Judgments Act 1982 (as amended by both the Civil Jurisdiction and Judgments Act 1991 and the Civil Jurisdiction and Judgments Order 2001), s 43(3).
117 Civil Jurisdiction and Judgments Act 1982 (as amended by both the Civil Jurisdiction and Judgments Act 1991 and the Civil Jurisdiction and Judgments Order 2001), s 43(4).
118 Article 4.

Regulation jurisdiction over contract

Having decided that the Regulation applies, unless the contract is classed as a consumer, insurance or employment contract or unless the contract has a jurisdiction clause, the defendant may be sued in the courts of his domicile[119] or 'in the courts for the place of performance of the obligation in question'[120].

Place of performance for sale of goods or supply of services

For sales of goods and supplies of services unless agreed otherwise, there are two presumptions as to the place of their performance. Where goods are sold (or should have been sold) under contract, the relevant court is in the place in a Member State where the goods were delivered or should have been delivered. In the case of services, a similar approach must be followed. The relevant court is the one in the Member State where the services were provided or should have been provided[121]. If neither presumption applies, one must look to resolve the more general question of where was the 'place of performance of the obligation in question'[122].

18. A website called StockTaken.de operates from and is based in Germany. It allows business users to specify what industrial equipment they need and at what price. Once sufficient numbers of buyers have pledged an interest in particular equipment, an invoice is issued to the buyers and the equipment shipped to them. There is no jurisdiction clause in the agreements between StockTaken.de and its buyers. A business in England receives the equipment it ordered, faulty. Despite StockTaken.de being based in Germany, it may be sued in the English courts as its principal obligation, breached, must have been to deliver non-defective equipment in England[123].

19. OurFastParts.com operates an EU business-to-business website allowing its members to barter parts for vehicles. No money changes hands. One member, the Seller, lists the parts he wants to 'sell' and other members, the Buyers, will bid for those parts using their own parts which they want to sell. After a certain period, the Seller may conclude his barter with a Buyer. To avoid disputes about which is the relevant court for this bilateral delivery of goods, the member agreement states that 'the Parties irrevocably agree that for the purposes of the Brussels Regulation, Article 5, the place of performance of the obligation to trade the Parts shall be the place in the Member State where the Seller delivered or should have delivered his Parts'.

119 Article 2(1).
120 Article 5(1)(a).
121 Article 5(1)(b).
122 Article 5(1)(c).
123 See *MBM Fabri Clad Ltd v Eisen Und Huntle werke Thale AG* (3 November 1999, unreported), CA.

Other obligations

Where the contract does not relate to sales of goods or supplies of services, one must concentrate on the 'obligation in question'. Lord Goff puts this as 'regard must be had to the contractual obligation under consideration and not to the contract as a whole'[124]. This may result in a court which does not have the closest connection with the dispute being seized of the action. It should therefore be obvious that the pleading of the contractual claim, or rather, the principal contractual obligation, is critical to any question of jurisdiction. Further, advisers should note that to determine what is the principal obligation, they might rely on what law would apply to the obligation[125].

Europe-based owners of websites who are concerned about being sued outside their home state should therefore be concerned to have jurisdiction clauses in their contracts if their principal obligations must be performed outside their home state[126] or if their ecommerce agreements are with consumers. As will be discussed, consumers can sue and can only be sued in their home state[127]. As many of the users of the Internet are consumers but the majority of website owners are suppliers or professionals, this application of jurisdiction will frequently occur. Those who own websites, therefore, may find themselves having to litigate and be sued away from home.

Consumer contracts

At first glance it may appear there is a straightforward answer to the question of which is the correct forum for a dispute over a contract made with a consumer. The Brussels Regulation (and the Convention more than 30 years older) contains rules to protect consumers in relation to consumer contracts, from being sued, or having to sue, otherwise than in the member state of their domicile[128]. What is important is that art 15 defines a 'consumer contract', inter alia, as one concluded which can be regarded as being outside the consumer's trade or profession[129] where the contract is:

(a) for the sale of goods on instalment credit terms; or[130]

124 *Union Transport plc v Continental Lines SA* [1992] 1 WLR 15 at 19H, referring to *Etablissements A de Bloos SPRL v Societes en Commandité par Actions Bayer* (Case 14/76) [1976] ECR 1497. Also see *Custom Made Commercial Ltd v Stawa Metallban GmbH* (C– 288/92) [1994] ECR I–2913, paras 14–23 and *Barry v Bradshaw and Co (a firm)* [2000] CLC 455, CA. Note the reluctance of Lord Justice Pitt to accept that: 'When a professional man is instructed to perform services in one jurisdiction he becomes liable to another Brussels Convention jurisdiction if the services include dealing with a public authority in that other jurisdiction.'

125 *Industrie Tessili Italiana Corp v Dunlop* (Case 12/76) [1976] ECR 1473, para 13; *Custom Made Commercial Ltd v Stawa Metallban GmbH* (C–288/92) [1994] ECR I–2913, para.26; *GIE Groupe Concorde v Master of Vessel Suhadiwarno Panjan* (C–440/97) [1999] ECR I–6307, para 32; *Leathertex Divisione Sinitetici SpA v Bodetex BVBA* (C–420/97) [1999] 2 All ER (Comm) 769.

126 See *MBM Fabri Clad Ltd v Eisen Und Huntle werke Thale AG* (3 November 1999, unreported), CA.

127 Articles 15, 16 and 17.

128 Brussels Convention, arts 13 and 14, and the Brussels Regulation, arts 15 and 16. The Civil Jurisdiction and Judgments Act 1982, s 8(1) and 8(2) (as amended by the Civil Jurisdiction and Judgments Order 2001) specifies that, in the UK, the courts where a consumer must be sued and can sue are those in the 'part' of the UK where they are domiciled. At the time of writing the three parts are: England and Wales, Scotland and Northern Ireland.

129 Brussels Regulation, art 15(1).

130 Brussels Regulation, art 15(1)(a).

(b) for a loan repayable by instalments, or for any other form[131] of credit, made to finance the sale of goods; or

(c) in all other cases, the contract has been concluded with a person who pursues commercial or professional activities in the Member State of the consumer's domicile, or, by any means, directs such activities to that Member State or the several states including that Member State, and the contract falls within the scope of such activities[132].

Article 15(1)(c) was introduced, after much negotiation and analysis, to ensure that consumers who transact, for example, over the Internet are protected by the special rules on jurisdiction[133].

Articles 15(1)(a) and (b) are self-explanatory and not 'Internet' specific. The same is not true for art 15(1)(c). This new addition to the Brussels rules of jurisdiction was meant to provide certainty to consumer and to businesses. As the following discussion will illustrate, it does not. Fortunately there are steps that businesses can take to minimise the risk of being sued in a Member State other than their own or one acceptable to them.

Article 15(1)(c) can apply in two situations. First, where the supplier 'pursues commercial or professional activities in the Member State of the consumer's domicile and the contract falls within the scope of such activities'. The second situation is where the supplier 'by any means directs commercial or professional activities to the Member State of the consumer's domicile or to several States including that Member State and the contract falls within the scope of such activities'. These two situations will be examined separately.

Pursuing activities in consumer's Member State

A key aspect to this situation is that the contract being litigated must fall within the scope of the activities being pursued in the Member State of the consumer's domicile. This is important. Many businesses conduct a great number of commercial and professional activities abroad. A website may promote employment opportunities for individuals living in the Member State. Glossy advertisements in financial newspapers within that Member State may also promote the business in a wider sense. On paper, the business may appeal to current and potential shareholders and stakeholders in the business. The business may also regularly attend trade fairs and exhibitions in the Member State to illustrate the business's success, almost as a way to ward off competitors. And all these activities may be actively pursued within the consumer's Member State.

What art 15(1)(c) requires, however, is something more. The pursuit of the activities within the consumer's Member State *must relate* to the consumer's contract under dispute[134].

131 Brussels Regulation, art 15(1)(b).

132 Brussels Regulation, art 15(1)(c).

133 See, for example, the various speakers reported in the Department of Trade and Industry's Consumer Affairs Report on the Revision of the Brussels Convention and the Proposals for a Community Regulation (2 November 1999).

134 The European Council and Commission's Joint Statement on arts 15 and 68 states that 'for Article 15.1(c) to be applicable it is not sufficient for an undertaking to target it's [*sic*] activities at the Member State of the consumer's residence, or at a number of Member States including that Member State; a contract must also be concluded within the framework of it's [*sic*] activities'.

20. Ratty-Ionise is an Italian company that operates a website selling its biochemical, free-standing, air-conditioning unit. The unit is expensive but is very popular in small offices in London. Ratty-Ionise regularly attend trade shows in the UK where it communicates with its local distributors. Without any other activity in the UK, consumers who order a unit for their home will not benefit from the additional protection afforded by the Brussels Regulation.

Many European businesses will wish to be selective as to which member states' jurisdictions they are subject. These businesses must examine *all* of their activities within each particular Member State of concern. They will need to ensure that any contracts entered into with consumers in that Member State are not related to any other commercial or professional activities pursued in those Member States.

By any means directs activities to several member states

This second leg of art 15(1)(c) begs the obvious question: when is a website 'directed' to several member states? Ultimately, it will be for the courts to decide this on a case-by-case basis. In the meantime, however, readers will not be helped by consulting the European Council, European Commission and DTI's musings on the issue. The Joint Statement issued by the European Council and Commission states:

> 'the mere fact that an Internet site is accessible is not sufficient for Article 15 to be applicable, although a factor will be that this Internet site solicits the conclusion of distance contracts and that a contract has actually been concluded at a distance, by whatever means. In this respect, the language or currency which a website uses does not constitute a relevant factor.'

One takes from this that it is the conduct of commerce in the member state that determines whether or not activities are directed to that member state. If those from the UK, for instance, cannot *transact* with the site (but can still view it) it would seem that the Council and Commission deem this not to be 'directed' at the UK. And this is even the case if the site is written in English and uses pounds sterling and not euros. This can be contrasted with the DTI's more ecommerce-friendly interpretation:

> 'We believe that [to determine whether a website falls within Article 15(1)(c)]:
> - it would be necessary to look at the nature of any given website;
> - websites giving information in different Community languages and currencies and offering to deliver to EU countries might well be covered by Article 15;
> - some websites (e.g. a site in English with prices in pounds and confining orders to UK customers) might be hard to describe as directed anywhere but the UK.'

The DTI here appears to be taking a narrower view than the European Council and Commission. It is essentially concluding that the mere fact that a transaction takes place on a site does not mean that the site has been directed at any particular member state. It is the 'nature' of the website that determines where, if anywhere, it is directed.

These are very different approaches. The Council and Commission explains that one must avoid *transacting* with consumers in a particular member state; the DTI explains that one must avoid *appealing* to consumers in a particular member state. This author sides with the DTI. Its interpretation is likely to be closer to a court's. The Article speaks of 'commercial and professional activities' being directed to the member state. It therefore is focused not particularly on the *contract* but on the *pre*-contractual enticement.

On this basis, how does one structure a website to avoid the bite of art 15(1)(c)? It is not trivial. Nevertheless, steps can be taken to reduce a business's chance of transacting over the Internet with consumers within a particular Member State. First, the business can operate a website which requests the user's jurisdiction from a 'drop-down' menu or a series of flags. This allows the business to shield out a consumer from a particular country. More sophisticated still, a business can make technical checks of the user's computer and connecting server. For example, the business can check for the server time zone and the language setting of the user's browser. In addition, the business can conduct a 'reverse DNS lookup' where the domain name of the user's service provider is used to locate the server. Not one of these steps is foolproof. Combined, however, these checks can provide a reasonable approximation of whether the user is based in a 'friendly' Member State. If they are not based in the 'friendly' Member States make sure not to transact with them after they access the site.

21. 'NotWeeMen' is a company arranging adventure activities in the Scottish Highlands. The company has two main types of clientele: businesses conducting 'away days' in the UK and men arranging stag nights in Glasgow city centre. It ensures that all of its advertising outside the UK is about 'corporate bonding' and is contained in business journals. Its website, in contrast, solely describes the stag activities, is written only in English and features a price list of 'stag activities' in pounds sterling. It also details the various trains and planes that fly from around the UK to Glasgow. The company does not pursue the 'stag' activities in the EU by virtue of its advertising.

Jurisdiction clauses

Most on-screen licences and contracts specify that the courts of one state have exclusive jurisdiction. If one of the parties is domiciled in a contracting state, and the term refers to the court of a contracting state then that court has jurisdiction[135]. This applies only for those contracts not considered by a court to be a 'consumer contract'; a jurisdiction clause can only add to but not derogate from the protection afforded to consumers[136].

135 Brussels Regulation, art 23(1).
136 Brussels Regulation, art 17. Also see *Benincasa v Dentalkit Srl* [1998] All ER (EC) 136.

22. A UK consumer downloads some software from a French website after selecting an icon labelled 'I Agree' at the bottom of a set of terms and conditions. The contract makes clear that no goods are being sent to the consumer and that, anyway, no title passes to the consumer; the consumer is gaining only a licence to use the software. The final clause of the contract, in capitals, is 'By clicking "I Agree", you submit to the French courts to resolve any dispute arising under or related to this licence'. The consumer at a later date seeks to sue in an English court the owner of the website for breach of contract as the software is defective. The French website owner may have some success in preventing the English courts from accepting jurisdiction because the contract was a licence of software not a contract for a sale of goods or supply of services. As a result the jurisdiction clause may apply despite the contract being with a consumer.

Common law jurisdiction over contracts

If the defendant to an Internet contract is not domiciled within a contracting state[137], the court must apply its domestic laws to determine jurisdiction[138]. The main method is considered below: service out of the jurisdiction with permission. The aspect of this is jurisdiction to serve out the next, the application of the courts' discretion[139]. Service by presence in England is not considered in any detail[140], readers are advised to more general texts on private international law.

SERVICE OUT

There are two separate and distinct aspects to serving out of the jurisdiction[141]. The first aspect is jurisdiction: does the claimant's claim fall within one of the sub-rules of CPR r 6.20(5) and (6). Although not yet deeply analysed by the courts, it is likely that this test does not need to be satisfied to any high degree of proof: a good arguable case that the claim is covered by the one of the sub-rules is probably sufficient[142]. The second aspect, which will not be covered here in great detail, is one of discretion: no permission to serve a claim out of the jurisdiction will be given unless the court is satisfied that England and Wales is the proper place in which to bring the claim. This is specified by CPR r 6.21(2A).

137 See 'Domicile of defendant', at p 48.
138 Article 4.
139 See 'Discretion under service out', at p 59.
140 See CPR, r 6.2
141 See *Seaconsar v Bank Merkazi Jomhouri Islami Iran* [1994] 1 AC 438, which applied, and it is suggested remains applicable, under the old Rules of the Supreme Court, Ord 11.
142 See *Attock Cement Co Ltd v Romanian Bank for Foreign Trade* [1989] 1 All ER 1189, which applied, and it is suggested remains still applicable, under the old Rules of the Supreme Court, Ord 11.

Jurisdiction under a contract sub-rule

The most common sub-rules that will apply in certain cases for ecommerce contracts entered over the Internet is CPR r 6.20(5). This is where[143]:

> 'a claim is made in respect of a contract where the contract . . .'

The rule then goes on to describe a number of contracts which will fall for consideration under this rule. These include: a contract made within the jurisdiction; a contract made by or through an agent trading or residing within the jurisdiction; a contract containing a term that the court shall have jurisdiction to determine any claim made in respect of a breach of contract within the jurisdiction. For the purposes of Internet contracts, however, the most contentious rule is where the contract was made within the jurisdiction.

Where a contract is made

The earlier part of this chapter focuses on when a contract is deemed to have been made when formed by email or over the World Wide Web. It is now appropriate to consider *where* such a contract is formed. The implications of where a contract is formed are great. For example, if contracts made over the web are made at the place of the server it will be simple for an organisation always to ensure that their contracts are formed outside Europe, or any other jurisdiction they wish to avoid. A server can be physically located anywhere in the world despite its owner and clients being elsewhere. Conversely, if a contract is deemed to be formed wherever a consumer is situated at the time of making a contract the owner of a website may find himself making contracts throughout the world.

There is no case law on this area although by analogy it is submitted that contracts made using email will be viewed as being made where the acceptance (not acknowledgement) email is sent and contracts made over the World Wide Web will be viewed as being made where the client is located.

Email contracts

It has been suggested that an emailed acceptance is very like a posted acceptance in the eyes of the law: it can go astray and it depends on the actions of a third party for proper delivery without the sender necessarily knowing of its arrival[144]. In such circumstances this chapter has suggested that the exception should apply to the general rule of 'communication of acceptance': the so-called 'postal rule' should apply deeming the time of making the contract the time of its posting, not its receipt. It follows that the contract is completed when the letter is posted, or for our purposes, when the email is sent. This author's view is that the Electronic Commerce (EC Directive) Regulations 2002 add little to the private international law question of where a contract is formed[145].

The 'postal rule' also applies if an acceptance is not simply delayed in the post but if the acceptance never reaches the offeror[146]. It must therefore be true that

143 Of course, CPR r 6.20(1) and r 6.20(8) may be more appropriate in some circumstances.

144 See 'Acceptances by email', at p 34.

145 See Electronic Commerce Regulations 2002, reg 5 and Electronic Commerce Directive, art 1(4).

146 See *Household Fire and Carriage Accident, Insurance v Grant* (1879) 4 Ex D 216.

the contract is also made at that place of posting; if this were not the case, a letter which becomes lost in the post may be deemed to form a contract at a place where it was meant to arrive at a time before it could have arrived and, in fact, at a place where it never arrives. To avoid such fictions, the rule applied by the English courts has been that 'acceptance is complete as soon as the letter is put into the letter box, and that is the place where the contract is made'[147].

For a contract made purely using email, it is submitted that the place where the contract is made is the place from where the acceptor sent the email; it is not from where the server which sends the email is located. Just as a postal contract is made from the place at which the acceptor no longer has control over the letter, ie the letterbox, so the place where an email contract is made is at the acceptor's computer.

23. An American, who uses a German Internet Service Provider, sends an email to an English property developer. The email contains a certain offer to buy the individual's holiday home in Florida. The English property developer firmly accepts the offer by sending an email from his London offices. Technically, this email acceptance is sent from London, to a French server and then on to the American's inbox located in Germany. The American reads the email using a laptop computer and a mobile phone while in Mexico. If the contract is deemed to be formed when the English email was sent, it will be formed at the place where it was sent: London.

Website contracts

Contracts made over the World Wide Web, as previously examined, differ considerably from email contracts[148]. On the assumption made earlier that the general rule applies, and that there is no binding contract until notice of acceptance is able to be accessed by the offeror, the contract is made at the place where the offeror could receive notification of the acceptance; where the offeror is[149].

24. A bookseller based in Chicago establishes a website within a portal which is based in New York. The portal uses a standardised online order form which ensures users make offers which are then accepted, if appropriate, by the individual stores. A teacher in England orders two books by American authors and the website responds with an acceptance notice that the books would be delivered to the teacher's address. This contract is made in England because the notification of acceptance, to the teacher, is received in England.

The conclusion that a website 'makes' contracts wherever its customers are, assuming the website accepts and properly acknowledges acceptance, accords with the case law and also accords with the business reality of the World Wide Web. The web, more than any other medium, allows vendors from around the

147 *Entores Ltd v Miles Far East Corpn* [1955] 2 QB 327 at 332, per Denning LJ. Emphasis added. See also *Benaim v Debono* [1924] AC 514. This common law rule should contrasted with the Electronic Commerce (EC Directive) Regulations 2002, reg 11(2) which specifies *when* an order (which may be the acceptance) is deemed to be received.

148 See 'Acceptances over the World Wide Web', at p 36.

149 See *Entores v Miles Far East Corpn* [1955] 2 QB 327 at 336 per Parker LJ; also *Brinkibon Ltd v Stahag Stahl GmbH* [1983] 2 AC 34 at 41 and 43 respectively, per Lord Wilberforce and Lord Fraser.

world to sell easily to English consumers. For a vendor, it is akin to having an agent in every town in the world who can visit every customer at home. A user only needs to make a local phone call to and receive acceptances from foreign vendors at home. The contracts being formed have every indication that they are being made in England.

The reason for discussing where a contract is made, it will be recalled, was to demonstrate that an English consumer could serve a claim form out of England to a foreign website owner in respect of a contract. However, even if a dispute falls within one of the sub-rules under CPR r 6.20 a court has discretion whether to permit the service out.

Discretion under service out

It is not sufficient simply to satisfy a court of a good arguable case under one of the sub-rules under CPR r 6.20. The claim must also be a proper case for service out under CPR r 6.21(1A). The discretion to serve out includes as a main factor, an assessment, perhaps not overtly, of whether England is the *forum conveniens*, the most suitable forum in which to hear the dispute. This will be considered briefly in the following section on staying actions[150]. This discretionary factor should not be overlooked by legal advisers: for a contract made over the Internet it may be difficult to persuade a court to serve out. If the defendant, in contrast, is domiciled in Europe, the court has far less discretion over jurisdiction[151].

Staying actions

It is always open to a putative defendant to apply to stay the common law jurisdiction of the English courts by pleading that it is not the most suitable forum in which to resolve the dispute[152]. Whether a court stays an action is decided with recourse to the principle of *forum non conveniens*. This principle is impressively explained and stated in the House of Lords' decision in *Spiliada Maritime Corpn v Cansulex Ltd*[153]. In a later case Lord Goff explains *forum non conveniens* as 'a self-denying ordinance under which the court will stay (or dismiss) proceedings in favour of another clearly more appropriate forum'[154]. A full discussion of this case is beyond the scope of this chapter, but an appreciation of its implications is worthwhile. Until courts approach electronic commerce and Internet disputes with the familiarity and understanding that they approach, say the telephone and telex, litigators must be prepared to argue that despite the transnational nature of the Internet, some forums are more suitable than others.

Lord Goff provided the leading judgment given in *Spiliada*. He set out a number of guidelines[155] that may guide a court as to whether England is a

150 The court's assessment is the same, although for service out, the plaintiff must ask the court to exercise discretion; for staying service as of right, the defendant must persuade the court to stay the action.

151 See the Court of Appeal's interpretation of the Civil Jurisdiction and Judgments Act 1982, s 49 in *Re Harrods (Buenos Aires) Ltd* [1992] Ch 72.

152 CPR, Pt 11 provides the necessary procedure.

153 [1987] AC 460.

154 *Airbus Industrie GIE v Patel* [1999] 1 AC 119 at 132C.

155 The necessary details of these guidelines can be found in specialist texts but readers are also directed to the very full judgments in *Lubbe v Cape plc* [2001] 1 Lloyd's Rep 139, CA.

suitable and appropriate forum: the court must, in effect, balance the suitability of England against that of another forum. This forum must be clearly and distinctly more appropriate: one 'with which the action [has] the most real and substantial connection'[156]. At this point, 'the court may nevertheless decline to grant a stay if persuaded by the plaintiff, on whom the burden of proof then lies, that justice requires that a stay should not be granted'[157].

This discretion, unlikely to be disturbed on appeal[158], may be of paramount importance in an Internet dispute. In contrast to most other means of communication, the Internet can make it appear that a defendant has little connection with any country. A server may be in a country far away from the defendant's domicile. Worse than this, a defendant may be using a hosting company situated on the other side of the world. The contract and possibly digital product that is the root of the dispute may have passed through as many as one hundred countries. Worse still, it is a question of technical semantics to resolve whether the digital product moved from the server to the claimant or whether the claimant 'collected' the digital product from the server.

These issues, and many more like them, may be used to cloud the answer to which is the forum conveniens for the dispute. The pivotal question before the courts should be: which is the suitable forum in the interests of all the parties and the ends of justice?

The answering of this question involves examining the mechanics of hearing the dispute as well as its geographical basis. In illustration, often it is important to know where the relevant evidence is held and where the relevant witnesses live[159]. For many Internet disputes, however, such factors may not be weighty enough to disturb the jurisdiction of the court. Computer files will often be the main evidence and often the party in England will be the sole human witness to the contract itself. So, for an Internet dispute, the jurisdiction of the English court may be less easily upset. As a further illustration, the issue of convenience, often a factor for the court, may be less convincing when all of the actual evidence is in a digital format. Such evidence can be sent to England, over the Internet, cheaply, quickly and accurately. Again, the actual nature of the Internet may lead to the conclusion that little is lost by hearing the dispute in England.

The court must consider all the relevant factors, such as where the defendant and claimant are and which law will apply to this dispute. It is discussed in the next section that, without a choice of law clause, English law will generally apply to contracts made over the web with English consumers. Even with a choice of law clause, protection for English consumers will apply in addition to the stated law. And Lord Goff in *Spiliada* notes that the law of the dispute will often be a relevant factor[160]. What can be concluded from all this is that presence of the Internet in a contract dispute will never create the situation where no court is appropriate to hear the case.

156 *The Abidin Daver* [1984] 1 All ER 470, at 478 per Lord Keith.

157 *Conelly v RTZ Corpn plc* [1998] AC 854 at 872A, per Lord Goff for the House of Lords restating the second stage of the *Spiliada* test.

158 [1986] 3 All ER 843 at 846–847 per Lord Templeman.

159 See [1986] 3 All ER 843 at 855.

160 With reference *to Crédit Chimique v James Scott Engineering Group Ltd* 1982 SLT 131. In this Scottish case, Lord Jauncy goes further and asks that a court look not simply at the fact that foreign law will be applied, but to look deeper at the nature of the foreign law. It may be that it is trivial for an English court to turn its mind to the foreign law, but it also may be that the law is so alien that the most appropriate court to consider the legal issues is a court which regularly deals with them.

CHOICE OF LAW

Even as long ago as 1980, debates were commencing around the problems of examining the choice of law over computer networks such as the Internet[161].

> 'T]he question of choice of law . . . is particularly difficult in the case of international computer networks where, because of dispersed location and rapid movement of data, and geographically dispersed processing activities, several connecting factors could occur in a complex manner involving elements of legal novelty.'

The following section is included because the Internet makes the questions of choice of laws more prevalent. As ecommerce expands, more contracts will be formed between parties in different jurisdictions[162]. It is essential that the law which applies to a contract is established before applying the reasoning in this chapter. Readers must not be confused into concluding that the Electronic Commerce Directive, and its implementing Electronic Commerce (EC Directive) Regulations 2002, address these questions of private international law. First, they only apply to those Information Service Providers which are established within the EU. Second, the statutes certainly do not determine which country's *law* will apply in a given situation. They merely prevent an Information Service Provider established in a Member State outside the UK being restricted from conducting activities inside the UK which would have been legal in their Member State[163]. This chapter therefore describes nothing wider than the application of English law to a contract.

The Rome Convention

Where the litigation over a dispute takes place in England, and its substance is a contractual obligation made over the Internet, the Rome Convention[164] will generally apply[165]. This section is concerned mainly with those contracts where

161 Organisation for Economic Co-operation and Development, Explanatory Memorandum, Guidelines on the Protection of Privacy and Transborder Flows of Personal Data, 13, 36 (1980).

162 It is, of course, correct to state that the telephone, telex and fax also allow transnational contracts to be made. The significant difference between the Internet and these other means of communication is that there are no temporal, financial or logistical problems with contacting a website abroad. The site is permanently switched on, time differences are not a relevant factor; the cost may be no more than that of a local phone call, and there is no increase in marginal cost, unlike fax, telex and telephone.

163 Regulation 4.

164 The Rome Convention is incorporated into the Contracts (Applicable Law) Act 1990. References to articles within the Convention can be located in the Schedules to the domestic statute. The Convention can be interpreted by recourse to the Giuliano and Lagarde report (OJ 1980, C282/10), see the Contracts (Applicable Law) Act 1990, s 3(3)(a).

165 The justification for this bold statement is that the Convention applies to contracts made after 1 April 1991 (art 17). In view of the youth of widespread electronic commerce it is presumed that contracts made using the Internet were made after this date. Attention is drawn to art 1(2) which lists the exceptions of its application. These include, among others, contractual obligations relating to wills and succession (art 1(2)(b)) obligations arising under negotiable instruments to the extent that the obligations arise out of their negotiable character (art 1(2)(c)) questions governed by the law of companies such as creation, legal capacity, and personal liability of officers and members (art 1(2)(e)) and questions as to whether an agent is able to bind a principal (art 1(2)(f)). To give definitive advice, therefore, advisers should consult a specialist text.

one party contracts using a website. Before considering the Convention in greater detail one must address the obvious, and logically, first question: what is a contract? The answer is not merely that which English Law considers to be a contract. The laws of some other Convention countries do not demand 'consideration' or 'privity'. As a consequence, courts (and litigants before them) 'must clearly strive to take a single, international or "autonomous" view of the concept of contractual obligations . . .'[166] and not merely rely on an English-law view of a contract.

For the purposes of the Rome Convention, and therefore English law, there are two possible types of contract that can be made over the Internet: one in which the law that will govern the contract is agreed, and one in which it is not. These two possibilities will be dealt with, but it is worthwhile noting here that there is little justification for not including an applicable law in a contract. It provides more certainty, and some insurance policies will only protect claims under contracts governed by English law.

Express choice of law

The first issue to understand is that although an ecommerce contract may contain an agreed choice of law, other laws may be applicable in addition. It will be seen below that certain mandatory laws of England will be applied despite choice, and that consumers benefit from certain other protections.

It is significant that no special words are required to choose a law for a contract. The Convention states that a choice can be express, or demonstrated with reasonable certainty by the terms of the contract or the circumstances of the case[167]. Both parties should be aware, therefore, that an express choice may be deemed to have been made even where a contract does not express 'The Law governing this contract will be the laws of England'. Where a contract entered into over the Internet does express the choice in such unambiguous terms, that law will apply to the contract. In certain circumstances a chosen law will be modified by English mandatory laws and consumer protective measures[168].

Demonstration of choice

The Giuliano and Lagarde report provides some guidance of what is a demonstration with reasonable certainty that a contract is governed by a particular law[169]. Where a standard form is used, such as Lloyd's policy of marine insurance, it can be taken that a choice of English law has been made. However, this does not suggest that a standard form of a lesser known company can suffice as a reasonably certain demonstration. This is especially the case when contracting over the Internet where it is possible, for example, unknowingly, to enter a contract to buy an American piece of software but from a French distributor. In this scenario there will not be sufficient certainty to demonstrate any choice of law for the contract.

166 *Raiffeisen Zentralbank österreich AG v Five Star General Trading LLC* [2001] 3 All ER 257, at 26, para 33.
167 Article 3(1).
168 See 'Modifications to express or demonstrated law', at p 63.
169 OJ 1980, C282/10 at C282/17.

Other indicators within the terms of the contract may demonstrate this certainty. For example, references to the courts of England. In a shipping dispute, an arbitration clause in favour of England provided a 'strong indication of the parties' intention to choose English Law as the applicable law'[170]. References to English statutes are also indicative. References to the Copyright, Designs and Patents Act 1988 or the Consumer Credit Act 1974, may leave a court in no doubt that English law was always intended to apply despite the lack of its expression.

25. A web-wrap contract expresses that the jurisdiction of California shall apply for all disputes but that this will not exclude the application of any consumer protection laws applicable in the consumer's place of residence. No express choice of law is made. This confusion over jurisdiction and choice of law, and the lack of other indicators, will be unlikely to demonstrate the reasonable certainty required that a particular law was deliberately chosen.

Modifications to express or demonstrated law

Mandatory rules

Even though an ecommerce contract may expressly state that the law of France should apply, if all the other relevant factors to the situation at the time of choice are connected with one country only, the mandatory rules of that country will remain applicable[171]. A mandatory rule is one that cannot be derogated from by contract[172]. Examples from English law include the Employment Rights Act 1996. The most relevant example for contracting over the Internet is the Unfair Terms in Consumer Contracts Regulations 1999 and the Unfair Contract Terms Act 1977 (UCTA), s 27(2)[173]. This particular Act is discussed below.

A mandatory law will apply in the limited circumstances that all relevant factors are connected with one country. This is a high burden and one which will be difficult to satisfy where the parties reside in different countries. In such a situation, clearly not all the relevant factors are connected with solely one country. And where downloading, or shipment, occurs from a country other than that of the purchaser's residence the mandatory rules will be unlikely to operate.

One more point must be made about mandatory rules. The mandatory rules that may apply need not be those from England. The first test is to establish a country with which all the elements of the situation are connected. This country may be somewhere other than England. And if the second aspect of the test is satisfied, that the laws are mandatory, the English court must apply them in addition to the chosen or demonstrated law of the contract.

170 *Egon Oldendorff v Libera Corpn* [1996] 1 Lloyd's Rep 380, QBD, per Clark J.
171 Rome Convention, art 3(3).
172 A statute may state that it applies only to contracts governed by English law. If it does not, it is a matter of statutory construction to establish whether the statute is a mandatory law.
173 Unfair Contract Terms Act 1977, s 27(2)(a) states that the Act will apply also if a term in a contract appears to have been included 'wholly or mainly' to avoid the operation of the Act.

26. A website, based in England and controlled by an English company, uses the same contract for all those who wish to download its software. The contract specifies that the law of New York will apply. If an American contracts with the website and is then sued in England, it is unlikely that English mandatory rules will apply. In contrast, if an English consumer contracts with the site, it may appear that all the relevant elements relate to England so that the mandatory rules will apply.

This difference in application depending on who makes a contract with a website can pose certain difficulties: the main one is that, if the same contract is used for all jurisdictions, its effect will differ for different consumers (as opposed to businesses). Web owners should be conscious that using one standard form contract, and allowing a person from any jurisdiction to complete that contract, may result in an unforeseen situation. Where possible a website should use a contract that is, at the least, predictable for each of the possible locations from where a consumer may contract. Some website owners have a home page where their viewers must select their residence from a list before a contract is presented for their acceptance.

Modifications by the Electronic Commerce Directive?

Some readers may be confused by the paragraph above: do the Electronic Commerce Directive and Regulations not do away with this issue? The Electronic Commerce Directive does introduce, within the EU, a so-called 'country of origin rule'. This can be summed up as: 'what is legal at home should be legal abroad'[174]. The Directive does, however, specifically avoid 'trumping' the Rome Convention. Article 4 states that 'this Directive does not establish additional rules on private international law nor does it deal with the jurisdiction of the courts'. And for consumer contracts, the 'country of origin' rule or 'internal market' is weakened further. Indeed, the Directive clearly avoids suggesting that any member state's law could trump the law that would otherwise apply to a consumer contract. For example, 'contractual obligations concerning consumer cont[r]acts'[175]. The Electronic Commerce Directive does not, therefore, eliminate the need to look first to the law governing the contract under the Rome Convention and then to any mandatory laws that may be 'layered' on top of the applicable law.

Application of UCTA

Where a court deems that the mandatory laws of England do apply to a contract it is necessary to check whether UCTA applies. The Act will apply to certain contracts governed by non-English law, where either or both

> 'the [choice of law] term appears to the court . . . to have been imposed wholly or mainly for the purpose of enabling a party impos-

174 Article 3(1) and 3(2).
175 Article 3(3), Annex, sixth indent.

> ing it to evade the operation of this Act; or in the making of the contract one of the parties dealt as consumer, and he was then habitually resident in the United Kingdom, and the essential steps necessary for the making of the contract were taken there, whether by him or by others on his behalf.'

It is important to realise that the operation of this does not strike down the choice of foreign law; it merely makes the operation of that law subject to the effect of UCTA.

Despite the above, not all the protection that UCTA provides to consumers and businesses will be applicable to certain contracts made over the Internet. This is because, if the contract is an 'international supply contract', UCTA's rules on 'excluding or restricting' liability[176] will not apply.

An international supply contract has three features[177]. First, it must be either a contract for the sale of goods or one under or in pursuance of which the possession or ownership of goods passes. Second, it must be made between parties whose places of business or residences are in territories of different states. The third feature is that there must be an international aspect to the contract: the goods must be carried from one territory to another; or, the acts constituting offer and acceptance must have been done in different states; or, the contract must provide for the goods to be delivered to a place other than where these acts are done.

So, although an English court may decide that UCTA applies to regulate a foreign contract, a foreign seller of goods who forms contracts over the Internet will not be bound by UCTA's restraints on exclusion of liability clauses. Applying the same reasoning, the operation of UCTA can prevent a foreign supplier of services from unreasonably excluding liability.

27. An American wine seller sets up a website with its standard form contract expressing no jurisdiction clause but an express choice that the law of New York shall apply to any disputes. A UK consumer is made ill by some corked wine delivered and understands that under the Unfair Contract Terms Act 1977 the supplier's contract could not exclude its liability. This Act will not apply to prevent this exclusion of liability because the contract is for the international supply of goods.

This contrast between the application of the Act to goods and services may be crucial to the supply of digital information over the Internet. The supply of software over the Internet is likely not to be classified as a sale of goods, indeed no title passes and there is no physical possession. Certainly, if the obiter dictum of Sir Iain Glidewell is followed[178], supplies of software made over the Internet will not be international supply contracts for the purposes of UCTA. As a result these contracts will be subject to UCTA's rules on the exclusions and restrictions of liability.

176 Unfair Contract Terms Act 1977, s 26(1).
177 Unfair Contract Terms Act 1977, s 26(3) and (4).
178 See *St Alban's City and District Council v International Computers Ltd* [1996] 4 All ER 481 at 492–494.

28. Two American software suppliers set up websites to provide software to English consumers. Both suppliers utilise an on-screen contract which excludes all liability and choose the contract to be governed by 'the Laws of the State of New York to the extent that all non-American consumer protection provisions will be inapplicable'. One supplier provides the software by shipping it on a CD-ROM to the English consumer. UCTA will not operate to restrict the application of the exclusion clause because this is an international supply contract. The other supplier decides to download the software to consumers using the Internet. UCTA will operate to restrict the application of the exclusion clause because the contract is not an international supply contract as no goods are passed.

Consumer contracts

Far more common than the application of a mandatory rule to a contract is the application of a particular mandatory rule, consumer protection laws. Article 5(2) expresses that in certain circumstances a choice of law made by the parties shall not deprive the consumer of the protection afforded by the mandatory rules from the law of his country of habitual residence. It was once thought that this provision will have very limited effect because English consumers generally buy from English suppliers under contracts governed by English law. This certainly was the case even for goods manufactured abroad. The Internet alters this though; the digital landscape is covered with foreign suppliers contracting directly with local consumers, missing out the domestic supplier. It is now relevant for these manufacturers to appreciate the effect of art 5. It will affect their decision whether to sell over the Internet and what legal advice they should take[179]. It should be repeated here that the Electronic Commerce Directive expressly does not reduce the applicability of the Rome Convention. It also does not reduce the mandatory protection afforded to consumers by the laws of their domicile.

Before considering these circumstances, which are usually satisfied over the World Wide Web, one must address what is a consumer contract. The courts may not consider a licence over copyright material to be a consumer contract as it is neither for the supply of goods or supply of services. The German Bundesgerichtshof held that a timeshare contract was neither a contract for the supply of goods nor services within the meaning of art 5[180]. On the basis that such a licence is classified as a consumer contract, parties contracting over the Internet should appreciate the conditions that must prevail for the consumer protection to apply.

Websites and consumers

Article 5(2) specifies that there are three ways in which the mandatory consumer protective laws will apply to a contract where a choice of law has been made or demonstrated appropriately. One of these ways directly concerns a contract made over the Internet:

179 It may not be enough simply to seek the advice of a domestic lawyer; to understand fully the possible effect of a web contract, legal advice should be solicited from other jurisdictions where potential contracting parties may reside.

180 VIII ZR 316/96, RIW 1997, 875, 19 March 1997.

> 'if in that country the conclusion of the contract was preceded by a specific invitation addressed to him or by advertising, and he had taken in that country all the steps necessary on his part for the conclusion of the contract . . .'

This chapter has explained that a court may view a website as a form of advertising. This is very likely where the website does not even attempt to block viewers from specified countries, either technically or by consent. It has also been explained that clicking a download button, or simply agreeing to a contract, will be sufficient to show that the consumer has taken all the necessary steps[181] in the country of his habitual residence. This provision will therefore often act to introduce consumer protective laws into a contract that a website owner never envisaged.

The fact that the similar provisions of the Brussels Convention have been amended in the Brussels Regulation begs one simple question: Does the current Rome Convention have a more narrow application than the Brussels Regulation? The answer to this question is found below under 'Avoiding certain consumers'.

Avoiding certain consumers

Avoiding the ambit of art 5 is difficult both technically and legally because it remains impossible to 'block' totally all access to a website from one particular jurisdiction. The website owner must make a decision: is he happy to contract with a consumer from every country in the world? If there is a jurisdiction that the owner seeks to avoid there are two methods to employ. First, technical solutions. Ensure that the web pages that precede the contract stress that the site is not intended for those consumers from the unwanted jurisdiction. This may be effective. The Giuliano and Lagarde report advises that[182]:

> '[i]f . . . the German replies to an advertisement in American publications, even if they are sold in Germany, the [art 5(2)] rule does not apply unless the advertisement appeared in special editions of the publication intended for European countries.'

One can also ensure that a web server establishes what language is 'set' for the consumer's Internet browser. This will allow the filtering of some jurisdictions by the unique languages spoken there. A further refinement of those filtered can be achieved by running a 'reverse DNS look-up'. This resolves the domain name of the Internet Service Provider being used by the consumer. A domain name ending in '.com' may indeed give little indication of the jurisdiction of the consumer. In contrast, an Internet Service Provider with a domain name ending in '.co.uk' gives a fair indication that the consumer using it is from the UK. Then the actual server being used to access the Internet can be located on the planet with a high degree of accuracy. Of course, the server may not be local to the consumer for a number of reasons. Although also not precise, one further check can

181 This careful drafting avoids the older problem of deciding where a contract was concluded. All that must be determined is where the consumer carried out all the steps necessary on his part to complete the contact. It will therefore make no difference whether the website is so constructed as to accept offers or make them. It is also submitted that the effect of the Electronic Commerce Directive's 'acknowledgement' is also irrelevant here. The relevant country will be identical.

182 OJ 1980, C282/10 at C282/24.

be made of the consumer's time zone. Collectively these solutions can weed out consumers from unsought territories.

The second method is to ensure, as is suggested, that the contract is not accepted by the consumer, but rather offered; the website should accept[183]. With this mechanism in place it becomes easy to ask consumers to complete details of where they are habitually resident or to where that want the goods, if relevant, shipped. The site can reject the offers from the unwanted jurisdiction. It can be seen that if the website made offers, even with conditional drafting as to habitual residence, it could be in breach of contract by refusing to supply to certain locations.

29. A website sells 'self-help' manuals. The website allows any consumer to fill in his details, including address and payment details. The contract chooses Swiss law. On clicking a button labelled 'Let me help myself' (an acceptance button), the manuals are sent to the consumer by mail. By fulfilling each order without checking the habitual residence of the consumer, the website may be leaving itself open to litigation or unexpected defences. It may be that the site should refuse to contract with consumers from certain jurisdictions.

These steps are also relevant, as explained above, to avoid the bite of art 15 of the Brussels Regulation. It remains relevant, therefore, to consider whether drafting differences between the Rome Convention, art 5 and Brussels Regulation, art 15, are commercially relevant. This author has always expressed the view that both the Brussels Convention, art 13 and Rome Convention, art 13 apply to protect most consumers accessing websites[184]. This author's view is therefore that the changes introduced by the Brussels Regulation were introduced not to *change* the law but to *clarify* it. The majority of the delegates of the Contracting States certainly had the view that changes to the Brussels Convention were not needed[185]. Website operators should not, therefore, assume that the current Rome Convention is now exposed as not protecting consumers. The Rome Convention, but more so, the Brussels Regulation, protects consumers who contract using websites that make no attempt to exclude them.

Absence of choice

Although it has been advised that a contract should always have a statement as to the law that will apply, there will be situations where a contract has no such statement. To cover these situations, rather than endorse them, the following section considers how a court will establish the applicable law. As above for an express choice, the section later goes on to address the radical difference made by contracting with a consumer without an express choice of law.

Without a choice under art 3, the general rule is that the applicable law shall be that of the country with which the contract is most closely connected[186]. There is a presumption, however, which is of direct relevance to website contracts. Article 4(2) makes the presumption that the contract is most closely connected with the country in which the person is located who effects the char-

183 See 'Website acceptance and acknowledgement', at p 28.
184 Gringras *The Laws of the Internet* (1st edn, 1997) pp 38 and 50.
185 European Commission Proposal, (1999) OJ C376/1.
186 Rome Convention, art 4(1).

acteristic performance. The following section breaks down this Article into two discrete elements: characteristic performance and location.

Characteristic performance

For a unilateral contract made over the Internet, the performance which is characteristic will always be straightforward. For a bilateral contract, as is recommended for the Internet, the answer may be more involved[187]. The Giuliano and Lagarde report illustrates the complexity over what is performance in a bilateral contract[188].

> 'It is the performance for which the payment is due, ie depending on the type of contract, the delivery of goods, the granting of the right to make use of an item of property, the provision of a service . . . which usually constitutes the centre of gravity and the socio-economic function of the contractual transaction.'

Where a viewer enters a website to download material or order its supply, the website owner will be the person effecting the characteristic performance. Providing money or digital cash is not, as seen, characteristic performance[189]. Where a business logs on to a business-to-business website to conduct electronic procurement or other corporate activity, again, it will be the website owner who effects the characteristic performance. For example, in a bidding contract, the provision of the bidder's professional services was considered to be the characteristic performance[190]. In a contract between a client and lawyer, the French court determined that the lawyer's provision of legal advice was the characteristic performance[191]. A distribution agreement, however, has a characteristic performance of supply to the distributor, not the supply to third parties by the distributor[192]. It can be said with some conviction that a website owner will usually be the contracting party making the characteristic performance.

Location

Once the characteristic performance of the contract is established, art 4(2) provides a separate test to determine the law that will apply to that Internet contract. It is vital not to make the wrong assumption that having determined

187 Article 4(5) explains that if the characteristic performance cannot be determined (not that *where* it is effected cannot be determined) the presumptions of arts 2, 3 and 4 will not apply and the court may choose the country with which the contract as a whole is more closely connected as the basis for the applicable law. This must be shown to the court by the party seeking to establish a country other than that determined by art 4(2). *Definitely Maybe (Touring) Ltd v Marek Lieberberg Kanzertagentur GmbH* [2001] 4 All ER 283.

188 OJ 1980, C282/10 at C282/20.

189 More involved transactions such as a contract for the provision of digital cash can result in strange results with this reasoning. It would appear that the location of the account determines the law of the contract rather than the bank's location: *Sierra Leonne Telecommunications Co Ltd v Barclays Bank plc* [1998] 2 All ER 821 at 827.

190 *HIB Ltd v Guardian Insurance Co* [1997] 1 Lloyd's Rep 412, QB.

191 *S v K* D 1983, J146, Tribunal de Grande Instance de Paris.

192 *Print Concept GmBH v GEW (EC) Ltd* [2001] ECC 36, CA.

the characteristic performance of a contract one has also found the law that will apply. The correct approach is to assess which party makes the characteristic performance and then to determine which law reflects this transaction. There are two possibilities: first, the contract has been entered into in the course of that party's trade or profession; second, the contract has been entered into otherwise.

Course of trade or profession

It is likely that those parties who own a website to make contracts will be considered to be acting within their trade or profession. In this situation, art 4(2) states that the law that shall apply is that of the country where the principal place of business is situated, with a proviso. If the terms of the contract specify that the performance is to be effected through a different place of business, the law of that place shall apply.

30. A Parisian clothes manufacturer sets up a website in Paris and allows retailers to place their orders over the World Wide Web. There is no choice of law made on the online order form. The clothes being shipped will constitute the characteristic performance of the contract. The manufacturer effects this performance, so the law of the principal place of business, France, will apply to the contract. If the contract specifies that the clothes shall be shipped from a German warehouse, the law of Germany shall apply being a place of business other than the principal one.

Website's place of business

Contracts made over the Internet grant freedoms to both parties: neither needs to be located in the same country as the website that takes and completes an order. It is possible that an order to acquire a digitised picture is made from England, and that the order is placed with a German company, trading out of Germany, but that the server which digitally effects the performance is located in the US. It would be equally easy if the server is located in Vietnam, or anywhere else in the world with a telephone network. The obvious question is therefore, does a server that can effect performance constitute a place of business? It is submitted, in the absence of any direct authority, that a server *per se* cannot constitute a place of business. This conclusion is drawn from a number of factors.

The wording of art 4(2) indicates that effecting the characteristic performance through a place does not necessarily constitute a place of business. This can be reasoned from the wording of the article that performance must be effected through a place of business other than the principal place of business. It does not merely state that performance through another place will trump the principal place of business[193].

The Giuliano and Lagarde report complements this point. It states that[194]:

193 It is admitted that such a literal analysis of a European Convention is, perhaps, inappropriate, and that a more purposive approach should be used. This follows.

194 OJ 1980, C282/10 at C282/20.

> '[t]he law appropriate to the characteristic performance defines the connecting factor of the contract from the inside, and not from the outside by elements unrelated to the essence of the obligation such as the nationality of the contracting parties or the place where the contract was concluded.'

This interpretation suggests that it is naïve to look solely at where a server is plugged in. What the Convention requires is to look to the reality of the transaction; the characteristic performance must be linked to 'the social and economic environment of which it will form a part'[195]. Indeed, the Giuliano and Lagarde report endorses this holistic approach by later stating: '[t]he place where the act was done becomes unimportant . . . Seeking the place of performance or the different places of performance and classifying them becomes superfluous.'[196] A company needs to do far more than simply connect a server abroad to have established a place of business there.

What and where is 'a place of business' is a vexed question for the purposes of choice of law and there are differing definitions concerning taxation and the service of proceedings. But there is little doubt that the policy considerations when establishing jurisdiction over a defendant differ from those to establish from where performance was effected. It is inappropriate and an over-simplification of the relevant factors to attempt to utilise a court's views on 'place of business' from one area of the law, say jurisdiction, to another, choice of law.

31. An Italian publisher charges viewers to read its newspaper which it uploads daily on to its two websites, one in Italy and one based in New York for speed purposes. Its contract with viewers has no choice of law clause, but does stipulate that, when demand is high, the American server may supply the information. When a viewer accesses the newspaper, and unbeknown to him, receives this information through the American server, the law of the contract will not be that of New York. A server simply based in New York is an insufficient link to constitute a place of business. The law that will apply is that of the place of the principal place of business: Italy.

Outside trade or profession

Where a party is not acting within his trade or profession but uses a website to make a contract, a slightly different, but more certain, rule applies. In this situation, art 4(2) states that the law that shall apply is that of the country where, for an individual, he habitually resides at the time. For a corporate or unincorporated entity, the law that applies is that of the place of its central administration.

The commercial reaction to this academic debate is short: where possible specify a law for any ecommerce contract made over the Internet. There is some truth in the statement that not providing a choice of law gives slightly more opportunity for argument at an interim stage as to which law will apply to a contract. This opportunity comes at the cost of distinctive uncertainty.

195 OJ 1980, C282/10 at C282/20.
196 OJ 1980, C282/10 at C282/21.

Modifications to applicable law

Consumer contracts

What constitutes a consumer contract under art 5(2) has already been addressed in some detail[197]. It was found that a contract made over the World Wide Web with a consumer will generally benefit from the protection afforded under the Convention[198]. Where the contract does not provide a choice of law, the effect of the transaction being a consumer contract is far more critical.

If no choice of law is made and art 5(2) is applicable, art 5(3) specifies that the law which governs the contract is that of the consumer's habitual residence[199]. This is in stark contrast to where a consumer contract does include a choice of law. In that situation, art 5(2) does not deprive the consumer of the protection afforded by the mandatory rules from his habitual residence.

32. A website sells 'self-help' manuals. The website allows any consumer to fill in his details, including address and payment details. On clicking a button labelled, 'Let me help myself' (an acceptance button), the manuals are sent to the consumer by mail. By fulfilling each order without checking the habitual residence of the consumer, the website will be forming contracts under many different laws all around the world. Its contracts may be unenforceable, or worse, they may be illegal. To avoid leaving itself open to these risks it must include a choice of law and refuse to contract with consumers from certain jurisdictions.

There is an elementary solution to the problem that any law could apply to a contract if any consumer is allowed to contract: choose a law for the contract. Then, to ameliorate the effect from the consumer's mandatory rules, apply the technical and legal precautions already described to 'block' certain jurisdictions[200].

CONSUMER CONTRACTS

It is rare for a contract to be concluded over the Internet *not* at a distance. The very nature and benefit of the Internet and the ecommerce that it facilitates is that parties no longer need to be in the same place to form a contract. Where one of the parties is an individual and a consumer, a new layer of protection is provided to that consumer.

Those who contract with consumers over the Internet need therefore to respect these particular 'at a distance' rules in addition to the more general

197 See 'Consumer contracts', at p 66.
198 See 'Websites and consumers', at p 66.
199 Subject to the two exceptions that the rule does not apply to a contract of carriage or a contract where the services are to be supplied to the consumer exclusively in a country other than that in which he has his habitual residence. See the Rome Convention, art 5(4).
200 See 'Avoiding certain consumers', at p 67.

substantive consumer protection regime[201]. The two specific pieces of legislation to be discussed below are the European Directive 97/7/EC on the protection of consumers in respect of distance contracts, implemented into English law as the Consumer Protection (Distance Selling) Regulations 2000, and the European Directive 2002/65/EC concerning the distance marketing of consumer financial services[202]. The more general Electronic Commerce Directive and Regulations also impose new requirements on those transacting with consumers; these requirements are discussed elsewhere in this chapter.

Non-financial consumer distance contracts

On 20 May 1997 Directive 97/7/EC on the protection of consumers in respect of distance contracts was adopted. The Directive certainly does[203] affect the practice of those who use the Internet to sell goods and non-financial services to European consumers[204]. It is implemented in the UK by the Consumer Protection (Distance Contracts) Regulations 2000[205]. The core issues are: what is a distance contract for the purposes of these Regulations; what information should be provided on websites prior to the contract's conclusion; what information should be provided in a durable medium on or before delivery or performance; what are the effect of cancellation rights; and, what are the risks of ignoring or breaching the regulations.

Distance consumer contract

There are three aspects to a contract falling within the Regulations. It must be a contract concerning a certain type of transaction. The second aspect is that a means of distance communication has to have been used exclusively up to and including the moment that the contract was concluded. Finally, the contract must be between a supplier and a consumer. Each aspect is discussed below.

Type of transaction

Not all contracts concluded using a website will fall within these Regulations. The excepted contracts[206] include those for the sale or disposition of an interest

201 General consumer protective measures include: the Consumer Credit Act 1974; the Unfair Contract Terms Act 1977; the Consumer Protection Act 1987; and the Unfair Terms in Consumer Contracts Regulations 1999. Readers should note that the European Court of Justice in the joined cases *Cape Snc v Idealservice Srl* (Case C-541/99) and *Idealservice MN RE SAS v OMAI Srl* (C-542/99) confirmed that the term 'consumer' in the Directive on Unfair Terms in Consumer Contracts (Council Directive 93/13/EEC) refers only to natural persons and not legal persons.

202 OJ 2002, L 271/16.

203 Choice of law clauses will not be effective in ousting the consumer's rights. See art 12.

204 This Directive has a similar cumulative effect as some of the US federal laws and regulations. See Federal Trade Commission 16 CFR 310, 16 CFR 435 and Federal Communication Commission Restrictions on Telephone Solicitations, 47 CFR 64.1200. Also Federal Trade Commission Mail or Telephone Merchandise Order Rule.

205 SI 2000/2334.

206 Regulation 5(1).

in land and construction contracts relating to the same[207]. The Regulations do not apply to contracts concluded at a genuine auction[208]. The Regulations also carve out a wide, non-exhaustive list of financial services which are subject to their own distance contracts regime discussed below[209].

Use of means of distance communication

The supplier must exclusively use, both prior to and for conclusion of the contract, a 'means of distance communication' on an organised (and not one-off) basis. This term is very widely defined as any means which, without the simultaneous physical presence of the supplier and the consumer, may be used for the conclusion of a contract between the parties[210]. There is no doubt that websites and email fall squarely within such a definition[211].

Suppliers and consumers

The final trait of a 'distance contract' is that it is between a 'supplier' and a 'consumer'. Suppliers are any person, whether legal or natural, who is acting in his commercial or professional capacity[212]. A consumer, in contrast, is any *natural* person acting outside his business[213]. Two issues become relevant here: one legal, the other commercial.

The legal issue is that, unlike the Brussels Regulation and the Rome Convention, a 'consumer' must be a natural person. Businesses ordering unusual supplies are not therefore covered by these Regulations. The commercial issue is that it is sometimes difficult to tell, using a website, whether an order has been placed by a natural person acting as a consumer on their own behalf or by a natural person acting as an employee tasked by their business to place the order. In some situations it will be relevant to distinguish between the two. Website operators could include a query on the ordering page which simply asks the question whether the order is being placed on behalf a business.

33. A hotel establishes a website to allow particular types of room to be searched for, reserved and paid for. A credit card must be used to reserve each room for which a billing address is required. The website does not require the person reserving the room to specify whether it is a corporate or individual booking. As a result, to be safe, the hotel must assume that every user of the website is a natural person.

207 Regulation 5(1)(a) and (b).
208 Regulation 5(1)(f).
209 Regulation 5(1)(c) and Schedule 2.
210 Regulation 3(1).
211 See Schedule 1 for a non-exhaustive list which at para 11 includes the term of art 'e-mail'. The Schedule does not refer to 'website' instead, somewhat amusingly, referring at para 10 to 'videotext (microcomputer and television screen) with keyboard or touch screen'.
212 Regulation 3(1).
213 Regulation 3(1).

INFORMATION TO BE PROVIDED PRIOR TO CONCLUSION OF CONTRACT

Having determined that a contract falls within these Regulations, one must consider the textual changes needed to be made to the website being used as the means of distance communication. These changes fall mainly within the remit of providing certain information to the consumer prior to the conclusion of the contract.

In good time prior to the conclusion of the contract, the supplier needs to provide certain information to the consumer[214]. The scope of the information to be provided is enumerated below. This is followed by a discussion of the manner in which the information must be provided.

Information to be provided

The scope of the information to be provided (discussed below) is straightforward. It is[215]:

1. * the identity of the supplier and, where the contract requires payment in advance, the supplier's address;
2. a description of the main characteristics of the goods or services;
3. * the price of the goods or services including all taxes;
4. * delivery costs where appropriate;
5. the arrangements for payment, delivery or performance;
6. the existence of a right of cancellation where appropriate;
7. the cost of using the means of distance communication where it is calculated other than at the basic rate;
8. the period for which the offer or the price remains valid;
9. where appropriate, the minimum duration of the contract, in the case of contracts for the supply of goods or non-financial services to be performed permanently or recurrently;
10. where appropriate, information that in the event of the goods or services ordered by the consumer being unavailable, the supplier will provide substitute goods or services (as the case may be) of equivalent quality and price; and information that the cost of returning any such substitute goods to the supplier in the event of cancellation by the consumer would be met by the supplier.

Manner of providing information

This information must be provided in a 'clear and comprehensible' manner appropriate to the means of distance communication[216]. On a website, therefore, it should be acceptable to use an obvious link from an ordering page to this prior information. In contrast, using a link from within any Terms and Conditions on the website may be burying the information too much.

Some of the information to be provided will also need to be provided under

214 Regulation 7(1).
215 Regulation 7(1)(a)(i)–(ix) and 7(1)(b) and (c).
216 Regulation 7(2).

the Electronic Commerce Regulations. This is preceded with an asterisk in the list above. These items of information are not required to be provided twice but website designers should ensure that the *manner* in which the information is required to be provided for both statutes is met. For example, the Electronic Commerce Regulations require that that the 'name of the service provider' is made available in a form and manner which is 'easily, directly and permanently accessible'. The Distance Contracts Regulations require the same information to be provided in a 'clear and comprehensible manner' prior to the conclusion of the contract. It is therefore prudent, for these dual-requirements, to observe the Electronic Commerce Regulation's stricter requirements relating to the manner of displaying this information.

34. A site's designer ensures that just before someone buys a particular product on his site they are shown a flashy animation summarising the price and delivery details. This cannot be printed but is rather impressive. Once the product is ordered one cannot see the price again. The designer may well have complied with the Distance Selling Regulations' requirement of providing the prices in a 'clear and comprehensible manner'. In contrast, being ephemeral, the animation is not likely to comply with the Electronic Commerce Regulations' requirement that the price be 'permanently accessible'.

Information to be provided on or before performance of contract

Either prior to the conclusion of the contract or during performance of the contract further information must be provided to the consumer. Unlike the information listed above, this information must be provided in durable medium. The nature of this provision is discussed below the scope of the information.

Information to be provided

There are two sets of information which must be provided. First, those items listed from 1 to 6 (inclusive) above[217]. As has been described above, this information must also be provided prior to the conclusion of the contract. Additional information is limited to the following[218]:

1. where appropriate, notification that the supplier intends that the consumer shall return the goods to the supplier in the event of cancellation;
2. where appropriate, information as to whether the consumer or the supplier is responsible for the cost of returning any goods to the supplier, or the cost of his recovering them, in the event of a cancellation;
3. the geographical address of the supplier's place of business of the supplier to which the consumer may address any complaints;
4. information about any after-sales services and guarantees;
5. the conditions for exercising any contractual right to cancel the contract, where the contract is of an unspecified duration or a duration exceeding one year;

217 Regulation 7(1)(a)(i)–(vi).
218 Regulation 8(2)(a)–(e).

6. where appropriate, prior to the conclusion of a contract for the supply of services, a statement that unless the parties agree otherwise, the consumer will not be able to cancel the contract once the performance of the services has begun with his agreement.

Cost of cancellation

It is financially important that suppliers pay particular attention to the second item of information listed above. In the event of a cancellation of a contract relating to goods, discussed below, the goods must be returned to the supplier. However, the supplier must specify whether he or the consumer should be responsible for the costs of returning the goods. Most suppliers will not wish to pay for goods to be returned to them. These suppliers should therefore ensure that they include a statement that the consumer pays.

Cancelling services

Services, such as the online provision of music, can be cancelled in just the same way as goods. This is discussed below. Suppliers need to be aware that, unless they state otherwise, consumers will be able to cancel a contract once performance of the services has begun. For obvious reasons, suppliers are advised to include a statement that once the services begin to be provided, the contract cannot be cancelled. Advisors are also warned to consider carefully the nature of the transaction between a supplier and a consumer. Many websites do not actually provide goods at all but rather perform a service. They should ensure that they exclude the right to cancel after performance of the services.

35. ToughSafe.co.uk runs a website that can be used to store documents and pictures on behalf of individuals. It is very secure and costs many hundreds of pounds each year, paid in advance. The website and online contract is silent as to whether the hosting can be cancelled after it has commenced. The site cannot prevent a user from lawfully using the site for a few days and then cancelling the contract. ToughSafe.co.uk will need then to refund the monies to the user.

Manner of providing information

The information above must be provided to a consumer 'in writing, or another durable medium which is available to and accessible to the consumer'[219]. It is important that consumer is able to retain the information. An email containing the information is therefore acceptable. A website may not be acceptable because, unless it remains always available, it does not have the quality of permanence envisaged by the legislation. Similarly, it is not likely to include 'instant messaging' messages; the Directive's recital 13 warns against 'ephemeral' information not received 'on a permanent medium'. Suppliers are advised to use email as their preferred method of providing the information.

219 Regulation 8(1).

The written material containing the information, in the case of goods, should be received at latest by the time of delivery. Including the material inside the packaging will therefore be sufficient. In the case of services, the information must be provided during the performance of those services.

Cancellation rights

The Distance Selling Regulations introduce a new right for consumers buying products and services at a distance to be able to cancel their contract within a certain time period following the receipt of the goods or performance of the services. The rationale for this is simple. Even the best websites cannot accurately portray what an actual product will be like. Consumers in a shop, in contrast, put on a watch, try on clothes, flick through a book; they can check they are happy with what they are buying. The Regulation aims to level this playing field and so encourage the take-up of consumer ecommerce activity. It can materially impact suppliers though. They should be aware under what conditions goods and services may be cancelled and, for cash-flow and stock control purposes, when this cancellation can occur. Finally they should be geared up to administer cancellations. These three critical ramifications are discussed below.

What can be cancelled

All goods and services can be cancelled unless they fall within one of two categories. The first category exhaustively defines those goods and services which are *by their nature* exempted from the cancellation regime. The second category is those goods which are by the way that they have been *used by the consumer* not capable of being cancelled.

Categories of goods that cannot be cancelled

Not all goods and services can be cancelled after a contract is formed with a consumer. The Regulations set out a limited number of exemptions[220]. For example, a contract for newspapers, periodicals or magazines cannot be cancelled after the goods are received[221]. This should be obvious; consumers could otherwise read them and then, within the allotted seven working days, send them back for a full refund.

A consumer also cannot cancel a contract for the supply of sealed audio, video recordings or computer software if the consumer has unsealed the goods[222]. Again, there is a common sense reason for this; consumers could watch the DVD a number of times over a weekend and then send it back for a full refund. This would end up being the cheapest way to rent DVDs! Again, for obvious reasons, goods which are made to a consumer's personal specification or are clearly personalised, cannot be returned for the full refund[223].

220 Regulation 13(1).
221 Regulation 13(1)(e).
222 Regulation 13(1)(c).
223 Regulation 13(1)(c).

36. MugMug.co.uk is a website which sells mugs onto which they will print a photograph supplied by a consumer. Apparently these are very popular for birthday presents and Mrs Jones sends a digital photograph of Mr Jones to MugMug.co.uk. Six mugs arrive a week later and Mrs Jones wraps them and gives them to Mr Jones as a present. He hates them. Mrs Jones cannot evoke her rights of cancellation; the goods were made to her specification.

There is also a set of goods and services which cannot be cancelled because their value is transitory. These include betting, gaming or lottery services[224] and goods or services where their price is dependent on fluctuations in the financial market if this cannot be controlled by the supplier[225]. Similarly, consumers cannot return goods which are liable to deteriorate or expire rapidly or those which, by their nature, cannot be returned, such as electricity[226].

37. A department store with a food hall establishes a website. The website includes a limited range of food for sale and delivery the next day. On a Wednesday a consumer orders a wheel of Brie for a party at the weekend. The cheese arrives on the Thursday but, sadly, noone turns up for the party. To add to his woes, he cannot return the Brie as it is perishable.

Finally, there is a category of services which cannot be cancelled. These are those which the supplier has, with the consumer's consent, started to provide before the end of the seven-working-day cancellation period. It is in the interests of most online providers of services to ensure that they therefore exclude the cancellation right in such circumstances in their contracts with consumers. Suppliers should also remember that this notice needs to be in a durable medium and delivered before conclusion of the contract[227].

Categories of goods which become unable to be cancelled

It has already been mentioned that a consumer can return for a full refund a *sealed* DVD but not an unsealed DVD. These goods were capable of being cancelled but for the use of them by the consumer. In a much broader context, the Regulation stipulates that consumers are under a duty to retain possession of the goods and take reasonable care of them throughout the period prior to cancellation[228]. The Regulation is silent as to what are the consequences of the consumer not retaining possession of or reasonable care of the goods.

Although untested by the courts, it is reasonable for suppliers to assume that they do not need to refund goods that have been treated unreasonably by consumers. It follows that suppliers should be clear to consumers as to what 'reasonable care' means in the context of the goods during the potential cancellation period and before return. Related to this, suppliers should ensure that the goods are covered by an insurance policy until the expiry of the cancellation period.

224 Regulation 13(1)(f).
225 Regulation 13(1)(b).
226 Regulation 13(1)(c).
227 See Manner of Providing Information, at p 77.
228 Regulation 17(2).

How and when cancellation can occur

There are three different deadlines before which consumers may give notice to cancel their distance contract and obtain a refund. The first deadline applies to goods; the second to services. A final deadline applies where a supplier has failed in its obligations to provide the consumer with the information in a durable medium[229].

How a consumer cancels

It is simple for a consumer to cancel a distance contract. All they need to do is to give the supplier a notice of their intention, in writing or another durable medium (including email)[230]. A format for the notice cannot be prescribed; 'however expressed' an 'indicat[ion] of the consumer to cancel the contract' is sufficient[231].

Consumers are not even obliged to send the notice by a certain means, such as email, to a particular person. The notice will be treated as properly given if the consumer leaves it, or posts it to the address last known by the consumer or to a company's registered address[232]. It should be made out for the attention of the supplier or other person by name. In these circumstances the notice will be deemed to have been given on the day it was left or posted[233].

Those more digitally-minded consumers may choose to fax or email the notice to the business fax or email address last known to them. In these situations, the notice will be deemed to have been given on the day it was left or posted[234].

Cancellation deadline for goods

A consumer may cancel a contract for the supply of goods by giving notice within the seven working days commencing on the later of the day after the date on which the goods were received by the consumer, or, the day after the date on which all the prior durable information was received.

38. Mark orders a book on Greek wines. It arrives on Monday morning. On the following Tuesday he sends an email to the supplier expressing his intention to cancel the contract and return the goods for a full refund. The supplier replies to the email saying that it is too late as seven days have elapsed. The supplier is wrong to say this. The first working day of the seven was the day after the good's arrival: Tuesday. The following Tuesday was actually working day six. Mark gave notice a day before he needed to.

229 See 'Information to be provided on or before performance of the contract', at p 76.
230 Regulations 10(1) and (3).
231 Regulation 10(3).
232 Regulations 10(4)(a), (b) and 5(a).
233 Regulation 10(4)(a) and (b).
234 Regulation 10(4)(c) and (d).

Cancellation deadline for services

A consumer may cancel a contract for the supply of goods by giving notice within the seven working days commencing on the later of the day after the date on which contract is concluded, or, the day after the date on which all the prior durable information was received.

Cancellation where supplier has not provided information in durable medium

Readers will note that for both goods and services, the cancellation deadline cannot occur until the prior durable information is received. What happens if the supplier never sends this; does the cancellation period extend forever? No, the Regulations impose a backstop date for any cancellation period. This is three months and seven working days from the consumer receiving the goods or the contract for services being concluded. Most businesses' balance sheets and stock control systems will not expect to reimburse and return three month old goods. It is therefore critical that suppliers send the necessary information to their consumers.

Effects of cancellation

There are two aspects to cancellation: the consumer's obligations and the supplier's obligations. As one would expect, a Directive strengthening consumer rights does not impose many new obligations on those consumers. Suppliers, in contrast, may find their new obligations quite onerous.

Consumer obligations on cancellation

Having provided a notice of cancellation, consumers must still look after the goods. If the contract is silent on the issue, the consumer simply needs to leave the goods at their premises to await collection. In the meantime, they must retain possession of the goods and take reasonable care of them[235].

Alternatively, the contract, or the supplier within 21 days of cancellation, can specify that the consumer must return the goods. This is good practice from a supplier's point of view. The consumer becomes obliged to return the goods at their own expense. If they do not return them at all, or do so at the supplier's expense, the supplier may charge the consumer for their 'direct costs' of collecting the goods[236]. Where a third party is involved in this collection, say a parcel delivery company, this amount will be easy to calculate. There can be difficulties for a supplier where the supplier's own staff and facilities are used to collect the goods. In such a situation, the direct costs may be no more than the incremental costs of recovery; these may be no more than the extra petrol to collect from the consumer's premises. Suppliers may therefore tend to use third parties to collect the goods.

235 Regulation 17(3).
236 Regulation 14(5).

Supplier obligations on cancellation

Having provided a notice of cancellation, suppliers are obliged to refund all the monies paid by the consumer within 30 days beginning with the date written notice of cancellation was given[237]. The supplier should also cancel any related credit agreement[238]. Suppliers should check the detailed provisions relating to withholding the portions of payment relating to interest paid in regs 15 and 16.

RISKS OF BREACHING REGULATIONS

On 21 March 2001, the Office of Fair Trading published a press release about the distance selling regime described above. The press release explained that the Office of Fair Trading and 28 Trading Standards Departments had conducted a 'mystery surf' of 637 UK websites. It deduced from examining these sites that 52% were in breach of the Distance Selling Regulations. Should these sites care? In short, yes. There are two types of sanctions for breaching the Regulations: extension of cancellation rights; and injunctions and 'Stop Now' Orders.

Extension of cancellation rights

If a supplier fails to comply with the information requirements of the Regulations, the cancellation period is extended to a maximum of three months and seven working days until they do comply with the requirements. If the supplier never provides the information, the consumer may return the goods or cancel the services (where appropriate) within three months and seven working days starting the day after the goods receipt or the conclusion of the contract for services.

39. A website is established by a retailer to supply Christmas crackers. The website guarantees delivery by 23 December. A family orders four dozen crackers at a cost of £48. They arrive in eight sealed boxes on 23 December. Neither the website nor the delivery contains the necessary information under the Regulations. The family enjoy the crackers. At the end of March, they discover under a couch that they still have three boxes left. Because the website failed to comply with the information requirements, the family may serve their cancellation notice during March and still be within the three months and seven working days.

Injunctions and 'Stop Now' Orders

The Director General of Fair Trading and the Trading Standards Departments have a duty to consider any complaint about a possible breach of the Regulations. Where they consider that a breach has occurred, they have the power to apply for an injunction in the courts or to apply for a Stop Now Order[239] against the supplier.

237 Regulation 14(1) and (3).
238 Regulation 15.
239 Stop Now Orders (EC Directive) Regulations 2001, reg 2(3)(i) and Sch 1, para 9.

Financial consumer contracts

On 23 September 2002 a Directive on the distance marketing of consumer financial contracts was adopted. The Directive had a hard passage through the European Commission and Council and was eventually published in the Official Journal on 9 October 2002. Together with marketing prohibitions on inertia selling, cold calling and 'spamming' the Directive also introduces a requirement to provide comprehensive information to consumers before a contract is concluded. Like the Distance Selling Regulations it also includes a new consumer right to withdraw from the contract during a cancellation period – except in cases where there is a risk of price fluctuations in the financial market.

As for the Distance Selling Regulations, the core issues are: what is a distance contract for the purposes of this Directive; what information should be provided prior to the contract's conclusion; what are the effects of cancellation rights; and, what are the risks of ignoring or breaching the regulations once implemented. At the time of writing the Directive was adopted at a European level, but certainly not yet implemented at a national level. Out of respect for the final, sometimes significant, drafting changes in national implementation, the following analysis is at a high level only.

Distance consumer contract

There are three aspects to a contract falling within the Directive. It must be a contract concerning a certain type of transaction. The second aspect is that a means of distance communication has to have been used exclusively up to and including the moment that the contract was concluded. Finally, the contract must be between a supplier and a consumer. Fortunately the Distance Marketing of Financial Services Directive borrows much language from the Distance Selling Directive. As a consequence, where relevant, readers are referred to the analysis of the Distance Selling Directive above.

Type of transaction

The Distance Marketing of Financial Services Directive defines the all-important 'distance contract' like the Distance Selling Directive but only one 'concerning financial services'[240]. These, in turn, are defined as 'any service of a banking, credit, insurance, personal pension, investment or payment nature'[241].

Use of means of distance communication

The Distance Marketing of Financial Services Directive defines 'mean of distance communication' in a similar way to the Distance Contracts Directive's definition of the same term. It is defined as being a means of communication which, 'without the simultaneous physical presence of the supplier and the consumer, may be used for the distance marketing of a service between those parties'[242]. Unlike the

240 Article 2(a).
241 Article 2(b).
242 Article 2(e).

Distance Selling Directive, there is no non-exhaustive list of such possible means. There is little doubt from reading the recitals that websites and organised email campaigns would fall into the ambit of this definition.

Suppliers and consumers

The definitions of 'supplier' and 'consumer' in the Distance Marketing of Financial Contracts Directive differ slightly to those in the Distance Contracts Directive. It is submitted that these differences have little legal impact; readers are directed to the discussion above on these definitions[243].

Information to be provided prior to conclusion of contract

As under the Distance Contracts Directive, sellers of financial services and products are obliged to provide consumers with a comprehensive set of information before a distance contract is concluded. This information must include specific information about the supplier, the financial service itself, the contract and redress available to the consumer in the event of a dispute[244]. Information on the technical quality and nature of the financial service must be provided in accordance with the rules of the other directives on credit, insurance and investment services or with relevant national rules for services not currently subject to EU legislation.

Manner of providing information

Like the Distance Contracts Directive, the information detailed above must be provided in a clear and comprehensible manner in any way appropriate to the means of distance communication used. In addition suppliers should have due regard to the principles of good faith in commercial transactions, and the principles governing the protection of those who are unable, because of the legislation of certain Member States, to give their consent, such as minors[245].

Cancellation rights

Cancellation rights are more complex under the Distance Marketing of Financial Services Directive than under its sister, the Distance Contracts Directive. There is an obvious reason for this. Financial services, often by their very nature, could not exist if consumers had a right to cancel them after a short period. For example, if a consumer were to purchase some foreign currency over the web from their bank, receive it and not spend it, can they return it if the exchange rate moves in their favour? Understandably, the financial services industry lobbied hard to eliminate such barriers to them providing online financial services. Indeed, it is apparent from the *language* of the Directive that the financial community has gained a very wide carve-out indeed.

243 See 'Suppliers and consumers', at p 74.
244 Article 3(1)–(4).
245 Article 3(2).

Which financial services cannot be cancelled

The right to cancel does not apply to financial services that may be subject to fluctuations in the financial market, such as sales of foreign currency and securities[246]. Member States may also choose to exclude mortgage or property credit from this right of withdrawal from a contract[247]. These two carve-outs are not only very wide but are also uncertain particularly to consumers. How many consumers are aware of those financial services which are not 'subject to fluctuations in the financial market'? This author believes this unbalance between the supplier's understanding of their services and the consumer's could lead to the unscrupulous financial service provider excluding the right to cancel when, in fact, it was appropriate.

In addition, in the event of fraudulent use of payment cards or other non-cash means of payment consumers will be able to cancel transactions and be entitled to reimbursement of any sums charged.

How and when cancellation can occur

Consumers have the right to cancel a contract within 14 calendar days after signing up. In the case of life insurance and pension plans this increases to 30 calendar days[248]. Suppliers should note that the Distance Contracts Directive provides a cancellation right of seven working days which will often be the equivalent of nine calendar days. Over the Christmas period, however, it is possible that 14 calendar days will be shorter than seven working days.

Like a cancelling consumer under the Distance Contracts Directive, a consumer can cancel by notifying the supplier on paper or on another durable medium available and accessible to the supplier. An email will suffice. The notification must be sent before the relevant deadline expires[249].

Obligations on cancellation

Unlike cancelling consumers under the Distance Contracts Directive, a consumer of financial services at a distance may be obliged to pay for 'part' of the financial services received. This amount must both be brought to the attention of the consumer prior to the contract being concluded and must not be a 'penalty'. In other words, it must be a genuine proportion of the full price to the extent that the service has already been provided[250].

From the day on which a supplier receives notification of a withdrawal, they have no more than 30 calendar days to return to the consumer any sums less any proportional deduction described above.

Risks of breaching Regulations

Sanctions are left for member states to decide and so, at this stage, are not known.

246 Article 6(2).
247 Article 6(3).
248 Article 6(1).
249 Article 6(6).
250 Article 7(1).

Chapter Three

Tort

'The difficulty and inconvenience of requiring operators to analyse either the message or the senders from either a factual or legal standpoint is manifest. The indispensability of the telegraph, on the other hand, is as unchallenged as the realisation that speed is the essence of its worth.'

William M Martin, 1940[1]

The open nature of the Internet and World Wide Web allows users to connect both intentionally and unintentionally with more people than ever before. A website created by an individual can be seen by all other Internet users. A message sent to a bulletin board or website chatroom can be read across the planet, almost simultaneously, by millions. Unfortunately, this global communication has its disadvantages. A computer file harbouring a computer virus can, in a matter of hours, spread across continents, damaging data and programs without reprieve.

The law of tort demands that, in certain circumstances, we are answerable for our actions and our inactions. Whether there is a contract between two individuals or not, the courts have the authority to make someone provide compensation for damage caused. Put simply, English law demands that users of the Internet operate with responsibility towards others.

This chapter considers these responsibilities in relation to three particular types of damage that can occur over the Internet. The opening section on negligence looks to the liability of those who, even accidentally, exacerbate the spread of a computer virus by particular conduct. The second section considers the possibility that if a person relies to their detriment on information provided by another over the World Wide Web, the provider of the information may, occasionally, be liable for the loss. The final tort that is then examined from the perspective of the Internet is defamation. The openness of the Internet brings benefits to those who wish to publish information, but sometimes the courts will deem them responsible for the damaging words of another.

This chapter examines the following issues.

1. How may someone be liable for the damage caused from accidentally spreading a computer virus?

1 'Telegraphs and Telephones – Qualified Privilege of Telegraph Company to Transmit Defamatory Message Where Sender is Not Privileged' 2 Wash & Lee L Rev 141 at 147 (1940).

2. From a legal perspective, what type of damage occurs when digital data is altered?
3. Might not using an anti-viral program, or not backing-up important data, be viewed by the courts as contributory negligence?
4. When may information published over the web be the basis of litigation over a negligent misstatement?
5. Can contracts and disclaimers prevent victims of these torts from having a right of action?
6. What are the risks of website operators and of Internet Service Providers being sued for defamation?
7. Which country's courts have the jurisdiction to adjudicate on these cases?
8. Which law will apply to resolve such a dispute?

NEGLIGENCE

Although malicious code spreads through the Internet and infects computers, it is humans who help this code to proliferate. Viruses circulate because people using the Internet upload and download the hosts that house damaging code. Most of the people who spread this code do so unknowingly. For example, the 'Nimda' virus, which prompted the FBI's National Infrastructure Protection Centre to issue an advisory warning[2], was spread by users simply viewing an infected webpage or opening an email attachment. The 'I Love You' virus used a similar 'automatic' means of spread. In these types of situations, particularly where an internal network becomes infected, that further spread can be halted by stopping all digital communication with the Internet. This section considers what the responsibilities are for users of the Internet when they are aware, or should be aware, of infection. This is of fundamental importance to system operators of internal networks and to designers of websites.

To examine negligence, this chapter focuses on its constituent parts: duty of care; breach of duty; type of damage; causation of damage. A defendant will only be liable in negligence where he breached his duty to the claimant resulting in a recoverable form of damage.

Duty of care

The Internet, more than any other medium, permits one person to affect almost every other person connected to it. Viruses can spread widely: it is possible for one person to make a fundamental difference to this spread. One only needs to alert potential victims of a virus where these people are one's legal 'neighbours', however.

An appropriate starting point to determine who is your neighbour on the Internet is the two-part test expressed by Lord Wilberforce[3]:

> 'First one has to ask whether, as between the alleged wrongdoer and the person who has suffered damage there is a sufficient relationship

2 The FBI issued its Advisory warning on 18 September 2001.
3 *Anns v London Borough of Merton* [1977] 2 All ER 492 at 498.

of proximity or neighbourhood such that, in the reasonable contemplation of the former, carelessness on his part may be likely to cause damage to the latter, in which case a prima facie duty of care arises. Secondly, if the first question is answered affirmatively, it is necessary to consider whether there are any considerations which ought to negative, or to reduce or limit the scope of the duty or the class of person to whom it is owed or the damages to which a breach of it may give rise.'

The first aspect of this test is therefore whether someone has a sufficient relationship of proximity.

Relationship of proximity: viruses

The law is less ready to impose a duty of care where damage to property results from a failure to act, rather than by action of the defendant. In other words, the law does not generally impose a duty to save a potential victim, but only a duty not to harm that person[4]. Of course, it is semantically possible for an infected claimant, and the court, to frame a system operator's activities as actions, rather than failures to act. A train driver was liable for failing to shut off steam, so allowing his train to run into a dead-end[5]. The court described the driver's conduct in the active terms of negligently managing the train to allow it to 'come into contact with the dead-end'[6].

1. A website controller is aware that one of the applets on its home page is capable of deleting data on computers that are using a particular browser. The site controller takes no precautions and then receives a claim form alleging damage as a result of his negligence. It is unlikely that a defence that he was not negligent, having performed no action, would succeed.

The courts have previously considered the duty that arises when storing biological viruses. Widgery J had little doubt that a defendant had a duty to those owners of cattle which would be affected by the spread of a virus[7].

> 'In the present case, the defendants' duty to take care to avoid the escape of the virus was due to the foreseeable fact that the virus might infect cattle in the neighbourhood and cause them to die. The duty of care is accordingly owed to the owners of cattle in the neighbourhood . . .'

4 Lord Diplock illustrates this by claiming that in the parable of the Good Samaritan, there would be no liability under English civil law for the conduct of the Levite and the priest who passed by the other side, 'an omission which was likely to have as its reasonable and probable consequence damage to the health of the victim of the thieves'. *Home Office v Dorset Yacht Co Ltd* [1970] 2 All ER 294 at 326. This stated, this section takes a slightly less forgiving view of the liability which may fix to a system operator. In short, it is assumed that a 'pure omissions' argument will not save an operator from all liability.

5 *Kelly v Metropolitan Rly Co* [1895] 1 QB 944.

6 [1895] 1 QB 944 at 947 per Rigby LJ.

7 *Weller & Co v Foot and Mouth Disease Research Institute* [1965] 3 All ER 560 at 570.

There appears little to suggest that, when a person is aware of a computer virus in his control, the operator may not owe a duty to potential victims; the Foot and Mouth Disease Research Institute owed a duty to all the farmers whose cattle were killed.

Like their biological counterparts, computer viruses will infect not only the direct recipients but also subsequent ones; this is well known. It may therefore be alleged that the controller of an infected system is in a sufficiently proximate relationship with the owner of any equipment which becomes infected by the virus emanating from his system. It is submitted that this is too wide. A system operator, like all tortious defendants, has a duty to a claimant not simply if the damage is foreseeable, but also where the whole concept of relationship demands it[8]. It is therefore impossible to speak generically of a 'system operator's duty to victims'; the law requires that the 'whole relationship' be taken into account.

Whole relationship

In an attempt to describe some of the relevant factors which may be present in this relationship, this section divides the duties of a defendant in respect of damage from email, forum and ftp sites, and websites.

Malicious code is as virulent when on a forum or website as on any other computer. This can have the catastrophic result that infection can spread exponentially through the Internet. An email with an attached virus could be sent from one person to another. This person, unaware of the infection, could then create another email, to which the virus could re-attach, and send this email to a group of individuals. Every one of these individuals may now be infected and be infectious. The more sophisticated viruses (or, strictly speaking, 'worms') send infected emails without the user even knowing. In May 2000, the so-called 'I Love You' worm outstripped by half the hundreds of thousands of infections caused by the Melissa virus; in days. It is this replication and spread that leads to two types of damage: primary and secondary. By primary damage this book envisages damage which results from direct contact with an infected computer[9]. Secondary damage is any damage that is 'one removed' from the primary damage.

The greatest concern for a defendant is not in respect of the limited number of primary infections, but in respect of the unlimited numbers of secondary infections.

Primary damage

Email infection

A person who is sent an email from an infected system is owed a duty by the sender if that sender knew the email was being sent and was infected. The situation becomes more complex where the sender is aware that the recipient has an

8 See the 'widening' of Lord Wilberforce's first test by the Privy Council in *Yuen Kun Yeu v A-G of Hong Kong* [1988] AC 175.

9 It is appreciated that this contact is not direct but that, in fact, the digital material is broken into packets and shunted between many computers before reaching their intended recipient.

anti-viral program that should cull the virus. Here, if the recipient's computer becomes damaged, one must ask whether the recipient is contributorily negligent.

The practical solution is obviously to test each outgoing email for viruses. If infection is suspected but the email must nevertheless be sent, operators should include a suitable warning in the email text. This will not negate the duty to the recipient, but it may provide a defence of *volenti non fit injuria* – voluntary assumption of responsibility – if the person goes on to open the email and is then infected[10].

In the workplace, many people other than the system operator send emails. If an internal network is infected, the system operator should block all emails from leaving the system until the suspected malicious code is treated. If it is technically difficult to block emails leaving, the system operator has a duty to external recipients to inform the employees not to send potentially infected material. As will be discussed below, viruses are often spread because system operators do not act quickly enough to prevent other users of the system from infecting others.

Forums, ftp sites and website hosts

The controller of one of these sites, such as an ISP, has two serious problems. First, all may allow other people to upload material to the site. This increases, dramatically, the risk from virus infection. A controller of one of these sites will be unable to rely solely on a disclaimer to avoid liability[11]. This is because the law tends to impose a duty to act to prevent harm where the defendant is in control of both the claimant and the injuring third party[12]. For the controller of an ftp site, forum or hosted website the controller has nominal control over the person who left the virus and no control over those who become infected with it.

The second legal problem for such a controller is that there will be a large number of people who experience primary damage. That is, many people will be directly infected by malicious code on a site, in contrast to an email where probably only one person suffers primary damage[13].

Technical solutions obviously include ensuring that no files can be uploaded before passing through the site's anti-viral program first. This will probably be sufficient to extinguish the controller's duty to his visitors, although it would be legally safer if a contractual disclaimer is also provided[14]. Additionally it may be evidentially useful for the controller to maintain a log of which person leaves which file. If a claim is brought against the controller, it may be crucial that the claimant can add, as co-defendant, the person who deposited the virus initially. Defences, however, are discussed later.

10 See 'Consent' at p 108.
11 See 'Contracts and disclaimers' at p 119.
12 *Ellis v Home Office* [1953] 2 All ER 149. See also *Cowden v Bear Country Inc* 382 F Supp 1321 (DSD 1974) in which it was held an operator of an animal park had to exercise a high responsibility to prevent damage to the zoo's visitors. Some may say that there is a higher duty where a site's visitors access it not to view viruses but to download safe code.
13 The Melissa virus primarily infected only 50 people. See p fn 9 on p 89.
14 See 'Contracts and disclaimers' at p 119.

Websites

Executable code and viruses such as Nimda which spread from websites are becoming commonplace on web pages and so the potential for sites to become infectious is great. Controllers of these sites, therefore, need to be cautious about the risks of distributing malicious code through their pages. Like controllers of ftp sites and forums, controllers of websites risk directly infecting a large number of people. Most website controllers have absolute power over the site: other people cannot easily leave malicious code on the site to infect others. It is difficult to 'write' to a website without permission from the controller. This is not the case for ISPs which permit their customers to upload onto their own websites.

A website should therefore operate a strict regime of checking all the material on the site and where possible attempt to disclaim, to some extent, liability for infecting viewers.

2. A software programmer distributes software from her website and is careful to include a disclaimer of liability in the licence downloaded with each item of software. Unless the programmer is sure that no damaging code can be distributed simply by viewing her site, say by executable code, a disclaimer should also be placed on the website.

It is an obvious and important point that any disclaimer of damage from the site must be shown on the home page and throughout the site. If the disclaimer is buried at the 'back' of a site's pages there is a risk that the viewer's computer becomes infected before liability is disclaimed. In this situation, the disclaimer will not operate as a contractual defence because notice is provided too late, and it will not be successful as evidence of *volenti* for similar reasons[15].

Secondary damage

The duty to prevent damage for secondary infections will be less onerous than for primary infections. This is because the law tends to avoid opening up the 'floodgates' to too many similar claims. Also the courts will only impose a duty where that is fair, just and reasonable. It is true that the infectious character of viruses is well known. It may therefore be difficult for a defendant to state that he did not reasonably contemplate his carelessness would damage secondary victims. It is the nature of viruses that they spread; it is not improbable and is not unreasonably foreseeable that a victim who is far removed from the source of the infection will be infected[16]. By Lord Wilberforce's test it may appear trivial for a victim of secondary damage to allege successfully that the system operator owed a duty of care. But, as mentioned, a duty is wider than mere foreseeability[17].

> 'As Lord Wilberforce himself observed in *McLoughlin v O'Brian* [1982] 2 All ER 298 at 303, [1983] 1 AC 410 at 420, it is clear that

15 See *Thornton v Shoe Lane Parking Ltd* [1971] 1 All ER 686.
16 Cf, the catalogue of unlikely events in, say, *Palsgraf v Long Island Railroad* 162 NE 99 (1928).
17 *Yuen Kun Yeu v A-G of Hong Kong* [1987] 2 All ER 705 at 710 per Lord Keith.

> foreseeability does not of itself, and automatically, lead to a duty of care . . . Foreseeability of harm is a necessary ingredient of such a relationship, but it is not the only one. Otherwise there would be liability in negligence on the part of one who sees another about to walk over a cliff with his head in the air, and forbears to shout a warning.'

This statement makes it clear that a claimant, having suffered secondary digital damage, will have to show more than simply that the system operator knew this would be possible. Each claimant will have to prove a close and direct relationship with the system operator. The court should impose the duty only where it is 'fair, just and reasonable'[18]. This will depend greatly on the facts before the court, the balance of powers of the parties, and the potential to open the floodgates to similar claims. In the main, few claims from secondarily-damaged defendants will be successful.

3. A famous brewery provides on its website a free screensaver program which mimics its television advertisement. Viewers are free to download this software. Unbeknown to the brewery, the program is infected with a virus. The program is very popular, so, to ease the strain on its web server, the brewery encourages owners of the program to copy it for their friends rather than direct them to the web site.

Some time after the promotion finishes, a virus infection breaks out on those computers which have the program. The brewery may owe a duty to those who downloaded the program from the website, and to those people who were directed to copy the program. Those claimants who became infected from the spread of the virus, rather than the program in which it incubated, are unlikely to be owed a duty: they do not have a sufficiently direct relationship with the brewery.

Standard of care

At this point it is useful to recap: negligence is where a defendant owes a duty of care and then breaches that duty causing damage as a result. Victims must prove that the defendant breached his duty; they must prove on the balance of probabilities that, say, a system operator was negligent in allowing a virus to be spread[19].

Reasonable man

To assess negligence the courts compare the actions and inactions of the defendant with those of a reasonable man 'guided upon those considerations which ordinarily regulate the conduct of human affairs'[20]. In the situation of a system

18 See *White v Jones* [1993] 3 All ER 481 at 502, CA; affd [1995] 1 All ER 691, HL. See also *Williams v Natural Life Health Foods Ltd* [1998] 2 All ER 577, HL.

19 Sometimes the evidential burden on the claimant can be lessened by the court accepting an allegation of *res ipsa loquitur*.

20 *Blyth v Birmingham Waterworks Co* (1856) 11 Ex Ch 781 at 784 per Alderson B.

operator, the court may take into account industry practice, CERT[21] alerts and warnings, anti-viral programs and their recent updates and the rapidly advancing sophistication of computer viruses.

Industry practice

Professional negligence cases can teach a system operator something about his obligations. The most important point is that the courts will construe the level of duty by reference to industry practice. This is not to say that a court will simply assume that the latest notice of advice from the CERT should be followed to avoid acting negligently[22]. The court may, however, draw an inference of negligence and reverse the burden of proof forcing the system operator, in effect, to argue against the industry[23]. In the converse situation, if a system operator does keep up-to-date with industry practice and current anti-viral programs, the victim will have a burden that is 'heavy'[24]. System operators should not have reliance solely on official industry statements; they should also aspire to reach the generally understood standards of Internet security[25].

Proportional precautions

The law does try to inject some proportionality into the standard that it expects from defendants. System operators will be judged not purely on the extent of risk but balanced with the difficulty of taking precautions to avoid that risk. Lord Denning put this succinctly[26]:

> '[T]his is an obligation which keeps pace with the times. As the danger increases, so must the precautions increase.'

The risk of a virus spreading is great. It is undoubtedly foreseeable[27] that if a virus is sent to a person connected to the Internet without an appropriate anti-viral program, that virus will infect the user's computer. From this point on, it is

21 The Computer Emergency Response Team is an American publicly-funded establishment that tracks Internet security issues.

22 In *Thompson v Smiths Shiprepairers (North Shields) Ltd* [1984] 1 All ER 881, Mustill J held that an employer was not in breach of his duty when advice was contained in the Lancet; breach occurred 12 years later when the government released an advisory note.

23 Of course, occasionally the industry practice itself is below the standard required by the law. See *Edward Wong Finance Co Ltd v Johnson Stokes & Master* [1984] AC 296.

24 *Morris v West Hartlepool Steam Navigation Co Ltd* [1956] 1 All ER 385 at 402 per Lord Cohen.

25 In *Aiken v Stewart Wrightson Members' Agency Ltd* [1995] 3 All ER 449 at 480, Potter J relied on the 'common ground' that in the US there was an escalation of asbestosis claims which would therefore increase the risk that the level of claims against Lloyd's would rise. Similarly, even without any industry guideline, it is 'common ground' that the move towards using executable code on web pages will escalate the amount of malicious code which can be transmitted. A system operator who seeks to avoid negligence actions should not wait for a reported 'Advisory' from CERT before employing precautions.

26 *Lloyds Bank Ltd v Railway Executive* [1952] 1 All ER 1248 at 1253.

27 There will be occasions where a system operator may view the spread of a virus as a slim possibility. For example, the better anti-viral systems are regularly updated to cope with the newer strains. There will be a chance that even the latest update will allow a new virus through its vetting procedures. It is unlikely that, without other factors, a court will be persuaded that this lag means that a system operator has not reached the required standard of care.

also foreseeable that further infection could occur. Whether the virus is damaging to any considerable extent is obviously something that will vary with the species. The more dangerous a virus, the greater obligation to take adequate precautions to prevent its spread.

The precautions that a system operator should take are unlikely to be expensive, but, as the aphorism prescribes, they must keep pace with the times[28]. System operators must ensure that the seriousness of virus control is understood by all users of a network. They should maintain equipment audits to check that the users of the network are not connecting modems; these may permit viruses to enter the system without passing an anti-viral program. The main precaution, of course, is to keep installed the latest anti-viral program while watching the industry press for any other security issues.

4. An owner of an old Apple computer traces the source of a viral infection to an email that was forwarded to him by a friend in an accountancy firm. It is discovered that this virus was present on all the computers in the firm as well. The reason that no symptoms were present on the firm's computers was that they are IBM-compatible computers, not Apples, and the virus was specific to the latter. The system operator will owe a duty of care to the owner of the infected computer, but it is unlikely that he breached this duty. It is a slim possibility that cross-infection can occur and one which has an expensive precaution: to have every system together with its anti-viral programs merely to prevent this unlikely occurrence.

Damage

If it is proved that a defendant has breached a duty of care, the claimant must then prove that this breach caused the complained-of damage. The law of negligence does not impose a burden on people to keep their duties to others; it imposes a duty not to harm others. In a virus-damage case, the claimant may have an additional burden: English law does not permit the recovery of damages for pure economic loss. There is an argument, explored below, that damage to data may be pure economic loss.

When malicious code infects a system it is often said that the code has 'damaged' the computer. For the purposes of litigation, a claimant must be more precise. It is very rare for code to damage the physical aspects of a computer. Simply because a computer or program may stop working does not mean that there has been any damage to the physical aspects of the machine, like the keyboard, the screen, the chips and the storage systems. What will more probably have occurred is that the so-called 'hardware' is prevented from working properly.

A claimant infected by a virus spread over the Internet may seek to claim for the cost of 'repairing' his computer[29]. In addition, claimants who rely on their computers for commerce will also seek to claim their wider losses such as loss of

28 In *Tutton v AD Walter Ltd* [1986] QB 61 a landowner sprayed a chemical on his yellow rape field which killed a neighbouring beekeeper's bees. The court held that the precautions he could have taken would have prevented the bees from dying and cost little. Similarly, a recently updated anti-viral program will prevent most malicious code leaving or entering: prevention at little cost.

29 Technically, this should read 'cost of cleaning of malicious code and the reinstallation of software and data'.

business and loss of profit. The relevant issue here is that the law will not permit the recovery of damages for pure economic loss. Recovery is permitted only where this economic loss is dependent on the negligently caused damage to property. Accordingly, it is initially necessary to establish that altering the orientation of magnetic particles, how programs and data are stored, is damage to property. Then, the question can be addressed as to what will constitute economic loss dependent on that damage.

Damage to digital media

The operating system of a computer is a complex program that digitally binds together the various aspects of a computer. For instance, it ensures that the central processing unit responds appropriately for each key pressed on the keyboard. It also allows the central processing unit to store data on the screen, the memory or on a storage device. Application programs, such as word processors and drawing packages run 'on top' of an operating system: they rely on the operating system to run; the operating system relies on the hardware. Data files are the raw information that are used, or shown through an application program. A word processing document or a list of client names would be classed as data files.

When any of these programs or data are 'damaged' the question arises as to exactly what has occurred. It will be recalled that computers work with and store only ones and zeros. Programs and data are stored as magnetic representations of zeros and ones either in memory or on a device, usually a disk. To damage a program or data, therefore, is not to cause any physical damage in the way in which it is normally considered: all that is occurring is that the magnetic particles are being altered. The memory or disk remains operative in a physical sense, what it was storing has been altered.

This discussion on technology suggests that a virus causes no property damage. It is more accurate to state that virus damage causes no physical damage: property is a wide term and encompasses more than 'that which can be touched'.

In two cases the criminal courts[30] decided, for the purposes of the Criminal Damage Act 1971, that altering magnetic media can be classed as damage to property[31]. The Court of Appeal, based on previous authorities[32], read widely the concept of damage[33].

Applying the reasoning that an impairment of the value or usefulness of a disk will constitute damage, it is clear that part of a damages claim could justifiably be for the price of the program or software which the disk held[34].

30 It is accepted that one cannot simply transpose the judgment on a point of law in a criminal case to answer a point of law in a civil dispute. However, here the transposition is not of the ratio, rather merely the judicial reasoning: it is persuasive, not authoritative.

31 By the Criminal Damage Act 1971, s 1(1): 'A person who without lawful excuse . . . damages any property . . . intending to . . . damage any such property . . . shall be guilty of an offence'; by s 10(1): '. . . "property" means property of a tangible nature'. This chapter does not suggest that tortious damage to property is restricted to tangible property.

32 *Cox v Riley* (1986) 83 Cr App Rep 54; *Morphitis v Salmon* [1990] Crim LR 48.

33 *R v Whitely* (1991) 93 Cr App Rep 25 at 29 per Lord Lane CJ. Lord Lane distinguished between tangible property being damaged and the damage itself being tangible: 'Where . . . the interference with the disc amounts to an impairment of the value or usefulness of the disc to the owner, then the necessary damage is established.'

34 See fn 29.

5. An accountancy firm distributes free tax assessment software from its website. An individual retrieves this software, which works well, only to discover that it had harboured a virus that crashed his word-processing application program which he had installed from CD-ROM. The firm admits its negligence, but disputes that its damages should include the cost of a new word-processing application. The firm is correct: there is no recoverable damage to the word-processing application; it can be easily reinstalled restoring the individual to the same position as he was in before the infection. The only new piece of software that the individual can claim damages for is the cost of an anti-viral program to clean his disk drive.

Economic loss

It has been seen that a claimant would be justified in claiming damages for the cost of repair, or if the program must be replaced by a new version, the cost of that[35]. What is questionable is the additional economic damages that the claimant can claim. For example, a claimant whose business is the quick design and production of leaflets may well lose trade as a result of his operating system being infected by a virus. But, strictly speaking, the virus has damaged the operating system and not the additional programs that the claimant uses for the design and printing. Whether the claimant can claim for this loss of business is partly a question of causation, but it is also one of economic loss.

In *Spartan Steel & Alloys Ltd v Martin & Co (Contractors) Ltd*[36] the plaintiffs manufactured stainless steel alloys. The power for this was supplied by cable from a nearby electricity station. The defendants damaged this cable stopping power to the factory for 14½ hours. They admitted their negligence, but appealed to the Court of Appeal on the sum of damages awarded by the judge at first instance. Three damages claims had been awarded: £368 for the value of the steel melt which was actually damaged in the furnace as a result of the drop in power; £400 for the profit which should have been made on this melt; and, contentiously, £1,767 for the profit which they would have made on four melts that they were unable to process.

Lord Denning was clearly unimpressed by the plaintiffs but he was able to decide the case on policy[37] rather than merely personality[38]. He stated that[39]:

35 It is unlikely that a new operating system would have to be purchased: it is usual that a user of an operating system will have a legal backup copy for just this sort of occurrence. Alternatively, the supplier of an operating system will often provide a free additional copy where it can be shown that the original is no longer able to be used. See the Copyright, Designs and Patents Act 1988, s 50A(1).

36 [1972] 3 All ER 557.

37 'At the bottom I think the question of recovering economic loss is one of policy. Whenever the courts draw a line to mark out the bounds of duty, they do it as a matter of policy so as to limit the responsibility of the defendant. Whenever the courts set bounds to the damages recoverable – saying that they are, or are not, too remote – they do it as a matter of policy so as to limit the liability of the defendant.' Per Lord Denning [1972] 3 All ER 557 at 561.

38 '[T]he cutting of the supply of electricity . . . is a hazard which we all run . . . When the supply is cut off, [most people] do not go running round to their solicitor. They do not try to find out whether it was anyone's fault. They just put up with it. They try to make up the economic loss by doing more work the next day. This is a healthy attitude which the law should encourage.' Per Lord Denning [1972] 3 All ER 557 at 564.

39 [1972] 3 All ER 557 at 564.

> 'it is better to disallow economic loss altogether, at any rate when it stands alone, independent of any physical damage.'

So the relevant question, policy aside, is when are the damages claimed by a claimant for infection by damaging code 'dependent' on physical damage? Applying Lord Denning's analysis above it would appear that the loss of business profit while an operating system is being repaired or replaced is irrecoverable, either as being too remote, or as pure economic loss. What would be recoverable is any work that at the time of infection is damaged by the virus.

6. A data warehouse performs online data processing operations on behalf of poll researchers for general elections. It is imperative that this processing is not delayed as such a delay would make the results inaccurate. Larger polls can take many hours to process. During the processing of one such poll, the entire system crashes as a result of a virus spread from a negligently operated Internet Service Provider. The warehouse will be able to claim damages in respect of the poll being processed, but probably not for the profit from the polls which it is unable to process during the disinfection. These damages will be pure economic loss.

Data damage

It has been mentioned that damage to programs is often cheap to repair[40]. Any damage caused to data may be expensive, with large consequential losses. For a business, damage to data may be catastrophic: orders may be unable to be fulfilled; research and development may have to be repeated; business may be lost through customers' qualms as to the security of the system. It will be recalled that economic loss not anchored to and resulting from physical harm to property is not recoverable.

If it is accepted that data being corrupted is damage to property it becomes easy to see that the economic loss, such as profits from the use of that data, will be recoverable. But it is vital to appreciate that this is the key to recovery: a claimant must hang any claim for economic loss on the corruption of the data being damage to property. Of course, a claimant must also be careful not to value the data twice: the 'value' of the data and business profits lost as a result of its damage can overlap in certain circumstances. It is this problem of calculation of which Lord Denning was wary[41]:

> 'It would be well-nigh impossible to check the claims. If there was economic loss on one day, did the applicant do his best to mitigate it by working harder next day?'

Ongoing damage

A program or data that is damaged by a malicious code will suffer repeated damage unless it is stopped by an anti-viral program which digitally cleans the

40 See fn 29.
41 [1972] 3 All ER 557 at 564.

infected computer. At law, without suitable settlement after initial damage, a claimant can bring numerous actions for each repeated damage caused by the defendant's negligence[42]. This, in theory, would suggest that a claimant infected by a virus spread through the negligence of another could bring a new claim each time the computer is prevented from working properly as a result of the ongoing infection. In practice, a claimant who became infected by a virus but attempted to continue working with that computer without cleaning it first would not have mitigated his damages. He probably would have made a voluntary assumption of risk so denying a cause of action.

Causation of damage

The final aspect to recovering for damage caused by the defendant's breach of duty is that the defendant caused the recoverable damage. A claimant whose software or data is damaged by malicious code must show that the defendant's negligent conduct was responsible for the loss. To show this the claimant must satisfy two tests: one factual and the other legal. The application of these tests to a virus victim does not greatly differ to any other type of claim. There are, however, a few issues that are specific to the Internet.

Factual test: causation

The first test is factual: did the defendant actually cause the damage? This is particularly relevant for the Internet because there is a chance that a person infected by a virus from one site was already infected by the same virus from another location[43].

Absolute nature of viruses

Viruses are rife on the Internet and, like viruses of a biological variety, a strain cannot be eliminated completely without destroying every last active virus and carrier. Unlike biological viruses, a computer virus can cause as much damage with one infection of a computer as with one hundred infections on the same computer. Having one copy of a virus on a computer at the time of a subsequent infection by the same virus may not alter the potential damage of that first virus. Also unlike biological viruses, a computer virus will generally act absolutely: if it is programmed to delete certain files on a certain date, those files will be deleted on that unfortunate date. No more files will be deleted by there being an additional copy of the virus infecting the system[44]. There is usually no

42 See *Hudson v Nicholson* (1839) 5 M & W 437.

43 This common occurrence on the Internet is a practical example of the three-house fire problem. This is where a house, sandwiched between two others, is burnt by a fire that has been started by the two separate negligent owners of each of the neighbouring houses. In the problem, each negligent owner may claim that, but for their actions, the middle house would still have burnt down.

44 It is admitted that there is possibility that malicious code could 'multitask', that is, run more than one copy at one time. In this situation it is technically possible that two copies of the virus will cause the same damage but more quickly than one copy of the virus.

increase of risk of damage, or damage, by there being two infections. These statements usually make a significant difference to the way that a defendant will approach the question of causation.

Previous infection: same code

One legal approach to whether the defendant factually caused the damage is to structure a question using the 'but-for' test. This is often employed by the courts. For example, but for the system operator's negligence would the user have suffered damage to data? Where the claimant can prove that the code which caused the damage was downloaded from a site under the control of the system operator the test will apply and the court will be able to decide that the operator actually caused the damage. It is common for a claimant to be infected more than once. A claimant may allege that but for the defendant's negligence her data would not have been damaged. The defendant could counter this by showing that the claimant was already infected from an unrelated site[45].

Because most viruses do not become more damaging in numbers and act absolutely, a defendant may simply be able to allege that because of a prior infection the claimant was destined to be damaged anyway. The negligence by the defendant may have allowed the virus to spread but, unless proved, it did not cause the damage. Such an approach has been successful in *Barnett v Chelsea and Kensington Hospital Management Committee*[46] in which a patient was admitted to hospital with arsenic poisoning. The doctor was negligent in taking so long to see the patient, but the court stated that even without this negligence, the patient had no reasonable prospect of living.

Although the courts should assess causation in fact as an issue divorced from duty there is inevitably some blurring of the two issues. This is why it may be considered unsafe to draw a principle from a medical negligence case to apply it to a computer virus infection. If anything though, the court in a medical negligence case, where the defendant has assumed responsibility and personal injury is in issue, would allow more generous causation than for a system operator who has assumed no such responsibility. It is, therefore, perhaps even less likely that a court would deem a system operator caused the damage where the claimant's computer was already infected.

7. A website system operator is sued for negligence in allowing an animation file to be infected with a virus which damages a viewer's browser on the first of the month. During the disclosure stage of the litigation, the defendant is able to see that the viewer's computer had already been infected by this virus five times previously. While the website operator may well have owed a duty of care to check his site for viruses, the breach of that duty did not cause the damage; the claimant's software would have been damaged with or without the negligence.

45 It may be possible using 'time-stamps' on infected code to assess exactly which virus caused which damage. Cf in *Cook v Lewis* [1952] 1 DLR 1, two hunters negligently shot through some trees. As a result of one of those shots, the claimant is hit by a bullet. The court, unable to prove absolutely which hunter was responsible for the wounding shot must decide whether the claimant can recover, and if so, whether from both or just one.

46 [1969] 1 QB 428.

Previous infection: different code

A claimant who has browsed the Internet considerably may be infected by more than one strain of virus. In such a situation the defendant may wish to allege that the claimant's software and data was going to be damaged in some way anyway, so, as above, the defendant is not liable. The problem with such a pleading is that with the help of expert evidence it should be easy to show which virus caused the damage. If it was not the virus contracted from the defendant's site, the defendant has not caused that damage and is not liable. If the virus was contracted from the defendant's site it is not relevant to the issue of causation that this is only one of the claimant's infections.

One final scenario is where evidence is adduced that the claimant was already infected with viruses which all caused roughly the same type of damage but it cannot be proved which virus caused the actual damage. There are two House of Lords authorities on which a claimant may rely to prove causation; both cases indicate the difficulties in proving causation.

Material increase of risk

The boiled-down rule from *McGhee v National Coal Board*[47] is that if a defendant is proved to have materially increased the risk of a claimant being damaged, the burden of proof moves to the defendant. The defendant must then prove on the balance of probabilities that the negligence did not cause the damage claimed. A superficial interpretation of this rule may indicate that the claimant needs only to prove that the presence of the 'defendant's' virus could have caused infection to reverse the burden of proof. But, any reading of the case must be far narrower than this: a claimant must adduce that the defendant's negligence materially increased the risk of suffering that damage. It is not enough to show that the claimant simply increased the risk of data damage per se.

8. A new word processor that integrates with online translation services on the Internet becomes the target of many virus writers. Three particularly vicious viruses attach to the program and scramble or delete any documents at the point of saving them. A firm's internal network, with a 'safe' connection to its main supplier, becomes infected with one variety of the virus. They sue their supplier for damages resulting from negligence. It is then discovered that the claimant's internal network is also infected with the other two strains. Because of poor retention of the evidence, the claimant is unable to show that the infection from the defendant is the actual cause of the damage complained of. But, the claimant does adduce that the defendant's negligence added to their risk of damage. They have not proved in fact that the defendant's negligence increased the risk of damage from the offending code.

47 *McGhee v National Coal Board* [1972] 3 All ER 1008.

Multiple possible causes

In *Wilsher v Essex Area Health Authority*[48] the House of Lords was faced with the case of a blind premature baby whose blindness could have been caused by a junior doctor's negligent insertion of a catheter into a vein rather than an artery. The problem of causation was that premature babies may be blind for four other reasons. The Lords judged that for the defendant to be liable the claimant would have to prove that the defendant's negligence was the most likely of all the reasons.

By cautious analogy it can be seen that if a claimant has a computer so riddled with infectious code that it cannot be said with certainty which code caused the damage, the claimant must prove that the 'defendant's' code was most likely to have caused the damage.

9. An unfortunate software programmer downloads the latest version of a programming tool from a supplier, only to realise that, on running the program, her hard disk is corrupted. The hard disk cannot be repaired and prevents the programmer retrieving any of her data. She sues the supplier who discovers that her hard disk was old and would have been prone to corruption at some point in the future. The court must take expert evidence as to the probability not merely of 'natural' corruption, but of data-caused corruption of the drive. If this is less likely to have caused the corruption at that point in time than the presence of the virus, the court must deem that the supplier is the factual cause of the damage.

Legal test: remoteness

After satisfying a court that a system operator's negligence actually caused the damage, the claimant has in addition to prove that the damage was not too remote. Remoteness is a judicial limit on liability. It is used by the courts to prevent a defendant being liable for 'all the consequences [of an act of negligence] however foreseeable and however grave'[49]. For malicious code damage 'remoteness' allows the liability of the defendant to be reduced by the actions of third parties or the claimant and condition of the claimant's equipment. This should be welcome news for operators whose systems are connected to the Internet. It may be perfectly possible that a system operator's negligence caused damage to thousands of computers through cross-infections; remoteness, however, will reduce the liability.

There are two types of situation that may require proper regard to the rules on remoteness. The first is secondary damage, that is, damage caused by subsequent infections of the virus after infecting the claimant's equipment. The second type of damage is where the claimant not only claims damages in respect of the damaged data but also of some apparently related event. As more computers that perform important tasks are connected to the Internet, more viruses will cause far-reaching effects. Hospital computers are now connected to the Internet; most financial institutions are connected; Parliament is connected. Every system

48 [1987] QB 730.

49 *Overseas Tankship (UK) Ltd v Morts Dock and Engineering Co Ltd, The Wagon Mound (No 1)* [1961] 1 All ER 404 at 413 per Viscount Simonds.

operator should be concerned to appreciate when the law will deem damage is too remote.

This author heeds the warning given by Lord Steyn in the House of Lords that[50]:

> . . . in this corner of the law the results of decided cases are inevitably very fact-sensitive. Both counsel [in this case] nevertheless at times invited your Lordships to compare the facts of the present case with the facts of other decided cases. That is a sterile exercise. Precedent is a valuable stabilising influence in our legal system. But, comparing the facts of and outcomes of cases in this branch of the law is a misuse of the only proper use of precedent, viz to identify the relevant rule to apply to the facts as found.'

With this in mind, what follows is a guide to the court's approach.This is provided by summarising the approach taken in one particular case[51]. The facts are unimportant for our purposes. Woolf J asked the pivotal question[52]:

> 'Are the damages that the claimant has to pay to his victims so remote that, although they are the consequence of the accident, they are not recoverable at law?'

To answer this question one general statement of remoteness was made together with three 'glosses'.

General statement: Wagon Mound

The general statement of the law on remoteness is drawn from the case *Wagon Mound*[53]. In that case the defendants allowed oil to pour from their ship onto the plaintiff's dockyard. The plaintiff's manager was assured by a manager of an oil depot that there was no reason to stop welding work; oil on the sea is not inflammable. The welding recommenced and some sparks fell onto some floating debris which in turn ignited the oil. The plaintiff's dockyard was burnt.

Viscount Simonds was convinced, as the courts have been since, that[54]:

> 'a man must be considered to be responsible for the probable consequences of his act. To demand more of him is too harsh a rule, to demand less is to ignore that civilised order requires the observance of a minimum standard of behaviour.'

So, the claimant in a digital damage case must show that it was reasonably foreseeable that the negligence by the system operator would lead to the damage. Where the claimant claims only for damage to the actual data or program it will

50 *Jolley v Sutton London Borough Council* [2000] 3 All ER 409, HL.
51 *Meah v McCreamer (No 2)* [1986] 1 All ER 943.
52 [1986] 1 All ER 943 at 945.
53 *Overseas Tankship (UK) Ltd v Morts Dock and Engineering Co Ltd, The Wagon Mound (No 1)* [1961] 1 All ER 404. The case remains supported by the House of Lords: *Jolley v Sutton London Borough Council* [2000] 3 All ER 409, HL.
54 [1961] 1 All ER 404 at 413.

be difficult for the defendant to rebut this claim with a statement that it was not reasonably foreseeable. For example, it is well known that if any executable files are sent over the Internet they can be hosts for malicious code. Not to screen for this malicious code before sending, or allowing the retrieval of this code, has the reasonably foreseeable consequence of damaging data or programs. The more difficult questions are addressed below, such as whether a system operator is responsible for events resulting from the data damage, and for secondary infections.

Glosses on remoteness

Cases following *Wagon Mound* have modified its effect on remoteness. Woolf J applied *Wagon Mound* together with these modifications; this section will do the same.

1. Thin skulls

In *Dulieu v White*[55] Kennedy J formulated the rule of English negligence law that a defendant takes his victim as he finds him[56]:

> 'it is no answer [to a negligence claim] that he would have suffered less injury, or no injury at all, if he had not had an unusually thin skull or an unusually weak heart.'

In *Smith v Leech Brain*[57] the court was asked to discount this rule in the light of *Wagon Mound*; if a claimant suffers from a rare condition the defendant should not be liable in relation to this condition as it is not reasonably foreseeable. The court was unconvinced by the defendant's argument and ruled that the thin-skull rule applied along with the *Wagon Mound* test.

The most relevant question for the damage caused by viruses is whether the thin-skull rule applies to property, not merely to the physical and mental condition of a claimant. If a victim's computer had an anti-viral program installed which would have eliminated the virus, but for some reason this program was not functioning properly, is the claimant able to rely on a rule akin to the thin-skull rule? This is an important question because it may be reasonably unforeseeable that an installed anti-viral program is not working which would mean that the damage is too remote to recover. But, if the thin-skull rule applies to property, this option will not be open to the defendant who must accept the claimant's faulty program as he finds it.

In the House of Lords case, *The Edison*[58], Lord Wright stated that the thin-skull rule was concerned only with actual physical damage[59]. This would indicate that the thin-skull rule may not apply to the state in which a claimant

55 [1901] 2 KB 669.
56 [1901] 2 KB 669 at 679.
57 [1962] 2 QB 405.
58 *Liesbosch, Dredger v Edison SS* [1933] All ER Rep 144, sub nom The Edison.
59 [1933] All ER Rep 144 at 159. See also *Bailey v Derby Corpn* [1965] 1 All ER 443 at 445 per Lord Denning.

leaves a computer. However, *The Edison*, although not overruled, has been heavily distinguished and will be unlikely to be followed[60]. It may therefore be said, with some conviction, that a fault or vulnerability of the claimant's computer to infection will not make the damage suffered too remote. A claimant may be able to rely on the thin-skull rule: this does not, as will be discussed, prevent the defendant alleging contributory negligence for the claimant not having a working anti-viral program[61].

2. Type, not kind, of damage

The second gloss on the *Wagon Mound* test distinguishes between the need for the type of damage to be foreseeable rather than the need to foresee the precise extent and manner of infliction. Lord Denning puts this as follows[62].

> 'It is not necessary that the precise concatenation of circumstances should be envisaged. If the consequence was one which was within the general range which any reasonable person might foresee (and was not of an entirely different kind which no one would anticipate) then it is within the rule that a person who has been guilty of negligence is liable for the consequences.'

Damage to programs and data, the very *modus operandi* of malicious code, will always seem to be reasonably foreseeable. What will entertain the courts is whether resulting damage from this data damage will be foreseeable.

3. Intervening acts

The final gloss, and one that may come into play when a claimant suffers secondary damage, is a general principle. The chain from breach of duty to damage can be broken by an intervening act by another person including the claimant. In a malicious code situation the main intervening act will be in relation to secondary damage: that is, it is the action of the first victim which allows the spread of the virus to a second victim.

The first point to make is that any intervening act by a third party in the chain of causation must reduce the probability that the defendant was responsible in fact for the damage suffered. Each new entrant into the chain of actions which finally result in the damage will decrease a judge's conviction that the defendant was liable for the harm. But when considering remoteness the court is posing a different question: are the actions of others so significant as to exonerate the defendant?

This area is one of substantial academic debate. There are cases that indicate a retreat from *Wagon Mound*[63] or a realignment of its terms[64] together with those suggesting *Wagon Mound* 'repay[s] full rereading'[65]. Here, it will be

60 In particular see the Court of Appeal's ingenious distinguishing of the case in *Dodd Properties (Kent) Ltd v Canterbury City Council* [1980] 1 All ER 928.
61 See 'Contributory negligence', at p 105.
62 *Stewart v West African Terminals Ltd* [1964] 2 Lloyd's Rep 371 at 375.
63 *Lamb v Camden London Borough Council* [1981] 2 All ER 408.
64 *Home Office v Dorset Yacht Co Ltd* [1970] 2 All ER 294.
65 *Delaware Mansions Ltd v Westminster City Council* [2002] 1 AC 321.

assumed that *Wagon Mound* and its glosses will apply to the question of third party intervention. A relevant question is, therefore, whether the interventions or their consequences were reasonably foreseeable by a person such as the defendant at the time of the accident. For damage occurring from secondary infection the answer is clear: it is foreseeable that a victim of a computer virus infection will pass the infection on to another *whilst their computer has not developed any symptoms*.

10. An Internet Service Provider admits negligence in allowing a virus to spread to its members' computers. One member refuses the *ex gratia* settlement offered by the Provider and sues for the damage done not simply to the connected computer but to the entire network of which this computer forms a part. One aspect of the damages claim is for the emotional distress suffered by the Head of the IT Department. On remoteness the Provider has two main arguments: first, it was unforeseeable that an entire network would be connected to an Internet computer without any firewall in place; second, it was unforeseeable that the virus would result in the emotional distress of the Head of IT. The first argument will probably fail as the Provider must take the company as found. This will not, however, preclude a defence of contributory negligence. On the second argument, it is possible that a court would view the damage to data and physical property as within the type of foreseeable damage. The court would be less likely to view the emotional distress to the Head of IT as within the same type.

Defences

There are two main defences to a negligence action for malicious code damage. The first, and one that will most commonly be invoked, is contributory negligence. This is where the defendant admits that he caused to an extent the damage but that the claimant also caused some of the damage himself. An analogy may be able to be drawn from an Internet user not having an anti-viral program and a car driver not wearing a seat belt. Not having a backup of important data may also be an issue of contributory negligence, although it is admitted that this blurs somewhat with mitigation of damages and remoteness issues. The second defence is that of consent or *volenti non fit injuria*. Not only has this defence lost much of the court's support, but also it is likely to be ineffective in a virus scenario.

Contributory negligence

The Law Reform (Contributory Negligence) Act 1945 provides the partial[66] defence of contributory negligence. The scope of the defence is clear from s 1(1):

> 'Where any person suffers damage as a result partly of his own fault and partly of the fault of any other person or persons, a claim in respect of that damage shall not be defeated by the reason of the

66 See the Court of Appeal's decision in *Pitts v Hunt* [1990] 3 All ER 344.

> fault of the person suffering the damage, but the damages recoverable in respect thereof shall be reduced to such an extent as the court thinks just and equitable having regard to the claimant's share in the responsibility for the damage.'

Anti-viral programs

Anti-viral programs are fortunately more effective than medical anti-viral treatments: they work absolutely, either preventing an infection or allowing an infection to take place. If a claimant had used an anti-viral program that covered the damaging strain, no damage would have occurred. The presence of an anti-viral program would have prevented the litigation being brought; the 'victim' may not even have known that his computer had been the object of an attack. Without an appropriate anti-viral program the computer will be infected; there are no proportions of damage. Similarly there are road traffic accidents where the victim's damage could have been completely prevented by the victim wearing a seat belt. Before moving to the law's treatment of this, it should be understood that a direct comparison between data damage and personal injury is not entirely appropriate. Clearly, whether the policy is stated or underlies a court's decision, a claimant with severe personal injuries will be looked upon more favourably than a computer user with corrupted data. This said, the comparison does reveal that a negligent defendant will not be able to avoid all damages merely by casting the aspersion that the claimant should have used an anti-viral program.

In *Froom v Butcher*[67], Lord Denning's analysis was given unanimous approval by the other members of the Court of Appeal. He said[68]:

> 'the cause of the accident is one thing. The cause of the damage is another. The accident is caused by bad driving. The damage is caused in part by the bad driving of the defendant, and in part by the failure of the claimant to wear a seat belt.'

This drawn distinction between accident and damage allowed Lord Denning to ensure that[69]:

> '[i]t should not lie in [the defendant's] mouth to say: "You ought to have been wearing a seat belt."'

This has parallels with negligence resulting in data damage. It too consists of an accident that would not have resulted in damage if the claimant had taken precautions. And it is submitted that, in these cases it is even less reasonable for the defendant to call for the claimant to have used an anti-viral program. In 1975 seat belts were fitted as standard on most cars and the Highway Code encouraged their use. Anti-viral programs are not installed as standard on Internet-connected computers and advisory statements are not included with each modem or computer[70].

67 [1975] 3 All ER 520.
68 [1975] 3 All ER 520 at 525.
69 [1975] 3 All ER 520 at 525.
70 'Everyone is free to [use] it or not, as he pleases . . . Free in the sense that everyone is free to run his head against a brick wall, if he pleases. He can do it if he likes without being punished by the law. But it is not a sensible thing to do.' [1975] 3 All ER 520 at 525 per Lord Denning.

Lord Denning said of those claimants who would not have been damaged at all, had they worn a seat belt[71]:

> 'Whenever there is an accident, the negligent driver must bear by far the greater share of responsibility. It was his negligence which caused the accident. It was also a prime cause of the whole of the damage . . . [Sometimes] the evidence will show that the failure made all the difference. The damage would have been prevented altogether if a seat belt had been worn. In such cases I would suggest that the damages should be reduced by 25 per cent.'

This reasoning is logically and equally applicable to the infection of a user's computer. The claimant is in no way to blame for the accident itself[72]. While it may be wise to use an anti-viral program, not to do so does not eliminate the defendant's duty not to cause an accident through negligence. The aspect of Lord Denning's judgment that cannot be so readily extrapolated is the level of 25% as the appropriate reduction in damages.

At the time of *Froom v Butcher* it was well known that one should wear a seat belt and the government encouraged it[73]. In a later endorsement of *Froom v Butcher* the Court of Appeal applied Lord Denning's guidelines to the situation other than an accident involving a seat belt. In this case, a moped rider failed to secure his crash helmet[74]. But it was a breach of the Motor Cycles (Protective Helmets) Regulations 1980 to ride a moped without securely fastened protective headgear. So the Court of Appeal's agreement with the guidelines was in relation to a similar obligation to protect oneself.

The use and regular updating of anti-viral programs by users is not at a similar level of awareness to wearing a seat belt or crash helmet. It is therefore submitted that a court should take this into account and apply Lord Denning's reasoning but reduce the upper boundary of 25% to allow for the lower level of awareness.

11. A corporation's network is infected by a virus and it claims over a million pounds in damages from its law firm which allowed the virus to pass through their 'safe' connection. The law firm is both shocked at the claim and at the fact that the infected corporation does not use a virus checker which would have prevented all the damage. The firm is advised to focus their attention on proving that they had no duty of care as it is foreseeable that a commercial organisation would have no anti-viral program. This is sensible because it is unlikely that even a successful defence of contributory negligence would reduce the damages by more than 50%.

Data backups

Where the damage caused by malicious code is purely loss of data there is a factual, and possibly legal, argument that if the claimant had backed up the data far

71 [1975] 3 All ER 520 at 528.

72 This is in the generalised scenario. Clearly a user who chooses to download some sample viruses will be unable to suggest that the defendant is wholly or even partially responsible.

73 Between 1972 and 1974 the government had spent millions of pounds on advertising to encourage people to wear seat belts.

74 *Capps v Miller* [1989] 2 All ER 333.

less damage would have occurred[75]. A legal basis for this argument could be based on contributory negligence, but it has less force than an argument that the victim should have used an anti-viral program. As to other arguments, the defendant could allege that the victim may have mitigated his damages by making a backup before the damage. It is submitted that such a claim is better pleaded as a remoteness issue: mitigation is usually a *post facto* issue.

CONSENT

It may be alleged by an operator of a website, forum or ftp site that, by a claimant choosing to use the site, he consented to the risk of virus damage. To plead such a defence is to rely on consent or *volenti non fit injuria*. Although a consent defence remains appropriate for intentional torts such as assault, particularly in sport, there is now some doubt as to the extent of the defence for negligence[76].

Whether or not the defence applies to negligence, what is certain is that if it does, a high degree of complicity is required by the claimant. Asquith J compared the degree of consent needed for a defence of *volenti* to 'inter-meddling with an unexploded bomb or walking on the edge of an unfenced cliff'[77]. For example, the Court of Appeal judged that a claimant who watched a pilot drink the equivalent of 17 whiskies would have his claim for negligent flying defeated by the defence of *volenti*[78]. Fox LJ stated, 'Flying is intrinsically dangerous and flying with a drunken pilot is great folly'[79].

12. A website acts as a depository of supposedly neutralised virus code. A claimant downloads one of the latest viruses with a view to writing an anti-viral code as an antidote. The code was not actually neutralised and the claimant's computer becomes infected, forcing him to lose one day's working time. On poor advice, he sues. Putting aside the inherent difficulties of establishing negligence, a court will probably allow the full defence of *volenti*: dealing with virus code is tantamount to dealing with unexploded bombs.

As for contributory negligence, it is difficult to extrapolate from a personal injury defence to one for data damage. If lessons can be learnt, clearly any defendant, who by negligence has caused data damage, will have a struggle to convince a court that the claimant was entering a dangerous area.

75 Some damage would have occurred owing to the time taken to restore the data from the backup and the loss of unrecoverable data having been created after the last backup.

76 See *Morris v Murray* [1990] 3 All ER 801 at 806 in which Fox LJ distinguishes between the dicta of Diplock LJ in *Wooldridge v Sumner* [1962] 2 All ER 978 at 988 and Asquith J's test in *Dann v Hamilton* [1939] 1 All ER 59 at 63.

77 [1939] 1 All ER 59 at 64. Applied by the Court of Appeal in *Morris v Murray* [1990] 3 All ER 801.

78 *Morris v Murray* [1990] 3 All ER 801.

79 [1990] 3 All ER 801 at 809.

Electronic Commerce Regulations' Hosting Defence

A host of damaging code may rely on two possible defences under the Electronic Commerce (EC Directive) Regulations 2002, reg 19. These defences ensure that service providers are not liable as a result of storing damaging third party material so long as they have no authority or control over the third party.

No actual knowledge, no awareness, no control

The first defence is essentially that the service provider must be unwittingly hosting the damaging code or virus[80]. This is expressed in three parts for damages claims. First, the service provider harbouring the virus must not have 'actual knowledge' that the transmission, or hosting, of the code was in breach of any law. The second part is that the host must *also* 'not be aware of facts or circumstances' from which it would have been apparent that the activity or information was unlawful. Third, and dealt with below, the host must have no authority or control over the third party.

No actual knowledge of breach of law

In the main, this part of the defence will be taken to mean that the hosting company or person has not been provided with 'notice' about the virus or other code. This notice need not, however, be in writing and it certainly need not originate from a court. There is no particular form which will provide the requisite 'actual' knowledge; it is a question of fact for the court. The court shall, however, have regard to whether the notice was sent to the Provider's published email address and the extent to which the notice identifying where the material is, why it is unlawful and whether the sender provides their name and address.

No awareness of facts or circumstances

This is the tough part of the defence. Even if the provider has no actual knowledge, for damages claims, they must still demonstrate that they have no awareness of relevant facts or circumstances which would lead them to believe the code is unlawful.

For viruses and other malicious code, this author believes a service provider will rarely meet this part of the defence. First, every service provider will be aware of security-monitoring organisations such as CERT which have 'live' information on their websites about computer viruses and other damaging code. CERT will even send out a warning email to those on a free mailing list. In addition, the objective service provider will be well aware that the release of damaging code or viruses is unlawful potentially under the tort of negligence and under the Computer Misuse Act 1990.

80 Regulation 19(a)(i).

The third leg of this defence is described below: the service provider must have no authority or control over the third party.

No authority or control and expeditious action

The second hosting defence concerns the actions of the service provider once they have knowledge or awareness. They will have the benefit of the defence if they meet two conditions. First, they must not be in control and they must have no authority over the person who left the virus. The second condition is that they must act expeditiously to remove or disable access to it as soon as they know about it[81].

No authority or control

The first condition to meet is for the third party who originally provided the virus for storage not to be acting under the service provider's 'authority' or 'control'[82]. Of course, often a service provider will have a contract with its members or customers. Will this constitute 'authority' or 'control'? This author and the DTI believe it will not.

The DTI states in its unbinding note on the Regulations that the concept of control or authority will be akin to 'effective control' under the Defamation Act 1996[83]. In other words, a mere contract to provide services to the third party will not be sufficient to bring the third party under the service provider's 'control' or 'authority'. The Regulations require a closer relationship such as between an employee, the third party, and an employer, the service provider.

An open question remains relating to whether or not the *ability* to control the third party will constitute control for the purposes of the first prong of the defence. After all, most, if not all service providers have the *ability* to remove material that is damaging. Indeed, in a worst-case scenario, a service provider can always simply disable *all* communication with the outside world; will that be 'control'?

US authority on a similar question is convincing that, were such an interpretation to be applied, it would be contrary to the spirit of the legislation itself. It would, in effect, state that those who are able to comply with the onus to remove material once notified must be able to remove the material and so are deemed to control it[84]:

> 'First, the "right and ability to control" the infringing activity, as the concept is used in the [Digital Millennium Copyright Act ("DMCA")], cannot simply mean the ability of a service provider to remove or block access to materials posted on its website or stored in its system. To hold otherwise would defeat the purpose of the DMCA and render the statute internally inconsistent. The DMCA specifically requires a service provider to remove or block access to materials

81 Regulation 19(a)(ii) and (b).
82 Regulation 19(a)(ii).
83 *A Guide for Business to the Electronic Commerce (EC Directive) Regulations 2002*, para 6.7(c).
84 *Hendrickson v Ebay, Inc* 2001 WL 1078981, CD Cal, 4 September 2001.

> posted on its system when it receives notice of claimed infringement. *See* 17 U.S.C. §§ 512(c)(1)(C). The DMCA also provides that the limitations on liability *only* apply to a service provider that has 'adopted and reasonably implemented . . . a policy that provides for the termination in appropriate circumstances of [users] of the service provider's system or network who are repeat infringers'. *See* 17 U.S.C. §§ 512(i)(1)(A). Congress could not have intended for courts to hold that a service provider loses immunity under the safe harbor provision of the DMCA because it engages in acts that are specifically required by the DMCA.'

Remove or disable expeditiously

The second condition is essentially that the service provider must act to stop any further harm as soon as they know about it. The Regulations state that 'upon obtaining such knowledge or awareness the service provider [must act] expeditiously to remove or to disable access to the information'[85].

The concept of 'actual knowledge' and the requisite 'awareness' is discussed above but 'awareness' in this context deserves more attention. The concept of 'awareness' is a wide one; it seems to encompass the service provider having a general 'sense' of the state of the technical and legal standards for unlawful material. Does this mean that a service provider unwittingly hosting a virus will be liable because a well-respected website publishes details of that virus? The answer is 'no' for two good reasons.

First, the Electronic Commerce Regulations implement the Electronic Commerce Directive. Article 15(1) states that:

> 'Member States shall not impose a general obligation on providers, when providing the services covered by [the] Articles [concerning mere conduit, caching and hosting], to monitor information which they transmit or store, nor a general obligation actively to seek facts or circumstances indicating illegal activity.'

This Article is not explicitly implemented in the Regulations. The reason for this must be that Parliament believed that nothing in the Regulations did impose a general obligation to monitor such facts and circumstances. It follows that the Regulations do not, in effect, force service providers to watch websites like CERT, to be able to benefit from the defence.

The second justification for the unwitting service provider not being liable is that, on awareness or knowledge, they are required to remove or disable access to the virus. Of course, if all they know is that the virus is 'in the wild', how are they to remove or disable the virus? They would need actively to search for it on their network. As explained above, a general obligation to seek or search for such information, is not envisaged within scope the legislation.

This leaves only the issue of how fast is 'expeditiously'. There is little doubt that this is quicker than 'reasonably quickly' but nevertheless will be assessed with reference to the facts and circumstances of the situation. It can be said with

85 Regulation 19(a)(ii).

some certainty that a service provider who is sent a specific notice about a virus on a Thursday evening will need to act well before the weekend to do so expeditiously.

Why negligence?

This section has dealt exclusively with using the law of negligence to claim for damage from a viral infection. For the sake of completeness, this final part of the section considers why a claim for occupier's liability, strict liability or nuisance may be inappropriate.

To understand the Internet, metaphors are often employed. A presence on the Internet is called a website. People using the Internet are said to browse it. Even the 'information superhighway' implies a tangible presence like a set of roads, the websites being like shops and billboards along the way. Such comparisons are useful to conceptualise the Internet, but they may not be reliable for legal analysis.

When one's data is harmed by a computer virus caught from browsing a company's website, nothing physical occurs. The site is no more than a collection of digital information, browsing is simply the transferral of information in the form of ones and zeros from one computer's memory to another's. Damage occurs, not because of faulty wiring or fire but because of inappropriate vetting of the digital information stored on the accessed computer. Laws, both statutory and common, that relate to occupier's liability, product liability and nuisance are likely to be inappropriate to apply.

Occupiers' liability

The Occupiers' Liability Acts 1957 and 1984 replace common law rules on occupiers' liability with a statutory equivalent. A website controller is liable only as an occupier of premises, which is any fixed or movable structure[86]. A website may be notional premises but the reality is that a person who browses a website has no physical presence there. The Act will not apply between website controllers and those who gain access to them.

Product liability

The Consumer Protection Act 1987 provides that almost anyone connected with the sale of a defective product may be liable for harm caused by the product[87]. The Act is unlikely to be applicable to digital materials transmitted over the Internet, but it will still apply to physical products conventionally sent. This is because the Act applies to defective products, and does not explicitly include information: incorrect information on a website is unlikely to be classed as a product, and even defective software, unless incorporated into a machine[88], is arguably not a product. In addition, there is a defence for new technologies

86 Occupiers' Liability Act 1957, s 1(3).
87 Consumer Protection Act 1987, s 2.
88 Consumer Protection Act 1987, s 3(2).

which may be applicable to exclude liability where the state of knowledge at the time was not such that a producer of the products might have been expected to discover the defect[89]. Arguably, using the latest anti-viral program is enough to be able to rely on this defence.

Nuisance

Comparisons seem reasonable between a reservoir owner allowing water to damage another's property and a website owner allowing code to damage another's property. However, in *Rylands v Fletcher*, in which the reservoir owner was liable for damage done owing to the escape of water, the House of Lords was careful to stress the ruling applied only to escapes from land[90]. This was affirmed by the House of Lords in *Cambridge Water Co Ltd v Eastern Counties Leather plc*[91] in which Lord Goff considered an earlier case[92] stating[93]:

> 'there can be no liability under the rule except in circumstances where the injury has been caused by an escape from land under the control of the defendant.'

It seems, therefore, that the ruling in *Rylands v Fletcher* is narrowly focused on escapes from land, and often to other land. It seems improbable that the courts will stretch its application to the Internet, particularly as the Law Commission has expressed misgivings about any generalised test for 'especially dangerous' activities[94]. Nevertheless, there does appear to be a glacially slow judicial movement to make nuisance indistinguishable from negligence[95].

NEGLIGENT MISSTATEMENT

The Internet allows wide, unfocused dissemination of information, and also concentrated, targeted distribution. For commerce this is special. The website that acts as a brochure for a mortgage adviser can also act as the ecommerce site to provide the quotes to be given to a customer. A stockbroker can host a web page that lists the current prices of stocks, allows customers to buy shares and provides, at an additional cost, tips on which shares to buy.

This ability easily to provide information, advice, and help to any person, anywhere in the world has massive potential. But this potential should be balanced with the law on negligent misstatements. In appropriate circumstances, a website controller or emailer may be found liable for the damage resulting from the

89 Consumer Protection Act 1987, s 4(1)(e).
90 (1868) LR 3 HL 330; affg *Fletcher v Rylands* (1866) LR 1 Ex 265.
91 [1994] 1 All ER 53.
92 *Read v J Lyons & Co Ltd* [1946] 2 All ER 471.
93 [1994] 1 All ER 53 at 76.
94 Civil Liability for Dangerous Things and Activities (Law Com no 32) 1970 in paras 14–16. Lord Goff stated, 'If the Law Commission is unwilling to consider statutory reform on this basis, it must follow that judges should if anything be even more reluctant to proceed down that path' [1994] 1 All ER 53 at 76.
95 See *Marcic v Thames Water Utilities Ltd* [2002] 2 All ER 55 at 70, para 55.

information he provides. This section considers the scope of this doctrine in relation to the Internet.

Hedley Byrne v Heller

Much has been written on negligent misstatements and this will not be repeated here[96]. What this section undertakes to do is to assess a stylised test for negligent misstatement considering the Internet. This section will only discuss the law where the peculiarities of the Internet affect the application of the test.

The ruling on negligent misstatements can be derived from *Hedley Bryne & Co Ltd v Heller & Partners Ltd*[97], but Lord Oliver in a later case summarises the position well[98]. He suggests that there are four factors that indicate a necessary relationship exists between the maker of the statement and the recipient who acts in reliance on the advice.

1. The advice is required for a purpose, whether particularly specified or generally described, which is made known, either actually or inferentially, to the adviser at the time when the advice is given.
2. The adviser knows, either actually or inferentially, that his advice will be communicated to the advisee, either specifically or as a member of an ascertainable class, in order that it should be used by the advisee for that purpose.
3. It is known, either actually or inferentially, that the advice so communicated is likely to be acted on by the advisee for that purpose without further independent inquiry.
4. The advisee acts upon the advice to his detriment.

Identity

There is a famous *New York Times*' cartoon that depicts one dog, sitting at a computer, talking to another dog sitting on the floor. The dog at the computer is saying, 'On the Internet, nobody knows you're a dog'. There is some truth in this. Without the use of encryption authentication, the Internet makes it difficult to establish who (or what) has sent an email and similarly who controls a website. This difficulty of identification does have legal ramifications.

The rules on negligent misstatement do not apply between all individuals. It has been said that the ruling applies only to those who are possessed of some special skill or expertise[99]. But this is not limited to particular categories of persons or situations. The dictum has been followed[100] which states[101]:

96 For the 'classic' professional advice issue, see *Law Society v KPMG Peat Marwick* [2000] 1 All ER 515.
97 [1963] 2 All ER 575.
98 In *Caparo Industries plc v Dickman* [1990] 1 All ER 568 at 589.
99 See [1963] 2 All ER 575 at 594, per Lord Morris.
100 *Esso Petroleum Co Ltd v Mardon* [1975] 1 All ER 203 at 219.
101 *Mutual Life and Citizens Assurance Co Ltd v Evatt* [1971] 1 All ER 150 at 163.

> 'when an enquirer consults a businessman in the course of his business and makes it plain to him that he is seeking considered advice and intends to act on it in a particular way, any reasonable businessman would realise that, if he chooses to give advice without any warning or qualification, he is putting himself under a moral obligation to take some care . . . [T]he principles established by the Hedley Byrne case . . . translate his moral obligation into a legal obligation.'

This wider statement suggests that the courts will not allow an adviser to discount his duty by stating that he was not actually qualified to provide such advice. If a website or an email gives the impression, without limitation or disclaimer, that advice or information is considered advice, a claimant may rely on that to establish a duty. It will be remembered that the claimant needs only to show that the defendant could have inferred that the advice was to be relied upon.

13. An individual establishes a home page with the domain name 'www.mpg.com'. This website, which is entitled 'Official Petroleum Institute' lists a number of supposed methods of increasing the fuel consumption of a car. Poor proofreading allowed one piece of advice to be published without specifying that the method applies only to unleaded vehicles. A claimant with a damaged engine sues. The defendant will not benefit from proving to the court that he was not qualified to provide the advice. The court will assess how the website appeared to the claimant.

Reasonable reliance on the Internet

The courts need to establish that the reliance made by the claimant was reasonable. There are two aspects to this. First, is it reasonable to rely on the Internet at all for particular advice? Lord Denning interpreted the term 'considered advice' as excluding informal situations such as casual conversation in the street; or in a railway carriage; or an impromptu opinion given offhand; or 'off the cuff' on the telephone[102]. There are analogies over the Internet.

'Instant Messaging' and Internet Relay Chat

'Instant Messaging' such as AIM and MSN Messenger and Internet Relay Chat are methods by which two or more users connected to the Internet can type messages to each other, these messages appearing as they are typed. It is like a telephone conversation using text not necessarily voice. This would appear to accord with the kinds of casual circumstances that Lord Denning envisaged. Other means of communication over the Internet are harder to pigeon-hole.

102 *Howard Marine and Dredging Co Ltd v A Ogden & Sons (Excavations) Ltd* [1978] 2 All ER 1134 at 1141.

14. A tenant worried about being evicted from her flat logs on to an Instant Messaging group. She locates an individual who purports to know her rights in this situation. He informs her that she can change the locks of the flat if she is worried about her landlady entering. The adviser's email address is rogerg@gbgb.com. The tenant changes the locks and is given notice for having breached her contract. The tenant is unlikely to have a right of action against rogerg@gbgb.com; it will be difficult to show that the advice was 'considered' and that it was reasonable to rely on it in the circumstances.

Bulletin Boards, Forums and Newsgroups

Certain Internet Service Providers, websites and bulletin boards or forums allow members to 'deposit' questions for all other members to read. These members are then free to reply by leaving another message, and so on. The collective group of questions and answers is called a conversation thread.

Some may consider that these conversation threads are as casual as Instant Messaging or Internet Relay Chat. This may not be the case. First, any forum or bulletin board is likely to have a name. A name such as the Cancer Forum or alt.advice.cancer gives a far stronger impression that the material being discussed and advised upon is serious and in no way casual. The courts should take account of these surrounding circumstances. The second factor that distinguishes a forum from the informal situation is that the advice provided, unlike Instant Messaging and Internet Relay Chat, does not have to be given immediately. Users of forums are free to read questions, research and then provide an answer in due course. It does not need to be 'off the cuff' at all. Some messages remain unanswered for numbers of days. This may influence a court into thinking that the advice was considered.

15. An individual accesses a website called AIDSAdvice. He is worried that he may have contracted HIV the previous night and seeks advice on how to assure himself that he hasn't. He leaves an appropriate question on the bulletin board and checks for a reply the next day. As he wanted, his question had been replied to. The reply advises him to carry on as normal for the next three months as it takes this long for the virus to incubate; he will place no one at risk during this 'window'. On checking the source of the reply, the personal details reveals a doctor's name and surgery. These circumstances should influence a court into thinking that the advice was not off the cuff, despite being incorrect.

World Wide Web

The name 'home page' for a portion of a website is quite an accurate description. The electronic documents stored on the World Wide Web are like pieces of paper. The authority of the information written on paper depends not on the fact that paper is used, but rather on the printing and the general impression given by the information. Similarly, a website may contain official and considered advice from professional sources or it may be no more than a collection of ramblings from an idiotic individual. This spectrum of information from a high quality to no quality at all often presents a problem for users of the World Wide

Web. If a site has a relevant domain name and looks official, is it reasonable to rely on the advice it provides? This is a question that can only be answered with the fullest understanding of the surrounding circumstances. Nevertheless, that the information was provided over the World Wide Web, without more, is inconclusive that it was reasonable to rely on the advice. Unlike Lord Denning's conversations in the street, the World Wide Web hosts a plethora of information; those who supply this information should be cautious of providing this information without appropriate warnings.

Reasonable reliance on information

The Internet, like any means of communication, can carry information of any quality; therefore, the medium itself is not conclusive as to whether it was reasonable to rely on that advice. As for any negligent misstatement, the courts should look to whether in the actual circumstances it was reasonable for the claimant to rely on the advice. This issue depends on the facts but some issues specific to the Internet can be mentioned.

Those who publish on the web may believe that no liability will attach to them if the words on their home page are not advisory but are merely informative or are stated as opinions. Certainly, one could arrive at such a belief by taking a superficial glance at Lord Denning's speech in *Candler v Crane Christmas & Co*[103]:

> '[A] scientist or expert . . . is not liable to his readers for careless statements in his published works. He publishes his work simply to give information, and not with any transaction in mind.'

However, this aspect of Lord Denning's much approved dissenting judgment does not classify what types of words are actionable, but rather, what types of transactions. It is perfectly possible for a scientist's published statement on the World Wide Web to be relied upon, with his knowledge, and to be the basis of a negligent misstatement suit. Lord Denning was attempting to provide an indication of to whom an adviser owes a duty, not over what he may owe a duty. Indeed, the court in a later case indicated that the operation of negligent misstatement is not restricted to a statement of fact or opinion, or even advice. It also applies where a notice should have been given but is not. The key is to establish whether a duty exists; if it does, it does not matter 'whether the breach takes the form of malfeasance or nonfeasance'[104].

Tailored websites

To create such a duty over the web, at first, appears difficult. The web can be seen as no more than a collection of documents aimed at nobody in particular and of such a generic nature as to prevent a duty arising. But many ecommerce sites are quite the opposite. Their supporting business plans clearly define a

103 [1951] 1 All ER 426 at 435.
104 *Midland Bank Trust Co Ltd v Hett, Stubbs & Kemp* [1978] 3 All ER 571 at 595.

market. Their advertising and material focuses on specific clients. Most sites use 'cookies' to tailor the experience. For example, an investor inputs their stock portfolio and the site not only allows the investor to trade in stocks but also advises the investor of stocks to add to balance the portfolio. It is likely that a duty to provide non-negligent advice will arise in this situation. The more 'focused' a website, the more they use software and specific content to make the site attractive for an audience, the more individuals will be owed duties by the controllers of those sites.

Finding or requesting

Advice provided from a tailored website raises a further issue that the courts have previously managed to avoid. In *Caparo Industries plc v Dickman* the claimant was considering making a takeover bid for a company[105]. To assess a good price it consulted the company accounts, prepared by auditors. Relying on the accounts, the claimant made its bid that was accepted, only to discover that the accounts were misleading. The claimant sued the defendant auditors but eventually lost in the House of Lords. One justification for the Lords taking this restrictive view of negligent misstatement was that the defendant should not be liable for information which the claimant, in effect, finds rather than requests.

When a user of the Internet requires to view information that is stored on a website, is this person 'finding' the document or are they requesting it from the controller? Certainly, where the site has no entry terms it may be analogous to picking up some company accounts from the foyer of a company: hardly the proximity required by the House of Lords. But where the viewer is required to enter some details as to who he is, where he heard about the information and why he requires it[106], the situation approaches one where the defendant will be unable to deny the necessary inferential knowledge.

16. Sites on the World Wide Web often host a collection of commonly asked questions and answers on a particular subject; they are called Frequently Asked Questions, or FAQ as an acronym. A website with the URL 'www.authors.co.uk' hosts an extensive FAQ on how authors can have their work published. It also contains a number of questions and incorrect answers on how to protect a work. If an author relies on these to her detriment, it will be difficult for the controller of the site to avoid having a duty to the author.

The Internet is an open source of information and material: if companies and individuals wish to avoid creating a duty with third parties they have two choices. First, they do not have to use the Internet for all types of material. Like any means of communication, the Internet is inappropriate for certain types of information. A more conservative attitude to the Internet will eradicate most of the glaring problems with negligent misstatements. The second choice is to publish the information but with a suitable contract and disclaimers. This is covered in the following section.

105 [1990] 1 All ER 568.
106 These type of questions are often asked, no doubt generally for marketing rather than legal reasons.

CONTRACTS AND DISCLAIMERS

Unlike a brochure or paper leaflet, well-designed websites allow themselves to be 'tailored' by their readers. This is achieved by using 'cookies' and other identifiers which allow a site to 'know' who is reading it. These features, and the lack of an 'order' to have to view web pages, alters the conception that a website is like a book. It may have many 'front covers' but individuals are no longer bound to view the pages in any particular order. Indeed, most websites allow an individual to jump straight to any one of the pages of a site, rather than passing through the home page[107]. The utilisation of frames that can be scrolled separately also adds to this fluidity. This creates a problem for legal advisers: to be effective, exclusions of liability are generally required before damage can occur; they should be the first text seen, but this hardly embraces the usual vogues in website design.

This section examines the exclusions required to reduce or exclude liability for digital damage.

Contractual exclusions

Digital damage

The safest way of excluding damage from malicious code is to incorporate appropriate terms in a contract, rather than to rely simply on an exclusion notice. Details of how best to form a contract with a viewer of a website are described in the chapter on contract.

A site should attempt to exclude any warranty as to the quality of any software downloaded on request or automatically by executable code and exclude its fitness for purpose[108]. In addition a disclaimer should be clear that the website controller is not liable for any damage caused by the software or code attaching to the software; this covers viruses and worms. The drafting for such a disclaimer must be carefully worded and should refer to indirect and consequential losses as well as specifically excluding damages from loss of data, profit revenue and contracts of business. It is all too easy purely to draft general sweeping exclusions that have the advantage of being concise, but have the distinct disadvantage of being ineffective.

If a viewer is permitted to download an executable file he should be warned before he can download the code that, although the code has been checked, he is at risk from digital damage and its consequences unless he first checks the code himself for viruses.

107 This is particularly influenced by search engines that will locate any given text in a website and permit the user to move straight to that page.

108 It is a moot point whether the Sale and Supply of Goods Act 1994 would include software as goods, or whether, in strict legal terms what is occurring is that the owner of the website is making a licence with a viewer over goods. Sir Iain Glidewell in *St Alban's City and District Council v International Computers Ltd* [1996] 4 All ER 481 at 493 states that 'the program is not "goods" within the statutory definition [of the Sale of Goods Act 1979]. Thus a transfer of the program [where it was transferred onto the computer by a third party] does not, in my view, constitute a transfer of goods'.

NEGLIGENT MISSTATEMENT

To disclaim responsibility for damages from a misstatement, a term or notice should state that the website or forum posting does not indicate any assumption of responsibility to the viewer or reader. The term or notice should ideally then address each element of the four-part test derived by Lord Oliver[109]. It should be stated that the wording and graphics on the site or posting are not provided for any specific or generally described purpose. To try to stop a third party seeing and relying on the advice[110] a notice or terms should insist that third parties are alerted to the same conditions. The last main disclaimer is that because the advice is not provided for any particular purpose it is assumed that no reliance will be made on the site or forum without having first taken specialised professional advice. Although strictly of no legal effect, for the avoidance of doubt, some sites and forums include a statement that the provider of information will not be liable for any loss caused as a result of doing or refraining from doing anything as a result of the wording, links or graphics.

NEGLIGENT LINKS

Often a site on the World Wide Web will feature links to other sites that may be of interest to its viewers; such is the nature of the web. In response to concerns that these links may increase liability, certain website owners are using notices to viewers that on them leaving a website the owners are not responsible for content outside their website. To some extent, such a practice addresses a risk that is almost non-existent.

There are two situations where such a notice is used: first, where the linked site is a 'subsidiary' of the main site, second, where the linked site is not associated with the first. Clearly, for the first situation, if the site is within the overall control of the website owner, say where a set of websites are collected together under the same domain, the controller will have some responsibility to viewers of the other sites. In the second situation, however, it is difficult to see how a duty would arise from providing a link to another's site.

The right of action against the first website owner who provides the link will, most probably, be based on negligent misstatement[111]. The claimant will have to claim that by relying on the advice to follow that link the claimant suffered damage (probably as a result of further relying on advice on that linked page). Putting aside the rather stretched notion of causation that the court would have to accept, the fundamental question must be answered: was there a duty to the viewer concerning the link?

The four rules stated by Lord Oliver must apply. First, the links would have to be rather specifically referred to for a particular purpose. Advice required for a purpose known by the website controller would not be satisfied by listing some links

109 See '*Hedley Byrne v Heller*' at p 114.

110 It is very common on forums for statements to be copied from one forum, or section, to another.

111 It is admitted that a case of negligent construction of a website could be brought, but it would appear easier for a claimant to satisfy the court as to the four rules of a negligent misstatement than to prove that a duty existed and that the website designer fell below the standard reasonably expected of website designers!

under the heading 'Other sites of interest'[112]. The site would have to use a special heading like 'Sites to consult for advice on swollen ankles'. The site owner would also have to know, either actually or inferentially, that as a result of the heading and the link that the viewer would not only follow the link but would take advice from the linked page without independent inquiry. It is submitted that it would be difficult for a claimant to convince a court that his reliance on the link could constitute reasonable reliance on the information contained in the linked site. In addition, there is the question of causation. It should be remembered that the advice is to follow the link; once at the linked page, the viewer will further have to act to be damaged. The courts will more readily break the chain of causation when the resulting damage depended on the claimant taking yet more negligent advice.

In short, although it is prudent to use markers such as 'You are now leaving our site' followed by a group of disclaimers as to the information on linked sites, it is submitted that it addresses a slim risk. A cleaner approach is merely to use a heading for the linked sites, 'Other sites of interest'. This simple statement distances the website owner from the other content and should be general enough not to form considered advice.

Effectiveness of exclusions

There are two factors that may limit the effectiveness of an exclusion or notice: incorporation and legal enforceability. The first is a factor which will have greatest impact on the World Wide Web.

Incorporation of exclusion

Unless an exclusion is within the terms of a contract, it must be otherwise incorporated to have binding contractual effect. On the World Wide Web such notices often are produced just before a viewer decides to download some executable code: 'If you proceed you agree that the file you are downloading may contain viruses and other damaging code which may damage your data and programs'. The controller of a website does not need to show a court that a viewer understood such a notice, or even that it was read; the controller must, however, show that he took reasonable steps to bring it to the claimant's notice. This does not require having the actual wording of the exclusion shown but its wording should be made available by a simple link.

17. A viewer uses a search engine to search for the websites that are supplying a free game. The search engine lists one particular page on a website. The viewer downloads the software advertised on the website's page by clicking a button labelled 'Download'. He sees no disclaimer because the website has only one link to its disclaimer notices and this is on the home page that was bypassed by the search engine. The site will be unable to rely on the disclaimer as they did not take reasonable steps to alert each person who downloads software of the disclaimer.

112 In the same vein, the footnotes in this book referring to other sources do not amount to a statement as to the reliability of the information contained in those sources.

Owners of websites must be careful not to assume that every viewer will read the pages on the site in a particular order. The very essence of the World Wide Web is that it is constructed with hypertext and that a portion of a site (unless blocked) can be 'framed' by another site thereby obscuring the disclaimer. A viewer is free to browse around a site or many sites in any order. The terms may need to be incorporated repeatedly throughout the site with a simple link called 'Disclaimer'.

Those who advise website designers should be conscious that drafting a contract or disclaimer may not be enough: they should ideally also have an input into exactly where on the website the disclaimer and links are placed. What is certain is that if the notice is intended to be incorporated into the web contract to exclude negligence, the viewer must have been able to view the notice or disclaimer before the web contract is made[113].

18. A software manufacturer decides to distribute its software utilities from its website. Before each utility is downloaded a notice is shown which excludes liability for negligently caused damage. After downloading some software from the site, a viewer's computer begins to slow down. It is discovered that some executable code that was on the website is retarding the computer. The notices provided before downloading the software will be inoperative: first, they relate to the downloaded software not the website's software; second, the poorly written executable code will have been downloaded to the viewer's computer before he had a chance to view the notice.

Limitations on exclusions

It is vital to pay due regard to the Unfair Contract Terms Act 1977 and successors and the Unfair Terms in Consumer Contracts Regulations 1999.

The Unfair Contract Terms Act 1977

Despite the title of the Act, the Unfair Contract Terms Act 1977 applies to simple notices which are not incorporated into a contract in addition to contractual terms. In the main, this Act makes ineffective the exemption clauses in contracts in relation to a 'business liability'[114], and with a person 'dealing as a consumer'[115]. However, as the World Wide Web contains many amateur sites that are not operated in the course of a business it is worthwhile checking whether the Unfair Contract Terms Act 1977 will apply. A term that seeks to exclude liability for damage resulting from negligence will operate only where it is reasonable[116].

113 See *Olley v Marlborough Court* [1949] 1 All ER 127, approved by the Court of Appeal in *Hollier v Rambler Motors (AMC) Ltd* [1972] 1 All ER 399 at 407.

114 Unfair Contract Terms Act 1977, s 1(3).

115 Unfair Contract Terms Act 1977, s 12(1)(a) and (b).

116 Unfair Contract Terms Act 1977, s 2(2). For guidance on what is reasonable, consult the Unfair Contract Terms Act 1977, s 11. This includes where the provider of information attempts to construct a notice as stating he has no duty at all. Section 13 prevents the exclusion or restriction of the duty itself unless it is reasonable.

It has been discussed that a term of a contract must be properly incorporated to be effective. A simple notice, in contrast, can be made at any point about the information being provided. The safest option, however, is to disclaim responsibility before a viewer has a chance to rely on any advice.

For a website, a viewer should be confronted with a page or frame of disclaimers or at the least a prominent notice that the viewer should follow the link to the disclaimers page of the site[117]. For the Unfair Contract Terms Act 1977, what is relevant is not the precise wording of a disclaimer but more its reasonableness regarding all the circumstances[118]. An adviser should not simply draft a form of wording and allow the client to place the words on the site or forum. The adviser should check that the format and construction of the site or forum makes it reasonably clear to all viewers that the controller is disclaiming responsibility. Position on a site may be as legally relevant as wording.

Unfair Terms in Consumer Contracts Regulations 1999

These Regulations strike at a more limited set of exclusions than those under the Unfair Contract Terms Act 1977. First, the Regulations apply only to contracts and only those contractual terms that have not been individually negotiated[119]. This will cover most contracts made over the World Wide Web. The second requirement is that the contract must be between a consumer and a supplier of goods or services[120]. The contract does not need to be for the supply of goods or services so it seems probable that the Regulations will apply to a licence over software. If applicable, the Regulations will exclude any term that is 'unfair'[121]. There is very little peculiar about the Internet which means that certain terms will be more or less fair. This said, terms must be incorporated before contracting with the consumer. The Regulations provide that a term may be regarded as unfair if it has the object or effect of 'irrevocably binding the consumer to terms with which he had no opportunity of becoming acquainted with before the conclusion of the contract'[122]. This may occur on the Internet where terms are flashed up on a consumer's screen without him actually having an opportunity to review or even repudiate their content.

DEFAMATION

A high proportion of Internet cases concern defamation. Part of the reason for this is that the Internet provides the man on the street with a unique opportunity to have his thoughts published instantaneously throughout the world. Moreover, the Internet, particularly in its early years, encouraged a spirit of unrestrained

117 See 'Incorporation of exclusion' at p 121.
118 This general approach was affirmed by the Court of Appeal in *Smith v Eric S Bush* [1988] QB 743.
119 See Unfair Terms in Consumer Contracts Regulations 1999, reg 3(3).
120 See Unfair Terms in Consumer Contracts Regulations 1999, reg 2(1). Unlike the Unfair Contract Terms Act 1977, a consumer must be a natural person.
121 For detailed advice, readers should consult specialist texts and the House of Lords' judgment in *Director General of Fair Trading v First National Bank plc* [2002] 1 All ER 97.
122 Unfair Terms in Consumer Contracts Regulations 1999, Sch 3, para 1(i).

comment or discussion. This often involved highly defamatory statements being made.

There is nothing special about the law as it relates to a person sending defamatory statements over the Internet. What is legally special is that to 'publish' on the Internet, one generally must submit the material in an electronic form to a third party; it is this third party that, in effect, publishes the material. The key legal questions in this section are therefore when will liability fix also to these intermediaries and to what extent must they disclose the identity of the author to the person being defamed.

Before September 1996, the answers to first of these questions was the subject of much speculation based on old English common law and analogies from abroad. The Defamation Act 1996 now provides for when a third party Internet 'publisher' will have no liability and when the party will have to rely on one of the limited defences. Unfortunately, the application of the Act particularly when combined with the Electronic Commerce (EC Directive) 2002 is not free from doubt.

This section will also address the practicalities of a case where the defamatory statement has been made across the Internet. These practicalities include how damages are to be assessed and the considerations in the collection of digital evidence to defend an action.

Before considering these legal issues, it is useful to appreciate the technical aspects of the Internet that may impinge on any defamatory statement made over it. First, defamation over the Internet necessarily involves a third party, usually an Internet Service Provider. Related to this is the issue that it is problematic to locate the person whose defamatory remark is published. A final issue is that defamatory remarks made over the Internet may be published extremely widely.

Technicalities

Third party

Information over the Internet cannot be sent single-handedly. In contrast to a poster that can be drawn and pinned to a wall without third party help, to publish on the Internet necessarily involves others. Forums that hold written conversation threads and websites that show material are stored in a digital form on a server computer. The same is true for electronic mail: it is not generally sent directly to the recipient's computer; it is sent to a 'digital pigeon-hole' from which the recipient downloads new messages. This reliance on a third party to publish the material has a significant impact on the analysis of a defamation action. In defamation, it is not only the writer of the statement who may be liable, but also those who are involved in its publication and distribution.

Identity of first defendant

Often it will be difficult to discover the identity of the person who typed the defamatory statement. It is easy and common to use a pseudonym when an email is sent to a person or a conversation thread. It is also possible to 'blind' an electronic message, making it impossible to tell even the source of the statement. This is achieved by sending an email to what is called an 'anonymous remailer' which is a computer program that automatically strips any message of any identifiers[123]. This difficulty of identification makes it attractive to litigate with the third party who actually distributed the message; this legal individual will be necessarily identifiable as the statement will be stored on the individual's equipment. In addition, the third party may be a substantial commercial organisation with deep pockets and more able to pay libel damages than the possibly impecunious real authors. This also makes them attractive targets for libel actions.

Extent of publications

To bring a defamation action, the statement concerned must have been published to at least one other person. The extent of publication is also a factor in the assessment of damages for a claimant. For a statement published on the Internet, this distribution has the potential to be global and numerous.

With a statement available on the Internet, there is no rebuttable presumption[124] that the statement has been read by a third party[125]. However, if publication is in dispute, the ISPs may be required to disclose all logs showing accesses to the page in question. A wise claimant will notify the ISP at the beginning of the action that if the fact and/or the extent of publication is likely to be in dispute, he will require this material to be disclosed and demand that it be retained.

The Defamation Act 1996

The Act does not alter what constitutes a defamatory statement; it addresses who should be liable for this defamatory statement and it introduces new procedures for claims[126]. For the sake of completeness, however, the following is a short summary of what constitutes a defamatory statement[127]; the issue of third party liability will then be tackled[128].

Defamatory statements

Material is defamatory if it tends to 'lower the claimant in the estimation of right-thinking people generally', or if the material causes people to 'shun or avoid' the claimant or, more narrowly, hold the claimant up to 'ridicule, hatred

123 See *Takenaka (UK) limited v David Frankl*, unreported 11 October 2000.

124 This contrasts with the position with publications in newspapers where there is such a presumption.

125 Ruling of Gray J in *Loutchansky v Times Newspapers Ltd (No 2)* [2001] EMLR 876.

126 Of particular relevance to Internet defamation are the new procedures of: Offer to make amends (ss 2–4); reduction of limitation period to one year from the date on which the cause of action accrued (ss 5–6); and Summary disposal of claim (ss 8–11).

127 There are two kinds of defamation: libel and slander. The importance of this distinction is that in a limited class of slander cases the claimant must prove 'special damage'; in libel the claimant does not need to prove any loss to succeed. Slander is where the defamation is in transitory form. It appears, therefore, that with the possible exception of Internet telephony, any defamatory material on the Internet will be a libel.

128 Specialist texts should be consulted in relation to what exactly can constitute a defamatory statement. The information provided here is the general position with application to some Internet specific issues.

or contempt'[129]. These tests are not entirely objective; part of the court's deliberations will be directed to the attitudes and likely response of the people who actually read the statement.

Similar interests

On Internet forums and newsgroups the individuals involved often have similar interests and an understanding of the frivolity of the messages posted. This may be a factor that a court should take into account. Internet forums and newsgroups[130] with names such as 'sci.anthropology' are made up of like-minded people who have an interest in common. This interest forms the title to the forum. Interested parties can view the messages that have been posted on the forum and reply to any message that they choose. Each reply is appended to the existing written conversations and so the thread expands.

The nature of the replies vary with each forum, rather as conversations may vary in different pubs across the country. A defendant should be prepared to emphasise the readership or likely readership of a forum either to demonstrate that the posting in question would not have been taken seriously or, even if taken seriously, it would not have lowered the person in the minds of its readers.

Types of defamatory material

It is not unique to the Internet that a person can be defamed by more than simply words. A defamatory statement means 'words, pictures, visual images, gestures or any other method of signifying meaning'[131]. Under this definition, it is possible that a computer-manipulated image posted on the Internet that shows a person performing a degrading act may be considered as defamatory. It is this wide scope of what is defamatory that makes it so difficult to operate automatic screening of potentially defamatory material.

Publication

A person who merely unwittingly contributes to the dissemination of a defamatory statement by providing an Internet service may claim that it is not publishing the statement at all. The cause of action in libel arises on publication rather than the writing of the defamatory material. The crucial questions for

129 Respectively: *Sim v Stretch* [1936] 2 All ER 1237 at 1240; *Youssoupoff v Metro-Goldwyn-Mayer Pictures Ltd* (1934) 50 TLR 581 at 587; *Thorley v Lord Kerry* (1812) 4 Taunt 355 at 364.

130 Generally, the word 'forum' refers to a collection of written conversations that are hosted by a commercial online service provider; a written conversation group with the nomenclature xxx.yyy is generally called a 'newsgroup' and is hosted on a non-commercial basis on the Usenet system; they are therefore less prone to editing.

131 Defamation Act 1996, s 17(1).

those who provide and store material on the Internet are therefore, can they be liable and, if so, what defences are available to them.

Mere Conduit

It has never been determined in English common law whether a telephone company or the Post Office could be held liable for communications they convey[132]. The Electronic Commerce Regulations, however, almost put this beyond doubt. A telecoms company usually acts as a true 'mere conduit' in that it does not initiate transmissions nor choose the final recipient of a transmission. It is the digital equivalent of a 'middle man'.

The Regulations provide that such mere conduits shall not be liable in damages for defamatory material sent over their 'pipes' (nor any other material) on three conditions: first, as discussed above, they must act as a true 'middle man' and neither initiate nor, second, determine the recipient of the transmission[133]. The third condition is that they must not select or modify the information contained in the transmission.

Of course, for very small periods of time, a telecoms company or other 'mere conduit' will be storing the material being transmitted. This short-term storage will still be classified as 'transmission' where it is necessary and quick. More particularly, this sort of storage must be 'automatic, immediate and transient' for no longer than is reasonably necessary and must take place for the sole purpose for the transmission[134].

However, where a company is providing an Internet hosting service which contains defamatory material, it will be deemed to be publishing the material if it fails to remove it once notified of the defamatory nature of it[135].

Storage Providers

Since the implementation of the Electronic Commerce (EC Directive) Regulations 2002, service providers have two possible defences to a defamation claim: first, under the Regulations, reg 19 and then, if appropriate, under s 1 of the Defamation Act 1996.

The reason for the potential of these 'two bites at the cherry' is that the Defamation Act 1996 provides, it can be argued, a wider defence than the Regulations. The Regulations do not repeal the Defamation Act, but rather provide the 'minimum' protection for service providers. And, of course, the

132 In the US, it has been held that a telephone company does not publish a message spoken down its lines – *Anderson v New York Telephone Co* 361 NYS 2d 913 (NYCA 1974).

133 Regulation 17(1).

134 Regulation 17(2).

135 *Godfrey v Demon Internet Ltd* [2001] QB 201. In his judgment, Morland J referred to the words of Greene LJ in *Byrne v Deane* [1937] 1KB 818 (a case which related to the failure of a golf club to remove a defamatory statement from a notice board under its control) as follows: 'The test it appears to me is this: having regard to all the facts of the case is the proper inference that by not removing the defamatory matter the defendant really made himself responsible for its continued presence in the place where it had been put?'

Regulations only benefit those service providers who are established in a member state[136], whereas the Act applies to all English defamation cases, whether or not the service provider is established outside the EU.

Defamation Act 1996 v Electronic Commerce Regulations

Before considering these two sets of defences separately, it is worthwhile giving a short précis of their potential differences.

1. The Defamation Act, s 1 defence applies only to those who are not authors, editors or publishers of the defamatory material; the Regulations are wider and apply to any service provider storing the material at the request of a recipient of their service.
2. The Defamation Act, s 1 defence applies only where the service provider took reasonable care in relation to the publication in question; the Regulations do not require a duty of care, they essentially require that the service provider 'unwittingly' published the statement, without knowledge or awareness.
3. The Defamation Act, s 1 defence will cease to apply where the service provider does not remove the material on notice, probably within a reasonable time period; the Regulations require that the service provider must act 'expeditiously' to remove or disable the material once notified.

The Defamation Act 1996, s 1 defence

If the provider of an Internet service is held to have published a defamatory statement, it may seek to avail itself of the defence contained in section 1 of the Act. To succeed, the third party Provider:

(a) must not be the author, editor or publisher of the material. Only if they are not considered to be one of these persons may they then rely on the defence;
(b) must take reasonable care in relation to the publication in question; and
(c) must not know or have no reason to believe that which it did caused or contributed to the publication of a defamatory statement[137].

Not authors, editors or publishers

The Act defines these individuals along with providing presumptions. If the third party's activities fall within one of the presumptions listed below, they may then seek to rely on the defence. If they do not fall squarely within the presumption, they will have to prove that their activities are not those of an

136 Electronic Commerce Directive, recital 19; Electronic Commerce Regulations, Reg 2(1).
137 In *Godfrey v Demon Internet Ltd* [2001] QB 201, the fact that a posting remained available on the defendant's servers some 10 days after the notification proved fatal for the defence. It is submitted that the courts will interpret 'expeditiously', a new import from the Electronic Commerce Regulations, to mean the defence is not lost where the material continues to be available an instant after notification. However, service providers should always err on the side of caution and remove the defamatory material as soon as possible after notification.

author, editor or the publisher as defined. If they do not fall within these definitions, ie they are not an author, editor or publisher, they may seek to rely on the defence.

Definitions

If a third party has been unable to convince a court that it falls within one of the presumptions or an analogous situation, it has one last chance of pleading that, in the alternative, it is not an author, editor or publisher within the definitions of the Act[138].

> '"author" means the originator of the statement, but does not include a person who did not intend that his statement be published at all;
> "editor" means a person having editorial or equivalent responsibility for the content of the statement or the decision to publish it; and
> "publisher" means a commercial publisher, that is, a person whose business is issuing material to the public, or a section of the public, who issues material containing the statement in the course of that business.'

It is clear from the definition of 'publisher' that the Act does not contemplate a person being a publisher where publishing is merely incidental to their business[139]. For example, many firms have internal networks or intranets on which various pieces of information are posted. Should defamatory material be posted on this internal network, by an employee, the employer is unlikely to be viewed as a publisher for the purposes of the Act. Their business is not the issuing of material to the public and they are not a commercial publisher; their business does not depend on the issuance of material on the intranet.

Presumptions

The relevant presumptions for the Internet are that a person shall not be considered the author, editor or the publisher of a statement if he is only involved[140]:

> '(c) in processing, making copies of, distributing or selling any electronic medium in or on which the statement is recorded, or in operating or providing any equipment, system or service by means of which the statement is retrieved, copied, distributed or made available in electronic form;
> ...
> (e) as the operator of or provider of access to a communications system by means of which the statement is transmitted, or made available, by a person over whom he has no effective control.'

138 Defamation Act 1996, s 1(2).
139 It should be noted that, although the words 'publication' and 'publish' retain their common law meanings, the word 'publisher' is specially defined for the purposes of s 1: Defamation Act 1996, s 17(1).
140 Defamation Act 1996, s 1(3)(c), (e).

The key to interpreting these sections is that the party must 'only' be involved in these activities. If a third party does no more than that described in s 1(3)(c) or (e) they may be able to rely on the defences described below. To illustrate the scope of these presumptions, this chapter applies them to the following issues: sending and forwarding emails; hosting a website; hosting a mirror site; designing websites; providing access to newsgroups; and providing forums.

Sending and forwarding emails

One safe example of an activity that falls within s 1(3)(c) is the facilities of a Provider to send and forward emails. When an email is sent to another individual, or a group of individuals, there are two third parties who are additionally often involved. The first is the defendant's Service Provider. The email is sent out onto the Internet from this Provider's server computers. There will also be a second third party, the Provider or Providers to which the defamatory email is sent. These Providers will pass on the email to their respective intended recipients.

The Providers to the defendant and recipients will not be viewed as editors or publishers under the presumption. They will only have provided a service by means of which the defamatory email statement is distributed (for the defendant) and retrieved (for the recipients)[141]. Each of the controllers of the intermediary computers on the Internet that automatically shunted the email nearer and nearer its destination will also fall within the presumption that they are not an editor or publisher. A server linked to the Internet has packets of zeros and ones 'passing through' every second. These packets originated as messages and data created and sent by other servers over which they have no control. What is more, the nature of the Internet is such that it may be impossible even to know who was the original sender of a message[142].

Hosting a website

Another safe example of an activity falling squarely within one of the presumptions is where a Provider rents out space on a web server to individuals to use as home pages. For example, many Internet Service Providers, by way of subscription, will provide a person with a website address at which he can leave material to be viewed by others. Again, such a provider has no hand in the actual content of the site and would be viewed as providing a service by means of which the material on the defamatory website is made available[143]. The Provider would be able to rely on the defences, as would the Provider used by the viewer of the website[144].

141 Defamation Act 1996, s 1(3)(c).
142 There is also the technical argument that the email is not even published by these intermediaries. Any email is broken into packets which are in a human unreadable form, and some of the packets will not pass through the same computer. It would be a momentous task to prove that one of the intermediary computers actually transmitted all of the packets in relation to one particular email, all in order.
143 Defamation Act 1996, s 1(3)(c).
144 Defamation Act 1996, s 1(3)(e).

Hosting a mirror site

A server that stores a website or ftp site must be able to cope with all the requests, sometimes simultaneously, from viewer's computers. Occasionally the most popular sites become so inundated with digital requests that they begin to slow. To solve this problem, a controller of a website will set up or rent space on a mirror site. As the name suggests, this site is an identical copy of the original site; it simply allows another route into the website so reducing the strain on the original. The controller of the mirror site appears not to be presumed to be an author, editor or publisher as he is only providing equipment by means of which the statement is retrieved, copied, distributed or made available in electronic form[145]. He would be able to rely on the defences.

Designing websites

The above examples should not be taken to indicate that all those involved in the website will not be viewed as authors, editors or publishers. There are many companies who design websites for other individuals, companies and advertising firms. These designers are involved in more than only making the statement available in an electronic form and have effective control over their contractor. Indeed, often these companies will amend text and include graphics to best represent the client's activities on the website. It is rare that a client will approach such a designer with the code ready to be used for the website. For website designers, therefore, it is important that they acquire an indemnity from their client over any defamation actions.

Providing access to newsgroups

Newsgroups exist on the Usenet network of computers. Like forums, they are collections of written conversations and files that are left for everyone to reply to or purely retrieve. Many of these forums have fairly specialised and often sexual subject matters; these run a great risk of holding defamatory material. To access these newsgroups, a viewer will generally have only to access his Provider's servers. This is because Service Providers store copies of the newsgroups on their local machines. Because of this, they may re-publish defamatory material so they should be careful to fall within one of the presumptions.

There is, however, a problem with attempting to persuade a court that, in relation to the newsgroups, the Provider is only providing a service by means of which a statement is copied or made available in an electronic form. This problem occurs because a Provider will rarely carry all the many thousands of newsgroups; they are selective. For example, many providers avoid the overtly pornographic groups. In doing so, it could be alleged that the Provider is doing more than only electronically distributing the material: they are censoring, for whatever reasons, certain of the newsgroups. In doing this, it is arguable that they are acting as an editor. That is they are assuming responsibility for the decision to publish a statement[146].

145 Defamation Act 1996, s 1(3)(c).
146 From the definition of an 'editor' in the Defamation Act 1996, s 1(2).

It is submitted that this reasoning relies on an excessively constrained view of the presumptions. The decision to exclude certain newsgroups without having seen their content should not be translated into having editorial responsibility for the content of the others: the Provider is still only making the copies of the newsgroups available in an electronic form[147]. Merely because there was certain material that the Provider chose not to make available should not indicate that the Provider has assumed some responsibility over the distributed newsgroups. It is when a Provider begins to edit or delete the actual text of the individual statements within a newsgroup that the Provider approaches the position of editor.

Providing forums

Many Service Providers and websites provide forums for their members. These are collections of written conversations and files that can be accessed by any member of the forum. The Providers of these forums face the greatest problem of liability. Rather than simply allowing anyone to post up anything on a forum, the Providers will often moderate the text and messages before or soon after they are posted. They do this, presumably, to protect the other members of the forum from vulgarities and irrelevancies. Of course, in doing this, just like a newspaper editor edits a reader's letter, they are, in effect, acting as an editor. The Provider is no longer only making the copies of the statements available in an electronic form; the Provider is editing the statement.

This would appear to indicate that the prudent Provider who attempts to screen out defamatory comments may not be able to benefit from the defence. In contrast, the Provider who turns a blind eye to defamatory comments and does not edit the messages will be able to rely on the defence[148]. There are two justifications for this seemingly counter-intuitive conclusion.

Stratton v Prodigy

The first is a commercial justification that is provided by the court in one of the first Internet defamation cases from America: *Stratton Oakmont Inc v Prodigy Services Co*[149]. Prodigy is a large Internet Service Provider; one of its services

147 The nature of the 'flooding algorithm' through which the newsgroups are distributed amongst Providers also gives the Provider little effective control over material.

148 An example of this is provided by the American case, *Cubby Inc v Compuserve Inc* 776 F Supp 135 (SDNY 1991). Compuserve carried a forum, 'Rumorville', that was managed by a company unrelated to Compuserve. A defamatory statement was published on this forum and Compuserve was sued. The court compared Compuserve to an 'electronic, for-profit library' (at 140) and stated that summary judgment should be given in favour of Compuserve. This was primarily because the claimants did not set forth any specific facts showing a genuine issue of Compuserve knowing or having reason to know of the forum's contents. (Cf Defamation Act 1996, s 1(1)(b) and (c).) Although this judgment and Compuserve's arguments were heavily steeped in the First Amendment, the case can be used to illustrate that the more distance a Provider puts between itself and the forum, the more likely it will be able to rely on the defence. Conversely, this imposes a burden on the claimant to adduce evidence that the Provider, by making this distance, was not taking reasonable care and should have known the risk of defamation. A forum name like 'Rumorville' must surely place the Provider on notice.

149 NYS 2d Index No 31063/94, 1995 WL 323710.

was a bulletin board called 'Money Talk'. An unknown individual posted a defamatory remark that the claimant company was guilty of fraud. The plaintiff sought partial summary judgment against Prodigy on two issues, namely: whether Prodigy may be considered 'publisher' of the statements[150]; and whether the Board Leader for the bulletin board on which the statements were posted was Prodigy's 'agent' for the purpose of the claims.

Prodigy was a prudent Internet Service Provider; it prides itself on exercising editorial control over the content of messages posted on its computer bulletin boards, differentiating itself from its competition and expressly likening itself to a newspaper. In the case, Prodigy is quoted as stating:

> 'We make no apology for pursuing a value system that reflects the culture of the millions of American families we aspire to serve. Certainly no responsible newspaper does less when it carries the type of advertising it publishes, the letters it prints, the degree of nudity and unsupported gossip its editors tolerate.'

It is precisely this editing, both manual and automatic, that the court reasoned brought the defendant within the realms of a publisher, or more widely, made the defendant responsible for the content. The court stated that:

> '. . . Prodigy is clearly making decisions as to content . . . and such decisions constitute editorial control . . . That such control is not complete and is enforced both as early as the notes arrive and as late as a complaint is made, does not minimize or eviscerate the simple fact that Prodigy has uniquely arrogated to itself the role of determining what is proper for its members to post and read on its bulletin boards . . . Prodigy is a publisher rather than a distributor.'

So the court was content to rule that, despite Prodigy's aim to protect its members, it should be liable when this protection fails. To the proposition that this decision will simply force Providers not to edit postings, so avoiding liability, the court drew on a 'market forces' argument.

> 'For the record, the fear that this court's finding of publisher status for Prodigy will compel all computer networks to abdicate control of their bulletin boards, incorrectly presumes that the market will refuse to compensate a network for its increased control and the resulting increased exposure . . . Presumably Prodigy's decision to regulate the content of its bulletin boards was in part influenced by its desire to attract a market it perceived to exist consisting of users seeking a "family-oriented" computer service. This decision simply required that to the extent computer networks provide such services, they must also accept the concomitant legal consequences.'

Looking strictly at law, the Prodigy case provides little authority for an English court. Under English law the Defamation Act 1996 is quite clear that editorial decisions, like those made by Prodigy, will bring the Provider into the realms of

150 In the case Prodigy were seeking to prove themselves as 'distributors' and thus able to rely on a defence of innocent dissemination.

an editor or publisher. This is particularly true where, like certain Providers, members are charged an extra rate to access certain 'moderated' forums. In this situation, the Provider appears to be within the definition of a 'publisher' under the Act[151].

> '"publisher" means a commercial publisher, that is, a person whose business is issuing material to the public, or a section of the public, who issues material containing the statement in the course of that business.'

What the case does illustrate is one justification for a court imposing a ruling that a prudent Provider should be liable whereas a reckless Provider has an opportunity to rely on a defence. This justification is that individuals will pay for quality and editing; too much of the Internet is of very dubious quality. This increase in income gained by being able to charge more to a discerning member has a concomitant legal risk.

There is a second explanation for the seemingly unjust rule that 'the prudent Provider is punished'. This is described below.

Strength of defences

In much of the discussion about the Defamation Act 1996 there seems to be an assumption that if a Provider is reckless as to content, the Provider has an easy task to plead a defence. This is not so. As will be considered below, a Provider who turns a blind eye to defamatory material will have difficulties in meeting the test of reasonable care. But there is also a commercial advantage in being a prudent Provider: you are sued less often and will have lower insurance premiums. A prudent Provider screening as much content as is feasible will eliminate many potential defamation actions. In contrast, a reckless Provider may find itself defending many law suits having to hope that they will be able to satisfy the defences. These two situations will obviously affect the level of insurance premiums payable by the two types of Provider.

This lengthy discussion on the liability for providing forums indicates that what at first appears as counter-productive legislation is explicable, even if not palatable, to those in the online industry.

The s 1(1) defence requires two hurdles to be cleared by the defendant. First, he must show that he took reasonable care in relation to the statement's publication. In addition, he must show that he did not know, and had no reason to believe, that what he did caused or contributed to the publication of a defamatory statement.

To determine what is reasonable and what should be known, the Act provides three considerations to which the court shall have regard. The first consideration is the extent of the responsibility for the content of the statement or decision to publish[152]. This provides little guidance for a Service Provider. The second and third considerations are more helpful. Regard shall be had to the nature or circumstances of the publication and the previous conduct or character of the author, editor or publisher[153].

151 Defamation Act 1996, s 1(2).
152 Defamation Act 1996, s 1(5)(a).
153 Defamation Act 1996, s 1(5)(b) and (c).

These last two considerations indicate that to take reasonable care one must first judge the care which is required in a given scenario. It will not be reasonable care simply to re-publish an entire Usenet newsgroup that has a reputation for being scurrilous and defamatory. It is no defence for the Provider to state that it did not know that a particular posting was defamatory. This is because the court is required to judge that the Provider did not know and had no reason to believe that the material would be defamatory[154]. Service Providers are advised not to turn a blind eye to the nature of the material that they publish. If a forum or newsgroup is known to carry postings of dubious veracity, a Provider is taking a risk to publish its material without vetting.

The prospect of vetting the contents of a newsgroup or forum raises two problems: one commercial, the other legal. The commercial problem is simply put: how can a Provider feasibly vet the thousands of postings that are posted up on newsgroups each day? The answer is also simple: the Provider cannot; it would be impossible. The question is whether the Provider is required to vet every posting. The Act and Electronic Commerce Reglations do not impose an absolute requirement that postings are vetted; it is more rational than that: reasonable care must be taken.

This does not mean vetting every posting, but it also does not mean blindly re-publishing dubious newsgroups and entertaining the postings made by known defamers. During the passage of the Bill through the House of Commons, Mr Streeter explained[155]:

> 'We must put distributors, printers, wholesalers and retailers on notice that they should have regard to the nature of a publication if they seek to rely on that defence.'

A commercial balance must be struck. Providers may choose to vet one hour of postings on a particular forum every day. Providers may also choose to allow members to alert them, by priority email, of a defamatory comment.

The legal problem that has been raised about vetting material is that it produces a circular argument. This goes as follows. To take reasonable care a Provider must occasionally edit some material. By editing some material the Provider cannot now be only involved with one of the five presumptive activities. This conclusion strips the presumption from the Provider that it is not an author, editor or publisher.

This legal problem is not as confusing as it appears. As this section has shown, a Provider can rely on a presumption that it is not an author, editor or publisher, but failing that, the Provider is not necessarily an author, editor or publisher. The Provider remains able to plead that it does not fall within the definitions of author, editor or publisher. So, by editing material the Provider is not prevented from relying on the defence, it is simply prevented from relying on the presumption. The

154 Defamation Act 1996, s 1(1)(c).

155 Parliamentary Secretary, Lord Chancellor's Department (promoter of the Bill), 280 HC Official Report (6th Series) col 119, 24 June 1996. This is added as an indication of the intention of Parliament; it is not mentioned as a statement upon which a court could rely under the strict criteria laid down in *Pepper (Inspector of Taxes) v Hart* [1993] 1 All ER 42 and *Melluish (Inspector of Taxes) v BMI (No 3) Ltd* [1996] AC 454. Although perhaps prejudicial to Internet Service Providers, it is this author's submission that the Bill does not meet the criteria of being ambiguous or obscure or its literal meaning leading to an absurdity.

court remains able to hear evidence that the Provider is not a publisher or editor under the definitions. And if convinced, the court can still allow the Provider to rely on the defence of reasonable care.

Of course, the ramifications of this analysis are that the Defamation Act 1996 has impaled many Service Providers on the horns of a dilemma. If they turn a blind eye to all content, they may be able to rely on the presumption that they are not a publisher. They will, however, be unlikely to convince a court that by doing nothing they took all reasonable care and so must rely on the Electronic Commerce Regulations only. Conversely, if they are prudent and edit out potentially defamatory material, they will not be able to rely on the presumption as they are now only involved in non-editorial activities. They will be left with convincing a court that they are not a publisher, which under the Act, as a person whose business is issuing material to the public, they probably are.

In this 'lose-lose' predicament a Service Provider should be aware of four practical issues. First, if the Provider does edit its content, it will be sued less frequently as it will re-publish defamatory statements less often. Ignoring content will increasingly lead one to a position of being unable to ignore litigation. The second issue is that insurance is available to Service Providers, but premiums will be significantly lower if the Provider takes some editorial responsibility. The third issue is one of identification. If a Provider ensures that each of its members provides a full name and address before entering a forum, it makes it more likely that a claimant may consider suing only the author of the statement. In *Prodigy* the offending posting was made by an unknown person[156]. The final issue is one of legal procedure. A court will often pay attention to whether the parties have 'clean hands'. In this respect, a court will not look favourably on a Provider who has deliberately avoided reading material to allow a technical plea of one of the presumptions.

Evidence

It is critical that Internet Service Providers appreciate the burden they are under, evidentially, to prove that they fall within the defence. It is the Provider, rather than the claimant, who must prove that it is not an author, editor or publisher. It is also the Provider that must meet the two tests to prove the defence[157]. It is therefore sensible for a Service Provider to maintain complete records of all its automatic or manual dealings with third party material. In particular, a Service Provider should be able to provide a court with evidence to satisfy the three issues to which the court will have regard to judge the level of care and knowledge of the Provider[158]. It is also worthwhile noting that the term 'reasonable care' introduces a relative test: Providers may find it useful to adduce expert evidence as to the reasonableness of their care in relation to industry practice.

156 This advice is applicable only to internal forums. Clearly, if a Provider re-publishes a Usenet newsgroup, many of the postings will be made from outside the control of the Provider.

157 This is in contrast, say, to secondary infringement under the Copyright, Designs and Patents Act 1988, s 23.

158 Defamation Act 1996, s 1(1)(b) and (c) and s 1(5)(a), (b) and (c).

Electronic Commerce Regulations' Hosting Defence

It was discussed earlier that the Electronic Commerce Regulations might provide an additional defence for service providers faced with a defamation claim. The reasoning is that the Regulations simply provide another defence; they do not repeal or amend existing legislation.

A service provider defending a claim of defamation may be able to rely on two possible defences under the Electronic Commerce Regulations 2002, reg 19. These 'hosting' defences ensure that ISP's and other such service providers are not liable as a result of storing defamatory material on behalf of a third party.

No actual knowledge, no awareness, no control

The first defence is essentially that the service provider must be unwittingly publishing the defamatory material[159]. This is in three parts. First, the host must not have 'actual knowledge' that the publication of the statement or material was in breach of any law, here defamation law. The second part is that the host must *also* 'not be aware of facts or circumstances' from which it would have been apparent that the activity or information was unlawful. Third, and considered below, the provider must have no authority or control over the defamer.

No actual knowledge of breach of law

This first part of the defence is akin to the Defamation Act 1996, s 1(1)(c). It should be taken to mean that the hosting company has not been provided with 'notice' about the defamatory material. This notice need not, however, be in writing and it certainly need not originate from a court. The court must, however, have regard to the extent to which the notice identifies its sender, the location of the material and the defamation. The court shall also factor in where the notice was sent.

In *Godfrey v Demon Internet Ltd*[160] on 17 January 1997, the defendant service provider's managing director was sent a fax from the claimant complaining about a posting on a Usenet news server hosted by them. This was enough for the court, under the Defamation Act 1996, to indicate that, at full trial, the defendant would be deemed to be 'on notice'; they had actual knowledge after 17 January 1997.

No awareness of facts or circumstances

If the service provider has no actual knowledge, they must then demonstrate that they have no awareness of relevant facts or circumstances which would lead them to believe the statement is unlawful. If they can do this, they will still need to prove that the defamer was outside their authority or control, described below.

159 Regulation 19(a)(i).
160 [2001] QB 201.

The courts may interpret this in a similar manner as the requirements in the Defamation Act 1996, s 1(1)(b) and (c). The nub of this part of the defence is that service providers who simply turn a 'blind eye' to a defamatory statement being on its service, cannot benefit from this aspect of the defence.

NO AUTHORITY OR CONTROL AND EXPEDITIOUS ACTION

The second hosting defence concerns the actions of the service provider once they have knowledge or awareness. They will have the benefit of the defence if they meet two conditions. They must not be in control and they must have no authority over the person who defamed. The second condition, as for the first defence, is that they must act expeditiously to remove or disable access to it as soon as they know about[161].

No authority or control

The first condition to meet is for the service provider not to have 'authority' or 'control' over the third party who originally published the defamatory statement on its service[162]. Of course, often a service provider will have a contract with its members or customers. If they defame, will this constitute 'authority' or 'control'? This author and the DTI believe it will not.

The DTI states in its unbinding note on the Regulations that the concept of control or authority will be akin to 'effective control' under the Defamation Act 1996[163]. In other words, a mere contract to provide services to the third party will not be sufficient to bring the third party under the service provider's 'control' or 'authority'. The Regulations require a closer relationship such as between an employee, the third party, and an employer, the service provider.

An open question remains relating to whether or not the *ability* to control the third party will constitute control for the purposes of the first prong of the defence. After all, most, if not all service providers have the *ability* to remove material that is defamatory. Indeed, in a worst-case scenario, a service provider can always simply disable *all* publication of the statement; will that be 'control'?

US authority on a similar question is convincing that, were such an interpretation to be applied, it would be contrary to the spirit of the legislation itself. It would, in effect, state that those who are able to comply with the onus to remove material once notified must be able to remove the material and so are deemed to control it[164]:

> 'First, the "right and ability to control" the infringing activity, as the concept is used in the [Digital Millennium Copyright Act ("DMCA")], cannot simply mean the ability of a service provider to remove or block access to materials posted on its website or stored in its system. To hold otherwise would defeat the purpose of the DMCA and render the statute internally inconsistent. The DMCA specifically

161 Regulation 19(a)(ii) and (b).
162 Regulation 19(a)(ii).
163 *A Guide for Business to the Electronic Commerce (EC Directive) Regulations 2002*, para 6.7(c).
164 *Hendrickson v Ebay Inc* 2001 WL 1078981, CD Cal, 4 September 2001.

requires a service provider to remove or block access to materials posted on its system when it receives notice of claimed infringement. *See* 17 U.S.C. §§ 512(c)(1)(C). The DMCA also provides that the limitations on liability *only* apply to a service provider that has "adopted and reasonably implemented . . . a policy that provides for the termination in appropriate circumstances of [users] of the service provider's system or network who are repeat infringers." *See* 17 U.S.C. §§ 512(i)(1)(A). Congress could not have intended for courts to hold that a service provider loses immunity under the safe harbor provision of the DMCA because it engages in acts that are specifically required by the DMCA.'

Remove or disable expeditiously

The second condition is essentially that the Service Provider must act to stop any further harm as soon as they know about it. The Regulations state that 'upon obtaining such knowledge or awareness the Service Provider [must act] expeditiously to remove or to disable access to the information'[165].

So, how fast is 'expeditiously'. There is little doubt that this is quicker than 'reasonably quickly' but nevertheless will be assessed with reference to the facts and circumstances of the situation. It can be said with some certainty that a Service Provider who is sent a specific notice about defamatory material on 17 January will need to act well before the 27th to do so expeditiously[166].

Damages

Extent of publication

The damages for defamation are based on a number of factors, although the extent of publication is very relevant: 'a libel published to millions has a greater potential to cause damage than a libel published to a handful of people'[167]. This statement leads some to presume that the damages for an Internet libel will be huge because so many people have access to it. This is false. That the Internet has potentially millions of people accessing it bears no relationship to the number of people accessing the defamatory piece. The jury should not be allowed to infer that the extent of publication must be great because the material is available over the Internet. What the claimant should adduce is the actual extent of the publication of the defamatory piece. On the Internet, it is far easier to estimate how many people actually viewed a particular piece than it is to prove how many people had access to a newspaper[168]. Figures should be able to be provided with quite a high degree of accuracy.

165 Regulation 19(a)(ii).

166 In *Godfrey v Demon Internet Ltd*, this was the timing of the fax from the claimant to the eventual removal of the statement from the servers.

167 *John v MGN Ltd* [1996] 2 All ER 35 at 48.

168 It can be said, in contrast with this, that it is difficult to tell the number of times a particular piece was copied and redistributed to other servers. This, it is submitted, is as far as one could go: it is difficult. It is not impossible and it is the claimant's burden to adduce the best evidence of circulation.

19. An Internet Service Provider defames an individual on a much used forum called 'GossipsVille'. Liability is not in issue. The individual claims that GossipsVille is the most popular forum on the Internet and hosts over 500,000 readers every day. Counsel for the Provider should attempt to provide evidence of the exact number of individuals who actually read the statement. It is very likely this will be significantly less than the 500,000 average so acting to reduce the award.

Reductions and recommendations

The general level of defamation damages is lowering. Since the Courts and Legal Services Act 1990 the Court of Appeal has been able to reduce the damages on appeal[169]. The most spectacular example was when the singer Elton John saw his £350,000 damages reduced by the Court of Appeal to £75,000[170]. Clearly, for Mr John, this was a significant reduction. What is of greater significance to all claimants is what the Court of Appeal said about future defamation cases. The first, almost revolutionary, point of law made was[171]:

> '[t]he time has in our view come when judges, and counsel, should be free to draw the attention of juries to these comparisons [between the awards for personal injury and awards for injury to reputation].'

The court called it 'offensive to public opinion' that the damages for injury to reputation may be greater than if the claimant had been rendered a 'helpless cripple or an insensate vegetable'[172]. To guide the jury from such offensive awards the court also added that the judge should be free to give indications to the jury as to the realistic bracket for the damages[173].

This judgment may have a chilling effect on claimants who seek to gain vast damages from Providers. In negotiation of settlement, defendants should be aware that awards in the hundreds of thousands of pounds will become increasingly rare.

Strategy

The area of defamation is problematic for Service Providers because the law appears to place them under a huge burden even after the Electronic Commerce

169 Courts and Legal Services Act 1990, s 8.

170 *John v MGN Ltd* [1996] 2 All ER 35. To avoid misleading the reader, the majority of the reduction is accounted for by the court's substitution of £50,000 for the awarded £275,000 for exemplary damages. This was justified by the statement of the law that exemplary damages are awarded where the publisher had no genuine belief in the truth of what he published, suspected that the words were untrue, yet deliberately refrained from taking the obvious steps to turn 'suspicion into certainty' (at 57–58). For Internet defamation, an exemplary damages award will only be appropriate where the Provider is not considered the author, editor or publisher of the statement. In these cases, the Provider would have had no real opportunity to read, let alone consider and investigate, the statements. The ruling on exemplary damages, therefore, will be applicable only where the Internet Service Provider is unable to field a defence because of being an author, editor or publisher.

171 [1996] 2 All ER 35 at 54 per Sir Thomas Bingham MR delivering judgment for the court.

172 [1996] 2 All ER 35 at 54.

173 [1996] 2 All ER 35 at 55.

Regulations. This section describes a strategy that may be of assistance in reducing their exposure to risk.

Withdraw quickly

Internet Service Providers should have a quick response policy for dealing with defamation allegations. They have the advantage over the paper publishers that they can withdraw the statement from circulation in a matter of seconds. This reduces their damages liability and can also increase the chance of settling the matter more quickly.

Grievance channel

The Provider must have a channel available to receive complaints. If a postal address is the only point of communication provided, the statement may have been published hundreds of thousands of times before the Provider is made aware. A special, not just the general, email address should be employed. Complainants should be requested to send a digital copy of the allegedly defamatory statement to the special email address for consideration.

Indemnity and identity

Two further strategies relate to the relationship between the Provider and the author of the alleged defamatory statement. There will be times where the defamatory material is authored by a person who has no relationship with the Provider. This is generally the case with Providers who host Usenet newsgroups: any person may have access to the groups from any Provider in the world. There will be other times where the Provider already has a contract with the author of the statement. It may be that the author is renting space on the Provider's server for a website, or that the author is a member of a particular forum hosted by the Provider.

In these contractual situations it is advisable to include a term in the contract that the member will indemnify the Provider against costs and damages as a result of any defamatory statement made by the author, published by the Provider. Of course, the problem with such a term is that it is worthless if the indemnifier is a man-of-straw. It may, however, provide some financial support in the wake of an action.

The second strategy is for the Provider to maintain records of the actual identity of a member. This can be used if there is litigation to provide, on request of the claimant, the identity of the actual author of the statement[174]. Although

174 The House of Lords in *Norwich Pharmacal Co v Customs and Excise Comrs* [1974] AC 133 provided that where a person had facilitated or become mixed up in the wrongdoing by another, that person is under an enforceable duty to disclose to a party harmed by the wrongdoing the identity of the wrongdoer in order to enable the party to sue the wrongdoer. This was followed in *Totalise plc v Motley Fool Ltd* [2002] 1 WLR 1233 where the service provider was required to disclose the identity of a defamer on a web chat site to the claimant. As with most *Norwich Pharmacal* applications, Aldous LJ stated that, in general, the innocent intermediary should have its costs met.

there is a likelihood that a claimant will prefer to pursue a wealthy Provider than an individual, the claimant will have no choice unless the Provider can supply the identity of the first defendant. For example, in the *Prodigy* case, Prodigy was unable to identify the individual who made the defamatory remark. This duty to provide litigants with the details of a defamer should be alerted to each member. They should be reassured that their details will be only provided in the light of a bona fide dispute[175].

JURISDICTION

The Internet allows digital material to be downloaded or seen simultaneously by individuals in every country in the world. If a person is damaged or aggrieved by the material, his claim will not necessarily fit neatly into a purely English legal dispute. The international growth of the Internet and its disregard for borders will probably introduce a number of non-English legal factors into the person's claim. More than any other means of communication, the Internet will produce truly transnational disputes. Users of the Internet and their advisers must therefore be fully conversant with the English court's rules on jurisdiction and choice of law and the impact of the country of origin rule in the Electronic Commerce Regulations. A deep understanding of private international law combined with the Internet's global dissemination can arm a litigator with additional causes of action and defence. It is crucial that advisers pay due regard to the conflict of laws that may be present in an Internet dispute before wading into an assessment of the substantive law.

This first section deals with jurisdiction: the English court's authority to judge a dispute.

The Brussels Regulation on Jurisdiction and the Enforcement of Judgments in Civil and Commercial Matters is the starting place for any tort committed over the Internet with a foreign element[176]. First, one must assess whether the Regulation applies or whether it 'transfers' jurisdiction to the English common law.

Brussels Regulation Jurisdiction

CIVIL AND COMMERCIAL MATTER

Many torts committed over the Internet will fall within art 1, that is, the resulting dispute is a civil and commercial matter. Before deciding that the Regulation applies, litigants are advised to consider specialist texts and cases from the European Court which highlight the broad scope of art 1 under the previous 1968 Brussels Convention.

175 Providers should be careful not to provide personal details without first consulting their data protection notification and their terms of confidentiality with each member.

176 This entered into force, replacing the Brussels Convention, on 1 March 2002 (2001 OJ L012, 16/01/2001).

Domicile of defendant

Subject to Articles outside the scope of this chapter, the fundamental issue is where the defendant is domiciled. Article 2 establishes that persons domiciled in a Member State[177] can be sued in the courts of that state, sometimes with the claimant having a choice of another forum. Articles 59 and 60 direct the English courts to consider the domicile of the defendant with reference to the UK's 'internal law'[178]. Even for multinational torts committed in a digital medium, jurisdiction hinges on 'domicile'[179], an essentially static concept which is mostly unrelated to the complex factors such as where a server is based.

For Regulation purposes, a defendant can be domiciled in one of two types of state: a Member State or a non-Member State. If the defendant is domiciled within a Member State, the Regulation rules apply; if outside, the common law rules will apply. These two outcomes are decided, currently, with reference to the Civil Jurisdiction and Judgments Act 1982, as amended.

Individual's domicile

UK domicile

An individual is domiciled within the UK only if he is resident in the UK and the nature and circumstances of his residence indicate that he has a substantial connection with the UK[180]. It is presumed, unless proved otherwise, that being resident for the last three months or more will constitute the requisite substantial connection[181]. The ownership, control or access to a website anywhere in the world is wholly irrelevant for the purposes of jurisdiction over an individual under the Regulation. If an individual is a UK resident nothing will be gained for jurisdiction purposes by locating a web server 'offshore'.

Member State domicile

If an individual is not domiciled in the UK for the purposes of the Regulation, one must decide whether the individual is domiciled within another member state. If he is not, the Regulation will not apply to the dispute; questions of jurisdiction will then be resolved at common law.

An individual is domiciled in a state other than the UK if that other state would view him as domiciled in that state. Therefore, to determine whether a defendant in an Internet tort dispute is domiciled within a Member State that person's domicile must be assessed from that state's legal perspective[182]. Failing this, the Civil Jurisdiction and Judgments Act 1982 (as amended), s 41(7)

177 Ie any Member State with the exception of Denmark.

178 Civil Jurisdiction and Judgments Act 1982 (as amended by both the Civil Jurisdiction and Judgments Act 1991 and the Civil Jurisdiction and Judgments Order 2001), ss 4 and 42.

179 Prescribed as being relevant tests by the Civil Procedure Rules 1998, rr 6.18(g) and 6.19(1).

180 Civil Jurisdiction and Judgments Act 1982 (as amended by both the Civil Jurisdiction and Judgments Act 1991 and the Civil Jurisdiction and Judgments Order 2001), s 41(2).

181 Civil Jurisdiction and Judgments Act 1982 (as amended by both the Civil Jurisdiction and Judgments Act 1991 and the Civil Jurisdiction and Judgments Order 2001), s 41(6).

182 Brussels Regulation, art 59 (2).

establishes the test to determine whether a defendant is domiciled outside Member States.

Non-Member State domicile

An individual is domiciled outside all the Member States if none of those states would deem him to be domiciled within their jurisdiction and if a further two-part test is satisfied. First, the individual must be resident in the non-Member State, and second, the nature and circumstances of his residence must indicate that he has a substantial connection with that state[183]. One is not required to consult the non-Member State's law on domicile.

> **20. An English academic who teaches in an English University defames a Dutch academic by posting a message to a forum. This forum is stored on a server in America and the Dutch academic has a substantial reputation only in Holland. The English courts will have jurisdiction over the dispute as the defendant is domiciled in England. The location of the server and the reputation are of little relevance for jurisdiction over the academic in the English courts.**

If the result of the domicile tests is that an individual defendant is domiciled within a Member State, the Regulation will apply to any other questions of jurisdiction. If the result is that the defendant is domiciled outside the Member State, the English common law rules on jurisdiction will apply[184]. These are described after the Regulation regime[185].

Company's or other legal person's domicile

A company or other legal person has its domicile in the state where it has its statutory seat, or central administration, or principal place of business[186].

UK domicile

A company or other legal person is domiciled within the UK if it was incorporated or formed under the law of a part of the UK, and its registered office or other official address is in the UK; or if its central administration or principal place of business is in the UK[187]. Again, the ownership, control or access to a website anywhere in the world is mostly irrelevant for the purposes of jurisdiction under the Regulation. A corporation that is, in effect, based in the UK will not be able to avoid the jurisdiction of the English courts simply by using an off-shore server.

183 Civil Jurisdiction and Judgments Act 1982 (as amended by both the Civil Jurisdiction and Judgments Act 1991 and the Civil Jurisdiction and Judgments Order 2001), s 41(7).
184 Article 4.
185 See 'Common law jurisdiction over torts', at p 151.
186 Article 60(1).
187 Civil Jurisdiction and Judgments Act 1982 (as amended by both the Civil Jurisdiction and Judgments Act 1991 and the Civil Jurisdiction and Judgments Order 2001), s 42(2).

Member State domicile

If a company or other legal person is not domiciled in the UK for the purposes of the Regulation, one must decide whether it is domiciled within another Member State. If it is not, the Regulation will not apply to the dispute; questions of jurisdiction will then be decided with recourse to the common law. A company or other legal person is domiciled in a state other than the UK if it satisfies two tests.

First, the English courts must be satisfied that the company or other legal person was incorporated or formed under the law of that other Member State, or, its central management and control is exercised in that State[188].

The second test that must also be satisfied, is that the entity shall not have been incorporated or formed under the law of a part of the UK, or, shown not to be regarded by the courts of the other Member State to have its seat within that Member State[189]. If either test is not satisfied, the common law rules on jurisdiction will apply[190]; these are discussed after the Regulation rules.

21. An estate agent company is incorporated and operates from France. It provides advice to wealthy Australians who are considering buying property in the South of France. Its server is physically based in Perth and the domain address has the suffix 'co.au' which indicates an Australian firm. An Australian arrives at a newly bought property to discover that the company's advice was negligent. Now having a base in France, the Australian decides that it will be cheaper to conduct the litigation from France. He will be able to do this as long as the French courts consider that the estate agent company has its seat within France.

Non-Member State domicile

If both of the previous tests fail to establish the defendant as domiciled in the UK or another Member State, the common law rules on jurisdiction will apply.

Regulation jurisdiction over torts

Having established that the defendant to an action is domiciled in a contracting state it can be said with certainty that the Regulation rules on jurisdiction apply. For matters relating to tort there are rules that supplement the main rule under art 2, that the defendant can be sued in the courts of his domicile. The tort rules provide a claimant with additional jurisdictions in which the defendant can be rightly sued. For example, a German individual may have defamed an English individual by posting a message on a Spanish Provider's bulletin board. Without more than the art 2 rule, the English claimant would have to sue in either Spain or Germany: a practice that may be expensive and complicated. The rules under the Regulation broaden the jurisdiction for tortious claims and specify[191]:

188 Civil Jurisdiction and Judgments Act 1982 (as amended by both the Civil Jurisdiction and Judgments Act 1991 and the Civil Jurisdiction and Judgments Order 2001), s 43(3).
189 Civil Jurisdiction and Judgments Act 1982 (as amended by both the Civil Jurisdiction and Judgments Act 1991 and the Civil Jurisdiction and Judgments Order 2001), s 43(4).
190 Article 4.
191 Article 5(3).

> 'A person domiciled in a Member State may, in another Member State, be sued: . . . in matters relating to tort, delict or quasi-delict, in the courts for the place where the harmful event occurred or may occur.'

What is a tort?

The heading above, 'What is a tort?' may surprise those who are unfamiliar with jurisdiction issues. The reason it is included is that the terms 'tort, delict or quasi-delict' in art 5(3) must be given an autonomous Community meaning; one cannot simply check whether the dispute would be included in an English text-book on torts. The European Court puts this[192]:

> '[T]he term "matters relating to tort, delict or quasi-delict" within the meaning of Article 5(3) of the Convention must be regarded as an independent concept covering all actions which seek to establish the liability of a defendant and which are not related to a "contract" within the meaning of Article 5(1).'

This approach has been endorsed by the House of Lords in *Kleinwort Benson Ltd v Glasgow City Council*[193]. For the purposes of this section, therefore, art 5(3) will apply in relation to digital damage, defamation and negligent advice[194].

Location of harmful events

A defendant domiciled in a contracting state who commits a tort may be sued in the court of the defendant's domicile or in the court where the harmful event occurred or may occur under art 5(3). Having examined above what constitutes a tort, it is now crucial to consider where a tort occurs.

The first European case to deal with this concerned a claimant who carried on the business of nursery gardening in the Netherlands and used water to irrigate the seed beds mainly from the Rhine[195]. The defendant mined in France and was alleged to have increased the salt content in the irrigating water by discharging from Alsace large quantities of residuary salts into the Rhine. On a reference from the national court the European Court held that the phrase 'the place where the harmful event occurred' could refer to two jurisdictions[196].

192 *Kalfelis v Schroder, Munchmayer* [1988] ECR 5565 at 5585 [18].
193 [1999] 1 AC 153 and *Agnew v Länsförsakringsbolagens AB* [2000] 1 Lloyd's Rep IR 317.
194 It is useful to note that Rix J correctly states in *Trade Indemnity v Försäkrings AB Njord* [1995] 1 All ER 796 at 820 that an action for misrepresentation or non-disclosures in making a contract is not covered by Art 5(1) which relates to contracts. One is therefore bound by *Kalfelis* (see fn 192 above) to conclude that art 5(3) will apply to misrepresentations. A misrepresentation made on a website may be therefore sued upon not only in the defendant's domicile but also in any state in which the claimant acted upon the representation on the web pages; an exclusive jurisdiction clause in the contract will, for this claim, be to no avail.
195 *Handelskwekerij G J Bier BV v Mines de Potasse d'Alsace SA* [1978] QB 708.
196 [1976] ECR 1735 at 1745–1747 [19].

> '[T]he claimant has an option to commence proceedings either at the place where the damage occurred or the place of the event giving rise to it.'

For an Internet tort, particularly one made over the web, this ruling has a significant effect. Defendants who are domiciled in a contracting state may face claims from any jurisdiction which is signatory to the Regulation. This is because it is technically difficult to prevent a server from being accessed from a particular place in the world. In illustration, malicious code on a website can infect any person accessing that from anywhere in the world; negligent misstatements made on a website or forum may be relied upon by any person anywhere in the world; and defamatory statements on a website or forum may be read by any person anywhere in the world.

The commercial effects of this are substantial. Companies and individuals domiciled in a Member State who use the Internet to provide information, services or products risk being sued in any jurisdiction party to the Regulation. Some more specific points are made below.

Digital damage

There are striking similarities between allowing a computer virus into the Internet and allowing pollutants into a water supply. Both cross borders. Both originate from a fixed source yet can spread in many directions, affecting many claimants. In one way computer viruses have more impact because they have a longer life owing to their perfect replication. These comparisons make it probable that, where the Brussels Regulation applies, a court will follow the European Court's ruling in *Bier*. Under art 2 the claimant will be permitted to sue the defendant in a court of the defendant's place of domicile. In addition, by art 5(3), the claimant can sue the defendant in the place of digital damage, probably the claimant's 'home' and also in the court of the place of the source of the virus. The claimant therefore has three options; the option to sue at home will generally be the most favourable.

22. A Spanish architect sent some unsolicited plans to an English property agent. The plans contained a computer virus which corrupted some entries on the agent's database. Were the agent to sue the architect for damage caused by negligence, the agent would have the jurisdiction of the English courts because the damage occurred there.

Secondary damage

It has been discussed that viruses and other malicious code will damage not only those directly in contact with the contaminated computer, but also those in contact with an already infected computer. This is coined 'secondary damage'. Such 'ricochet' damage has been criticised as a basis for ousting the right that any defendant has to be sued in the courts of his domicile.

In *Dumez France v Hessische Landesbank (Helaba)*[197] two French parent

197 [1990] ECR 49.

companies sued in France two German banks. The claim was for compensation for damage arising out of the winding up of their two German subsidiaries. The subsidiaries, it was claimed, had to be wound up because the German banks had withdrawn credit facilities to one of the subsidiary's customers. The European Court was asked whether the 'place where the harmful event occurred'[198] can be interpreted as including damage claimed by a claimant that is the consequence of harm suffered by other persons who were direct victims[199]. An affirmative answer would have allowed the French companies to sue the German banks in France, as that was the place where they claimed the harmful event occurred.

The court accepted the approach made by the Advocate General that a victim 'by ricochet' cannot bring an action in the courts of the place of that damage. The court is looking not for where damage is suffered, but rather where it occurs. As seems to be obvious, this ruling may often be applicable for digital damage by viral infection. The application is more difficult for economic loss that may occur as a result of viral damage or negligent misstatement.

23. A company based in Holland, through the negligence of a supplier also based in Holland, becomes infected by a logic bomb which damages important data. Before the logic bomb is triggered, the infected company sent an infected file to a customer in England. The customer's computer was damaged and there was no indication that the Dutch company was negligent in sending the file. The English customer's action must be solely against the Dutch supplier but the jurisdiction of the English courts will be not be supported by art 5(3). The English customer's damage was the consequence of harm suffered by direct victims.

Negligent misstatement

An individual or company domiciled in a contracting state providing negligent advice on a website risks being sued in a court within any contracting state. This is because application of the judgment in *Bier* establishes that a claimant can sue the defendant in a state of his domicile, or, where the server was situated, or where the damage occurs. The damage will usually occur where the claimant accesses the negligent advice.

24. A luxury boat mortgage company is incorporated in and operates from Italy. It provides mortgages and advice to wealthy Italian-Americans who are considering buying a boat moored in Italy. The company rents web space on a server that happens to be based in Ireland; its domain name 'moorings.com' clearly gives little indication of its base. An American mortgages a boat through the site that turns out to be far from sea-worthy and sinks off the coast of Spain. The Spanish courts will not have jurisdiction over the tort; the damage from the negligent advice occurred in Italy where the mortgage report was relied upon; that the actual damage was suffered in Spain is not relevant for art 5(3).

198 See [1976] ECR 1735.
199 [1996] All ER (EC) 84 at 94[8].

Often negligent advice results in economic loss as one of the heads of damage. Apart from the domestic question of whether such loss is recoverable, there is the issue of where economic loss occurs. If a claimant's bank account is in England but the claimant accesses and relies upon information on a website from Germany, will the English courts have jurisdiction purely because the bank account was situated there?

A similar question was answered by the European Court in *Marinari v Lloyds Bank plc (Zubaidi Trading Co intervening)*[200]. Mr Marinari, domiciled in Italy, sued Lloyds Bank plc, whose registered office is in England. His claim was that he had deposited promissory notes with a value of $750 million with a Manchester branch of the bank. The bank staff suspected that the notes were bogus, kept them and advised the police who arrested Mr Marinari. He sued in Italy for compensation for the payment of the notes, damage to reputation and loss of contracts. Lloyds Bank objected to the jurisdiction of the Italian courts arguing that the damage occurred in England.

The court derived from *Mines de Potasse d'Alsace* and *Bier* that the choice generally afforded to a tort claimant could provide a significant connecting factor from the point of view of jurisdiction. But, the choice must not be extended, so negating the general principle in Art 2, to encompass any place where the adverse consequences of an event that has already caused actual damage has occurred[201]. In short, it affirmed that one must look for where damage occurs (and now, where it may occur), not where it is suffered.

Whatever the flaws in the court's solution, it does have the quality of certainty for torts committed over the Internet. By focusing on the tangible and fixed aspects of damage the court is able to ensure that the court with jurisdiction is appropriate to determine the legal dispute. The court was particularly wary of the fluidity of damaged assets and therefore the possibilities of 'entirely inappropriate' courts having to take the relevant evidence. It is submitted that this is correct. Although the Internet does allow intellectual property, advice and funds to be moved and accessed from any jurisdiction in the world, it is not necessarily in the interests of justice that any court in Europe could govern the relevant dispute. The rules on jurisdiction attempt to delineate which cases are appropriate to be heard and decided by which courts; it is naive to suggest because the Internet has no technical boundaries to the flow of digital material that the law should drop its boundaries also.

25. A Russian entrepreneur owned a number of shares in an English company, held by an English bank. From Russia he logged on to a French investor's web page, and on the basis of information there, sold the shares in the English company. The information was provided negligently. Under the Brussels Regulation, the Russian will be able to sue only in France under art 2: the damage occurred in Russia, which is not a contracting state, and where the damage was suffered is irrelevant under art 5(3).

Defamation

The Internet and associated technologies allow the whole world to have access to information about one individual; it is now possible to have a truly global

200 [1996] All ER (EC) 84.
201 [1996] All ER (EC) 84 at 95 [10–15].

reputation. For the same technical reasons it is possible for a defamatory statement to be read from anywhere in the world; it is possible to defame someone on a global scale. These two conclusions present the law with an issue as to a court's jurisdiction over defamation. If a celebrity is defamed on a worldwide forum, which court is appropriate to hear the dispute between the claimant and defendant?[202] There are a number of options. Two main ones are: first, only ever in one jurisdiction, the so-called 'single publication' rule; second, in multiple jurisdictions, wherever the claimant has a cause of action. We shall see, both at common law and under the Brussels Regulation, that the highest courts in Europe agree that there is no such 'single publication' rule in European jurisprudence[203].

The answer for defamation claims falling under the Brussels Regulation is provided by the European Court in *Shevill v Presse Alliance SA*[204].

Presse Alliance SA, a French company, published its daily newspaper with an article that mentioned the claimant's name in relation to a drug trafficking network that was raided by the drugs squad. The claimant was in England at the time of the raid, having only been in France for three months. 237,000 copies of the newspaper containing the defamatory article were sold in France; 230 were sold in England. The claimant asserted that the English courts had jurisdiction over the dispute by virtue of art 5(3); the defendants objected, eventually appealing to the House of Lords. The Lords then referred seven preliminary questions to the European Court.

The important answer provided by the Court was that the claimant in a defamation action may sue in the courts of the defendant's domicile, under art 2, and under art 5(3) may sue in the courts of the place from where the libel was issued and circulated. And any one of these courts have jurisdiction to hear the action for damages for *all* the harm caused by the unlawful act. Alternatively, the claimant may sue in the courts of any Member State in which the defamatory publication was distributed and in which the victim claims to have suffered injury to reputation. These courts have jurisdiction only to rule on the injury caused to the victim's reputation in that state. The 'single publication' rule, which would force a claimant to choose, is not therefore European law.

Again, this answer takes due account of justice to the parties: the courts best suited to consider damages must include those which are territorially the best placed to assess the libel committed in the state and determine the corresponding level of damages. That the claimant has the option of suing once for all the damages in the court of the defendant's domicile accords with the basic rule of the Brussels regime: 'defendants should be sued at home'.

Of course for the Internet such a decision has a great impact. Without careful deployment of certain technologies, a website or a forum will be available throughout the world. A victim defamed on one of these globally accessible

202 It is not assumed that the defendant is necessarily an individual and may well be the host of the website, discussion board or forum itself. If the host is not domiciled within a contracting state it may still be brought within the regime of the Defamation Act 1996 where the actual defamer is domiciled in England. In this situation the claimant would be relying on art 6(1) of the Regulation.

203 This is in sharp contrast to the long-standing US rule preventing such a multiplicity of suits. See *Ogden v Association of the United States Army (a corpn)* 177 F Supp 498 at 502, (1959).

204 [1995] All ER (EC) 289.

sites needs only to find a very limited number of 'hits' from a particular contracting state to be able to litigate there[205]. In most cases of Internet defamation the claimant will be able to sue in the courts of their domicile; a scenario that was to be avoided under the Brussels Convention and Regulation. It is a scenario, however, which makes legal sense.

There are advantages and disadvantages with every form of communication. The Internet's advantages include that there is little increase in marginal cost to distribute information throughout the world. If it is useful information, the *global* reputation of the provider will increase; if it is defamatory information, the *global* reputation of the victim will decrease. That this is somehow 'unfair' or 'prejudices the Internet', does not take into account that one cannot expect to reap the rewards from cheap global distribution without bearing its risks.

26. A UK resident soap star is defamed on a French bulletin board by an Australian co-actor who had since left the programme. The bulletin board operator included the Australian's comments in a highlighted section of the bulletin board called 'Celebrity Clangers'. The victim can sue the French bulletin board in England as long as it can be proved that the board was accessed from England. This will be sufficient to establish that damage occurred in England giving the English courts jurisdiction under art 5(3).

Common law jurisdiction over torts

If the defendant to an Internet tort is not domiciled within a contracting state[206], the court must apply its domestic laws to determine jurisdiction[207]. The main method of service abroad with leave is examined below.

Service out

There are two separate and distinct aspects to serving out of the jurisdiction[208]. The first aspect is jurisdiction: does the claimant's claim fall within one of the sub-rules of CPR r 6.20(8)(a) or (b). These are where the tortious damage was sustained within the jurisdiction, or, the damage sustained resulted from an act committed within the jurisdiction. Although not yet deeply analysed by the courts, it is likely that this test does not need to be satisfied to any high degree of proof: a good arguable case that the claim is covered by the one of the sub-rules is probably sufficient[209]. The second aspect,

205 In *Shevill* less than 0.1% of the distribution was in England. There presumably must be some *de minimis* amount although the court did not appear to take notice that less than a thousandth of the distribution occurred in England. This said, the amount of distribution in absolute terms may reduce the possible damages which may be awarded.

206 See 'Domicile of defendant', at p 143.

207 Article 4.

208 See *Seaconsar v Bank Merkazi Jomhouri Islami Iran* [1994] 1 AC 438, which applied, and it is suggested remains applicable, under the old Rules of the Supreme Court, Ord 11.

209 See *Attock Cement Co Ltd v Romanian Bank for Foreign Trade* [1989] 1 All ER 1189, which applied, and it is suggested remains still applicable, under the old Rules of the Supreme Court, Ord 11.

which will not be covered here in great detail, is one of discretion: no permission to serve a claim out of the jurisdiction will be given unless the court is satisfied that England and Wales is the proper place in which to bring the claim. This is specified by CPR r 6.21(2A).

Jurisdiction under tort sub-rule

The head that will apply for most torts committed over the Internet is CPR r 6.20(8)(a) or (b)[210]:

> 'the claim is made in tort where the damage was sustained within the jurisdiction, or the damage sustained resulted from an act committed within the jurisdiction.'

Until 1987 the provision used to relate only to a claim 'founded on a tort committed within the jurisdiction'. This was amended in the light of the *Bier* case[211] and the amendment carried through from the Rules of the Supreme Court to the Court Procedure Rules. A claimant is now required to satisfy two requirements. First, the claim must be made in tort. Second, the damage must be sustained in the jurisdiction or have resulted from an act committed in the jurisdiction. The second question has been discussed in relation to the Brussels Regulation and it would appear that the reasoning given there is equally applicable[212]. What must be considered here, in contrast, relates to the first question: simply put, what is a tort?[213]

The answer to this question can be found by considering the main precedent in this area: *Metall und Rohstoff AG v Donaldson, Lufkin & Jenrette Inc*[214]. In this case the defendants whilst in New York had sent to English persons inducements to break contracts which subsisted with other English persons. The tortious claim was for inducing breach of contract in which the damage was sustained in England. The court permitted service abroad, but not before making an analysis of this complex area. It is submitted that this remains good law.

Choice of law under jurisdiction

The court decided that to determine whether a 'tort' has been committed[215], one had to consider the choice of law rule in *Boys v Chaplin* to ascertain whether the

210 Of course, CPR r 6.20(2) may be more appropriate in some circumstances.
211 See 'Location of harmful events', at p 146.
212 See 'Location of harmful events', at p 146. This said, the English courts appear keener to look for a 'substantial act' rather than merely any tortious act. See *Metall and Rohstoff AG v Donaldson, Lufkin & Jenrette Inc* [1989] 3 All ER 14 at 25; *Schapira v Ahronson* [1999] EMLR 735.
213 This was discussed in relation to the Brussels Regulation but it is clear that the autonomous meaning under the Convention is inapplicable for an English court to adopt in these circumstances. See 'What is a tort?', at p 146.
214 [1989] 3 All ER 14. Readers should note that the overruling of this decision in *Lourho plc v Fayed* [1992] 1 AC 448 was on other aspects.
215 It should be noted that the sub-rule 6.20(8) head refers not to a 'wrong' but to a claim made in 'tort'; this is therefore a legal question that is distinct from the question of where, in substance, a wrong is committed.

relevant events would have given rise to liability in tort under English law[216]. The court expresses this ruling as[217]:

> 'if [the court] find that the tort was in substance committed in some foreign country, they should apply the [*Chaplin v Boys*] rule and impose liability in tort under English law, only if both (a) the relevant events would have given rise to liability in tort in English law if they had taken place in England, and (b) the alleged tort would be actionable in the country where it was committed.'

In short, the court must consult the choice of law rules first to check that the 'wrong' is actionable here as a tort; it must be a claim capable of being pleaded as a tort. But, as the following section explains, the choice of law rule for torts other than defamation, is no longer that expounded in *Chaplin v Boys*. It is contained in the Private International Law (Miscellaneous Provisions) Act 1995; s 10 of the Act abolishes the common law rules in *Chaplin v Boys* replacing them with the rules in ss 11 to 13[218].

Proving jurisdiction under tort head

For a 'wrong' committed over the Internet, it would appear that the convoluted scheme for determining whether one can serve out is as follows.

1. Check whether damage was sustained within the jurisdiction or whether the damage resulted from an act committed within the jurisdiction[219]. If neither apply, the claimant will be unable to serve out under CPR r 6.20(8).
2. Check whether, under English law, the claim relates to issues arising in any defamation claim, including claims for slander of title, goods or other malicious falsehood[220].
3. Looking back over the series of events establish where in substance the cause of action arose[221].
4. If the cause of action arose in England, the claimant will have established jurisdiction under CPR r 6.20(8).
5. If the cause of action arose outside England and Wales, the claimant will have to prove that the 'wrong' is actionable in England as a tort:

216 [1971] AC 356. Apologies are made to those who are unfamiliar with the conflict of laws. It is correct but confusing that in *Metall und Rohstoff* the court conflated the usually distinct considerations of jurisdiction and choice of law. If a reader is unfamiliar with choice of law in tort it is advised, at this point, to read this chapter's following section on these rules. Normally one can consider jurisdiction separately from choice of law. For service out on a tortious claim, however, one must decide whether the 'wrong' is a tort in the first place and this is only achievable with recourse to English choice of law rules. The circularity of this section is regretted but unavoidable.

217 [1989] 3 All ER 14 at 32.

218 Readers unfamiliar with the operation of the new Act are advised to read this chapter's following section on choice of law. Issues arising in relation to defamation are still governed by the common law.

219 As confirmed by *Metall and Rohstoft AG v Donaldson, Lufkin & Jenrette* [1989] 3 All ER 14.

220 Private International Law (Miscellaneous Provisions) Act 1995, s 13.

221 See *Distillers Co (Biochemicals) Ltd v Thompson* [1971] All ER 694 at 699 per Lord Pearson with refinement in *Castree v ER Squibb & Sons Ltd* [1980] 2 All ER 589; and also *Schapira v Ahranson* [1999] EMLR 735.

5.1. If the claim relates to a defamation claim (see 2) the claimant will have to apply the old common law test in *Boys v Chaplin* satisfying the court that both the relevant events would have given rise to liability in tort in English law if occurring in England, and that the alleged tort is actionable in the country where it is committed[222].

5.2. If the claim does not relate to a defamation claim (see 2) the claimant will have to apply the Private International Law (Miscellaneous Provisions) Act 1995 satisfying the court that the 'wrong' is actionable under the law of the country where the tort occurs[223], or if more than one country is involved, the law of the country in which the most significant element of the events occurred[224].

6. If points 1 and 4, or points 1 and 5, are satisfied, the claim falls within CPR r 6.20(8).

30. Revealing pictures of a British film director and his mistress are released onto the Internet by an American journalist. Under English law, the director has no legal redress against the journalist, but under American law a law of confidence would protect him. The director has a good arguable case that the dispute falls within CPR r 6.20(8). Damage to the director's reputation has occurred in England, and the cause of action arose in America where the 'wrong' is actionable as a tort. The director may have the jurisdiction of the English courts to serve out to the journalist suing him under American law.

Discretion under service out

It is not sufficient simply to satisfy a court of a good arguable case under sub-rule (8) under CPR r 6.20. The claim must also be a proper case for service out under CPR r 6.21(1A). The discretion to serve out includes as a main factor, an assessment, perhaps not overtly, of whether England is the *forum conveniens*, the most suitable forum in which to hear the dispute. This will be considered briefly in the following section on staying actions[225]. This discretionary factor should not be overlooked by legal advisers: for a tort committed over the Internet it may be difficult to persuade a court to serve out. If the defendant, in contrast, is domiciled in a Member State, the court has far less discretion over jurisdiction[226].

222 It is admitted, but ignored for the sake of simplicity, that the flexible exception in *Red Sea Insurance Co Ltd v Bouygues SA* [1995] 1 AC 190 may be invoked allowing a defamation-type claim which is not actionable in England to be actionable here. This said, in the light of Parliament's intention to prevent the Act applying to defamation claims, a strong case would have to be put to invoke the *Red Sea* exception.

223 Private International Law (Miscellaneous Provisions) Act 1995, s 11(1). This country will probably be the same as that decided for point 3.

224 Private International Law (Miscellaneous Provisions) Act 1995, s 11(1). This country will probably be the same as that decided for point 3.

225 The court's assessment is the same, although for service out, the plaintiff must ask the court to exercise discretion; for staying service as of right, the defendant must persuade the court to stay the action.

226 See the Court of Appeal's interpretation of the Civil Jurisdiction and Judgments Act 1982, s 49 in *Re Harrods (Buenos Aires) Ltd* [1992] Ch 72.

Staying actions

It is always open to a putative defendant to apply to stay the common law jurisdiction of the English courts by pleading that it is not the most suitable forum in which to resolve the dispute[227]. Whether a court stays an action is decided with recourse to the principle of *forum non conveniens*. This principle is impressively explained and stated in the House of Lords' decision in *Spiliada Maritime Corpn v Cansulex Ltd*[228]. In a later case Lord Goff explains *forum non conveniens* as 'a self-denying ordinance under which the court will stay (or dismiss) proceedings in favour of another clearly more appropriate forum'[229]. A full discussion of this case is beyond the scope of this chapter, but an appreciation of its implications is worthwhile. Until courts approach wrongs committed over the Internet and Internet disputes with the familiarity and understanding that they approach, say the telephone and newspapers, litigators must be prepared to argue that despite the transnational nature of the Internet, some forums are more suitable than others.

Lord Goff provided the leading judgment given in *Spiliada*. He set out a number of guidelines[230] that may guide a court as to whether England is a suitable and appropriate forum: the court must, in effect, balance the suitability of England against that of another forum. This forum must be clearly and distinctly more appropriate: one 'with which the action [has] the most real and substantial connection'[231]. At this point, 'the court may nevertheless decline to grant a stay if persuaded by the plaintiff, on whom the burden of proof then lies, that justice requires that a stay should not be granted'[232].

This discretion, unlikely to be disturbed on appeal[233], may be of paramount importance in an Internet dispute. In contrast to most other means of communication, the Internet can make it appear that a defendant has little connection with any country. A server may be in a country far away from the defendant's domicile. A defendant may have mirror servers, identical websites, scattered throughout the world. The information or product that is the root of the dispute may have passed through as many as one hundred countries. Worse still, it is a question of technical semantics to resolve whether the digital information moved from the server to the claimant or whether the claimant 'collected' the digital information from the server.

These issues, and many more like them, may cloud the answer as to which is the *forum conveniens* for the dispute. Of course, one may take the more pragmatic approach and look at the dispute trying to ignore the Internet complexities. To describe computer virus damage, one may state that, say, an individual's property in England was damaged as a result of the negligence of an individual, whose property was in America. While this may appear a precis of the dispute, it does not address the question before the courts: which is the suitable forum in the interests of all the parties and the ends of justice?

227 CPR, Pt 11 provides the necessary procedure.
228 [1986] 3 All ER 843.
229 *Airbus Industrie GIE v Patel* [1999] 1 AC 119 at 132C.
230 The necessary details of these guidelines can be found in specialist texts but readers are also directed to the very full judgments in *Lubbe v Cape plc* [2000] 4 All ER 268, HL.
231 *The Abidin Daver* [1984] 1 All ER 470 at 478 per Lord Keith.
232 *Conelly v RT2 Corpn plc* [1998] AC 854 at 872A, per Lord Goff for the House of Lords restating the second stage of the *Spiliada* test.
233 [1986] 3 All ER 843 at 846 to 847 per Lord Templeman.

To answer this question involves examining the mechanics of hearing the dispute as well as its geographical basis. In illustration, often it is important to know where the relevant evidence is held and where the relevant witnesses live[234]. For many Internet disputes, however, such factors may not be weighty enough to disturb the jurisdiction of the court. Computer files will often be the main evidence and often the claimant in England will be the sole human witness to the tort itself. So for an Internet dispute, the jurisdiction of the English court may be less easily upset. As a further illustration, the issue of convenience, often a factor for the court, may be less convincing when all of the actual evidence is in a digital format. Such evidence can be sent to England, over the Internet, cheaply, quickly and accurately. Again, the actual nature of the Internet may lead to the conclusion that little is lost by hearing the dispute in England.

A court will also consider the residence of the defendant. The claimant, no doubt, will attempt to persuade the court that the Internet allows persons to have no residence as such. In this sense, those who use the Internet have no claim over one country any more than another. The defendant's argument may take a more common sense view: the Internet is a means of communication that operates from one fixed point to another. In addition, the defendant who would be forced into the English courts has a fixed residence; that the defendant is alleged to have committed a tort over the Internet which is difficult to locate may not be relevant as to where is the most appropriate place to litigate the dispute.

For the purposes of jurisdiction, the defendant's argument is the more realistic. If a tort committed over the Internet seems to have no geographical locus then, presumably, any court is equally suitable to gather evidence on the Internet aspects of the dispute. What will tip this finely balanced situation is the fact that the court is judging which is the natural forum: which is the forum with the closest and most real connection to the dispute. This is a relative not absolute requirement: the forum need not be close, but simply the closest out of many; the forum need not have a real connection, but simply the most real out of the other connections. The court is seeking, at times, the 'best out of a bad bunch'. The court must consider all the relevant factors, such as where the defendant and claimant are and which law will apply to this dispute.

Under the Private International Law (Miscellaneous Provisions) Act 1995, except for defamation issues, the law that generally will apply to a tort dispute is the law of where the tort occurred. And Lord Goff in *Spiliada* notes that the law of the dispute will often be a relevant factor[235]. What can be concluded from all this is that presence of the Internet in a dispute will never create the situation where no court is appropriate to hear the case. All the Internet may complicate is the question of where the tort occurs; there are numerous other factors that will, despite this complication, prove that England is, or is not, the natural forum.

234 See [1986] 3 All ER 843 at 856.

235 With reference to *Crédit Chimique v James Scott Engineering Group Ltd* 1982 SLT 131. In this Scottish case, Lord Jauncey goes further and asks that a court look not simply at the fact that foreign law will be applied, but to look deeper at the nature of the foreign law. It may be that it is trivial for an English court to turn its mind to the foreign law, but it also may be that the law is so alien that the most appropriate court to consider the legal issues is a court which regularly deals with them.

28. A publisher resident in Calcutta publishes an online newspaper. In one edition an Indian domiciled in England is gravely defamed. He seeks to serve a writ out of the jurisdiction against the Indian publisher. Evidence is adduced that the newspaper has 73,000 subscribers in India but only 15 in England. The court in deciding whether England, or Calcutta, is the appropriate forum may consider that the courts of the place where the publisher is resident, publishes and has the greatest distribution, is the place with the most real connection with the dispute.

Extent of circulation

The last scenario is included for a number of reasons. First, it relates to a real case involving not online newspapers, but paper newspapers[236]. Second, the result is supported by the House of Lords in a similar precedent in *Berezovsky v Michaels*[237] in which 780,000 copies of a Forbes magazine were circulated containing a defamatory article about a Russian businessman. However, only 6,000 readers were in the jurisdiction of the English Courts. The third reason is that it acts as a nice comparison with *Shevill* and other defamation claims heard under the Brussels Convention and Regulation[238].

What is clear from these cases, and others[239] is that the extent of circulation is in no way conclusive as to where an action may commence. In both *Shevill* and *Berezovsky*[240], one under Brussels Regulation rules and the other under common law rules, the concept of a 'global tort' or a 'single publication rule' is rejected. Since the *Duke of Brunswick v Harmer*[241] in the late 1800s each communication is a separate libel. This applies across borders (for the purposes of jurisdiction assessment) as in *Berezovsky* and *Shevill* and at any time in the future (for purposes of limitation periods and damages).

Under the Brussels Regulation, in fact, circulation seems not to be a factor at all. At common law, circulation figures and 'hits' on websites are merely one of the factors relevant for the *Spiliada* test.

This section has shown that, if a defendant of an Internet tort is domiciled within a Member State, a claimant will have little difficulty in suing in the English courts. In contrast, if the defendant is not domiciled in a Member State, a claimant will have to concentrate on convincing the court of their substantial connection with England; the number of 'hits' or downloads may not influence the court either way.

CHOICE OF LAW

Establishing that the English courts have jurisdiction over an Internet tort dispute does not determine which law they must apply to resolve the dispute. This

236 *Pillai v Sarkar* (1994) Times, 21 July.
237 [2000] 2 All ER 986.
238 See 'Defamation', at p 149.
239 See *Kroch v Rossell* [1937] 1 All ER 725; *Schapira v Ahranson* [1999] EMLR 735 at 745; *Chadha & Discom Technologies Inc v Dow Jones & Co Inc* [1999] EMLR 724; and the judgment pending in the Australian case *Gutnick v Dow Jones & Co Inc* [2001] VSC 305 (28 August 2001).
240 See Lord Hoffman at [2002] 2 All ER 986 at 1005.
241 (1849) 14 QB 185.

is a separate issue decided by reference to English law's choice of law rules for foreign torts. It may be a complex issue because the court must determine where the tort occurs before deciding which law will apply. Over the Internet, such geographical issues may be difficult to resolve, but, it is submitted, of no increased difficulty over other transborder torts. What the Internet will increase is the frequency with which courts are pressed on these issues of choice of law.

Common law choice of law

The Private International Law (Miscellaneous Provisions) Act 1995 leaves in place the old common law rules to determine the law to apply to the determination of issues arising in any defamation claim[242]. Defamation claims include not only libel and slander but also slander of title, slander of goods or other malicious falsehood and their equivalents[243].

Double-actionability test

The common law rules are well covered in specialist texts so what follows is a short introduction to their vestigial application to an Internet defamation claim. The basic rule is that the claimant must have a cause of action under English domestic law[244] and under the law of the place where the tort occurred[245]. Without this 'double-actionability' the claim cannot be brought unless it falls within the exception. This is that, in the interests of justice, single-actionability may suffice. In *Boys v Chaplin* the exception was 'created' and invoked by the House of Lords to permit a claimant to recover in England that which he could not recover under the foreign law[246]. In *Red Sea Insurance Co Ltd v Bouygues SA* the Privy Council invoked the exception to allow the claimant to recover under the foreign law for a claim not actionable under English law[247].

29. An Internet Service Provider in Spain publishes a web page for a known libellous sports commentator. As could be expected, this individual uses the web page to defame an English football player. The player seeks to sue in England the individual and Provider. The player has the jurisdiction of the court under art 5(3) of the Brussels Regulation. Under English law, the Internet Provider may be liable not having taken reasonable care considering the author's previous conduct. Under Spanish law, however, the Provider may be liable for defamation only where the publisher knew that the material was defamatory. Unless a court becomes convinced of the need to invoke the exception, the player will have no right of action against the Provider in the English courts.

242 Private International Law (Miscellaneous Provisions) Act 1995, s 13(1). See *Lukowiak v Unidad Editorial SA* [2001] EMLR 1043.
243 Private International Law (Miscellaneous Provisions) Act 1995, s 13(2).
244 See *The Halley* (1868) LR 2 PC 193.
245 See *Phillips v Eyre* (1870) LR 6 QB 1.
246 [1969] 2 All ER 1085.
247 [1994] 3 All ER 749. See approval of rule by House of Lords in *Kuwait Airways Corpn v Iraqi Airways Co* (No 3) [2002] UKHL 19, [2002] 3 All ER 209.

Statutory choice of law

Applicable law: general rule

The Private International Law (Miscellaneous Provisions) Act 1995 introduces a regime for choice of tort law. It abolishes the common law test of double-actionability[248] and instead looks primarily to the law of the place where the events constituting the tort occurred[249]. To aid the courts in assessing where this place is when events occurred in different countries[250], the Act provides two rules of relevance to the Internet[251]. The first is that the applicable law for a cause of action in respect of damage to property is the law of the country where the property was when it was damaged[252]. The second is that in any other case, the applicable law is the law of the country in which the most significant element or elements of the events occurred[253]. The European Commission is currently consulting on a European-wide statute of similar effect: a European Council Regulation on the law applicable to non-contractual obligations. This author believes that one of the reasons for the UK's refusal to be bound by the Regulation[254] is that there is no demonstrated requirement for the new Regulation.

30. A controller of an American website knowingly and maliciously allows virus code to be transmitted to its viewers' computers. One English corporation suffers huge data damage and sues the American controller in the English courts. The American seeks to prove that the law of the State of New York should apply as it is from there that the virus spread. This is incorrect. The property that is damaged is in England; English law will apply. There is no real conflict of laws.

31. A controller of an English Website provides dubious financial advice on which reliance is placed by a Canadian company with offices around the world. The company suffers loss and decides to sue the controller in England. The applicable law for resolving the dispute will not be English law. The significant elements of the tort occurred in Canada. It is there that the company received, acted upon and was damaged by the negligent advice. Canadian law will be the applicable law. That the dispute is brought in the English courts is of no consequence to which law applies.

248 Other than for defamation claims as discussed, Private International Law (Miscellaneous Provisions) Act 1995, s 13(1).
249 Private International Law (Miscellaneous Provisions) Act 1995, s 11(1).
250 Private International Law (Miscellaneous Provisions) Act 1995, s 11(2).
251 The Act provides three rules in total; the other rule is excluded from this discussion as it relates to personal injury (s 11(2)(a)). It is assumed, at least for now, that a rule relating to personal injury is generally irrelevant to the Internet. This said, the Act does specifically define 'personal injury' to include 'any impairment of physical or mental condition' (s 11(3)). Therefore, the recovery for nervous shock as a result of seeing or hearing about a tragedy provides a possibility that the Internet will be messenger of such bad news and that claims will be brought blaming the Provider or creator. Cf *Alcock v Chief Constable of South Yorkshire* [1991] 4 All ER 907 at 921 per Ackner LJ: 'I agree, however, with Nolan LJ that simultaneous broadcasts of a disaster cannot in all cases be ruled out as providing the equivalent of the actual sight or hearing of the event or its immediate aftermath'.
252 Private International Law (Miscellaneous Provisions) Act 1995, s 11(2)(b).
253 Private International Law (Miscellaneous Provisions) Act 1995, s 11(2)(c).
254 Article 1(3).

Applicable law: displacement of general rule

A court is not entirely bound by the rules in s 11; it can displace the general rule where it appears from a number of factors that there is a substantially more appropriate law for determining the issues[255]. Section 12 contains three factors to consider which are persuasive, not definitive, as to when it is appropriate to displace the general rule. This is not meant to be invoked regularly, it is an exception and should be treated as such. Litigants should be conscious of the fact that the general rule in s 11 is 'not to be dislodged easily'. The word 'substantially' is meant as a high hurdle for those seeking to displace s 11[256].

255 Private International Law (Miscellaneous Provisions) Act 1995, s 12.
256 *Roerig v Valiant Trawlers Ltd* [2002] 1 All ER 961 at 968, per Waller LS for the Court of Appeal.

Chapter Four

Intellectual property

'[T]he Internet is the world's biggest copying machine.'
Marybeth Peters, Register of Copyrights, 1995[1]

The material stored and transmitted through the Internet is intangible and much of it will be protected by intellectual property rights. These rights can protect the intangible but substantial assets of companies and creative products of the mind from damage and unauthorised use. This chapter focuses on two of these rights: trade marks and copyright. Patents are gradually becoming of greater significance in protecting aspects of the Internet often as 'business method' patents[2]. Regrettably the grant of these patents does not benefit patent-applicants in the UK. The Patents Act 1977 severely limits the protection of computer programs as such and the Government seems reluctant to change the law or introduce business method patentability[3]. In contrast to the US, IBM alone has been awarded 900 patents including software-related technologies that were fundamental to its ecommerce strategy[4].

A trade mark or a brand name is increasingly important to businesses and consumers. For businesses the goodwill built up through sales under a brand can be extremely valuable. For consumers, a trade mark indicates the source of a product can so indicates its quality. It is therefore crucial that where ecommerce takes to the Internet, where it is easy to fake an identity, the law protects trade mark owners and consumers from imposters. This is crucial in the area of domain names.

Copyright protects almost all the material used and transferred over the Internet and the World Wide Web. This right can protect emails, websites and the programs and content shipped across the Internet. It is therefore relevant for users and Internet Service Providers to understand the ambit of these rights and what activities will lead to their infringement.

1 US News and World Report, 23 January 1995, p 59.

2 See Amazon's US Patent No 5,960,411 which protects its one-click technology; also see US Patent 5,848,396 which would appear to strike at the heart of using a user's profile to select the banner advertisements shown to them – the basis of sophisticated Internet advertising.

3 *In the matter of Application No 9204959.2 by Fujitsu Ltd* [1997] RPC 608, CA. But see Neuberger J's judgment in *Kirin-Amgen Inc v Roche Diagnostics GmbH* [2002] RPC 1, at 536–540. Then see Patricia Hewitt's announcement, 'Patents for Internet Trading and Computer Software' on 12 March 2001.

4 The US patent office received about 10,000 business-method patent application for Fiscal Year 2001 having increased from 7,800 application filings in the previous year. They issued approximately 433 business-method patents in Fiscal Year 2001, a slight fall from the previous year's 899 patents.

This chapter examines the following issues:

1. What is the relationship between trade marks and domain names?
2. What are the legal remedies against those who use another's trade mark as a domain name?
3. What is the best way to protect a domain name?
4. What are the legal issues involved in using trade marks on a website and as metatags?
5. What are the legal issues involved in search engines using trade marks?
6. What is the reach of the English court's jurisdiction over trade mark infringers?
7. Where must an Internet work be created to be protected by copyright?
8. What is the nature of copyright protection over emails, conversation threads, file collections, and websites?
9. How do moral rights protect material published on the Internet?
10. How may those who store and cache internet material be liable?
11. What are, and what are the legal ramifications of, peer-to-peer networks?
12. What are the legal restrictions over the use of frames, deeplinks and spiders?
13. What is the English courts' jurisdiction over those who deal with copyright works from abroad?

TRADE MARKS

Most television and newspaper advertisements detail not only conventional addresses, but also the website address of the advertiser. Sometimes this website address, or domain name, is recognisable as the name of the company itself. For example, McDonalds can be reached at the address 'www.mcdonalds.com'. A central registry that allocates names on a first-come, first-served basis provides this domain name. In addition, the registry is able to provide only one user with a particular domain name. There is only one 'pobox.com' and there will not be another until the company that owns it decides to release its rights over this domain name. This situation has resulted in and will continue to lead to many clashes between companies. This chapter considers when a domain name will infringe a trade mark and what a company should do to protect itself having registered a domain name.

The greatest use of trade marks is on a website itself. Signs, sounds, animations and static graphics are all capable of being registered under the Trade Marks Act 1994. This chapter therefore examines whether there are any special conditions that may apply for the use of registered trade marks on the web. Clearly related is this section's analysis of trade mark infringement using a website as an infringing medium.

As the Internet grows, the need to make one's website known to the public becomes harder and more expensive. It is estimated that most search engines only have a searchable catalogue of less than 20% of the sites available[5]. It is not

5 Lawrence S Giles, CL, NEC Research Institute, Princeton, US as published in *Nature*, September 1999. Others, such as Michael K Bergman, correctly state that many websites supported by databases do not reveal all their pages to most search engines: the 'deep web'. This deep web is calculated to be between 1,000 and 2,000 times larger than the websites available to most search engines. Giles' 20% therefore reduces to 0.03% of the web. (See Bergman, MK 'The Deep Web: Surfacing Hidden Value' The Journal of Electronic Publishing, July 2001).

surprising, therefore that companies are including hidden-from-humans 'metatags' in their websites so that a user of a search engine may be drawn to their site even if their site does not mention the word searched for. This chapter considers the consequences for a website to include another's trade mark in their 'metatags'. The chapter also addresses the possibility of infringement when a search engine 'sells' one particular search word so that, when entered, a particular banner advertisement is shown above the search results.

A registered trade mark in the UK placed on a website in the UK can infringe a trade mark registered elsewhere in the world. Although trade marks protect only within a defined territory, the web operates across all territories so permitting infringement in all. A corollary of this is that a trade mark registered in the UK may be used to prevent a website anywhere on the globe using that trade mark, if such use would infringe the UK trade mark. The advantages in reaching an audience in every country are in equal measure with the respect that must be paid to the legal regimes of those countries.

Rights in domain names

Every presence on the web has a unique address called a domain name. Usually these domain names begin with the prefix, 'www' and end with a two- or three-letter suffix that indicates which type of organisation runs the site. For example, a business will often have a 'com' or 'co' suffix. In addition, there may be a two-letter suffix that indicates the country of registration.

A full example of this is the domain name for *The Times* newspaper: 'the-times.co.uk'. This indicates that the owner of this website is a company and that its name was registered in the UK. It does not mean that the company which owns the website or the server computer storing the web pages are in the UK. The domain name address, once obtained, may be utilised from anywhere in the world. So, unlike a postal address that necessarily changes when one moves to another town, a domain name may remain the same wherever one moves; it is like a PO Box address. This is possible because the domain name is actually an alias for a large, unique number called an Internet Protocol Address. It is this number that corresponds to the computer that stores the digital material. If that material is moved to another computer, the unique number will be altered but the domain name can remain the same. It only refers to the unique number. Just as the post office will forward any post from a PO Box to a 'real' address, so the Internet forwards digital information from a domain name to the storing computer[6].

Domain names are truly international. Not only can any domain name be reached from anywhere in the world, but the computer to which that domain name refers can be located anywhere in the world. Seeing the domain name, 'www.harrods.co.uk' gives a strong impression that it is an English website, but

6 Because the domain name which humans remember and type merely 'refers' to a unique number, it is possible to expand the quantity of IP addresses without having to alert consumers to the change. This is clearly different from telephone numbers where, if extra numbers are required to allow for growth, every existing number must change. For example, IP addresses (at the time of writing) are 32 binary numbers long. The Internet Assigned Numbers Authority decided in July 1999 to extend the underlying IP address from these 32 binary digits to 128 digits. It is estimated that this will equate to four billion billion addresses for each square metre on the planet's surface.

this cannot be confirmed until the Internet Protocol Address is geographically located.

Domain names, like company names, are not simply taken; they are registered. Many registration companies do not check that an applicant has the right to use a particular name as a domain name and so allocates them on a first-come, first-served basis. In relation to the domain name 'pitman.co.uk', the Vice-Chancellor was asked to adjudicate over whether or not the first-come, first-served basis of dishing out domain names was appropriate[7]. Because the plaintiff, Pitman Training Ltd had no rights to proceed for passing off or any other tort, the Vice-Chancellor ruled that Nominet (responsible for 'co.uk' domain names) was entitled to register domain names as and when they are requested by an applicant.

Types of domain name

There are various families of domain name each with different suffixes. Those with a suffix 'org' refer to charitable organisations; those ending 'gov' are governmental domains. There are also a number of different suffixes for companies: 'com' was the first; 'co.uk' was the first UK domain name but there are now others such as 'uk.com' and 'com.uk'. There are many suffixes and more are due for creation under the auspices of the Internet Corporation for Assigned Names and Numbers (ICANN) and the Domain Names Supporting Organisation (DNSO): 'biz', 'info', 'name' to name a few are operational and available for registration. This does not eliminate the fundamental legal problem with domain names: they are unique. This is considered below by comparing domain names with trade marks.

Trade marks v domain names

For every computer connected to the Internet from every country in the world there is only one 'apple.com'. It is obvious that Apple Computers and Apple Records would both like to use that name, but it is impossible for them to share the name. This creates serious conflicts because there is no compromise available. In contrast, the law generally allows two companies to own the same trade mark but in respect of differing classes of products or service offerings. Trade marks are also protected only within a defined territory; there is no one system which provides worldwide rights. Two individuals in different countries may therefore own the same mark. This creates the situation where two users of a trade mark in the same class but in different countries may be fighting over the same domain name. The important questions in such a dispute are: who is entitled to the name and is it infringement for one to use the name within the other's territory.

This section also addresses the practice of trafficking in domain names. This is where a person registers a domain name purely to sell it.

7 *Pitman Training Ltd v Nominet UK* [1997] FSR 797.

Trademarking domain names

One common issue concerning domain names is whether they are protected by an existing trade mark registration. The Trade Marks Act 1994 specifies that in order to be registered, a trade mark must be a sign capable of being represented graphically which is capable of distinguishing goods or services of one undertaking from those of other undertakings. Unless the mark has acquired a distinctive character through use before application, a trade mark cannot be registered if it has no distinctive character, or serves to designate the characteristics of goods or services. This basic background is useful to appreciate the tension between choosing a domain name and trying to protect that name by registering it as a trade mark.

Descriptive domain names

In some industries, it is often better to be listed under one's services than under one's name. For example, it may be more profitable for a chemist to be listed under 'pharmacies' than under his name. It may appear that the same is true for the Internet: the domain name, 'flowers.com' may appear to be worth far more than 'lindasflorist.com'. The legal difference between these two domain names is that one is descriptive, so probably unregisterable as a trade mark while the other, though less memorable, may be more distinctive so is more likely to be registerable. The advantage of registering a descriptive domain name, however, shall not be overstated: most viewers on the web use search engines to find sites of interest.

Search engines, unlike, say directory enquiries for a telephone number, do not simply search for particular words within a domain name; they can search almost every word in billions of documents appearing on the web[8]. So, searching for the word 'florist' would identify the sites which sell flowers, sites which contain an article about florists, and so on. For each of the sites, the viewer is presented with a collection of domain names and their site's descriptions to choose from[9]. Because of this common way of searching for information on the Internet, the advantages of acquiring a generic domain name are not as great as they might otherwise be.

Those individuals who are considering acquiring a domain name are therefore advised to use a distinctive name: this has few disadvantages on the web but has the obvious advantage of being registerable as a trade mark.

Registered trade marks

There will often be occasions where an owner of a registered trade mark over a name seeks to use that name as a domain name. For a name to gain protection as a registered trade mark it must fulfil two tests.

8 Search engines also permit sites to have words indexed which are not mentioned in their pages. For example, a florist may design a website to include rotating pictures of floral displays. These displays could be used for many occasions including birthdays, weddings, funerals, parties etc. Rather than visibly include such a list on the site, the florist may include the list in 'metatags'. These are words read by the search engine, searchable by a user, but not shown on the site itself.

9 This author used the Google search engine to look for the word 'florist'. Within less than half a second Google had found about a million sites that included the word 'florist'.

Capable of being represented graphically

To be registered as a trade mark, the sign must be capable of being represented graphically. This is essentially a procedural requirement and is one always met by a domain name[10].

Capable of distinguishing undertakings' goods or services

The Trade Marks Act 1994 requires that the sign is capable of distinguishing goods or services of one undertaking from those of other undertakings[11]. This sign must be registered within a particular class of goods or services[12]. It is important not to confuse uniqueness with being capable of distinguishing. Each domain name is necessarily unique. This uniqueness alone does not make the name capable of distinguishing its goods or services from those of another.

1. A data recovery company registers the domain name 'data-recovery.co.uk.' It is the only owner of this domain name; it is unique among not only all data recovery companies, but also all domain name owners. This does not mean that the name is capable of distinguishing the services of its owner from any other company. Without more the company will be unable to register a trade mark over the name.

Additional trade mark classes

Practically, there will be few occasions when a registered trade mark proprietor will need to broaden the scope of his trade mark registration when using the name as a domain name. It is wrong to think that because the medium of exploitation is the Internet that the trade mark registration needs to be expanded into this class as well.

2. Artsake Ltd is a manufacturer of artists materials within the UK. It has a trade mark registration in class 16 to reflect the use of its name Artsake in relation to paper, cardboard goods and other artists' materials. It now wishes to expand its business by setting up a website through which customers can place orders. It chooses the domain name 'artsake.co.uk' and is concerned that it will require additional trade mark protection for the domain. It does not; its existing registration will equally protect its domain name in respect of artists' materials sold over the Internet.

There may be times where an individual already has a trade mark registration but is providing new goods or services through a website. In this circumstance there may be a reason to broaden the number of classes or specification for

10 Trade Marks Act 1994, ss 1(1) and 103(2). The UK Trade Marks Register takes the view that domain names may be registered as trade marks, subject to the usual criteria: The Trade Marks Registry Guide, Ch 6, para 6.5.2.
11 Trade Marks Act 1994, s 1(1).
12 Trade Marks Act 1994, s 34.

which a trade mark is registered. Some websites are, in trade mark terms, still little more than a digital billboard or leaflet. In contrast, true ecommerce solutions which allow the site to obtain information about the viewer and take payment from a user may lead to an increase in the activities provided through a website. An illustration is where the proprietor of a small local paper newspaper newly allows and charges for sophisticated searching of its archives from its website. A change in the nature of the business may be taking place. This trade mark owner should not simply rely on a registration for paper products, but should widen it to include the use of computers to search and access data.

3. A car manufacturer that uses its trade mark as a domain name decides to make its website more than merely a digital version of its paper brochures. To do this the dealer includes on its website an ActiveX program that acts as a route finder: individuals may type in where they are and where they wish to go and the program generates a map of the quickest route. The map also includes the miles per gallon that the dealer's car would use on the same route, so promoting the fuel economy of the car. The business now involves not only the sale of cars but also the provision of a route-finding service. It would be prudent to broaden the trade mark protection accordingly.

Similarly there will be times where the trade mark owner continues to use the registered trade mark in a slightly different market of goods or services. For example, a travel agent may well have a trade mark registered in classes including class 39 for travel services. If, however, the agent expands its business to include taking bookings over its website, it may want to consider carefully its existing specification on the trade marks register. In this situation it may be wise to ensure its registration covers the provision of travel services by means of a global network.

The UK Trade Marks Registry has warned that specifications in the service classes of 'electronic trading in goods' will not be accepted[13]. Specifications, in contrast, covering the specific goods or services are acceptable to the Registry if the trade mark application covers the appropriate goods or service classes. What this means is that, for example, a class or specification should cover selling of software.

New trade mark

The Internet has spawned a great number of new businesses seeking to gain a foothold in the ecommerce market of goods and services. Because the barriers to setting up a website are so low, there is a need to differentiate oneself in that market and then to protect that differentiation. To register a trade mark that protects a domain name will provide substantial reinforcement. What follows are not the words of a trade mark attorney touting for business, but that of Mr Justice Laddie extolling the virtues of trade marks:

13 *Registration of Internet Domain as Trade Marks*, The Patent Office, 2 April 1998.

> 'If a trader wishes to bring passing off proceedings he has to prove the existence of a reputation in his mark with potential customers. In the majority of cases this means that his common law rights will wither and disappear unless he continues to market and advertise his goods under the mark. Furthermore his rights are only breached if there is, or is likely to be, confusion in the marketplace which will cause him substantial damage. *This should be contrasted with the rights acquired by a proprietor who registers a mark*. His registration gives him a true monopoly. Subject to certain statutory defences, the proprietor will be able to restrain any trader who uses the same or a sufficiently similar mark on the goods covered by the registration. This is so even if, in the marketplace, no confusion is being caused. Indeed he will be able to sue for infringement even if he is not using his own registered trade mark (subject to it being removed if prolonged non-use is proved). Furthermore, with little effort any competently advised proprietor will be able to keep his registration in force indefinitely.'[14]

Little more needs to be said of the power of trade marks and their worth in such a fiercely competitive market such as the provision of Internet-related services. Companies, such as eBay and Amazon, have used a very distinctive name both as their company name and domain name. From a protection point of view, this is helpful to gain a trade mark registration over the domain name or the company name.

Registering a domain name as a trade mark

Some individuals and companies may wish to register as trade marks their actual domain name, prefix, suffix and all. This is opposed to registering as a trade mark only the name making up the domain name. For example, in America, MovieFone Inc registered as a trade mark the domain name 'moviefone.com' as well as 'movielink.com'[15]. From a pragmatic perspective, there seems little reason to register as a trade mark a domain name including the suffix, rather than purely the name element of the domain name. Registering as a trade mark the name element of the domain name will also protect the name's use within a domain name.

If all the other registration criteria are met, there seems little that would prevent a domain name being registered as a trade mark[16]. When examining a domain name applied for as a trade mark, the UK Registry will 'strip' the trade mark of the 'domain name' elements when assessing whether or not it is distinctive[17]. In applying to register 'www.sckoolz.com' as a trade mark, Examiners and Hearing Officers would consider whether the 'sckoolz' remainder is descriptive or otherwise non-descriptive. If it is, the sign as a whole, 'www.' and all, is likely to be open to objection. In short, sandwiching an otherwise descriptive sign between 'www.' and '.co.uk' will not, alone, make the sign registrable.

14 *Mercury Communications Ltd v Mercury Interactive (UK) Ltd* [1995] FSR 850 at 864. Emphasis added.

15 4 November 1994: applications 74/595, 293 and 74/595, 294.

16 See *Application No 2182437a By Cable And Wireless plc* (14 October 2000, unreported). The Register refused to register 'CAN AND WILL' but accepted the registration of 'CAN AND WILL.COM'.

17 The UK Trade Marks Registry Guide, Examination, para 6.5.3.

4. Phillip Jones Ltd is a one-man company that specialises in repairing old hi-fi equipment. As the company grows in experience its owner realises that there is a market in repairing old computer equipment for a pre-determined quotation. The company sets up a website on which restored equipment is offered for sale and on which viewers may enter details of their ailing equipment to receive and emailed repair quotation. The domain name for the site is 'www.compair.com'. To provide added protection for this sign, Phillip Jones Ltd may seek a trade mark registration over the word 'compair' in the appropriate classes.

Computer software class

Software and Internet-related firms need to consider the extent of the trade mark protection they require for the trade mark. It is too easy but wrong to suggest that the registration over a domain name that references a search engine should be within class 38 for telecommunications. Class 38 should be considered as only appropriate for the infrastructure providers for the Internet. AT&T as the owners of some of the Internet's conduits would be appropriately registered in class 38[18]. It is submitted that the owner of a website that acts as a search engine may be more appropriately registered for computer programs and information services. Authority to this effect can be found in the case *Mercury Communications Ltd v Mercury Interactive (UK) Ltd*[19].

> '[T]he defining characteristic of a piece of computer software is not the medium on which it is recorded, nor the fact that it controls a computer, nor the trade channels through which it passes but the function it performs'.

Controllers of websites need to consider carefully whether a registration outside the computer software class 9 is actually warranted or whether it is an incorrect understanding of their goods and services.

Computer software classification

Once it is decided in which class a trade mark should be obtained, an appropriate specification within that class must be provided. Here, again, those who provide a website should rein in their delusions of grandeur: a specification that includes the generic term 'computer programs' is likely to be viewed as too wide. 'Electronic communication apparatus' may be more appropriate[20].

18 In contrast, a controller of a website, without more, would not be appropriately registered in class 38. Similarly, the companies who rent out storage space on web servers may often be inappropriately registered in class 38; they should be within class 42. See the Trade Marks (Amendment) Rules 2001 which came into force on 1 January 2002 widening the number of classes from 42 to 45.

19 [1995] FSR 850 at 865.

20 In *Second Sight Ltd v Novell Inc and Novell UK Ltd* [1995] RPC 423 an overly wide specification in class 9 for 'computer software' was the cause of a clash between two rights-holders in different fields both asserting rights over the same trade name.

In *Mercury*, Laddie J was able to comment on the trade mark in Class 9 held by Mercury Communications Ltd. The specification was in broad terms, including both 'computers' and 'computer programs'. Mercury Communications Ltd alleged that Mercury Interactive was infringing its trade mark as Mercury Interactive analysed and bug-tested computer software. Laddie J held that the term 'computer software' or 'computer programs' is normally far too wide as a specification. It would cover any set of digitally recorded instructions used to control any type of computer. This would include software in the medical diagnostic field, software for controlling the computers on the London Underground and software for designing genealogicial tables[21]! Clearly such a wide registration provides an excessively broad monopoly over goods and services that are unconnected with the true trading interests of the applicant.

It was Laddie J's opinion that such a registration is ripe for having its registration removed entirely on the grounds of non-use, or at the least, having the specification of the goods dramatically pruned during rectification proceedings.

In *Avnet Incorporated v Isoact Ltd*[22] Mr Justice Jacobs was required to assess, in trade mark terms, the services offered by Internet Service Providers to those subscribers who use their websites as a means of advertising their businesses. Avnet was the registered proprietor of the 'Avnet' trade mark under class 35 (advertising and promotional services etc, all included within class 35). The defendant was an ISP using 'Avnet' in the course of business as a domain name and trading name. This mark was used to promote its usual ISP services of: providing email addresses and providing server space to customers on which they could host their own websites.

Jacob J refused Avnet's application for summary judgment. The main reason for his refusal teaches important lessons for those applying to register trade marks in relation to their activities on the Internet. Jacob J was convinced that the provision of ISP services did not fall within 'advertising and promotional services' within class 35, even where the ISP allowed its subscribers to use its services for this purpose. This decision, of course, defeated the plaintiff's claim. However, it also indicates that ISPs must choose their trade mark specifications with care. A registration in class 35 may well be inappropriate and therefore worth little[23].

The lesson that website owners can learn from these cases is clear. If the name within a website domain name is registrable, a trade mark may provide additional protection against those who would seek to emulate the name of the site. But the registration of the trade name must be in respect of a suitable specification in respect of goods and services. In *Avnet*, Jacob J warned that:

> 'specifications for services should be scrutinised carefully and they should not be given a wide construction covering a vast range of activities. They should be confined to the substance, as it were, the core of the possible meanings attributable to the rather general phrase.'

21 Examples provided by Laddie J in his judgment: [1995] FSR 850 at 864.

22 [1997] 8 ETMR, 26 July 1997.

23 Although for differing reasons Avnet was also denied a transfer of 'avnet.net' by the WIPO Arbitration and Mediation Centre under the ICANN Uniform Domain Name Dispute Resolution Policy: *Avnet Inc v Aviation Network Inc* Case No D2000–0046, (24 March 2000, unreported).

5. BetaBlockers Ltd are the pioneer testing company for unreleased software, often called beta versions. They have established a website with the domain name 'BETABLOCKER.CO.UK'. They then discover that another site exists, also controlled by a beta-testing company, with the domain name 'BETABL0CKER.CO.UK'. Knowing that two identical domain names cannot exist, they investigate further to discover that the copycat has used the number zero instead of the letter 'o'. If BetaBlocker was appropriately registered as a trade mark, this would permit an action of trade mark infringement; if no trade mark was registered, the company would have a harder and more expensive task proving passing off.

PROTECTING DOMAIN NAMES

This section contains numerous examples of clashes over domain names. Since the first edition of this book domain name disputes either in court or in other fora have become commonplace. This should come as no great shock. First, as mentioned previously, domain names are unique. If you want a domain name owned by someone else you have but three choices. Wait for the domain name to become available if the owner chooses not to renew it; buy it from the owner or litigate for it. With domain names registered for a year or two at a time, still changing hands for vast sums, such as the possible top price $7.5 million paid for 'Business.com' on 30 November 1999, it is hardly surprising that so many turn to litigation.

The Internet Corporation for Assigned Names and Numbers, ICANN, is one of the key domain name bodies. It represents the interests of those who register 'com', 'org' and many other so-called top-level domain names. The World Intellectual Property Organisation made the first adjudication under its dispute resolution policy on 14 January 2000. Since then, over five thousand decisions have been made resulting in over seven thousand domain names being transferred to a new owner and a couple of thousand staying put.

The most common type of dispute is where a person with a legal right to a trade mark seeks to use it within a domain name but discovers that someone already has registered that name as a domain name. More complex are the examples of companies already with a domain name who object to another domain name that has a different suffix.

This section, with reference to the facts of actual disputes, considers in detail how the English courts determine such suits. The section also considers possible clashes such as where a trade mark and domain name owner objects to the use of its domain name as a link on another website or in a 'metatag' provided to a search engine. Finally, this section prescribes the safest way of legally and technically protecting a domain name as well as the best way of resolving a dispute.

Infringement of a registered trade mark can occur where there is unauthorised use in the course of trade of a sign that is identical or similar to that trade mark. This use may be in respect of goods that are identical to or similar to the goods for which the trade mark is registered. This chapter considers two real examples of trade mark infringement with domain names: first, between a registered trade mark and an identical domain name in respect of the same services; second, between a registered trade mark and an identical domain name in respect of dissimilar services. The chapter also considers what rights of action the trade mark owners would have against the domain name owners if their trade marks were not registered.

The English case of *British Telecommunications plc v One in a Million Ltd*[24] is an essential starting place for any domain name dispute brought before the English courts. This is for two reasons. First, the case was appealed from the summary judgment given in the High Court to the Court of Appeal. It still serves as the highest authority on the way in which English trade mark law applies to domain names. Second, the facts of the case are those most commonly encountered in practice: where a domain name is registered for the purpose of selling it to a third party, rather than for own use. Rather than merely rehearse the case and others that have followed it, this section considers two 'case studies'. It applies the lessons from the Court of Appeal to two American situations to illustrate the vital aspects of the case. Initially, however, the facts of the case are given below.

British Telecommunications v One in a Million

The defendants were dealers (or directors of companies which deal) in Internet domain names. They registered domain names and sold them to potential users, rather like company registration agents. The defendants also specialised in registering domain names comprising the names of trade marks similar or identical to well-known commercial or other enterprises without the consent of those enterprises. Examples of these include 'burger-king.com', 'cadburys.com' and 'macdonalds.com'. It was admitted by the defendants that all of their registered domain names were either actually on the market or else potentially available for sale. One of the defendant's websites listed the domain names 'available for sale or hire'.

One of the defendants wrote to Burger King after acquiring the domain name 'burgerking.co.uk' and offered to sell the name for £25,000, or the domain name would be available for sale to any other interested party. Burger King was not a party to the action but a similar, although less explicit, attempt had been made by one of the defendants to sell the domain name 'bt.org' to British Telecom for £4,700.

The plaintiffs, listed below, alleged passing off and infringement of their trade marks by the registration of the following domain names, shown in brackets: Marks and Spencer plc (marksandspencer.com, marksandspencer.co.uk); J Sainsbury plc (j-sainsbury.com, sainsbury.com, sainsburys.com); Ladbroke Group plc (ladbrokes.com); Virgin (virgin.org); British Telecommunications plc (bt.org) and Telcom Securicor Cellular Radio Limited (cellnet.net).

Technical rights v legal rights

Even in 1994 domain name disputes were starting to appear in courtrooms. In *MTV Networks v Adam Curry*, Adam Curry had beaten the famous Music Television Network to a domain name[25]. Before August 1993 he had registered and operated a website with the domain name 'www.mtv.com'. This site pro-

24 [1999] FSR 1.
25 867 F Supp 202 (SDNY 1994).

vided information about the music business and dovetailed with the television business of MTV. On 19 January 1994 MTV sought to reacquire the domain name owned by Adam Curry. By Spring 1994 millions of Internet users had accessed the 'www.mtv.com' site.

This is a common scenario in domain name clashes. The only right which Adam Curry had over the site was a technical one: he was the owner of the domain name alias: he was not the owner of any legal rights to use the name MTV in relation to the same business. Under English law there are three main legal attacks that could be used to acquire the domain name: trade mark infringement; passing off; and deliberate damage to goodwill.

Trade mark infringement

On the assumption that 'MTV' is registered as a trade mark under the Trade Marks Act 1994 in respect of music information and broadcasting, the use of the letters in a domain name of a site providing similar services seems a blatant infringement[26]. Section 10(1) states that it is an infringement for a person to use in the course of trade a sign which is identical with a registered trade mark and in relation to goods or services which are identical with the goods or services for which the trade mark is registered. It appears that s 10(1) was not even mentioned at first instance in *One in A Million* and in the Court of Appeal, the respondents 'did not press their claim that the appellants had infringed their trade marks by carrying out acts falling within s 10(1) of the Trade Marks Act 1994.' This section considers this, therefore, without assistance from judicial authority. The two relevant questions are: is the use of the domain name use of a sign in the course of trade, and is the defendant's sign identical or similar to the registered trade mark?

Use of a sign in the course of trade[27]

The two concepts to examine are therefore the simple question of what is 'use' of a sign and then, the more complex concept of what is 'use' of a sign in the course of trade.

A person uses a sign *in particular* when he[28]:

26 A suitable defence may be that the domain name is the actual name of the defendant: Trade Marks Act 1994, s 11(2). See 'Misrepresentation by defendant', at p 180 for an example and the passing off equivalent of the defence.

27 Some have attempted to read into s 10(1) that the sign must be used as a trade mark. One argument is that s 9(1) states that exclusive rights in a trade mark are infringed by the use of the trade mark without consent. To this argument, Jacob J in *British Sugar plc v James Robertson & Sons Ltd* [1996] RPC 281 at 291 stated, 's 9(1) is really no more than a chatty introduction to the details set out in s 10, itself adding no more than that the acts concerned must be done without consent.' To this he added that the Directive, art 5 does not use this language: 'For reasons which baffle me our parliamentary draftsman did not simply copy this. He set about re-writing it. So the argument based on s 9(1) involves a departure from the Directive. This is wholly improbable. I reject it.' Some years later, in *Euromarket Designs v Peters* [2001] FSR 288, Jacob J reaffirmed his view on this issue. The High Court and the Court of Appeal in *One in A Million* similarly did not accept that the sign must be used as a trade mark.

28 Trade Marks Act 1994, s 10(4).

'(a) affixes it to goods or the packaging thereof;
(b) offers or exposes goods for sale, puts them on the market or stocks them for those purposes under the sign, or offers or supplies services under the sign;
(c) imports or exports goods under the sign; or
(d) uses the sign on business papers or in advertising.'

The relevant examples for this scenario are (b) and (d). Adam Curry was offering and supplying services under the sign 'www.mtv.com' where 'www' and 'com' are entirely generic or are not part of the name. In addition, the sign could be seen as advertising for Adam Curry's activities within the goods and services covered by MTV's trade mark registration.

'In the course of trade' should not be taken to mean 'in the course of taking money'. To be trading, money need not change hands; it does, however, imply the use of the trade mark in relation to the trading activities of the defendant. If the site is serving some commercial purpose, be it for money or money's worth, it may be classed as trading[29]. However, merely because the site is serving a commercial purpose need not mean that the domain name is being *used* in the course of trade.

Ultimately, clients will be unhappy to hear, whether use is 'in the course of trade' is a question of answered only by interpreting the facts and economics of the situation. Two European cases from 2002, both decided by the European Court of Justice, address what is meant by 'use in the course of trade'. These two cases illustrate that the facts make all the difference.

In the decided case, *Hölterhoff v Freiesleben*[30] Mr Freiesleben is the proprietor of two registered trade marks, Spirit Sun and Context Cut, covering, respectively, 'diamonds' and 'precious stones' for further processing as jewellery. Mr Hölterhoff deals in precious stones of all kinds. He cuts them himself or buys them from other dealers. He markets both his own stones and stones from third parties. In illustration, in 1997, he offered for sale, and took an order from a fellow jeweller for some stones which he described by the names Spirit Sun and Context Cut. Mr Freiesleben sued Mr Hölterhoff and the case eventually reached the European Court of Justice. A question had to be answered about whether this situation described, 'use in the course of trade'.

The Court decided that there was no use of the trade marks in the course of trade. Their decision was supported by the fact that the customer was professional and would not believe that the use of the Spirit Sun and Context Cut trade marks indicated that Mr Hölterhoff was the originator of the stones. Mr Hölterhoff was merely using the brand names to convey the particular characteristics of the stones.

In contrast, the European Court in *Arsenal Football Club plc v Matthew Reed*[31] was convinced that Mr Reed's obviously unauthorised sale of Arsenal Football Club scarves involved use of a sign in the course of trade. They were clear that even though a fan (or otherwise) may know that the scarf is not authorised,

29 In *Panavision International v Toeppen* (CV 96–3284 DDP, 1 November 1996) the Californian district court held that the defendant's 'business' was to 'register trade marks as domain names and then to sell the domain names to the trade marks' owners.'
30 Case C–2/00 [2002] All ER (EC) 665.
31 Case C–206/01, (12 November, unreported).

they are buying it because it bears the registered trade mark. This is use of the (registered) sign in the course of trade.

So how can these two contrasting precedents be applied to our MTV dispute? Arguably, the MTV situation is closer to the *Arsenal* situation than the *Hölterhoff* one. The first indication of the existence of a particular website is its domain name. There is no way of knowing, before one sees the website itself, that the domain name may not be owned by its registered trade mark proprietor as in the *Hölterhoff* case. In this MTV dispute, the domain name is not only the attractive force that brings in viewers. It is also the sole mechanism for these viewers to see the site: the name 'www.mtv.com' must either be clicked on as a link or typed to reach the site.

What if Adam Curry had not yet used the 'mtv.com' domain name in conjunction with a website, but merely had registered it and had offered it to MTV; would that have been use of a sign in the course of trade? Rather like the Californian District Court[32] almost two years before, the High Court and Court of Appeal in *One in a Million* judged, respectively, that 'The use of a trade mark in the course of the business of a professional dealer for the purpose of making domain names more valuable and extracting money from the trade mark owner is a use in the course of trade.' The Court of Appeal put this '[The trade marks] will be used in relation to the services provided by the registrant who trades in domain names.'

These quotations should not be taken out of context: in *One in a Million*, the defendants 'offered' to sell the domain names. If they merely had registered the domain names and instead of approaching the plaintiffs, had waited for the plaintiffs to contact them, it is less certain this would have been 'use in the course of trade'. In this situation a putative claimant may have to 'draw' the domain name owner into offering to sell the name.

For example, the putative claimant can write to the domain name owner asking for his undertaking that he will either sell the domain name to the claimant for the amount of money it cost him to register the domain name or undertake not to sell or transfer it at all. If the domain name owner does not confirm this, or offers to sell it for more than the mere registration cost he is, arguably, threatening to use the domain name in the course of trade. In *Tropical Resorts Management Ltd v Morgan*[33], Mr Morgan did just this. He registered a domain name incorporating the claimant's trade mark 'Banyan Tree'. When approached about the domain name, he tried to bargain for a higher price than the claimants would pay. And when they refused to pay, he threatened to auction the domain name. Were the case brought under the Trade Marks Act 1994, this would have been use, or at least threatened use, in the course of trade.

In *Britannia Building Society v Prangley*[34], Mr Prangley was a little more circumspect. Having registered the domain name 'britanniabuildingsociety.com' (apparently for the purposes of a new business providing services to British builders in Iran!) he refused to sell it to the claimants. He did not threaten to sell it to anyone else, unlike Mr Morgan. In these circumstances where there appears no use of a sign *at all*, let alone use of a sign in the course of trade, Mr Justice Rattee admitted that there is some doubt over a cause of action in infringement of a registered trade mark.

32 See footnote 29, above.
33 [2001] All ER (D) 38 (Jul).
34 [2000] IP & T 1419.

Next we must assess whether the defendant's domain name is identical or similar to the claimant's trade mark.

6. RRZ Ltd is a well-known stockbroker with a registered trade mark over the mark 'RRZ' in the appropriate classes. It wishes to register the domain name 'RRZ.co.uk' and instructs a domain name agent accordingly. The agent reports back that RRZ.co.uk is already registered as a domain name but that no website is 'pointed' to the domain name. Without some indication of trade from the domain name owner, RRZ Ltd will have a difficult task to sue the owner for registered trade mark infringement as the domain name (the sign) does not appear to be being used in the course of trade.

Identical sign to registered trade mark

For this case, let us assume that the registered trade mark is the letters 'mtv' and the defendant used as its domain name 'www.mtv.com'. These two strings of characters are not identical character for character, but are they identical for the purposes of s 10(1)?

The Court of Appeal in *One in a Million* does not address how one should determine whether a registered trade mark is identical to a domain name. Advocate General Jacobs, however, provides a general solution *SA Société LTJ Diffusion v SA SADAS* that is likely to the followed by the Court of Justice[35]. The French court, in essence, asked him how to construe 'identical'. He determined that a strict interpretation is necessary: 'identical' covers 'identical reproduction without any addition, omission or modification other than those which are either minute or wholly insignificant'[36]. He goes onto assist national courts with a methodology to assess what is minute or wholly insignificant[37]:

> 'In reaching its decision in such cases, the national court must first identify what is perceived by the average, reasonably well-informed, observant and circumspect consumer as the relevant mark and sign, then assess globally the visual, aural and other sensory or conceptual features of the mark and sign in question and the overall impression created by them, in particular by their distinctive and dominant components, in order to determine whether the two would be perceived by such a consumer as the same in the sense that any differences are minute or wholly insignificant, or whether the two would be perceived rather as similar in the sense that the differences are greater than that.'

Bearing this in mind, it is submitted that the courts should consider the trade mark 'mtv' and the domain name 'www.mtv.com' as identical. The characters both before and after 'mtv' are standard and do not form part of the sign. Just as the Trade Marks Registry usually strips off the suffixes when comparing marks, so should the English courts when considering whether a mark is identical[38].

35 Case C–291/00 (17 January 2002, unreported).
36 At para 53.
37 At para 53.
38 The issue of where two domain names are identical bar the prefix and suffix is discussed at 'Legal and technical rights v legal and technical rights', at page 186.

What is at issue is whether a consumer would consider the sign and mark as identical; it is submitted that the 'average, reasonably well-informed, observant and circumspect' consumer familiar with the Internet would see them as identical[39].

This issue becomes particularly relevant where the domain name 'appears' identical but actually incorporates a typographical, or technical error. When a domain name is registered the string of characters, excluding any punctuation, is combined with a suffix to make the entire domain name. In illustration, a company may wish to use 'www.company.com' but they will only actually register 'company.com'. The common 'www.' prefix is a matter of choice for the domain name owner when establishing the website. If they desired they could use 'the.company.com' instead of 'www.company.com'. This said, although it is not required most domain names are *used* after a 'www.'

Some enterprising individuals have preyed on this common but voluntary use of 'www.' before a domain name. They have registered a domain name *including* three 'w's'. Of course, because no punctuation is permitted in a domain name their registrations appear as 'wwwcompany.com' with no 'dot' after the triple 'w'[40]. In *Painewebber Inc v wwwpainewebber,com*[41] US District Judge Claude Hilton was sure that the mere lack of the 'dot' was not sufficient to distinguish the trade mark 'Painewebber' from the domain name 'wwwpainewebber.com.'

It is submitted this reasoning should follow under English law. What the court must try to do is to consider the mark and sign from the perspective of a customer of the trade mark owner, not a 'Domain Name Server resolving the domain name into an IP Address.'

In relation to goods or services

The sign purportedly infringing the trade mark must be used in relation to goods or services. Like its equivalent in the 1938 Act, this requirement of use is interpreted widely and will generally be satisfied whenever used as a domain name. This is because most websites are used in this way; they may appear to be purely providing information but usually they also have links to other pages that advertise or provide goods or services. Few sites are no more than an electronic poster. If the site were used for interaction with customers then the domain name would appear to be used in relation to goods or services. There is no other route to access the website than by using the domain name[42]. Where the domain name is not yet pointed to a website, so does not display a website on being

39 Indeed, most browsers now 'understand' the typed characters 'www.site.com' or even 'site.com' as 'http://www.site.com'. This is a further indication that the letters before and after the name should be discarded when comparing the claimant's mark with the defendant's sign.

40 For example, Data Art Corp of St Petersburg, Russia, used to own, amongst others, 'wwwdisney.com', 'wwwsony.com', 'wwwamazon.com' and, relevant here, 'wwwmtv.com'.

41 ED Va 99–0456–A, 9 April 1999.

42 Of course, off the Internet, the domain name may be used not in relation to registered goods or services. For instance, a designer of the Harrods website may set up his own website to advertise his previous commissions including Harrods'. The presence on his website of the domain name 'www.harrods.co.uk' would not be the use of the trade mark in relation to goods or services for which Harrods had a trade mark. See *Harrods v Schwartz-Sackin* [1986] FSR 490. In contrast, Harrods were granted an injunction against defendants who registered the domain name 'harrods.com' when Harrods had already registered 'harrods.co.uk' (unreported, Mr Justice Lightman, 9 December 1996).

entered, there is a question as to whether it is being used at all and certainly whether this use is in the course of trade. There must, therefore be a greater question as to whether the domain name is being used in 'relation' to anything. In *One in a Million*, the High Court assessed that when not pointed to the domain name owner's website there are 'four uses' to which domain names registered could be put:

> 'The first and most obvious is that it may be sold to the enterprise whose name or trade mark has been used, which may be prepared to pay a high price to avoid the inconvenience of there being a domain name comprising its own name or trade mark which is not under its control. Secondly, it may be sold to a third party unconnected with the name, so that he may do or attempt to do the same thing or to use it for the purposes of deception. Thirdly it may be sold to someone with a distinct interest of his own in the name, for example a solicitor by the name of John Sainsbury or the Government of the British Virgin Islands, with a view to its use by him. Fourth it may be retained by the dealer unused and unsold, in which case it serves only to block the use of that name as a registered domain name by others, including those whose name or trade mark it comprises.'

It is clear that the first three of these 'uses' could be construed as being 'use[s] of a sign in the course of trade in relation to goods or services'. The fourth 'use' is, however, misconceived and was recognised as such by the Court of Appeal. The registration of a domain name does not actually block the brand owner from exploiting its brand name as a domain name. All the plaintiffs in the *One in a Million* action already had at least one domain name which reflected their brand names; they simply wanted to prevent any *other* confusingly similar domain names from existing. The Court of Appeal puts this as follows:

> 'The registration [of a domain name] only blocks the identical domain name and therefore does not act as a block to registration of a domain name that can be used by the owner of the goodwill in the name.'

It would therefore appear that a domain name could be registered but not 'used' for the purposes of registered trade mark infringement if it is retained unsold and unconnected to the Internet's IP addresses. It would appear that it is nevertheless difficult to persuade a court that one does not intend to 'use' the domain name having registered it. Despite the prejudicial evidence adduced as to 'One in a Million's previous conduct'[43] their approaches to the plaintiffs in the action had all been careful to pre-empt any suggestion of illegal use of the domain names. To J Sainsbury plc, one defendant wrote: 'We are not trading under the name Sainsbury nor do we intend to trade under the name Sainsbury. We have

43 In September 1996, one of the defendants wrote to Burger King: 'Further to our telephone conversation earlier this evening, I confirm that I own the domain name burgerking.co.uk. I would be willing to sell the domain name for the sum of £25,000 plus VAT. In answer to your question regarding as to what we would do with the domain name should you decide not to purchase it – the domain name would be available for sale to any other interested party.' The threat to sell the inherently deceptive name possibly to a person passing off the trade mark is explicit. It should not be forgotten that Burger King was not a plaintiff in the action.

merely purchased the Internet domain names j-sainsbury.com, sainsbury.com and sainsburys.com as part of our personal collection.'

Identical goods or services

The last test is that the use of the purportedly infringing sign must be in relation to identical goods or services for which the trade mark is registered. This is a question of fact, although in this scenario it appears likely that a UK court would deem Adam Curry's site to be in the identical services of MTV's registrations[44].

Trade mark infringement remedies

Having established a prima facie case of infringement, MTV would have to think carefully about the remedies it seeks. Unlike usual trade mark infringement where an injunction and delivery up of infringing articles is possible, for a domain name the issues are more complicated. MTV would prefer that Adam Curry not only stop using the domain name, or any similar, but also allow MTV to take over the domain name[45].

For this reason, in addition to any claim for damages and injunction, MTV should seek delivery up of the infringing materials[46]. These materials are essentially the domain name registration in the name of Adam Curry; the actual content of the site may, or may not, be infringing material. Section 17(4) defines 'infringing material' to include material bearing a sign identical or similar to the infringed mark which either is used for advertising goods or services in such a way as to infringe the registered mark, or is intended to be so used and such use would infringe the registered trade mark.

Under this definition it appears possible that a domain name registration could be delivered up. This said, a domain name does not fit comfortably into 'infringing materials'. The High Court and Court of Appeal in *One in a Million* accepted this is not an 'unjust' remedy but, should a court take the view that a domain name cannot constitute 'infringing materials', the claimant should seek an Order that the defendant 'takes all steps as lie within its power to release or facilitate the release and/or transfer or facilitate the transfer to the claimant of the domain name' and appeal to the court's general discretion to grant 'all such relief' to the claimant under s 14(2). It may be also relevant to the court that the High Court in *One in a Million* accepted that 'assigning the domain name' is the equivalent, in this particular context, of the delivery up of infringing goods.

44 It should be remembered that the services can be identical despite MTV providing its services over the television and the site providing the same services over the Internet.

45 The right to an interlocutory injunction under the Trade Marks Act 1994, s 14(2), like all interim injunctions must be sought expeditiously. In the real facts of *MTV v Curry*, it would appear that MTV would have been too late to be awarded with an interin injunction. The MTV Network Vice-President discussed Curry's use of the MTV site in June 1993 and allowed him to continue at Curry's expense. 867 F Supp 202 (SDNY 1994), at 203–204, Counterclaim 9.

46 Trade Marks Act 1994, s 16(1).

Passing off claim

If MTV does not have a registered trade mark that it can use as the basis of trade mark infringement proceedings, it may seek to rely on its common law rights: namely a passing off claim. The ingredients of passing off have been classified as a 'classical trinity': goodwill of the plaintiff; misrepresentation by the defendant; and consequent damage[47]. Because of an anomaly which will become apparent, unlike for registered trade mark infringement, the mere registration of a domain name can constitute passing off.

Goodwill of plaintiff

The concept of 'goodwill' is succinctly defined by Lord MacNaghten in *IRC v Muller & Co's Margarine Ltd*[48]:

> 'It is the benefit and advantage of a good name, reputation and connection of a business. It is the attractive force which brings in custom.'

If a company has customers who would think of using its name, or the name of a product, as a domain name, there appears little to suggest that the company does not have goodwill in the domain name. And as businesses have pervaded the World Wide Web many businesses have to advertise and provide goods and services to their customers using the Internet. This, in turn, increases the chances of a company extending its goodwill from merely its name to the domain name of the company.

In the *MTV* case there is indubitable goodwill in the domain name 'mtv.com' by virtue of the existent goodwill in the name MTV. The claimants should be able to prove this element of the passing off classical trinity.

Misrepresentation by defendant

The term 'misrepresentation' does not imply any malice or intention; it is more a statement of the perception of the public[49]. Using a domain name may therefore be bona fide. The court, however, will look to whether potential customers are misled into thinking that the defendant's goods are those of the claimant [50]. In a passing off case concerning the use of similar telephone numbers, Aldous J said[51]:

47 *Consorzio del Prosciutto di Parma v Marks & Spencer* [1991] RPC 351, per Nourse LJ. Cf the five characteristics of passing off presented (and followed) by Lord Diplock in *Erven Warnink BV v J Townend & Sons (Hull) Ltd* [1979] FSR 397 at 405. Advisers should be wary of using the three- (or five-) part test as the definitive answer whether one website passes off a plaintiff's reputation. Lord Diplock warns, at 405, 'It does not follow that because all passing off actions can be shown to present these characteristics, all factual situations which present these characteristics give rise to a cause of action for passing off.'

48 [1901] AC 217 at 223–224.

49 Innocence does not provide a defence to an injunction. The court will simply assess whether on an objective basis injury was a reasonably foreseeable consequence of the misrepresentation. See *Taittinger v Allbev Ltd* [1993] 2 CMLR 741 at 751 [21]–752 [25].

50 *Frank Reddaway & Co Ltd v George Banham & Co Ltd* [1896] AC 199.

51 *Law Society of England and Wales v Griffiths* [1995] RPC 16 at 21.

> 'The defendants are right that a misrepresentation must be established, but are wrong in believing that it requires an express statement. A person who adopts the mantle of another can by his silence misrepresent that he is that other. Thus a person who selects a confusingly similar telephone number or a similar name may well represent that he is that other by either saying so or by failing to take steps when telephoned or called to disabuse the person who is making the telephone call.'

This can be applied to domain names. If instead of Adam Curry setting up the copycat website, Martin Trevor Vantram had established the site with his initials as a domain name, the facts of such a case may be far more persuasive there may not have been a misrepresentation[52]. Indeed in *MBNA America Bank NA v Stephen Freeman*[53] the court was not convinced either way that the abbreviated domain name 'mbna.co.uk' for Mr Freeman's new business 'Marketing Banners for Net Advertising' was a misrepresentation by Mr Freeman of the MBNA America Bank's unregistered trade mark, MBNA. What is important is whether the misrepresentation, intentional or not, leads, or is likely to lead, the public to believe that goods or services offered by the defendant are those of the claimant[54].

Without more, the domain name 'mtv.com' gives the impression that the site is under the control or licence of MTV networks. Of course, the suffix of the domain name may go some way to indicate the business of the owner: 'www.oxford.ac.uk' is an academic institution as shown by the suffix 'ac'.

This raises the question as to whether anything could be done to disabuse the public of this misrepresentation. Certainly the defendant, in the knowledge that its domain name is confusingly similar to another's name, may seek to distinguish its site from the potential claimant's. It may be thought that, by using the words, 'Unofficial MTV Site' the misrepresentation is stopped. In certain circumstances this may be true. It is submitted, however, that often the misrepresentation is the domain name *itself* and its mere registration.

The Court of Appeal in *One in a Million* goes so far as to rule that: 'The placing on a register of a distictive name such as marksandspencer makes a representation to persons who consult the register [a WHOIS search] that the registrant is connected or associated with the name registered and thus the owner of the goodwill in the name.' So, unlike mere registration under registered trade mark law, mere registration for passing off purposes makes a representation which is false.

After the domain name has been entered into a browser and the site is seen through the web, information on the site may make clear the true nature of the site, but this may be too late to defeat the misrepresentation element of passing off[55].

52 That this may be a misrepresentation does not mean there is passing off. Indeed, it has been said, 'a man must be allowed to trade in his own name and, if some confusion results, that is a lesser evil than that a man should be deprived of what would appear to be a natural and inherent right': *Marengo v Daily Sketch* (1948) 65 RPC 242 at 251 per Lord Simonds.

53 [2000] All ER(D) 995.

54 A paraphrasing of Lord Oliver in *Reckitt & Colman Products v Borden Inc* [1990] 1 All ER 873.

55 Its effect may be to defeat the element of consequent damage, or at the least reduce the damages awarded if the claimant is successful at trial.

What is key to a passing off case is the influence of the defendant's representations at or prior to the point of sale not later[56]. The court will consider whether the 'public is moved in any degree to *buy* the article because of its source'[57]. It may be of no relevance that after entering the site the viewer is instructed that it is not the one expected.

Because domain names and their owners are put on a public register held on the web by the registration companies, avoiding litigation may be difficult. A defendant may seek to introduce 'true' distance between its site and that of the claimant by using disclaimers. Associations could be avoided, but even so, the domain name and representation is at large on the public register. This said, if concerned, a defendant might be able to persuade the domain name registrar who controls the register to include a disclaimer on the record itself. Of course, there will always be some individuals who will remain confused as to the source of a website because of the domain name. Gibson LJ addresses this issue bluntly[58]:

> 'It is not right to base any test on whether a moron in a hurry would be confused, but it is proper to take into account the ignorant and unwary[.]'

Consequent damage

Misrepresentation in respect of another's goodwill does not provide the basis for a passing off action. The third aspect of passing off is that the claimant must show that he has suffered, or is likely to suffer, damage to the property in his goodwill because of the misrepresentation. This requirement to show damage, however, is not onerous in quality or quantity.

Quality of damage

If the infringing website is selling goods or services, the test will be easy to satisfy. But the World Wide Web contains many sites that serve not as shops but as shop fronts. A website under the domain name 'mtv.com' may not provide products and services for payment; it may merely provide useful information such as the latest releases and Top 20 sales. The damage therefore cannot be equated to lost sales but to a 'dilution' in the distinctiveness of the name MTV or harm to the reputation attaching to it. This will have the likely consequence that the goodwill in the name MTV will be reduced. Lord Justice Aldous in *One in a Million* in relation to the famous mark 'Marks & Spencer' held that: '[R]egistration of the domain name including the words Marks & Spencer is an erosion of the exclusive goodwill in the name which damages or is likely to damage Marks & Spencer plc.'

56 See *Bostik v Sellotape GB Ltd* IPD 17029.

57 *Crescent Tool v Kilborn & Bishop* 247 F 299 (1917), per Judge Learned Hand. Emphasis added. Cited with approval by Jacob J in *Hodgkinson and Corby Ltd v Wards Mobility Ltd* [1995] FSR 169 at 178.

58 *Taittinger v Allbev Ltd* [1993] 2 CMLR 741 [20]. See *Singer Manufacturing Co v Loog* (1882) 8 App Cas 15 at 18, per Lord Selborne LC.

Quantity of damage

The level of damage need not be high. In fact, the level required is expressed in terms of a presumption that there will be damage unless proved to be below a *de minimis*[59].

> 'The question is whether the relevant activities of the defendants are on such a small scale leading to such a small injury that it can be ignored.'

Instrument of fraud claim

Although not in the MTV dispute, the *One in a Million* case shows that there are occasions where an individual with no legal rights over a name acquires a domain name incorporating that name and then offers to sell the domain name to a more *bona fide* owner. This practice can work where the policy of the domain name registration company permits such arbitrage. Such a practice is common for company names[60] and the Court of Appeal confirms that precedents from that area may be applicable for domain names. Before describing one such case, a word of warning: each case turns on its facts. In *One in a Million* the court was clear the defendants were dishonest. For occasions where the case is not simply one of obvious extortion, the courts may be more conservative[61].

Glaxo plc and Wellcome plc v Glaxo-Wellcome Ltd

On 23 January 1995, a press release was issued announcing that if Glaxo plc's bid for Wellcome plc was successful, the new merged company would be called Glaxo-Wellcome. The next day a company registration agent filed an application for Glaxo-Wellcome Ltd. After Glaxo's bid was accepted the two companies discovered that the limited version of the name had already been registered; they offered the going rate of £1,000 to buy the name. The agent together with his mother refused and demanded £100,000 with the implicit threat of exploiting the name of the newly merged company to its prejudice. The companies sought an injunction, urgently needing to resolve the issue before the adoption of the new name on 1 May 1995[62].

Lightman J was convinced that the defendants were dishonest[63] and that they were abusing the system of company name registration by attempting to extort a substantial sum for not damaging the plaintiff's goodwill. As a result of this he not only granted the obvious injunction against the company and its subscribers to be restrained from continuing to be registered; he was also prepared to order

59 *Taittinger v Allbev Ltd* [1993] 2 CMLR 741 at 753 [27] per Gibson LJ.

60 See *Habib Bank Ltd v Habib Bank AG Zurich* [1981] 2 All ER 650; *Exxon Corpn v Exxon Insurance Consultants International Ltd* [1982] Ch 119; *Fletcher Challenge Ltd v Fletcher Challenge Pty Ltd* [1982] FSR 1; *Direct Line Group Ltd v Direct Line Estate Agency Ltd* [1997] FSR 374.

61 See *Ben & Jerry's Homemade Inc v Ben & Jerry's Ice Cream Ltd* (19 January 1995, unreported).

62 *Glaxo plc v Glaxo Wellcome Ltd, Cullen, and McDonald* [1996] FSR 388.

63 The defendant's allegation that the choice of the name 'Glaxo-Wellcome' was 'merely an interesting combination of words' was sternly rejected: 'All I need say in regard to these suggestions is that there are limits to judicial credulity.' [1996] FSR 388 to 391.

an express mandatory injunction specifically requiring the company and subscribers to change or facilitate the change of the company name.

In *One in a Million*, the Court of Appeal considered this case and others[64] and discerned a jurisdiction to grant injunctive relief where a defendant is equipped with or is intending to equip another with an instrument of fraud. Advisors should note that, as with all passing off cases, the facts are everything: whether any domain name is an instrument of fraud depends upon all the circumstances.

The first consideration is whether or not by reason of the similarity between the domain name and the brand name, there will inherently be passing off. The more famous and distinctive the brand name, therefore, the greater the likelihood that a similar domain name will lead to passing off. The second consideration arises if the domain name does not inherently lead to passing off. The Court of Appeal was certain that the domain name might still be an instrument of fraud. In this situation the court may look at the 'wider' issues such as the intention of the defendant, the type of trade and all the surrounding circumstances.

Claimants should therefore investigate the past conduct of the defendants. The fact that the defendants had previously offered to sell domain names to Burger King, although not plaintiffs, was utilised to great effect to illustrate the defendants' 'intention'. Advisors should therefore check to see what other domain names have been registered by the defendants.

Many domain name disputes have parallels with this situation. An individual selects a domain name on the basis of selling that name to a company for an extortionate price. It is discussed above that Mr Prangley provided evidence to the High Court that he was looking to set up a business serving British builders in Iran[65]. He registered the domain name 'britanniabuildingsociety.com' seemingly being unaware of the Britannia Building Society in England. As in *One in a Million*, the court was not inclined to believe this version of events. Mr Justice Rattee said:

> '. . . I regard the evidence as wholly incredible, and I have no doubt that the defendant registered the [domain] name that he did having regard to the fact that it represented the name of the claimant, a very well known British trading organisation, and the fact that the first defendant regarded such a domain name as being a commercially usable instrument is apparent from . . . his particulars of defence . . .'

In these situations, where the defendant is clearly trafficking in a domain name with the intention of, in effect, holding to ransom the rightful owner of the name, it would appear that analysing the domain name as an 'instrument of fraud' is an appropriate claim on which to base an injunction.

Passing off remedies

Like the remedies for trade mark infringement, the key order that the claimant should seek is to restrain the defendant from providing or describing any

64 See *Habib Bank Ltd v Habib Bank AG Zurich* [1981] 2 All ER 650; *Exxon Corpn v Exxon Insurance Consultants International Ltd* [1982] Ch 119; *Fletcher Challenge Ltd v Fletcher Challenge Pty Ltd* [1982] FSR 1; *Direct Line Group Ltd v Direct Line Estate Agency Ltd* [1997] FSR 374.

65 *Britannia Building Society v Prangley* [2000] IP & T 1419.

website, email access or other Internet access under or by reference[66] to the domain name 'www.mtv.com' or any other domain name colourably similar. The injunction will be unlikely to be awarded in a form wide enough to prevent the use of the material on the website itself, as long as, subject to the main restraint, it does not use the domain name. This is, of course, unless it too passes off the claimant's reputation. Whether the court would order the domain name to be transferred to the claimant is a matter of debate. It is not necessary to restrain the passing off. The situation therefore may theoretically result in no one being able to use the domain name; the court may refuse to grant mandatory relief on motion[67].

Unable to find domain name owner

The technical nature of domain names is such that, presently, one may not know who owns a domain name. Even if one knows the owner, pinpointing them on the planet to issue proceedings against them can be complex. The domain name registrars do not necessarily require, and certainly do not check, whether the name and address of the registrant is correct. WIPO has advised that 'wilful' provision of inaccurate ownership data should trigger domain name cancellation. Where, for whatever reason, one cannot locate the defendant, how can one prevent the infringement from occurring?

If the domain name is 'pointed' at a website, there is a good argument that, once on notice, the host of the website may be jointly liable. If the domain name is not yet pointed to a website, the plaintiff may choose to pursue the domain name itself 'in rem'.

Certainly, before 1873, the High Court of Admiralty used the concept that a ship could be the defendant in an action in rem. The ship was ascribed personality. She was regarded as the wrongdoer. If this arcane and ancient concept could be applied to a domain name, one could sue the 'domain name itself' rather than bother trying to sue its owner. This is what Porsche cars attempted in its action *Porsche Cars North America v Porsche.com*[68].

Like other brand owners, Porsche attempted to sue those who registered domain names which infringed their trade marks. This said, 'Porsche correctly observes that some of the domain names at issue have registrants whose identities and addresses are unknown and against whom *in personam* actions would be fruitless.' Porsche's action against the domain names themselves failed because of US constitutional grounds.

It is submitted that a similar action would also fail under English law. The only surviving English action 'in rem' is the Admiralty action. The only action *in rem* which may therefore be brought must specifically relate to a question or claim defined by statute as being within the Admiralty jurisdiction[69]. Suffice it to say that the Supreme Court Act 1981 does not refer to domain names nor to any similar property. Indeed, the courts have shown that an 'in rem' action is

66 This will include the use of the domain name in a page of links on which viewers click rather than retype into their browser.

67 In such a case, after a given time, the registration authority would reclaim the name at which the 'truer' owner could register it.

68 No 99–006–A (ED VA, June 8, 1999).

69 Supreme Court Act 1981, ss 20 and 21, as amended.

construed very narrowly. In one case, despite the statute covering 'aircraft' in three paragraphs this was not enough to cover a 'glider'[70]. It is consequentially inconceivable that a domain name could be brought within the *in rem* jurisdiction of the English courts.

Legal and technical rights v legal and technical rights

Although there can be only one '.com', there has always been the risk that there may be many variations of the domain name with different suffixes. For example, in November 1993, Merritt Technologies Inc was granted the domain name 'mit.com'. From 30 December 1993 Merritt used the domain to provide free Internet access to the handicapped, disabled and elderly. On 6 May 1996, Merritt received a letter from the Massachusetts Institute of Technology asking Merritt to select an alternate domain name. Their rights to insist upon this were based on their use of the MIT trademark since 1861, having a worldwide reputation and five registered trade marks in classes unrelated to Merritt's use of the mark. They also relied upon the amended US Trademark Act, s 43(c) providing rights for famous trade mark owners against those who might 'dilute' their marks. The Institute already owned the domain names 'mit.org' and lit.edu'. There was no crossover in fields of activity: the Institute was simply worried that its trade mark was being used at all.

This is a scenario that is occurring more and more frequently. This is because the naming committees both here and elsewhere are expanding, and will continue to expand, the numbers of suffixes available. But as the late Jon Postel of the Internet Assigned Name Authority wrote[71]:

> '[T]he trademark issue is just a mess. McDonalds is going to want to have mcdonalds.com, mcdonalds.biz, and other domain names involving McDonalds.'

What follows, as for the MTV dispute, is an assessment of English law's reaction to the MIT dispute. Unless a mark is famous, English law does not provide a total monopoly over *every* use of a word.

Trade mark infringement

Unlike the MTV dispute where the domain name was used in relation to identical goods and services, Merritt's domain name is used in relation to dissimilar goods and services. The Institute has registered its mark only in relation to clothing; coffee mugs, cups, etc; pencils, notebooks, etc; computer programs and manuals; educational courses. With the assumption that these registrations were under the Trade Marks Act 1994, the use of 'mit' in Merritt's domain name seems possibly to be an infringement of a registered trade mark over the

70 *The Glider Standard Austria SH 1964, Schenipp-Hirth Kommandit-Gesellschaft (owners of The Glider Standard Austria SH 1964) v Persons Having Possession of The Glider Standard Austria SH 1964* [1965] 2 All ER 1022.

71 Information Law Alert, 02/09/96, 'Antidilution trademark law gets first court case'.

identical or similar name but with dissimilar goods or services[72]. Section 10(3) states that it is an infringement for a person to use in the course of trade a sign which is identical or similar with a registered trade mark[73] and in relation to goods or services which are identical with the goods or services for which the trade mark is registered[74].

Use of a sign in the course of trade

As already discussed, s 10(4) provides four presumptions for when a person uses a sign[75]. The relevant presumptions in this scenario are again (b) and (d). Merritt was offering and supplying services under the sign 'www.mit.com' and advertising for Merritt's other business activities. Assuming that Merritt's use was in the course of trade, despite being for a charity, it is certainly arguable that the sign was used in the course of trade[76].

Identical or similar sign to registered trade mark

The Institute's trade mark is the acronym 'mit' and the sign used by Merritt is 'http://www.mit.com'. It has already been discussed that despite these two strings, character for character, not being identical they may be identical for the purposes of the Act[77]. One reason for this is that the characters before and after 'mit' are generic for domain names or are not considered to be part of the sign at all[78]. But, as this heading suggests, s 10(3) is wider than s 10(1): it may operate on more than purely an identical sign, but also a similar one[79].

72 Here a suitable defence may be that the domain name is the actual name of the defendant used according to honest practices in commercial matters: Trade Marks Act 1994, s 11(2). Countering this, of course, the Institute may allege that the name of the defendant is not MIT, but Merritt Technologies Inc.

73 Trade Marks Act 1994, s 10(3)(a).

74 Trade Marks Act 1994, s 10(3)(b).

75 See 'Use of a sign in the course of trade', at page 176.

76 For deeper reasoning see, in relation to mtv.com, 'Use of a sign in the course of trade', at page 137.

77 See generally, 'Identical sign to registered trade mark', page 173.

78 When comparing marks most trade mark offices, US and UK included, ignore the prefixes and suffixes.

79 One needs to identify the defendant's sign for the purposes of comparison. Occasionally, the sign will not be within the domain name, but within the hierarchical folders on the server holding the website. For example, one could register a domain with the name, 'www.complete.com' with few complaints from the domain name registry. But, once the site is in use, one can create series of hierarchical folders that store the various pages on the website. If the top level of these folders is name 'paq' and contains a page called 'computers', a link on a website to that folder will look like 'http://www.complete.com/paq.computers'. Once the words 'compaq computers' are identified it becomes simple to allege that this sign is identical or similar to Compaq's trade mark. *In Patmont Motor Werks Inc v Gateway Marine Inc* (18 December 1997, unreported) DC N Calif, No C 96–2703 TEH, the use of the trade mark 'goped' in the path name of the URL ('www.idiosync.com/goped') was held under US trade mark law not to infringe the trade mark. Similarly, one can use a domain name as an address for email. Usually the 'www' is replaced with a person's name followed by an '@' sign. Bill Gates has the email address, 'billg@microsoft.com'. Someone could also register the domain name 'soft.com' and publish the contact email address as 'micro@soft.com'. Again, once the sign is identified it can be seen that the sign is identical or similar to Microsoft's mark. This said, one is humorously reminded by Jacob J that 'No one but a crossword fanatic, for instance, would say that "treat" is present in "theatre atmosphere"': *British Sugar plc v James Robertson & Sons Ltd* [1996] RPC 281 at 294.

Similarity of sign to mark

The requirements in s 5(2) for non-similarity are generally considered to be equivalent to the 1938 Act's prohibition on registering trade marks that 'nearly resemble' another's mark[80]. The court's assessment of this section is notoriously dependent on the facts of each case, but if there is one common theme it is that the court is looking to establish the 'gist' of the two trade marks as the public would perceive them, not as the Registry lists them[81]. In this context, the sign 'www.mit.com' as compared with the mark 'mit' does appear similar if not identical. The millions of people who use the Internet and World Wide Web are unlikely to be aware of the conditions that must be met to be granted a 'com' domain name; they are likely to view the sign as similar to the mark[82].

In relation to dissimilar goods or services

The difficult aspect to this test is not proving that the goods or services are dissimilar; Merritt's use of the domain name is clearly not covered by the Institute's registrations. The hurdle is that the trade mark must be used in relation to some goods or services. Certainly, Merritt was utilising its site as more than merely an information board: it was a self-promotional website with a purpose not entirely altruistic. It will therefore be assumed that this aspect of the section was met. This brings us to the most uncertain aspect of a s 10(3) infringement: the defendant must have used the mark without due cause and by doing so must have taken unfair advantage of or been detrimental to the distinctive character or repute of the trade mark[83].

Due cause

The concept that the defendant must have had 'due cause' to use the sign is vague. The Act does not expand upon the term and its extent remains debatable, although jurisprudence is now helping to explain the term. Neuberger J in *Premier Brands UK Ltd v Typhoon Europe Ltd*[84] adopts the approach taken in the Benelux Court[85] to the term 'without justifiable reason'. In short, the user of the mark must be under a compulsion to use the mark so that he cannot honestly be asked to refrain from using the mark, whatever the damage to the trade mark owner.

80 Trade Marks Act 1938, s 12(1). Also the similar infringement provisions under the 1938 Act, as amended, s 4.

81 See *Kerly's Law of Trade Marks and Trade Names* (12th edn), paras 17.08 and 17.09.

82 Such an argument can be tempered with the view that the mark should not be divided but viewed as a whole when being compared to another: *Bailey (William) Ltd's Application 'Erectico'* (1935) 52 RPC 136. This does not sit comfortably with the more common view that the marks should be assessed for their 'feel' rather than their strict spelling and syntax. See generally *Wagamama Ltd v City Centre Restaurants plc* [1995] FSR 713.

83 The mark must also have a reputation in the UK; this contrasts with the situation where a trade mark is registered without a reputation in the UK. For the purposes of this English law analysis of the MIT dispute, it is assumed that the Institute does have a reputation in the UK.

84 [2000] FSR 767.

85 *Lucas BAS* [1976] IIC 420 at 425.

For a domain name dispute, this phrase may become pivotal. Merritt may well also have a trade mark over the letters MIT but in a different class altogether. It may be for this reason that they applied and used the domain name 'mit.com'[86]. The intention to use one's trade mark as a domain name appears to be due cause and justifiable reason[87]. It should be noted that the infringement is only made out by the claimant if the use is without due cause. It certainly does not appear to be without due cause to use one's trade mark as a domain name[88].

It appears from the above discussion that, without strong opposing reasons, it will be due cause to use as a domain name one's own name for which one has a registered trade mark.

Unfair advantage or detriment

Even without due cause, the claimant must establish that the use of the sign takes unfair advantage of, or is detrimental to, the distinctive character or repute of the registered mark. It is important not to overlook that this section is not available to all registered trade marks: they must have a distinctive character or repute.

Unfair advantage

Taking unfair advantage conveys a theme of free-riding: that one cannot reap the benefits of another's labour in building up goodwill in a trade mark. To defeat this in a domain name dispute, one would have expected to be able to 'distance' one's sign from the registered trade mark. For instance, one could use an opening disclaimer on a website that 'this is not the Massachusetts Institute of Technology official site which can be found at http://www.mit.org'. It is submitted that, by doing this one is gaining little to no advantage, other than people passing through one's site on the way to another. To class this as an unfair advantage is perhaps to misconceive the Web. The very nature of the web is a number of documents that are interlinked. Using a site as a thoroughfare to another is no more taking unfair advantage of the destination site as is walking into one shop on the high street while on the way to another. Clearly, any use of such a disclaimer must not be a sham; the courts will look beyond the words and coding and concentrate on any ulterior motives in choosing the domain name.

What should concern those with a domain name registration similar to a well-known brand is that in *One in a Million*, there is a suggestion that a domain name is not merely used (in the course of trade) on a website but also simply on the domain name register. Consequently, even if a disclaimer is issued on the website, a WHOIS search[89] will still represent the domain name

86 These arguments justifying use are similar to those which can be put forward as a defence in s 11(2).

87 See *Fry's Electronics Inc v Octave Systems* (No C95–2525 CAL ND Cal). Frenchy Frys, a Seattle-based seller of french fry vending machines, registered the domain name 'frys.com'. Fry's Electronic alleged that Frenchy Frys wrongly appropriated the Fry's trade name. Fry's Electronics did not have a Federal trade mark. Frenchy Frys remains at 'frys.com'.

88 As noted by Neuberger J in *Premier Brands UK Ltd v Typhoon Europe Ltd* [2000] FSR 767 in the Uniform Benelux Trademarks Law 1971, art 132, 'due cause' has been construed narrowly, and even that article embraces the idea of prior rights in the sign.

89 A WHOIS search reveals the owner of a particular domain name.

as being owned by an individual other than the owner of the well-known mark. This said, the domain name owner should nevertheless do all *possible* not to take unfair advantage of their domain name. They should make it clear to their site's viewers that they may be at the wrong site owing to a contingency of the domain name system, rather than any motive of the site controller. It will be a sign of good faith to include on the home page a link to the 'other' site.

Detriment

Fair wider than the requirement that the domain name not take unfair advantage of a registered trade mark is the alternative requirement. A sign that is detrimental to the distinctive character or repute of the registered trade mark, all other conditions met, is infringement[90]. Despite the fact that a trade sign must be *used* in the course of trade, to be capable of infringing a trade mark, it appears that the English courts are not concerned to see the use of the domain *in relation* to a website. The fact that a domain name has been registered *at all* may constitute adequate use. Consequently, the content of a website may simply worsen the risk of infringement.

This was obvious in the dispute between Hasbro, owners of the Candyland trade mark, and Internet Entertainment Group[91] who owned the domain name 'candyland.com'. IEG used the domain as a website offering sexually explicit material. Hasbro's trade mark was used in relation to children's toys and activities. The two uses could not be more dissimilar. The detriment to the trade mark is clear and was clear to the court who injuncted IEG from using the domain name[92]. In contrast, Warner Brothers, which had registered 'Road Runner' as a trade mark for toys, objected to Roadrunner Inc using the domain name 'roadrunner.com'[93]. Roadrunner Inc was a provider of Internet access services. In this situation it will be harder than in the Hasbro situation to suggest that the use of the Roadrunner sign will lead to the detriment of the trade mark. It may be more appropriate, but still hard, to allege unfair advantage.

From *One in a Million* it would appear that proving 'detriment' is not a high hurdle. The High Court merely suggests 'It seems to me to be equally clear [that the trade mark Marks & Spencer has a reputation in the UK] that the Defendant's use of it is detrimental to the trade mark, if only by damaging the Plaintiff's exclusivity.' The Court of Appeal relies on the circular notion that: '[The] domain names were registered to take advantage of the distinctive character and reputation of the marks. That is unfair and detrimental.' These statements rely more upon the perception by the courts that the defendants were fraudulent and so should release the domain names, than on the strict legal analysis of what constitutes 'unfair advantage' and 'detrimental' use of a domain name.

90 See *Premier Brands UK Ltd v Typhoon Europe Ltd* [2000] FSR 767.

91 After, IEG.

92 *Hasbro Inc v Internet Entertainment Group Ltd* (No C96–130WDE, 9 February 1996) United States District Court, WD Washington.

93 Some may recall that this is not the first time that the Road Runner has been involved with litigation. In *Duracell International Inc v Ever Ready Ltd* [1989] FSR 71 one of the advertisements that was claimed to be infringing used a monochrome picture of the cartoon Road Runner with the Road Runner emitting a 'beep-beep' sound (at 74).

This may be contrasted with a US Court of Appeals judgment in the case *Avery Dennison v Jerry Sumpton*[94]. Avery Dennison, not unlike Marks & Spencer, is a distinctive brand name constructed from common-use surnames. The defendant, Mr Sumpton, 'rented' vanity email addresses to individuals. For example, the defendant had a collection of surnames that individuals could 'rent' together with a first name. In illustration, say, Phillip Jacobs may be able to rent for $19.95 the email address Phillip@Jacobs.com for the period of one year. Two of the surnames for rent included 'Avery' and 'Dennison'. This offering formed the basis of the action by the office product supplier. The court considered the 'motivation' of the defendant was actually to 'capitalise on the surname status of "Avery" and "Dennison".' For this and other reasons, Avery Dennison lost the appeal.

Being under US law, little of direct application to an English case can be drawn from this appeal. However, it is clear that courts on both sides of the Atlantic are prepared to look at the 'intention' of a domain name registrant, rather than merely basing their decisions on typographical comparisons between trade marks and domain names. Indeed, both in *One in a Million* and *Avery Dennison* the courts relied upon how the defendant acted in relation to *other* domain names not in issue.

For the present case study, between MIT and Merritt, it appears that the Institute under English law would have a hard task to prove trade mark infringement. This reflects the commercial decision taken by the Institute on 23 July 1996 to withdraw its complaint and accede to Merritt's use of the domain on two conditions[95]. First, the rights should not be transferred to a third party. The second condition was that Merritt agreed to forward to the Institute all communications that are intended for the Institute.

This second condition was met by Merritt using a link on its website to the Institute's. As indicated by this section, this forwarding link may not compromise either party; it is common to arrive at the wrong address on the Internet. Such a commercial solution should be contemplated before legal action is taken; John Gilmore of the Electronic Frontier Foundation sums up the issue well[96]:

> 'Trademarks are registered in a system that permits many companies to share a name legitimately without interfering with each other, such as Sun Photo, Sun Oil and Sun Microsystems. Domain names only permit one user of a name; there is only one sun.com, which Sun Microsystems registered first. *Neither lawyers nor governments can make ten pounds of names fit into a one-pound bag.*'

Repute of the trade mark

In *General Motors Corpn v Yplon SA*[97] the European Court of Justice was asked what the proper construction is of the term 'repute of the trade mark' – in effect, what is the meaning of 'has a reputation' in art 5(2) of the Trade Mark Directive[98]. The court ruled that this means that the 'trade mark must be known

94 Ninth Circuit, Appeal No 98–55810, 23 August 1999.
95 Letter dated 23 July 1996 from Director of the MIT Technology Licensing Office.
96 *The Economist*, Letters, 13 July 1996. Emphasis added.
97 C–375/97 [1999] All ER (EC) 865.
98 First Council Directive (89/104/EEC) of 21 December 1988 to Approximate the Laws of the Member States Relating to Trade Marks (OJ 1989 L40/1).

by a significant part of the public concerned by the products or services which it covers.'[99] There is no percentage of the public at which point the court will deem the trade mark has repute. The key is therefore to prove that a significant part of the public knows the trade mark. In the current scenario, MIT is very well-known by those in scientific academia and, with a registration concerning academic-related services, is likely to be known by a significant part of *that* public.

Trade mark infringement remedies

As for the MTV dispute, MIT would have to think carefully about the remedies it seeks. In the interest of the balance of convenience between the parties it may be useful to allow a 'hand-over' period in any injunction order. For this the defendants should immediately remove all the content from the site, but post a referral notice on the site to the new location of the defendant's content. This notice should not be a hypertext link, thus cutting down the risk that viewers may unwittingly pass through the trade mark domain name site to the detrimental or unfairly advantageous site. This non-linked referral notice should remain for a fixed time after which the defendants should discontinue any use of the domain name or any similar to it.

This allows the intentional viewers of the infringing site to locate the new location, so not damaging too much the legitimate trade of the infringing site. It also stops dead any further infringement under the infringing sign. It does not stop the potential infringement, as suggested by the Court of Appeal in *One in a Million*, which occurs where the WHOIS search reveals that the trade mark owner does not own the domain name.

Passing off claim

If the Institute did not have a registered trade mark on which they could base trade mark infringement proceedings, they may have sought to rely on a passing off claim. The 'classical trinity' has been discussed in relation to the MTV dispute[100]. What is different from that situation is the consequent damage.

Consequent damage

Assuming that the first two requirements of misrepresentation and goodwill are satisfied, the Institute must prove the final requirement of passing off: it must have suffered, or be likely to suffer, damage to the property in its goodwill because of the misrepresentation. Although the requirement to show damage is not onerous, as discussed[101] it may be difficult to establish where the defendant's site is in a different field of activity.

The damage claimed cannot be equated to lost sales but to a 'dilution' of a trading name; a reduction in the distinctiveness and repute of the MIT name. In

99 At para 31.
100 See 'Passing off claim', at page 180.
101 See 'Consequent damage', at page 182.

Taittinger v Allbev the Court of Appeal was of the opinion that the use of the name 'champagne' in relation to an elderflower drink caused the requisite damage[102]. This was based on the fact that[103]:

> '[a]ny product which is not champagne but is allowed to describe itself as such must inevitably, in my view, erode the singularity and exclusiveness of the description champagne and so cause the first plaintiff's damage of an insidious but serious kind.'

Could the Institute, or any company with a distinctive name, claim similar damage? It is submitted not. First, champagne is a special and unique product, 'a reference to champagne imports nuances of quality and celebration, a sense of something privileged and special'[104]. As such the goodwill can be damaged merely by its use on other products. The same may not be true for a domain name. It is understood by users of the Internet that domain names are limited; damage is rarely caused by simply using another's domain name. Where there may be damage is if the site using the claimant's name will somehow benefit from the connection or prejudice the defendant[105]. This is a question of fact and of the cross-substitutability of the claimant's customers with the defendant's. In this situation, it is suggested that the Institute's goodwill in its abbreviated name suffers no such damage as that in the *Taittinger* case[106].

Deliberate goodwill damage

To rely on the *One in a Million* precedent it is clear that a court will have to find that the defendants abused the domain name system by attempting to use it in their favour to extort from the claimants [107]. This is not the situation with MIT: both users of the MIT domain names are 'rightful owners with prior legal and common law rights in the name'. For these situations, it is inappropriate to cite *One in a Million* as authority that the domain name should be relinquished.

Protective domain name measures

This examination of domain names allows the deduction of a series of measures which may be beneficial to those who wish to register a domain name. As has been discussed, registering a domain name which is protected by another's

102 [1993] 2 CMLR 741 at 762 [62]–763 [64].
103 [1993] 2 CMLR 741 at 763 [63].
104 [1993] 2 CMLR 741 at 763 [64].
105 See 'Detriment', at page 190.
106 In *Panavision International v Toeppen* (CV 96–3284 DDP, 1 November 1996) the court stated that '[a]s a result of the current state of Internet technology, Toeppen was able not merely to "lessen [. . .] the capacity of a famous mark to identify and distinguish goods or services" 15 USC 1127, but to eliminate the capacity of the Panavision marks to identify and distinguish Panavision's goods and services on the Internet'. This is not strictly true, as the Court of Appeal realised in *One in a Million*: Toeppen had registered only 'Panavision.com' leaving Panavision International able to register 'panavision-int.com' and any other unregistered domain name which is not exactly 'panavision.com'.
107 See 'Investment of fraud claim', at page 183.

registered trade mark can lead to problems. Conversely, registering a domain name and then protecting that domain name with a registered trade mark can provide additional security over the domain name. Potential applicants for domain names should therefore first perform some clearance exercise over the name they wish to register as a domain name. Having registered a domain name they may then seek to protect it from third parties and the registration authorities.

1. Check availability of domain name

Domain names are not simply taken. Like company names, they are registered. Over 100 Registrars have registered more than 20 million domains ending in '.com'. For domains ending 'co.uk', 'ltd.uk', 'net.uk', Nominet UK is the provider. All these companies charge a small fee to register a domain name and generally sell the domain names through agents, rather like Companies House 'sells' companies through formation agents. The difficulty arises because the Registrars do not have the resources to check that an applicant has the right to use a particular name and so allocates them on a first-come, first-served basis. Because of this policy, many names are already registered. The first step is therefore to use online searches to check whether the intended name has been registered. Companies should try to consider variations of their names and attempt to register these also.

2. Register domain name

Increasingly, domain names which are desired have been registered. This is as a result of the first-come, first-served system. But it is also as a result of the huge increase in domain names being registered. Over nineteen '.com' domain names are registered each second. This does not lend itself to careful selection and 'mulling over' of a number of possible brands before 'plumping' for the best. Having searched and found that a number of domain names are free, any delay in registering one of them could lead to disappointment if the desired domain name is registered in the meantime.

To be safe, therefore, each *possible* domain name should be registered (up to a commercially sensible number). Once these 'possibles' are secured, each should then be 'cleared' to reduce the risk of trade mark infringement. It should be understood that even the registration of a domain name can give rise to a claim for passing off a trade mark infringement. This is a risk that, unfortunately, must be taken to avoid seeing a 'cleared' brand registered as the domain name during the clearing process. Registrants may therefore like to register the domain name, pre-clearance, in a shelf company and then assign the domain out of the limited liability shell when the clearance is positive. This has two advantages. First, thoughtful naming and corporate structuring of the shelf company should ensure that noone gets wind of a new product launch or branding strategy before time. Second, if the mere registration does infringe a trade mark, the liability arising from this is restricted.

It is admitted that it is not ideal for a company to spend hundreds, if not thousands, of pounds registering domain names it may not use because of later rejection at the 'clearance' stage. When hundreds of thousands of domain names are being registered during the 24 hours of each day across the planet, however, registering pre-emptively may be the safest option.

3. Clear use of domain name

Registering a domain name does not provide any legal rights over the domain, only technical rights. A company that seeks a particular domain name should search to see whether or not a third party is using the intended domain name as a trade mark. As far as practicable and economically justifiable, this search should be performed on an international basis to take account of the transnational nature of the Internet, and so the multinational nature of any rights claims[108].

4. Protect domain name with trade mark registration

As described earlier, an applicant's domain name may already be protected under its existing trade mark registrations. If this is not the case, the domain name owner should seriously consider obtaining a trade mark registration in respect of the trade mark within the domain name. It has been illustrated that a trade mark registration provides significant rights against a user of a commercially-impinging domain name. Even without a registration, the use of a domain name may build up trade mark rights in the name. To signify this to the 'world' the domain name can be followed with the ™ symbol on the website content[109].

5. Consider domain name dispute rules

Each domain name is bought from a commercial third party. The majority of these purchase contracts (certainly those relating to .com, .net, .org) incorporate the Uniform Domain Name Dispute Resolution Policy[110]. This Dispute Resolution Policy regulates how, without resorting to the courts, an applicant may defend the use and ownership of their domain name. It replaces an earlier Dispute Resolution Policy[111] which was often unjust, with a policy which is vague and also, potentially, unjust.

Advisors are recommended to weigh up the costs and benefits of this grievance procedure with those of the courts. The overly-complex logistics and timing of the Resolution Policy are as follows:

1. An individual or corporation may complain about the ownership of a domain name by submitting a complaint to a nominated Provider[112] in hard copy and electronic form.
2. The complaint must address three types of issue. First, formal issues; second, factual issues; third, legalistic issues[113].

108 See *JackSpade.com* (WIPO D2001–1384) para 6.9.

109 One should pay particular attention to the fact that it is a criminal offence to use in relation to an unregistered trade mark any word, symbol or express or implied reference that the trade mark is so registered. Use of ® should be carefully monitored – it is not akin to misuse of © for which there is no criminal sanction: Trade Marks Act 1994, s 95.

110 Can be seen with explanatory notes at www.icann.org. This has been in force since 1 January 2000.

111 NSI Domain Name Dispute Policy Statement (Revision 03, effective 25 February 1998).

112 Rules for Uniform Domain Name Dispute Resolution Policy, para 3(a) and (b).

113 Rules for Uniform Domain Name Dispute Resolution Policy, para 3.

Formal issues

The complaint must[114]:

1. request that the complaint is to be submitted for a decision in accordance with ICANN'S Policy and Rules;
2. provide the hard copy and email contact details of the complainant and representatives;
3. specify with whom and on what medium the provider should conduct the Dispute Policy; elect for either a single member, dispute panel or select the three members for a three-member panel;
4. state that the copy of the complaint and copies of Rules have been sent to the domain name holder;
5. state that the complainant will submit to the jurisdiction of the domain name holder's local court or the registrar's local court to resolve any challenges to the application of the Rules. Complainants should note that this does not prevent either party suing in any other court of competent jurisdiction;
6. state verbatim the waiver of all claims against the dispute resolution panelist(s), registrar, ICANN and their representatives and officers; and
7. state that the complaint has been made in good faith and is complete and accurate etc.

Factual issues

The complaint must[115]:

1. specify domain names subject to the complaint;
2. specify the Registrar with whom the domain names are registered;
3. specify, with supporting evidence, the trade mark or service mark upon which the complaint is based;
4. specify the goods or services with which the mark is used or is intended to be used;
5. identify any other legal proceedings that have been commenced or terminated in connection with the domain names.

Legalistic issues

The complaint must:

(1) Describe the three grounds on which the complaint is made, in particular:

(a) The manner in which the domain name is identical or confusingly similar to a trade mark or service mark in which the complainant has rights[116].

First, one must address what is encompassed by a 'trade mark or service mark'.

114 Rules for Uniform Domain Name Dispute Resolution Policy, paras 3(b)(i), 3(b)(ii), 3(b)(iii), 3(b)(v), 3(b)(xii), 3(b)(xiii), and 3(b)(xiv).

115 Rules for Uniform Domain Name Dispute Resolution Policy, paras 3(b)(vi), 3(b)(vii), 3(b)(viii), 3(b)(xv), and 3(b)(xi).

116 Rules for Uniform Domain Name Dispute Resolution Policy, paras 3(b)(ix)(1).

Having established this, one can consider when a domain name is 'identical' and when it is merely 'confusingly similar'.

The cases on the ambit of a 'trade mark or service mark' show that the panellists view the term generously. Certainly a registered trade mark falls within its scope, even where the trade mark is registered in one jurisdiction but the respondent was in another[117]. Beyond registered trade marks, the panellists have also accepted unregistered rights under common law[118].

Difficulties have arisen where the well-known have been concerned that their famous names have been used as a domain name. Here, it would appear, the more uncommon the famous name, the more likely it is for the panellists to deem the name is a trade mark or service mark. So, for example, Julia Roberts[119] and Jeannette Winterson[120] were able to assert their common law rights in their names. The, arguably more famous, pop singer Sting, was not able to assert his common law rights because his name 'is in common usage in the English language, with a number of meanings'[121].

Having established that the complainant has these necessary rights, one must then determine whether the domain name is identical to or confusingly similar to the name over which the complainant has rights. Under the first ever case[122] the panel had little difficulty in determining whether this ground was met: the domain name was 'worldwrestlingfederation.com' and the registered trade marks were 'World Wrestling Federation'. The panellists have seemingly accepted, as it is believed will the courts, that the '.com' or suffix should be disregarded when comparing the domain name with the trade mark[123].

Further, in *Draw-Tite Inc v Plattsburgh Spring Inc* the panel held that the addition or deletion of a hyphen or a space does not necessary affect the confusing nature of the domain name and mark[124]. Where, however, the domain name and trade mark are not alphanumerically identical but are phonetically similar under a particular language, the panel will doubtlessly seek to rely on trade mark law of the relevant jurisdiction. This view is supported by the fact that the panel is able to decide a complaint using any rules and principles of law that it deems appropriate[125] and in the above case relies on two US court decisions.

Complainants and their advisors are therefore well-advised to support all their legal arguments with court decisions from, it would appear, any relevant jurisdiction.

(b) That the domain name holder has no rights or legitimate interests (other than technical ownership) in the domain name[126].

Guidance is given as to three non-exhaustive issues that should be discussed to support this claim. Each of these three elements must be proved by the complainant.

117 *thetimesofindia.com* (WIPO D2000–0015).
118 *48hours.com* (WIPO D2000–0379).
119 *JuliaRoberts.com* (WIPO D2000–0210).
120 *JeannetteWinterson.com* (WIPO D2000–0235).
121 *Sting.com* (WIPO D2000–0596) at para 6.6.
122 *WorldWrestlingFederation.com* (WIPO D99–0001).
123 See *kcts.com* (WIPO D2001–0154).
124 *DrawTite.com* (WIPO D2000–0017).
125 Rules for Uniform Domain Name Dispute Resolution Policy, para 15(a). See *AmericanVintage.com* (WIPO D00–0004) and *MusicWeb.com* (WIPO D00–0001).
126 Rules for Uniform Domain Name Dispute Resolution Policy, para 3(b)(ix)(2).

First, prior to the dispute, the domain name holder should have no use or preparations of use of the domain name in connection with a *bona fide* offering of goods or services[127]. Only in rare circumstances will offering to sell the domain name to the complainant be considered a *bone fide* use of the domain name[128]. In the main, unless the domain name is particularly descriptive or generic, offering to sell the domain will not get the respondent off the hook.

Second, the domain name holder must be proved not to be commonly-known by the domain name[129]. Each of these three elements must be proved by the complainant. If the domain name holder proves that they have, say, been commonly known by the domain name, the dispute is lost. The domain name will remain with its holder. For example, Anand Ramnath Mani registered the domain name 'armani.com'. This matched his business cards which, since 1982, displayed the name A. R. Mani. The owners of the Armani fashion brand complained to the WIPO panel and lost[130]. The panel stated: 'This is therefore not a case of the type sometimes encountered, where an opportunistic registrant adopts a name which is intended to give a spurious air of legitimacy to an otherwise questionable registration.' Having unregistered rights, even as against a complainant's registered rights may constitute 'rights' under this section[131].

Third, the domain name holder must be shown to be making illegitimate non-commercial or unfair use of the domain name with intent to make commercial gain to misleadingly direct consumers or to tarnish the trade mark at issue[132]. This third issue is often relied upon by those who register domain names, often finishing off the trade mark with the word 'sucks', to criticise the company or product. It may come as no surprise that 'natwestsucks.com' and 'dixonssucks.com' were domain names registered, apparently, to condemn those companies[133]. It is rare for such variations on a trade mark to be deemed to be legitimate uses and therefore, presumably, hardly worth registering in the first place[134].

(c) The domain name has been registered in bad faith and is being used in bad faith[135]. Again guidance is provided as to evidence that may constitute bad faith in registration and in use. This is important: the domain name must not only be registered in bad faith but subsequently also used in bad faith[136]. The Dispute Policy provides a non-exhaustive list of what constitutes registration and use in bad faith.

Registration in bad faith includes[137]:

(i) registration in circumstances indicating the registration was primarily for

127 Rules for Uniform Domain Name Dispute Resolution Policy, para 4(c)(i).
128 See the oft-cited, rarely followed decision in *Allocation.com* (WIPO D2001–0537).
129 Rules for Uniform Domain Name Dispute Resolution Policy, para 4(c)(ii).
130 *Armani.com* (WIPO D2001–0537).
131 *SixNet.com* (WIPO D2000–0008).
132 Rules for Uniform Domain Name Dispute Resolution Policy, para 4(c).
133 *natwestsucks.com* (WIPO D2000–0636) and *dixonssucks.com* (WIPO) D2000–0584.
134 See *Wallmartcanadasucks.com* (WIPO D2000–1104), *NatWestFraud.com* (WIPO 2001–0212) and the unprintable domain name disputed in *Ford Motor Co v 2600 Enterprises* US District Court for Eastern District of Michigan, 20 December 2001.
135 Rules for Uniform Domain Name Dispute Resolution Policy, para 3(b)(ix)(2).
136 The strict logic of this dual requirement is applied in disputes. Consequently, even pointing a domain name to a pornographic site seemingly to harm the complainant's reputation may constitute bad faith in use, but necessarily in registration: *Telaxis.com* (WIPO D2000–0005).
137 Rules for Uniform Domain Name Dispute Resolution Policy, para 4(a)(b)(i)–(iii).

the purposes of selling, renting or otherwise transferring the domain name to the owner of a trade mark or service mark over the name or their competitor for a sum greater than the out-of-pocket expenses to acquire it;

(ii) registration in order to prevent the owner of a trade mark or service mark from reflecting the mark in a corresponding domain name, having engaged in a pattern of such conduct;

(iii) registration in order to disrupt the business of a competitor;

(iv) use of the domain name intentionally to attempt to create a likelihood of confusion as to the sponsorship, affiliation or endorsement of the website or location or product or service on the website or location.

Point (i) makes clear that any offers to sell the domain name at greater than cost will automatically lead to an inference of bad faith[138]. Domain name registrants are therefore advised to be careful when negotiating the sale of a domain name. Even though they may have registered it in good faith, a high offer to sell it will indicate bad faith. Without prejudice communications should therefore be used at all times during negotiation[139]. Conversely, a complainant should try to draw out from the registrant an open offer to sell the domain at a high cost[140].

Point (ii) is a very wide requirement. This ensures that 'flavours' of a trade mark are also protected by the policy. The domain name need not be identical (as in the previous policy) to the trade mark relied upon.

7. Arrgh Inc is the owner of a registered trade mark, 'Arrgh', which it licenses to its European-based group of pain therapists. It also owns the domain name 'Arrgh.com'. Since registering the trade mark a competitive anaesthetist has registered the domain name, 'Arrh.com', and publishes at that website distressing stories of why pain therapy can be damaging. Under the previous domain name resolution policy, Arrgh Inc would have no recourse as the domain name was not identical their trade mark; under the new current policy, they have a right to dispute the ownership of 'Arrh.com'.

Trade mark holders and their advisors should note that (iii) is not merely concerned with disruption of business but disruption by a competitor of that business.

8. Ladybird Ltd runs an extremely successful children's book-publishing business and catches on, perhaps a little late, that it could use its reputation and warehouse for an ecommerce website. It has a registered trade mark which covers its activities and attempts to register the domain name. It discovers that Ladybird.com, Lady-bird.com, LadyBird.com and many other such variants have been registered by a pornographic website. Despite the perception of the damage caused by children accessing 'Ladybird.com', Ladybird Ltd will have difficulty in proving the bad faith requirement, particularly as it does not compete with Ladybird.com.

138 Of course, where a domain name owner has legitimate rights to a domain name, offering to sell it for more than out-of-pocket expenses may, nevertheless, be acting in good faith: *Avnet.net* (WIPO D2000–046).

139 No guidance has been given as to whether 'without prejudice' communications may be relied upon in such proceedings but it is expected that this is likely to be the case.

140 There is a suggestion by the panel that an offer to sell a domain name for a six-figure amount 'was clearly' bad faith: *Easyjet.net* (WIPO D2000–0024).

Use in bad faith also includes[141] using the domain name in an intentional attempt to attract, for commercial gain, Internet users to the website or another online location, by creating a likelihood of confusion with the complainant's trade mark as to the source, sponsorship, affiliation or endorsement of the website or locating or of a product or service on the website or location. This is a significant requirement: the domain name must not merely be registered but also used. It is therefore relevant to consider whether, if a website is not established under a domain name, whether or not the domain name is being 'used'.

This matter has been already considered in relation to UK trade mark 'use in the course of trade' and by analogy with US domain names. Jurisprudence is apparent from these two jurisdictions and the *World Wrestling* dispute that offering to sell the domain name (ie 'offline' use of it) constitutes 'use' of the domain name. Where this offer to sell is at a price in excess of the out-of-pocket expenses, there is a suggestion that the domain name is being used in bad faith. A good example of this is where a domain name is 'posted' on a domain name auction site such as 'GreatDomains.com' as in *Ellenbogen v Pearson*[142].

9. 2L8.com is a company which registers the '.com' domain names of newly merged companies. Websites are not established for each domain name. 2L8.com lists all the domain names it has for sale and conducts auctions as soon as each corporate merger is officially announced. Even though the domain names are not pointed to operating websites, this is use of the domain names and use in bad faith.

The concept of 'use' is also encapsulated by actually doing nothing in relation to a domain name, or merely being passive, or inactive in relation to a domain name[143]. Indeed, even not filing evidence in relation to a lodged domain name dispute has been held to constitute use of a domain in bad faith[144]. It should be obvious, therefore, that the requirement of 'use' is easily met.

Interestingly, there are now strong precedents that the registration and use of a domain name by a legitimate re-seller of a particular product under that name does not necessarily constitute bad faith. In *Draw-Tite Inc v Plattsburgh Spring*, Plattsburgh Spring was a legitimate promoter and seller of Draw-Tite trailer accessories. This was enough to allow it to be seen as using the domain name 'Draw-Tite.com' in good faith despite being registered as a trade mark by Draw-Tite[145].

(2) Provide a statement of remedies

Having set out the legal basis for the complaint, the remedies sought must be stated[146]. These are either cancellation of a domain name or transferral of the domain name to the complainant[147]. It is difficult to conceive of a complainant who does not wish for the transfer of the domain name but who would rather

141 Rules for Uniform Domain Name Dispute Resolution Policy, para 4(a)(b)(iv).
142 WIPO D00–0001.
143 *Telstra.org* (WIPO D2000–0003).
144 *AmericanVintage.com* (WIPO D00–0004).
145 (WIPO D2000–0017). But see *heelquick.com* (NAF 92527).
146 Rules for Uniform Domain Name Dispute Resolution Policy, para 3(b)(x).
147 Rules for Uniform Domain Name Dispute Resolution Policy, para 3(b)(i).

cancel it. Cancelling it would appear to leave open the chance that another usurper will register the name.

(3) Specify any connected legal proceedings

Finally, the complainant must specify any legal proceedings in connection with the domain name[148]. In its absolute discretion, the panel may use such proceedings to decide not to proceed to its decision or suspend or terminate its proceedings[149]. Clearly, it is therefore in the interests of any domain name holder to initiate declaratory legal proceedings prior to a trade mark holder commanding a complaint under the Rules. This may dissuade or delay the panel from adjudicating over the domain name.

The provider will then review the complaint and then either:

(i) Within three calendar days, forward the complaint to the respondent ('commencement date')[150]; or
(ii) Inform the complainant and respondent that the complaint is administratively deficient, allowing the complainant five calendar days to correct the deficiencies[151].
(iii) Within 20 days of the commencement date the respondent must submit a response akin in all requirements to the complaint[152].
(iv) Within no more than a further 15 days (35 days post commencement date) the constitution of the panel is decided[153].
(v) Within 14 days of its appointment (49 days post commencement date) the panel will decide the dispute and inform the provider[154].
(vi) Within three days of the provider receiving the decision (52 days post commencement date) the provider informs the parties of the decision[155].
(vii) If the complainants wins and the domain name is to be cancelled or transferred, the domain name holder has ten business days (at least 62 days post commencement date) to start legal proceedings so halting the implementation of the decision[156].

In summary, it would appear that a domain name holder has little to lose by using the approximate two months to prepare legal proceedings to retain the domain name.

6. Protect domain name from registration companies

All registration companies would prefer to remove themselves from any disputes as quickly as possible. Indeed the ICANN policy states that it 'will not participate in any way in any dispute between you and any party other than us

148 Rules for Uniform Domain Name Dispute Resolution Policy, para 3(b)(xi).
149 Rules for Uniform Domain Name Dispute Resolution Policy, para 18(a).
150 Rules for Uniform Domain Name Dispute Resolution Policy, para 4(a).
151 Rules for Uniform Domain Name Dispute Resolution Policy, para 4(b).
152 Rules for Uniform Domain Name Dispute Resolution Policy, para 5.
153 Rules for Uniform Domain Name Dispute Resolution Policy, para 6(b)–(f).
154 Rules for Uniform Domain Name Dispute Resolution Policy, para 15(b).
155 Rules for Uniform Domain Name Dispute Resolution Policy, para 16(a).
156 Rules for Uniform Domain Name Dispute Resolution Policy, para 4(k). See *Jay D Sallen v Corinthians Licenciamentos* No 01–1197 (1st Cir, 5 December 2001).

regarding the registration and use of [the] domain name'[157]. Because of this, and worries of liability, some domain name owners have found these 'middle men' a little too willing to transfer, cancel or 'hold' a domain name where there is an indication of a dispute. This may have served one party, but it can be extremely inconvenient if unwarranted.

For this reason domain name owners have attempted to injunct registration companies from suspending the domain name *until* the outcome of any parallel trade mark dispute is settled. Data Concepts sued both Network Solutions and Digital Consulting for attempting to interfere with its domain name, 'dci.com'[158]. On this basis, Data Concepts sought a declaratory judgment establishing its right to use the domain name and an injunction preventing Network Solutions from interfering with that use. Network Solutions has agreed to maintain the status quo by letting Data Concepts continue use of the domain name. Roadrunner Computer Systems and Clue Computing Inc have also sought to injunct Network solutions on a similar basis[159].

Despite Network Solutions' desire to avoid being drawn into litigation it is not always successful in remaining out of court[160]. In *WorldSports Networks Ltd v ArtInternet SA*[161] Network Solutions was ordered never to allow the defendant to register another similar name as the plaintiff's trade mark. In the main however, Network Solutions and other registrars have been remarkably successful, and tremendously committed to convincing courts that they should not be involved in domain name disputes. Conversely, the courts are content to hear and decide a dispute while a registrar is carrying out investigations[162].

7. Monitor Dispute Resolution Policies

Over the past five years, domain name authorities have developed and honed their dispute resolution policies. InterNIC, Network Solutions and now ICANN, published the first policy in November 1995, the second in September 1996, the third in February 1998 and the current more generic policy since 24 October 1999. Each differs from the previous one both in the substance of what is considered to be a 'dispute' and the formalities required to conduct the regulation of the dispute. Nominet, the registry for '.uk' domain names released its new policy on the 24 September 2001.

Advisors and brand owners should therefore regularly check the effective policy at any material time. Changes to the policy are not brought expressly to the notice of a domain name owner and certainly are not brought to the attention of potential complainants. It should therefore be part of any domain name litigation first to check which resolution policy currently binds the domain name owner.

157 ICANN Uniform Domain Name Dispute Resolution Policy, para 6.

158 *Data Concepts Inc v Digital Consulting Inc* (MD Tenn, filed 8 May 1996).

159 *Roadrunner Computer Systems Inc v Network Solutions Inc* Civil Docket No 96–413 A (ED Va, filed March 26, 1996); *Clue Computing Inc v Network Solutions Inc* No 96 CV 694 (Boulder City, Colo. June 12, 1996) – this was based on contractual claims.

160 Owners of registered trade marks should be careful in threatening those who apply a registered trade mark as a sign to a website or as a domain name. If worded without care, a warning letter or 'letter before action' may fall within the 'groundless threats' provisions of the Trade Marks Act 1994, s 21. See *Prince v Prince plc* [1998] FSR 21.

161 US District Court for the Eastern District of Pennsylvania, Civil Action No 99–CV–616, 27 April 1999.

162 *Lawyers Online Ltd v LawyerOnline Ltd* (7 July 2000, unreported).

Trade marks on the World Wide Web

The World Wide Web can present text, pictures, sounds, music, movies and animations. The Trade Mark Act 1994 does not, of itself, prevent any of these items being protected by a trade mark. The only limitation on the nature of a mark is that it must be[163]:

> 'capable of being represented graphically, and capable of distinguishing goods or services of one undertaking from those of other undertakings.'

The condition that the mark used on the Internet be capable of graphic representation is unlikely to present much of a hurdle, even in unusual cases.

10. To signify that a program is being used to secure websites, its designer uses a small Java applet on every secure site. This applet shows an animation of a keyhole being secured by a red thumb. The programmer can apply to register this applet as a trade mark. Both a frame-by-frame 'storyboard' of the animation and the applet code should be sufficient to represent the trade mark graphically[164].

Sounds or music can also, in appropriate cases, be registrable. A sound can be represented graphically both as a description and as a series of notes or frequencies. With the increased use of jingles on websites, this may be a useful way of protecting the goodwill in a website.

Apart from these new forms of trade mark, the use of symbols, graphics and words remain registrable and will probably form the greatest number of trade marks on the web.

It has already been explained that in registering a trade mark for use on the World Wide Web one needs to be careful about for which goods and services those registrations are made[165]. It has also been explained that for owners of existing trade marks often there will be no need to expand the scope of their protection, although there may be a need to encompass its use for electronic goods or services[166].

Infringement on the web

There are two stages to every trade mark infringement alleged to have been committed over the web[167]. The first is whether the wrong complained of occurred within the jurisdiction of the English courts[168]. The second stage is

163 Trade Marks Act 1994, s 1(1).
164 The Derbyshire Building Society has registered in class 36 the gesture made by a person tapping one side of his or her nose with an extended finger, normally the index finger: No 2, 012, 603 on 28 February 1995.
165 See 'New trade mark', at page 167.
166 See 'Additional trade mark classes', at page 166.
167 This chapter focuses on a trade mark that is infringed by a sign present on the Web, rather than a trade mark on the web that is infringed on some other medium.
168 See page 211 et seq.

whether the use of the sign constitutes infringement of the registered trade mark. For this section's analysis, however, the substantive issues will be taken first: what is infringement on the web?

Examples of infringement on the web

Websites are used for marketing as well as for actually providing goods and services; true ecommerce rather than mere advertising. Sites can act as a billboard, an agent, and a shop and till. All these activities will involve the use of a variety of words, symbols and other signs that could potentially conflict with others' trade mark rights[169]. The US 9th Circuit Court of Appeals warned of future disputes occurring on the Internet: 'We now reiterate that the Web, as a marketing channel, is particularly susceptible to a likelihood of confusion since, as it did in this case, it allows for competing marks to be encountered at the same time, on the same screen.'[170] This section examines what activities on the Internet can constitute *trade mark* infringement. This includes an examination of the use of 'metatags' and an analysis of the use by search engines of 'key words'.

Infringement on website

A person who offers or exposes goods for sale, or puts them on the market under a sign, or offers or supplies services under that sign, may infringe a registered trade mark if that sign conflicts with the trade mark in question[171].

11. A website lists various programs for sale under the Microsoft logo and uses the Microsoft logo on the small icons that represent each program itself. The name of each program begins 'Microsoft' or 'MS'. Microsoft is not the developer of any of these programs. It is of little legal consequence that this is on a website: this is use of a sign by exposing and offering goods for sale under a registered trade mark.

Section 10(4)(d) provides another example of the use of a sign that can constitute infringement, all other things being equal. This is where a person uses the sign in advertising. Trade mark owners will not be able to sue successfully all those on the web who merely use their trade marks. Having proved 'use' the harder proof is that there was infringement.

Trade mark infringement by metatags

A metatag is a statement on a website which can be read by a search engine but is not displayed when one views the website. Metatags are there to help search

169 It is submitted that the Internet as a medium does not alter the legal tests needed to establish infringement of a trade mark by a sign on a web page. Trade mark texts should be consulted in this respect; but see 'Protecting domain names', at page 171 for illustrations of the scope of s 10(1) and (3).

170 *GOTO.com v Disney* (US 9th Circuit Court of Appeals, No 99–56691, DC No CV–99–01674–TJH).

171 Trade Marks Act 1994, s 10(4)(b).

engines understand which sort of visitors may appreciate the website in question. For example, the following could be included in the HTML code making up a law firm's website: <META name="keywords" content="law, legal, lawyer, litigation">. This code will not be visible to most visitors to the website[172]. The law firm includes this code to ensure that, even if the words 'law', 'legal', 'lawyer' and 'litigation' are not actually used within any articles on the website, someone entering 'lawyer' into a search engine may still be directed to the firm's website.

Metatags may be used to 'trick' search engines to display details of a site that is not actually connected with the metatag used. In illustration, one may enter into a search engine, the brand name 'Microsoft'. If a competitor had used that registered trade mark as a metatag on their website, one may be shown a link to that competitor's site when in fact, one may have been searching only for Microsoft. This 'bait and switch' is vexing courts on both sides of the Atlantic for one main reason. Are there any occasions when one can legitimately use such a metatag or will it always constitute trade mark infringement?

Infringement of registered trade mark

The US case *Playboy Enterprises v Terri Welles*[173] provides a good example of legitimately using a metatag which is identical to a registered trade mark. Terri Welles was Playboy's Playmate of the Year for 1981. She was sued by Playboy Enterprises Inc for, amongst other issues, having certain metatags on her personal erotica website. These metatags were identical to the Playboy Enterprises Inc's registered trade marks, 'Playmate' and 'Playboy'. In short, were this dispute under English law, this would be a case concerning use of a sign identical to a registered trade mark in relation to identical goods and services.

The Court of Appeals rejected the District Court's previous decision. It said:

> 'Forcing Welles and others to use absurd turns of phrase in their metatags, such as those necessary to identify Welles, would be particularly damaging in the internet search context. Searchers would have a much more difficult time locating relevant websites if they could do so only by correctly guessing the long phrases necessary to substitute for trademarks. We can hardly expect someone searching for Welles' site to imagine the same phrase proposed by the district court to describe Welles without referring to Playboy – "the nude model selected by Mr. Hefner's organization . . ." Yet if someone could not remember her name, that is what they would have to do. Similarly, someone searching for critiques of Playboy on the internet would have a difficult time if internet sites could not list the object of their critique in their metatags.'

Were this case heard under English law, the Trade Marks Act 1994 could be applied. As discussed above, s 10(1) states that it is an infringement for a person

172 Some, of course, will use the 'View Source' command from their browser to see this, and other, hidden code.

173 US Court of Appeals, 9th Circuit, No 00–55009, DC No CV–98–00413–JNK, 1 February 2002.

to use in the course of trade a sign which is identical with a registered trade mark and in relation to goods or services which are identical with the goods or services for which the trade mark is registered. In this situation, there is little doubt that the metatags used by Ms Welles are identical to the trade marks registered by Playboy Enterprises Inc. It is also clear that Ms Welles' website operates in relation to identical goods and services for which the trade marks are registered.

What remains to be examined is whether or not the use of a metatag is use of a sign in the course of trade. There are two main elements to this issue. First, in general, can a metatag *ever* be a sign used in the course of trade; it is, after all, meant to be invisible to the human eye. Second, is Ms Welles using the metatags as signs in the course of trade? We will ascertain that metatags can indeed be signs used in the course of trade but that Ms Welles' sporting of 'Playmate' as a metatag is unlikely to be deemed as use in the course of trade.

The legislation directs courts to determine whether there is 'use' of a sign in the course of trade. It is, however, true that most of the cases focusing on the question of what is 'use' look to a customer's perception. This seems to indicate that the sign complained of needs to be seen by the customer. The legislation does not direct courts to determine whether there is 'display' of a sign in the course of trade, however. It just so happens that the types of 'uses' complained about in the majority of cases so far are where the sign *is* visible to the customer.

A metatag, while not seen by the user, is seen 'on behalf' of the user by the search engine. Indeed, a user of a search engine positively relies on a search engine to interpret the metatags. Users of search engines want to be shown sites that are as close to the ones they would choose themselves if they had time to read the 2,500 million or so web pages. With this in mind, it seems arguable that the use of a metatag may constitute use of a sign even though most users will never see the sign itself; they will, however, see the impact of its use. In a case discussed below, Mr Justice Pumfrey said: 'The sign in a metatag is being used to suggest that this site is to be treated in a manner appropriate to the way in which the trade mark owner's site should be treated'[174].

Having concluded that the use of a metatag may well be use of a sign (for the purposes of registered trade mark infringement), it is then time to examine Ms Welles' metatags to establish whether they have been used 'in the course of trade'. It has been discussed that whether a sign is used 'in the course of trade' is determined more by the facts of the situation than any clear legal distinction. Certainly, if one reads the European Court decision in *Hölterhoff v Freiesleben*[175] it seems arguable than an English court would permit Ms Welles to use the metatags on her website. Ms Welles is merely using the brand names to convey her pedigree as a model.

Passing off

The 'classical trinity' needed for a passing off claim has been discussed above. Let us assume that Playboy has the first aspect of that trinity: goodwill. Next we must consider whether there is any misrepresentation, resulting in damage.

174 *Reed Executive plc v Reed Business Information Ltd* [2002] 29 LS Gaz R 33.
175 Case C–2/00 [2002] All ER (EC) 665.

Misrepresentation

'Misrepresentation' is a statement of the perception of the public; the public should be moved to believe that the defendant's goods or services are those of the claimant. It should not matter whether or not the perception of the public is altered *directly*, say by a confusingly similar domain name, or *indirectly*, by using an identical metatag to a brand with goodwill.

In the *Reed v Reed* case mentioned above, both parties used the brand name 'Reed' in relation to a variety of products and services[176]. The defendant used the metatag 'Reed' on its recruitment site, 'Totaljobs.com'. Mr Justice Pumfrey paid considerable attention to the claim that this metatag infringed the claimant's registered trade mark claim but did not deeply consider the passing off claim. He stated: 'So far as the invisible uses [being the metatag uses], the answer [to whether or not there is passing off] seems to turn on the question whether the defendants can be said to be responsible in any way for the appearance of the site in response to a search against "Reed", and, if so, what the nature of that responsibility is.' On the question of registered trade mark infringement he succinctly frames the issue: 'The short test, which must be applied with caution, is whether the sign tells the truth about the site.'

This author believes that such a low-hurdled test cannot be applied with enough caution. One must take into account the *context* of the search results. Albeit in relation to the different issue of infringement of a registered trade mark by the use of a domain name, Jacob J in *Avnet Inc v Isoact* sensibly observed[177]:

> 'It is a general problem of the Internet that it works on words alone and not words relating to goods or services. So, whenever anyone searches for a word even if a searcher is looking for the word in one context, he will, or may find, Web pages or data in a wholly different context. This may be an important matter for the courts to take into account in considering trade mark and like problems.'

When bearing in mind this commercial reality of search engines' results, it seems apparent that Ms Welles' metatags *do* 'tell the truth about the site'. She was indeed Playboy's Playmate in 1981 and is honestly referring to that to describe the stature of her modelling career.

Damage

Where there is misrepresentation one must still ascertain whether there is damage from the use of a metatag? It has been mentioned above that the

176 In an earlier English case, *Roadtech Computer Systems Ltd v Mandata (Management and Data Services) Ltd* [2000] ETMR 970, Master Bowman also was asked to address the question of whether or not metatags can result in passing off. For the purposes of this chapter it is regrettable that he stated 'no positive defence [was] put forward but the necessary ingredients for a claim in passing off and the evidence in the claimant's application are nowhere challenged in the defendant's evidence and have not indeed been the subject of serious challenge before me.' Little can therefore be derived from this case and, in the area of metatags, reliance on it is not recommended.

177 [1998] FSR 16 at 18. Cf US Court of Appeals decision in *Brookfield v West Coast* 174 F 3d 1036, 1063–64 (9th Cir 1999).

required quantity of damage is not great: 'The question is whether the relevant activities of the defendants are on such a small scale leading to such a small injury that it can be ignored.'[178]

On the one hand, the use of a metatag will simply ensure that the defendant's site is listed in the search results together with the claimant's site. There may be no damage at all. The metatag will not *exclude* the claimant's site. On the other hand, websites fight to be placed by search engines at the top of the list of results, and certainly on the 'first page'. The more rogue entries, such as from those with infringing metatags, the greater the risk of the genuine site being displaced. This author therefore would suggest that the use of a metatag does not *per se* cause damage but that it will not be unusual to cause such damage. This does not entirely accord with the view of Mr Justice Pumfrey in *Reed v Reed*.

Albeit in relation to loss resulting from registered trade mark infringement, Mr Justice Pumfrey seems to lean towards it not being 'normal' to suffer such loss or damage. He states:

> 'Furthermore, it seems to me that it will not normally be possible to prove loss merely by virtue of the fact that the [defendant's] site appears on a particular search, it nothing in the search results or in the site itself uses the infringing sign. Merely to present the site at some point in a list of results should not be sufficient.'

This certainly does not accord with the commercial reality. Websites will pay substantially to be ranked on the first page, and at the top of the first page, of any search listings. Indeed, some search engines make a virtue out of being 'even-handed' and not permitting the purchase of higher rankings. It follows that damage may well be caused by being relegated below a certain position on the listings page. The facts and statistics of the search results for the many search engines need to be investigated (and retained by the relying party) to determine the extent, if any, of the damage.

12. Deftly is a well-known manufacturer of ultrasound equipment. It competes with another manufacturer called GUB Equip. They each have a website. GUB Equip's contains many articles that objectively compare its equipment with Deftly's. Deftly is concerned that these articles may lead to a search engine displaying a link to GUB Equip's website when someone is searching for Deftly's website. In response it includes the distinctive metatag 'GUB Equip' on its website. This may well result in passing off whereas GUB Equip's honest use of the Deftly brand is likely to be legal.

Sale of key words by search engines

Search engines rank the results for any given search in one or both of two ways: objectively or subjectively. The objective method strictly utilises an algorithm or program to rank the results in some decreasing order of relevance. Depending on the particular interests of the user, the most relevant results should be shown at the top of the listing. Most users of search engines are familiar with this ranking and may favour search engines that seem to 'know' what they are searching for.

178 *Taittinger v Allbev Ltd* [1993] 2 CMLR 741 at 753 [27] per Gibson LJ.

The alternative search method is subjective in that ranking depends on whether a given website has purchased a 'key word' from the search engine. In such a situation, the search engine will bestow the purchasing website with a greater relevance than it otherwise may have had. Complaints occur because some search engines may sell key words that are not generic but are in fact trade marks owned by entities other than the purchaser.

It follows that when a user searches for a brand name, an 'accurate' search engine will display the brand owner's website together with the other highly ranked search results. In fact, users performing search queries for a company's trade names and marks are clearly relying on the goodwill inherent in the name or mark, and are likely searching for the source of the goods corresponding to those names or marks. Conversely, a search engine may skew the ranking of the results towards those sites that have purchased the searched-for brand name. This is sometimes called 'paid placement' or 'bid for location'. In this situation, the search engine may be accused of registered or unregistered trade mark infringement.

In *Body Solutions v AltaVista, FindWhat, Kanoodle and Overture*[179] the plaintiff, Mark Nutritionals, owned the registered trade mark 'Body Solutions'. It claimed that when these words were typed into the defendants' various search engines, rival sites using the trade mark appeared first on the resulting list of relevant sites. In illustration, PerfectHealth4Life.com paid Overture 72 cents each click to be at the top of the results list when someone searched for 'Body Solutions'. As a clear indication of PerfectHealth4Life.com's true intent, it is worthwhile stating that it did not even sell the plaintiff's product.

The plaintiff claimed that the search engines, for example Kanoodle, profited by using the trade mark. Kanoodle charged the plaintiff's rivals a sign-up fee and a small sum of money each time users of its search engine click on a search result to direct them to the website. Similar allegations were made in *Playboy Enterprises v Netscape and Excite* in June 1999 in which Playboy claimed the defendants used the sale of key words, including 'Playboy' and 'Playmate', to generate banner advertising above the displayed results[180].

These two cases, and others like them, indicate that brand owners are concerned over the trading of 'key words' incorporating their trade marks. What follows is an analysis under both registered and unregistered trade mark law of a brand owner's legal arguments.

Infringement of registered trade mark

Were the 'Body Solutions' case heard under English law, the Trade Marks Act 1994 could be applied. As discussed above, s 10(1) states that it is an infringement for a person to use in the course of trade a sign which is identical with a registered trade mark and in relation to goods or services which are identical with the goods or services for which the trade mark is registered. In this situation, there is little doubt that the key words used by both the search engine and potentially the purchasers of the key words are identical to the trade marks

179 Complaint filed in February 2002 in United States District Court for the Western District of Texas, San Antonio Division.
180 55 F Supp 2d 1070 (CD Cal, 1999).

registered by Mark Nutritionals. It is also likely to be the case that the key word purchasers operates in relation to identical goods and services for which the trade marks are registered.

What remains to be examined is whether or not the 'sale' of a key word is use of a sign in the course of trade. This seems free from doubt to this author. The key words themselves, in contrast to a metatag, are actually discussed, negotiated and form the subject of a contract between the search engine and a purchaser. They are certainly used as a 'sign'. Further, it must be difficult to argue that it not use in the course of trade to 'sell' or 'rent' or claim any fiscal benefit from a series of words in directly in relation to a registered trade mark. The search engine, in treating a sign identical to the trade mark as a commodity, is using it in the course of trade. And, rather like a metatag, the sign in the keyword is being used by the search engine to suggest to its users that the site that purchased the keyword is to be treated in the same way as the trade mark owner's site.

Passing off

The 'classical trinity' needed for a passing off claim has been discussed many times above. As for the examination of metatags, let us assume that Mark Nutritionals has the first aspect of that trinity: goodwill. We now consider whether there is any misrepresentation, resulting in damage.

Misrepresentation

'Misrepresentation' is a statement of the perception of the public; the public should be moved to believe that the defendant's goods or services are those of the claimant. It does not matter whether or not the perception of the public is altered *directly*, say by a confusingly similar domain name, or *indirectly*, by linking a description and address of a website to a brand name with goodwill.

As for our discussion of passing off through use of metatags one must determine, with caution, two issues. First, are the defendants responsible in any way for the appearance of the site in response to a search against the trade mark? Clearly the search engine *is* wholly responsible for the appearance of the interloping site. The second element of the test is, what is the nature of that responsibility? A search engine 'selling' words identical to a brand name with goodwill is trading off the reputation, and hence value, of those words to someone *other* than the site to whom the goodwill would otherwise attract.

Damage

Where there is misrepresentation one must still ascertain whether there is damage from the use of a keyword. As for a metatag, the sale of a keyword may simply ensure that the imposter's site is listed in the search results *together* with the claimant's site. In the Mark Nutritionals case, the sale of the key words put this company seventeenth in the list of websites on one search engine. This may be no damage at all. The key words will not *exclude* the claimant's site. On the other hand, not being on the first page may be tantamount to not being listed at all. Just as with metatags, this author believes such sale of key words does not per se cause damage but that it will not be unusual to cause such damage[181]. Just as for metatag cases, the claimant must research and retain copies of the facts and statistics of the search results for the search engine to determine the extent, if any, of the damage.

Jurisdiction over infringement

Private international law and intellectual property law have an uneasy coexistence. What is uneasy is that the older rules of jurisdiction and choice of law rely on tangible 'things' being dealt with by people in fixed locations. These older rules are now layered with newer rules which, regrettably, themselves do not adequately address intellectual property. The Internet in particular highlights these inadequacies. A web developer in America may knowingly put a UK trade mark on a website maintained in Holland but accessible throughout the world. In this situation do the English courts have any jurisdiction to hear complaints of infringement from the UK trade mark proprietor? The proprietor may complain that the American web developer was a secondary infringer and that the Dutch controller was a primary infringer of the trade mark by using the sign in an infringing manner. Our courts are being faced with many problems like this; it is therefore important to examine the issues for the judges who sit in those courts, and for the litigants who deserve reasoned judgment.

The Brussels Convention became part of the UK's domestic law in 1982 and was then replaced by the Brussels Regulation which, for the purposes of intellectual property, is very similar[182]. Laddie J observed in *Coin Control Ltd v Suzo International (UK)*[183]: 'One of [its] purposes . . . is to replace the differing domestic rules, at least in relation to forum, by a simple set of rigid provisions forcing litigation into the courts of one country and out of the courts of others.'

Readers somewhat familiar with this area must not be confused into concluding that the Electronic Commerce Directive, and its implementing Electronic Commerce (EC Directive) Regulations 2002, address such questions of private international law. First, they only apply to those Service Providers which are established within the EU. Second, the statutes certainly do not determine which country's *courts* will decide a particular dispute and certainly not which country's *law* will apply in a given situation. They merely prevent in particular circumstances a Service Provider established in a Member State outside the UK being restricted from conducting activities inside the UK which would have been legal in their Member State[184]. However, these particular circumstances do not extend to intellectual property issues[185]. The Electronic Commerce Directive

181 See the Dutch Appeal Court's decision in *VNU Business Publications BV v Monster Board BV* [2002] ETMR 1, 1. In this appeal, the Court determined that not only was the key word not inherently distinctive but that its purchase merely prevented the claimant from having its banner advertisement shown above the search results.

182 This entered into force on 1 March 2002 (2001 OJ L012, 16.01.2001). This chapter relies upon cases heard under the Brussels Convention to construe the manner in which similar cases will be heard under the Brussels Regulation. Consequently, there are occasions when this text will use extracts from cases heard under the Brussels Convention as though the court were addressing the Brussels Regulation.

183 [1997] FSR 660.

184 Regulation 7.

185 Regulation 4(4)(1) and art 3(3), Annex, first indent.

and Regulations therefore have absolutely no influence over the jurisdiction and applicable law rules applied to intellectual property disputes.

The Brussels Regulation provides simple rules on where a claimant can sue when 'choosing' between the member states. Article 2 sets out the primary rule: defendants must be sued in the courts of their domicile unless another article derogates from this rule[186]. In the words of Mr Justice Laddie 'ie the plaintiff must play away'. Article 5 provides a list of particular types of proceedings that may be brought in additional courts. Article 5(3) states that in matters relating to tort one may sue in the courts of the place where the harmful event occurred or may occur. It is clear from the Regulation, and clarified by the courts' consideration of the Convention, that intellectual property infringements fall within this article[187]. These two rules, but art 2 especially, appear to provide the foundation for a foreign intellectual property infringement, indeed a multiplicity of infringements, to be brought before the UK courts. However, art 22(4) (and art 16(4) under the older Convention) states that proceedings concerning the validity of patents and other registered rights must be determined in the country of registration.

This distinction is extremely important for trade mark infringements committed over the Internet because, as will be seen, infringement of registered trade marks may be treated differently to infringement of unregistered trade marks, such as passing off actions. Two types of case can illustrate the impact of this distinction. Then we will consider under what circumstances the display of an English trade mark on a foreign website can bring the website owner within the jurisdiction of the English courts.

INFRINGEMENT OF UNREGISTERED RIGHTS ACROSS EUROPE

Mecklermedia Corporation was a Delaware corporation whose subsidiary, Mecklermedia Limited, had been involved in the organisation of trade shows in the UK. These shows used the name 'Internet World' and were organised in conjunction with a licensee. The shows were widely advertised and well attended. DC Congress was a German company which organised trade shows also called 'Internet World', but in Germany. To promote these shows, DC prepared a letter and brochure in English which were sent out to prospective attendees, including in the UK. They also established a website to promote their show at www.internetworld.de.

Mecklermedia alleged that DC committed the English tort of passing off and sought relief in relation to the tortious activities of DC originating from Germany. DC Congress applied inter alia for an order setting aside the writ on the grounds that the court does not have jurisdiction over it under the, then in force, Brussels Convention and thereby forcing Mecklermedia to litigate the UK issues in Germany[188].

Jacob J considered the general rule in art 2 that '[I]n footballing terms the plaintiff must play away', but art 5(3) permitted derogation from this in matters relating to tort where a defendant is sued in the courts of the place where the

186 *Fort Dodge Animal Health Ltd v Akzo Nobel* [1998] FSR 222.
187 *Mölnlyke AB v Procter & Gamble (No 4)* [1992] 4 All ER 47 at 52f–j, per Lord Justice Dillon.
188 *Mecklermedia v DC Congress* [1997] FSR 627.

harmful event occurred. This left the question: where did the harmful event occur?

Jacob J stated that, for English passing off, the harm is to the goodwill in England and to the effect of the reputation in England; the direct effect is of harm to the plaintiff's English property. He was confirmed in this view by extensively referring to the European Court of Justice's decision in *Dumez France v Hessiche Landesbank*[189] and *obiter* made by Knox J in relation to a hypothetical supposition in *Modus Vivendi v British Products Sanmex Co Ltd*[190].

Although the case tangentially concerned the Internet, Jacob J was keen to play down the novelty of his judgment:

> 'when an enterprise wants to use a mark or word throughout the world (and that may include an internet address or domain name) it must take into account that in some places, if not others, there may be confusion. Here it is clear that [the defendants] knew that [the plaintiffs] used the name "Internet World" and I do not think it is surprising that it is met with actions in places where confusion is considered likely.'

So, where unregistered intellectual property rights are in issue, such as passing off or copyright, a claimant within the EU may sue where those rights subsist.

Infringement of registered rights across Europe

Coin Controls Limited was the proprietor of three national patents which arose out of a single patent application made to the European Patent Office. Patents, like registered trade marks, are applied for to a central authority, examined and either granted or refused. The subject matter of the patents was a so-called 'Coin Hopper', a device used to dispense winnings from fruit machines. The four defendants were each in the same market as Coin Controls and the first defendant Suzo International (UK) Limited sold in England a coin dispensing device called the Cube Hopper. The plaintiff alleged this fell within the claims of its UK patent. It was also alleged that the Cube Hopper's offer for sale in Germany and Spain infringed the plaintiff's German and Spanish patents respectively.

The plaintiff was seeking interlocutory injunctions against all four defendants to restrain them from infringing the three patents in England, Germany and Spain[191]. The defendants applied to strike out all but Suzo UK from the proceedings and to strike out of the statement of claim all assertions relating to the infringement of the German and Spanish patents. For this chapter's purposes, the crucial question to be decided was whether infringement of the German and Spanish patents was to be heard in the UK High Court.

189 Case C–220/88 [1990] ECR 49.

190 [1996] FSR 790 at 802.

191 [1999] Ch 33. One could equally demonstrate the application of the Brussels Convention/Regulation to registered intellectual property rights by examining *Fort Dodge Animal Health Ltd v Akzo Nobel NV* [1998] FSR 222.

In relation to jurisdiction, art 16(4) of the Brussels Convention was considered. It could have been considering art 22(4) under the current Brussels Regulation. This, it may be recalled, states that proceedings concerning the validity of patents, and other registered rights, must be determined in the country of registration. In addition, art 25 of the Regulation states that a court of a contracting state should declare that it has no jurisdiction where it is seized of an action principally concerned with an art 22(4) matter. Of course, validity is often a major issue on UK patent and registered trade mark cases. So once the defendant raises validity, then court must hand the proceedings, of infringement and validity, over to the courts having exclusive jurisdiction over the issue.

Laddie J acted on this basis and threw out all the claims in relation to the foreign patents. He did not hide his unhappiness at reaching this conclusion, however. As he stated 'a defendant can, within limits, forum shop by deciding to attack on validity'. Were it not for art 22(4) (and then art 16(4)) or an attack on validity, there would be nothing to stop the UK courts adjudicating on a foreign patent or trade mark. So, where registered intellectual property rights are at issue, such as registered trade marks, a plaintiff within the EU may sue only where the trade mark was granted. In Mr Justice Laddie's words: 'The fact that registered and unregistered rights (eg passing off and registered trade mark proceedings) may be subject to different regimes could well produce a proliferation of litigation rather than the opposite.'[192]

This author would not wish to stand in the way of such a long line of authorities. But, it is important that the authorities are not applied out of their historical and technical context: on the Internet many acts done in relation to UK trade marks, even though appearing to originate from overseas, will be actionable in the UK. The excerpts above consider the situation where the activity occurs outside the UK. The courts are attempting to resolve the conflict of laws where the intellectual property right is dealt with in a territory other than the one that granted the right initially. For example, to apply a UK trade mark to a product in America is clearly outside the jurisdiction of the English courts: the action that constitutes the infringement occurs outside the UK. In contrast to this, there are situations where the action takes place outside the UK, but the infringement occurs within the territory. What follows is a consideration of the manner in which the courts decide when a claimant may sue in the UK for trade mark infringement.

Jurisdiction over trade mark infringement over the Internet

It has already been discussed that a UK-based website may sport a particular sign, which, under English law infringes a registered or unregistered trade mark. Like all disputes, however, one must first determine whether the English court will hear a particular case; the court must have jurisdiction. And we have seen that the English courts view their jurisdiction over registered and unregistered rights differently. The following section considers the related and critical issue of when an English court may decide that a *foreign* website infringes an English trade mark therefore leaving its owners open to being sued here.

192 [1999] Ch 33 at 53.

Nothing new under the sun

The fact that an English trade mark owner may try to sue a foreign defendant is nothing new. The Internet may have increased the prevalence of such cases but it certainly has not introduced them. In the 1950s in *R J Reuter Co Ltd v Ferd Mulhens*, the plaintiff was the registered proprietor of a number of English trade marks over the perfumes and associated products called '4711'[193]. The defendant, in Germany, was exclusively associated with the manufacture there and elsewhere of '4711' eau de cologne. On 23 October 1951, the defendant addressed a letter to the export agents for the plaintiff's product: the letter's envelope featured a '4711' that was in all respects identical with the plaintiff's trade mark. Reuter sued for trade mark infringement, inter alia, under the Trade Marks Act 1938, s 4(1)(b). Under this section if the registered mark is used in an advertisement issued to the public as importing a reference to some person having such a right, there may be infringement.

The Court of Appeal was convinced that sending the envelope, even from abroad, was an advertisement within the Act. The court disagreed that to infringe there must be an intention to use the mark in the UK in relation to goods in the course of some transaction in the UK[194].

> 'Since, admittedly, the device on the envelope was advertising matter, the use of the envelope constituted . . . an infringement of the plaintiffs' rights under section 4 if they are in other respects entitled to succeed.'

Merely because a website is accessible within the UK and uses a sign identical or similar to a registered or unregistered trade mark does not necessarily mean that there is infringement or passing off here. Certainly, in *Mecklermedia*, Mr Justice Jacob did not think it surprising that when an enterprise uses a domain name throughout the world it is met with actions in places where confusion is considered likely. Three US and UK cases, discussed below, have shown that the mere fact that a website is accessible in a particular country, however, may not be enough to bring the website owner before its courts[195]. Before finally leaving this discussion of trade marks and moving to copyright, we examine the key factors influencing these differing decisions.

Playboy v Chuckleberry Publishing

On 1 April 1981, Playboy Enterprises Inc, publishers of the magazine *Playboy*, were awarded an injunction against an Italian company called Tattilo, the publisher of *Playmen* magazine. The injunction prevented Tattilo from using the word 'playmen' or any confusingly similar word anywhere on the cover of a 'male sophisticate magazine' that is published, distributed or sold in the US. It should be noted that this injunction has no extra-territorial effect: it operates only against activities in the US. Indeed, in Italy, the Italian courts had ruled

193 [1954] Ch 50. The case was complicated by the Trading with the Enemy Act 1939, s 7(1), but the court was able to divorce that Act from the issue of infringement.
194 [1953] 2 All ER 1160 at 1174. Admittedly, this aspect has been subject to academic criticism.
195 Also see *Bonnier Media v Greg Lloyd Smith* (2002) Times, 10 July; and *V&S Vin & Sprit Aktiebolag v Absolut Beach Pty Ltd* [2001] All ER (D) 199 (May).

that 'Playboy' was a weak mark and was not entitled to protection there. Tattilo continued, not breaching the injunction, publishing *Playmen* in printed form in Italy.

Around 22 January 1996, Playboy discovered that Tattilo had created a website with the domain name 'www.playmen.it'. This site provided free access to moderately explicit images. By email subscription, viewers were able to access the Playmen Pro version of the site. Playboy Enterprises Inc moved for a finding of contempt in the US Courts against Tattilo for violating the injunction[196].

The court discovered that, as is true for most websites:

> '[t]he Playmen Internet site is widely available to patrons living in the United States. More to the point, *anyone* in the United States with access to the Internet has the capacity to browse the Playmen Internet site, review, and obtain print and electronic copies of sexually explicit pages of *Playmen* magazine.'

The first issue for the court was whether the 15-year-old injunction could have been violated despite the fact that the Internet was not contemplated at the time. The court was under no doubt that the injunction still had force to prevent distributions by the Internet into America.

To decide that the injunction was violated, the court had to find three conditions. First, that the word 'Playmen' had been used as part of any trade mark, service mark, brand name, trade name or other business or commercial designation. This condition was met partly by the domain name and partly by the Playmen logo being present on each page of the website. The second condition was also met: the use had to be in conjunction with an English language publication or related product. The final condition was the most analytically difficult for the court but the most pertinent for similar English disputes: the use had to be made in connection with sale or distribution within the US.

Before continuing with the court's analysis, it is worthwhile reconsidering the UK position. Under the Trade Marks Act 1994, s 10(4), a sale or distribution of a product under a sign will constitute use of that sign. And as the sign 'Playmen' is similar to 'Playboy' and is clearly being used in the course of trade, there is a strong likelihood that such use would infringe Playboy's trade mark in England. The court's analysis of whether the product was sold or distributed in the US is therefore as relevant to whether it would have been sold or distributed in the UK.

'boarding a plane, landing in Italy'

Tattilo argued that it was not distributing the pictorial images within the US. It argued that it was merely posting the images on a server in Italy. A computer operator who wished to view these images must, in effect, transport himself to Italy to view Tattilo's pictorial displays. The court summed up this analogy as,

> '[t]he use of the Internet is akin to boarding a plane, landing in Italy, and purchasing a copy of *Playmen* magazine, an activity permitted under Italian law. Thus the defendant argues that its publication of

196 *Playboy Enterprises Inc v Chuckleberry Publishing Inc* 939 F Supp 1032 (SDNY 1996).

> pictorial images over the Internet cannot be barred by the injunction despite the fact that computer operators can view these pictorial images in the United States.'

This reasoning will continue to be repeated by many defendants in cases involving the Internet. The logic of the argument works by stressing the passivity of those who host websites. First, the technology must be explained: a web server does not broadcast information of its own volition. A web server will only distribute information if another person actively requests it. This explanation allows the controller of a website to claim that he had no active role in distributing the information; the website owner may even highlight to a court that the computers that view websites are called 'clients' while those that store them are called 'servers'. The second limb of the argument is to suggest that this passivity indicates that it is the viewers of a site who move into the website's jurisdiction, not the website owner into the client's.

The court in this case was unconvinced by this passive bystander defence:

> '[the] defendant has actively solicited United States customers to its Internet site, and in doing so has distributed its products within the United States.'

The court was not legally concerned that the Internet site could be accessed from around the world; it is that the defendant accepted subscriptions from American customers that proved distribution in the US.

> 'While this court has neither the jurisdiction nor the desire to prohibit the creation of Internet sites around the globe, it may prohibit access to those sites in this country. Therefore, while Tattilo may continue to operate its Internet site, it must refrain from accepting subscriptions from customers living in the United States. In accord with this holding, an Italian customer who subsequently moves to the United States may maintain his or her subscription to the Internet site.'

Amongst other orders, the court ordered that Tattilo refrain from accepting any subscriptions from customers residing in the US. The order was backed up with a fine for non-compliance of $1,000 each day.

1-800 Flowers v PhoneNames

On 13 February 1993 a US-based trade mark applicant applied to register the trade mark 800-FLOWERS in respect of the services receiving and transferring orders for flowers and floral products. The application was opposed on a number of grounds including one relating to the Internet. The applicant argued that since 1992 it had a website under the domain name 1-800 FLOWERS. Interestingly, the applicant was not able to ascertain how many times the website has been accessed from the UK. Nevertheless, it alleged that the mere fact of internet activity is enough to establish an intention to use the mark in the UK for the purposes of registration. The Internet-aspect of the case therefore concerned whether a website accessible in the UK establishes actual use of the mark, or a bona fide intention to use the mark.

On 17 December 1998 the Trade Marks Registry rejected the grounds of opposition relied on by the opponent so accepting the mark for registration. The opponent then appealed to Mr Justice Jacob in the High Court[197] and subsequently to the Court of Appeal[198].

'putting a tentacle into the computer user's premises'

Jacob J allowed the appeal and rejected the argument that a website merely accessible in the UK was enough to prove 'actual use' of the mark on the website. Jacob J questioned the applicant's notion that placing a trade mark on a website was 'putting a tentacle' into the computer user's premises in the UK. Indeed, he was certain that 'the mere fact that websites can be accessed anywhere in the world does not mean, for trade mark purposes, that the law should regard them as being used everywhere in the world.'[199]

He contended that two of the relevant factors to determine 'use' in the UK were the intention of the website owner and what the reader will understand if he accesses the site.

The Court of Appeal followed the High Court's reasoning and rejected the fact of the website being merely accessible as being enough to constitute use[200]. The Court, *obiter*, stated[201]:

> 'There is something inherently unrealistic in saying that [a website owner] "uses" his mark in the United Kingdom when all he does is place the mark on the internet, from a location outside the United Kingdom, and simply wait in the hope that someone from the United Kingdom will download it and thereby create use on the part of [the website owner].'

EUROMARKET DESIGNS V PETERS

The claimant in this case was a US company which owned US stores trading under the brand 'Crate & Barrel'. It mainly sells household goods. Since 1988, it has owned a registered trade mark in the UK in relation to the words 'Crate & Barrel'. On the other side of the Atlantic, the defendants owned a store in Dublin called 'Crate & Barrel' which, since 1994, sells home furnishings and accessories. The claimant alleged two acts of infringement by an advertisement in a UK magazine and by their trade mark being used in the UK on defendants' website and applied for summary judgment[202].

The defendants contended that the paper advertisement and website did not constitute 'use' of the mark in the UK, or, was not 'use in the course of trade in the UK'. Jacob J dismissed the application for a summary judgment.

197 [2000] FSR 697 at 705.
198 [2001] EWCA Civ 721, [2001] 28 LS Gaz R 42.
199 [2000] FSR 697 at 705.
200 It also seems apparent that the scant facts of trade being conducted within the UK did not help the applicant. The Court of Appeal mentioned on more than one occasion that there was no evidence as to the extent of which the website had even been 'accessed' from the UK, let alone traded in the UK.
201 [2002] FSR 191 at para 137.
202 [2001] FSR 288.

Again, the courts (and Mr Justice Jacob) were required to determine what sort of actions for trade mark infringement involving use on a website fall within the jurisdiction of the English courts. And, again, counsel in the case resorted to 'real world' analogies to support their case.

'focussing a super telescope into the site'

Jacob J was not prepared to accept that the mere fact the 'crateandbarrel.ie' website was available in the UK suggested that the defendant was 'trading' in the UK. The business was local to Dublin and the website was actually being used to advertise their shop in Dublin. Were this not the case, the judge reasoned that the absurd conclusion would be that this little local business would be using the words 'Crate & Barrel' in every country of the world. The defendants only intended to sell to and in the Irish market; they did not seek trade in the UK. Mr Justice Jacob liked the defendant's counsel's analogy that: 'using the internet was more like the user focussing a super-telescope into the site concerned . . . the very language of the internet conveys the idea of the user *going to* the site – "visit" is the word.'[203]

Jacob J was keen to distinguish this case from one in which an overseas trader had not only advertised on the Internet but also in other ways, and offered and operated a real supply or goods or services in this country.

Factors under English law

These cases illustrate the relevant jurisdiction factors under English law. The starting point is that English courts and litigants must accept that the Internet permits access from any country in the world. This does not, without more, give the English courts jurisdiction over the contents of every server in the world. To gain jurisdiction under trade mark law, the owner of the server must infringe a UK trade mark within the UK.

The first factor is that the 'passive provider' argument has been rejected: telescopes trump tentacles. In contrast to criminal law, merely *permitting* a website to allow material to be distributed will not be viewed under English trade mark law as an active transmission or 'use'. The courts must look to the nature of the website: if its content is focussed on UK customers, there may be infringement. In *Flowers* particular attention was paid to the commercial audience of the website complained of in the case. A site which 'faces' the UK and possibly trades with UK consumers is more likely to find itself infringing a UK trade mark than one which both is clearly not directed at a UK audience and which does not permit trading with UK consumers.

The second factor is that non-Internet based advertising in the UK is likely to influence the decision that there is use within the jurisdiction. In *Mecklermedia*, *Euromarket* and *V&S* the courts took into account the nature, if any, of advertising within the UK. Advertising and other similar acts within the jurisdiction go to the intention of the defendant *to* trade with consumers in the UK.

The third relevant factor is blocking. That the Internet, technically, permits worldwide distribution does not necessarily mean that this limitless dissemination must be utilised. The customers of certain countries can be blocked out by

203 [2001] FSR 288, at 295–296.

the suffixes of their email addresses, the settings of their browser and other clues such as time zone. Those who pass through this net can be warned to go no further if they are from a particular jurisdiction. Finally, if services or goods are provided over the Internet, consumers from certain jurisdictions can be screened out at the contractual stage. If defendants from foreign jurisdictions do this, not as a sham, but with deliberate intent not to use a sign in the course of trade in the UK, they may avoid the jurisdiction of the UK trade mark courts. This can be learnt from the *Playboy v Chuckleberry* case. If the defendant does not, and freely advertises and sell goods throughout the world, they must appreciate that with profits of worldwide distribution they are accepting the potential risks of litigation in every court on the planet.

COPYRIGHT

Most material on the Internet is protected by copyright. It protects emails sent from one person to another and protects all the elements of an intricate website including all its mini-programs or executable code. Copyright can also protect the underlying material beneath that which appears on a screen: it protects say the original drawings which were converted into a digital animation on a home page. This width and depth of protection means that everyone using the Internet should be aware of their rights as creators of copyright works and their obligations as users of others' works. Users must also be aware of the forthcoming implementation into English law of the EC Directive on Harmonisation of Certain Aspects of Copyright and Related Rights in the Information Society, which addresses aspects of copyright and the Internet[204]. In addition, the Copyright, Designs and Patents Act 1988 grants not only a 'right to copy and not be copied' but also certain 'moral rights'.

This section considers the exact extent of copyright protection of material on the Internet. It examines the copyright in emails and postings to websites, and the copyright that protects websites. This examination of websites reveals that, although copyright protects the whole website, its constituent elements are also protected: a separate copyright attaches to the text, the graphics, and more active elements such as animations and sounds. Copyright even protects the complex executable programs embedded within a website.

Having discussed that copyright protects most material on the Internet, this section goes on to show that most material on the Internet is copied on a regular basis. Through a clashing of technology with older legislation, all information retrieved by a computer is deemed to have been copied. This width of copying results in a simple conclusion. Copyright disputes involving the Internet will rarely turn on the existence of copyright or if copying took place: the key will be whether or not the copier was explicitly or implicitly permitted to copy the work and whether the Electronic Commerce Regulations provide them with a suitable defence. This is particularly important when considering peer-to-peer copying groups facilitated by programs like Kazaa, Morpheus and the erstwhile Napster.

204 Where possible, this chapter alludes to the Patent Office and Department of Trade and Industry's Consultation Paper (7 August 2002) on the implementation. As ever, however, even with EU-originated legislation, the devil in such implementation is in the detail of the final statute.

The Internet works by copying. Emails are not actually sent and web pages are not purely viewed: they are both broken into packets and copied from one computer to another. Emails therefore are copied at least once – the original exists on the sender's computer and the recipient holds a copy. Web pages are also necessarily copied – the server computer hosts the original and each client computer stores another copy. Internet Service Providers who host chat rooms do not simply store people's original postings: like emails, the Internet Service Provider stores a copy of the posting. Even the executable code that livens most web pages is automatically copied from its host to a client computer. Although this indicates that all those involved in the Internet copy copyright material, they do not all infringe those copyrights. Much of the copying that takes place on the Internet is impliedly authorised by those who hold the copyright: the law implies a licence. This section focuses on the types of copying that regularly occur on the Internet and attempts to partition that which is legitimate or defensible copying from that which is infringement of copyright or moral rights.

The final section on copyright considers the force of English law on a telecommunications medium which facilitates infringements around the world. It is as easy to copy an English copyright work on the Internet from Brazil as it is from England. This section therefore concludes by examining the conflict of copyright laws that exist on the Internet. It then summarises the disputes that will be actionable in the English courts and those which may have to be litigated elsewhere.

Copyright works

There are two important questions that must be answered at the outset. First, is the work itself protected by copyright at all? Second, who owns the copyright? This is a query that is always relevant to a copyright issue, but particularly relevant for the Internet. More than any other medium, the Internet allows many individuals to interact to produce a copyright work. Taking the most simple of examples: a website company selling books hosts a 'Review and Rant' board on its website to which customers may post reviews, about which other customers may comment. This is repeated over many days creating a 'thread' that is shown on the website and stored on its Internet Service Provider's server. What rights have the individual customers who have posted up their reviews and comments? What rights has the website owner in relation to the entire thread, and the individual postings? These questions, and many more like them, will be examined but first there must be some analysis of what works are protected by copyright.

Elements for protection

Types of work

The Copyright, Designs and Patents Act 1988, s 1(1) states nine different types of work that can qualify for protection as a copyright work[205]. These are:

205 The Patent Office and Department of Trade and Industry's Consultation Paper (7 August 2002) on the implementation of EC Directive on Harmonisation of Certain Aspects of Copyright and Related Rights in the Information Society, indicates that cable programmes will be removed as a species of copyright work from the Act.

'(a) original literary, dramatic, musical or artistic works,
(b) sound recordings, films, broadcasts or cable programmes, and
(c) the typographical arrangement of published editions.'

Before moving to discuss which categories of work encompass which aspects of the Internet, an important point should be noted. The work which appears on the screen of someone viewing a website is not simply one copyright work, it is a collection of works, some side-by-side and some underlying the work shown on screen. For example, a home page consisting of graphics, text and which plays a recorded tune has at least four discrete copyright works that are evident and others underlying those. Separate copyrights will attach to the text on the page, the graphics and the sound recording. In addition, the copyright that protects computer programs may protect the entire home page. However, deeper than this is the protection that may attach to the musical score that was composed to play the recorded tune. Controllers of websites in particular must therefore understand that their servers are not holding simply one copyright work, but a montage of works. They should ensure that they have the right to use all the works and understand that a visually small aspect of a website may represent an entire copyright work.

Fixation

A requirement for most copyright works distributed over the Internet is that they are fixed on a material form; if a work is not fixed, even indirectly, then it is no more than an idea or concept. The Copyright, Designs and Patents Act 1988, s 33 provides a specific endorsement of this principle:

> 'Copyright does not subsist in a literary, dramatic or musical work unless and until it is recorded, in writing or otherwise[.]'

Copyright does not protect ideas; it protects the skill, labour and judgment exercised in converting an idea into something tangible. Merely recording an idea, however, does not provide protection over that idea.

13. Four individuals use a special instant messaging service which allows them to type messages to each other in real time; they can see one another's typing on their own screen as each letter key is pressed. The controller of the website realises that one of the individuals is a famous actor and keeps a copy of everything typed by the actor with a view to publishing it. Without a licence or assignment, the controller does not have the copyright to do this; the actor's typing is a copyright work that was formed when he converted his ideas into expressions through his keyboard.

Every copyright work has an author[206]. The person who is the author is the person who creates it. Generally, the first owner of a copyright work is its author[207]. This is, however, a general statement and those who work for others

206 Copyright, Designs and Patents Act 1988, s 9.
207 Copyright, Designs and Patents Act 1988, s 11(1).

in creating websites and online graphics should be aware that works made in the course of employment are first owned by their employer, subject to any prior arrangement[208].

> **14. A designer is employed by a bank for general design work and is asked to create a website for the bank: the site looks like the inside of a bank with graphics of cashiers counting money, help-desks and other features. Some months later the designer resigns from his post and starts working as a freelancer. He is asked to design a similar website for a building society. He reuses the graphics of the cashiers and help-desks. Unless this is provided for in his contract, he does not own the copyright in those graphics. He may be the *author* of the works, but having created them during his employment, the bank is the copyright *owner.***

Original works

Most copyright works must be original to be protected. The term 'original' does not mean novel or new; it refers to the fact that the work must *originate* from its author. It will therefore not be original if it is purely copied from another work and no independent skill, labour or judgment was used to produce the copy.

This requirement of originality has a second effect: because a work need not be novel or unique to acquire protection it is possible that two identical works are both protected by copyright and owned by different authors. In most areas identical works are rare and are the result of copying; on the Internet, there are instances of works being identical without copying. The most common example of this is the use of search engines. These are programs that can search for a given word or phrase amongst many websites with the engine producing a list of every occurrence of the searched term. Two different search engines both searching for the same term may well both produce identical lists. That these lists are identical does not mean that the works are not original; it is simply a quirk of digital precision and both may attract a separate and equally valid copyright[209].

> **15. A budding journalist 'cuts' an article he finds on a website (by pressing two keys) and 'pastes' it into an email. He sends this email to an editor of a newspaper claiming to have written the article. The editor publishes the article without paying the journalist. The journalist, however, may not be entitled to payment: he had no copyright in the email sent to the editor as it did not originate with him.**

Skill, labour or judgment

Until 1990 the aphorism, 'what is worth copying is worth protecting' was much in vogue. It originated from Peterson J's statement in a 1916 case, *University of London Press v University Tutorial Press*[210]. It seems to suggest that if a person

208 Copyright, Designs and Patents Act 1988, s 11(2).
209 It is, however, unlikely.
210 [1916] 2 Ch 601 at 610.

seeks to copy a work then the law will ensure that the work has sufficient protection to prevent that copying. This *post facto* attribution of rights has been doubted; the House of Lords in *Re Smith Kline & French Laboratories* said it was 'not the law'[211]. What English law requires is that some skill, labour or judgment must have been utilised to convert the idea into the fixed expression. The level of skill and labour needed to qualify is low[212]. Unlike the US, which looks more for creativity than mere labour, the fact than an author expends 'sweat of the brow' is generally enough to be granted copyright's protection over that work[213].

This has the legal result that most works that are original in the copyright sense will also have the minimal level of skill and labour required to enjoy protection. This becomes important where individuals on the World Wide Web have generated lists of useful sites for others to view. Under American jurisprudence there may be an argument that the list does not possess the 'minimal degree of creativity'[214]. Under English law, in contrast, copyright may be granted over such a list without the courts having significant recourse to the effort, or creativity of its author[215]. What is even more certain is that the list will qualify as a 'database' and, hence, be protected by the database right.

Types of protection

Copyright provides copyright owners with protection in the form of economic rights. These differ slightly for each particular category of copyright work but can be broadly summarised as follows: the owner of the copyright in a work has the exclusive right to copy it, issue it to the public in any form and adapt the work[216]. In addition the authors of certain types of copyright work enjoy moral rights which protect the integrity of the work and the right to be identified as the work's author. The implication of these rights on the Internet will be discussed under each aspect of the Internet considered below.

Qualification for protection

This book considers only when English law will grant copyright and moral right protection. This section also only deals with the law as it applies to works created after 1 August 1989. The section is concerned with the rights afforded to copyright works created *for* the Internet, rather than the wider rights afforded to copyright works that can be *used* on the Internet.

There are three alternative routes for a work to qualify as protected under the Copyright, Designs and Patents Act 1988:

211 [1990] 1 AC 64 at 106.

212 *Autospin (Oil Seals) Ltd v Beeline Spinning (a firm)* [1995] RPC 683 at 694 per Laddie J.

213 See *Feist Publications Inc v Rural Telephone Service* Co 499 US 330 at 364 (1991).

214 *Feist Publications Inc v Rural Telephone Service* Co 499 US 330 at 345 (1991).

215 Cf *CCC Information Services Inc v Maclean Hunter Market Reports Inc* 44 F 3d 61 (2nd Cir 1994).

216 The Patent Office and Department of Trade and Industry's Consultation Paper (7 August 2002) on the implementation of EC Directive on Harmonisation of Certain Aspects of Copyright and Related Rights in the Information Society, indicates that a new restricted act of 'communicat[ing] a work to the public' will be introduced at s 16(1)(d).

1. in relation to its country of first publication;
2. by reference to its author;
3. where applicable, by reference to the place from where it was broadcast[217].

If any one of the routes is satisfied, the work benefits from protection.

Place of publication

The question of where the work is first published[218] is complicated in an Internet environment. It is made available simultaneously throughout the world but where is it published? To address this question it is initially important to understand the stages in creating and 'publishing' a website.

When people speak of 'designing a website' they are technically creating a computer program. Either the designer creates the program by typing commands or uses another program visually to design the site and then allows that program to generate the appropriate commands. These programs that represent websites are written in special computer languages called HTML, Java, Flash and increasingly in XML. For copyright purposes, these languages describe to a computer what a particular web page should look like and how it should operate[219]. The program is then 'run' through a viewer's browser (maybe thousands of miles away) which interprets the commands and converts these back into a visual layout for the website. Similarly, any executable code embedded in the code is written on the designer's computer and then interpreted by the viewer's. For example, a designer may create some executable code in the form of a Java applet. This is stored on the designer's computer in and interpreted on the viewer's computer.

The 'publication' of a website is only when a viewer's computer is provided with a copy of the code from the server computer and the viewer's browser program converts this into a visual representation.

So a website is not published as such; it is made available on a server for the public to access over the Internet. It is published by means of an electronic retrieval system rather than an electronic distribution system. The Act construes this as being 'publication'[220]. But this still leaves open the issue of where that publication takes place. It is submitted that the old principles apply and that publication takes place not in the place of receipt of a copy but where the publisher invites the public to view the copies. Were this not the case, 'a periodical which is offered to the public by postal subscription and has 10,000 subscribers would have 10,000 places of publication'[221]. Applying this to the web, the

217 Copyright, Designs and Patents Act 1988, s 153. NB The Patent Office and Department of Trade and Industry's Consultation Paper (7 August 2002) on the implementation of EC Directive on Harmonisation of Certain Aspects of Copyright and Related Rights in the Information Society indicates that acts of 'broadcasting' are likely to be replaced by appropriate references to 'communication to the public'. This is likely to be the situation in s 153(3) although the section was not included in the Consultation's non-exhaustive list of references.
218 Copyright, Designs and Patents Act 1988, s 153(1)(b).
219 Copyright, Designs and Patents Act 1988, s 153(1)(b).
220 Copyright, Designs and Patents Act 1988, s 175(1)(a).
221 *British Northrop Ltd v Texteam Blackburn Ltd* [1974] RPC 57 at 66.

relevant place is from where the site material is made available[222]. If this is located in the UK or in another country to which the section extends[223], UK copyright will protect the site. This important question of place of publication for a website is therefore answered by where the server is located. This will be the physical location of the web server which may be located by reference to its Internet Protocol Address (the unique number which has a domain name as its alias).

16. An Iraqi company establishes a website, stored on a server based in Iraq, to publish anti-English propaganda aimed at Iraqis living in England. This propaganda is printed, verbatim, in a scathing newspaper article in an English newspaper. It will not be deemed to have been first published in England, even if the only accesses to the website are from England. England is the place of receipt; Iraq is the place of first publication under English law.

Simultaneous publication

In view of the conclusion that the place of the server is the place of publication it is vital to address how this rule works for a website on more than one server. These are called 'mirror sites' and are server computers holding identical copies of the website code so allowing more people to access the code at once. Website designers who wish to benefit from the English copyright regime must ensure that their porting of website code to such servers will not constitute first publication outside the requisite countries.

Simultaneous publication, for the purposes of the Act, appears reserved for when two separate distribution channels exist in separate countries. This will be the situation for two or more mirror sites. The rule that applies to this situation is simple: as long as material on one server inside a requisite country was made available within 30 days of the site's publication on another server, the site will qualify for copyright protection[224].

17. An individual establishes a website based on a server outside the requisite countries. After a couple of months the popularity of his site has grown so much as to warrant renting space on a server based in London. Unfortunately, one week after establishing this mirror site, a copycat site springs up also in London. The individual has missed by one month having his work qualify for protection.

The lesson of this is obvious: it makes little practical difference where a website is hosted. The server can physically be based anywhere in the world. Those web designers outside the requisite countries can therefore be advised to publish

222 See *McFarlane v Hulton* [1899] 1 Ch 884; and *British Northrop Ltd v Texteam Blackburn Ltd* [1974] RPC 57 as applied in *Television Broadcasts Ltd v Mandarin Video Holdings* [1984] FSR 111. This also accords with the definition that both 'publication' and 'commercial publication' refer to the issuing of the work to the public: Copyright, Designs and Patents Act 1988, s 175(1)(a) and (2)(a).

223 Copyright, Designs and Patents Act 1988, ss 155 and 157.

224 Copyright, Designs and Patents Act 1988, s 155(3).

simultaneously their site material on two servers, one within a requisite country. It is hard enough preventing worldwide infringement, but it is easier if rights over the work are gained in as many countries as possible.

Author qualification

There is another method to fall within the Copyright, Designs and Patents Act 1988 for copyright protection: if at the time the work was created its author was a 'qualifying person'[225].

A wide spread of people qualify, including[226]:

> 'a British citizen, a British Dependent Territories citizen, a British National (overseas), a British Overseas citizen, a British subject, a British protected person within the meaning of the British Nationality Act 1981, an individual domiciled or resident in the United Kingdom or a British dependency, a body incorporated under the law of a part of the United Kingdom or a British dependency.'

This is in addition to those citizens and subjects of the extra countries provided by the Copyright (Application to Other Countries) Order 1993[227].

18. An American web designer does not get a chance to publish her work before it is copied onto a London-based server. The copyright work in question, the Macromedia Shockwave animation, has not been published but the author is resident and domiciled inside one of the requisite countries. The work is, therefore, protected in the UK.

Broadcasts or cable programmes

The Copyright, Designs and Patents Act 1988, s 153(1)(c) includes a qualification for broadcasts and cable programmes which is the country from where the broadcast was made or the programme sent. The forthcoming changes to the Act as a result of the EC Directive on Harmonisation of Certain Aspects of Copyright and Related Rights in the Information Society is likely to alter this section of the Act. It is likely that cable programmes are to be removed altogether and that the country from where the broadcast was made will be supplemented by the place from where communication to the public was made. Unfortunately, the Patent Office and Department of Trade and Industry's Consultation Paper is silent on the qualification aspects of broadcasts. It is this chapter's assumption that other than truly live streaming (such as say a live concert being shown on a website) the Internet and the World Wide Web are not broadcasts or, as a rule, cable programmes. This is certainly the attitude being taken by the UK Government in consulting on the Communications Bill. It is also the view seemingly being taken by the Patent Office and Department of

225 Copyright, Designs and Patents Act 1988, s 154.
226 A paraphrasing of the Copyright, Designs and Patents Act 1988, s 154(1) and (2).
227 SI 1993/942.

Trade and Industry[228]. A website may qualify as a broadcast when it is genuinely published by broadcasting.

Definition of 'broadcast'

Section 6(1) currently defines a broadcast as being, essentially, a transmission by wireless telegraphy of visual images, sounds or other information[229]. Wireless telegraphy refers to sending electro-magnetic energy over paths not provided by a material substance constructed or arranged for that purpose[230]. The optical fibres and telephone wires that constitute the Internet are clearly arranged for the purpose of sending such energy: the Internet does not therefore facilitate broadcasts in the copyright sense.

The Patent Office and Department of Trade and Industry have suggested amendments to this section which confirm the exclusion of websites from the definition. The new proposed definition excludes: '[a]ny transmission included in an interactive service which operates in such a way that members of the public may at their individual request access a transmission from its commencement at a time they select or determine'[231]. What is intended by this amendment is to exclude online or broadcast activities where the public are not 'forced' to watch particular aspects at particular times. So, because the pages of an ecommerce website can be viewed in any order at any time, it falls within the exclusion. Nearer the 'edge' of the exclusion is a website which features 'streaming' of a particular archived news report. Here, the website 'plays' the old footage from the beginning until the end (unless stopped earlier). In contrast to the live news report, the viewer may start the streaming when they desire; it too falls within the proposed exception and so outside the proposed definition of broadcast. Where a website features live news footage and no archive, the viewer cannot choose the starting time; if they are late and miss the start of the footage they will have missed that section. Broadcasts wait for no man.

Definition of 'cable programme'

A 'cable programme' is soon to be removed from the species of copyright works under the Act. Nevertheless, a case concerning this old species highlights some important concepts, and misconceptions, about the Internet. So while the definition remains law or even the Internet continues to operate as it does today, the following remains very relevant.

A cable programme refers to any item included in a cable programme service; this is defined as a service which consists wholly or mainly in sending visual images, sounds or other information by means of a telecommunications system, otherwise than by wireless telegraphy, for reception in one of two ways. First, at

228 The Patent Office and Department of Trade and Industry's Consultation Paper on the implementation of EC Directive on Harmonisation of Certain Aspects of Copyright and Related Rights in the Information Society.

229 Proposed changes to s 6(1) widen the means of transmission from wireless telegraphy to a concept of 'electronic means' which would include wireless telegraphy.

230 Copyright, Designs and Patents Act 1988, s 178. The Copyright and Related Rights Regulations 1996 alteration of this definition does not change its application to the Internet.

231 Proposed s 6(1A).

two or more places whether for simultaneous reception or at different times in response to requests. The second way is for presentation to members of the public[232].

Sending information

It is submitted that few websites or presences on the Internet will be within this definition. First, a website does not 'send' material; if anything it is collected. As with dialling someone's telephone number, the person answering the 'phone does not 'send' audio information back to the caller. In disagreement with this, Lord Hamilton, in a Scottish interim interdict, decided that a website did send information[233]. He agreed that the information 'passively awaits access being had to it by callers' but stated that this did not preclude the information being 'conveyed to and received by the caller'. It seems semantic, but is important to analyse this statement closely.

Material available over the Internet is retrieved by a viewer, not generally pushed to a viewer from the site server. To prove this one needs only to question what occurs when no one accesses a website: no information is conveyed. In contrast, if no one accesses a terrestrial or satellite television broadcast, the programme is still conveyed but it is not seen. So Lord Hamilton's description of a website's operation is technically dubious: websites do not 'send' information, it is requested and then is drawn from them.

Two or more places

The second aspect of a cable programme is that it is intended to be received at two or more places whether for simultaneous reception or at different times in response to requests. Lord Hamilton did not consider that this definition of a cable programme service attempts to encompass multicasting or broadcasting. That is, it is defined in terms of 'two or more places'. The inclusion of these words eliminates one-to-one communication. But this is communication that is perfectly possible over the Internet, for example emails and instant messaging.

Interaction

So without looking further in the Act, a cable programme service does not appear to encompass every website. Subsection (2) of s 7, however, provides a number of exceptions which can be clearly demonstrated to exclude the majority of websites from the definition of a cable programme service:

> '(2) The following are excepted from the definition of "cable programme service": a service or part of a service of which it is an essential feature that while visual images, sounds or other information are being conveyed by the person providing the system there will or may be sent from each place of reception, by means of the same system or (as the case may be) the same part of it, information (other than signals sent for the operation or control of the service) for reception by the person providing the service or other persons receiving it[.]'

232 Copyright, Designs and Patents Act 1988, s 7(1).
233 *Shetland Times Ltd v Dr Jonathan Wills* [1997] FSR 604.

Mr Butcher, the Bill's proponent, explained the ambit of this exception during its debate in the House of Commons[234]. He stated that the exception does not exclude from the definition of 'cable programme service':

> 'any element of the service capable of purely passive reception, even though it may be used interactively, so that, to take the example of teleshopping, the sending of the catalogue pages to subscribers will be a cable programme service, even though each subscriber may then order goods and receive confirmation of the order; it is only the latter aspect that is taken out of the definition.'

In the *Shetland Times* interdict, Lord Hamilton stated that '[w]hile the facility to comment or make suggestions via the Internet exists, this does not appear to me to be an essential element in the [website], the primary function of which is to distribute news and other items'. Lord Hamilton did admit that final resolution of the legal issues 'may in the end turn on technical material not available . . . at the hearing'. This hearing did not occur as the case settled beforehand.

Technically speaking, few sites on the Internet consist of only one page. They are a collection of pages and material referenced usually from the home page which acts like a contents page for the site. To move from this contents page to another page the viewer must so instruct the site's server – subsequent pages do not simply follow one another like the frames of a cable television film. The viewer interacts with the site by sending requests for new data[235]. Viewing a website is therefore not a one-way experience, as believed by Lord Hamilton or as indicated by the soon to be removed definition of a cable programme. It is possible while downloading one page of a website to select a link to commence downloading another page. This is what is special about the World Wide Web: viewers can select what they want to see and when they want to see it. A website therefore falls within the exception to a cable programme service.

Nevertheless, if a website is classified as a cable programme, its services will qualify for protection if they were 'sent' from qualifying country. Being a cable programme for qualification therefore has the same result as if publication only is considered. The place will be that of the location of the server.

It is now possible to consider the copyright protection that may vest in various aspects of material available over the Internet.

Emails

Electronic mail will be protected as a literary work if it meets the hurdle of originality and the lower hurdle of the requisite skill, labour and judgment used in its creation. The Copyright, Designs and Patents Act 1988 defines, rather widely, a literary work as any work, other than a dramatic or musical work, which is written, spoke or sung[236]. Emails are not generally spoken or

234 Hansard (Commons) 12 May, 1988, cols 51–52.

235 Such interaction is over and above 'signals sent for the operation or control of the service'. This exception (to the exception) refers to checksums that are sent by the receiving equipment so the transmitting equipment 'knows' the material has been received correctly. Even 'push' technologies require these checksums to be sent.

236 Copyright, Designs and Patents Act 1988, s 3(1).

sung[237], they are typed. Typing, in any language, even using symbols, appears to fall within the Act's definition of 'writing' that includes any form of notation or code. And this may be by hand or otherwise regardless of the fixing medium. This presumably includes the use of 'emoticons' which are little pictures made from the characters of the email viewed from the side[238]. It will also encompass an email which is not written but dictated to a voice recognition or dictation system. If the author is an employee creating the email in the course of employment, the first owner will be deemed to be the employer[239].

To individuals and others

Unless there are agreements to the contrary, sending an email to someone does not alter its copyright owner or its owner's rights over that copyright. So, for most emails sent to other individuals, the ownership and exclusive rights remain with the sender of the email. Receivers of emails, therefore, unless they are aware of an implied licence or have an express one, should not forward the email to others. By forwarding an email one is not simply performing the equivalent of putting a letter in another envelope (which would not constitute a breach of copyright, but perhaps only one of confidence). By forwarding an email one is involved in copying and therefore may infringe its copyright. This, and the issue of moral rights, is covered below[240].

Term of protection

Copyright subsists in an email as an original literary work, for the life of the author plus 70 years from the end of the calendar year in which its author dies[241].

Forums

A 'forum' is the term used by this chapter to encompass Usenet newsgroups, commercial bulletin boards controlled by Internet Service Providers and website-based chat rooms. Forums contain a variety of digital information. Some contain only postings and replies from members, called conversation threads; others contain digital files such as pictures, movies and sounds deposited by members. These two types of posting will be considered separately.

Conversation threads

A conversation thread is a collection of postings by individuals collected together as a written conversation. An individual, instead of sending an email to

237 The emailing of digital recordings of messages is more appropriately protected as a sound recording under s 1(1)(b).

238 For example, ;-) is a smiling, winking man when turned sideways. Whether such a symbol would qualify as an original literary work is another question. See *Exxon Corpn v Exxon Insurance Consultants International Ltd* [1982] RPC 69.

239 See fn 208 at page 223.

240 See 'Email', at page 266.

241 Copyright, Designs and Patents Act 1988, s 12(2).

another person, sends the email to the forum and a particular thread. Anyone else who also accesses the particular thread may then read this email. These readers can either reply to the public email or can simply read the emails and their replies. Over time, sometimes minutes, a conversation thread emerges in which questions are asked and answered and those answers prompt other questions.

The controller of the thread maintains this collection of emails in one of two ways. First, the conversation thread may be 'moderated'. This means that the controller, or his agent, takes an active part in the management of the thread: certain parts of messages or whole messages may be deleted and certain conversations may be 'steered' in their content. The controller acts as an editor. The second way is where the controller does not manage or oversee the content of the thread in any way. The controller, in such a system, is simply providing a storage system for a group of individual's emails.

Compilation of conversations

A collection of emails sent to a forum is a compilation. Compilations of emails may themselves be subject to protection as copyright works[242]; the Act explicitly mentions this[243]. However, it will be recalled that copyright does not protect 'literary works' but 'original literal works' for the creation of which the author expended skill, labour or judgment[244]. This raises the issue of whether a conversation thread is original and whether it has the requisite level of skill, labour or judgment.

It may be thought that a conversation thread falls at the first hurdle of originality; after all, the thread is simply a copy of others' emails. In fact, the subject of protection is not the individual emails but *their collection*. The copyright and database right protection extends to the collecting, the arrangement and the selection of the emails. For an unmoderated conversation thread, however, it is unlikely that there will be sufficient skill, labour or judgment or warrant copyright protection. Database protection is, however, likely to protect the collection.

It is admitted that the tests for skill, labour and judgment are not particularly onerous[245], but it is nevertheless submitted that a thread that is created without any human interaction cannot possibly be a copyright work. Of course, those who would wish to claim copyright in a conversation thread may seek to allude to their skill, labour and judgment in setting up the conversation thread[246] or in writing the computer program which allows the individuals to post their email messages. Again, it is submitted that such underlying skill, labour and judgment are not that which is required to create a copyright work[247].

242 'There will be copyright in the database as a compilation in the same way as there is in, for example, a street directory': Lord Beaverbrook for the government proposing the Copyright, Designs and Patents Act 1988, 489 HL Official Report (5th Series) col 1533, 12 November 1987.

243 Copyright, Designs and Patents Act 1988, s 3(1)(a).

244 See 'Original works', at page 223; and 'Skill, labour or judgment', at p 223.

245 See *University of London Press Ltd v University Tutorial Press Ltd* [1916] 2 Ch 601 at 609.

246 Another option is for the controller to claim that the conversation thread is a computer-generated work under the Copyright, Designs and Patents Act 1988, s 9(3). Also see 'EU Database Rights' at p 275.

This should be contrasted with the situation where a moderator has a hand in editing and guiding the stored conversations. In this situation, the moderator does add that element of human skill, labour and judgment. Moderated conversation threads therefore probably do have protection as literary works.

What is true for either type of thread is that, without an agreement to the contrary, the controller does not own the copyright in the individual postings. It will be examined below as to what rights the controller does have in the individual postings[248].

19. A Usenet newsgroup is unmoderated and is published through many different Internet Service Providers. One Internet Service Provider objects to a particular competing Internet Service Provider also publishing the newsgroup. One aspect to the Provider's objection is breach of copyright. This is groundless. The Provider has no rights in the newsgroup. Simply storing the postings is not enough to warrant copyright or database right-protection.

File collections

In the same way as some controllers of conversation threads simply store emails for members, others store files for members. Often these are sound recordings or movies in a compressed format such as MP3 or DivX that a member wishes to share with others; often the files themselves are infringements of copyright. What is of concern here is what copyright a controller has over the collection of files. The fundamental question is whether the collection of files could constitute a copyright work at all; compilations, to be protected by copyright, must constitute literary works in their own right. Case law indicates that the concept of a literary work, however, is wide enough to embrace collections of sound recordings or pictures in certain contexts[249]. The widest point in this reading of a literary work came in *Anacon Corpn Ltd v Environmental Research Technology Ltd*[250]. The question facing Jacob J was whether a circuit diagram could constitute a literary work under the Copyright, Designs and Patents Act 1988. Like most people's initial reaction to such a question, Jacob J said[251],

> 'My first thought was that it would be absurd to regard a circuit diagram as a literary work . . . [.]'

247 An Internet Service Provider may allude to the protection afforded to the journalist in *Walter v Lane* whom the court decided had copyright in his verbatim transcript of Lord Rosebery's speech: [1900] AC 539 (still good law, see [1990] FSR 359). Of course a written transcript is very different in character to the transcribed oral speech and also takes judgment and skill. An Internet Service Provider who does not moderate a forum or newsgroup simply re-publishes the text typed by others, formatted by others. The Internet Service Provider does not even select the order to re-publish the various postings; the poster decides whether to 'follow' a thread or create a new one. There is little that the Internet Service Provider adds to alter the quality and character of the raw material (see *Macmillan & Co Ltd v Cooper* (1923) 40 TLR 186 at 188 per Lord Atkinson).

248 See 'Forums', at page 231.

249 *Geographia Ltd v Penguin Books* [1985] FSR 208.

250 [1994] FSR 659.

251 [1994] FSR 659 at 663.

He continued to state that on further thought it becomes apparent that the Act's use of the expression 'writing' encompasses almost anything[252]:

> 'provided it is all written down and contains information which can be read by somebody, as opposed to appreciated simply with the eye[.]'

This may well serve as a protection for a collection of meaningful symbols that are grouped together, or a series of instructions in the form of diagrams. It does not serve as any indication that the group of sorted pictures, sound recordings, animations and messages found on bulletin boards benefit from protection as literary works. These files are simply to be appreciated with the eye or ear.

It is certainly arguable, therefore, that controllers of collections of assorted files do not hold any copyright over the unsorted collection as such. If they wish to prevent others copying the collection they must rely upon establishing a contract with their viewers that prevents this copying or create something worthy of database rights protection. Such a contract, as all, suffers from the limitation on privity: it may serve to restrict contractually primary copiers, but those who duplicate the copy will not be bound by the contract. They, and the controller, may also be restricted by the copyright vested in the individual files themselves.

Commercial forums and newsgroups

So far this section has discussed the copyright that subsists in the conversation threads as compilations. It is also important to highlight the issue of who owns the copyright in the individual postings to the conversation threads. As this section has stated, without prior agreement, the copyright to a posting is vested in its author. Certain commercial forums controlled by websites and Internet Service Providers ensure that all members to a particular forum accept a contract which grants a wide licence to the website or Provider over any postings made to the forum. Often such licences permit these Providers to 're-post' conversation threads on other forums or even further afield. Members of these forums should be careful to read the licence agreement if they are concerned that their postings may be read outside the forum.

Usenet houses the largest collection of bulletin boards on the Internet. Its bulletin boards are called newsgroups and there are many many thousands of different varieties. But no one individual owns or controls any of the conversation threads. In fact, every Internet Service Provider who seeks to provide its members with access to the newsgroups is only responsible for adding messages posted by its own members. Once posted the message is slowly and methodically copied to each of the other Internet Service Providers who are also hosting that newsgroup. This so-called 'flooding' eventually reproduces the posted message on all the different Internet Service Providers' copies of the newsgroup.

From a copyright point of view there are two conclusions from this. The first is that one Internet Service Provider has no exclusive rights over the compilation. At best all the thousands of Internet Service Providers who host the newsgroup are joint copyright owners[253]. In addition, it is this author's submission that with

252 [1994] FSR 659 at 663.
253 Copyright, Designs and Patents Act 1988, s 10(1).

no skill, labour and judgment involved to produce the thread, there is no copyright over which to have joint ownership anyway[254]. The second conclusion is that the individuals who post their messages must be posting their messages with a very wide implied licence. This will be discussed in more detail below, but at present it is enough to state that individuals who are concerned that their postings may be copied into many different forums should not post them to a newsgroup. The system only works on the basis of implied licences to copy all the messages to anyone who wishes to host the same newsgroup.

Term of protection

If a conversation thread is deemed to be an original literary work, copyright subsists in the compilation for the life of the author plus 70 years from the end of the calendar year in which its author dies[255].

WEBSITES

Websites are the most legally complicated of all works on the Internet. Websites consist of many overlapping and adjacent copyright works each of which may have protection separate from the whole and each of which may have a different owner. To appreciate these many copyright works it is perhaps useful to outline how one creates a website.

Creation of a website

To most website designers what is important is how the site looks, how it interacts and how quickly it can be displayed[256]. The first stage is usually to create a scheme that shows how each of the different pages of a site fit together. For example, the first page, or home page, will generally link to many pages, rather like a contents page of a book. Each one of these connections will be drawn either on paper or on a computer screen. Eventually the designer will have built up a skeleton for all the various pages of the site. For the most complex sites, it is at this stage that a designer concocts some animations and may draw in some frames within each one of the pages. Animations may be used. Frames allow some information to remain on the screen even though the viewer chooses a new page. Candidates for frames are contents sections and legal disclaimers; these then remain on the screen for any page of the website.

The second phase of the site's design is the preparation of the individual pages. A designer must be aware of where every element of a page will be placed. This is because the language used to store the site eventually is a layout language, and like all computer programming languages demands certainty.

Designers do this 'storyboarding' either on paper (converting it subsequently by eye into programming commands), or on a computer screen using a special program that performs the conversion.

254 See 'Compilation of conversations', at page 232.
255 Copyright, Designs and Patents Act 1988, s 12(2).
256 This section refers extensively to web designers in the sense of a person or company, who creates the code to put on a server. The legal conclusions reached, however, are equally applicable to anyone who designs a website whether for themselves or their company.

A page may consist of many discrete, individually designed elements. The most basic of these is the text: this is the line of characters from the first letter to the last, rather than the layout that is concerned with how the characters are portrayed, in which typeface[257] and in which format. The other common element is graphics. These are digitally stored pictures but it is crucial to realise that their digital nature refers only to the method of storage. A picture on a website could just as easily have been an oil painting on canvas as a digitally created picture made using a computer-painting software package. Each graphic is stored on the website and 'anchored' into the page at the correct place. Unlike a newspaper, the graphics are stored and are accessible separately from the main page. All the page holds is a link to the graphic.

Certain websites use a particular script or include an executable program which allows interaction with the viewer of the site. At its simplest, viewers can enter their name and other details to receive information. More involved scripts allow certain areas of the screen to become 'hotspots' which respond to a viewer's clicks on those parts.

The most complex element to websites is executable code. These 'applets' and 'objects' are, in short, whole computer programs that are automatically run whenever a website is viewed or an event is triggered. Some executable code may perform a simple task such as playing a three-note tune. Other code is more intricate and displays animations and allows viewers to play games. For instance, some websites will allow their viewers to draw pictures, others to write letters. Many ensure that an entered credit card is both valid and subsequently debited. Of course the effort which goes into coding one applet may be extensive involving the work of many people including designers and programmers.

Having explained this factual background it is now possible to examine the copyright that will, inevitably, protect not only the whole website, but also its constituent parts.

Preparatory material

Most websites start life as a few sketches on paper or computer. The Copyright, Designs and Patents Act 1988 protects original artistic works being[258] any painting, drawing, diagram, map, chart or plan, engraving, etching, lithograph, woodcut or similar work, and photograph, sculpture or collage, irrespective of artistic quality. So, the visual chart of how the website fits together, even though not on computer, if fixed and originating from its author, will be protected by copyright as an original artistic work. Each of the individual graphics, even as rough sketches, are protected as original artistic works.

This underlying protection cannot be ignored: if the designer is not the owner or the licensee of the underlying protected works, he will probably infringe their copyright by incorporating them into a website. This is dealt with below. What should be noted is that those who design websites cannot simply scan, say, a photograph[259] from a magazine and legally use it on their website without being

257 Or 'font' in computer parlance.
258 Copyright, Designs and Patents Act 1988, s 4(1)(a) interwoven with s 4(2)(a) and (b).
259 See *Bauman v Fussell* [1978] RPC 485.

the owner or licensee of the copyright in the photo[260]. Web designers cannot hide their work, as a website is available for viewing by anyone who wants to type the corresponding URL. Designers must be wary of using infringing works as they can easily be spotted.

20. Many websites use a backdrop that gives each page a patterned background. One designer decides that the patterned wallpaper on his office walls would be appropriate for a particular background. He uses a digitised version as the backdrop. Although he may have incorporated the graphic and designed the other portions of the site, he is not entitled to use the textured background to the site. The wallpaper can be protected as an original artistic work and he may face infringement proceedings for copying it.

Constituent elements

The lesson that a website may infringe copyrighted elements *underlying* the main site is even more serious for elements that are obvious to any viewer. This is because the more similar a work is to an alleged copy, the greater the inference of copying. This should not be taken to mean that a distorted copy that is unrecognisable as such is not an infringement; it simply may be harder to prove.

Text

The text that is used on a website is clearly a literary work and as such will probably be protected by copyright. The web designer, by simply retyping the text, gains no copyright over it unless a contract specifies this.

21. A web designer is employed to create a site for a law firm. As to be expected, the firm supplies a page of carefully drafted disclaimers to put on the site in a frame. Months later the designer is approached to design a site for an accountancy firm and offers them a site, 'including web-specific disclaimers'. If the designer uses the same disclaimers on the accountant's site, without permission from the lawyers, he is copying a literary work protected by copyright. He may be sued for doing so.

Term of protection

If the text on a website is an original literary work, copyright subsists in it for the life of the author plus 70 years from the end of the calendar year in which its author dies[261].

260 In July 2000, Rodney Fitch & Co Ltd was sued for a summary judgment that, in designing an antiques website it had infringed the copyright in photographs from a well known antiques encyclopaedia, [2001] FSR 345. The defendant used small copies of the photographs to form icons and other graphics. The claimant was entitled to summary judgment on the basis that there was copyright in the photographs which had been infringed by the claimant.

261 Copyright, Designs and Patents Act 1988, s 12(2).

Links

The Scottish *Shetland Times* case may be thought to indicate that there is copyright in a link to one's site[262]. The implications of this interim decision could be serious if it allows one site to prevent another linking to it. This is unlikely to be followed and was settled in November 1997 before appeal.

The *Shetland News* was a website, like many others, which provides its readers with access to web pages on other sites by including links to those pages. These included links to CNN's website and other major newspapers. At no time did the *Shetland News* provide its readers with copies of the articles themselves. The links are simply listed on the website as series of headlines from the other websites.

The *Shetland News* had included among the links on its home page a number of headlines appearing in issues of the *Shetland Times*' website. The headlines on the *Shetland Times'* website were identical to those on the *Shetland Times*' list of links. If a viewer were to select one of these headlines from the list, the Internet would then connect the viewer to the *Shetland Times'* website at the point of the headline. The *Shetland News* did not copy nor provide the copy of the relevant article. The *Shetland Times* sought declarator that the *Shetland News*' actions constituted an infringement of copyright in the headlines.

On 24 October 1996 Lord Hamilton granted the *Shetland Times* an interim interdict (the Scottish equivalent of an interim injunction) for copyright infringement. Without being referred to any authority on the point, Lord Hamilton rejected the defendant's submissions that a headline was not an original copyright work. His opinion was that there was copyright in the newspaper headline and that it is an infringement to copy it in an electronic form or to incorporate it in a cable programme. What is important here is to assess whether copyright vests in the headline and then assess the relevance of this.

There are a number of cases which indicate that it will be rare for there to be copyright in a headline, or indeed any other single line of text[263]. This, perhaps, does not reflect the position accurately. A page of text on a website may well be protected by copyright as a literary work. To infringe the copyright in the work one must copy the whole or a substantial part of the work[264]. One line of text, or one link, is clearly not a 'whole' copyright work. The question then is, is the line or link a substantial part of the copyright work of which it makes up a part? The House of Lords has addressed this question[265]:

> 'No doubt [headlines] will not as a rule be protected, since alone they would not be regarded as a sufficiently substantial part of the book or other copyright document to justify the preventing of copying by others.'

For the web a distinction should be made between including the text from another's website in your own and including a link to that website. A link is no

262 *Shetland Times Ltd v Dr Jonathan Wills* [1997] FSR 604.
263 *Dicks v Brooks* (1880) 15 Ch D 22; *Francis, Day and Hunter Ltd v Twentieth Century Fox Corpn Ltd* [1940] AC 112.
264 Copyright, Designs and Patents Act 1988, s 16(3)(a). See 'A substantial part', at page 253.
265 *Ladbroke (Football) Ltd v William Hill (Football) Ltd* [1964] 1 WLR 273 at 286 per Lord Hodson.

more than a reference to other material, rather like the first footnote on this page. The typical codes in HTML include 'HREF' and 'IMG' followed by the URL reference to the linked material. HREF generally refers the user to text and does not usually 'incorporate' this text within the referencing website. IMG, in contrast, tends to be used to display an image 'inline' so that the referencing website actually incorporates the referenced image within its 'four corners' creating a digital patchwork quilt of images from other's. It is submitted that there is either no copyright in such a link by virtue of it not taking skill, labour and judgment to create, or that by itself it cannot form a substantial part of its embodying copyright work[266]. Including the text from another's site is subject to all the usual checks and balances in copyright law. If a substantial part of that site is included on one's site, without defence, the copyright in the work is infringed[267].

Graphics

Web designers are often approached by companies and firms who already have graphics to put on their site. These may include logos and photographs already used on the commissioner's paper literature. Sometimes the designer will have to go to considerable trouble to convert these paper graphics into a suitable format for viewing on a website. For example, a website may use just 256 colours, whereas a supplied photograph may be full-colour[268]. The labour and judgment expended by the designer in creating a new, 256-colour artistic work could possibly lead to the designer having a new copyright over the digital version of the photograph. But this right should not be confused with the right to copy the original photograph: the designer's right is in the fixed conversion not in the underlying photograph. The designer should therefore seek explicit permission if he seeks to re-use the digitised photograph on another website.

22. A well-known petrol company commissions a web designer to produce a website for it. It supplies the designer with its logo which is a small yellow fish. The designer sets about writing a Java applet that will appear to rotate this fish in three-dimensions on the screen. Some time later the designer is approached by a high-class seafood restaurant which also wants a website. The designer, rather than 'reinventing the wheel' colours the fish grey and uses the same Java applet on the restaurant's site. If copyright subsists in the fish logo, the designer can be prevented from displaying the copy even though his skill, labour and judgment went into the production of the animating applet.

266 In addition, there may be a fair dealing defence that the justification for including a link to another's website must have been for the purposes of the viewer reviewing that website: Copyright, Designs and Patents Act 1988, s 30(1).

267 See 'A substantial part', at page 253.

268 One can presumably imply a licence from the commissioner to make the adaptation (Copyright, Designs and Patents Act, 1998 s 16(1)(e)) although the web designer should ensure that the commissioner has the right to grant this licence. The photographer may hold the copyright and have granted a limited licence to the commissioner that does not extend to its use on a website.

Term of Protection

If the graphics on a website are original artistic works, copyright subsists in them for the life of the author plus 70 years from the end of the calendar year in which its author dies[269].

Music and sounds

Websites often play or 'stream' music. They allow a sound recording to be played. But the technical conversion from a musical score to a recording or MIDI file should not be confused with any legal rights over that underlying musical score. If original in the copyright sense, a musical score is protected as an original musical work[270]. That does not translate into having a legal right to reproduce the tune of a musical score on a website. Again, therefore, a web designer must look to the owners of the rights in the underlying works for permission before reproducing them in another form on a website.

It is more common on websites to hear sounds and recordings than music, however. For example, a site advertising a new film set in space may open with the sound of laser fire. The 'sound' is recorded in a digital format called a 'sample'. This sample is sent from the website server to the client computer. The browser program on that computer then interprets the sample's series of binary codes as pitch and amplitude variations and will play the sound back in perfect quality.

This sample will be a sound recording in a copyright sense. A sound recording means either a recording of sounds from which the sounds may be reproduced, or a recording of the whole or any part of a literary, dramatic or musical work from which sounds reproducing the work or part may be produced. This *is regardless of the medium on which the recording is made or the method by which the sounds are reproduced or produced*[271]. This definition is wide enough to protect both digital recordings on a computer, stored in a digital format, and a MIDI file, storing the music in a special musical notation that allows the computer to 'play' the music directly.

No rights subsist in a sound recording that is a copy of another[272]. This may also be an infringement of the copyright in the copied recording.

> **23. The owner of a news website decides to use a sound recording of Big Ben chiming one o'clock. The owner digitally records BBC Radio's use of the same chime on its one o'clock news programme. The website owner not only may have infringed the copyright in the BBC's own recording, but also, the owner has no copyright in his own recording. If the owner had stood beside Big Ben and digitally taped the chiming himself, he would have a copyright in the sound recording.**

Term of protection

If the music used on a website is an original musical work, copyright subsists in it for the life of the author plus 70 years from the end of the calendar year in

269 Copyright, Designs and Patents Act 1988, s 12(2).
270 Copyright, Designs and Patents Act 1988, s 1(1)(a).
271 Copyright, Designs and Patents Act 1988, s 5(10).
272 Copyright, Designs and Patents Act 1988, s 5(2).

which its author dies[273]. The copyright in a sound recording expires 50 years after it was released as long as this release was within 50 years of being made[274]. It seems currently acceptable to assume that when a sound recording is present on a server that is connected to the Internet, this will be its first publishing, and hence its release[275].

Commercial point

This discussion of the individual elements of a website serves two purposes. First, it shows that those who design websites should be careful to form explicit arrangements with their commissioners. They should ensure that they are indemnified from any copyright infringement by virtue of using material supplied to them by those who commissioned them. They should, conversely, be sure to indicate what rights are to pass back to the commissioner and what is to remain vested in the designer.

There are a number of cases[276], albeit not concerned directly with the Internet, which indicate the necessity of explicitly specifying which party owns what works and what each party is entitled to do with the works. The most scathing comment is rightly given by Mr Justice Lightman in relation to the rights over a database created by a consultant[277]:

> 'This litigation springs from the failure of the parties (and more particularly the advisors who were then acting for them) at the time that the parties entered into the Consultancy Agreement to consider, or provide for, the intellectual property rights that would arise in the course of the engagement of the Plaintiff. This expensive lesson of this litigation is the vital necessity for provision for these rights in such agreements.'

Programming a general-purpose Java applet that, say, animates a graphic may be something that the designer would wish to use again. Without a contract stating this explicitly, the law can imply that the owner of the copyright is the designer[278].

The second purpose of looking at the copyright that subsists in the elements of a website is that it is trivial for infringers to copy only those elements. It is better to show a court that one owns the copyright in a graphic that is copied than to have to demonstrate that the graphic copied constitutes a substantial part of the whole website so is an infringement[279].

273 Copyright, Designs and Patents Act 1988, s 12(2).
274 Copyright, Designs and Patents Act 1988, s 13A(2). This subsection is likely to be amended by the implementation of the EC Directive on Harmonisation of Certain Aspects of Copyright and Related Rights in the Information Society to take account of the new right of 'communication to the public'.
275 Copyright, Designs and Patents Act 1988, s 13A(3). This subsection is likely to be deleted by the implementation of the EC Directive on Harmonisation of Certain Aspects of Copyright and Related Rights in the Information Society.
276 *Pierce v Promco SA* [1998] EWHC Patents 275; *Fylde Microsystems Ltd v Key Radio Systems Ltd* [1998] FSR 449.
277 *Ray v Classic FM plc* [1998] FSR 622.
278 Cf Copyright, Designs and Patents Act 1988, s 11(2).
279 See the Copyright, Designs and Patents Act 1988, s 16(3)(a). This will be addressed in greater detail under 'Infringement', at page 247.

Encompassing aspects

Although a website is built up from a number of smaller elements, the whole site is the code which is stored on the server computer. This is the website absolute. This section explains the assumption that a website is a computer program within the Copyright, Designs and Patents Act 1988.

Websites as programs

The Copyright, Designs and Patents Act 1988, s 3(1)(b) states that computer programs should be considered as literary works. The same requirements of originality and skill, labour and judgment apply, and it will be assumed that they are met for most websites that are created independently.

'Program or computer', for this section of the Act, is wisely left undefined by the draftsman; there are too many examples of legislation serving only a bygone technology. So, the term should be given its reasonable meaning. There would be few programmers or lawyers who would disagree that a program is a set of instructions that can be interpreted by a computer into a set of functions. So is HTML or XML code a program? It is a set of instructions which when read by a browser program produces functional, visual and or audible changes in the operation of the computer[280].

Protection for programs

In *Ibcos Computers Ltd v Barclays Mercantile Highland Finance Ltd*, Jacob J considered the extent to which copyright protects programs[281]. There are two critical aspects to his lucid judgment: first, the American case of *Computer Associates v Altai*[282] relied on by a previous judgment[283], is not 'particularly helpful' and its main concept 'merely complicates the matter so far as our law is concerned'[284]. The second aspect of the judgment of direct relevance is that copyright may protect not simply the whole program but also the sub-programs which make up the complete program.

Copyright protects the program at two levels: one, the actual words, symbols

280 It will be rare for sites also to have protection for their typographical arrangement under the Copyright, Designs and Patents Act 1988, ss 1(1)(c) and 8. The reason that only few sites will benefit from this protection is that most web pages allow the area in which they are viewed to be resized and allow the viewer's browser to re-align and re-set the information to fit inside this resized area. For these cases, it would be difficult for the coder of such re-sizable websites to assert that the layout has been fixed and so is capable of copyright protection. For sites that do not allow such re-formatting, their term of copyright protection over the layout is 25 years from the end of the calendar year of first publication on the World Wide Web: Copyright, Designs and Patents Act 1988, s 15. See *Newspaper Licensing Agency Ltd v Marks & Spencer plc* [2001] 3 All ER 977 for a discussion of the strict nature of typographical arrangement copyright protection.

281 [1994] FSR 275.

282 982 F 2d 693 (2nd Cir 1992).

283 *John Richardson Computers v Flanders* [1993] FSR 497 at 526.

284 [1994] FSR 275 at 302. This author is in full agreement with this assessment: the US Copyright Code 102(b) actively excludes from copyright protection any 'process, system, method of operation'. This is partly the reason why the court in *Altai* developed the 'filtration' of such aspects from protection, eventually to reduce the work to a 'core of protectable material'. The Copyright, Designs and Patents Act 1988 does not exclude these aspects of a work.

and numerals of the code[285] and two, the compilation of the various smaller programs or elements within the whole. These are both literary works.

Protection of websites

For a website this is no mean protection. The entire coding from the first instruction to the last is protected as a pure literary work. In addition, the individual programming elements are also protected as smaller literary works. This becomes particularly important for websites that use a considerable amount of executable code. If a person copied one small applet without licence there is an argument that, in relation to the whole HTML or XML listing, the applet is insubstantial so its copying is not infringement[286]. If the programmer of the code can claim that the copyright work is not the whole website but is the copied applet only, an argument of insubstantiality will fail. The whole work is copied.

24. An insurance company establishes a website over which it conducts business. One aspect of the site is a form to fill in one's personal details. The website has over 200 graphic-rich pages of information taking up 20 Mbytes of storage space; the form takes up half a page and less than one Mbyte. The form is copied, no doubt for its neatness and compactness. If the company claims copyright only in the whole site, the taking of the form may be viewed as not substantial. The company can, however, also claim a separate literary copyright in the code for the form for which the 'defence' of insubstantiality will surely fail.

Term of protection

If a website is classified as a computer program, and then as an original literary work, copyright subsists in it for the life of the author plus 70 years from the end of the calendar year in which its author dies[287].

Website copyright by remote control[288]

Having examined the significant protection for websites it is necessary to touch again on who benefits from that protection. It will be remembered that every copyright work must have an author, but a copyright work can have joint authors[289]. This is particularly relevant for website designers who often work with their clients' in-house designers. In illustration, a designer of a brochure may instruct a website designer to create a website similar to the brochure[290]. As the design of the website

285 Some might use the word 'source code' to refer to this listing. This is perhaps not strictly accurate as the distinction between source and object code for HTML and XML code is not as pronounced as for compiled computer languages.

286 Copyright, Designs and Patents Act 1988, s 16(3)(a).

287 Copyright, Designs and Patents Act 1988, s 12(2).

288 A phrase seemingly coined by Mr Hobbs QC in *Cala Homes (South) Ltd v Alfred McAlpine Homes East Ltd* [1995] FSR 818 at 835. The implications of this case are discussed below.

289 Copyright, Designs and Patents Act 1988, s 10(1).

290 This is common practice for firms who wish to maintain some coherence between all their publicity and products.

progresses, the in-house designer may contribute to the design process, recommending different typefaces, providing extra illustrations and other input.

In providing this guidance, the in-house designer may allege that he provided skill, labour and judgment into the creation of an expression from a mere idea. In short, the designer is partially responsible in an 'investment' sense for the finished product. The website designer, in contrast, could claim that copyright vests in an author who expends skill, labour or judgment in fixing an idea into an expression. On these lines, a helpful idea or suggestion from a third-party is not a copyright work; it is a mere idea to which copyright affords no protection.

Joint authorship of website

The Act is of little guidance in this area, demanding only that joint authorship requires both collaboration and contributions that are indistinct[291]. Fortunately, the case law now provides some useful guidance on the requirements for joint authorship[292].

In *Cala Homes (South) Ltd v Alfred McAlpine Homes East Ltd* the requirements for joint ownership were examined[293]. Employers of Crawley Hodgson were the sole draftsmen of some architectural drawings. However, Mr Date, a designer who worked for the client often provided the ideas for the drawings, even to very small details. The draftsmen of Crawley Hodgson worked to Mr Date's brief but, for the drawings in question, he did not 'move the pen on the paper'[294]. This should not detract from the fact that most of the design features of the drawings came from and were insisted to be included by Mr Date. The question before Laddie J was whether Mr Date could be viewed as the joint author of these drawings. He was sure that he could[295].

> 'In my view, to have regard merely to who pushed the pen is too narrow a view of authorship. What is protected by copyright in a drawing or *a literary work* is more than just the skill of making marks on paper or some other medium. It is both the words or lines and the skill or effort involved in creating, selecting or gathering together the detailed concepts, data or emotions which those words or lines have fixed in some tangible form which is protected. It is wrong to think that only the person who carries out the mechanical act of fixation is an author.'

This conclusion in *Cala Homes* has been applied in the context of computer programs and their creations. In *Fylde Microsystems Ltd v Key Radio Systems Ltd*[296] Mr Justice Laddie suggested that the court must check that a plaintiff has the 'right kind of skill and labour' and then that the contribution is 'big enough'[297].

Clearly it is not simple to decide whether a web designer or in-house designer contributed to the 'right kind of skill and labour' to the creation of a detailed idea. This, therefore, highlights the need for both parties in a website design

291 Copyright, Designs and Patents Act 1988, s 10(1).
292 Previously, the cases have been indicative but not guiding: *Murray v King* (1983) 2 IPR 99; *Prior v Lansdowne Press Pty Ltd* [1977] RPC 511.
293 [1995] FSR 818 at 834–836.
294 [1995] FSR 818 at 833.
295 [1995] FSR 818 at 835. Emphasis added.
296 [1998] FSR 449.
297 [1998] FSR 449 at para 25.

agreement to make explicit who owns what and what can be done with the works one owns.

Specific websites

This final section on protection examines the copyright considerations for special websites. With the use of frames, it is increasingly common for these special types of website simply to become parts of a larger site. The same conclusions will then apply, but the protection that will be afforded will be in addition to the protection for the site as a compilation.

Search engines

Certain websites are devoted to searching for other websites. These sites allow a viewer to enter a string of words or even one word and then be presented with a complete list of every site containing the searched-for words[298]. When the word or words are found the search engine presents a list of all the sites and their addresses in which the word appears.

Computer-generated list

Clearly, the copyright to the program which searches the web is owned by or licensed to the search engine owners. But who owns the copyright to the outputted list of 'found' sites? The list is a literary work; it is a compilation like many other protected lists. If done by hand, its author would be the poor person who had to wade through the documents searching for the given word. But this searching, this labour and judgment, is performed by a computer program; who is its author, and owner, in this situation?

The Act states that a computer-generated work is one that has been generated by computer such that there is no human author of the work[299]. This is the case with a list generated by a search engine. The Act provides that the author of the computer-generated work must be the person by whom the arrangements necessary for the creation of the work are undertaken. This is probably the search engine company who have compiled the database of words and materials from the web. The list is also likely to be protected by database rights[300].

Nevertheless, search engines are advised to enter a licence with every user of the site. This may provide that the generated list is provided only on a non-commercial basis and that any list created by the engine must display also a link to the search engine that created it (in a non-copyright sense).

25. A search engine is used to find every art gallery in Manchester that has a website. The resulting list is simply ported onto a website and advertising is sold on that website to the galleries listed. The search engine site has a right to object to the use of the list.

298 The engine is searching its own *index* of these pages. See 'Sale of key words on search engines', at p 208 for more details.
299 Copyright, Designs and Patents Act 1988, s 178.
300 Copyright, Designs and Patents Act 1988, s 9(3). See 'EU Database rights' at p 275.

Term of protection

If a search engine creates a computer-generated compilation, copyright subsists in it for 50 years from the end of the calendar month in which it was made. The database rights over the underlying index protect for 15 years from the earlier of the end of the calendar year of first making, or, first being made available to the public[301]. A human-made list, as an original literary work, has copyright protection for the life of the author plus 70 years from the end of the calendar year in which its author dies[302].

Link lists

While some people prefer to search for websites using a search engine, others prefer to use the equivalent of an index or contents page. The most famous example of this sort of site is Yahoo!'s. This site does allow searches to be conducted but it is better known for its lists of selected sites in categories. For example, one may wish to look for lawyers who specialise in construction law. A list of suitable lawyers could be found under say both: 'Lawyers: Construction' and under 'Building: Construction: Services'.

These sites, far from being boring, are colourful and are able to make revenues through advertising and listing space sold on their site. Not surprisingly, they wish to protect the information on their site with the full force of copyright. There seems little reason why this should not be possible. English law, in contrast to American law, has always protected lists of information where only a slim amount of skill and judgment is required to construct them[303]. The copyright in such a listing is in the compilation, the collection of the links. It is not in the links themselves. There is therefore nothing stopping an individual copying one interesting link or using a link from a link list. First, it is unlikely that copyright subsists in a URL; second, it would be unlikely that one link could form a substantial part of a list to form the basis for an infringement action under either copyright or database right.

The rights in a link list that is commercially available are the same as those that are publicly available.

26. Over a period of months, a Bonsai tree expert compiles a list of useful Bonsai-related sites on the Internet. He lists these on his personal site. A commercial link list receives a number of emails requesting a list of bonsai sites and a number of gardening centres indicate that they would be happy to pay for advertising near such a link list. The commercial link list copies the expert's list, reformats it in a different typeface and posts it up on their own site. They do not own the copyright in this list and may be infringing by copying it for this purpose. They would not have infringed copyright by simply providing a link to the expert's list.

301 Copyright, Designs and Patents Act 1988, s 12(7), and, Copyright and Rights in Databases Regulations 1997, Reg 17.

302 Copyright, Designs and Patents Act 1988, s 12(2).

303 See fn 242 at page 232.

Term of protection

If a link list is a computer-generated compilation, copyright subsists in it for 50 years from the end of the calendar month in which it was made. Database rights protect the list for only 15 years from the earlier of the end of the calendar year of completion or making it available to the public[304]. As a human-made list, as an original literary work, it has copyright protection for the life of the author plus 70 years from the end of the calendar year in which its author dies[305].

INFRINGEMENT

Copyright works are protected in two main ways. First, certain ways of copying the work are deemed to be copyright or database infringement. The second way, for certain works, is to have the protection of moral rights.

Copying and infringement

It is vital to understand that not all copying is infringement and that not all infringement is copying.

Not all copying is infringement

To infringe[306] a copyright work by copying it one must, without licence of the copyright owner[307], reproduce[308] at least a substantial part[309] of it in any material form[310]. If one has the licence to copy a copyright work, one does not infringe it. If one copies only an insubstantial part of a copyright work, one does not infringe the copyright in the work. These two non-infringing methods of copying are particularly relevant. This is because the only way to use the Internet involves copying.

Not all infringement is copying

It is not only unlicensed substantial copying that infringes a copyright; visually presenting a work in public may also infringe the copyright in the work[311]. One

304 Copyright, Designs and Patents Act 1988, s 12(7), and, Copyright and Rights in Databases Regulations 1997, Reg 17.
305 Copyright, Designs and Patents Act 1988, s 12(2).
306 Copyright, Designs and Patents Act 1988, ss 16(1)(a) and 17(1).
307 Copyright, Designs and Patents Act 1988, s 16(2). NB The Patent Office and Department of Trade and Industry's Consultation Paper on the implementation of EC Directive on Harmonisation of Certain Aspects of Copyright and Related Rights in the Information Society, indicates that acts of 'communicat[ing] the work to the public' are likely to replace the restricted act of broadcasting or inclusion in a cable programme service.
308 Copyright, Designs and Patents Act 1988, s 17(2).
309 Copyright, Designs and Patents Act 1988, s 16(3)(a).
310 Copyright, Designs and Patents Act 1988, s 17(2).
311 Copyright, Designs and Patents Act 1988, s 19(2)(b).

also infringes a copyright by authorising anyone to perform an act restricted by copyright[312]. In addition the law provides for secondary infringements where one deals in a restricted way with an infringing copy of a work[313].

Copying and infringement

Copying technically

A copy is made each time one views a website, or accesses a bulletin board, or even forwards an email. This is because, unlike the postal system, any material of any form that is sent over the Internet or viewed over it is copied. What occurs is that the viewer's computer transmits a request to the server computer to forward a duplicate of some particular material it is storing. This duplicate material is not passed directly to the viewer's computer. It is broken into packets, each with a delivery address, and sent across the Internet. It is passed from one computer on the Internet to another until all the packets are eventually received at the viewer's computer. In reality, each of these intermediary computers has made a copy of the packet that it received and forwarded.

When the material is finally received by the viewer's computer it is stored in the computer's memory – another copy. This transfer does not physically alter the information held by the server, rather it reproduces in the memory of the viewer's computer the material held by the server. The material on the server remains unchanged. The material now held in the viewer computer's memory is then 'interpreted'[314] or 'executed'[315]. This will allow the viewer to experience the website. But this is the result of another copy. The computer's main memory translates the material received from the server into graphic images and sound and these are sent to the screen memory – further copies.

Copying legally

The Act defines copying widely. A copy is made by reproducing the whole, or any substantial part, of the work in any material form. This includes storing the work in a medium by electronic means[316]. As has been examined, all material on the Internet and World Wide Web is, or had underlying it, a work protectable by copyright. The Act goes further and makes explicit that any reproduction will be deemed to be copying. This is even where the copying is indirect[317], and even where it is transient or incidental to some other use of the work[318].

This wide ambit of what is copying can be translated into one simple truth: using the Internet creates copies. Sometimes, the retention, and further copying or distribution is coined 'caching'. When a website is viewed, all the server computers on the Internet that pass on the packets will be deemed to have

312 Copyright, Designs and Patents Act 1988, s 16(2).
313 Copyright, Designs and Patents Act 1988, ss 22–26.
314 For pure HTML or XML.
315 For executable code.
316 Copyright, Designs and Patents Act 1988, s 17(2).
317 Copyright, Designs and Patents Act 1988, s 16(3)(b).
318 Copyright, Designs and Patents Act 1988, s 17(6).

copied the site. Their copying is transient and incidental to another's use, but this still remains copying under the Act. The computer that finally receives the copies will also be deemed to have copied the site. The computer's copy may not be on paper, but storage by electronic means is sufficient to constitute copying under the Act. When emails are sent, received, even viewed, copies are made in a similar way as described above.

As almost all use of the Internet involves copying, the main legal issue in copyright actions will be whether the copying constitutes infringement[319]. The issues of licensing, defences and substantiality will be generally discussed before addressing the infringement of moral rights.

Temporary copies: licences and defences

It will be recalled that it is not an infringement to copy the whole or a substantial part of a copyright work with licence from the copyright owner[320]. A licence does not need to take any particular form. Licences can be implied from statute[321] and by the courts from the circumstances in which the copyright work or part of it is transferred[322]. What will be at issue in most Internet cases is the existence, scope and duration of these implied licences. It should also be kept in mind that the Electronic Commerce Directive introduces a new defence for those who make temporary copies on behalf of others. This defence is examined in some detail below.

Common law licence

Some licences can be readily implied for dealings over the Internet. For example, the intermediary computers involved with an Internet dealing would seem to be impliedly licensed to copy the packets being passed to the end user. This can be inferred from the fact that the copyright owner made the information available over the Internet, so, surely a licence must be implied for business efficacy. If the owner of every server computer on the Internet infringed any packet that passed through it, the Internet would collapse because no one would want to connect to it. It seems also fair between the parties that the licence is implied only to the extent that the intermediary can pass on the packets. It would be outside the scope of the implied licence to retain copies of the packets after they are confirmed to have been accurately sent.

Copyright Directive 'licence'

The EC Directive on Harmonisation of Certain Aspects of Copyright and Related Rights in the Information Society confirms this 'licence' to make such

319 Of course, there may be many factual disputes as to whether the defendant actually *did* copy the work.

320 Copyright, Designs and Patents Act 1988, s 16(2).

321 Copyright, Designs and Patents Act 1988, ss 50A–50C.

322 *Springfield v Thame* (1903) 89 LT 242; *Hall-Brown v Iliffe & Sons Ltd* (1928–35) Macq Cop Cas 88; *Blair v Osbourne & Tomkins* [1971] 2 QB 78; *Solar Thomson Engineering Co Ltd v Barton* [1977] RPC 537 at 560–561; *Barnett v Cape Town Foreshore Board* [1978]; *Roberts v Candiware* [1980] FSR 352; *Anvil Jewellery Ltd v Riva Ridge Holdings Ltd* (1985–87) 8 IPR 161.

temporary copies at art 5.1. The Patent Office and Department of Trade currently intends to implement this mandatory provision by proposing draft language for s 31A as follows:

> 'Copyright . . . is not infringed by the making of a temporary copy which is transient or incidental, which is an integral and essential part of a technological process and the sole purpose of which is to enable –
> (a) a transmission of the work in a network between third parties by an intermediary; or
> (b) a lawful use of the work;
> and which has no independent economic significance.'

Consequently, following the implementation of this section, the technologically necessary copies of works made every second across the Internet will no longer be possible infringements. Of course, where an intermediary temporarily copies a work for the purposes of generating advertising revenues, or direct revenues, that intermediary may then infringe the work. One should also note that the Copyright Directive expressly excludes its application to computer programs. Consequently, this proposed s 31A exception also does not apply to computer programs whereas this chapter concludes the majority of websites will be classed as computer programs. Does this mean that the necessary temporary copying of a website purely for transmission of the work is possibly an infringement? Here s 50 of the unamended Copyright, Designs and Patents Act 1988 assists.

The Copyright, Designs and Patents Act 1988, s 50C provides that it is not an infringement of copyright for a lawful user of a copy of a computer program to copy it provided that is necessary for his lawful use and is not prohibited by contract. As a website is a computer program and the only way to 'use' the website is to copy it, it is implied that a lawful viewer of a website and the intermediaries working on behalf of the website owner are entitled to copy it. It will be examined below whether a user or server may also store a copy on a disk and for how long this copy may be stored.

The caching defence

A web cache is a computer with vast storage capacity which holds copies of the most popular pages on the World Wide Web. If this cache is located on the local network, users can be saved the delay of gaining access to the over-burdened site. It also means that the network can restrict access to the Internet, thus reducing the risk from hacking and viruses.

Commercially, a web cache may be unwelcome for a website owner, few companies publish on the web out of charity; they wish to advertise, to sell to and to find the demographics of those who visit their site. A web cache may hide this information from companies. Companies whose sites are cached may be unable to establish exactly how many people are 'hitting' their site, and also they cannot find out who makes up their audience. These statistics are an attractive aspect of the Internet.

Caching can also adversely affect companies whose income comes from selling advertising space on their pages. To increase this income, these companies often show a different advertisement each time the site is viewed; they 'roll' a number of adverts. This multiples each page's earnings. Unfortunately, the caching computer stores just one copy of the popular pages. So there may be just one advertiser who is getting their money's worth. Clearly then, these companies have a commercial objection to caching.

The EC Directive on Certain Legal Aspects of Electronic Commerce in the Internal Market introduced a defence for intermediaries who make temporary copies of material under six conditions[323]. The Electronic Commerce (EC) Regulations 2002 implement this defence at reg 18. The defence is absolute and the intermediary is not liable for damages or for any other pecuniary remedy or for any criminal sanction as a result of the storage and subsequent transmission.

Automatic, intermediate and temporary

This defence applies where the copyright work in question is both the subject of automatic, intermediate and temporary storage and where that storage is for the sole purpose of making more efficient onward transmission of the work to other recipients of the service upon their request[324]. In essence, therefore, the storage of the copyright work must not be an end in itself; the work must be stored automatically to transmit it to others.

> **27. ForeverThere.com spots a gap in market for search engines. It realises that other search engines' index of websites become inaccurate in a matter of weeks because websites continually update the web addresses on which they store pages. This leads to 'broken links' where an individual is unable to relocate the page indexed by the search engine. As a strategy, ForeverThere.com takes full copies of websites as it indexes them to allow its users to locate the information requested, even if the website moves the page in question. This may be automatic and intermediate but it is not temporary; ForeverThere.com may not be able to rely upon the caching defence.**

No modification

This second condition is that the intermediary must not modify the 'information', here a copyright work, to benefit from the defence[325]. This is self-explanatory.

No technical interference

The following three conditions are similar[326]. Each addresses the manner in which the information, or copyright work, is to be treated by the intermediary web cache. First, the intermediary must comply with conditions on access to the information. An example of this is where a password is required to access the

323 Article 13.
324 Regulation 18(a).
325 Regulation 18(b)(i).
326 Regulation 18(b)(ii)–(iv).

copyright work and the web cache stores a copy of the pages *beyond* the password point. As a result this website would allow those without passwords to access the copyright work. Such a tactic would bring the intermediary outside the scope of the defence.

Second, the intermediary temporary copier must comply with any rules regarding the updating of the information, specified in a manner widely recognised and used by industry. Some websites include 'objects' which cannot be cached as they are defined as 'PRAGMA:No Cache' or must be dynamically retrieved each time they are accessed, say, from a database. If a web cache were to circumvent these well-known strategies, it would, again, lose the benefit of the defence.

Third, the intermediary must not interfere with the lawful use of technology, widely recognised and used by industry, to obtain data on the use of the information. Again, certain websites are concerned with the number of visits that they receive. There are certain ways of allowing the majority of one's website to be cached but ensure that a small element is required to be accessed from the original site. This allows the website to be cached but still to be able to know how many visits there have been to the site. Interference with this important data will be enough to prevent the cacher from relying on the defence.

Act expeditiously on obtaining actual knowledge

The final condition to permit legal temporary copying is that the intermediary must act expeditiously to remove or to disable access to the copyright work he has stored upon obtaining actual knowledge of the fact that the information at the initial source of the transmission has been removed from the network, or access to it has been disabled, or that a court or an administrative authority has ordered such removal or disablement.

In the main, this part of the defence will be taken to mean that the caching company has not be provided with 'notice' about the ordered or actual removal or disablement. This notice need not, however, be in writing and notice of actual removal or disablement certainly need not originate from a court. The court shall, however, take into account whether the cacher received the notice through its published email address, and whether the notice contains its sender's name, address, details and location of the unlawful information. The web cache need not, however, monitor those websites it caches from to check whether material has been removed.

Article 15(1) from the Electronic Commerce Directive states that:

> 'Member States shall not impose a general obligation on providers, when providing the services covered by [the] Articles [concerning mere conduit, caching and hosting], to monitor information which they transmit or store, nor a general obligation actively to seek facts or circumstances indicating illegal activity.'

This Article is not explicitly implemented in the Regulations. The reason for this must be that Parliament believed that nothing in the Regulations did impose a general obligation to monitor such facts and circumstances. It follows that the Regulations do not, in effect, force those who cache or take temporary copies for other justifiable reasons to monitor for changes on the websites they copy from, to be able to benefit from the defence.

This leaves the issue of how fast is 'expeditiously'. There is little doubt that this is quicker than 'reasonably quickly' but nevertheless will be assessed with reference to the facts and circumstances of the situation.

A SUBSTANTIAL PART

To infringe a copyright work by copying it one must not only have no licence so to copy the work, but also the copy must be of a substantial part of the claimant's work[327]. There is no statutory definition of what constitutes a 'substantial part'. This absence is complicated further by the two senses of the word 'substantial'. The *Concise Oxford Dictionary* defines the word both qualitatively as 'of real importance or value' and quantitatively as 'of considerable amount'. The courts have indicated that the test is more one of quality than one of quantity but it appears that even aspects of a claimant's work that are quantitatively small may still constitute part[328]. What constitutes a substantial part of a conversation thread may be a familiar issue for a court to assess; what constitutes a substantial part of website may be more difficult.

A website may consist of 200 individual instructions to the computer and a copier may copy 100. But whether this quantitatively substantial taking is substantial in a copyright sense may depend on how the 100 lines appear on interpretation. If the lines are part of some executable code that merely animates a small graphic on a many-page website, this may not be substantial. This said, the courts must not forget that copyright protects not the expression itself but the skill, labour and judgment that was expended in creating that expression. So, if the animation of the graphic was a very complex and time-consuming piece of programming it may be a substantial part of the whole copyright work[329].

Assessing substantiality is a question that will always rest on the facts of a case[330]. The last word on its determination is left for Jacob J in *Ibcos Computers Ltd v Barclays Mercantile Highland Finance Ltd*[331]:

327 Copyright, Designs and Patents Act 1988, s 16(3)(a). 'The question is whether the defendants' [work] reproduces a substantial part of the [plaintiff's work], not whether the reproduced part of the [plaintiff's work] forms a substantial part of the defendant's [work]': *Warwick Film Productions v Eisinger* [1967] 3 All ER 367 at 385 per Plowman J. Approved by the House of Lords in *Designer Guild Ltd v Russell Williams (Textiles) Ltd* [2001] 1 All ER 700.

328 '[T]hough it may be that it was not very prolonged in its reproduction, it is clearly in my view, a substantial, a vital, and an essential part which is there reproduced': *Hawkes & Son v Paramount Film Service* [1934] Ch 593 at 606, per Slesser LJ; '[I]t is quite clear that the question of substantiality is not determined solely by any process of arithmetic': *Joy Music v Sunday Pictorial* [1960] 2 QB 60 at 68, per McNail J; '[T]he question whether he has taken a substantial part depends much more on the quality than on the quantity of what he has taken. It will, therefore, depend not merely on the physical amount of the reproduction but on the substantial significance of that which is taken': *Ladbroke (Football) Ltd v William Hill (Football) Ltd* [1964] 1 All ER 465 at 469, per Lord Reid, and at 473 per Lord Evershed.

329 In such a case, the claimant should not overlook the issue that the website, although a computer program, is also a compilation. He may therefore be advised also to plead infringement of the Java applet by itself. This then eliminates the question of whether the taking is a substantial part of the website. This can be compared to the approach used in *Ibcos*. See 'Protection of websites', at page 243.

330 See the Court of Appeal in relation to substantiality in drawings: *Biotrading & Financing OY v Biohit Ltd* [1998] FSR 109 at 122, per Aldous J.

331 [1994] FSR 275 at 301.

> 'Even in the case of technical drawings it is possible to examine the parties' drawings to see whether a substantial part of the plaintiff's work is to be found in the defendant's. In a computer program case, however, the court cannot so readily assess the question of substantial part unaided by expert evidence. I believe I should therefore be largely guided by such evidence.'

In illustration, a large parcel delivery company sets up a website. It consists of information about the company, parcel-tracking facilities and lists of all its services. It amounts to over 30 pages of web pages and just under 1,000 lines of code. It features animations, sound jingles and forms to be filled in where appropriate. One such form was copied from a newspaper's site on the Internet. The form takes up one-third of one page and the coding is about 30 lines. The company admits unlicensed copying but deny that it is a substantial part when the form amounts to only 3% of the code on their page and 1% of the visual reproduction of their site. This is focusing on the wrong work and the wrong concept. The question should be how much of the newspaper's site has been lifted (even this question should not be answered with percentages); the significance of the form in programming terms should determine its substantiality. Merely because the code creating this form, if removed, would prevent the whole newspaper's site from functioning does not prove that it is a substantial part. Indeed, most computer programs are created using many modules and without any one module, the program would not operate. This is not, by itself, enough to prove the module or element is substantial[332].

Infringers suing infringers

It is the nature of the Internet that on a frequent basis copying and inevitably infringement occurs. This raises an issue more relevant to the Internet than any other medium: can an infringer of a copyright work sue for infringement of his copyright work?

The fundamental point to make is that even if a work infringes another, the work may still benefit from copyright protection[333]. Conversely, it is not a defence for a defendant to claim that the claimant's work is a copy[334]. What is proposed by Lightman J, and accepted by the Court of Appeal in *ZYX Music GmbH v Chris King* is that where there is no obvious public policy ground[335] the claimant can pursue infringers of his work with an obligation to account to the original author for his share of the recovery[336]. Infringement of a third party's copyright is not sufficient to refuse to enforce the copyright on public policy grounds. Lightman J added that the court[337]:

332 *Cantor Fitzgerald International v Tradition (UK) Ltd* [2000] RPC 95.

333 *Redwood Music Ltd v Chappell & Co Ltd* [1982] RPC 109 at 120.

334 *British Leyland Motor Corpn v Armstrong Patents Co Ltd* [1982] FSR 481 at 502.

335 For example , a 'dishonest and misleading work' (*Slingsby v Bradford Patent Truck and Trolley Co* [1906] WN 51) or an exploitation of a breach of confidence 'reeking of turpitude' (*A-G v Guardian Newspapers Ltd (No 2)* [1990] 1 AC 109 at 262H, 276H–277A and 294A–D).

336 [1995] FSR 566 at 576–578 and Court of Appeal, [1997] 2 All ER 129. This issue had been the subject of much academic debate, and Lightman J chose to endorse the view taken in Laddie, Prescott & Vitoria *The Modern Law of Copyright and Designs* Volume One (2nd edn, 1995, Butterworths, London).

337 [1995] FSR 566 at 577–578.

'may require that the copyright owner whose rights the plaintiffs have infringed should be notified of the proceedings and given the opportunity to be joined, make representations or otherwise protect his rights before judgment is given or enforced.'

28. A software developer uses some executable code on his website to make the viewer's mouse cursor appear to shine a beam of light on the current web page like a torch. A manufacturer of high-durability torches copies the code and uses it on its site. It does not credit nor pay for its use of the code. Some time later a small retailer copies the majority of the manufacturer's site substituting its details on the contact page. This retailer is sued for infringement of copyright and passing off. It should not rely on a defence that the manufacturer has also copied a copyright work; as long as the manufacturer has notified the software developer and undertakes to account for the developer's proportion of the damages, the claimant has a valid claim of copyright infringement.

Moral rights and the Internet

The Copyright, Designs and Patents Act 1988 does not purely provide economic rights to copyright owners. It also provides certain 'moral' rights to the authors of copyright works[338]. These rights include the right to be attributed as author of a copyright work, the right to object to derogatory treatment of a copyright work and the right not to be falsely attributed as the author of a copyright work. This section considers the first two of these rights: the so-called rights of 'paternity' and of 'integrity'.

The two rights do not apply to computer programs or computer-generated works, so much of the work on the Internet is excluded from protection. The rights attach only to literary, artistic, musical and film works. This does not mean that a site on the World Wide Web cannot *infringe* a work's moral rights. What this means is that those who construct web pages, and those that control forums, should be wary of infringing the moral rights in one of the works they are using.

Paternity

The author of a literary work has the right to be identified as the author of that work whenever it is published commercially, broadcast or included in a cable programme service[339]. The author of an artistic work has the right to be identified as the author of that work whenever the work is published commercially or exhibited in public[340]. It has been discussed that putting a work on a website will constitute commercial publication; money does not need to change hands[341].

338 The rights do not apply where the work was created by an employee in the course of employment: Copyright, Designs and Patents Act 1988, ss 11(2), 79(3), 82(1)(a).
339 Copyright, Designs and Patents Act 1988, s 77(1) and (2)(a).
340 Copyright, Designs and Patents Act 1988, s 77(4)(a).
341 See 'Place of publication', at pages 225 to 227 especially, fn 222.

Assertion

To rely on the right, an author needs first to assert it[342]. This is achieved in relation to general or specific acts on an assignment of copyright or by an instrument in writing signed by the author[343]. A relevant question for those who see their works commercially published on the Internet is, therefore, whether this right can be asserted *over* the Internet.

Certainly, in this context an email can constitute a written instrument. The term 'writing' is widely defined as including any form of notation or code, whether by hand or otherwise and regardless of the method by which, or the medium on, in or on which, it is recorded[344]. Whether a signature can be included within an email is another, and more difficult question. What is certain is that the term 'signature' is interpreted widely by the courts[345] as a means 'as personally to authenticate the document'[346] and 'any mark which identifies it as the act of the party'[347]. This broad interpretation, no doubt, may, in certain circumstances, permit an encrypted message to serve as a written signed instrument[348]. But it is a risk until the appropriate Government minister makes specific provision in the Copyright, Designs and Patents Act 1988 in accordance with his power under the Electronic Communications Act 2000. In the meantime, if authors truly are concerned that their moral rights on the Internet are respected, they should revert to paper and pen to make their assertion.

29. An individual posts an email to a commercial forum and ends the email with the words 'This author asserts his right to be identified as the author of this work under the Copyright, Designs and Patents Act 1988'. This is unlikely to be a valid assertion and, subject to copyright infringement, the forum and others using the forum may reproduce his email without reference to his authorship.

Artistic works may have their paternity right asserted simply by being identified on the original or copy of the work in relation to a public exhibition[349]. For this method of assertion it appears likely that the assertion may be made over the Internet. Most websites that show artistic works may be considered as public exhibitions and it is easy to include on a digital copy of a work a typed or 'signed' name.

342 Copyright, Designs and Patents Act 1988, s 78(1). See *Christoffer v Poseidon Film Distributors* [1999] All ER (D) 1063 per Park J.
343 Copyright, Designs and Patents Act 1988, s 78(2).
344 Copyright, Designs and Patents Act 1988, s 178. Cf Law of Property Act 1925, s 40 which is silent on what may constitute 'writing' forcing a court to rely, therefore, on the Interpretation Act 1978, Sch 1. This provides that '[w]riting includes typing, printing, lithography, photography and other modes of representing or reproducing words in a visible form . . .'
345 See also *Baker v Dening* (1838) 8 Ad & El 94; *Cohen v Roche* [1927] 1 KB 169.
346 *Goodman v Eban (J) Ltd* [1954] 1 All ER 763 at 766.
347 *Morton v Copeland* (1855) 16 CB 517 at 535.
348 See *Clipper Maritime v Shirlstar Container Transport, The Anemone* [1987] 1 Lloyd's Rep 546 in which there are dicta that the 'answerback' of the sender of a telex would constitute a signature.
349 Copyright, Designs and Patents Act 1988, s 78(3)(a).

30. A website serves as an advertising medium for young artists. One artist posts up on the site a computer-generated graphic that he designed. He includes on the graphic his name and is perturbed when he sees his work republished on a website without payment and without acknowledgment. He may well have a strong case of copyright infringement. He would have a similarly strong case of infringement of his moral rights but there are no moral rights over computer-generated artistic works. A hand-generated work digitised and posted on the Internet, in contrast, could be protected by a paternity right.

Infringement

The right of paternity applies to the whole or any substantial part of the work[350]. This right is infringed where the work is commercially published or exhibited without the author's identity being brought to the notice of a viewing person[351].

Integrity

In appropriate circumstances, the author of any literary or musical work has the right not to have the work subjected to derogatory treatment[352]. Similarly, in appropriate circumstances, the author of any artistic work has the right to object to any derogatory treatment of a copyright artistic work in a commercial publication or public exhibition[353]. In comparison to the right of paternity, the right of integrity is far more powerful: it does not need to be asserted, it applies to any part of the work not merely substantial parts[354] and it has far wider scope for infringement.

Infringement

Treatment on the Internet

A 'treatment' of a work means any addition to, deletion from or alteration to or adaptation of the work. It does not include a translation of a literary work or a transcription of a musical work involving no more than a change of key or register[355]. As should be apparent, this is a very wide definition. It may include the re-colouring of an artistic image to look appropriate on a website with a limited palette[356]. It will also include the reduction in size of an artistic work, or cropping of an artistic work to fit in a particular space on a website. More technically, an artistic work will also be 'treated' where it is converted into a digital format with a lower resolution so that the picture appears more grainy or

350 Copyright, Designs and Patents Act 1988, s 89(1).
351 Copyright, Designs and Patents Act 1988, s 77(7)(c).
352 Copyright, Designs and Patents Act 1988, s 80(1).
353 Copyright, Designs and Patents Act 1988. s 80(4)(a).
354 Copyright, Designs and Patents Act 1988, s 89(2).
355 Copyright, Designs and Patents Act 1988, s 80(2)(a).
356 See the analogous French judgment of *Angelica Houston v Turner Entertainment* [1992] ECC 334.

'pixelated'. Literary works may be treated by over-zealous editing or 'snipping' as it is termed in conversation threads. Obviously, literary works are also 'treated' when they are blatently altered.

Derogatory treatment

A treatment is derogatory if it amounts to distortion or mutilation of the work or is otherwise prejudicial to the honour or reputation of the author[357]. This has not been tested at full trial, so it is difficult to guess how favourably the courts will interpret the phrase. Some indication can be provided by a summary judgment given by Rattee J. In *Tidy v Trustees of the Natural History Museum*, Bill Tidy, a well-known cartoon artist, objected to a 16% reduction in size of his cartoons when displayed[358]. The plaintiff claimed that this reduction constituted derogatory treatment as a distortion of the work or by being prejudicial to his honour or reputation.

Rattee J decided that it would be difficult to decide that a treatment was prejudicial to an author's honour and reputation without recourse to evidence from the public as to how the reduction affected the plaintiff's standing in their eyes[359].

If anything can be drawn from this summary judgment it is that the opinion of the author, while sometimes persuasive, is not the final arbiter of whether treatment is derogatory. What can outweigh the author's opinion, when reasonably arrived at, is the reaction of the public. On the Internet, therefore, the public may be aware that a computer screen does not always faithfully represent the artistic works it portrays. Often this lack of quality is as a result of the quality of the viewer's screen or computer specifications; something for which the owner of a server or website cannot be legally responsible.

For literary works, the result is less than clear. Those who edit conversation threads should therefore be careful to treat with respect the postings made by others.

Waiver of rights

The uncertainty and scope of moral rights should make every user of another's copyright on the Internet think carefully about obtaining a waiver from each contributing author. It is not an infringement of the moral rights if the author waives those rights[360]. Unlike assertions, a waiver does not have to meet any formal requirements and can be in relation to any works for any purposes[361]. The waiver can also be made unconditional[362].

Web designers would therefore be wise to obtain such a waiver in respect of any work that they use for a site and Internet Service Providers can also be advised to obtain a waiver on all works submitted by their members. Finally, the terms and conditions for any site should include an express wavier in relation to any posting.

357 Copyright, Designs and Patents Act 1988, s 80(2)(b).
358 [1996] 3 EIPT D–81, 29 March 1995.
359 Rattee J was not clear that the opinion of the author was essential to decide the point, so doubting the application of the Canadian decision *Snow v Eaton Centre Ltd* (1982) 70 CPR (2d) 105.
360 Copyright, Designs and Patents Act 1988, s 87(1).
361 Copyright, Designs and Patents Act 1988, s 87(3)(1).
362 Copyright, Designs and Patents Act 1988, s 87(3)(b).

THE INTERMEDIARY'S POSITION

The text below describes the way in which works may be infringed over the Internet. Perhaps more pertinently it discusses how infringing works may be stored and distributed using the Internet. It will become clear that individuals and corporations who *choose* to infringe material and post it up on websites or pass it to others are left with little or no defence to their actions. Previously 'middle men' such as those companies who host websites or forums together with Internet Service Providers were once forced to rely on older, less 'well-fitting' legislation to exonerate themselves. Since August 2002, these intermediaries have a 'hosting defence' introduced by the Electronic Commerce (EC Directive) Regulations 2002.

Position without the hosting defence

This section considers the existing law of when an Internet Service Provider or other intermediary will be liable for infringing material uploaded onto its servers by one of its members or subscribers. In the same way as someone can post an email to a forum or bulletin board, a person can equally as easily post material to be viewed on a website. This material may be a work in which the poster owns, or has a licence over, the copyright. In this situation, the intermediary has little to fear. There are other times where the poster of the work is depositing an infringing copy of the work on the servers for publication to, potentially, the world. This section concentrates on this situation as this demonstrates how welcome the hosting defence is for intermediaries.

SECONDARY INFRINGEMENT

Reproducing without licence a substantial part of a copyright work is a copyright infringement. The Copyright, Designs and Patents Act 1988, ss 22 to 26 also provide circumstances where other dealings with a copyright work with a 'guilty mind' will constitute secondary infringements of copyright[363]. These dealings include the possession in the course of business of an article which is an infringing copy of a copyright work; a dealing that may be satisfied by a hosting company storing a copy of an infringing work. The requisite guilty mind is where the defendant knows or has reason to believe that the article is an infringing copy. These two aspects to a secondary infringement are discussed below with specific reference to those service providers, usually Internet Service Providers or web hosting companies, who store and transmit digital material on behalf of others.

Dealings

Sections 22 to 26 of the Copyright, Designs and Patents Act 1988 provide the types of dealings in a copyright work that, together with a guilty mind, will

363 It is not dealt with here, but it also should be considered that there can be secondary infringement of a derogatorily treated copyright work: Copyright, Designs and Patents Act 1988, s 83.

constitute a secondary infringement. This section illustrates those dealings by examining them with reference to a website hosted for an individual.

Section 23 provides four situations where, with the requisite guilty mind and without licence of the copyright owner, a person will infringe the copyright in a work, as follows:

1. in the course of business he possesses an article which is an infringing copy of the work;
2. if he sells or lets for hire, or offers or exposes for sale or hire an article which is an infringing copy of the work;
3. in the course of a business he exhibits in public or distributes an article which is an infringing copy of the work; or
4. otherwise than in the course of a business, he distributes an article which is an infringing copy of the work to such an extent as to affect prejudicially the owner of the copyright.

Infringing copy

An article is an infringing copy if its making constituted an infringement of the work in question[364]. It is presumed that an article was made at the time that copyright subsisted in the work if it is shown that the article is a copy of the work and that copyright subsists, or has subsisted, in the work at any time[365].

Course of business

A business is defined by the Act to include a trade or profession[366]. A question arises as to under what circumstances will a person 'dealing' with an infringing copy not be seen as doing so in the course of business. The cases which have considered the meaning of 'course of business' all point to the conclusion that an Internet Service Provider hosting a website or even a newsgroup will do so in the course of business[367]. It has been stated that 'transactions which are only incidental to a business may not be possessed in the course of that business'[368]. It is clear that the Internet Service Providers that provide web space for its customers to host their sites do so very much as part of their business. It costs the Internet Service Provider in terms of support and, albeit marginally, in terms of storage costs. Storing third party data and material is not incidental to the business of any Internet Service Provider and some websites: attracting customers to pay rental charges or to bolster advertising is integral to its business.

It is less likely that an individual who hosts a bulletin board purely as an amateur does so in the course of business; of course, even if he does not, he may still be caught under s 23(d) where his distribution is to such an extent as to affect prejudicially the owner of the copyright.

364 Copyright, Designs and Patents Act 1988, s 27(2).
365 Copyright, Designs and Patents Act 1988, s 27(4).
366 Copyright, Designs and Patents Act 1988, s 178.
367 *L A Gear Inc v Hi-Tec Sports plc* [1992] FSR 121 (re copyright); *Davies v Sumner* [1984] 3 All ER 831 (re trade descriptions); *R & B Customs Brokers Ltd v United Dominions Trust Ltd* [1988] 1 WLR 321 (re Unfair Contract Terms Act 1977).
368 *Pensher Security Doors Ltd v Sunderland City Council* [1999] EWCA Civ 1223, [2000] RPC 249 per Aldous J.

Exhibit, distribute and possess

The four subsections of s 23 use the words 'exhibits', 'distributes' and 'possesses' in relation to infringing articles. There appears to be little doubt that the word 'possesses' carries a wide connotation; the presence on a hard disk drive or memory of a computer would seem to constitute possession. It is for this reason that even if an Internet Service Provider is able to show that no person viewed a website or downloaded a particular file, so that there was no distribution, there may still be secondary infringement by virtue of its storage of the file. Of course, with no distribution any damages will probably be minimal, s 23(a) will therefore probably be appropriate for any infringement in the course of Internet business[369].

Knowledge or reason to believe

This is the most important aspect of secondary infringement and is relevant for the hosting defence: the claimant must prove that the defendant knew or had reason to believe that the article is an infringing copy of the work in question. The proof, for the purposes of this chapter, can be rephrased as: did the controller of the digital depository know or have reason to believe the file was an infringing copy of the copyright work?

Clearly, in most cases, a claimant will be seeking only to show 'reason to believe'; proving knowledge is more onerous than proving a reason to believe. In *LA Gear Inc v Hi-Tec Sports plc* Morritt J decided that 'reason to believe'[370]:

> 'must involve the concept of knowledge of facts from which a reasonable man would arrive at the relevant belief. Facts from which a reasonable man might suspect the relevant conclusion cannot be enough. Moreover, as it seems to me, the phrase does connote the allowance of a period of time to enable the reasonable man to evaluate those facts so as to convert the facts into a reasonable belief.'

On appeal the court upheld this decision for, in Nourse LJ's words, substantially the same reasons as those given by Morritt J. The principle has again been applied by the Court of Appeal in *ZYX Music GmbH v Chris King*[371]. The test would be applied as follows: the claimant should prove that the facts known by or brought to the attention of the controller would have made the reasonable *controller of such a server* believe that the file or element of the site perhaps is infringing. This need not be immediate; a period of time may elapse during which the reasonable controller may come to the belief. If this is satisfied, the actual controller may rebut the allegation by proving that facts in his knowledge made him believe that the article was not infringing.

369 It is perhaps an anomaly of the digital world that it is impossible to distribute a digital file without first possessing it.

370 [1992] FSR 121 at 129.

371 [1997] 2 All ER 129, CA.

Reasonable belief on the Internet

The application of this test to the Internet is vexed. On the one hand, Internet Service Providers are fully aware that pirated software and copyright-infringing images, sound recordings and movies are posted on their servers. In some situations, this will be enough to indicate that a posting is an infringing article. On the other hand, this general knowledge may not be enough to prove a reasonable belief: the very 'work in question' must have been reasonably thought to be infringing[372]. Also, knowing that many files on a server are infringing does not translate into a reasonable knowledge that a *particular* file is an infringement[373].

Electronic Commerce Regulations' Hosting Defence

It should be obvious from the discussion above that an Internet-specific defence will be very welcome to those intermediaries who find themselves unwittingly storing and distributing others' infringing material. These intermediary hosts of such material may be able to rely on two possible defences under the Electronic Commerce (EC Directive) Regulations 2002, reg 19. These 'hosting' defences ensure that ISPs and other such service providers are not liable in any manner for storing the material.

No authority or control

The common element for both defences is that the third party who originally provided the infringing material for storage is not to be acting under the service provider's 'authority' or 'control'[374]. Of course, often a service provider or website will have a contract with its members or customers. Will this constitute 'authority' or 'control'? This author and the DTI believe it will not.

The DTI states in its unbinding note on the Regulations that the concept of control or authority will be akin to 'effective control' under the Defamation Act 1996[375]. In other words, a mere contract to provide services to the third party will not be sufficient to bring the third party under the service provider's 'control' or 'authority'. The Regulations require a closer relationship such as between an employee, the third party, and an employer, the service provider.

An open question remains relating to whether or not the *ability* to control the third party will constitute control for the purposes of the first prong of the defence. After all, most, if not all service providers have the *ability* to remove material that is infringing. Indeed, in a worst-case scenario, a service provider can always simply 'pull the plug' and prevent *all* communication with the outside world; will that be 'control'?

372 Copyright, Designs and Patents Act 1988, s 27(3)(b).
373 See *Columbia Picture Industries v Robinson* [1986] FSR 367.
374 Regulation 19(b).
375 *A Guide for Business to the Electronic Commerce (EC Directive) Regulations 2002*, para 6.7(c).

US authority on a similar question is convincing that, were such an interpretation to be applied, it would be contrary to the spirit of the legislation itself. It would, in effect, state that those who are able to comply with the onus to remove material once notified must be able to remove the material and so are deemed to control it[376]:

> 'First, the "right and ability to control" the infringing activity, as the concept is used in the [Digital Millennium Copyright Act ("DMCA")], cannot simply mean the ability of a service provider to remove or block access to materials posted on its website or stored in its system. To hold otherwise would defeat the purpose of the DMCA and render the statute internally inconsistent. The DMCA specifically requires a service provider to remove or block access to materials posted on its system when it receives notice of claimed infringement. *See* 17 U.S.C. §§ 512(c)(1)(C). The DMCA also provides that the limitations on liability *only* apply to a service provider that has "adopted and reasonably implemented . . . a policy that provides for the termination in appropriate circumstances of [users] of the service provider's system or network who are repeat infringers." *See* 17 U.S.C. §§ 512(i)(1)(A). Congress could not have intended for courts to hold that a service provider loses immunity under the safe harbor provision of the DMCA because it engages in acts that are specifically required by the DMCA.'

Having determined that the person storing the infringing material was not so acting under the authority or control of the service provider, one can look to the key elements of the two hosting defences.

No actual knowledge and no awareness

The first defence is essentially that the service provider must be unwittingly hosting the infringing material[377]. This is expressed in two parts. First, the service provider hosting the material must not have 'actual knowledge' that the storage of was in breach of any law. The second part is that the host must *also* 'not be aware of facts or circumstances' from which it would have been apparent that the activity or information was unlawful.

No actual knowledge of breach of law

In the main, this part of the defence will be taken to mean that the hosting company or person has not been provided with 'notice' about the infringing material. This notice need not, however, be in writing and it certainly need not originate from a court. Indeed, an email to a published email address about the damaging code, or even a telephone warning, is likely to be enough to put the provider 'on notice' and so be fixed with actual knowledge. There is therefore no

376 *Hendrickson v Ebay Inc* 2001 WL 1078981, C D Cal, 4 September 2001.
377 Regulation 19(a).

particular form which will provide the requisite 'actual' knowledge; it is a question of fact for the court. This said, a court will, however, have particular regard to whether a service provider received the notice through an email address published on the provider's website. The court will also have regard to the extent to which the notice includes the sender's full name and address, details of the location of the dubious material and the details of the unlawful nature of the activity or information in question[378].

In the well-publicised US summary judgment *Religious Technology Center v Netcom Online Communications Services Inc*, a member of the Centre left the religion and then published the centre's materials through a Netcom Internet connection on a Usenet newsgroup: alt.religion.scientology[379]. The Centre sued Netcom for both direct and contributory infringement of copyright. While the court was sure that there was no direct infringement, it was clear that the plaintiffs[380]:

> 'raised a genuine issue of fact regarding whether Netcom should have known that Erlich [the former member] was infringing their copyright after receiving a letter [fixing them with notice] from plaintiffs, whether Netcom substantially participated in the infringement, and whether Netcom has a valid fair use defense. *Accordingly, Netcom is not entitled to summary judgment on plaintiffs' claim of contributory copyright infringement.*' [381]

In this case, therefore, the letter from the plaintiffs was the means by which the Service Provider was put on notice. This is relevant. Even though the Regulations state that a court shall take into whether or not email was used to serve the notice, the Regulations do not prescribe that email must be used. Indeed, Service Providers and other intermediaries should ensure that all their 'official' addresses, in particular registered office addresses, are staffed with individuals who can spot, and act upon, such notices.

No awareness of facts or circumstances

Even if the Service Provider has no actual knowledge, to act as a defence to claims to damages, they must still be able to demonstrate that they have no awareness of relevant facts or circumstances which would lead them to believe the material was unlawful. If they cannot do this, they will need to rely on the second defence to escape liability.

For much infringing material stored with Service Providers, this will be very difficult to prove. Most sound recordings are still not available in a digital format which can be stored on a website; CDs remain the main form of their distribution. Consequently, the storage of a well-known sound recording on a website is very likely to be infringing and also likely to be within the awareness of the service provider once alerted. Admittedly, certain material is encrypted or given

378 Regulation 22.
389 No C–95–20091 RMW (ND Cal, 21 November 1995).
380 Emphasis added.
381 The action was entirely settled on 22 August 1996.

coded titles; here it is more difficult to prove awareness. In most situations, however, a service provider will therefore be unable to demonstrate the necessary level of unawareness to 'pass' this second test. As a consequence, they will also not benefit from the first hosting defence.

Expeditious action on notice

The second hosting defence, again as a pre-requisite requires the infringer not to be acting under the authority or control of the intermediary. Once this is satisfied, the service provider will have the benefit of the defence if they act expeditiously to remove or disable access to it as soon as they know about[382].

Remove or disable expeditiously

This requirement is essentially that the service provider must act to stop any further harm as soon as they know about it. The Regulations state that 'upon obtaining such knowledge or awareness [the service provider must act] expeditiously to remove or to disable access to the information.'[383]

The concept of 'actual knowledge' and the requisite 'awareness' is discussed above but 'awareness' in this context deserves more attention. The concept of 'awareness' is a wide one; it seems to encompass the service provider having a general 'sense' of the state of the technical and legal standards for unlawful material. Does this mean that a service provider unwittingly hosting infringing material will be liable because a well-respected website publishes details of the infringement of the copyright work? The answer is 'no' for two good reasons.

First, the Electronic Commerce Regulations implement the Electronic Commerce Directive. Article 15(1) states that:

> 'Member States shall not impose a general obligation on providers, when providing the services covered by [the] Articles [concerning mere conduit, caching and hosting], to monitor information which they transmit or store, nor a general obligation actively to seek facts or circumstances indicating illegal activity.'

This Article is not explicitly implemented in the Regulations. The reason for this must be that Parliament believed that nothing in the Regulations did impose a general obligation to monitor such facts and circumstances. It follows that the Regulations do not, in effect, force service providers to watch the press and websites for details of possible infringements to be able to benefit from the defence.

The second justification for the unwitting service provider not being liable is that, on awareness or knowledge, they are required to remove or disable access to the infringing material. Of course, if all they know is that the material is being copied 'somewhere', how are they to remove or disable access to it? They

382 Regulation 19(a)(ii).
383 Section 19(a)(ii).

would need actively to search for it on their network. As explained above, a general obligation to seek or search for such information, is not envisaged within scope the legislation.

Of course, where the service provider acts to *facilitate* the infringement, they will be deemed to have the requisite knowledge but not to have acted quickly enough. In the US case *Playboy Enterprises Inc v George Frena*, Frena operated a bulletin board on a subscription basis[384]. The board stored copies of Playboy's pictures but these were not posted there without Frena's knowledge or awareness: he actually removed from the photographs Playboy's own text and substituted his own name and contact details! Under the Electronic Commerce Regulations, any operator who did such an activity would then certainly have (or be deemed to have) the requisite awareness that the uploaded images infringed Playboy's copyright. They will then need to remove or disable access to them expeditiously.

This then leaves the issue of how fast is 'expeditiously'. There is little doubt that this is quicker than 'reasonably quickly' but nevertheless will be assessed with reference to the facts and circumstances of the situation. It can be said with some certainty that a service provider who is sent a specific notice about an infringing movie file on a Thursday evening will need to act well before the weekend to do so expeditiously.

EMAIL

Infringement by recipient

This section considers what might constitute infringement of the copyright in someone's email. It is assumed that there is copyright in the email. When an email is received, it has already been copied; it is copied into the memory and probably hard disk drive of the receiver's machine. That much copying will certainly be implied by the common law (and after the implementation of the Copyright Directive, statute) not to be infringement: it is necessary for business efficacy and can be implied by sending it over the Internet rather than, say, by post. What is not implied is for an individual (rather than a server because that is likely to be an essential part of a technological process)[385] to forward the message without either an express or implied licence to do so. A good example of this is any email that is headed 'Private & Confidential'.

31. Paul sends an email to Robbie. It ends, 'Actually, you should tell Charlotte about this.' Robbie forwards the email to Charlotte who then replies to Paul. Paul is upset that Charlotte read the email, but he has no legal redress in copyright. His end-note was an implied licence that Robbie would not infringe the copyright by copying the whole message to Charlotte. Charlotte also does not infringe Paul's copyright; her licence is implied by the common law.

384 839 F Supp 1552 (MD Fla 1993).

385 See the discussion above at page 249 relating to the Directive on Harmonisation of Certain Aspects of Copyright and Related Rights in the Information Society, art 5.1.

Infringement by Internet Service Provider

It has been described that an Internet Service Provider may legally hold a copy of all its member's emails until they are collected by the member. But there are times, say for backup or security purposes, that the emails are retained for longer. Internet Service Providers are advised to alert members to this additional copying by including such a statement in their terms and conditions with each member. The legal difficulty is that, while a member can provide a licence to their Internet Service Provider in respect of emails authored by them, the member cannot provide a licence on behalf of others for emails sent to them. Of course here, the Internet Service Provider can rely on its hosting defence in reg 19 of the Electronic Commerce Regulations 2002.

Infringement by forums

There are two discrete issues concerned with controllers of bulletin boards and storage website infringing copyright. The first is the issue of what the controller can do with copyright material owned and posted by its members. This will be discussed presently. The second issue is the liability a controller of a forum has in respect of copyright material *not* owned by its members but nevertheless posted on the forum. This issue of infringing material is discussed in the section below.

Every email posted by its author to a forum, bulletin board or conversation thread carries with it an implied licence, from common law. In addition, the Electronic Commerce Regulation's hosting defence provides a defence for the host in respect of any unwitting infringement[386]. This licence and defence permit the copying of the email or message on the server itself and also onto any other viewer's computer that is legitimately permitted *by the controller* to access the email. What is uncertain is the extent to which the controller may re-post or authorise re-posting to other forums. This uncertain issue can be more easily addressed by considering separately commercial forums from Usenet newsgroups.

Usenet newsgroups

A Usenet newsgroup can be republished by any Internet Service Provider. Consequently there is an implied licence by those who post emails to a newsgroup that their work is free from publishing restriction[387]. This is implied from the course of trade with Usenet. This might not mean that the email is free to be published in newsprint or in a medium other than the Internet. It is clear that authors of newsgroup postings wish their work to be distributed as widely as possible. Of course, any implied licence can be rebutted by an express provision to the contrary within the email or posting.

386 See 'Electronic Commerce Regulations' Hosting Defence' at page 262.
387 Licences to 'all the world' have been upheld as valid. See *Mellor v Australian Broadcasting Commission* [1940] AC 491.

32. Mr Smith is a contributor to alt.female.erotica and ends all his postings with 'Not for re-posting or redistribution on any other newsgroup.' Ms Jones re-posts his messages to a forum dealing with women's exploitation. That re-posting constitutes an unlicensed copy of the whole of a copyright work; it is an infringement of Mr Smith's copyright.

This scenario allows two distinctions to be drawn. First, between a 'human' infringer, ie the user who re-posts the message, and the owners of the server 'computers' who *store* the re-posting.

Human 'requests' to infringe

When a message is posted to a Usenet forum, it enters the forum at the 'request' of a human. So, Ms Jones will have used her connection to the Internet to provide Mr Smith's message, in digital form, to an Internet Service Provider which hosts the forum. Because this message is, or contains a large part, of a copyright work without licence from Mr Smith (the owner), Ms Jones will infringe copyright in the work.

Server 'response' to infringe

As soon as Ms Jones clicked the 'send' or 'OK' icon to post Mr Smith's message, this message was sent to the forum automatically. Many computers were involved in the request. These include: the first Internet Service Provider; possibly a second Internet Service Provider hosting a copy of the Usenet forum; all the other Internet Service Providers hosting a copy of the forum and the intermediary servers acting as conduits between the previous three 'families' of server.

We have seen that the posted message infringes Mr Smith's copyright. It can also be said with reasonable certainty that each of these computers has copied a substantial part of the work without licence from Mr Smith. However, the Electronic Commerce Regulation's hosting defence will provide a defence for the host in respect of any unwitting infringement until they receive a possible complaint from Mr Smith or are otherwise put 'on notice'.

Commercial forums

A controller of a commercial forum may attempt to assert copyright in the compilation that constitutes each conversation thread, and generally by express agreement, a licence over any individual's postings. As a result of such an express agreement it is likely that there will be terms that prevent any re-postings by individuals of others' emails. An individual is unlikely to be contractually restricted from posting his own message elsewhere[388].

To re-publish an entire conversation thread to another forum may be an infringement of the copyright over the compilation. This depends on whether the conversation thread as a compilation is actually protected by copyright.

388 Or rather, such a contractual term would have to be drawn to the attention of a new member to be enforceable as it would be unusual.

33. A member of the Mechanics Forum is also a member of the Engineers Forum. These are operated by two rival Service Providers. The member re-posts from the Mechanics Forum to the Engineers Forum a conversation between him and another mechanic. This lasts about 15 lines out of a thread that is made up from over 200 lines from 40 different contributors. The controller of the Mechanics Forum threatens the mechanic with an action for copyright infringement. The controller has three significant legal hurdles. First, it must be proved that there is a copyright in the compilation; second, that it, rather than all the 40 contributors jointly, own the compilation; and third, that the taking is a substantial part of the copyrighted conversation thread.

Even if the conversation thread is not protected by copyright, for want of skill, labour or judgment, it is possibly protected as a database. Even if not, the Service Provider may still be able to assert its contractual rights. This is achieved by ensuring that every person who is allowed to access a conversation thread enters a contract which stipulates that no material, other than the member's own, will be re-posted elsewhere. A person that does re-post the material will be in contractual breach. Re-posting a thread from a commercial forum to a Usenet newsgroup will almost always be a clear copyright infringement of the compilation right, if present, and more certainly of the rights held by the individual author of the posted messages.

Infringement using peer-to-peer networks

This chapter has already considered the manner in which a central repository of files may be liable if these files infringe copyright. However, there is more than one way to store a group of digital files for access across the Internet. Another way is to *distribute* the storage and spread the files out across more than one computer. This method has spawned a huge number of programs and websites, singularly created, to facilitate the storage and distribution of infringing sound recordings, pictures, programs and even movies. The English law that could apply to these systems is described below; first, the technology.

Peer-to-peer storage systems

Suppose we wanted to store two files, 1 and 2. We could, as mentioned, put them both on a central server. A person could access the central server, search for one of the files, and with permission, download it. The alternative distribution method could work as follows. We could use two servers, A & B, each storing one of the files only but *both* holding details of where the files are stored. Let us say that server A stores file 1 and server B stores file 2. Each server will also store an 'index' which indicates that file 1 is found on server A and file 2 on server B. If one now wanted to download one of the files one could contact *either* server and it would either supply the download itself, or, use its index to direct you to its neighbour.

Now imagine that there are hundreds of thousands of servers and many millions of files spread amongst them. Now add to that network a more sophisticated index. Instead of each of the servers holding an index of the files held across the network, they each hold an index of their own files *and the locations of their neighbours* in the network. Now search for a file, say, 231. The first server you contact, say AAA, will search for the file on its hard drive. If it is there, you may download it. If not, server AAA will ask the same request of each of its neighbours, say, BBB, ABC, and FGH. Again, if they hold file 231, they will allow you to download it. If they too do not store the file they will ask their few neighbours the same request. Within seconds the search for file 231 will propagate across the network until it is found or all the servers have failed to find it.

Finally, instead of thinking of these servers as being special computers such as those used by Internet Service Providers, think of them as any old PC hooked up the Internet used by a regular individual. Suddenly you will be imagining a huge network of individuals who can distribute files amongst themselves without any central body either 'regulating' them or knowing the complete scope of the files stored. Try to picture about 62 million people currently. And, unfortunately for copyright owners, think of the files as software, movies, and sound recordings. Suddenly you are thinking of the proliferation of a peer-to-peer network just like Napster, now gone[389], and some of its replacements such as Morpheus, LimeWire, Audiogalaxy and KaZaA.

User infringement

Users of such peer-to-peer systems generally conduct two activities. They copy their own material and store it on their own hard drive. They also download material from others' hard drives to their own and play it. Without a defence close at hand, these two activities would constitute infringement of the works. When one loads material onto one's hard drive, say a sound recording, the recording is copied and this copy is substantial. This therefore amounts, without more, to an infringement of the copyright in the sound recording. There is no appropriate defence to this despite it being such a widespread activity.

Of course, users of a peer-to-peer network not only copy such works, they also title them and position them on their computer in such a way as to allow other members of the network to copy the works.

The Copyright, Designs and Patents Act 1988, s 16(2) states:

> '[c]opyright in a work is infringed by a person whom without the licence of the copyright owner does, *or authorises another to do*, any of the acts restricted by copyright.'

In a peer-to-peer network, the restricted act that would be complained of is the copying and issue of copies of the work to the public[390]. An authorisation has been defined as[391],

389 Napster was ultimately a victim of its own success. Its massive index of users' infringing sound recordings drew the attention of the record industry and its lawyers. After numerous cases it was eventually forced by the US courts to select out infringing material from its *central* index of stored files. In March 2001 the record industry duly supplied Napster with a list of 135,000 songs to be removed from its service. Napster was not able to comply and after an abortive acquisition by Bertelsmann, moved into a bankruptcy liquidation in September 2002. See *A&M Records v Napster Inc* 239 F 3d 1004 (9th Cir 2001).

390 Copyright, Designs and Patents Act 1988, s 16(1).

391 *CBS Songs Ltd v Amstrad Consumer Electronics plc* [1988] AC 1013 at 1054 per Lord Templeman, HL.

> 'a grant or purported grant, which may be expressed or implied, of the right to do the act complained of.'

Indeed, users, with great care, specifically include some files within one 'folder' allowing others to copy them ensuring, presumably, that their personal and private files are kept well away from this published folder. It follows that the users are purporting to confer on all the other users of the network the right to copy the infringing works.

Other infringement

Apart from the innocent Internet Service Providers and telecommunications companies who pass these infringing works to and fro (only storing them for a short period), and benefit from the Electronic Commerce Regulations, regs 17 and 18, who else is involved in these peer-to-peer networks? The programmers of the peer-to-peer software and those who distribute it, of course.

There will be difficulties in suing these individuals and companies for the same reasons as CBS had such difficulty in successfully suing Amstrad for its tape-to-tape recorders. In that case the defendant manufactured and sold music systems including a double cassette deck for copying tapes. There was little doubt in the minds of the House of Lords that a number of members of the public used them for copying pre-recorded tapes, so infringing the copyright in the works recorded on the copied tape. The House of Lords nevertheless held that the defendant had not authorised the infringements which would be committed by the public.

Lord Templeman gave the leading speech stating[392]:

> '. . . an authorisation means a grant or purported grant, which may be express or implied, of the right to do the act complained of. Amstrad conferred on the purchaser the power to copy but did not grant or purport to grant the right to copy.'

The same can be said of peer-to-peer software and its sellers. It is well known that the software can be used to copy copyright works, so infringing them. What cannot be said is that the software is purporting to grant rights to copy *a particular* file. And without this specificity all the software confers is the 'power to copy' but no purported right to copy.

Websites

This section now looks to the other side of the coin and considers how the copyright in a website may be infringed. This is an issue often overlooked by those who deal with the World Wide Web; merely because a site is available for all to view does not mean that all the images and applets and text can be used at

392 *CBS Songs Ltd v Amstrad Consumer Electronics plc* [1988] AC 1013 at 1054 per Lord Templeman, HL.

will. It is all too often said that, because a website is in the 'public domain' (whatever that term legally means) that the website can be freely copied. This is a classic misunderstanding of the nature of copyright: merely because a copyright owner chooses to publish his work in a particular way does not entitle the rest of the world to copy the work without permission.

Framing, linking and searching are integral aspects of the World Wide Web. For this reason, many have sought to deny the application of the law to prevent it. Of course, there are many circumstances when the activities may be illegal. A prior contract, maybe even one at the 'entry' to the site, may be breached. The use of a frame or particular link may infringe the claimant's trade marks leaving viewers confused into whose text they are reading. After examining backup copies of websites, this section considers the way in which copyright and database rights may be utilised to prevent such framing and repeated searching.

Backup copies

Some users believe that a website comes complete with an implied licence to take a backup copy, on disk rather than the normal memory only[393]. Indeed, the 'offline viewing' facility standard with Microsoft's Internet Explorer makes it trivial to create these copies. There are also useful websites that allow one to make a perfect copy of a website and to hold that copy on its servers. This is unlikely to be implied by either the courts or the law. It has been discussed that a website is a program for the purposes of copyright. Under the Copyright, Designs and Patents Act 1988, s 50A(1) lawful users of a computer program do not infringe copyright by making a backup copy of it *which it is necessary for him to have for the purposes of his lawful use*. It will rarely be necessary to take a backup copy of a website. The material that is being backed up is already available 24 hours a day on the website that originally supplied it. It may be *convenient* not to have to re-access a website but is seldom *necessary*. And as more owners of websites compete for advertising income they are increasingly aware of the need to have viewers re-accessing their pages to have 'sticky' content. The more 'hits' on a page each hour, the more one may be able to charge advertisers for space.

Increasingly, however, websites have explicit restrictions on copying in certain situations. Viewers and users of websites should be cautious of these restrictions which may be found in the context of a positive licence. Some prevent viewers from even making a printed copy of a site. Other sites prevent the use of their graphics[394]. These explicit licences are not added on sites as rhetoric. If contravened they will have the result that the viewer has infringed copyright. If this infringement is then 'advertised' by, say, posting a copied graphic on one's own website, the copyright owner may well take action.

393 A website viewed but not saved will not be available for re-viewing after the computer is switched off and then on again. A website saved to disk will be re-viewable even after the computer has been switched off.

394 The popular browsers allow users to copy a graphic to be used as the computer screen's backdrop; even this may be infringement by the viewer.

34. An online newspaper has a classified adverts section which allows a user to search for a particular item for sale. Where this item is not currently advertised, the newspaper automatically searches its competitors online classifieds and provides a link to suitable items for sale on their sites. No doubt many sites linked-to will be happy to benefit from this seemingly altruistic link. They are receiving additional traffic to their site. However, if their terms and conditions bar such 'deep-linking' the online newspaper will be infringing the database right which subsists in the collection of adverts by utilising the database as an unlawful user.

Framing

The World Wide Web was created to link together documents in a seamless fashion. Like a 'live' footnote, a link on one document can be clicked upon and the linked document is then retrieved. The browser replaces the linking document with a freshly retrieved document; this new document may have been stored on an different web server. A browser can also be instructed to display on one screen a collage of images and text all from different web servers at the same time. This appears to the viewer as one document from one source; in fact and at law there are a number of different owners of the copyright in these images and some of them may see this selective copying as an infringement of copyright.

The commercial concern at this framing is evident from the US case *Washington Post Co v Total News Inc*[395]. Total News operated a website deriving its revenue from selling advertising on the site. To attract advertising, the site provided its audience with news articles published by the plaintiffs. Each article enclosed had been within a 'frame' around which was the totalnews.com logo and advertising. There is one commercial issue which needs to be highlighted before discussing the legal aspects of the case. Each of the plaintiffs also sold advertising on their site next to their articles. The defendant, therefore, was competing for this advertising revenue but was not troubled with first having to write the content; it merely had to gather the stories together.

The plaintiff's complaint included allegations of trade mark infringement but also copyright infringement of the text of the articles. The case was settled and the defendant agreed not to re-publish material from the plaintiff's sites as long as it was entitled to link to this material without passing off or infringing the plaintiff's trade marks. Paragraph 4(d) of the Settlement Order provides:

> '[P]laintiffs agree that Defendants may link from Totalnews.com website or any other website to any Plaintiff's website, provided that: . . . (d) each Plaintiff's agreement to permit linking by Defendants remains revocable, an IS business day's notice in accordance with [manner of providing notice] at each Plaintiff's sole discretion. Revocation by any Plaintiff shall not affect any other terms and conditions set forth herein.'

395 97 Civ 190 (PKL) (SDNY complaint filed 20 February 1997).

This clause indicates that the plaintiffs believed that at law they were entitled to prevent a mere link being made to their sites. It is submitted, as has been discussed, that a link of itself does not infringe the copyright in the title, or headline of the article because it is likely not to qualify for protection. Further, it is submitted that there is also no work qualifying for protection in a single URL which points to the content-bearing site and article. It is therefore conceivable that only trade mark issues would entitle the blocking of a link to one's site as has been discussed earlier. No doubt for these and other reasons, the Settlement Order continues:

> 'If Defendant refuse [sic] to cease linking upon notice, and any Plaintiff brings an action to enforce its rights under this subparagraph, it shall be an affirmative defense that Defendant's conduct does not otherwise infringe or violate Plaintiff's rights under any theory of any intellectual property, unfair competition or other law.'

Making an unlicensed article

The copyright owner of a computer graphic used within a website has the right to license, or choose not to license, almost any use of the image and material. What is questionable is whether it is an infringement, not to copy another's graphics or text, but instead to include a command that instructs the *viewer's* computer to copy those graphics. Although this is untested in the UK courts, it is submitted that, inclusion without permission of the owner of these in-line graphics or other frames may infringe their copyright. There is certainly copying; no website can be viewed without there being copying. The question that arises is who is doing the copying? From a technical perspective the copying is actually being conducted by the viewer *with the instruction* from the framer's website.

The Copyright, Designs and Patents 1988, s 24(1)(a) provides that it is a secondary infringement to make an unlicensed article specifically designed or adapted for making copies of the copyright work when the maker knows or has reason to believe that it is to be used to make infringing copies. It is submitted that a line of code can be an article and that as the URL refers to a specific graphic or element on a specific website this article is specifically designed for making copies of a work[396]. The final requirement is a guilty mind that the article would be used to make infringing copies. This also is satisfied. Unless the viewer turns off the automatic loading of images, the framer's programmer knows that a copy will be made of the material. As the programmer is the person who has electronically contacted the material's true site, this person will know that the copy will infringe. It will be outside the bounds of most implied or explicit licences on websites. It is clearly arguable that using in-line links or frames without a licence is secondary copyright infringement.

DEEP LINKS AND SPIDERS

Occasionally, a website finds its links being systematically 'searched' by another website. This is often conducted so that the searching website can keep abreast

396 Unlike a tape recorder that makes copies per se rather than makes copies of specific CDs.

of, say, the prices on the harvested website. This may allow the harvesting website to conduct 'comparison' shopping across many similar websites. It is often called 'spidering'. Further, a series of link from the harvested site may then appear on the other site, so-called 'deep links'.

In *Ticketmaster Corpn v Microsoft Corpn*, Ticketmaster, the world's largest provider of computerised ticket services, complained that Microsoft, the world's largest software company, was operating a website which contained various links to Ticketmaster's website[397]. Many of these links were created automatically by Microsoft repeatedly searching the Ticketmaster site for particular items of interest.

One could imagine that Ticketmaster would be flattered and would benefit financially from this link. Instead, Ticketmaster suggested that Microsoft was 'feathering its own nest at Ticketmaster's expense.' Microsoft, however, merely 'referenced' Ticketmaster's site; it did not include on its site any of Ticketmaster's content, only its brand. As a consequence, Microsoft was not infringing the significant copyright held by Ticketmaster. Ticketmaster's complaint therefore focused only on trade mark issues.

Under English law, this case and others like it, may well involve an application of database rights to the facts.

EU database rights

Database rights were introduced into UK law by the Copyright and Rights in Databases Regulations 1997. This short statute implemented Directive 96/9/EC. At the time of writing only one case has been heard under the legislation; the case, unfortunately, is inconclusive as the Court of Appeal referred the key questions to the ECJ for determination. At this time, therefore, the judgment given by Mr Justice Laddie stands in limbo.

In the case, *British Horseracing board v William Hill*[398], the British Horseracing Board complained that their database of details relating to horseracing and horses was infringed by William Hill, the bookmakers. The claimants spent in the region of four million pounds each year to obtain, verify and present the contents of its database. Each year would see 800,000 new records or changes made to the database. The claimant provides the data from this database to many participating elements of the racing industry, including bookmakers. The defendant has and pays for a licence to use this data in its licensed betting shops, on television's Ceefax service and for telephone betting. It did not have a licence to publish the data on its website and yet each day, it repurposed its existing non-Internet data feed to re-publish pertinent data on its website.

Databases

A database is defined as a collection of independent works, data or other materials which are arranged in a systematic or methodical way, and are individually

397 CV 97–3055 RAP (CD Cal filed 28 April 1997).
398 [2001] 2 CMLR 215.

accessible by electronic or other means[399]. It is submitted that most websites, or at least most websites worth framing, deep linking or spidering, store a high degree of data in a systematic or methodical way. Indeed, most large websites use content management systems or other applications to arrange the content from their site into a database (in the computer sense). It is also relevant that the Directive indicates a database may be more than merely text or digits. It may also encompass sounds, images, and other data[400].

In usual circumstances, the maker of the database is the person who takes the initiative in obtaining, verifying or presenting the contents of a database and assumes the risk of investing in that obtaining, verification or presentation[401]. It is vital here to appreciate that the maker of a database takes the initiative and risk of investing in the *database* but not necessarily its contents. A database is a collection of *other* works and data. The maker of the database may have had no hand in the creation of these underlying elements. To be a maker of a database one needs only to have taken the initiative and risk of obtaining, verifying or presenting the underlying data. Databases are therefore more about 'contents pages' and 'indexes' than chapters and sentences.

Many complex websites utilise the skills of database architects and other computer programmers to ensure that the database supporting a website functions correctly. This is an ongoing and expensive task; most websites, in particular ecommerce websites, have a continually changing structure and appearance to keep both stock and the look of the website fresh. These websites are likely to qualify as a database.

Database rights

A database is protected by a database right if there has been a substantial investment in obtaining, verifying or presenting the contents of the database[402]. The concept of investment, however, is wider than mere financial investment. It also includes human or technical resources[403]. It follows, again, that most websites supported by 'back office' databases or content management systems are likely to have the requisite investment to justify the database right protecting their databases.

The database right protects the database for 15 years from end of the calendar year in which the making of the database was completed or, if earlier, 15 years from the end of the calendar year in which the database was first made available to the public. In addition, a new 15 year period will commence if there are any substantial changes made to the contents of a database, including a substantial change resulting from the accumulation of successive additions, deletions or alterations, which would result in the database being considered to be a substantial new investment[404]. The databases supporting even the oldest websites will therefore be protected for some time to come.

399 Copyright, Designs and Patents Act 1988, s 3A(1).
400 Recital 17.
401 Regulation 14(1).
402 Regulation 13(1).
403 Regulation 12.
404 Regulation 17.

Infringement of database rights

A person infringes a database right if, without the consent of the owner of the right, he extracts or re-utilises all or a substantial part of the contents of the database[405]. The term 'extracts' means the permanent or temporary transfer of those contents to another medium by any means or in any form[406]. It therefore does not necessarily entail the contents being visible to the public nor does it mean that the copied database remains permanently. It may serve a short-term purpose, be deleted, and yet still have been extracted. Extracted can therefore be contrasted with re-utilises which means making the database contents available to the public by any means[407]. It is critical to understand that a 'substantial part' need not be extracted or re-utilised all at once: repeated and systematic extraction or re-utilisation of insubstantial parts of the contents of a database may amount to the extraction or re-utilisation of a substantial part of those contents[408]. And substantial may mean in terms of quantity or quality or a combination of both[409].

Finally, a lawful user of a database which has been made available to the public in any manner is entitled to extract or re-utilise insubstantial parts of the contents of the database for any purpose[410].

Deep links, spiders and database rights

It is argued above that many websites will be supported by databases. And because of the investment in these databases, they will be protected by database rights. What remains to be answered is how these database rights may be infringed by taking deep links from them and spiders over them.

Often those who deep link to websites do so both automatically and often. As in the *Ticketmaster* case these individuals and companies are trying to 'fill' their website with links from others. Where this is prevented by terms and conditions applicable to the website, these individuals will not be lawful users. They are therefore re-utilising (and probably have extracted) the various links that they sport on their site. These links form part of the database that is protected by the database right. All that remains for factual analysis is whether or not the parts re-utilised and extracted form a substantial part of the database. One will recall that the concept of 'substantial' here is defined by the legislation (unlike for copyright) as being qualitative or quantitative or both. Where the links copied, time and time again, are those most pertinent or most important, there will be a good basis to plead that the links form a substantial part of the whole database.

405 Regulation 16(1).
406 Regulation 12.
407 Regulation 12.
408 Regulation 16.
409 Regulation 12. The first English case concerning this and other aspects of database rights, unfortunately, leaves us with no clear precedent as to their application. In *British Horseracing Board Ltd v William Hill* [2001] EWCA Civ 1268, [2001] All ER (D) 431 (Jul) Mr Justice Laddie's judgment was appealed to the Court of Appeal who were unsure enough of the correct application of the law to refer a number of significant questions to the European Court of Justice.
410 Regulation 19(1).

35. A meteorological website is funded by advertising and features seven day forecasts for about 50 popular holiday destinations. One can search the site with reference to a city name, a country and even a desired temperature. A travel website creates a program that automatically 'grabs' ten relevant links from the weather website and inserts them next to its descriptions of its package holidays. The weather site uses a database to drive its sophisticated search engine. The travel website is not only extracting from the database but also re-utilising it by publishing the links on its own site. Bearing in mind the travel website systematically and repeatedly copies ten links, it is likely to be a substantial extraction from the database.

JURISDICTION OVER INFRINGEMENT

This section considers the type of situation where a UK copyright work on the Internet is dealt with abroad in a way that would be an infringement if here. The sort of situation considered is where a web developer in the US uses a UK copyright graphic on his website that is maintained in Holland but accessed throughout the world. In this situation do the English courts have any jurisdiction to hear complaints of an infringement from the UK copyright owner?

Infringement abroad

The English courts' approach to foreign infringement of English intellectual property has already been met in relation to trade marks[411]. Some of the conclusions reached there will be equally applicable here. Infringement is a legal term in relation to a legal right granted within a territory. One cannot infringe a UK copyright abroad because 'abroad' is outside the width of the monopoly granted by the UK legislation[412].

> 'The owner of the copyright in a work has, in accordance with the following provisions of this Chapter, the exclusive right to do the following acts *in the United Kingdom* . . .'

One can perform actions in relation to a UK copyright work that are the descriptive equivalent of infringement but those actions will not be infringement unless within the UK territory. Courts have been restraining the rights of copyright holders in this way for many years.

> 'It is therefore clear that copyright under the English Act is strictly defined in terms of territory. The intangible right which is copyright is merely a right to do certain acts exclusively in the United Kingdom: only acts done in the United Kingdom constitute infringement either direct or indirect of that right.'[413]

411 See 'Jurisdiction over infringement', at page 211.
412 Copyright, Designs and Patents Act 1988, s 16(1). Emphasis added.
413 *Def Lepp Music v Stuart-Brown* [1986] RPC 273 at 275.

The dicta above are with reference to an activity carried on *outside* the UK that is purported to be an infringement *inside* the UK. The courts are attempting to resolve the conflict of laws where the intellectual property right is dealt with in a territory other than the one that granted the right initially. To illustrate, to copy in the US a UK literary work is clearly outside the jurisdiction of the English courts: the action that constitutes the infringement occurs outside the UK. But these are not the only types of infringement. There are situations where the *action* takes place outside the UK, but the action may still be litigated in the UK, because the Civil Jurisdiction and Judgments Act 1982 permits the trial of the nevertheless *foreign* infringement in the UK's courts. This is discussed below[414]. There are other situations (as opposed to 'rights to sue') where the action takes place outside the UK, but the infringement occurs within the territory[415].

Authorise to infringe

In *ABKCO Music and Records Inc v Music Collection International Ltd* the Court of Appeal was faced with an authorisation to infringe made from abroad[416]. ABKCO claimed a British copyright over certain sound recordings made by Sam Cooke. The second defendant was a Danish company that carried on no business in the UK but that did grant a licence to the first defendant to manufacture and sell copies of the sound recordings in the UK.

ABKCO sued under the Copyright, Designs and Patents Act 1988, s 16(2) that states[417]:

> '[c]opyright in a work is infringed by a person who without the licence of the copyright owner does, *or authorises another to do*, any of the acts restricted by the copyright.'

The restricted act complained of being authorised was the copying and issue of copies of the work to the public[418]. The Court of Appeal had to consider two discrete legal issues: could an authorisation made abroad be litigated within the jurisdiction of the English courts? The second issue was the substantive one: was the granting of a licence an authorisation under the Act?

Hoffmann LJ was clear, even in the fact of the general authority, that for authorisations of infringement the Copyright, Designs and Patents Act 1988 did apply to foreigners[419]:

> 'It does not matter that the acts which preceded that consequence [of infringement] all took place abroad. It is I think sufficient that the definition of a tort requires an act and that that act is performed within the United Kingdom, however it may be linked to the preliminary act performed abroad.'

414 See 'Actionable foreign infringements', at page 281.
415 It is also possible that, because of the Brussels Regulation arts 2 and 6(1), an infringer is sued in a contracting state other than the state which vested the copyright in the claimant.
416 [1995] RPC 657.
417 Emphasis added.
418 Copyright, Designs and Patents Act 1988, s 16(1).
419 [1995] RPC 657 at 660. Agreed to by Neill LJ.

As a final indication of the common sense of this approach Lord Justice Hoffman added[420],

> 'I think that a territorial limitation on the act of authorising would lead to anomalies. Anyone contemplating the grant of a licence to do an act restricted by copyright would be able to avoid liability simply by having the document executed abroad.'

This case teaches that for authorisation the place of communication is irrelevant so long as the authority is to do an infringing act within the jurisdiction. This reasoning can be applied to the Internet, specifically, the World Wide Web[421].

Bounds of authority

An authorisation has been defined as[422]:

> 'a grant or purported grant, which may be expressed or implied, of the right to do the act complained of.'

This raises an interesting issue which can best be illustrated with the following scenario.

36. A programmer in Brazil copies an entire applet from an English website. As the copying takes place outside the UK, the UK copyright is not infringed. The Brazilian then places the applet onto his own website which can be accessed around the world. An individual accesses the website from the UK. Necessarily the applet is copied onto the individual's own computer. This will constitute a copy under the Copyright, Designs and Patents Act 1988. As the applet's copyright owner has not provided a licence to copy this work the Brazilian is actually providing an authorisation to infringe a UK copyright. This is an infringement within the jurisdiction of the English courts.

This scenario indicates that one who copies a UK copyright work from elsewhere but then specifically allows it to be retrieved over the Internet will be providing authority to infringe the copyright. The reason for this is that the Internet does not transport copyright works; it allows them to be copied. So specifically to put an infringing work on the Internet should always be viewed as an authorisation to copy the work, infringing it once more. To counter this, a foreign defendant would have to resist the court's jurisdiction, or prove that the work was not copied within the UK[423]. This may appear to some as being a conclusion that strikes at the heart of the Internet itself. To intellectual property owners, on the other hand, it is serious and worrying if a work can be copied without permission outside the

420 [1995] RPC 657 at 660–661.

421 There is a risk that infringement actions based on the Copyright, Designs and Patents Act 1988, ss 17, 18, or 19 will be viewed by the courts as 'occurring' outside the jurisdiction.

422 *CBS Songs Ltd v Amstrad Consumer Electronics plc* [1988] AC 1013 at 1054 per Lord Templeman, HL.

423 The mere existence of the infringing work on a website that *can* be accessed from the UK should be enough on which to base a *quia timet* action unless the site can be blocked from access from the UK.

UK but then freely distributed within the UK without fear of litigation. The law will apply to the individual abroad where that individual seeks to erode, using the transnational scope of the Internet, the rights that an owner has over a work within the territory. The law will certainly apply to those domiciled in contracting states who seek to infringe UK copyright works[424].

Other 'foreign' infringements

The reasoning used in relation to authorisations may also apply to other types of primary infringement. A claimant may allege that the issuing of copies occurs where the copies are received. By this reasoning, a website holding material infringing a UK copyright can be construed as issuing the copies within the UK, so within our courts' jurisdiction[425]. This author doubts the strength of such a pleading[426]. The location of the activity of issuing copies is more likely to be construed as being the place from where copies are issued, rather than where they are received[427].

ENFORCEMENT OF COPYRIGHT ABROAD

To sue the authoriser of the infringement over the Internet is simply a case of viewing the authorisation as a tort and proceeding on the basis of a tort committed within the jurisdiction. The defendant will have to be served with the proceedings outside the jurisdiction.

Actionable foreign infringements

The Brussels Regulation permits an action being brought in and heard by the English courts in relation to infringement of a signatory country's copyright by acts done in a signatory country. Set in a commercial Internet context, a possible scenario could be as follows:

37. A Dutch architect opens a sophisticated ecommerce website which permits, for a fee, any of its plans to be downloaded and utilised as the basis of a building. The server hosting this site is based in Holland. A Dutch builder pays the fee, downloads a plan, builds an office to the specification and is promptly approached by a UK company wishing to open an office in Holland. Contrary to the terms of the site he passes the plans, for a fee, to the UK company who build their office in Amsterdam. Knowing that the builder has few funds to pay damages, the Dutch architect sues the builder and UK company in England.

424 See fn 415 at page 279.
425 Copyright, Designs and Patents Act 1988, s 18(2).
426 It is submitted that it is also a weak allegation that a visual or acoustic presentation, a primary infringement, occurs where it is seen or heard: Copyright, Designs and Patents Act 1988, s 19(2)(b).
427 See fn 211 at page 225. Cf the concept of 'distributes' in *Playboy Enterprises Inc v Chuckleberry Publishing Inc* 939 F Supp 1032 (SDNY 1996). The reasoning in this case would be applicable to a secondary infringer under the Copyright, Designs and Patents Act 1988, s 23(c) or (d).

The chapters of this book on contract and tort describe how the Brussels Regulation permits actions to be commenced in England even though the dispute relates to activities which occurred abroad. Despite the Convention (now Regulation) there has been considerable uncertainty[428] that an English court could nevertheless adjudicate on matters of foreign copyrights being infringed abroad. The two issues raising this uncertainty[429] are now issues of historical legal interest following a robust judgment given by the Court of Appeal in *Pearce v Ove Arup Partnership*[430]. The Court of Appeal makes clear that the English court will hear an action for infringement of copyright where the work is protected under a signatory country's copyright law and is infringed in that signatory country.

For Internet users and abusers, this is significant. Infringers may not avoid the English courts merely because their activities take place abroad. If they are domiciled in the UK[431] or a co-defendant is[432] they may find themselves facing claims under a foreign law but in the English courts.

The Private International Law (Miscellaneous Provisions) Act 1995, s 11(1) provides that the general rule is that the applicable law is the law of the country in which the events constituting the tort in question occur. As the work is protected by one country's copyright law and the acts complained of occurred in that country, it will be that country's law which will apply. Further reasoning is given by relying upon s 11(2)(b) which provides that the applicable law for a course of action in respect of damage to property is the law of the country where the property was when it was damaged. Because copyright is a territorial property right (it cannot cross borders) it must be 'damaged' in the country in which it is infringed. Where advisors seek to base an action on this possibility, they must clearly plead the foreign law or laws on which they rely. There is strong authority that the English courts will not entertain the fiction that English law also applies in other countries. Mr Justice Ferris states 'it is simply not realistic to suppose that the Plaintiffs intend to go to trial on the basis that the copyright of every Convention country is the same as the law of England.'[433]

428 *Pearce v Ove Arup Partnership* [1997] 3 All ER 31 at 34; *Mother Bertha Music Ltd v Bourne Music Ltd* [1997] EMLR 457.
429 First, is an action under a foreign copyright law actionable in the English court; second, is such an action justiciable?
430 [2000] Ch 403.
431 Brussels Regulation, art 2.
432 Brussels Regulation, art 6.
433 *Mother Bertha Music Ltd v Bourne Music Ltd* [1997] EMLR 457.

Chapter Five
Crime

> *'It is easy to run a secure computer system. You merely have to disconnect all dial-up connections and permit only direct-wired terminals, put the machine and its terminals in a shielded room, and post a guard at the door.'*
>
> *Grampp FT and Morris RH, AT&T Bell Laboratories Technical Journal*[1]

Unauthorised access to property, damage to property, theft, distribution of obscene and indecent material are all familiar crimes. Under new guises all are possible using the Internet. This chapter considers these crimes in the context of present and future Internet developments.

Unauthorised access to computer material is becoming more prevalent, and with our increasing reliance on computers, more serious. The US Computer Security Institute reported in April 2002 that 90% of its 503 respondents (primarily large corporations and US government agencies) had detected computer security breaches since April 2001. The average reported financial loss was over $200,000. The UK's Department of Trade and Industry's Information Security Breaches Survey 2002, also in April 2002, revealed that 78% of large UK businesses have fallen victim to some kind of electronic attack. In February 2000 the very largest websites were attacked to paralysis. These were: Yahoo!, CNN, eBay, Buy.com, Amazon, E*Trade and ZDnet[2]. Even the mighty Microsoft admitted on 27 October 2000 that its corporate network was penetrated and accessed by an intruder for over 12 days. But it is not merely civilian computers that are at risk. In February 1998, the US Pentagon reported that 'fairly heavy cyber attacks occurred'. All military services suffered 'penetration to some degree'. By June 1998, the chief of the US National Infrastructure Protection Centre of the FBI announced that, since the attacks on the Pentagon that February, 'half dozen of what I would call substantial' attacks had been launched against US government computer systems.

It is also clear that the proliferation of ecommerce is being matched by an expansion of crime on the Internet. The use of credit cards over the Internet provides a greater incentive to hack than ever before. Raphael Gray, in July 2001,

1 UNIX operating system security. *AT&T Bell Laboratories Technical Journal*, 63 (8, Part 2): 1649–1672, October 1984.

2 The 16-year-old perpetrator, known as Mafiaboy, was arrested in Quebec on 15 April 2000 and, having pleaded guilty to 55 counts of 'mischief to data', was sentenced on 17 September 2000 to eight months in a youth detention centre.

pleaded guilty to a number of charges related to his hacking of ecommerce sites and subsequent obtaining of some 23,000 credit card details. He claimed his motivation was to 'expose and publicise the fact that the e-commerce retailers were not security conscious'[3].

This chapter also considers the corresponding rise in the spread of computer viruses. This is because of a technical change in the material being sent over the Internet. There has always been a threat from computer viruses which are spread over the Internet. However, the growth in Internet transmission of executable code provides an increased number of hosts from which viruses may be contracted.

What is more distasteful is that the Internet is also being extensively used by paedophiles who take advantage of the ease with which images and movies, encrypted from the prying eyes of the authorities, can be transmitted in a matter of seconds. One shocking case in this area is of a Catholic priest who utilised an 'instant email' service called ICQ to access indecent images and stored them on a computer at a Catholic girls' school where he used to teach. He was put on two years' probation and on the national sex offenders' register[4].

All of these crimes, and the evidence needed to support their prosecution, are examined as follows.

1. When does one commit the computer misuse crime of unauthorised access using the Internet?
2. How does the more serious computer misuse offence of unauthorised access with ulterior motive address the wrongful interception of credit card numbers or digital cash?
3. What are the laws and how do they control the electronic spread of viruses, logic bombs and other malicious code?
4. For crimes committed over the Internet, what is the special significance and difficulty of adducing computer-generated evidence?
5. Those who gain unauthorised access to computers often follow the same pattern; what are the key legal issues involved in their techniques?
6. What is the English courts' jurisdiction over criminals who use the Internet and how may they be extradited?
7. What are the criminal laws that apply to obscene digital articles, and more serious indecent photographs?

This chapter does not address the Council of Europe's Draft Convention on Cyber Crime[5]. This rather ambitious all-encompassing Convention attempts to create an international 'cyber-crime' framework for the Council of Europe's member states and non-member states. The Convention enters into force[6] when five states ratify it. Unusually, the Convention cuts across a number of substantive and procedural areas of law, including hacking, virus-spreading, copyright infringement, child pornography, extradition, interception of data and many other issues. Such is the complexity and scope of its recommendations that this author doubts that it will be ratified by the UK in the short to medium term.

3 *R v Gray* (6 July 2001, unreported).
4 *Evening Standard*, 13 August 1999.
5 Strasbourg, 29 June 2001, CDPC (2001) 17. As at 19 October 2002, 32 States had signed the Convention but only Albania and Croatia had ratified it.
6 Article 36, para 3.

TYPES OF COMPUTER MISUSE

Broadly, there are three main types of computer misuse. First, there is unauthorised access, or 'hacking'. This is where a person without authority physically or electronically penetrates a computer system. This may be compared with breaking and entering, where no further offence is intended or then committed. The second type of digital crime is the more serious form of unauthorised access. This is where a person without authority accesses a computer with the intention to commit a further offence such as theft. Distinct from unauthorised access is the third type of digital crime: destruction of digital information, or the impairment of access to digital information. A common example of this is a computer virus which may prevent a computer from working.

The unique legal question in relation to all these three crimes is who or what is actually the victim? Everything which exists in a computer is represented as zeros and ones. These binary digits, or bits, are generally stored using a magnetic medium. So, to destroy a computer file a person may only have to change the state of, say, 100 bits from one, on, to zero, off. Before the Computer Misuse Act 1990, courts were forced to wrestle with older statutes which concerned physical property to fit the misuse of new technology before them[7]. Even where this was successful, there was an obvious need for legislation to take account of computers. Prosecutions were troublesome[8].

The legislative solution

To counter the distrust of computers which was emerging, stemming from the ineffectiveness of the criminal law to deal with computer viruses and hacking, Parliament introduced the Computer Misuse Act 1990; an Act[9]:

> 'to safeguard the integrity – what I call the trustworthiness – of computers.'

The Act introduced three new criminal offences[10]:

1. digital browsing through a computer without authority;
2. such unauthorised browsing with intent to commit or facilitate the commission of further offences;
3. unauthorised modification of computer material.

This section also briefly touches on the Terrorism Act 2000 which may be utilised for the most serious of computer misuse. In relation to the Computer

7 For example, Forgery and Counterfeiting Act 1981 in *R v Gold and Shifreen* [1988] 2 All ER 186.

8 In an obvious signal to Parliament, Brandon LJ in *R v Gold and Shifreen* said, 'there is no reason to regret the failure of what [Lord Lane CJ] aptly described as the Procrustean attempt to force the facts of the present case into the language of an Act not designed to fit them'. [1988] 2 WLR 984 at 991.

9 Michael Colvin MP, *Hansard* 166 HC col 1134. Despite statements in April 2001 by the then Home Secretary, Jack Straw, to consider 'whether (the Act) needs to be reviewed, the Computer Misuse Act 1990 remains the United Kingdom's key statute addressing general hacking and malicious code'.

10 Computer Misuse Act 1990, ss 1, 2 and 3. The CPS broadens the scope of the Act by bringing cases of conspiracy to commit an offence 'with persons unknown'.

Misuse Act 1990, this section takes a split approach to examine the role and strength of this legislation in practice. First, the prohibitions are dissected in relation to the Internet in particular. Second, a typical hacking scenario is analysed. One general point about this Act is relevant throughout the chapter. There are numerous suggestions from experts that the Computer Misuse Act is weak and out of date[11]. Nevertheless, in July 2001, Raphael Gray, mentioned above, who accessed credit card details on commercial websites, pleaded guilty to charges under the Act. The legislation still remains effective, therefore, in persuading hackers such as Mr Gray that they would lose their case if scrutinised by the courts.

TERRORISM ACT 2000

The Terrorism Act 2000, which came into force on 19 February 2001 and is amended by the Anti-terrorism, Crime and Security Act 2001, bolsters the Computer Misuse Act 1990 for the most serious of computer attacks. The Terrorism Act addresses, inter alia, the use or threat of an '[action] designed seriously to interfere with, or seriously to disrupt an electric system'[12] where two other conditions are met. First, the use or threat of the action must be 'designed to influence [any] government or to intimidate the public or a section of the public [including public of a country other than the United Kingdom]'[13]. The second pre-condition which must be met is that the use or threat must be made for the 'purpose of advancing a political, religious or ideological cause'[14].

1. A British-based cult from the UK threatens to disrupt the computer systems and power supplies in every US hospital that practices abortions. It threatens to do so in accordance with its governing religious doctrine that 'all life is sacred'. This serious threat, despite being targeted at a non-UK, non-governmental section of society, will fall within the provisions of the Terrorism Act 2000.

COMPUTER MISUSE ACT 1990

Unauthorised access

The following discussion of hacking over the Internet focuses on the Computer Misuse Act 1990. The Terrorism Act 2000 is not discussed further. It is crucial to understand that it is often easy to prove the conduct aspect of the offence, the *actus reus*. The structure of the Act is such that, where the Internet is involved, it is almost impossible for a defendant to interact in any way with a victim computer without satisfying the physical requirements of the section of 'causing the

11 See *Computer Weekly*'s 'Lock down the Law' campaign and the private member's Computer Misuse (Amendment) Bill, 1 May 2002.
12 Terrorism Act 2000, s 1(2)(e).
13 Terrorism Act 2000, ss 1(1)(b) and (4)(c).
14 Terrorism Act 2000, s 1(1)(c).

performance of a function'. The tough burden on the prosecution lies elsewhere. It is proving the necessary intention and satisfying the rules to admit computer-generated evidence. Before considering these burdens it is necessary to appreciate the ambit of the activity required to satisfy the conduct aspect of the offence.

Section 1: conduct or *actus reus*

Section 1 creates the summary offence. The details of the *actus reus* are set out in full in s 1(1) of the Computer Misuse Act 1990:

> '1. (1) A person is guilty of an offence if –
> (a) he causes a computer to perform any function with intent to secure access to any program or data held in any computer;
> (b) the access he intends to secure is unauthorised; and
> (c) he knows at the time when he causes the computer to perform the function that that is the case.'

There are two main questions which must be addressed in relation to this section. First, what is required to cause a computer to perform a function? Second, what is entailed in securing access to any program or data?

Computer, data and programs

The conduct element of a s 1 offence is causing a computer to perform any function with intent to secure access to any program or data held in any computer. At an early stage it should be noted that the words 'program', 'data' and 'computer' are not defined by the Act[15].

Computers on the Internet

The Computer Misuse Act 1990 does not define 'computer'. This will no doubt cause problems for the prosecution seeking to prove, say, that a car's computerised braking system which has been tampered with has been the victim of a s 1 offence. The absence of the definition will not cause any difficulties, however, for proving unauthorised access over the Internet. For a machine to be a victim or conduit of hacking over the Internet, that machine must be a computer within any reasonable definition. The very nature of the Internet is that it joins together networks of computers[16]. For the purposes of this chapter, therefore, where the

15 Mr Harry Cohen MP did attempt to amend the Act at the Committee Stage with a definition of the word 'computer'. This was unsuccessful. Cf Law Commission No 186 on the Computer Misuse at para 3.39: 'it would be unnecessary and indeed might be foolish, to attempt to define computer . . . We cannot think that there will ever be serious grounds for arguments based on the ordinary meaning of the term "computer".'

16 It is not doubted that the *future* of ecommerce is away from the conception of simply linking computers as such but more towards connecting together 'intelligent appliances' such as Personal Digital Appliances and wireless devices and even household appliances such as fridges!

hacking is conducted over the Internet, the functioning 'machine' and accessed 'machine' will both be considered as computers within the ambit of s 1.

Programs and data on the Internet

The terms 'program' and 'data' within s 1 are also left undefined by the Act. As with 'computer' these terms were left undefined for fear of a definition becoming outdated by technological developments. That said, it remains crucial for a computer misuse prosecution that the conduct element of the offence, the *actus reus*, is proved and, therefore, that the two terms are understood in a reasonable context.

The main difficulty with these terms is appreciating what, other than 'a program' or 'data', *can* be accessed in a computer. The answer is that the terms program and data do encapsulate all that can be accessed *digitally* in a computer. But if the terms were absent from the section, one could commit a s 1 offence by turning off a computer before prising open the casing. Turning off the computer causes it to perform a function, and opening its metal casing would be accessing the computer in the physical sense.

In summary, the absence of definitions should not concern a court where the accused has used the Internet to gain access to information which resides in a digital form. In this form, the information will constitute data or a program within the ambit of the relevant section.

2. A company runs a mobile phone and WAP-enabled website which tracks business news stories on particular companies. Users pay a subscription fee and, in return, are given a password to grant them access to the site. A hacker attempts to use a password which he has not paid for in order to enter the site to read the stories. The home page is mainly constructed using a computer language called Java, and much of the site's content is data. The hacker is intending to secure access to a program and its associated data without authority.

Held in any computer

Before examining the remainder of s 1 and its application to the Internet, this section analyses the notion of data or programs being 'held in a computer'. A computer can be reasonably thought as to include the processing unit, its memory and storage devices. Computers are simple machines; they are so simple that they can purely store and work with two numbers: a zero and a one. But that sentence illustrates one division which exists within a computer: it *stores* and it *works*; it executes instructions on those numbers. The central processing unit of a computer is able to store very few of these numbers at one time but is able to process them very quickly: it is where all the real work is performed. However, certain other physical parts of the computer cannot process or work with these numbers: they can only store them. Examples of these are the computer's hard disk drive and its memory. These are purely components of a computer that can store vast quantities of digital information.

Section 17(6) clarifies the phrase 'held in a computer' by providing that it includes references to data or programs held in any removable storage medium which is in the computer for the time being. This particular inclusion refers to the possibility of obtaining access to the data or program which is stored on a floppy disk: these allow the storage of small quantities of data, but are physically small and portable. A CD-ROM is a further example of a removable storage medium. Section 17(6) does not define the term and seeks only to clarify the phrase 'held in a computer' with one example, one inclusion. 'Held in a computer' may therefore also be reasonably read to include data or programs which are stored away from the processing unit of a computer, but accessible by it.

3. A hacker uses an authorised person's password to log in to a UK insurance company's computer. The hacker is hoping to gain access to the company's customer details. The computer to which he logs in stores these details in a huge data storage unit which is located elsewhere. The data itself is stored on a magnetic tape. The processing unit of the computer retrieves this information through fibre-optic cables. The computer would be thought to include the magnetic tape, and so the data would still be considered as being 'held in a computer'.

Performing any function

If it is concluded that any machine which is connected to the Internet will fall into the category of 'computer' in s 1(1), it is then necessary to establish how one causes that computer to perform a function. The word 'function' is also undefined within the Act, but the interpretation section of the Act provides some indication of the wide scope of the term. It appears that there is no activity which one can perform in relation to a computer which does not cause a function to be performed. Even typing on a computer's keyboard or using an input device, such as a mouse, will alter the state of the computer's processor. This alteration has been effected by the person causing the computer to perform a function.

Function on any computer

The computer performing the function does not need to be the same computer on which the data or programs are stored. So, a client computer, being made to perform a function, which is intended to secure access *to the server computer*, falls within the ambit of s 1(1). Section 1(1) also encompasses the use of a home computer to login to an Internet Service Provider's server from which the user intends to penetrate another computer. The home computer is caused to perform a function, and so is the Internet Service Provider's computer.

Where a hacker uses the Internet to attempt to gain access to a victim computer, signals may pass through many computers, as described in this book's introduction, before reaching the victim. Indeed, when Yahoo.com, one of the busiest sites on the Internet, was brought down in February 2000, it was attacked from a vast number of other computers. Each had been made to act in concert having been themselves infected with a 'daemon' program. Each of these infected computers was then under the control of a 'master' program (generally without the computer owners' knowledge). In the case of Yahoo!'s attack, the 'master' program probably instructed its 'daemons' to simultaneously bombard Yahoo!'s servers with a flood of requests to be sent data or web pages: a 'SYN flood'. This was probably combined with a set of other attack procedures variously called 'spoofing', 'smurfing' and 'fraggle'. In short, a vast range of computers, all compromised in the same way, were made to focus their attentions on one victim computer, this time Yahoo.com. This so-called Distributed Denial of Service attack illustrates the way in which the computers made to perform the function are often not the same computers on which the data or programs being attacked are stored.

What is important to the prosecution though, is that each of these intermediary computers is caused to perform a function. And the cause of the performance of this function is the instructions which the hacker has provided to the first computer in the chain. This allows the prosecution to rely on the functioning of any computer in the chain to establish this aspect of the *actus reus*. What is difficult for the prosecution to prove is that the *accused* was the cause of the performance of this function. This difficulty is considered in greater depth below[17].

4. A hacker uses a set of software tools called a 'root kit' to break into an insecure computer on the Internet. A 'master program' is installed onto this computer with a view to controlling a large number of 'daemon' programs installed on other computers. Using a program called 'Tribal Flood Network' the hacker remotely calls on all the 'daemon' computers to launch a distributed attack on a well-known sports site. For a s 1 offence, the prosecution does not need to prove that the hacker's own computer was made to function: all the computers involved, 'daemons' and 'masters' will suffice. The prosecution may have a problem in proving that it was the accused who caused these functions.

Unsuccessful attempts

The broad drafting of s 1 has the effect that even unsuccessful hackers can be guilty of the offence. Usually to gain unauthorised access a person must enter a login procedure, and masquerade as another, or attempt to bypass the login procedure altogether. In the first instance, if the victim computer rejects the unauthorised login, the person has caused at least two computers to function: his own, and the victim computer. The victim computer has performed a function: it rejected the hacker. Where the hacker attempts to login with the requisite intention, a guilty mind, despite being unsuccessful the hacker may have committed the offence.

Of course, the difficulty for the prosecution in such a situation is proving that the victim computer did foil the attempt, and proving that the attempt was made by the accused. This will be hard unless the victim computer maintains a log of all unsuccessful logins as well as successful ones[18]. It is more technically complex to prove the source of an unsuccessful login, weakening further a prosecution.

If the person is somehow able to bypass the standard login procedure, this bypassing itself will constitute the function. If the standard procedure for the victim computer is to ask for login details from each person wishing to gain access, by avoiding this the person must be causing the computer to perform a function.

17 See 'Evidence', at p 309.

18 Evidence used to convict one hacker consisted of a log which his computer maintained of all functions!

5. A hacker oversees a password being entered by someone logging-in to a remote computer. The login prompt specifies that you must be authorised to access the computer. Later, the hacker then attempts to use the password himself. Because the remote computer only allows one login each day, the unauthorised login attempt is rejected by the computer. This would still constitute a s 1 offence: the rejection constitutes a function and this function was caused by the hacker using a password at the wrong time.

AUTOMATIC CAUSATION OF A FUNCTION

Most hackers will automate part of the process of unauthorised access. Distributed Denial of Service attacks rely on automotive co-ordination between computers. As another example, a home page may require two items of information from each of its users to allow them to enter the site. The first may be the person's name, followed by the second, their password, which is say a number seven digits long. To penetrate this site digitally a hacker may write an automatic login program. Its first task is to enter a common name, 'John Smith'. The hacker's program then tries to enter the password. First the password 0000001 is tried. If the victim computer rejects this as being incorrect, the login program will simply move the password number to 0000002. Often after a number of unsuccessful attempts, the victim computer will reject the attempting client.

As automation usually plays some part in hacking, it is necessary to address whether this may constitute a s 1 offence[19]. The key question is whether a computer has been caused to perform a function. The running of the hacker's program would constitute the conduct element of the offence. It is at the point of executing that code that a computer is caused to perform a function, so the physical element of the offence can be made out. Establishing the intention for this automated hacking is less straightforward.

Securing access

The Computer Misuse Act 1990 prescribes that securing access to a program or data is established where the defendant, by causing a computer to perform a function[20]:

> '(a) alters or erases the program or data;
> (b) copies or moves it to any storage medium other than that in which it is held or to a different location in the storage medium in which it is held;

19 A similar program can be used to search automatically for the vulnerable hosts on the Internet, which, once discovered, may be probed further. See Cheswick WR and Bellovin SM, *Firewalls and Internet Security* (Addison-Wesley Publishing Company, Wokingham, 1995) at p 145. Similar programs were used to scan a range of telephone numbers to test whether they were connected to a modem, and are thus potential targets. Such a program is described in the now deleted book, *The Hacker's Handbook* by Hugo Cornwall (Century Communications, London, 1985).

20 Computer Misuse Act 1990, s 17(2).

(c) uses it; or
(d) has it output from the computer in which it is held (whether by having it displayed or in any other manner).'

The purpose of considering this aspect of s 1 is to establish the *intention* of the defendant to secure access to any program or data held in any computer[21]. That the defendant actually *did* secure such access, a question of fact, may bolster the case that the defendant has the requisite intention; it is not a prerequisite of proving this intention.

WHICH COMPUTER?

It is helpful to consider to which computer s 1(1)(a) refers. Section 1(1)(a) states 'to secure access to any program or data held on *any* computer'[22]. The access does not need to be directed at the computer on which the hacker caused performance of the function. It will now be illustrated that the Computer Misuse Act 1990 leaves very little scope for interacting with a computer over the Internet without that interaction being classified as securing access.

6. A hacker uses a Telnet connection to attempt to gain unauthorised access to a company's Intranet. Three main computers are used to attempt the access: the hacker's own computer and the computer to which he connected to by Telnet. This 'distance' alone will not prevent a successful hacking prosecution. There are two computers caused to function: the hacker's own and the Telnet computer. That the hacker sought to secure access to data held on a third computer is not a bar to a conviction: it is still 'any computer'.

Copying or moving programs and data

Section 17(2)(b) defines securing access as a person copying or moving data or programs to any storage medium other than that in which it is held or to a different location in the storage medium in which it is held. The word which widens this section dramatically is 'copies'. Computer data and programs cannot even be viewed on a screen without there being copying. To show characters on a screen, the characters making up the program or data are copied from the storage unit, be that memory or a hard-disk drive, to the video memory of the computer. The same is true of a hacker who uses the Internet to view the content of programs or data which are held on a victim's computer. By being able to view their content, a part of those data must have been copied into the memory of the hacker's computer. It therefore appears that viewing files which are held on any computer will constitute securing access to those files.

21 The author submits that no emphasis should be placed on the Act's use of the word 'secure'. It is the author's understanding that this verb is introduced because, while using the word 'access' as a verb is grammatically dubious, it also makes the word ambiguous. Cf USC, Title 18, Pt I, Ch 47, 1030(a)(1).

22 Emphasis added.

7. A hacker makes a connection to a secured part of a server. Once within this portion of the server the hacker views the contents of a password data file. To avoid drawing attention to the breach in security, the hacker does not make a digital copy of the data file. Nevertheless the hacker has secured access to the file by having read it: to view the file it must have been copied from the storage unit on the server to the memory of the hacker's computer.

Using a program

Section 17(2)(c) states that one secures access to a program if one 'uses it'. The Act elaborates on the meaning and context of this word 'use'. Section 17(3)(a) explains, first, that one uses a computer program if the program is executed. This is, pragmatically, covered by subsection (2)(b). Section 17(3) explains that running a program indicates the gaining of access to that program. This will therefore cover programs executed on a client computer, having been copied there, or programs executed on the server computer.

8. An employee uses her firm's intranet to attempt to read the online diary of her supervisor. She is unable to read the diary because the program requests her to enter a password which she does not know. That the diary program is able to reject her attempt shows it had, at the least, been executed. The employee did intend to access the diary program.

In *Ellis v DPP*[23], John Ellis, a graduate of the University of Newcastle appealed to the Divisional Court against three convictions under s 1. He had used computers left logged on by others to access certain websites. The evidence was that he used already-running Internet Browsers on the computer and that he accessed already-'activated' sites. Nevertheless, and technically correct, the Divisional Court unanimously judged that he did 'use' the computers knowing that use to be unauthorised.

Output of programs or data

Section 17(1)(d) expands the term 'access' by not only including executing a computer program, but also *reading* a computer program. A computer program is made up from a list of instructions. Each instruction tells the computer to perform a function. Some functions are imperceptible, such as moving a byte from one storage area to another. Others make a perceptive difference, for example clearing the screen. Section 17(1)(d) defines securing access as including 'ha[ving the program or data] output from the computer in which it is held . . .'. Section 17(4)(a) refines this section by further defining 'output' as including the instructions of the program being output. So, executing a program over the Internet is deemed to be securing access to it. This therefore compromises the 'classic' thin-client where the server executes the program but outputs the *results* to the client computer. This was explained above[24]. In addition, merely looking at the instructions which make up the program will also be securing access.

23 [2001] EWHC Admin 362, [2001] All ER (D) 190 (May).
24 See 'Using a program'.

It is crucial that a court appreciates the mischief at which this section is aimed. It is concerned with the 'integrity'[25] of programs and data. It is not directed at subsequent use, or utility, of the digital information compromised. For this reason, s 17(4)(b) clearly expresses that the form of output, whether executable or otherwise, is immaterial. This expression applies also to data: it is of no concern that, say, the data is unusable. The fact that it has been output *per se* is sufficient to constitute securing access.

9. A company, worried about data security, encrypts all data held on its network. Each individual who is permitted to gain access to the data is provided, on disk, with a de-encrypting key. The network security is breached and a hacker prints out some of the encrypted data. The hacker has still gained access to that data despite the issue that the output is unreadable. In addition, the data will be deemed to have been copied onto the hacker's computer for printing; this also denotes securing access.

Erasure or alteration

Subsection (a) of s 17(2) illustrates the final type of access to programs or data: alteration or erasure of programs or data. This would constitute a 'classic' hack: data are deleted and programs are altered. Complex issues of proving the program has been altered, where the program itself is the source of that proof (an activity-logging program for example), are covered below[26].

Section 1: intention or *mens rea*

The prosecution must prove the two limbs of the intention aspects of the offence. The first, that the defendant intended to secure access to any program or data held in any computer, has been considerably examined above[27]. Nevertheless, a few additional points are mentioned below. The second limb is that at the time of causing the computer to perform the function the defendant knew that the access intended to secure was unauthorised. This can be a difficult intention to prove where the defendant had limited authority, but is accused of operating outside this authority. A common example of this is where the defendant is an employee of a company and is accused of using the company's intranet outside their authority.

Intention to secure access

Any computer

Much has been explained about what constitutes securing access; a little needs now to be added to what is an *intention* to secure access. First, it should be reiterated that this intention can be directed at *any* computer. The defendant does not need to have been aware of exactly which computer he was attacking. This

25 See fn 9 at p 285.
26 See 'Proof of modification', at p 316.
27 See 'Securing access', at p 291.

suits the Internet: often it is complicated to prove that a person intended to log in to a specific computer. This is particularly true where the defendant used a program to check automatically the security, or otherwise, of a computer.

Any program or data

The intention to secure access also does not need to be directed at any particular, or particular kind of, program or data. It is enough that an individual intends to secure access to programs and data *per se*. The section encompasses the hacker who intends to access a computer with no clear perception of what data or programs will be held on the computer.

UNAUTHORISED

The second limb of intention is focused on the authority of the defendant to secure access. Section 1(1)(b) prescribes that the access the defendant intends to secure be unauthorised. Section 1(1)(c) makes it clear that the person must have the relevant knowledge that the access is unauthorised at the time the computer is forced to perform a function. One can envisage arguments arising as to whether a defendant had the relevant knowledge but it seems that the subsection is relatively restricted in operation.

Outsider

The question of authority is generally not difficult to prove when an 'outsider' to a system uses the Internet to attempt to secure access to any programs or data on the system. Where a person must resort to using 'techniques' to gain access to programs or data, it can be readily inferred that it is an insecure defence to claim he did not know he was unauthorised.

Partial authority

The concept of authority is elaborated, but thinly, by s 17(5). This section states that access is unauthorised if the person is not entitled to control access of the kind in question, and the person does not have the consent of the person who does control access.

A person must *know* that he is unauthorised in this sense. The question of fact as to whether the individual knew the limits of his authority will often be a finely balanced one.

10. An art gallery uses a website to advertise forthcoming displays. On its home page it states that the graphics which follow on subsequent pages may not be downloaded to a storage medium. A person saves one of the graphics to his hard disk. The person has authorised access to copy the file to memory, but not to his hard disk. Access was unauthorised; the issue would be whether the evidence would be strong enough to prove that he did not see the limitation to disprove he had the necessary intention.

This raises an issue of relevance for advisers to server operators. Where a server seeks to provide limited authority, say with an extranet site, the boundaries of this authority must be clearly stated[28]. If not, it will be doubtful an offence has been committed. If publicly available but subject to a limitation, a court will be unenthusiastic to hold that an offence has been committed. What is more, because the intention must have been formed at the time of causing the function, the stipulations of any limitations should be obvious at all times. An ftp site appears to a user as a catalogue of the files and directories on the particular computer. Unless security is in place, a user can secure access to any file without having to pass through any limitations statement. Similarly, if poorly constructed, it is possible that a person may select a single page of the website to view, missing the opening page altogether[29]. A viewer may not have seen a limitation statement.

Insiders

The ubiquity of intranets and extranets within organisations creates a potential arena for insiders to secure unauthorised access to programs and data. Disgruntled employees, temporary staff and even happily employed staff may all attempt to read information which is actually out of their authority to view. This is possible where there are various strata within a system each for different users of the network. For example, personnel files may be uploaded to the intranet but only made available to the personnel department. Before considering the problems of an insider's unauthorised access it is necessary to mention how an insider may access the files.

Direct access to server

An insider can secure access to unauthorised information held on an intranet through a connected computer, or through the actual server on which the information is held. A legal point must be made about this second technique; it is covered by the Act, despite only one computer being involved. In the early case, *R v Cropp*[30], Sean Cropp, without authority, entered a discount into a computerised till to obtain key-cutting equipment at 30% of cost. This is a straightforward example of unauthorised access.

Aglionby J, after consulting the statute, held that there was no case to answer. Section 1(1)(a) refers to:

28 A website may state the following on its terms and conditions page: 'Permission to use, copy and distribute documents and related graphics available from this server ("Server") is granted, provided that . . . (2) use of the graphics available from this Server is for non-commercial purposes . . . (4) no graphics available from this Server are used, copied or distributed separate from accompanying copyright notices.' Accessing the site with the intention to use the graphics in a commercial brochure would therefore constitute a s 1 offence, if these disclaimers were known at the time of downloading the graphic.

29 This is a very common occurrence where a person uses a search engine to search for a particular term. If the term is found the engine returns not only the site which features the term, but also the exact *page*. It is a regular occurrence that a site's pages will not be viewed in their sequential order.

30 *R v Cropp* unreported although see [1991] 7 Computer Law & Practice 270.

> 'causing a computer to perform any function with intent to secure access to any program or data held in any computer.'

He construed this wording did not apply where only one computer is used; he felt the word 'any' referred to any *other* computer. To confirm this interpretation, Judge Aglionby considered s 17 of the Act. Here, a s 3 offence is described as only addressing[31]:

> 'the computer concerned or *any other* computer . . . It seems to me to be straining language to say that only one computer is necessary.'

Concern at this decision was so widespread that an opinion on a point of law was sought from the Court of Appeal[32]. The question was asked, to commit an offence under s 1(1) does the computer caused to perform a function have to be a different computer to the one in which unauthorised access is intended? The Court of Appeal set the Act back on course[33]:

> 'In our judgment there are no grounds whatsoever for implying, or importing the word "other" between "any" and "computer" . . .'

This leaves no doubt that, all things being equal, insiders who gain access to unauthorised files through the computer on which they are stored can commit the offence.

So, an insider may be as culpable as an outsider. It should be noted that it is easier for an insider to gain unauthorised access. By definition an insider is behind the firewall so already beyond security measures. In court, proving an insider was acting outside of their authority can be arduous.

Authorisation

For an insider to be convicted the prosecution has two hurdles to prove intention. The first is that the person intended to secure access to any program or data. This may not be disputed. What will often be disputed is the second, higher hurdle, that the insider knew that he was unauthorised to secure this access at the time of causing the computer to perform a function[34].

In a perfect organisation the boundaries of each employee's actions are clear and known. In practice, an employee's role changes over time. This is especially the situation for a temporary worker who may work for many different sectors

31 Per Aglionby J in *R v Cropp*. Transcript of Shorthand Notes, page 9F. Emphasis added.

32 *A-G's Reference (No 1 of 1991)* [1993] QB 94 under s 36 of the Criminal Justice Act 1972. While explaining s 1 offences to the House of Commons, Michael Colvin MP added, '[The section] is also aimed at insiders who try to get into parts of the system where they know that they should not be'. *Hansard* 166 HC col 1138. Parliament's intention is confirmed by the unanimous opposition to and later withdrawal of Harry Cohen's amendment proposing that 'any computer' be replaced by 'another computer'.

33 [1992] 3 WLR 432 at 437.

34 A 'bootstraps' approach to this question is to assess whether the ultimate purpose of the access was unlawful. As unlawful, it must, necessarily, have been unauthorised by the controller of the programs or data. That this was *known* by the defendant remains a question of fact but, an unlawful purpose, will indicate such knowledge.

of an organisation within a short period. It will therefore often be important for the prosecution to show clear guidelines which were made known to the employee at the time of causing the computer to perform the function.

On this point the Law Commission has provided the following guidance[35].

> 'We think there is some importance in requiring the court, in a case where there is a dispute about authorisation, to identify, and to be clear about the status of, the person alleged to have authority to control the access which is in issue.'

Unclear company guidelines, or none at all, in relation to the use of the intranet can only weaken the prosecution's case that a person knew they were acting outside of their authority. Conflicting authorisations will also weaken any case.

11. An employee secures access to the personnel section of her company's intranet. She copies her personnel file using a stolen password. Clearly the employee does not have authority to enter the personnel section of the intranet, but her intention was to gain access to her own personnel file. The relevant knowledge and intent may be inferred from her stolen password.

Without a clear indication of boundaries, the defence is at liberty to question whether the defendant actually knew of these limits[36].

This discussion highlights the theoretical applicability of the Computer Misuse Act 1990 to insider access, but also the practical difficulty of satisfying the criminal standard of proof in such a case.

Usual authority in unusual circumstances

The most complex situation concerning insiders is where they are carrying out their duties with 'technical authority' but without 'actual authority'. The *Bignell* case illustrates this concept.

Paul and Victoria Bignell were police officers and lived together. A dispute arose in relation to two cars owned by the new partner of Mr Bignell's former wife. On six occasions between December 1994 and May 1995 the Bignells instructed police computer operators to extract from the Police National Computer details of the two cars. Such instructions would have been perfectly legal were the Bignells discharging genuine police duties. However, they were not.

35 Law Commission No 186, para 3.37.

36 This said, the defence should be wary that 'it is always open to the tribunal of fact, when knowledge on the part of a defendant is required to be proved, to base a finding of knowledge on evidence that the defendant deliberately shut his eyes to the obvious or refrained from inquiry because he suspected the truth but did not want to have his suspicion confirmed'. Per Lord Bridge, *Westminster City Council v Croyalgrange Ltd* [1986] 2 All ER 353 at 359. This 'wilful blindness' approaches a subjective recklessness threshold of intention. It is the author's opinion that this lower level of intention was not intended by Parliament. Emma Nicholson's Bill, proposed but rejected, included recklessness; the Computer Misuse Act 1990 does not. Further, the proponent of the Act explained, '[Section 1] is also aimed at insiders who try to get into parts of the system where they *know that they* should not be'. *Hansard* 166 HC col 1138. Emphasis is added to indicate the use of the qualifier, 'they know that', rather than solely, 'should not be'.

On 28 June 1996, the Respondents were convicted by a Stipendiary Magistrate and fined under the Computer Misuse Act 1990, s 1[37]. They each appealed against these convictions to the Crown Court. The appeals were heard on 19 September 1996 and the Crown Court upheld their submission that, even if their use of the police computer was for private purposes, it was not within the definition of 'unauthorised access' under s 17(5) of the Act because the *access* was with authority even though the authority was used for an unauthorised purpose.

The DPP appealed, its main question to Pill LJ and Astill J being whether or not it was correct in law to conclude that a police officer does not commit an offence contrary to s 1 of the Computer Misuse Act 1990 if he intends to secure access to the Police National Computer for purposes other than policing[38].

Mr Justice Astill gave judgment for the court in a systematic manner. Access is unauthorised if it meets the conditions in s 17(5): one is not entitled to control access of any kind in question, and, one does not have consent to access from any person so entitled. Section 17(2)(a) to (d) sets out four ways in which a person secures access, including altering data, copying data, using it, or outputting it. Section 17(5), however, is drafted in terms of access 'of the kind in question'. This, the court judged, referred to the four kinds of access set out in s 17(2)(c) and (d) at least. The court felt this indicated that as the respondents were authorised to secure access by s 17(2)(c) and (d) they had not committed the s 1 offence. In short the respondents had authority to access even though they did not do so for an authorised purpose.

The effects of this ruling would have been devastating. It would suggest that, because all employees have authority to touch the keys connected to a computer, any employee may use the computer to gain unauthorised access to material in the computer without criminal sanction.

The Bignells instructed that a false 'Reason Code' be typed into the Police National Computer[39]. Why? They wanted the computer to perform this function to allow them to gain access to data which was 'not necessary for the efficient discharge of genuine police duties'[40]. In other words, they were not authorised *in those circumstances* to secure access to the data. The offence should have been made out. The reason that the court did not come to this conclusion was because they did not restrict their analysis of the facts to the precise wording of the statute. The Act is drafted in terms of 'causing a computer to perform a function' together with the intention to 'secure unauthorised access to any program or data'. It is therefore an error in law for the court to have provided a judgment littered with references to 'accessing a computer'. The Act does not sanction those who access computers, it sanctions those who use computers to secure access to data and programs.

37 In a remarkably similar case, the CPS prosecuted a police officer, David Keyte, of conspiring to commit 'misconduct in a public office'. The officer was found guilty and jailed for two years. See *Computing*, 10 July 1997.

38 *DPP v Bignell* [1998] 1 Cr App Rep 1.

39 A question remains whether when *a third party* touches the computer this is sufficient for the offence. Certainly, precedent suggests it is: *R v Pearce, Farquharson* (unreported, Croydon Magistrates' Court, 9 December 1993). Mr Farquharson was convicted under s 2 for instructing Ms Pearce to access her employer's computer system to obtain details of numbers and electronic codes which would have facilitated the cloning of mobile phones. Mr Farquharson did not touch the computer.

40 Directions on the use of the Police National Computer, para 3.8.

Unfortunately, this ruling was relied upon by Kennedy, LJ and Blofeld, J in *R v Governor of Brixton Prison exp Adeniyi Momudu Allison*[41]. Allison was accused by the US government of conspiring when in England with an employee of American Express (then in Florida) to defraud the credit card company. The committal had sought that Allison, within the jurisdiction of the US, conspired with this US employee to secure unauthorised access to the American Express computers with intent to commit theft, forgery and to modify their computers' contents. The employee had access to accounts of American Express cardholders and relayed the secret information about these accounts to Allison. This permitted them to forge credit cards and obtain substantial sums of money.

The court relied upon the ruling in *Bignell.* It decided that the US employee was, under more usual circumstances, entitled to access the data about the American Express accounts. Consequentially, the court determined that the access was not 'authorised' access within the Computer Misuse Act 1990, s 17(5).

The case was appealed from the Divisional Court to the House of Lords[42]. Lord Hobhouse delivered judgment for all five Lords and was clear that the Divisional Court fell into error by relying on the *Bignell* judgment. Indeed, the House of Lords ruled that the *Bignell* case wrongly elided 'kinds of access' and 'kinds of data'. The Act is not concerned with authority to access kinds of data. It is concerned with authority to access the *actual* data involved. The 'level' of security that an individual has is therefore largely irrelevant; the question is whether, given the circumstances, the individual had authority to access the data.

In short, Allison's accomplices, although no doubt trusted employees of American Express at the time, were not authorised to provide data to third parties to allow frauds to be committed. Similarly, by disapproving of the decision made in *Bignell*, the House of Lords was also impliedly stating that the police officers in that case had accessed data without authority.

12. Cleerdz.com operates a credit card clearance system for other websites. It allows a website to offer credit card payment facilities to customers without having the capability themselves. Cleerdz.com is entitled to debit from the entered card where the card's 'fraud score' is below an agreed maximum. An operator at Cleerdz.com re-enters old customer details to pay for a holiday for himself. Even though his usual job and usual level of authority would have permitted him to enter card details, he was not authorised to do so in those particular circumstances. He accessed a computer and data without authority.

HACKING TO OFFEND FURTHER

The s 2 offence applies to someone seeking to access a computer for a further criminal purpose. That is, where a s 1 offence has been committed with the further intent to commit a serious criminal offence[43].

41 [1999] QB 847.
42 [2000] 2 AC 216.
43 No exhaustive list of these further offences is provided by the Computer Misuse Act 1990. The offence must carry either a fixed sentence penalty, such as murder, or be punishable with imprisonment of five years or more. This appears to cover the majority of serious offences.

The growth of ecommerce will lead to an increase in the reliance on this section. It will be discussed below that this section applies to interception of digital cash and credit card numbers. It also applies to the interception of goods or services which are delivered over the Internet, for example software[44].

Further offence

If a s 1 offence is made out, the s 2 offence may be proved by establishing that the defendant committed that offence with the intention to commit a further offence. This type of further offence is defined as one punishable by at least five years' imprisonment. This covers theft and fraud, and most other dishonesty offences[45]. Importantly it now covers an offence of dishonestly obtaining a money transfer by deception[46].

13. A hacker gains unauthorised access to a computer and takes a copy of an encryption key used for Internet-safe ecommerce transactions. The hacker then uses the key to pay for services without the permission of the account owner. The hacker may be convicted of the s 2 offence because the s 1 requirements are met and the defendant intended to commit the further offence of obtaining a money transfer by deception.

Intention

The hacker is not required actually to commit the further offence. Simply committing a s 1 offence with the intention of committing the further offence is sufficient. Where the hacker is accessing encryption keys to digital cash accounts, it seems probable that the secondary intention will be inferred. Gaining access to another's email account though, with no other evidence of intent, would not appear to provide sufficient evidence to make out a conviction.

Towards the end of 1999, an individual accessed without authority a database of 300,000 accounts held by CD Universe, a leading online music retailer. The individual demanded $100,000 in ransom from the company. CD Universe refused and the individual threatened to post 25,000 credit card account details on the Internet. This is a classic example of a s 2 type offence[47].

If a hacker is found not guilty under s 2, the jury may still find the defendant guilty under s 1[48]. Of course, where this takes place in the Crown Court, the powers of sentencing are those which the magistrate would have under s 1[49].

44 The application of the Computer Misuse Act 1990 to such a mischief, however, may not always be possible. In that scenario, the Law Commission has concluded that if a service (not product) is deceitfully obtained, no offence would be committed because no human mind would be deceived: *Law Commission Report on Fraud and Deception*, May 1999.

45 In illustration, although Cropp was acquitted for other reasons (discussed at 'Direct access to server', at p 296, Aglionby J stated, 'There is no doubt that false accounting contrary to s 17(1)(a) of the Theft Act 1968 falls within the statutory definition of "further offence"'. *R v Cropp* Transcript of Shorthand Notes, p 7G.

46 Theft Act 1968, s 15A as inserted by the Theft (Amendment) Act 1996.

47 For details, see *Observer*, 12 February 2000.

48 Computer Misuse Act 1990, s 12(1)(a).

49 Computer Misuse Act 1990, s 12(2).

Future intention

Section 2(3) states:

> 'It is immaterial for the purposes of this section whether the further offence is to be committed on the same occasion as the unauthorised access offence or on any future occasion.'

This eliminates difficult issues for the prosecution of whether the subsequent offence was sufficiently connected in time with the s 1 offence. It also creates a wider frame of culpability for the defendant: the intention may be to use the data at some time in the future.

Impossible further offence

Similar to the House of Lords' ruling in *R v Shivpuri*[50] in relation to the Criminal Attempts Act 1981, 'objective innocence' does not save a hacker who attempts a factually impossible crime. A hacker may be guilty of an offence under s 2 even though the facts are such that the commission of the further offence is impossible[51]. But the Computer Misuse Act 1990 is wider than the existing provisions under the Criminal Attempts Act 1981 and, say, the Theft Act 1968. This is because, even under the *Shivpuri* wider reading of the Criminal Attempts Act 1981, the defendant must still have done 'an act which is more than merely preparatory to the commission of the offence'[52]. In contrast, under the Computer Misuse Act 1990, an act less than merely preparatory may suffice as evidence of the additional intention needed for a s 2 offence.

14. A hacker uses a computer to obtain another person's encryption key with which he intends to access the owner's online bank account. The hacker does not know that the bank will only allow access through its own dial-up connection and not over the web. The hacker's attempt would fail. Despite this the hacker may have committed a s 2 offence, although he would probably not have made sufficient preparation for a statutory attempt.

This illustrates two crucial issues for would-be hackers and their lawyers. Almost any unauthorised dealing over the Internet with digital cash or other secure electronic transmissions will fall within s 2 of the Computer Misuse Act 1990. As a result of a conviction under this section, hackers may face up to five years' imprisonment. The same warnings extend to almost any dealing with intent to gain services or products using the Internet.

UNAUTHORISED MODIFICATION

In 1865 Mr Fisher was convicted of damaging a steam engine by plugging up the feed-pipe and displacing other parts to render the engine useless[53]. There was no

50 [1987] AC 1, especially at 21.
51 Computer Misuse Act 1990, s 2(4).
52 See Lord Bridge, [1987] AC 1 at 21; cf *Anderton v Ryan* [1985] AC 560 at 582–583.
53 (1865) LR 1 CCR 7.

removal of any part, no cutting and no breaking. Pollock CB upheld the conviction stating[54]:

> 'It is like the case of spiking a gun, where there is no actual damage to the gun, although it is rendered useless . . . Surely the displacement of the parts was a damage . . . if done with intent to render the machine useless.'

Malicious computer code is similar to Mr Fisher's feed-pipe plug. Often the victim computer program remains intact, as does the data it generates or uses; what alters is the computer's 'usefulness'. Before the Computer Misuse Act 1990 courts were forced to rely on the Criminal Damage Act 1971 to reason that the value of a computer's storage medium was impaired by altering the storing magnetic particles[55].

Prosecutions are more straightforward under s 3 of the Computer Misuse Act 1990.

> '3. (1) A person is guilty of an offence if:
> (a) he does any act which causes unauthorised modification of the contents of any computer; and
> (b) at the time when he does the act he has the requisite intent and the requisite knowledge.
>
> (2) For the purposes of subsection (1)(b) above the requisite intent is an intent to cause modification of the contents of any computer and by so doing:
> (a) to impair the operation of any computer;
> (b) to prevent or hinder access to any program or data held in any computer; or
> (c) to impair the operation of any such program or the reliability of any such data.'

This s 3 offence is triable either way. The section covers a vast range of acts and programs. That is the first key point to the section: it covers both a person who directly impairs the workings of a computer and also the distribution of a program which does such an activity. It is worthwhile appreciating the range of modifications which can be made by rogue programs. Each type of modification has acquired a suitably descriptive tag which will be used in the remainder of this chapter.

Virus A computer virus is actually a generic term for computer code which replicates, not only throughout the storage medium in which it incubates, but also across the network to which that computer is connected. Without anti-viral software a computer connected to the Internet poses a threat to all other computers also connected, and risks infection from those other computers. The ability to infect a home page with a virus, and even a word processing document, makes the

54 (1865) LR 1 CCR 7 at 9.

55 See *Cox v Riley* (1986) 83 Cr App Rep 54; also *R v Whiteley* (1991) 93 Cr App Rep 25. The Criminal Damage Act 1971 is no longer applicable owing to the Computer Misuse Act 1990, s 3(6).

Internet capable of spreading malicious code widely and rapidly. David L Smith's 'Melissa' virus was first discovered on a Usenet group on Friday afternoon, 26 March 1999. By 30 March 1999, 233 organisations were infected, involving over 81,000 computers[56]. The court which convicted Mr Smith in December 1999 determined that the virus had caused more than $80 million in damages.

Worm A worm is a program which replicates and grows in size[57]. This reproduction and expansion can cause a computer storage system to run more slowly and can also cause the computer itself to slow down. Legally it is important to note that it does not attach itself to the operating system of the computer it infects; it does not *directly* impair the workings of a computer. The most infamous example of such a program is Robert Morris's Internet Worm. This was released on 2 November 1988 and within a couple of days had almost crashed the entire Internet which existed at the time including NASA and the US Defense System. Morris was convicted of violating the Computer Fraud and Abuse Act[58]. More recently the Code Red worm attacked on 19 July 2001 and within nine hours had infected 250,000 systems. *Computer Economics* estimated that the total economic impact of Code Red was $2.6 billion.

Trojan horse A trojan horse is a seemingly innocent program which, true to its name, carries something more sinister. It harbours a further sub-program which is usually used for a special purpose such as capturing passwords or secretly copying and forwarding data. The vital legal issue is that the main program is executed by the user of the computer not the writer of the trojan horse. The 'Inner Circle', a sophisticated group of hackers, hid a trojan horse inside a chess program which was used in a large computer in Canada[59]. A trojan horse was used to penetrate one of Russia's gas suppliers. The Interior Ministry reported that the central switchboard of gas flows was 'for some time' under the control of the hackers[60].

Logic bomb A logic bomb, like a trojan horse, is a hidden program which, when triggered by a particular event, performs a function. Often this function is something rather destructive, such as wiping a storage medium, or crashing the computer on which it resides. Again, a significant legal factor is that such a program remains dormant until the triggering event. The most famous, still rife, is the Code Red Worm which spreads for the first 20 days of a month and then conducts all infected computers to mount attacks on certain sites.

Unauthorised modification: conduct or *actus reus*

Any act which causes an unauthorised modification of the contents of a computer can be the necessary conduct for a s 3 conviction[61]. As for a s 1 conviction,

56 Subcommittee on Technology, Committee on Science, US House of Representatives, 15 April 1999.
57 Not to be confused with the acronym WORM. See Glossary.
58 *United States v Morris* 928 F 2d 504 (2nd Cir 1991). For additional details see Hafner K and Markoff J, *Cyberpunk* (Corgi, London, 1993).
59 For additional details see Landreth B, *Out of the Inner Circle* (Microsoft Press, Washington, 1985).
60 *Associated Press*, 26 April 2000.
61 Computer Misuse Act 1990, s 3(1)(a).

it is useful to examine the pivotal words in this section. It will be shown that the *actus reus* aspect of the offence is quite wide, but the scope of the offence is tightened because specific intent must be proved.

MODIFICATION

Modification is exhaustively defined as taking place where, by the operation of any function, any program or data held in a computer is altered or erased or is added to[62]. The concept of this is widened by defining 'any act which *contributes* towards causing such a modification shall be regarded as causing it'[63].

15. A programmer is commissioned to write a Java applet which will show an animation on a home page. Without authority he also includes a logic bomb which downloads to each client computer and wishes them 'Happy Christmas' on 25 December. The logic bomb will not directly alter any program or data as it does not attach to other code stored on the computer. On the set date, however, the program will alter the contents of data held in the computer. The applet causes a modification.

Proving modification

Defence counsel should be alive to the fact that it is not unlawful to possess virus code. Further it is not prohibited to write malicious code[64]. The hard task for the prosecution is therefore to prove that the defendant distributed or contributed to the release of malicious code. This is the case for two reasons.

First, viruses are often spread by people other than those who wrote them initially. It can therefore be difficult to prove to the high burden of criminal proof that the source of the infection on the victim computer was the defendant's action. The existence of the virus on other systems *prior* to the alleged infection can weaken the prosecution's case by suggesting someone other than the defendant caused or contributed to the modification. The second difficulty for the prosecution is that, at present, there is no equivalent of a DNA fingerprint test for computer code. It will often be impossible to state categorically the source of an infection other than by extrapolating the code's dissemination. Occasionally, though, the prosecution will be able rely on evidence gained from the defendant's own computer. In *R v Pile* the defendant surreptitiously stored programs on his computer which he used to write and distribute the viruses[65]. The FBI was helped by 'globally unique identifiers' (such as the embedding of Ethernet adaptor addresses in Microsoft Office 97 documents) to capture David L Smith, the Melissa virus writer.

62 Computer Misuse Act 1990, s 17(7)(a) and (b).

63 Computer Misuse Act 1990, s 17(7). Emphasis added.

64 Sadly, there are countless examples of 'macro virus construction kits' for large programs such as Microsoft Office. Use of inchoate offences to prosecute such virus writers, while possible, has never been tested in the UK's courts.

65 (May 1995, unreported) Plymouth Crown Court. See *The Guardian*, 16 November 1995.

Unauthorised modification

The second aspect to the *actus reus* is the issue of authority. As for ss 1 and 2, lack of authority is rarely a difficult factor to prove when the malicious code is spread from outside an organisation[66]. Under s 3 a modification is unauthorised if two conditions are met. First, the person who causes the act must not be entitled to determine whether the modification should be made[67]. The second condition is that the person must not have consent from any person who is entitled to provide the authority[68]. Sometimes within an organisation the malicious code and tampering are so obvious that the defence can raise no serious questions of authority. Two real case examples should suffice. A male nurse pleaded guilty to two charges under s 3. He had altered prescriptions and treatment of various patients in his hospital[69]. In *R v Spielman* the defendant, a former employee of an online financial new agency, tampered with and deleted employee emails[70]. He pleaded guilty to the charge under s 3.

There can be other situations where the modification of code over an Intranet does not pose a difficult question of authority. As stated previously, the more vague the internal guidelines on such authority, the more difficult it may be to prosecute an individual who is regarded to have acted outside such authority[71]. Of course, employers may not resort to calling the police when the employee can be dealt with internally for gross misconduct[72].

Section 3(1): intention or *mens rea*

There are two limbs of a 'guilty mind' for s 3: the defendant must have the 'requisite intent' and the 'requisite knowledge'[73]. Logically, requisite knowledge must be considered first.

Requisite knowledge

Simply put by the Act, the 'requisite knowledge' under s 3(1)(b) is that any modification intended to be caused is unauthorised. The examination under s 1 of the degree of 'knowledge' is equally relevant for this section[74].

Requisite intention

The defendant must not only have intended to modify the contents of a computer, but also this modification should have at least one of four results set out

66 See 'Unauthorised', at p 295.
67 Computer Misuse Act 1990, s 17(8)(a).
68 Computer Misuse Act 1990, s 17(8)(b).
69 (December 1993, unreported) *R v Rymer* Liverpool Crown Court. See *The Guardian*, 21 December 1993.
70 (March 1995, unreported) Bow Street Magistrates Court. See *Computer Weekly*, 2 February 1995.
71 See 'Authorisation', at p 297.
72 In *Denco v Joinson* an employee's unauthorised access was stated by the Employment Appeal Tribunal to be gross misconduct [1992] 1 All ER 463.
73 Computer Misuse Act 1990, s 3(1)(b).
74 See fn 36 at p 298, the dicta of Lord Bridge, *Westminster City Council v Croyalgrange Ltd* [1986] 2 All ER 353.

below[75]. This does not indicate that the defendant must have intended one particular kind of modification: an intention to modify is sufficient[76]. These results are considered below with specific reference to potential rogue code which may be spread over the Internet. It is not a defence that the results were intended to be merely temporary[77].

Impair the operation of any computer (s 3(2)(a))

To impair the operation of a computer *per se*, without impairing the operation of any program, would suggest that this subsection caters for a worm. As explained, this type of code does not need to attach itself to a program or data[78]. Its presence in a computer, in multiple copies, alone may be enough to slow down a computer's processing speed.

It should be stated that, in certain circumstances, the prosecution may have problems in establishing that the worm's presence constitutes a modification. A worm may operate adequately without actually altering or adding to a program or data held in the computer. Too much should not be made of this technicality. Counsel should take expert evidence concerning both the nature of the worm, and also of the range of computers which it may infect. It may be that for one type of infected computer, programs and data *are* altered. The range of computers connected to the Internet and the increasing compatibility of these machines increases the likelihood that the operation of a computer is modified for the purposes of the Act.

Prevent or hinder access to any program or data (s 3(2)(b))

A worm will hinder access to a program or data, indirectly, but there are three other types of code which will cause this. A virus which obstructs the use of a computer will certainly fall within this section. One of Christopher Pile's viruses, Pathogen, after infecting a computer 32 times would at a particular time on a Monday evening show a message, 'Smoke me a kipper, I'll be back for breakfast. Unfortunately some of your data won't'[79]. This virus certainly hinders the access to the program being used at the time.

This type of result is also satisfied where a programmer seeks to use a logic bomb to 'lock out' an individual from accessing a program or data. Again, disgruntled employees appear to be the prime candidates for causing this. Mr Hardy, an IT manager, added a program to his company's system which encrypted stored data, and de-encrypted it on retrieval. One month after he left the firm the program stopped unscrambling the data. This left his former company hindered from accessing its stored information. He pleaded guilty[80].

75 Computer Misuse Act 1990, s 3(2).
76 Computer Misuse Act 1990, s 3(3)(c).
77 Computer Misuse Act 1990, s 3(5).
78 See 'Worm', at p 304.
79 See *The Guardian*, 16 November 1995. See also fn 65 at p 305.
80 *R v Hardy* (November 1992, unreported) Old Bailey.

16. As a joke a person attaches a virus to a word processing document which he forwards to a friend at work. The virus was intended simply to play a rude sound when the machine was next switched on. Owing to a special sound device attached to the friend's machine, the computer, and then the entire network, crashed. The more limited result intended by the joker is not relevant to the issue of culpability; it may be relevant for sentencing.

Impair the operation of any such program (s 3(2)(c))

This subsection focuses on how a program executes when some code has run. The 'operation' can be taken to mean how the program should function without the malicious code. It should not be read narrowly to mean the use that the victim makes of the program. The Melissa virus would automatically 'send itself' to the first 50 addresses listed in the address book of the Microsoft Outlook program. The operation of Microsoft Outlook was impaired on the infected computer.

17. A website has a virus which is downloaded secretly and automatically to any computer which accesses the site. This virus reduces the security of any credit card transactions which the user makes using their browser. It is of no importance that the only victims of the virus do not actually use their browser for such a purpose. The operation of the browser, as it was originally designed, has been impaired by the unauthorised modification.

Impair the reliability of any such data (s 3(2)(c))

This should be viewed by defence counsel as an objective notion of reliability. It is not enough for an infected-computer owner to claim that he now cannot rely on the data because he feels it may be unreliable. The prosecution must prove the alteration or reduction in quality of the data on an objective basis[81]. This approach is supported in a case mainly concerning the extradition of two Kazakstan hackers[82]. The facts of the case concerned the hacking of the Bloomberg financial computer system, so allowing the appellants to send messages that appeared to come from someone else; they were, in effect, forging the messages. The Divisional Court was asked whether or not *adding new* data to a computer system would fall within the section. Mr Justice Wright's terse judgment pointed out that s 17(7) of the Act provides that any addition of data to the contents of a computer amounts to a modification of the contents.

81 This approach is confirmed in *A-G's Reference (No 1 of 1991)* [1993] QB 94. Lord Taylor stated *obiter* that it is questionable whether it is correct to 'giv[e] the word "reliability" the meaning of achieving the result in the printout which was intended by the owner of the computer. It may not necessarily impair the reliability of data in the computer that you feed in something which will produce a result more favourable . . . than the [owner] intended'. [1992] 3 WLR 432 at 438.

82 *Zezev and Yarimaka v Governor of HM Prison Brixton and Government of the United States of America* [2002] EWHC 589 (Admin) [2002] 2 Cr App Rep 515.

Any program or data

The intention to modify does not need to be directed at any particular computer, or particular program, data or kind of program or data[83]. It is enough that an individual intends to modify the contents of a computer in general. The drafting of s 3(3) was essential to encompass fully the mischief which it addresses. Computer viruses and other malicious codes are disseminated in a random manner. The initial release of the code then results in it being passed to, and perhaps replicated by, any number of computers anywhere on the Internet. The prosecution would not be able to show a defendant had the intent to infect each victim of his code[84].

EVIDENCE

The defence counsel of any alleged computer misuser must focus his attention on the weaknesses of the evidence put before the court. Almost all relevant evidence will be computer-generated evidence. This evidence is treated differently from other evidence[85]. It is trusted less and requires a certificate as to the authenticity of the evidence. The prosecution should be aware that the existing rules on computer evidence are not easily applied to an Internet case.

Police and Criminal Evidence Act 1984

Like the Civil Evidence Act 1968, s 69 of the Police and Criminal Evidence Act 1984 will only admit computer evidence that satisfies certain requirements. Section 69 has two tests which must be satisfied before evidence from a computer can be admissible as a fact recorded by the evidence.

First, there must be no reasonable grounds for believing that the statement is inaccurate because of improper use of the computer[86]. Second, the computer must have been operating properly at all material times or at least the part that was not operating properly must have not affected the production of the document or the accuracy of its contents[87].

The House of Lords in *DPP v McKeown*, Jones explained that there can be 'a relevant malfunction and an irrelevant malfunction'. Lord Hoffman defined these terms: 'A malfunction is relevant if it affects the way in which the computer processes, stores or retrieves the information used to generate the statement

83 Computer Misuse Act 1990, s 3(3)(a) and (b).

84 This is confirmed by the conviction in *R v Pile*. Mr Pile's viruses were placed on bulletin boards and then spread by other people. Unreported, Plymouth Crown Court, May 1995. See *The Guardian*, 16 November 1995.

85 The Law Commission Consultation Paper 138 at para 14.32 proposes repealing the special rules on computer evidence without replacement. Before such repeal, the defence may take the benefit of the special rules alluded to at para 14.20: 'The complexity of modern systems makes it relatively easy to establish a reasonable doubt in a juror's mind as to whether the computer was operating properly. Bearing in mind the very technical nature of computers, the chances of this happening with greater frequency in future are fairly high.'

86 Police and Criminal Evidence Act 1984, s 69(1)(a).

87 Police and Criminal Evidence Act 1984, s 69(1)(b).

tendered in evidence. Other malfunctions do not matter [to whether the document can be adduced in evidence]'[88].

High authority on the actual operation of s 69 is given in *R v Shephard*[89]. Mrs Hilda Shepherd was alleged to have stolen some items from a Marks & Spencer store. She admitted to having thrown her receipt away, but every item in a Marks & Spencer's branch has a Unique Product Code. So, a store detective was able to ascertain whether those items had been sold by examining all the codes on a till roll from the day in question. As a central computer issued a date on each till roll the question was whether this evidence should satisfy the Police and Criminal Evidence Act 1984, s 69(1).

The Lords answered this with clear statements as to what evidence falls within the section, who can certify that evidence, and how.

Certifiable computer evidence

Lord Griffiths made the following statement[90]:

> 'if the prosecution wish to rely upon a document produced by a computer they must comply with s 69 in all cases.'

Examples of computer evidence

Evidence of a fact which is generated by a computer must clear the s 69 hurdle. Moreover, a critical analysis made of the types of evidence used in a digital crime case reveals that there will be little evidence which will *not* be required to meet the criteria of s 69. This evidence may include logs stored on the client's, host's, victim's or accused's computers[91]. It will also possibly include data or programs to which the prosecution alleges the defendant gained access. In this situation, the prosecution may, unwisely, also rely on 'date stamps'. As their name suggests, these dates show the last time that a computer file was modified or even viewed[92]. These date stamps may appear useful to the prosecution to show the exact time and date when, say, a program was infected with a virus. The evidential difficulty with these stamps is that they are notoriously unreliable and this can be challenged by the defence.

88 [1997] 1 All ER 737 at 744.

89 [1993] 1 All ER 225.

90 Per Lord Griffiths, [1993] 1 All ER 225 at 230. This is not strictly correct. Some computer evidence may be adduced not for 'any fact therein', but as actual fact. Professor Smith gives the example of a bank statement showing an entry of £100 into a bank account: [1983] Crim LR 472. This evidence is not a statement that the account is credited, rather the fact. As will be discussed, under a s 3 prosecution a computer program which is alleged to have been modified may be brought before the court without clearing the s 69 hurdle. In such a circumstance the code is adduced not as evidence of the fact therein, but as the fact itself.

91 This author has been informed of one prosecution where the *accused's* computer held a log of all the attempted and actual hacking which took place!

92 See Haber S and Stornetta WS, '*How to time-stamp a digital document*', Advances in Cryptology: Proceedings of CRYPTO '90 (Springer-Verlag, 1991).

18. The prosecution seek to adduce as evidence of unauthorised modification a computer file which is alleged to have a date stamp showing an alteration during the weekend. All employees are forbidden from logging in outside office hours. Two discrete pieces of evidence are being adduced: the file itself with the modification apparent and, second, the date stamp of the file indicating the time of modification. To adduce this latter, temporal, evidence the prosecution must satisfy s 69. Adducing the file is not evidence of any recorded fact, but the actual fact itself: no certificate is needed.

The defence and prosecution should remember that s 69 poses a negative requirement: *unless* the evidence sought to be adduced meets the criteria it is inadmissible. Section 69 is therefore a powerful tool to ensure that the other side relies only on appropriately reliable evidence.

How to certify

There are two ways to prove that the generating computer is reliable for the purposes of producing a certificate: call oral evidence, or tender a written certificate in line with the Police and Criminal Evidence Act 1984, Sch 3, para 8.

Signed certificate

A certificate must be from a 'person occupying a responsible position in relation to the operation of the computer'[93]. To rely on this certificate, Lord Griffiths stated that[94],

> 'it should show on its face that it is signed by a person who from his job description can confidently be expected to be in a position to give reliable evidence about the operation of the computer.'

If the defendant is not satisfied by the certificate, he can ask the judge to require oral evidence which can be challenged in cross-examination. Indeed, in *R v Koltun*[95], the Court of Appeal admitted documents made in Romania together with a statement made by a non-cross-examined Romanian official.

Oral evidence

Where oral evidence of the reliability of computer evidence is given the court does not need to insist on hearing the testimony given by an expert in the 'proper workings of the computer'. Indeed, in *R v Shephard* the court instead was prepared to accept the testimony of the store detective as proof that the central computer was working. Lord Griffiths went on to indicate that the burden of s 69 may vary from case to case[96]:

93 Police and Criminal Evidence Act 1984, Sch 3, para 8(d).
94 [1993] 1 All ER 225 at 230.
95 [2000] All ER (D) 454.
96 [1993] 1 All ER 225 at 231. Emphasis added.

> '*The evidence must be tailored to the needs of the case*. I suspect that it will very rarely be necessary to call an expert and that in the vast majority of cases it will be possible to discharge the burden by calling a witness who is familiar with the operation of the computer in the sense of knowing what the computer is required to do and who can say that it is doing it properly.'

The House of Lords indicated that the simpler the computer, the less technically qualified the witness needs to be. In all but the most straightforward Computer Misuse Act 1990 prosecutions it is suggested that no less than an expert familiar with the system should be accepted as having the requisite understanding of the computer's trustworthiness[97]. In *DPP v Barber*[98] the magistrate's court was found to have wrongly concluded that a custody sergeant and operator of an intoximeter was not an expert on its operation. The court held that an expert witness in these cases was merely a person who was qualified by education, training or experience and who thereby had greater authority on a subject than those not so qualified.

The House of Lords in *Shephard*, Divisional Court in *Barber* and Court of Appeal in *Koltun* should indicate that the defence will rarely be able to attack the expert nature of the prosecution's expert witness and will need instead to concentrate on the weight of their testimony.

Degree of reliability

The final question which must be addressed, particularly in oral evidence, is what is the necessary level of reliability of computer evidence? This is of paramount importance in hacking cases where very often a hacker will attempt to 'clean up his fingerprints' by tampering with logs of his activities. It is also important where a modification is alleged to have occurred, but it is the time of this modification which is disputed.

Vigilant counsel for a computer misuse defendant should concentrate on the strength of the expert witness's testimony. They should certainly be more pressing than those in *R v Shephard*. In evidence-in-chief Mrs McNicholas, the store detective, was asked, 'And what about the master computer? Did that malfunction?' Her reply was less than convincing, 'Touch wood, no. I have never known it to break down since we have had it'. She was not cross-examined on the

97 The defence should also be conscious of the ease of manipulating digital data without trace; this is sometimes called 'chain of custody' evidence. The Committee of Experts on criminal procedural law problems connected with information technology notes honestly, 'Adequate safeguards must be taken by the investigating authorities to guarantee the integrity of data between its copying during the investigation and its presentation at court proceedings . . . [C]ourts may demand that the proponent of a digital picture, for example, be ready to establish a complete chain of custody. A hand-to-hand chain from the photographer to the person who produced the printout may, in some circumstances, be the only way to adequately ensure the integrity of an exhibit': Final Activity Report, Recommendation No R(95) 13 Concerning Problems of Criminal Procedural Law Connected with Information Technology (Strasbourg, 2 October 1995) at para 161.

98 (1998) 163 JP 457.

point[99]. It is submitted that such a weak affirmation in a computer misuse case should certainly be tested under cross-examination.

This background understanding of the interaction between the Computer Misuse Act 1990 and the Police and Criminal Evidence Act 1984 is fundamental to the following examination of the evidence used in a computer misuse case.

Evidence of computer misuse

There are two main issues prevalent in a computer misuse case that may create an evidential burden on the prosecution. First, there must be continuity of evidence from the first computer used by a hacker to the final victim computer; second, hackers rarely use their own names and addresses to log in to a victim computer.

Continuity of access evidence

To prove beyond reasonable doubt that the defendant was responsible for the unauthorised access of the victim's computer, the prosecution can be forced to prove continuity of evidence. That is, the prosecution should be able to 'follow' a line of access from the hacker's own computer to the victim's. Any discontinuity may raise the court's reasonable doubt that the defendant in the court was not the person responsible for the final unauthorised access. Only the most simple Internet hacking cases will feature two computers and an identifiable abuser. More regularly a hacker's commands to his computer will pass through many different computers spread across the Internet. It is also usual that a hacker will attempt to disguise his true identity: he is unlikely to attempt unauthorised access using an electronic signifier which can identify him. This poses an evidential difficulty for the prosecution.

Fragmentation of Internet hacking

It has been explained that messages and commands sent over the Internet do not pass directly between the sender and receiver computer. Instead the message is broken into small packets, each with a destination address. Each packet is shunted from one computer on the Internet to another, and from that computer to the next; gradually moving the packet towards its destination. Eventually, all the packets arrive at their final resting computer in a matter of seconds.

Hackers' messages and commands are no different. Each message will be broken into packets and shunted through many different computers. The prosecution will have to establish that a hacker's message did travel to an unauthorised computer.

In addition, hackers rarely attempt to gain access to their victim computer directly. Their preferred method is to log in to one computer on the Internet and

99 (1991) 93 Cr App Rep 139 at 143.

from there to log in to another. This process is repeated many times; it is the digital equivalent of speeding around many corners to shake off a chasing police car. And each new login made by the hacker presents another piece of evidence which the prosecution may have to prove to establish continuity from the first to the final unauthorised access[100].

These computers can be contrasted with the thousands of computers which shunt data from the victim computer to the hacker's computer. In a sense, there are many computers involved with any hacking which merely act as 'conduits' – they do not 'process' the data passed between them. This must be contrasted with computers which carry out functions or process the data involved in a hacking prosecution.

In *R v Waddon* both the Crown Court[101] and Court of Appeal[102] were clear that the many computers involved in the downloading of obscene images by one individual from one website did not necessitate having s 69 certificates for each one. Hardy J refers to the numerous computers in the chain as 'mere post boxes'. The Court of Appeal, unanimously giving judgement through The Vice President, Lord Justice Rose, draws a distinction between the computers that 'produce' the evidence and those that 'transmit' the evidence. Only the former are addressed by the Act.

False identification – spoofing

The situation for the prosecution may be more complex. A hacker logging in to a computer on the way to his victim will often log in under a different identity. This is called 'spoofing'. The hacker is able to do this by having previously obtained actual passwords, or having created a new identity by fooling the computer into thinking he is the system's operator. Whatever the technical method, the legal result remains the same. The prosecution must establish that the hacker at his own computer was the person who has logged in to countless other computers.

Evidential implications

There are many s 69 implications of fragmented and spoofed access. Many certificates from many jurisdictions can be required. Also, hackers will often tamper with the evidence which recorded the details of their activities.

Obtaining certificates

Multiple certificates

Unlike the one certificate in *R v Shephard*, a hacking prosecution may have to rely on numerous certificates, and possibly produce the witnesses for oral examination.

100 *R v Cochrane* [1993] Crim LR 48 illustrates the utility of focusing on one computer in a chain to 'break' the continuity. This must be contrasted with more than one computer 'transmitting' the same evidence but only one computer 'producing' the evidence (*R v Waddon* 6 April 2000, unreported, CA). In such a case, only the computer 'producing' the evidence is subject to the hurdles of s 69.

101 His Honour Judge Hardy, (30 June 1999, unreported).

102 (6 April 2000, unreported).

While this, in itself, is not a bar to a conviction, each certificate must adequately verify the proper workings of the computer. Each certificate is therefore potentially a weak link in the continuity chain[103].

Multiple jurisdictions

The computers which a hacker may journey through to arrive finally at the victim computer will be scattered throughout the world. A hacker will often search for an insecure computer and then, using software tools called a root kit, use this compromised computer as a starting base to begin the real nuisance[104]. It will be recalled that there is one cost of accessing a computer anywhere on the Internet; there are no financial restraints on crossing borders and continents. Again, this is not a bar to a conviction but it does raise the possibility of a judge requiring that one of these witnesses be orally examined[105].

Refusal to certify

This author has been informed of at least one Internet Service Provider who has refused to supply details from any log for a computer misuse investigation. The prosecution needs only one such stubborn system operator to produce a potential flaw in the continuity of evidence[106].

Not working reliably

A hacker will often not only spoof his identity but also attempt to tamper with the logging software actually used by the system. This poses two problems: first, technically it may be impossible to prove that the defendant in the court was the hacker modifying the log. Second, to admit that the log has been tampered with at all raises the suspicion that the computer was not operating properly at the material time[107]. Any admission by the prosecution of tampering should be met

103 '[F]orging computer logs is trivial. The same commands that let us obscure the names of attacking sites for [the referenced] book would let us insert any names we wished in our logs, including yours . . . [E]ven assuming an absence of malice on our part, computer systems have a less-than-sterling reputation for reliability. The hardware is almost certainly working properly; the software though, is another matter entirely.' Cheswick WR and Bellovin SM, *Firewalls and Internet Security* (Addison-Wesley Publishing Company, Wokingham, 1995) at p 200. Cheswick and Bellovin designed AT&T's Internet gateway and are established experts.

104 Most Distributed Denial of Service attacks use these techniques.

105 Subject to the Criminal Justice Act 1988, ss 23 and 24. Often a log of accesses will have been prepared for the purposes of the trial. In such a situation, s 26 may be applicable. Section 29 assists both sides in obtaining evidence from a witness residing abroad. Section 32 allows a witness from abroad to give evidence using a video conference.

106 The Computer Misuse Act 1990, s 10, as amended by the Criminal Justice and Public Order Act 1994, s 162, now ensures that law enforcement officers will not be committing a s 1 offence by gaining unauthorised access to programs or data for investigation purposes.

107 The defence should, however, remember that Lord Hoffmann stated: 'A malfunction is relevant if it affects the way in which the computer processes, stores or retrieves the information used to generate the statement tendered in evidence. Other malfunctions do not matter': *DPP v McKeown* [1997] 1 All ER 737 at 744.

by the defence with a question as to whether the evidence still deserves a certificate, or at least that the operator should be orally examined[108].

Proof of modification

The prosecution of a s 3 offence may be faced with similar difficulties under s 69. To convict a person under s 3 the prosecution may seek to show that, following modification, the operation of a computer is impaired[109]. Evidence of this impairment, that the unauthorised modification caused the improper operation, must satisfy the Police and Criminal Evidence Act 1984, s 69(1)(b): the computer must have been operating properly at all material times. But this may be the very fact that the prosecution cannot prove because of the modification itself. This loophole has been addressed by the Law Commission, who provide a less than satisfactory solution for the Crown[110].

> 'We see no reason in such a case for exempting the prosecution from the general requirement imposed by s 69 of showing that the computer was, apart from the alleged interference of which evidence will be given, *otherwise* operating properly.'

It is submitted that this may sometimes be impossible. A malevolent piece of code or modification can affect the very aspect of the computer which allows it to produce reliable data. For example a program which corrupts all time-stamps on files, including its own, will make it impossible for the prosecution to rely on any time-stamp. The defence should be aware that the more serious the modification alleged, the more likely it is that the prosecution will find their evidence unreliable.

In *R v Vatsal Patel*[111], a s 3 prosecution, the Crown wished to rely on file time-stamps which were admitted to be inaccurate. The defence properly objected to the admission under the Police and Criminal Evidence Act 1984, s 69. After hearing expert evidence from both sides Slack J ruled that the evidence was admissible. He stated that any doubts as to its reliability should go to weight. Under the cross-examination of prosecution witnesses it was heard that other members of the team used the defendant's computer and that these members knew how to alter time-stamps. The jury found Mr Patel not guilty on all three counts under s 3. This case indicates that even where modification evidence is ruled admissible, the defence may still successfully challenge the evidence.

108 For commercial logging programs, often the software writer will be the most appropriate witness to testify as to the log's authenticity. He knows the weaknesses of a particular system and may be able to give evidence that, 'yes' the log has been modified, but 'no', this modification or unreliability 'was not such as to affect the production of the document or the accuracy of its contents'; Police and Criminal Evidence Act 1984, s 69(1)(b).
109 Computer Misuse Act 1990, s 3(2)(a).
110 Law Commission Paper 186 para 4.9. Emphasis present in original text.
111 (July 1993, unreported), Aylesbury Crown Court. See Turner M, *Case Report* Computers and Law, May 1994. See also *DPP v McKeown* [1997] 1 All ER 737 at 744.

COMMON DIGITAL CRIME

What follows is a brief legal analysis of the ploys used by hackers in gaining unauthorised access to computers over the Internet[112].

Destroy evidence

Having gained unauthorised access to a computer, a common hacking goal is to destroy the evidence of this access. This itself is an offence under s 3 of the Computer Misuse Act 1990. It will make more onerous the burden on the prosecution to prove the unauthorised access occurred, when it occurred and who was responsible. Nevertheless, a s 69 certificate or oral testimony of the workings of the computer does not need to prove that the computer was operating properly *in all respects*. It is open to the prosecution to admit that the computer's reliability has been reduced, but not in respect of the evidence relied upon. In illustration, an activity log which is stored on a Write Once Read Many[113] (times) device is far less likely to have been adversely modified.

Obtain further passwords

Obtaining further passwords is the first step to being able to 'spoof', to pretend you are someone else. To do this a person must be acting out of his authority because he knows that he is not the person whose password he obtains. The person is therefore within the ambit of a s 1 offence by making the computer perform a function to gain this password. Where it is a commercial system, his use will be charged to the real owner of the password. This may be enough to permit the prosecution to bring charges under s 2 also.

Evidentially, the prosecution have to prove that the hacker, not the rightful owner, was using the password. This will pivot on the facts, but it should be remembered that a log from the rightful owner's computer showing he was not connected shows merely that. It does not show that the hacker wrongly using the password was the defendant.

Open security holes

A hacker will often attempt to open up new security holes in the attacked system in case their present 'entrance' is discovered and sealed. They may use a 'root kit' to assist. Doing this necessarily involves both unauthorised access under s 1 and unauthorised modification under s 3. The interesting legal point is to consider which subsection of s 3(2) will be 'intended' by the hacker. It is submitted that

112 This metastasis is reproduced with kind permission from William Cheswick and Steven Bellovin. For their technical examination see Cheswick WR and Bellovin SM, *Firewalls and Internet Security* (Addison-Wesley Publishing Company, Wokingham, 1995) at p 152.

113 WORM. As the source of this acronym suggests, this device permits data to be stored but does not allow it to be altered thereafter. A good example of this is a CD-ROM. On this medium, like a music compact disc, one can record only once; users are able to retrieve but not modify its contents.

the hacker necessarily must intend to restrict access or impair the operation of at least the program or code he has introduced into the system. The very reason for introducing the hole is that, without it, the present entry point may be discovered. The introduced code therefore impairs the operation of the program which would have discovered his entry.

Little more needs to be said about the evidential difficulties in proving a modification where the very program which is to be used to prove this fact has itself been modified[114]. It is enough to reiterate that the Law Commission saw no reason why the s 69 evidential burden should be lifted for the Computer Misuse Act 1990, s 3; the court and defence should also be cautious before lowering it.

Obtain root access

The ultimate goal of any hacker is to burrow to the root of a computer system, giving him as many rights as the authorised system operator. Gaining access to this level of power clearly steps into unauthorised territory and any modifications will, as above, be designed to secure that position for the hacker. As such, the modifications will be intended to hinder access to programs or data, namely the programs or data which establish the hacker with system operator rights.

The caveats of computer-generated evidence apply even more strongly to penetration to this level. With the same rights as the system operator, a hacker can delete any trace on a log, or otherwise, of his presence on the system.

JURISDICTION AND EXTRADITION

Jurisdiction and extradition can be fundamental to an Internet-based case. The Computer Misuse Act 1990 operates within tight jurisdictional confines. Computer misusers do not. It has been discussed that a hacker will often log in to computers across the globe in a bid to disguise his true location and identity. Malicious code, such as viruses, can spread across the whole Internet, and are therefore capable of modifying any data or program in any jurisdiction.

The physical location of the hacker is not an indication of where the crime is committed. And what may not be legal here, may well be caught by the laws of another jurisdiction. These other laws are not considered in this chapter, but the rules on extradition *to* those countries are.

Jurisdiction

The Computer Misuse Act 1990 provides its rules on jurisdiction in ss 4 to 7[115]. They are complex and they apply differently to each of the three offences. If the

114 See above, 'Proof of modification', at p 316.

115 Readers unfamiliar with rules as to jurisdiction are warned not to conflate the assessment of jurisdiction with assessment of culpability under the offence itself. The rules described below are necessarily wider than the rules for a conviction. It is perfectly possible that the courts have jurisdiction over a person, who at trial, is found not to be guilty of the offence itself. Nevertheless, the defence should be prepared to fight on jurisdiction, without which there will be no trial in England at all.

English court does not have jurisdiction over the offence the offender may still face charges from abroad.

Section 1 jurisdiction

The court will have jurisdiction over a computer misuse offender under s 1 where the offence has at least one 'significant link' with England[116]. For a s 1 offence, a significant link can be either[117]:

1. that the accused was in England at the time when he did the act which caused the computer to perform the function; or
2. that the computer containing any program or data to which the accused secured or intended to secure unauthorised access by doing that act was in England at that time[118].

Location of accused

Neil Woods and Karl Strickland were convicted and sentenced to six months' imprisonment under s 1. They had used UK computers, mostly academic, to break into databases in 15 countries outside the UK[119].

19. A French postgraduate at university in England logs in to his former university computer in France. From this computer he runs an automated hacking program which fails to gain access to a further computer in America. The English court has jurisdiction even though the computer caused to function was outside England, as was the victim computer. The act causing the function was made while the postgraduate was in England.

Location of victim computer

The nub of this subsection is that the hacker secured access or intended to secure access to *any* computer situated in England. It is of no consequence that the hacker was only using an English computer as a 'stop' on the way to a victim computer outside the jurisdiction. Jurisdiction can result from the victim computer or any computer through which the hacker journeys being within England.

116 Computer Misuse Act 1990, s 4(2).
117 Computer Misuse Act 1990, s 5(2).
118 A 16-year-old pleaded guilty to 12 s 1 offences. All the unauthorised accesses were performed from his north London home. The victim computers were top security military computers based in the US. The Senate said that 'he had caused more damage than the KGB': *R v Pryce* (21 March 1997, unreported) Bow Street Magistrates.
119 (21 May 1993, unreported) Southwark Crown Court.

20. A programmer based in America has for some time been plotting to hack into an English oil company's computer. He is caught by American police having secured access to an American computer which has a secure line to the English computer. The English court, perhaps not alone, has jurisdiction over the American. It is sufficient that his intentions were directed to an English computer.

21. A hacker based in a country with no extradition treaties gains unauthorised access into a computer with weak security in Bolivia. She uses this computer to plant daemon programs in countless other computers across the globe. Finally, she uses a program called Tribal Flood Network to launch attacks at a UK newspaper's websites. It is brought down by the attack in seconds. The English court has jurisdiction over the hacker as her intention was to impair a UK computer.

SECTION 2 JURISDICTION

The jurisdiction over s 2 offences is wider than that for s 1. Either or both of two rules give the court jurisdiction:

1. subject to 'double criminality' below if the accused intended to do or facilitate anything outside England which would be a s 2 offence if it took place in England *and* the offence has a significant link to England for a s 1 offence[120];
2. if the accused gained unauthorised access to a computer abroad with the intent to commit the further offence in England.

Double-criminality

Not only the English courts must view the conduct as falling within the ambit of the offence. The relevant country abroad must also view the conduct as criminal, although the offences here and abroad need not be the same[121]. The further offence must involve the commission of an offence under the law in force where the whole or any part of the further offence was intended to take place[122].

Defence counsel must note that the onus is on them to serve a notice on the prosecution stating that the double-criminality is not satisfied. Full facts and grounds for that opinion must be included in the notice[123].

120 Computer Misuse Act 1990, s 4(4).
121 Computer Misuse Act 1990, s 8(4).
122 Computer Misuse Act 1990, s 8(1).
123 Computer Misuse Act 1990, s 8(5) and (9).

22. An American bank protects its records by storing them with an English data warehouse, fully encrypted. From a mobile device, a hacker, at the time in Switzerland, gains access to this data warehouse and appropriates a number of confidential files, still encrypted. After cracking the encryption, the hacker intends to steal electronically from the American bank. The English court has jurisdiction over the hacker having both a significant link with England, constituting an offence if in England and being punishable in the US.

SECTION 3 JURISDICTION

The court will have jurisdiction over s 3 computer misuse where the offence has at least one 'significant link' with England[124]. For a s 3 offence, a significant link can be either[125]:

1. that the accused was in England at the time when he did the act which caused the unauthorised modification; or
2. that the unauthorised modification took place in England.

It has been mentioned on numerous occasions that a virus may spread throughout the entire Internet. It is possible to affect computers in multiple jurisdictions. An effect of the 'significant link' is to allow the English courts to prosecute a person who disseminates malicious code from England, even if no computer in England is modified. Also, the significant link contemplates a computer modifier from anywhere in the world being prosecuted for a computer in England being modified.

Location of accused

23. An English public schoolboy uses his school computer to post on a French Internet bulletin board a logic bomb which corrupts an important part of any computer it infects. It is of no consequence that the logic bomb is 'defused' before it reaches a computer in England. The act constituting the offence was committed within the jurisdiction.

As previously stated, executable code which is on a website may cause an unauthorised modification. The act of uploading this code to the website will constitute the relevant act for the purposes of jurisdiction.

124 Computer Misuse Act 1990, s 4(2).
125 Computer Misuse Act 1990, s 5(3).

Location of victim computer

The jurisdiction of the court is triggered by any computer situated in England affected by an unauthorised modification. It does not matter that the modifier had no intention to infect an English computer.

Extradition

The law concerning extradition is involved and it is considered more appropriate that readers consult a specialist text in the field before providing or acting on any advice. The following is a brief indication of the aspects of digital crime over the Internet which should be factored into any extradition evaluation.

The Extradition Act 1989 defines an 'extradition crime'. This is conduct which is both an offence in England and in the other country which has a minimum sentence of 12 months' imprisonment[126]. As for the rules of double-criminality for jurisdiction[127], it is irrelevant how the offence is defined in the other country[128]. In addition to the application of the Extradition Act 1989, the Extradition Act 1870 remains in force in respect of countries with which Britain has established extradition treaties.

The Extradition Act 1989's requirement of a maximum sentence in excess of 12 months excludes any extradition for a s 1 offence, but ss 2 and 3 offences are covered. The Extradition Act 1870 is also suitably amended to include ss 2 and 3 offences[129].

Extradition for hacking

The following discussion of an actual extradition case illustrates the way a hacker from abroad may be extradited to a place where his actions were illegal.

In *R v Governor of Brixton Prison, ex p Levin*, the US government sought the extradition of a Russian expert computer programmer who had gained access to Citibank's computer in New Jersey, America[130]. Levin, using his skill as a computer programmer, was able to monitor the transactions of substantial customers and insert unauthorised instructions to make payments from those accounts into those of a Russian accomplice. If the scheme had been successful, sums in excess of $10 million would have been obtained. Levin was detained on 3 March 1995 in execution of a warrant under s 1(3) of the Extradition Act 1989 at the request of the US government. He was accused of having committed in the US offences of wire fraud and bank fraud and of conspiring to commit those offences. No single criminal offence under the law of England and Wales equates to the offence of wire fraud or bank fraud.

126 Extradition Act 1989, s 2.
127 See 'Double-criminality', at p 320.
128 Extradition Act 1989, s 2.
129 Computer Misuse Act 1990, s 15.
130 [1997] QB 65; affd [1997] 3 All ER 289, HL.

The prosecuting authority gave details of acts and conduct which translated into 66 offences under the criminal law of England and Wales including unauthorised access to a computer with intent to commit or facilitate further offences, conspiracy to commit offences under the Computer Misuse Act 1990 and unauthorised modification of computer material.

The applicant challenged his committal on the main grounds that the computer print-out records could not be admitted under s 69 of the Police and Criminal Evidence Act 1984 since that section did not apply to extradition proceedings, because they were not criminal proceedings within s 72 of the Act.

The Divisional Court and House of Lords held that as the extradition crimes had conduct punishable under the criminal law, they were criminal proceedings for the purposes of the Police and Criminal Evidence Act 1984. Evidence of the computer print-outs in extradition hearings should be, and was rightly in this case, admitted in evidence under s 69 of the Act.

One of the other grounds was that as the appropriation took place in Russia, where the computer keyboard was situated, the English courts have no jurisdiction. For the purposes of the Theft Act 1968 the Divisional Court had to decide where the actions of Mr Levin took place. They said[131]:

> '[T]he operation of the keyboard by a computer operator produces a virtually instantaneous result on the magnetic disk of the computer even though it may be 10,000 miles away. It seems to us artificial to regard the act as having been done in one rather than the other place. [T]he fact that the applicant was physically in St Petersburg is of far less significance than the fact that he was looking at and operating on magnetic disks located in [America]. The essence of what he was doing was done there.'[132]

Mr Levin's extradition to the US took place in September 1997. In January 1998 Federal Prosecutors announced that they had reached a plea agreement with Mr Levin; three years in prison together with $240,000 payable in restitution.

OBSCENE AND INDECENT MATERIAL

It has always been possible to acquire by mail order obscene and paedophilic material from abroad which would be illegal in England. The Internet has made this process easier, it may have also made this activity more prevalent; it has not, however, altered the legal ramifications of the activity[133].

131 [1996] 3 WLR 657 at 671.

132 In *Zezev and Yarimaka v Governor of HM Prison Brixton and Government of the United States of America* [2002] EWHC 589 (Admin) [2002] 2 Cr App Rep 515 the Divisional Court also judged that the UK court could extradite two hackers who committed computer misuse from Kazakstan against Bloomberg LP in New York.

133 See also Telecommunications Act 1984, s 43 and Indecent Displays (Control) Act 1981.

Obscene Internet material

The Obscene Publications Act 1959, as amended by the Criminal Justice and Public Order Act 1994, covers material which has the effect of depraving and corrupting.

Publication over the Internet

An offence is committed if a person publishes an obscene article: merely possessing an article is not an offence[134]. Possessing an obscene article for publication for gain is an offence[135]. Often those who use the Internet for these purposes do not pay money for obscene articles, rather, they exchange them for other articles. This too will be seen as 'for gain'[136]. It is for the possessor of the article to prove that it was not for gain.

An amendment to the Obscene Publications Act 1959 introduced the concept that it is publication to transmit electronically stored data which is obscene on resolution into a viewable form[137].

> **24. A person sends an email attached to which is an encrypted graphics file depicting an obscene activity. Only the recipient has the unlocking key. The person will have transmitted the obscene material: it does not matter that the data is encrypted; when de-encrypted it will be obscene.**

Transmission or retrieval

Often obscene material is not transmitted to an individual. It is uploaded to a website or an ftp site. Interested parties download this material by instructing their computer to issue a command to the holding site. It is clearly an important question whether this constitutes transmission, and thereby constitutes publication.

This question was addressed by the Court of Appeal in *R v Fellows; R v Arnold*[138]. The appellants appealed that publication within s 1(3) requires some form of active conduct and that providing the *means* of access to a website or ftp site is passive only. In short, putting obscene pictures on a website, although no doubt *seen* by many people, is not publication of those pictures; technically it is each viewer who retrieves the picture.

The Court of Appeal was prepared to accept that some form of activity is required for publication. In this case they thought that there was ample evidence of such conduct: the first appellant:

> 'took whatever steps were necessary not merely to store the data on his computer but also to make it available world-wide to other computers via the Internet. He corresponded by e-mail with those who

134 Obscene Publications Act 1959, s 2.
135 Obscene Publications Act 1959, s 2.
136 Obscene Publications Act 1959, s 1(5). See *R v Fellows; R v Arnold* (unreported, Court of Appeal, 27 September 1996).
137 Obscene Publications Act 1959, s 1(3), as amended by Criminal Justice and Public Order Act 1994, s 168 and Sch 9.
138 [1997] 2 All ER 548.

> sought to have access to it and he imposed certain conditions before they were permitted to do so.'

This 'activity' prior to the actual offence appears to have satisfied the court that the storage of the material alone would be distribution[139].

Publication abroad

It has been stated that possessing an obscene article is not an offence. However, where a person possesses an article and then transmits this *abroad* where it is there published, a question arises as to whether this is an offence.

In *R v Waddon* the Crown Court[140] and Court of Appeal[141] were asked whether a UK resident creating obscene articles in the UK and uploading them to non-UK websites was 'publishing' for the purposes of the Obscene Publications Act. The courts reasoned that 'publishing' an article includes 'transmitting' that data[142]. Transmitting, the Crown Court held, means to send on from one place or person to another. Consequently, the transmission by the defendant to his UK Internet Service Provider took place within the jurisdiction. The Court of Appeal added that there was not one publication but rather 'further publication when the images are downloaded elsewhere'. The fact that the appellant would not have been directly responsible for any downloads into the UK, so therefore could not have been prosecuted for them, is ignored by the Court of Appeal. This author prefers the arguments of the Crown Court as being more a more robust application of the law to the known facts.

In a similar case, *R v Perrin*[143], the Court of Appeal was asked to consider an appeal to a conviction of publishing an obscene article. The article in question was a sexually obscene web page, able to be viewed by anyone, and a further much larger set of sexually obscene material only viewable by subscribing with a credit card. The site was, in part, managed from outside the UK. The appellant appealed the conviction on a number of grounds. One was that it was necessary for the Crown to show where the major steps in relation to publication were taken. The Court of Appeal rejected this as being a necessary pre-cursor to any prosecution. Instead, they deemed it enough to rely on a strict application of *Waddon*: there was 'transmission' within the jurisdiction.

These cases illustrate the rather parochial (and maybe morally justified) application of the Obscene Publications Act to published material on the Internet. Perhaps not unreasonably, in *Perrin*, the appellants sought to convince the Court of Appeal of the legal consequence of 'the sites [being] legal where they were managed'. In effect, the appellants unsuccessfully tried to appeal to the Court's commercial sense: 'Community standards as to what tends to deprave and corrupt are not Europe-wide, and the court should look at the problem from the point of view of a publisher who is prepared to comply

139 See also *R v Pecciarich* (1995) 22 OR (3d) 748 at 765.
140 (30 June 1999, unreported) Southwark Crown Court.
141 (6 April 2000, unreported).
142 Obscene Publications Act 1959, s 1(3)(b), as amended.
143 [2002] EWCA Crim 747, [2002] All ER (D) 359 (Mar). It should be noted that the Court of Appeal also rejected the various pleas that the European Convention on Human Rights, arts 7 and 10, were sufficient to overturn the conviction.

with the law.' Of course these arguments are neither novel nor unique to English Internet jurisprudence. In the US, the Court of Appeal (Third Circuit) has (reluctantly) judged that only where the 'major' steps in relation to publication take place in the jurisdiction should the court take jurisdiction over a prosecution[144]. The US court in that case noted that 'web publishers cannot restrict access to their site based on the geographic locale of the internet user visiting their site'[145].

It is clear from these cases that the UK criminal courts' jurisdiction in cases of this kind will not be upset by the careful placing of servers or 'management' abroad[146].

25. A woman living in Manchester establishes a Dutch company which operates a series of servers in Holland. The servers host a website which, after a credit card is entered, shows a number of obscene pictures involving sexual acts with animals. These obscene articles are uploaded to the Dutch servers from her home in Manchester. By transmitting the obscene articles from within the UK she is publishing obscene articles in the UK. She will not be able to avoid the jurisdiction of the UK courts by pointing to the 'major' steps being taken outside the UK.

Indecent material

Section 1(1) of the Protection of Children Act 1978[147], as amended by the Criminal Justice and Public Order Act 1994, makes it an offence:

> '(a) to take, or permit to be taken, an indecent photograph of a child (meaning in this Act a person under the age of 16); or
> (b) to distribute or show such indecent photographs or pseudo-photographs; or
> (c) to have in his possession such indecent photographs or pseudo-photographs with a view to their being distributed or shown by himself or others . . .'

Although the circumstances will be rare, there may be occasions where an individual possesses such items without knowledge of them. This is possible because most Internet browsers automatically store a copy of every graphic file viewed, called a 'cached' copy. In *Atkins v DPP*[148] the defendant was not convicted of

144 *ACLU v Reno (No 3)* [2000] F 3d 162. The case concerned the preliminary injunction against the Attorney-General to prevent the enforcement of the Child Protection Act.

145 *ACLU v Reno (No 3)* [2000] F 3d 162, at 176. Cf *Groppera Radio AG v Switzerland* (1990) 12 EHRR 321.

146 In *Gold Star Publications Ltd v DPP* [1981] 2 All ER 257, the House of Lords was asked to consider whether thousands of hard core pornographic magazines due for *export* from the UK would fall within the jurisdiction of the courts. Only Lord Simon dissented, taking the narrow view that the Obscene Publications Act 1959 should not be interpreted to grant UK courts powers to prevent activities abroad.

147 This legislation remains unaffected by the coming into force of the Human Rights Act 1998, and therefore the European Convention of Human Rights, arts 8 and 10. In *R v Smelhurst*, the Court of Appeal were clear that the exception in art 10(2) covers the Act and it does not contravene the provisions of the Convention.

148 [2000] 2 All ER 425.

the offence where he was not aware that his computer's cache held copies of the illegal photographs he had once viewed. This can easily be contrasted with 'making' by downloading and or printing indecent material, which does constitute and offence[149]. Downloading and printing are intentional acts and so may constitute 'making'. Even the deliberate copying of such material in the process of deleting it, may constitute the offence[150].

Photographs and pseudo-photographs

Photographs

The changes brought by the Criminal Justice and Public Order Act 1994 have been implemented to address the use that paedophiles make of computers. The term 'photographs' includes data stored on a computer disk or by other electronic means which is capable of conversion into a photograph[151]. This includes digital graphic images. The court will take a 'purposive approach': if the data can be converted into an indecent image, the data will be classed as a photograph[152].

Pseudo-photographs

This means an image, whether made by a computer graphic or otherwise, which appears to be a photograph[153]. This inclusion, apparently, reflects the practice of paedophiles who use pornographic images of adults and then digitally alter them to look like indecent photographs of children. In *G v DPP*, two paper photographs taped together were not held to be a pseudo-photograph as they did not 'appear' to be a single photograph[154]. This can surely be contrasted with two digital graphic images which, when aligned, do appear as one.

Transmission or retrieval

As in the case for obscene material, *R v Fellows* indicated that it will be distribution simply to allow such images to be transmitted. Similarly, having been warned that certain newsgroups contain indecent material it will be difficult to rely on the defence that one had no knowledge or reason to suspect that the material was indecent.

Liability of Internet Service Providers

As a starting point, because publication can be 'passive', an Internet Service Provider who facilitates, by storing, the transmission of an obscene file may be culpable as the publisher of obscene material. Similarly, under the Protection of Children Act 1978, mere possession on a server may be an offence under s 1(1)(c).

149 *R v Jonathan Bowden* [2001] QB 88.
150 *R v Mould* (6 November 2000, unreported), CA.
151 Protection of Children Act 1978, s 7(4)(b), as amended.
152 See the US Court of Appeals for the Sixth Circuit, *United States v Thomas* 74 F 3d 701 (1996).
153 Protection of Children Act 1978, s 7(7), as amended.
154 *R v DPP* (8 March 2000, unreported) Divisional Court.

Internet Watch Foundation

The high risk of liability where 'blind eyes are turned' together with an interest in the 'common good' led Internet Service Providers to concoct a remarkably impressive system of self-regulation and authority co-operation. The Internet Watch Foundation (IWF) was formed in October 1996. It is independent and aims (and succeeds) in restricting the availability of criminal content on the Internet. It operates a hotline and a 'notice and take down' procedure for Internet Service Providers. The IWF works closely with relevant authorities forwarding child or adult pornography details on UK servers to the Metropolitan Police. Child pornography on foreign servers is forwarded to the National Criminal Intelligence Service.

Demonstrating the effectiveness of this 'hotline' together with 'notice and takedown' and 'authority notification' is the case of Leslie Bollingbroke. The IWF discovered that an individual using the pseudonym 'Sammy' was posting illegal images of children on the Internet and discussing them on newsgroups. The IWF forwarded the information to the Metropolitan Police. 'Sammy' was discovered to be one Leslie Bollingbroke who was subsequently jailed for four years. Between January and June 2002 the IWF's hotline received 8,414 reports – an increase of nearly 65% on the previous year. Amost 25% of these reports were, indeed, judged to be potentially illegal and, in 2000, 2,498 items hosted in the UK were taken down.

A second reason for the effectiveness of this 'self-regulation' is the interaction between the Internet Service Providers Association (ISPA) and the IWF. Both are independent bodies but the ISPA acts, among other objectives, to represent and lobby for ISPs before government and the public. Consequently, most ISPs are ISPA members. However, their Code of Practice[155] obliges members to register with the IWF and receive and act upon 'take down' notices. On 15 February 2002 the IWF strengthened its role yet further by recommending to all UK ISPs that they do not carry newsgroups which IWF identifies as regularly hosting child pornography and which have names that appear to advertise or advocate paedophile content or activity[156].

Electronic Commerce (EC Directive) Regulations 2002

The Electronic Commerce (EC Directive) Regulations 2002[157] now provide Internet Service Providers with a 'global' defence to their liability under the Obscene Publications Act 1959 and the Protection of Children Act 1978 together with other criminal statutes. Four conditions must be met: ISP has no actual knowledge; ISP is not aware of unlawful nature; ISP acts expeditiously to remove or disable on knowledge; ISP has no control[158].

155 Adopted 25 January 1999.

156 This approach has echoes of the approach taken by New Scotland Yard in 1995 when they, in effect, put all Internet Service Providers 'on notice' of the newsgroups which mainly carry illegal material: *Independent*, 20 December 1995.

157 Implementing the Directive 2000/31/EC of the European Parliament and of the Council of 8 June 2000 on certain legal aspects of information society services, in particular electronic commerce, in the Internal Market (Directive on electronic commerce) (OJ L 178, 17.7.2000, p 1).

158 Regulations 19 and 22.

The first condition is that the Internet Service Provider must not have actual knowledge that an activity or information was in breach of any law[159]. This 'actual knowledge' is likely to involve the Internet Service Provider knowing, with some precision, about the activity or information. This precision, particularly relating to the location of the offending material, is essential because the defence envisages the Internet Service Provider needing to 'remove or disable' the information[160]. If the ISP is not able to locate the material, it does not have sufficient knowledge.

26. A very popular UK-based Internet Service Provider has over 500,000 users, most of whom have a website which the ISP hosts. It provides a freephone answerphone for any complaint about the material on these websites. A young girl leaves a message on the answerphone that there are 'horrid pictures of me on a website', bursts into tears and then puts down the phone. While the Internet Service Provider may well have very serious concerns about this complaint, it does not have 'actual knowledge' of any breach law. It neither knows the nature of the breach nor the identity or location of the complained-of material.

The second condition, wider than the first, is that the ISP is also not aware of facts or circumstances from which it would have been apparent to the service provider that the activity or information was unlawful[161]. The IWF's notification to ISPs of suspicious newsgroups will doubtlessly move ISPs into being in the position of being 'aware of facts or circumstances' from which it will be apparent that information on those newsgroups is unlawful.

The third condition is that upon obtaining such knowledge or awareness the service provider acts expeditiously to remove or to disable access to the information[162]. There are two issues that arise from this. First, how quickly must an ISP act to ensure that they are removing or disabling 'expeditiously'? Neither the Regulations nor the originating Directive provide a definition. The courts will initially rely on the dictionary's definition if pressed to judge an ISP's 'reaction time'. The dictionary talks of the concept of 'speedily'. The ISP must therefore treat the knowledge or awareness with some urgency and not merely as some 'housekeeping' that can wait.

A second issue arising from the obligation to remove or disable access to the material is the ISP's risk of doing so. What if the 'notice' to the ISP was malicious or plain wrong but, in good faith, the ISP removes the material anyway? The Regulations are silent on this very real possibility. In contrast, this exact situation is considered by the US Digital Millenium Copyright Act. In that Act the ISP has a 'good samaritan' defence to such an act[163]. UK ISPs are therefore advised to state in their contracts with users that they reserve the right to remove or disable access to material in these circumstances. In addition, ISPs must ensure that their contracts exclude any of their liability for so removing or disabling access to such material.

159 Regulation 19(a)(i).
160 See below, reg 19(a)(i).
161 Regulation 19(a)(i). Cf 'Once it is or should be appreciated that the material is indecent then its continued retention or distribution is indecent then its continued retention or distribution is subject to the risk of prosecution': *R v Land* [1998] 1 All ER 403 at 407, CA.
162 Regulation 19(a)(ii).
163 47 USC §§ 230(c)(2)(A).

The final condition of the defence, obviously, is that person responsible for the storage or transmission of the illegal material must not have been acting under the 'authority or the control' of the Internet Service Provider[164]. It is submitted that for an ISP to have 'authority or control' over someone, they would need to have gone further than merely having a usual member contract with the individual. In this sense the concept of 'authority or control' is akin to the concept of 'effective control' in the Defamation Act 1996[165].

164 Regulation 19(b).
165 Section 1(3)(e).

Chapter Six

Data protection

'And while serious – very serious – the privacy issues we're dealing with today are trivial compared to what's ahead. What are the implications for individual privacy in a world where millions of people are driving Internet-enabled cars that have their movements monitored at all times? What happens to privacy for millions of people with Internet-enabled pacemakers?'

Lou Gerstner, Chairman & CEO of IBM[1]

Commercially, businesses demand that their digital presences, including websites, collect and analyse personal data. They collect it, not only to ensure that simple things are performed correctly, such as delivering goods to the right address. They also collect to predict their customers' needs. The more sophisticated collect personal data to sell or rent to *other* businesses to help *them* predict *their* customers' needs. In short, businesses now view personal data as a critical asset. In the UK, the Information Commissioner ensures these businesses respect the individuals whose data is being harvested.

The Commissioner has the power to prevent the transfer of personal data outside 'adequate' territories. It is this possible prohibition on overseas transfers that makes the Internet a closely watched medium for transferring personal data. There are few aspects of the Internet that someone cannot access from anywhere else in the world. Potentially therefore, personal data that are readily accessible over the Internet are necessarily accessible from a data area with inadequate protection for UK citizens.

The Commissioner also ensures that users of data comply with seven other data protection principles. One of the most salient for the Internet is that all personal data must be kept secure. This is in stark contrast to the Internet, which is inherently open to all to access. Without specific security measures in place, the Internet does not discriminate between different people accessing its data. Without, say, password control, it is difficult for a controller of a web site to prevent access by a particular person. This is in contrast to the controller of an ftp site, who can provide passwords to selected users. The data protection legislation therefore imposes minimum levels of security on Internet users of personal data.

This chapter deals with the following issues concerning data protection and the Internet:

1 eBusiness Conference Expo, New York City, 12 December 2000.

1. What types of data are regulated?
2. What types of activity over the Internet are regulated?
3. Are Internet Service Providers, Application Service Providers and users of websites classed as data controllers or data processors?
4. What are the obligations of notification for Internet data controllers and processors both in the UK and abroad?
5. What are the recommended principles for obtaining and processing personal data over the Internet?
6. What are the recommended principles for keeping personal data up-to-date and accurate?
7. With the Internet often lacking security, what are the principles for adequate data security over the Internet?
8. In such a transnational medium, to where in the world may personal data in the UK be transferred?
9. What are the requirements for sending unsolicited marketing messages over the Internet?
10. What is the extent of the Information Commissioner's jurisdiction over UK and overseas data controllers?

BACKGROUND

History

The Council of Europe's Convention for the Protection of Individuals with regard to the Automatic Processing of Personal Data[2] sought to eradicate the hazard of a data-haven operating data banks outside national jurisdictions. To do this, ratifying countries of the Convention could withhold personal data from countries which did not have equivalent protection. In fear of this information exile, the UK signed the Convention.

First European Convention on Data Protection

The Convention consisted of three main parts: general principles; rules on transborder data flow; and mechanisms for mutual assistance and consultation between contracting states. The central aspects of the Convention were the 'common core' principles[3]. These ensured that all individuals in all signatory countries had the same minimum protection from misuse of automated personal data[4]. The theory was that this would eradicate the fear of data havens and decrease possible conflicts over data protection between states.

2 European Treaty Series, no 108, Edition January 1981. After, First European Convention on Data Protection.

3 See art 5, Quality of data; art 6, Special categories of data; art 7, Data security; art 8, Additional safeguards for the data subject.

4 The European Parliament recommended that the Convention should cover both automated and manual data, but the Council rejected this suggestion. See Official Journal of the European Communities, number C 140/37, 5 June 1979, para I.1, and European Council Explanatory Report on the Convention for the Protection of Individuals with regard to automatic processing of personal data, Strasbourg, 1981, para 1.

The Data Protection Act 1984

The Data Protection Act 1984 came into force on 1 October 1985. The Act fixed new civil rights for individuals on whom computerised data was held; it also created complementary civil and criminally sanctioned responsibilities for those persons who used that data. A Data Protection Registrar oversaw those new rights and responsibilities and could verify that registered users of data complied with the eight data protection principles.

Two types of computer user were required to register: any UK data user who automatically held or processed personal data; and any UK computer bureau providing services in relation to personal data.

Second European Convention on Data Protection

As is so often the case, member states interpreted and implemented the First Convention in divergent ways. The aim of harmonisation remained just that, an aim. The Commission reacted by pushing through, over the course of five years, a new Directive[5].

For our purposes, the differences between the two regimes include: individuals have new rights and powers of enforcement; the flow of data outside the EU or to countries with 'inadequate' data protection regimes is prohibited, and the need for security over processing is strengthened.

The Data Protection Act 1998

This chapter considers electronic commerce and use of the Internet within the framework of the Data Protection Act 1998 ('the Act'). Those familiar with its 14-year-old predecessor should notice a number of trivial and not so trivial differences. First, the trivial. The Data Protection Registrar, albeit the same lady, became the Information Commissioner. A further nomenclature change sees 'registrations' become 'notifications'. What is more significant to Internet users and businesses is the widening of a number of the principles and the inclusion of a new eighth principle to restrict dataflows to countries with inadequate protective regimes. Also, new rights of individuals redress the balance between the respect expected by citizens and the increasingly common perception by businesses that 'personal data is a commodity and a valuable asset'.

The Telecommunications Regulations 1999

The Telecommunications (Data Protection and Privacy) Regulations 1999 came into force on 1 March 2000 implementing the European Telecoms Directive 97/66/EC. They set out the rules for sending unsolicited direct marketing messages using publicly available telecommunications services (eg telephone fixed or mobile, fax and Internet). These rules vary according to how a marketing message is sent and to whom it is sent. The Regulations also contain provisions dealing with

5 Directive 95/46/EC.

limitations on processing of traffic and billing data, line identification and directories of subscribers.

The Telecoms Directive has been implemented differently across the EU. This is an inevitable consequence of uncertainties as to key definitions, particularly relating to consent requirements and whether or not the concept of 'calls' includes email. Those sending email messages to recipients in different countries across Europe must be aware therefore that different approaches may be necessary. This has sparked ongoing debate and confusion on when, and in what form, 'opt in' as opposed to 'opt-out' consent is required, terms which are not even used in the legislation.

Electronic Communications Directive 2002

In an attempt to try and clear this up, the European Institutions have debated the scope of an Electronic Communications Directive[6]. This covers three contentious issues: the regulation of unsolicited communications, in particular 'spam' email; the use of website cookies used to harvest users' personal data; and the extent to which users' traffic and billing data may be lawfully retained by a Service Provider after a communication has ended.

TYPES OF DATA

Before investigating the application of the Data Protection Act 1998 to the Internet, it is vital to set out the main aspects to the legislation. It is unfortunate that the Act is particularly definition-based: to appreciate the responsibilities of a data user one must appreciate a great number of separate concepts: data, personal data, relevant filing system, processing of data, data subject and recipient. For ease of understanding, therefore, this chapter attempts to simplify the legislation by referring to these issues. This chapter describes each of these issues with specific Internet examples; the remainder of the chapter considers the application of these issues to commonplace ecommerce transactions and activities on the Internet.

Personal data

Data

The Act applies only to personal data and those dealing with it. Assessing whether digital information is personal data is the starting point for all data protection questions. The word, 'data', is circularly defined with reference to further defined terms which themselves refer to 'data'[7].

This wide definition is:

6 European Parliament and Council Directive concerning the processing of personal data and the protection of privacy in the electronic communications sector.

7 Data Protection Act 1998, s 1(1). This definition is not drawn from the body of the Directive but rather its preamble.

> 'information which
> (a) is being processed by means of equipment operating automatically in response given for that purpose;
> (b) is recorded with the intention that it should be processed by means of such equipment;
> (c) is recorded as part of a relevant filing system or with the intention that it should form part of a relevant filing system;
> (d) does not fall within paragraph (a), (b) or (c) but forms part of an accessible record as defined by s 68 [including health records, education records and accessible public records].'

There are three, often overlooked, aspects to this pivotal definition. First, the definition includes reference to 'intention'. In the ever-changing world of ecommerce and the Internet, this is particularly relevant. Business plans and marketing forecasts drive web designers and database architects to create forms and data structures ready for data. Often this data is collected but then never used. The fact that the commercial intentions were not executed does not mean that this collected data will not fall within the definition. 'Automatically' is the second aspect of the definition which needs consideration. In contrast to the 1984 Act, the 1998 Act envelopes paper-based data storage systems as well as the digital ones, which are the focus of this book. The definition therefore allows for both computerised processing (ie automatically in response to instructions) and for human processing. This is key because it ensures that, even if a human operator processes data instead of a computer, that data falls within the definition.

1. RemCom gathers salary data from recruitment agents to allow prospective employees to gauge their potential remuneration package in a given job. When an employee gains employment they are encouraged to feed back into RemCom their new salary and benefits package. Even though some of this information is taken from the happy employees by telephone operators, it will be classified as data.

The third important concept is that information is 'data' if it is recorded. For the Internet, this will generally be the case. Any data that is flowing through, or stored on, the Internet must necessarily be recorded. Email is stored on a host computer. Even a page on the web that features sound, music and animation has these data stored at the server, and then downloaded and stored on the accessing computer. The short point is that all data that can be accessed via the Internet will be classified as data for the purposes of the Act. It is not always true that these data are personal data; this is considered next.

PERSONAL DATA

The word 'personal' refers to the data[8]:

> 'which relate to a living individual who can be identified:
> (a) from those data; or
> (b) from those data and other information which is in the possession

8 Data Protection Act 1998, s 1(1).

> of, or is likely to come into the possession of, the data controller and includes any expression of opinion about the individual and any indication of the intentions of the data controller or any other person in respect of the individual.'

While this definition is fundamental to whether or not one has data protection obligations, personal data may not be fundamental to a successful Internet or ecommerce initiative.

2. An individual repeatedly visits a website and always downloads from it the latest screensaver of a particularly attractive tennis star. Because the individual has entered data into an on-screen form, the website 'knows' four items of data about the individual. The individual is male, between 25 and 35 years of age, earns over £45,000 a year and likes tennis. Each time the individual visits the site, the site confirms it is him by placing on his computer a small file containing a unique identifier. The site, therefore, 'knows' what he looks at, what he downloads, how often he visits etc. All this data is useful and helps the site target the individual with new relevant screensavers when he visits. Without more, however, the site holds no personal data.

This technique of using 'non-personal' data has led ecommerce businesses to explore whether or not they can avoid entirely the obligations of the Act[9]. To consider this avoidance of the Act, one first needs to appreciate the scope, and purposive interpretation, of the definition.

What follows is a set of four cumulative tests that can establish whether data could be personal data. These are then examined with reference to use and availability of data on the Internet and in ecommerce businesses:

1. living individual;
2. identification;
3. possession or likely to come into possession of other information;
4. expression of opinion.

1. Living individual

The Act focuses on the data, not the individual to whom it relates. As long as the individual is living and is not a body corporate, the Act can apply. This includes all individuals whether resident abroad or of foreign nationality.

3. A UK software supplier forms contracts with users and distributes software to them over the Internet. When considering the Data Protection Act 1998, the supplier need not ascertain the residence or nationality of each customer. The Act will apply to all the customers if the data held are classed as personal.

9 Of course, companies still need to ensure they comply with the Act in relation to their other personal data: personal, supplier, contacts etc.

4. A foreign national enters his personal details into an online form required to access a UK newspaper's website. The individual is now concerned that these personal data are being misused. All things being equal, he has rights under the Act to prevent this misuse because he is a living individual and the data held are personal. The individual's nationality is largely irrelevant to the newspaper's obligations.

The definitions of personal data in both the Act and Directive refer to 'person' and 'individual' and not 'people' and 'individuals'. A question therefore arises whether or not the Act applies to processed data about 'joint' individuals. Certainly, joint bank account holders are likely to be considered each as an individual under the Act, as are joint tenants of property. More difficult 'joint' entities are legal constructs like 'partnerships' (limited or otherwise).

5. A well-known department store establishes an online wedding site for couples to create a 'micro-site' before their happy day. As well as displaying directions to the venue and a ceremony of service, the micro-site also provides the chance for guests to make purchases from the couple's gift list. Together with their address and wedding day, the department store does possess data relating to an individual.

2. Identification

For data to be personal is a subjective notion, not an objective one. To one data controller the data may be personal, but to another data controller, who possesses less 'other information', the data may not be personal: the data controller may be unable to identify the individual. In this respect, one resolves whether an individual can be identified by examining the relationship between the data controller and the data themselves.

Identification should be considered as being able to process data to distinguish that data subject from any other individual. This has a consequence that most, but not all, email addresses will be personal data.

This author's main personal email address, clive@pobox.com, does not have the quality of 'identification'; there are other 'Clive's. The author's other personal email address, Clive@Gringras.com, at first glance appears to be more 'identifiable' to a particular individual. This appearance, however, may be illusory. It is based upon two assumptions: first, that the 'Gringras' portion refers to a second name rather than the name of a company. If 'Gringras' was the name of a company of 10,000 employees, it is unlikely that there would be only one person called 'Clive' working there. The second assumption is based on knowing that the first name 'Clive' is rare and the second name 'Gringras' is even more rare. One therefore assumes that there is unlikely to be another individual called Clive Gringras.

Now swap the word 'Clive' for 'John' and 'Gringras' for 'Smith' in the paragraph above. It is obvious that not all *types* of email addresses permit identification of a particular individual and whether or not identification is positive turns on the information available to the data user. However, given the uncertainties, Internet and ecommerce businesses would be unwise to assume their collection of email addresses does not constitute identifiable data about living individuals.

3. Possession of other information

The definition of 'personal' data refers to identification in conjunction with other information in possession or likely to come into the possession of the data controller[10]. The Directive's recital 26 illustrates the likely width of 'possession'. It states:

> 'To determine whether a person is identifiable, account should be taken of all the means likely reasonably to be used either by the controller or by any other person.'

It follows that merely because one does not physically possess data does not mean that one does not, for the purposes of the Act, 'possess' the data permitting identification. When assessing whether or not one is processing personal data, one must therefore examine data which is publicly available (which would 'confirm' the identity of the individual) and data available from a third party under contract or other relationship.

6. SecuriFirst and Last is a security firm which generates digital 'safes' for people who wish to store digital data off their own hard drives. To do so, one must provide one's first name, date and place of birth to SecuriFirst and Last. One pays for the safe through a third party which takes one's full name and residential address. This third party then provides a password to enable 'unlocking' of the safe. The third party clearly can identify each customer using information in its possession; SecuriFirst and Last also is likely come into possession of this information because of its relationship with the third party.

4. Opinions on individuals

The final test to establish whether data is personal data is to ascertain the nature of the data: if the data is an expression of opinion or indication of intention about the individual, then the data can be personal.

The definition also includes an intention being expressed by a third party. For this reason, repeating the intention of another with respect to a living individual will still fall within the definition; the data may still be personal.

Anonymous data

The Directive explicitly states that: 'the principles of protection shall not apply to data rendered anonymous'[11]. In addition, the Act refers only to living individuals who can be identified from the data processed. This has led many website operators and ecommerce businesses to seek to force (technically or legally) their data into being anonymous and so avoid the regulation of the Act. This is easier said than done. The legal analysis of this follows.

When businesses talk of 'anonymised', 'aggregated', 'generic' or even 'neutered' data, they may be referring to a number of situations. What follows are the common explanations of anonymous data.

10 Data Protection Act 1998, s 1(3).
11 Recital 26.

1. 'My business cannot identify living individuals from information we have in our possession. If we wanted to obtain extra information to do so, we could.' This business only possesses anonymised information. It will still be classified as personal data because reasonable enquiries would enable them to turn the anonymised data into identifying data.

2. 'My business cannot identify living individuals from information we have in our possession. We have come to an arrangement with a third party; they hold the personal data, we merely hold a unique identification number which allows them to resolve the identities.' This business only possesses anonymised information. Unless their contract with the third party is unambiguous, it is likely that their relationship will allow them to resolve the identification number into identifying a living individual. It is likely that the business will be classified as possessing personal data[12].

3. 'My business can no longer identify living individuals from information we have in our possession. We have stripped out any information from our data which would allow us directly or indirectly to identify any living individual. Even other data sources would not assist us to identify particular individuals.' If the business truly has destroyed the identifiable features of its data, and even with reasonable enquiries, could not identify individuals, then it is no longer able to be classified as processing personal data. The key words, however, are 'no longer'. The Act and Directive do not apply to anonymised data but the process *of* anonymising the formerly identifiable data would have been considered to be processing it under the Act. All the usual pre-conditions would have applied to such processing. One such pre-condition may well be 'consent' by the individuals *to* allow their personal data to be anonymised[13].

In *R v Department of Health, ex p Source Informatics*, Source Informatics alleged that it was entitled to anonymise patient prescription data gained from general practitioners to sell to pharmacists. No supplied data could identify patients. Latham J in the Queen's Bench Division considered, inter alia, the Data Protection Act 1998 and suggested Source's use of the anonymised data was contrary to the Act[14]. On appeal, Simon Brown LJ, for a unanimous Court of Appeal, disagreed. He stated that the Directive does not apply to anonymised data[15].

4. 'My business does not even collect identifiable data from individuals; our systems even ensure that the collected data is insufficient to permit us to combine the data with other data to identify any individual.' This challengeable statement means that the Act does not apply to this particular dataset; the Act will apply to other datasets such as credit card processing, order or service fulfilment[16].

12 On 11 November 2000, *The Economist* wrote: 'Unlike DoubleClick's data, which is entirely anonymous, Abacus had 88m real names and addresses. Mr O'Connor [the chairman and founder of DoubleClick] realised that, by marrying the two, he could identify individual web users and not only track, but also predict their behaviour – making online advertising even more science than art . . .' Had this integration of anonymised and identifiable personal data occurred, DoubleClick would have had personal data.

13 A consent of this type should be included in privacy policies to ensure such anonymisation is permitted.

14 [1999] 4 All ER 185 at 192.

15 [2000] 1 All ER 786 at 798–199.

16 The search engine company Google openly admitted that its new toolbar application permitted Google to monitor the sites frequented by its toolbar users. It stated 'By using the Advanced Features version of the Google toolbar, you may be sending information about the sites you visit to Google.' Google spokesman David Krane said 'We're looking at data en masse, not going record by record' (ZDNet News, 11 December 2000). Google's revised general 2002 privacy policy does not, however, contain this wording.

Relevant filing system

The Act applies only to a 'relevant filing system'. Section 1 of the Act defines this as:

> 'any set of information relating to individuals to the extent that although the information is not processed by means of equipment generating automatically in response to instructions given for that purpose, the set is structured as by reference to individuals or by reference to criteria relating to individuals, in such a way that specific information relating to a particular individual is readily accessible.'

The vast majority of computer databases storing information relating to individuals will fall within the scope of this definition. In this author's opinion, the only computer databases outside the definition are those that store personal data *incidentally* and *unsearchably* in relation to other data.

7. A website in its launch phase invites visitors to comment on the site using a 'comment page'. This page asks a number of precise questions which are answerable using a limited number of options. The final question invites visitors to type in any general comments about the site. Some visitors, impressed by the site, complete this section and, uninvited, include their name and email address. This section is stored as one 'field' in the website's database. The website is unlikely, therefore, to be using a relevant filing system for these purposes.

Questions do arise as to whether relational and object-orientated databases would qualify as 'relevant filing systems'. The pivotal issue for 'relevant filing systems' is not the nature of the files, but rather the structure of the database. And, when assessing structure, do not be confused by technical structures such as 'relational' or 'object-orientated'. The question is whether or not the personal data is readily accessible by virtue of its structure. This raises the academic question of whether or not a relevant filing system would include unstructured datasets which are searchable using search engines or algorithms? The answer to this lies in how 'readily accessible' this search technology is.

DATA PROTECTION ACTIVITIES

It will be recalled that the Act only impinges on certain activities in relation to data with a particular quality: it must be personal. Having defined personal data and relevant filing system, it is possible to consider two main activities regulated by the Act. These are processing and disclosure. Processing is regulated directly; disclosure is not defined but is one of the main activities relevant for notifications. These two terms are vital to decipher the main restrictions on dealing with personal data over or from the Internet. Although the restrictions will be explored in greater depth below it is worthwhile setting the terms in their applied contexts.

Processing

The Act defines processing as performing one of a defined set of operations on personal data. In contrast to the 1984 Act's definition of personal data, it is also no longer necessary that one must perform these operations with reference to a data subject to fall within its remit; it is now wider. It is now enough simply to perform the digital processing on personal data even if not combined with reference to a data subject.

Processing operations

Section 1(1) defines processing as:

> 'in relation to information or data, means obtaining recording or holding the information or data carrying out any operation or set of operations on the information or data, including:
> (a) organisation, adaptation or alteration of the information or data;
> (b) retrieval, consultation or use of the information or data;
> (c) disclosure of the information or data by transmission, dissemination or otherwise making available; or
> (d) alignment, combination, blocking, erasure or destruction of the information or data.'

The above list of what constitutes processing is non-exhaustive. The Directive's definition uses the magic words 'such as' and the UK's definition the similarly widening word 'including'. It is therefore difficult to imagine what operations or activities in relation to personal data would not constitute processing it. Bearing in mind that even holding the data is processing, it is likely that all personal data is processed at some point by someone.

As if the definition of processing was not extensive enough, the Act confirms that the terms 'obtaining', 'recording', 'using' and 'disclosing' all include those activities in relation to the information contained in the data, not merely the data[17]. Suffice to say, therefore, that it is a brave litigant who seeks to explain why their data is personal but they do not process it.

Disclosure

One relevant activity on the Internet for data protection is disclosure: the Internet, especially the World Wide Web and email, is heralded for the ease with which information can be disclosed to others. The novel legal issue for the Internet is whether there is disclosure when information is not actively distributed but is merely 'left' on a server for collection.

Disclosure of data occurs where the data or information from the data is divulged to another person or recipient[18].

17 Section 1(2).
18 Defined in s 70.

8. An Internet Service Provider maintains a log of its members' log-in times. The Provider allocates each member a unique number and stores log-in times in conjunction with this number; in another database, the Service Provider stores a list of the unique numbers for each member.

The Service Provider seeks to use this log to inform the local telephone networks of the most popular access times. It will be a disclosure for the Service Provider to supply only the log to the network, even when the members' numbers database remains unseen. The ISP is disclosing the information gleaned from the personal data.

Disclosure on a home page

One of the keys to the commercial success of the Internet is that it is very cheap to 'distribute' information to many recipients. There are two main ways: first, using a mailserver to emailshot[19] a list of email addresses; the second way is to 'leave' information in a readily accessible area of the Internet, be that as an upload on an ftp site or published on a website. The commercial difference is that in the second scenario, it is the receiver of the information who acts to retrieve that information; the Provider remains passive. Receivers may pay the online or connection charges to locate and download the posted information. By contrast, when emailing the Provider takes the active role, by sending the information, the recipients cannot help but receive it, they remain passive.

Disclosure or dissemination

This distinction makes little difference for the purposes of the Data Protection Act 1998. Certainly, there are technical differences between posting personal data on a website and emailing it. Technically, the data are not provided to a third party when uploaded onto the website. Data are copied onto a second computer, called a server. It is only after *the third party accesses* the site that the data may be revealed to an outside source, and by no action of the data user. The data user has no active role in the reading of and reacting to those data.

A likely definition of disclosure

There are strong reasons to conclude that disclosure is effected by publishing personal data on a web page or uploading it to an ftp site. Unlike under the 1984 Act, the term 'disclosure' is not defined. The *Oxford English Dictionary* defines the verb 'to disclose' as, 'remove cover from, expose to view; make known, reveal'. With this definition it becomes clearer that publishing personal data on a web site or uploading them to an ftp site will be disclosure for the purposes of the Act. There can be little doubt that publishing data on a website is exposing

19 It is common to find that the information technology industry elides nouns and verbs. This example, to 'emailshot' should be read to mean 'to send a mailshot of emails'.

to view or revealing those data. Under the 1984 Act, in the case *R v Brown*, Lord Goff considered the concept of 'disclosure', albeit then with reference to a definition to assist his interpretation. He said[20]:

> '[I]t may be readily inferred that the person effecting the transfer was inevitably therefore disclosing the data to another person or persons who, as he well knew, would retrieve the information from the second database and so have the information disclosed to him.'

9. A UK firm of advisers to wealthy individuals seeks to advertise its work for clients. It chooses to use a website featuring lists of clients, each with a link to a further page describing the nature of the work undertaken for the person. Notwithstanding issues of professional conduct and confidentiality, the firm will be disclosing this personal data.

DATA PROTECTION NOTIFICATION

The impact of the Data Protection Act on users of the Internet has been shown to be great. All information sent over the Internet will constitute data, and if personal, providing those data over the Internet will be viewed as processing. Those persons falling within the Act's ambit are required to register with the Information Commissioner. If a person should notify but does not, this constitutes a criminal offence[21].

The Data Protection Act 1998 regulates two types of computer users: data controllers and data processors. It is important both for users of data and for individuals concerned over their personal data to understand this distinction. This does not mean that a person cannot fall into both categories: often a data processor will, on closer inspection, fall within the category of a data controller *as well*. Persons who are acting as data processors are not required to notify; data controllers are required to notify a range of information related not only to themselves but also related to the type of data being held and their intended use.

Data controller

A data controller is[22]:

> 'A person who (either alone or jointly or in common with other persons) determines the purposes for which and the manner in which any personal data are, or are to be processed.'

It is necessary to deconstruct two of the conditions listed above. First, determining the purposes and the manner of processing; second, alone or jointly.

20 [1996] 1 All ER 545 at 549.
21 Data Protection Act 1998, ss 17(1) and 21(1).
22 Data Protection Act 1998, s 1(1).

Determines

One of the two conditions of being a data controller is that one determines the purposes for which and manner in which the personal data are or are to be processed. This determination may be jointly or in common with others.

Determination of purposes and manner of processing

'Determines' can be distinct from processing. It is possible that one person compiles personal data, another processes it and a third person then uses the data. This differentiation separates data controllers from data processors: data controllers (potentially with others) make the final decision as to the purpose of processing the personal data and how it is to be processed. Of course, where a data controller delegates any decisions to a third party, as is often the case with third party database architects, that third party becomes a data controller too. Because the obligations on data controllers are more onerous than those on data processors it is important to understand what the Act means by 'determines'. If an Internet Service Provider is doing more than only processing personal data and is actually deciding the ways in which it is processed, he may be committing a criminal offence by acting as an unnotified data controller. The relevant criteria therefore is not what a person or body does with the data or the means he uses, but the individual's capacity to make decisions in relation to the purposes and means of the processing. This said, it is not easy to distinguish between determining the nature of data processing and actually effecting the processing. It is especially difficult because 'processing' is such a broad term and includes the organisation of the data.

10. A UK bookseller maintains a website which allows customers to read rated reviews of selected books online and then place an order if desired. The bookseller seeks to establish whether there is any correlation between placing an order and reading a highly rated review. To establish this, the bookseller divulges all the data to a market researcher. The bookseller determines the purposes of the data and their use but is unlikely to know how the data will be correlated and analysed. The market researcher will, being the expert, determine the manner in which the customer data is processed. Both therefore have the relevant capacity to make decisions.

Jointly or in common

The terms 'jointly' and 'in common' broaden the ambit of 'determine' not only by including data that are under the absolute control of the data controller, but also by including the data partially under the instruction of the data controller. Similarly, where many persons share one collection of data, each person will be classed as determining the use of that collection in common. The inclusion of these terms is particularly relevant to the Internet because it is rare that a single-entity will deal on the Internet with data: most organisations use one person to design a website, another to host it and perhaps even a third to provide access to the server.

11. A UK business rents space on a website to a number of retailers and service providers, rather like a shopping mall. The website collects personal data on each of the entrants to the mall. At the end of each day, the business provides to its 'tenants' a full list of each of the entrants to the mall. Each of the tenants uses the data at its discretion. The business and each of its tenants are data controllers in common.

12. An organisation maintains a website that allows any person's name to be entered and searched for to provide the email address for the person, where applicable. This information is extracted from any postings to Usenet newsgroups and chatrooms. While the owner of the website does not absolutely determine how the data is utilised on the site, the owner is a data controller.

Of course, determinations exerted over a collection of data may vary with time. It is conceivable that a person who previously had no input over the content of data or processing of data, could begin determining issues as trust between the parties develops and expertise grows. The varying involvement of a web designer who takes an administrative role is one example. This variance of determination does create uncertainty: those individuals who consider that they only process data under instruction, without discretion, should maintain careful records of their activities to ensure that they can justify their position as a mere data processor.

13. An airline already using an online reservation system seeks to research the use of its system. To do this, it provides a list of its users' email addresses to a market researcher for the purposes of sending out a questionnaire. The market researcher reasons that geographical and age data will be useful to focus the questions. If the reasoning is accepted, the researcher has contributed to the content of the data and so may have determined the purposes of the data and manner of processing controlled and so used the data jointly with the airline.

Actual or potential processed data

After processing data, where a data controller has a specific intention to re-process the data he will continue to process that data even if the data are converted into another format.

If the Information Commissioner would class say, a web developer, as processing personal data but the developer is not notified as a data controller, the developer may be prosecuted. The scope of processing is therefore significant and should also not merely be considered once; a change in circumstances may change an activity into processing. To be safe, data users should consider that they are processing the data if the data *can* be processed; converting the data into a non-processible format, such as a printout, may even still be classed as processing the data.

Data processors

As discussed, the Data Protection Act 1998 applies to data controllers who process personal data. Those individuals who either allow users access to their equipment to process data, or perform the processing for them are data processors and need not notify their activities to the Commissioner. More specifically, a person is a data processor if he:

1. not being an employee of the data controller;
2. processes data on behalf of the data controller[23].

Before considering the scope of this legal definition of these persons, it is useful to appreciate the types of storage and manipulation of data over the Internet.

Remote access

Data-warehousing

The ease of transmitting data over the Internet provides an opportunity to store information not on a client computer, but on a remote computer. Certain members of the computer industry consider that, in the future, home users will store information not on a home or office computer, but in a 'data warehouse' which will charge a rent for the amount stored[24].

Large corporations, fearing data corruption, already store backups of their data with data-storage corporations. Similarly for websites, an owner of data can rent space on a web server, rather than investing in his own hardware.

Internet Service Providers already perform a data-warehousing function for their members by storing emails until they are collected. Websites are stored on servers, but there are often occasions where the owner of the website only rents space on the storing server. Indeed, many of the Internet Service Providers rent a fixed amount of storage space for each personal or corporate user to create and store their website with augmentary databases.

Remote manipulation

Certain corporations provide facilities for remotely manipulating data. Clients may choose this because the remote computer is extremely powerful and is able to perform tasks far more quickly than the client computer. There are two ways in which this manipulation can be performed: one, where the client computer communicates directly with the remote computer, giving instructions over the Internet or using a direct line; for the second way, owners of the remote computer are actually given instructions as to how to manipulate the data. It should be clear that the risk of a security breach is lower in the first way than the second.

23 Data Protection Act 1998, s 1(1).
24 This, combined with Application Service Providers, would be true, remote working.

REGULATION OF DATA-WAREHOUSING

This chapter divides data-warehousing into two sections: archives and servers. The archives section contemplates the legal regulation of organisations who simply store backups for data controllers. The servers section contemplates the Internet industry's widespread use of servers to store data, applications, emails or websites for users.

Archives

A mere provider of equipment for backing-up a data controller's data will be a data processor. This is because it is usual that the data are stored and are also accessible by the data user if there is a breakdown or emergency. This access is likely to fall within the broad scope of processing; as such, the owner of the data warehouse is processing data on behalf of the data controller. It is rare that those persons may determine the nature of the data processing. In addition, the means have arguably been determined by the data user in selecting that provider. Those who merely archive are therefore more likely to be data processors rather than controllers.

Another common scenario is that the owner of the data warehouse, on request, will perform actions on the data on the data controller's behalf. For example, where a data controller urgently requires a list of names and addresses from a particular database, the owner of the data warehouse will usually, on request, provide these data. In doing so, that person is taking on the role of data processor. The person is performing processing on behalf of the data controller.

The short and important point is that when storing another's data one should carefully assess whether one is acting as a data processor. The difficulty with such an assessment is that processing, as has been discussed, is a subjective term and who 'determines' is more a matter of opinion than fact.

Servers

The following discussion considers a few examples of server warehousing.

Internet Service Providers

Internet Service Providers may provide their customers with an area of storage space which could be used to store personal data. In itself, such storage makes an Internet Service Provider a data processor. Internet Service Providers are likely also to hold personal data on those customers who use their service making them a data controller for this purpose.

14. An Internet Service Provider holds emails for each of its members until the member logs in. At this point the member is informed that mail is being stored and is given a choice: either continue to store the mail, or, download the information. On choosing to download the mail, the mail is deleted from the Provider's server. One copy only ever exists. Because the Service Provider cannot determine the processing of the data, but requires its members' instructions, the Provider will not be a data controller but merely a data processor.

15. An Application Service Provider prides itself on allowing its members to access their accounts from anywhere in the world, on any computer they choose. To facilitate this, one of the features of their system is that its members do not store their address book of email addresses contacts on their own computer, but on the Provider's server. This has the result that its members can process personal data using the Provider's equipment. This makes the Provider a data processor in respect of these personal data but probably a data controller in relation to the personal data held about the members themselves.

REGULATION OF REMOTE MANIPULATION

Remote processing

Access to the Internet allows use of some of the most powerful computers in the world. Under certain conditions the owners of these and other computers will permit remote usage. Where the owner of a computer does permit remote access and manipulation, it may fall within the ambit of a data processor. The most common scenario is that a data user provides a batch file to a remote computer together with instructions for its processing. This arrangement will make the owner of the remote computer a data processor under the Act.

Search engines

The above situation differs from the use of *search engines* on a remote website. In this instance, the search engine is searching data that is unlikely to be determined by the person requesting the search. They are therefore not a data controller. As a result, the owner of the search engine is not acting as a data processor.

NOTIFICATION FORMALITIES

The Act requires more than compliance; it also requires, in most circumstances, formal 'notification' with the Information Commissioner.

Notification exemptions

Certain data controllers are not required to notify as they are exempt. Nevertheless, they may notify voluntarily[25] and in all cases are still bound by the other provisions of the Act[26]. The main exemptions extend to processing only for:

25 Data Protection Act 1998, s 18(1).

26 Voluntary notification is not available to the following exempt persons, being those who: hold personal data for personal, family or household affairs; hold personal data exempt under national security exemptions; hold personal data exempt under transitional provisions for payroll, unincorporated members' clubs and mailing list usage. Data Protection Act 1998, Part IV.

1. personal, family or household affairs[27];
2. maintaining a public register[28];
3. a non-profit organisation processing only for establishing or maintaining membership or providing or administering activities for individuals who are members of the organisation[29]; or staff administration, or, advertising, marketing and public relations, or, accounts and records but no other processing at all[30].

Time of notifications

The date of notification is the date on which it is received by the Commissioner, unless sent by registered post in which case the day after the day on which it is received for despatch by the Post Office[31].

Even where notifications are completed online, this form will need to be printed off, signed and submitted by post.

Use of the notifications

The Register of notifications is a public document. Any member of the public can access a specific entry using the www.dpr.gov.uk website. This right differs from the right of a data subject to see his personal data. The register contains details of the data controllers and the use of the data, but not the actual data.

Format of notification

Data controllers must complete an application, whether pre-filled by the Commissioner or starting as a blank form. This provides the Commissioner with details of the data controller and a description of the processing of personal data, being: purposes, data subjects, data classes, recipients, transfers outside the EEA and security provisions. As has been mentioned, it is a criminal offence to process personal data without an adequate notification.

Data controller identity

The notification must contain details of the actual legal identity of the data controller. Companies are advised to include not only the name and address of their registered office, but also include their number in the Register of Companies. Where the data controller is not a company, it should include an appropriate address, such as a home or business address. A suitable contact address (for the Commissioner, not the Register) is also required. It is not obligatory to provide a trading name, which is often relevant for online businesses, although the Information Commissioner says that such information is 'helpful'.

27 Data Protection Act 1998, s 36.
28 Data Protection Act 1998, ss 17(4) and 70.
29 Data Protection (Notification and Notification Fees) Regulations 2000, Sch, para 15.
30 Data Protection (Notification and Notification Fees) Regulations 2000, Sch, paras 1-4.
31 Data Protection (Notification and Notification Fees) Regulations 2000, reg 8.

Description of processing

This is a general description of the processing of personal data. The Commissioner may provide applicants with a pre-filled section appropriate to that general business description. Check this is accurate. This part of the forms will include multiple purposes, each of which conforms to a set format.

Purpose

Data controllers should pay much attention to any partially completed template received from the Commissioner. This delineates the responsibilities of the data controller to its subjects. Data controllers should also ensure that their application includes 'free-text' references to the Internet, where appropriate. If this section does not accurately describe the ambit of a data controller's purpose for processing the data, that may expose the data controller to prosecution.

The Notification Handbook contains a large number of possible purposes for which a data controller is processing data. Each purpose-type has a title and a full description of that purpose. Because there are a limited number of purposes to choose from, there will be some purposes that, while envisaged by the data controller, are not encompassed by a standard purpose.

The Commissioner has only provided *typical* examples of each purpose in its corresponding description. It is perfectly feasible that a data controller's intended purpose, while appearing to fall within one of the purposes, is not specifically mentioned in the descriptions. This is currently the situation where a data controller wishes to highlight the use of the Internet to achieve a particular purpose.

It is open for a data controller to define a personalised purpose to complete the form. This said, the many pre-defined purposes should cover the majority of anticipated purposes, especially where a data controller amends slightly the corresponding description. Data controllers should also be aware that the processing of an application with standard purposes will be quicker than one with unique self-defined purposes.

Internet purposes

16. A UK company currently uses one free-standing computer to store and process the biographical details of its staff. Now that the company is expanding out of the UK, it wishes to port these data onto a website, to allow any member of the overseas operation to access the details. The company's notification should reflect this. For, say, the purpose of 'Maintaining and publishing biographical details of staff', the description should be expanded to stress this is 'over the Internet and World Wide Web'. An example of needing to amend the description of a purpose is where the Internet is integral to the purpose.

Often it will not be as straightforward as simply including the words 'over the Internet' to expand properly the description. Data controllers may wish to be more specific as to exactly what aspects of the Internet they will use.

17. An online UK car retailer has always sold its customer details to car insurance companies; appropriately, its registration notification included the P018 purpose of Trading in Personal Information. Previously, it provided its lists of personal data to the insurance company on disk. To keep the lists more up-to-date, it now has installed a server which acts as an ftp site for any person with the correct password. Despite this purpose remaining the same, the retailer should update the relevant description to reflect the change in provision.

Data subjects

Each purpose refers to a type of data. Data controllers should include in their notification the description of the data, not the actual data. For this, the form provides standard subjects to whom the purpose refers. Again, the form also allows data controllers to expand the descriptions of any standard data subject. The use of the Internet should not affect a data controller's assessment of the data subjects about whom personal data is held.

Data classes

The 'C' section for each purpose refers to the 'description' of data to be or being processed. C200, 'Personal details', is likely to be included in most notifications. This author advises that if email addresses are held and or processed, C200 should always be selected. Data controllers should note that the Commissioner's examples within each data class are non-exhaustive.

Recipients

The recipient's section is one which requires a deep understanding of the controller's business: just who will have access to the data? A recipient is defined by s 70 as:

> 'any person to whom the data are disclosed, including any person (such as employee or agent of the data controller, a data processor or an employee or agent of a data processor) to whom they are disclosed in the course of processing the data for the data controller, but does not include any person to whom disclosure is or may be made as a result of or with a view to a particular enquiry by or on behalf of that person made in the exercise of any power captured by law.'

What should strike data controllers immediately is that its employees are considered to be recipients if data is disclosed to them. It will therefore be rare that a notification does not include R406, 'Employees and agents of the data controller', for at least some of the purposes. Similarly, R400, 'Data subjects themselves' will usually be included against most purposes. Where a data controller publishes personal data on a website, notwithstanding any password control, the possible recipients are effectively any person with access to the Internet. Where technical barriers are in place, such as passwords or client identifiers, there is an obvious reduction to the number of recipients.

Shared email addresses

Data controllers should not overlook that more than one person may share one email address. It is therefore possible that a data controller's recipients are more numerous than a mere list of email addresses portrays. To allow for this, like sending confidential information, data controllers should check whether the disclosing email is available to more than one person, be that a legal or natural person.

> **18. A recruitment agency is concerned that one of its larger clients has a central email address, allowing all employees in the organisation to access its email. The agency wishes to email to the personnel officer a list of potential candidates for a new position. To avoid broadening its disclosure section of its registration the recruitment agency encrypts the email with public-key cryptography. This ensures that disclosure is solely to the personnel officer who controls the unlocking private key.**

TRANSFERS OF PERSONAL DATA

If personal data are able to be freely exchanged with territories where data protection safeguards are weak, the effect is that the domestic regime is compromised. It is essential for data protection that 'data havens' are exiled from any personal data transfer. In this respect the Act includes protective measures to prevent personal data from being transferred into an impotent jurisdiction.

The first protective measure is that data users must complete the 'Transfers of personal data' section which describes the scope of their overseas transfers outside the European Economic Area[32]. This is described in greater detail below, but it is worth noting at this point that the section provides three main options including a worldwide choice. The consequences of choosing the worldwide category, as will be inevitable for many Internet data controllers, are considered below also. The second protective measure to prevent personal data seeping into data havens is the Commissioner's power to prevent a breach of the eighth principle.

Transfer

'Transfer' is undefined by the Act. It is essential for Internet users, though, to appreciate the ambit of this term. Indeed, it is a more important concept under this Act than the 1984 Act. Under the 1984 Act, s 5(2)(e) it was an offence directly or indirectly to transfer data held by a data user to any country or territory outside the UK other than one named or described in its entry in the data protection register. The eighth principle now changes the emphasis of the prohibition: one can only transfer data to certain countries or to other countries in certain circumstances. This is discussed in relation to the eighth principle.

32 Currently: Austria, Belgium, Denmark, France, Finland, Germany, Greece, Iceland, Ireland, Italy, Liechtenstein, Luxembourg, The Netherlands, Norway, Portugal, Spain, Sweden and the UK.

19. A UK company circulates a list of candidates for appointment to a new management position to the company directors by email for their comments. The directors' distribution list on the company's email system includes two non-executive directors resident in the US. This will be a transfer outside the UK.

The concept of transfer has ramifications for multinational organisations. A seemingly internal transfer of personal information between an English and overseas branch of a company may not include an additional recipient as it may not be between two legal persons. The same actions may be deemed a 'transfer' as this concept focuses also on the place of receipt not identity of recipient. This is particularly relevant for transnational companies who utilise a company-wide Intranet to transfer personal data.

Internet-wide transferrals

It has been mentioned that the choice to publish on the Internet is not simply a technical one, nor even solely a commercial one; there are also important legal considerations. These legal considerations are most evident where the law specifically addresses jurisdictional issues. Transfers include posting information on a website that can be accessed from overseas[33]. Therefore, without appropriate security measures in place, any territory in the world can access any page on the World Wide Web, any file on an ftp site, any computer through Telnet. So, if the data that identifies a living individual is retrievable by these methods the data controller must be making worldwide transferrals. They should therefore select the 'Worldwide' category.

Worldwide notification

The notification form allows for data controllers to select a 'Worldwide' category for potential transferrals. It is suggested that data controllers with personal data on a website without security measures in place do select this category. They cannot predict where in the world their data are being accessed from or in which territory the data are being retrieved. Similarly, if there are more than 10 transferee countries outside the EEA, data controllers must select the 'Worldwide' choice.

The controller of a server without security cannot predict from where the accesses to that server will originate. It is also technically extremely difficult to restrict access from a particular territory to a particular server. The nature of the Internet is that data packets are routed around the world making it complex to predict the final destination of a retrieval. The presence of a firewall en route may make it impossible to establish from where a retrieval will finally be made. These security devices can act like a one-way door, allowing data packets to move in one direction, but preventing the data's final destination being divulged in the opposite direction. Even if requests from certain territories could be prevented, there is nothing stopping an individual from that territory accessing

33 The Notification Handbook, Office of the Information Commissioner.

through Telnet a computer in an acceptable territory: the data would appear to be retrieved to an agreeable jurisdiction, when in fact this territory is simply the *penultimate* stop before the unacceptable territory. On similar principles, there is little preventing an individual dialling long-distance from an unfit territory to an Internet Service Provider based in a more appropriate territory. For these reasons, it often cannot be predicted to where data on the Internet will be retrieved. Therefore, use of the 'Worldwide' category will be relevant in many circumstances.

A data user's inability to predict the destinations of data transfers over the Internet is discussed above in that most Internet disclosures are passive: the data controller, and controlled server, have little regulation over the retrieval of data. The retriever of the data, the client, accesses and instructs the server to transfer the data; the data controller is not directly involved in this process. A data controller's knowledge of transfers is, necessarily, at best historic, not predictable. Clients do not give any notice of their access to a website or log in at an ftp site.

Putting personal data on the Internet, without security measures, allows any person, from any place in the world, at any time, to gain access to those data. These Internet data controllers must select the 'Worldwide category'; anything narrower may leave them open to committing offences by falsely completing the notification. However, by alerting the Commissioner to transfers to potentially inadequate regimes, controllers leave themselves open to allegations of breaching the eighth principle. This author suggests that in order to make this less ominous, a free-text entry is made stating that since use of the Internet and a company website is an integral part of the business, some data may potentially be accessed worldwide.

Security statement

Highlighting the importance of the seventh principle, data controllers must give a general description of the security measures to be taken to protect against unauthorised or unlawful processing of personal data and against accidental loss or destruction of, or damage to, personal data. Often this description will be very sensitive for the data controller and, as a consequence, is not published in the public register.

Data controllers need to provide the necessary comfort regarding physical security, technical security and organisational security. Further details relating to security are discussed below in relation to the seventh principle.

Renewing and amending notifications

The notification period is one year. Renewals do not occur automatically unless the renewal fee of £35 has been arranged to be paid by direct debit payment. Otherwise, the renewal notification and fee must be submitted prior to the expiry date of the entry. Although the Information Commissioner's office sends out notices before the expiry date of a notification, it is essential to be alert to this date and to have arrangements in place to effect the necessary administration. Where a notification has passed its expiry date, notifications cannot be renewed and data controllers will be obliged to make a new notification.

Any changes to a notification must be notified within a period of 28 days from the date on which the entry becomes inaccurate or incomplete. Failure to do so is a criminal offence. Changes can be made free of charge by post using the specific form to add an additional purpose or a second form covering other amendments. These forms are available from the website www.dpr.gov.uk.

PRINCIPLES OF DATA PROTECTION

All users of personal data must abide by the eight principles of data protection which are set out in Sch 1 of the Act.

Eight principles of data protection

1. Personal data shall be processed fairly and lawfully and, in particular, shall not be processed unless:
   (a) at least one of the conditions in Sch 2 is met, and
   (b) in the case of sensitive personal data, at least one of the conditions in Sch 3 is also met.
2. Personal data shall be obtained only for one or more specified and lawful purposes, and shall not be further processed in any manner incompatible with that purpose or those purposes.
3. Personal data shall be adequate, relevant and not excessive in relation to the purpose or purposes for which they are processed.
4. Personal data shall be accurate and, where necessary, kept up-to-date.
5. Personal data processed for any purpose or purposes shall not be kept for longer than is necessary for that purpose or those purposes.
6. Personal data shall be processed in accordance with the rights of data subjects under this Act.
7. Appropriate technical and organisational measures shall be taken against unauthorised or unlawful processing of personal data and against accidental loss or destruction of, or damage to, personal data.
8. Personal data shall not be transferred to a country or territory outside the European Economic Area unless that country or territory ensures an adequate level of protection for the rights and freedoms of data subjects in relation to the processing of personal data.

Consequences of breach

The eight principles are enforced by the Commissioner serving an enforcement notice[34]. Unlike the bizarre situation under the 1984 Act, the Commissioner may now bring such enforcement proceedings against any data user, and not merely those who have registered (now 'notified'). In short, there is no longer a protective loophole for those who breach the principles. This said, the Commissioner must at least take into account whether the breach has or is likely to cause damage or distress to any person[35]. Non-compliance with an enforcement notice

34 Data Protection Act 1998, s 40.
35 Data Protection Act 1998, s 40(2).

is an offence[36]. Subject to a limited defence of 'due diligence', non-compliance with such a notice can result in prosecution. The bad publicity generated by any action taken against a company could, of course, be one of the most damaging effects.

Reach of principles

It is vital for almost every user of personal data in relation to the Internet to understand what is entailed in complying with the principles.

1. Processed fairly and lawfully and satisfies additional conditions

> 'The information to be contained in personal data shall be obtained, and personal data shall be processed, fairly and lawfully.'

This principle will be particularly relevant for all Internet data users who use their websites or other digital activities to collect and then utilise personal data from visitors. In short, the principle attempts to ensure those individuals who access a service or send information understand, and consent to, what will happen to their personal data. Such a concept can run contrary to the 'marketeers' plans for collected data: there may be a temptation to collect data today and then decide what to do with it tomorrow. Such an approach is contrary to the protection provided by the first principle. Well-established companies have been served with notices under this principle, damaging both consumer confidence and profitability. The Act protects data subjects, not users of these data. One must bear in mind that 'processing' encompasses the stages of first 'obtaining' data and then utilising it, by, say, organising, consulting or disclosing[37]. It is therefore important to consider, initially, whether a site is 'obtaining' data fairly and lawfully and then consider the method of fuller exploitation. The Act also specifies that 'In determining . . . whether personal data are processed fairly, regard is to be had to the method by which they are obtained . . .'[38].

Data obtained fairly

There is no one test to establish that a data user has fairly obtained information from personal data, but there are a number of factors that the Commissioner will take into account. One key factor prescribed by the Act is that the individual was not deceived or misled about the purpose for the data[39]. A data controller should try to indicate to the data subject the full potential use of that information. It is not enough to direct the subject to the notification or to assume that the subject knows the scope of a data controller's notification. To be

36 Data Protection Act 1998, s 47.
37 Data Protection Act 1998, s 1(1).
38 Data Protection Act 1998, Sch 1, Pt II, para 1(1).
39 Data Protection Act 1998, Sch 1, Pt II, para 1(1).

safe, a data controller must make explicit the purpose to each potential data subject at the point of collection: a data user may breach this principle even where the data subject was misled unintentionally[40]. Unless it is obvious from the method to obtain the information, data controllers should inform their subjects of the potential disclosures and transfers of the information, and the purpose for processing that information.

A good, albeit US, example of the concept is the US Federal Trade Commission Complaint against Geocities[41]. Geocities operated a website consisting of 'virtual communities' of free and fee-based personal home pages. At the time of the complaint, it had more than 1.8 million members. Each member had the option to enter certain personal data with the various provisos that[42]:

> 'We will not share any information with anyone without your permission'
> '[W]e will NEVER give your information to anyone without your permission'
> 'We assure you that we will NEVER give your personal information to anyone without your permission'

Despite such assurances, Geocities did disclose the personal information to third parties. They, in turn, used the information to target Geocities members. In its consent order with the Federal Trade Commission (FTC), Geocities admitted these 'facts' as true. This blatant misrepresentation as to the use of personal data should amount to 'unfair' obtaining under the first principle. Under the US FTC codes, Geocities settled the Complaint.

Identity of data user

Potential data subjects should be made aware of to whom they are providing their personal data. The seamless way that a viewer of a website can move between different websites may cause data protection problems. For example, many commercial sites outsource any payment mechanisms to a third party who also operates a website. A viewer of the commercial site will be taken through the various stages of choosing a product to purchase. The final stage in this process is for the viewer to enter his personal details and payment particulars. To do this the viewer will often be instructed to click on a certain icon, one say labelled, 'Payment'. At this point, unbeknown to the viewer, the viewer is connected with the payment website. The only way for the viewer to discover this, unless made clear, may be to watch the URL alter at the top of their browser. Where framing or imbedded applications are used, even the URL may not alter.

It is certainly unfair obtaining of data where the provider of that data is not alerted to the identity of the person obtaining that data. Controllers of websites that interact with others for the collection of personal data should make it clear to their viewers that this is the case. It is particularly important that data

40 This was decided in the *Innovations (Mail Order) Ltd v Data Protection Registrar Data Protection Tribunal* case DA/92 31/49/1.
41 File No 9823015, 1998.
42 Respectively: New Member Application Form Privacy Statement, Geocites Free Member E-mail Program Privacy Statement, World Report Newsletter 1997.

controllers at the very least make this information 'readily available' to the potential data subject[43].

Non-obvious purposes

Often a data controller will have more than one contemplated purpose for personal information. Where a purpose could not reasonably be expected, the data user must inform the subject prior to obtaining the data. Data controllers must give each individual the informed chance to refuse to become a data subject[44].

Data controllers should assume that there is a need to inform the data subject of the intended use. Data controllers should alert their data subjects to any processing prior to obtaining. This is the case even where the data, once obtained, will be used solely by the data controller.

When and how to inform

A data controller's obligations are not to deceive or mislead the user about the likely processing of the data *prior* to processing the data or disclosure to a third party[45]. In practice this is likely to entail the data controller informing the potential subjects of all relevant information prior to obtaining the data. Otherwise, the data controller will be obliged to conduct the embarrassing and costly activity of re-contacting data subjects to ask their permission to exploit their data in a new undisclosed manner.

For commercial and legal reasons, therefore, data controllers are advised to inform their potential data subjects of all relevant information before the subject has opportunity to enter their data. A US import to achieve this is the 'privacy policy' which is often used to explain the 'who, why, what and where' of processed data. Despite the Information Commissioner stating that privacy policies are 'good practice'[46] they are not legally required. They are merely a common (and excessive in the eyes of the author) way of ensuring that *prior* to obtaining the data, the data controller has 'made available' to the subject all the relevant information.

Where a data controller needs to do this, to broaden its purposes, silence should not be taken to be a data subject's consent. In *Midlands Electricity plc v Data Protection Registrar*[47] it was made clear to Midlands Electricity that:

> 'For the avoidance of doubt . . . consent shall not be inferred from the failure of any person to return any other documentation containing an opportunity to opt-out.'

This clarification is also repeated in the undertaking made by London Electricity

43 Data Protection Act 1998, Sch 1, Pt II, para 2(1)(a).
44 This is specifically discussed below at 'Prior consent', p 359.
45 Data Protection Act 1998, Sch 1, Pt II, para 2(2).
46 Internet: Protection of Privacy, Data Controllers, Version 4, January 2000. This document is published by the Office of the Information Commissioner.
47 Final form of the enforcement notice (as approved by the Data Protection Tribunal) 20 July 1999, at para 9.5.

plc[48] and Thames Water Utilities Ltd[49] both given to avoid the Commissioner enforcing its sanctions.

Data controllers would be prudent not to rely upon a data subject's silence.

20. An online pencil procurement website has fairly collected the email addresses and personal data of the stationery budget holders in the country's largest companies. Pressure from its venture capitalist investors leads it to expand into advertising conferences and jobs in the procurement field. It emails all its customers explaining this expansion and asking them to return the email if they have any objections to this new processing. Merely because noone returned an objection does not mean that the site's personal data is now fairly obtained.

Changed purposes

Often a data controller will obtain personal data with one intention in mind, and then later decide to use the information for another purpose. Unless this new purpose is within the scope of the purpose reasonably contemplated or disclosed to the data subject, strictly speaking, the data user should seek new consent.

Prior consent

In the fiercely competitive ecommerce sector, it is important to keep open one's options for future business ventures. Unfortunately, it is not advisable to attempt to keep open one's options of dealing with personal data. A data controller can not try to get around this by making the initial description of the purposes vague in order to encompass future purposes for which they may later choose to use the data. Data controllers must make their intentions clear to potential data subjects before soliciting their personal data.

21. Fat?No! a web-based health and fitness magazine informs its online subscribers that their personal data is held in order to 'send you details of competitions, events and articles that may be of interest to you and for any other related purposes'. The company is not generating enough income through advertising revenues on its site. It approaches a sponsor who requires that they directly send subscribers weekly promotions for its range of fat-free ice-cream. This is not within the scope of the original purposes stated and even without this new purpose, the original notice is arguably unfair.

The Innovations case

In *Innovations (Mail Order) Ltd v Data Protection Registrar*[50], under the 1984 Act, the appellant collected individuals' names and addresses for completing

48 London Electricity plc Undertaking, 1 January 2001.
49 Thames Water Utilities Ltd Undertaking, 1 January 2001.
50 DA/92/31/49/1.

order requests by them. After completing the order Innovations sent an acknowledgement on the back of which was a statement informing the customer that Innovations rents out its names and addresses. The company gave an address to its customers to write to if they objected to their data being used in this way. The Data Protection Tribunal held that this was too late: to be fair, data users must give their subjects the chance to consent to the use of personal information before it is taken. It upheld the enforcement notice served by the Registrar on 9 April 1992.

Surreptitious obtaining

One quality of the Internet is that a data controller may technically collect personal data without a data subject being aware. 'Cookies' can be deposited on a data subject's hard drive which, when combined with personal data knowingly entered by the subject, can create new personal data. If a site 'records' all the movements one makes within a site, and is able to link those movements to data identifying a living individual, it is obtaining personal data about *use* of its site. Controllers must only obtain such covert data, albeit valuable, where the data subject has been given clear information about the use and purpose of cookies. The Electronic Communications Directive addresses this issue.

Given that 'cookies' and other data such as IP addresses must be processed to be linked to the personal data collected on the site (say by a form) the 'relevant time' is arguably *prior* to the 'cookie' being deposited on the hard drive, or the IP address, or whatever, being collected. This would have required that, *before* such activities are conducted, subjects be told or data controllers risk breaching the first principle. Companies which sell banner advertising onto third party sites will find such a requirement next to impossible to comply with; they will therefore need to ensure that they do not process personal data, ie stay well away from data which may identify a living individual. The Electronic Communications Directive tones down such an onerous requirement so that data subjects do not necessarily have to be informed of the use of cookies prior to using the site in question. They merely must be given 'access to clear and comprehensive information' about the cookies and other information[51].

22. A successful version of browser software allows each site visited to store a small quantum of data about the visitor accessing the site. This data, or 'cookie', is stored on the visitor's hard disk and is used to compile data about each visitor when they revisit any site. If the visitor has no knowledge of this surreptitious method of obtaining information, be it stored at the client or server, it may be unfair obtaining of data. If the server then processes the information, again, without the client's tacit consent, this may also be a breach of the first data protection principle as unfair processing.

51 Article 5, para 3, also see recital 25. See Agreement between the Attorney General of the States of Arizona, California, Conneticut, Massachusetts, Michigan, New Jersey, New Mexico, New York, Vermont and Washington and Doubleclick Inc, 26 August 2002.

Disingenuous consent

It is likely to be unfair where a data subject has no choice but to provide consent to additional uses of his personal data. This is the situation where the data controller informs all potential subjects that their order or transaction will not be processed unless they agree to the secondary uses of the data. While the data subject does still have a nominal choice, to stop dealing with the data user, for certain dominant data controllers it will not be a genuine choice.

Information obtained lawfully

The first hurdle for the Commissioner to prove unlawful obtaining is to prove that the obtaining of the information was in breach of a law. Possible candidates for grounds for unlawful obtaining in the normal course of dealing with personal data are breach of confidence and breach of contract. In the Internet sphere the most likely law to be broken is not civil, but criminal: the Computer Misuse Act 1990[52]. Unauthorised access, an offence under the Computer Misuse Act 1990, may result in the obtaining of information unlawfully under the Data Protection Act 1998. Along with these more general laws by which data users must abide, certain data users are bound by rules specific to their industry. *British Gas Trading Ltd v Data Protection Registrar*[53] is a good illustration of this. In this case the Registrar (as she then was) viewed the use of customer data to provide non-gas services was ultra vires. The Tribunal disagreed but concurred with the concept of an *ultra vires* act of a corporation being 'unlawful' under the first principle.

Whatever the unlawful activity alleged, it will always be open to the data subject or Commissioner to argue that, in the alternative, even if the obtaining was not unlawful, it was nevertheless unfair[54]. The protection for data subjects under the first principle of data protection is certainly broader when the accusation is unfair obtaining as compared with unlawful obtaining.

Data processed fairly

Fair processing is directed at protecting data subjects from treatment that may be described in a data controller's notification but is, nevertheless, prejudicial use of the personal data. The first question is necessarily to establish that processing itself has occurred. It will be recalled that 'processing' is an extremely wide and far-ranging concept. It includes, in relation to data, 'obtaining, recording or holding' and also organising, adapting or altering it; retrieving, consulting or using it; disclosing it in any manner; aligning, combining, blocking, erasing or destroying it[55]. As has been discussed, it is therefore close to impossible to

52 See Chapter 5 on Crime.

53 [1998] Info TLR 393.

54 There will be many situations where obtaining is both unfair and unlawful under the Unfair Terms in Consumer Contracts Regulations 1994/9 which make unenforceable against a consumer certain unfair contractual terms. A contracting party which by its unequal bargaining power is able to coerce a consumer into agreeing to supply personal data may be acting unfairly under the Regulations. The obtaining of those data may be outside the enforceable terms of the contract and classed as unlawful and, by virtue of the disparity in bargaining strength, unfair.

55 Data Protection Act 1998, s 1(1).

consider any action or activity in relation to personal data that will not be deemed to be processing. As has also been discussed, the concept of 'fairly' is also very wide. Despite such a 'catch-all' provision, the Act further raises the hurdle for a data controller.

Additional conditions necessary for the first principle

The first principle stipulates both that data shall be processed fairly and lawfully 'and, in particular, shall not be processed unless . . . at least one of the conditions in Sch 2 is met'. Despite practitioners familiar with the 1984 Act choosing often to ignore this additional wording, data controllers must not. The additional conditions are discussed below in the context of Internet data controllers.

Data subject has given his consent to the processing

The consent condition under Sch 2 should not be confused with the specific requirement to obtain consent where data is being put to certain uses, as for example under the Telecoms Regulations in relation to direct marketing (see below). The factors in considering how this consent can be obtained over the Internet are the same, however.

On the Internet, just as in the offline world, one may consent in a number of ways. One may 'positively' consent by continuing to conduct oneself in a particular way. One may also actively consent by signing a particular document at a particular place.

On a website, data controllers and their web designers are faced with the difficulty of 'what is consent?'. Is it an opt-in box, pre-ticked? Is it an opt-out box[56] in a small font size and 'below the fold'?[57] There is no definition of 'consent' in the Act. In the House of Lords debate on the Act Lord Williams was adamant that there was no need to include a definition as existing law and the courts were enough[58].

Further guidance can be drawn from the Act's spawning Directive at art 2(h). This states a person's consent is 'freely given, specific and informed indication of his wishes by which the data subject signifies his agreement to personal data relating to him being processed'. It is worthwhile considering the elements of this definition in the Internet context.

Freely given

This will rarely be a difficult challenge for most data controllers. Even if a data subject must provide consent as an obligation under the contract with the data controller, the data subject does not need to enter into the contract. Consequently, it is acceptable to deduce the 'consent' was freely given. Difficulties can arise where, without acting in an anti-competitive or collusive

56 See discussion on the meaning of opt-in and opt-out consent below.
57 The hidden part of the current web page which is available for viewing by scrolling down the web page. This is, in part, a factor of the resolution of the viewer's screen.
58 Vol 586, No 108, col CWH 15, 23 Feb 1998.

way, a great number of organisations within a particular sector require consent to process certain data. In such a situation, a data subject may be unable to enter this type of contract with *any* supplier without giving 'consent'[59].

23. A large group of airlines that fly from London to Paris each have websites and independently choose to allow bookings to be taken only over their respective websites. Each ticket sale contract includes a term to the effect of 'You agree that we may use your personal data to provide you with details of great hotel offers during your flight'. There is no opt-out box. Because it is impossible to fly directly to Paris without giving this 'consent' it may be deemed not to be freely given.

Specific

This aspect of 'consent' is the one which causes most clashes between the marketing team behind a site and its legal advisors. Specific means just that; general is not enough.

Wording next to a text box stating: 'You agree to us using your personal data for other exciting promotions', is poor for a number of basic reasons. It does not explain 'who' the 'us' is: if a subsidiary company is collecting data, it is not by law allowed to pass that data to its subsidiary companies or associated companies. If this is the intention, it should be specified in the fair collection notice. The aforementioned example wording also does not explain with particularity 'what' is that type of activity. Is it 'marketing' for 'exciting promotions' or 'research' for 'exciting promotions'? Again, this intended activity should be specified. Similarly, for how long may this activity continue? The temporary or permanent nature of the activity is also an integral aspect of being specific.

As discussed below, the nature of the consent required depends on how any particular communication will be sent.

24. A fireplace installer establishes a website which allows customers to design and order their fireplaces. The 'fair collection' notice states: 'By ordering this fireplace you will also agree to allow one of our group of companies to contact you by email, yearly, to enquire only whether or not you require your chimney to be swept for your comfort and safety.' Such a notice is specific and leaves the data subject in no doubt as to the precise purpose of collecting their data.

Informed

Allied to 'specific' is the concept of 'informed': simply put, one cannot consent unless one knows what one is consenting to. For data protection purposes online, companies have taken to producing 'privacy policies'. These detail every possible activity that may be contemplated in relation to the data. Despite their almost viral, widespread usage across websites, this author is unconvinced that most 'privacy policies' have their intended effect. This is not down to their

59 See Mr Lamidey's (Assistant Registrar under the 1984 Act) concern at high street bank practices: *Financial Times*, 2 February 1993.

content wanting; it is because their *position* and *incorporation* is often so hidden that they are not immediately visible. Websites with unusual uses of personal data would be advised not merely to include details of the uses in their privacy policy. They must also bring the policy to a user's attention, not bury it at the bottom of a web page.

25. An individual complains to the Information Commissioner that a certain website has used their personal data in a non-obvious manner. When approached, the website's owner directs the Commissioner to click on a tiny 'Terms of Use' link at the base of the home page followed by a further link on that page to the 'Privacy Policy'. The page on which personal data was collected has had no such links. Whatever the contents of the privacy policy, it is likely that its hidden position will mean no informed consent was given.

Indication and signifies

These two terms have been prised out of the Directive's definition to support the Commissioner's view that:

> 'Data controllers cannot infer consent from non-response to a communication, for example by a customer's failure to return or respond to a leaflet.'[60]

This approach to 'silence' is endorsed by the undertakings given by London Electricity plc and Thames Water Utilities Ltd[61] in relation to alleged breaches of the first principle. In both undertakings the statement is made:

> 'consent shall not be inferred from the failure of any person to return any leaflet or other document containing an opportunity to opt out.'[62]

Similarly, in the Final Form of the Enforcement Notice (as approved by the Data Protection Tribunal on 20 July 1999) against Midlands Electricity plc consent is stated to include where:

> '[the individual customers] have returned a document to the [data] user or, by other means of communication received by the data user have indicated that they consented to, or by not filling in an opt-out box or other means have indicated that they do not object to such processing.'[63]

These cases do show that the Commissioner believes (and just as important, the Tribunal supports the view) that silence or acquiescence is unlikely to be an 'indication' of consent. The commercial lesson to draw from this is simple.

60 *The Data Protection Act 1998 – An Introduction*, Office of the Data Protection Registrar, October 1998, at p 10.
61 7 January 2001 and 11 January 2001.
62 Paragraphs 1.5(iii) and 5(3) respectively.
63 Clause 9.2(ii)(bb).

Wherever possible, ensure that a data subject has to 'do' something having read the privacy policy or fair collection notice. This may be clicking in a box or clicking 'I Accept'. It may even be clicking the privacy policy link and then going ahead to order the goods.

Evidence of consent

If 'consent' is being relied upon to comply with Sch 2, websites should ensure that they retain evidence of this consent. If a database contains only the email address of data subjects, how can this be used to prove that all their owners did consent, by say, ticking a box? If a privacy policy contains some unusual uses for data, how can its website owner prove that there was a specific, informed indication of the data subject's consent?

To answer these questions, the customer database needs to be constructed to record not merely the collected personal data but also the data relating to the consent itself. In addition, with websites under constant re-design flux, data users should maintain a secure, date-stamped copy of the main data protection aspects of the site to allow them to prove how the site was configured at the time that a data subject keyed in their details and consent.

Processing necessary for the performance of or entering into a contract[64]

At first glance, a data user could be forgiven for assuming that all that is needed to satisfy this paragraph is publishing an appropriate term in the data subject's contract. The correct focus, however, is on the word 'necessary'. An ancillary use of the data will not be necessary for the performance of the contract. The word necessary must be construed very narrowly and objectively.

26. NeuPub2 is a radical new type of online publisher: writers submit their manuscript and NeuPub2 distributes their work having edited the manuscript to include 'product placement' from well-known brand names. In return, NeuPub2 pays its writers a royalty on copies sold. For writers that do not sell well, NeuPub2 states: 'From time to time we will pass your details to experienced writing coaches who can help your next project be even more successful.' Processing the data for this ancillary purpose is not necessary for the performance of the contract.

Processing necessary for compliance with a data user's non-contractual legal obligation

This paragraph of Sch 2 relates to a statutory obligation on the data user to process the data in a particular manner. Owners of websites should take specific sectoral legal advice before relying only on this paragraph to satisfy their compliance with Sch 2.

64 Data Protection Act 1998, Sch 2, para 2.

Processing necessary for data subject's vital interests

It is clear both from the recitals to the Directive[65] and the Commissioner's guidance[66] that this condition is concerned with life and death situations for the data subject.

Processing necessary for public functions

This related to the administration of justice, functions of the Crown, minister, government department and related functions of a public nature exercised in the public interest. Again, this is narrowly construed because of the limiter 'necessary'. This condition should not concern private bodies and should not be confused with non-contractual obligations.

Processing necessary for a data controller's legitimate interests

This is an ambiguous condition. It requires the Commissioner, Tribunal and possibly the courts to balance the data user's legitimate interests with those legitimate interests of the data subject[67] particularly his right to privacy[68].

This author strongly believes that this condition does not allow in, through the back door, anything that a private body does for profit because 'profit making is a legitimate interest'. Legitimate interest in this context must mean those interests protected by the Treaty of Rome and other enabling provisions. It does not mean, in effect, any vires act a company chooses to conduct.

Even if such a wide interpretation were afforded to this condition, one must not forget why the condition needs to be met. To comply with the first principle, *first* the data must be processed fairly *and* then *also* it must satisfy one of the conditions.

Web businesses and their advisors are warned not to trust this condition as their way unfairly to process data and to avoid providing the data subject with the 'specific information' relating to the processing.

27. SpamMethods Ltd is established as a company whose sole function is to harvest Director-level email addresses from corporate websites and then sell access to these email addresses to financial advisors. Such harvesting and processing, without the data subjects' knowledge, is obviously unfair. That the activity is the only reason SpamMethods was established does not make it a 'legitimate interest'. And, even if it were a 'legitimate interest', being 'unfair processing' it remains illegal.

65 Recital 31.

66 '[R]eliance on this condition may only be claimed where the processing is necessary for matters of life and death . . .'

67 Data Protection Act 1998, Sch 2, para 6.

68 Directive 95/46/EC of the European Parliament and of the Council, art 7(f) and art 1(1).

28. A manufacturer creates a sophisticated home page that records the number of hits to its site and the email addresses of its members who view the site. This information is then analysed and certain addresses are targeted with 'follow-up' emails. Without a method for an individual to avoid being included in the emailshot, the processing, and obtaining, may be unfair, and therefore a breach of the first data protection principle[69].

Data processed lawfully

An obligation to process lawfully is narrower than fair processing and the fact that a data controller has satisfied at least one of the Sch 2 conditions does not, of itself, mean that the requirement for lawful processing is necessarily satisfied. If processing breaches another legal duty, including both criminal and civil duties, or would lead to such a breach, then it will also be a breach of the first data protection principle. The Registrar under the 1984 Act indicated three areas of law particularly relevant to breaches of the first principle of data protection[70]. It is submitted the same areas will be considered under the 1998 Act.

> 'Confidentiality, arising from the relationship of the data user with the individual;
> The ultra vires rule and the rule relating to the excess of delegated powers, under which the data user may only act within the limits of its legal powers;
> Legitimate expectation, that is the expectation of the individual as to how the data user will use the information relating to him.'

29. A data subject supplies to a data controller personal data encrypted using a public key. This encryption may be enough to give the subject the legitimate expectation that the personal data will be used by only the holder of the private key. Wider processing may be unlawful and constitute a breach of the first data protection principle.

2. Obtained for specified and lawful purposes

> 'Personal data shall be held only for one or more specified and lawful purposes.'

69 It is a moot point, and discussed earlier, whether simply processing an email address can constitute processing under the Act as personal data must relate to a living individual. An email address may not actually relate to an individual and may not permit identification of the living individual. A similar point was raised by Equifax in a Data Protection Tribunal inquiry. Equifax processed purely in relation to an address. The Tribunal gave a purposive answer to the point saying that one should look to the purpose of the processing. Where that processing was to determine information in relation to the living individual, the processing will fall within the definition of the word in the Act.

70 Data Protection Guideline 4, para 1.18.

Obtained for specified purposes

To comply with this second principle is simply a matter of ensuring that all purposes for which a data controller obtains data are properly and accurately notified to the Commissioner[71], and are properly specified to the data subject in accordance with the first principle[72]. Data controllers should be vigilant over their databases and appreciate that including an additional field against a set of personal data or using a database in a new way may constitute a new purpose which their notification to the Commissioner and specification to the data subject must reflect. A data controller must also be aware that obtaining is widely encompassing: newly received personal data may alter the capacity in which other data are being processed. And, the Interpretation Schedule of the Act states that 'regard' has to be had to the intended processing[73] when determining compatible obtaining. These other data may then become part of a collection of data which are intended to be processed. As such, these data will fall within the scope of data held.

30. A university has a list of academics who have applied for a new post. To gain more information on them, it enters each academic's name into a search engine that searches both the World Wide Web and Usenet. From these additional data, the university appends to its database two new entries: first, personal details gleaned form the search; second, opinions on the nature of each academic's postings on Usenet. To comply with the second data protection principle the university must check that their current notification and method of obtaining covers the newly held data.

Obtained for lawful purposes

As for the first data protection principle, the word 'lawful' relates both to criminal and civil laws. Depending on the intention for obtaining the data, it is feasible that an accurate notification is still in breach of the second data protection principle for being unlawful. It would, for example, be unlawful for an online travel agent to compile names and addresses of its customers to provide those details to criminals to burgle the customers' properties while they are on holiday.

Value of personal data database, including on insolvency

Attention economy

Increasingly, corporations are realising (in both senses of the word) the value of personal data. Personal data allows marketers to target more accurately products and services at individuals. The more a marketer 'knows' about an individual, the higher likelihood that the individual will be interested in the offering. This necessarily increases the return on (marketing) investment. Because of this real value, corporations are also beginning to understand the utility of *their* customers' personal data to *other* corporations.

71 Data Protection Act 1998, Sch 1, Pt II, para 5(b).
72 Data Protection Act 1998, Sch 1, Pt II, para 5(a).
73 Data Protection Act 1998, Sch 1, Pt II, para 6.

It is this author's opinion that there are three main reasons why personal data is now viewed as a commodity. First, on the Internet, as the good joke tells 'no-one knows you are a dog'. In other words, unlike in the corner shop, the website cannot tell whether you are a regular customer, a new customer or even a troublesome schoolchild with no pocket money to spend. Consequently, websites have been forced into collecting information about a visitor to ensure they can greet them appropriately and even recommend purchases to them based upon previous interactions. The second main reason is that many websites have subsisted only on advertising revenues, not direct revenues. As detailed here, the more a marketer knows about an audience and its individuals, the higher price it will pay to access those 'eyeballs'. The third, and more recent, reason is the increasing demise of 'dot com' companies; investors, insolvency practitioners and creditors are needing to extract the greatest possible value from a company's assets. One such asset is the personal data database. And, for the first two reasons, this database has a value well worth paying for (or worth selling). Companies and their advisors or insolvency practitioners are, however, worried that the 'open market' value of the database may not be accurate; the company may be prevented by data protection law from selling the database at *any* price.

The second principle prevents a company from obtaining data and then, without having told the individual, processing it for the purposes of selling it to a third party. This absolute prohibition applies whether the selling company is on the verge of insolvency or not. The Toysmart bankruptcy is a good US illustration.

Toysmart.com bankruptcy data sale

Since September 1999, Toysmart.com had posted a privacy policy stating 'When you register with Toysmart.com, you can rest assured that your information will never be shared with a third party'. By 19 May 2000, Toysmart had officially ceased operations having run into dire financial difficulties. It was prompted to sell its principal remaining asset, its customer information database. By 21 July 2000, the Federal Trade Commission had blocked the sale to 'any' buyer[74] saying: 'Customer data collected under a privacy agreement should not be auctioned off to the highest bidder'. The FTC were only prepared to permit the entire website and data to be sold off to the 'highest bidder' who operates a 'family-orientated website'.

It is submitted that, under the UK's regime, the Commissioner would construe the word 'never' as just that. She would therefore determine that the Toysmart data, having been obtained for processing by Toysmart, could not merely, because of bankruptcy, be transferred to another entity. The second principle would have been breached. Indeed, the US FTC's Commissioner Swindle, in the minority, was of the strong opinion that:

> '. . . I do not think that the [Federal Trade] Commission should allow the sale [of Toysmart customer data]. If we really believe that customers attach great value to the privacy of their personal information and that consumers should be able to limit access to such information

74 *Federal Trade Commission v Toysmart.com LLC* (US District Court of Massachusetts, Civil Action No 00-11341-RGS, 10 and 21 July 2000).

> through private agreements with businesses, we should compel businesses to honor promises they make to customers to gain access to this information . . . In my view, such a sale should not be permitted because "never" really means never.'

In a twist of fate, no appropriate buyers came forward for Toysmart. Eventually, by January 2001, a Walt Disney company subsidiary bought the company for $50,000 but was forced to destroy the customer records as the FTC had indicated.

Advisors and data controllers (and banks who believe they have security over customer databases) should take a few lessons from the Toysmart incident. First, never say never. It is this author's strong belief that once the word is uttered in a fair collection notice or privacy policy, no other processing changes may be introduced without explicit data subject consent. Each and every customer would have to be contacted for permission to 'purpose creep' and their silence would *not* mean that they had consented. Second, very few privacy policies should not allow for the transfer of personal data to a third party who will operate under the same privacy policy and terms and conditions. This, at least, allows consensual transfer to a third party seeking to continue to operate the business of the data controller. The third lesson is for those who lend money to companies taking security over customer databases. Conduct detailed due diligence to ensure that this database *could* have a value to a third party.

3. Adequate, relevant, not excessive

> 'Personal data shall be adequate, relevant and not excessive in relation to the purpose or purposes for which they are processed.'

The Act does not define the limits of this principle and does not interpret it. In relation to the similar principle under the 1984 Act, the Registrar (as then titled) suggested that one method of determining the correct quota of data is to decide the absolute minimum amount of data needed to achieve the registered purposes. The Data Protection Tribunal has established that it will look closely at exactly what information is necessary for the specified purpose[75]. Information should not be held simply on the basis that it might come in useful one day with no clear idea how and when.

31. A sports website runs a competition to win two tickets to an important football game. The winner will be selected at random from the correct answers received to three simple questions. Email answers must be sent by contenders on the standard email form stating the dates on which they would be available for travel and the name of the individual who would accompany them if they win. This is excessive, since the company would only need this information from the winner.

75 The Tribunal held that it was excessive for the Community Charge Registration Officers of the local authority of Rhondda to hold the date of birth of an individual. This seemingly innocuous piece of datum was sufficient to warrant the Tribunal deciding that the local authority had breached the relevant data protection principle: Case DA/90 25/49/2.

Living individual focus

It is wrong to assume that the necessary quotum of data can be assessed purely in relation to the purpose. The principle applies to each living individual on which the data user holds personal data. What might be the minimum quantum of data for one individual may be excessive for another. To establish a breach, the Commissioner may well examine the data held on each individual for each purpose as specified. This assessment is conducted from an objective viewpoint; it is of little relevance to a breach whether a data controller had reasoned it was holding acceptable amounts[76].

32. An online software supplier uses a standard online form for its customers to complete their order details. Owing to programming technicalities each field of the form must be filled in before the user can select the 'Okay' button to complete the order. This has the result that all users are required to include their home address, even users who will be sent the software by downloading it directly from the site. The supplier will be holding excessive data on all customers who wish their software to be delivered online: a breach of the third data protection principle.

P3P

The World Wide Web Consortium continues to promote the Platform for Privacy Preferences (P3P). This allows a user to set a maximum criteria for the personal data his browser will share with any website. For example, this author may be happy to allow a website automatically to feed cookies onto his browser and automatically to store his name, but no more.

This technology is a great advance in solving privacy problems; it is not, unfortunately, the data controller's way of avoiding obtaining excessive personal data. Whether data is excessive or not is an objective test and not subjective for either the data controller or data subject.

Future business models

The web lends itself to flexing and changing business models. This creates a tendency and a temptation to 'hedge one's bets' when collecting personal data and to collect personal data *in case* it may be useful at some point in the future. From a commercial prospective this makes sense: ask for all a person's personal data in one go; having collected the data, then decide how it can be utilised. Such a policy for obtaining personal data will be a breach of the third principle. One must have, at the time of obtaining, a view as to how the personal data will be used.

76 See Part A of 1984 Guidance Note 25.

33. Office@Home sells high-quality home office furniture for home workers. Its Marketing Director observes that many of their purchasers are actually high-powered office executives who are buying office furniture for their studies at home. Office@Home changes its sign-up page to also collect details of the purchaser's work address, status and work type. Office@Home risks this additional data being viewed as excessive for the purposes of selling furniture for use at home.

4. Accurate and up-to-date

'Personal data shall be accurate and, where necessary, kept up-to-date.'

Accurate personal data

The definition of 'accuracy' is:

> '[D]ata are inaccurate for the purposes of this section if incorrect or misleading as to any matter of fact.'[77]

This definition excludes a mere opinion which does not include, or purport to be, a statement of fact. This may appear to be an onerous requirement for data users, especially using the Internet, where one search engine may provide links to reams of personal data, each of which would have to be checked independently. However, the interpretative schedule to this principle excludes the data obtained and accurately recorded from a third party, including the data subject, under two circumstances[78]. These are that the data controller has taken reasonable steps to ensure the accuracy (with regard for the purpose or purposes for which the data were obtained and further processed) and, if relevant, the data user records an appropriate indication of the data subject's notification of alleged inaccuracies. So, a data controller must be careful when trawling, say, the Internet for personal data to buttress an existing data record. One should certainly record details of the source of the data.

Internet data sources and locations

Particularly on the World Wide Web, the location of data may be only one aspect of its source. For example, the data held on the home page at http://www.allserve.com/ourhome/coolhome are stored on the Allserve server in the coolhome directory that is within the parent directory, ourhome. This is its location. Its source, in contrast, will include the person who uploaded that data onto the home page. This will probably be the owner of the Allserve account, coolhome. This person's identity, together with the URL, will form the source of the information.

The reason for insisting on this distinction is two-fold. First, the relevant

77 Data Protection Act 1998, Sch 1, Pt II, para 7.
78 Data Protection Act 1998, Sch 1, Pt II, para 7.

section refers to receiving or obtaining data from the 'data subject or a third party'[79]. Both these terms refer to natural or legal persons. The source required under the section is therefore not the place where the data are stored, or from where they are retrieved, but the person who supplied the data to the data user. In illustration, if a data user obtains personal data from a particular book, it will not be enough to include as its source its location in a library; the publisher and author will be its source. By analogy, if personal data are obtained from a particular home page, it will not be enough to include as the source the URL on the Internet; the controller and creator of the home page will be the source.

The second justification for the source to be the person not the URL is that it is trivial to alter a URL. Indeed, the greatest difficulty for home pages on the web is that their links to other sites may become outdated. The person who created the site is therefore a more stable and certain source than the location of the data in question.

Notification of inaccuracy

If a data subject finds personal data inaccurate he may commence an action under s 14 for the court to order rectification, blocking, erasure or destruction of the data. The court may also order a verification enquiry, a supplementary statement and/or a communication order.

Database construction

This section of the book concentrates only on these final three remedies. What is relevant is the need with any of the section's orders to be able to identify all data relating to an individual from that individual's details. Databases, simple, relational, object-orientated or whatever type, must therefore be carefully constructed. It must be trivial for any of the data relating to an individual to be able to be:

(i) rectified, ie corrected without necessarily deleting the previous data;
(ii) blocked, ie presented in the database structure but obscured from viewing or processing unless under certain restrictive conditions;
(iii) erased, ie erasure of reference to data and also erasure of data itself;
(iv) verified, ie investigation of the source of the data being queried by the data subject; certainly contentious data must be recorded together with its source;
(v) communicated to third party recipients, ie, the data controller may be required to alert all subsequent recipients of the queried data as to the inaccuracy; this order, made under extreme circumstances, blocks the 'flow' of inaccurate data.

Reliability of Internet sources

One of the advantages of the Internet over other information sources is that it is quick and simple to retrieve vast quantities of data about almost any subject, including living individuals. There is no quality control, however, over this data.

79 Data Protection Act 1998, Sch 1, Pt II, para 7(a).

It is as easy for individuals to publish unsubstantiated personal data on the World Wide Web as it is for organisations who prudently vet their data. It is therefore unwise, and probably unreasonable, for a data controller to compile data about individuals using unsubstantiated material from the Internet. This reinforces the issue that the important details about data extracted from the Internet are the actual sources, which can be checked for the irreliability, potentially under a verification enquiry, not simply the URL of the material on the Internet.

Up-to-date, where necessary

The fourth data protection principle does not require that data users keep all their data up-to-date at all times; they must do this if it is *necessary*.

There will be circumstances where data held on an individual does need to be updated. Under the 1984 Act, the Registrar included data used to decide whether to grant credit or to confer or withhold some other benefit[80]. These are examples where what is required is a reflection of the data subject's current status or circumstances.

34. An online cinema-ticket agency establishes an account for each new customer. To set up an account a data subject must enter, among other details, his age in years and months on 1 January next. If the purpose of these data are to ensure that customers do not attend films under the required age, it must be updated each month to ensure that these data do not exclude individuals who have had a recent birthday.

5. KEPT NO LONGER THAN NECESSARY

> 'Personal data processed for any purpose or purposes shall not be kept any longer than is necessary for that purpose or those purposes.'

Data users should be diligent in deleting data when they have already served their purpose. Each set of data should have a life-span. At the end of this time, the data should be reviewed and assessed against the specified purpose for holding that data. If the data no longer appear necessary to complete or continue the purpose, data users have one of two options. They can either delete the data, or they can obtain consent from the data subject and amend their notified purposes to reflect the reason for extending holding the data.

Contrary requirement to retain data

It should be noted that data controllers can no longer approach this issue simply in terms of deleting data when it has served the purpose for which they collected them. Acknowledgement will also need to be had to codes of practice which are drafted under the Anti-Terrorism, Criminal and Security Act 2001. Although

80 Data Protection Guideline 4, para 5.3.

only a code of practice, holders of personal data should be warned against assuming that compliance will be truly voluntary. The effect will be that Internet Service Providers and other businesses will be required to retain certain data so that they are available to law enforcement authorities for the purpose of investigating and criminal activities and potential breaches of national security.

Of particular concern to Internet Service Providers at the current time are the cost consequences of storing and retrieving such data. An open question is whether in view of the conflict with the Act, it is in fact 'lawful' under the first principle to be retaining such data contrary to the Act pursuant to a voluntary code of practice. In truth, however, this is likely to be an academic question only. If forced, most ISPs would prefer to suffer the sanctions (if any) under the Data Protection Act 1998 than those under the Anti-Terrorism, Criminal and Security Act 2001.

Multiple purposes

There will be many occasions when one set of data is held for more than one purpose. Consequently, there will be occasions when, for one purpose, a data user should delete data, but for the other purposes the data remain necessary and relevant. The principle's use of both the singular 'purpose' and the plural 'purposes' clearly envisages this situation. The solution is to attempt to segregate the use of the data into their various purposes and to ensure that all data which are not necessary for a purpose are deleted.

35. A firm publishes biographical data about its employees on its home page. One of these employees leaves the firm. The firm is able to hold on an internal database the necessary information about the former employee for many years for, say, legal claims. In contrast, it should, to comply with the fifth data protection principle, remove the personal data being held on the home page as soon as the employee leaves.

The ease with which data may be published and obtained on the World Wide Web acts also as a reason continually to check the relevance of data published on the World Wide Web. Data users should regularly check their website and other Internet sites to delete data which has served its purpose and is past its life-span. It is therefore not simply good commercial practice to update one's website; it may be required under data protection, and possibly other, laws.

Holding historical data

Data users are at liberty to hold indefinitely data that they will purely use for historical, statistical or research purposes[81].

81 Data Protection Act 1998, s 33(3).

No one or fixed rule

Too often, a general 'purge rule' is set for a personal data database. This cannot be correct unless all the data serves the same purpose and all the data subjects have an identical relationship with the data controller. Databases need to be constructed to allow deletion at particular times of particular types of data relating to particular types of data subject. No one or fixed rule can be adequate.

6. PROCESS IN ACCORDANCE WITH DATA SUBJECT RIGHTS

'A person is to be regarded as contravening the sixth principle if, but only if:

(a) he contravenes [a data subject's right to access personal data];
(b) he contravenes [a data subject's justified right to prevent processing likely to cause damage or distress];
(c) he contravenes [a data subject's right to prevent processing for the purposes of direct marketing];
(d) he contravenes [a data subject's justified rights in relation to automated decision making].'

Data subject access

Validity of requests

If a subject access request is ignored or is incorrectly complied with within the usual 40-day period[82], the Commissioner may make an access order forcing the data controller to reveal the data held on the subject. What is more serious, though, is that the *Commissioner* may also inspect the data held by the controller.

A valid subject access request must be made in writing[83] and to any valid address for the data controller. The request need not be in any particular form or style, and, data controllers may not impose a special format upon a data subject. The request is valid only when the appropriate fee is paid (being no more than £10.00).

36. A website is concerned that its staff may 'miss' a data subject access request being sent to them and so devise an online form, to allow requests to be made. Despite the form, an elderly gentleman sends a request (together with a £10 cheque) on paper to the website owner's registered office where it is ignored for two months. The website owner is at risk of an action, even though the gentleman utilised another medium to make his requests.

82 Data Protection Act 1998, ss 7(8) and 7(10) subject to any variation by the Secretary of State under s 7(11).
83 Data Protection Act 1998, s 7(7).

Data controllers need also only process a request where the data subject supplies him with the appropriate information both to satisfy himself as to the identity of the requesting person and the information being sought[84].

Frequency of requests

Part (a) of this sixth data protection principle is essentially duplicated by the rights accorded to data subjects in the Data Protection Act 1998, s 7. This section is relevant for data subjects whose data is stored on or off computers connected to the Internet[85].

A data subject may enforce their rights to access personal data where a data controller has not provided the personal data appropriately. Even then, the data controller has a discretion over what is a reasonable interval between requests[86]. Clearly, a website attracting over 500,000 unique users each day, and holding information on each of them, would be unable to satisfy the requirements of the principle if each individual made a request each week. The data controllers, when refusing for reasons of frequency, must have regard to: the nature of the data; the purpose of processing the data; and the frequency of altering those data[87].

37. An online secure spreadbetting site updates its 'credit risk' analysis on each of its members every 20 minutes. This allows it to extend the maximum line of credit to its customers at all times. Phillip makes a subject access request and within two days of making the request, he discovers that the site has now deemed his credit line to be zero. Bearing in mind the nature of the data, why the data is processed and the frequency of updating, it would be reasonable for Phillip to make a further request to discover what had changed.

When to provide data

Little of the Data Protection Act 1998 forces an Internet data controller to act in a particular manner with personal data. Generally the Act simply prohibits acting in that manner without having previously notified and sought consent to that effect. The consequence of a request under the sixth data protection principle, however, does force the data user to act. He must supply to the data subject the relevant information under s 7. In addition, data users must supply this information promptly, but at least within 40 days from receiving a request[88].

Data users should pay respect to this sixth principle by ensuring that, on constructing and programming their database, there is a simple way of extracting all the data relating to one individual. It is important for data users to note that

84 Data Protection Act 1998, s 7(3).
85 Readers should consult specialist texts on these general rights.
86 Data Protection Act 1998, s 8(3).
87 Data Protection Act 1998, s 8(4).
88 Data Protection Act 1998, ss 7(8) and 7(10). This 40-day period begins on the first day on which the controller has both the fee and request.

merely because a particular record has no reference to an individual's name does not mean that the information should not be provided to the subject. If the data user possesses sufficient information, wherever held or stored, to identify the individual, then the data can be classed as personal data, and so be requested by its subject. Where the data held on individuals are spread throughout many databases, throughout many buildings, it can be expensive and time-consuming to locate all the necessary data within the period set by the Act. This said, 40 days is the maximum period and so systems should be established early which allow a request to be processed rapidly.

Information disclosed on other individuals

A problem may arise where a data controller in complying with a subject access request would be disclosing information relating to an individual other than the individual making the request. The Act recognises this problem. In such circumstances a data controller is obliged to comply with the subject access request in only two situations. The first is where the other individual has consented to the disclosure of the information. The second situation is where it is reasonable in the circumstances to comply with the request without the consent of the other individual.

38. Teenze FM, a website for teenage girls, runs a feature called 'nightmare date of the month'. It invites its members to send in photographs and stories of disastrous dates to be posted on the site. June's 'winner' is horrified to see his picture appear on the site together with a totally fictitious story. He submits a subject access request in order to find out who nominated him without his knowledge. The site would arguably be breaching the confidentiality of the sender if it disclosed the nomination email containing these details without the consent of the sender.

What to provide

Data controllers cannot simply 'print out' their database entry for an individual. Indeed, doing merely this, complies with only one of seven requirements. These are listed and described below.

(i) Data controller to inform subject whether or not processing is being carried out in relation to data subject

In effect, the data controller must reply to a data subject whether or not they are holding or processing data. Because of potential difficulties involving misspelt or mistyped names, it may be safer for a data controller not merely to search on the precise details given by the subject, but also to use 'fuzzy logic' to search wider[89].

89 Data Protection Act 1998, s 7(1)(a).

39. Jane Isaacs is worried that an auction site has retained her personal details. She sends an email from her home email address together with £10 to constitute a subject access request. The data protection officer at the company incorrectly searches for the name 'Jane Isaac' and for her home email address; both searches return a negative result. The auction site would have been better advised to reply to Jane, seeking, as they are entitled under s 7(3) the reasonable information they need to search for Jane's personal data.

(ii) Data controller to give subject description of personal data

This can be thought of as a requirement to 'put the data into context'. It is an obligation to explain what the data 'means' to the data controller.

(iii) Data controller to give subject description of purposes for which data is processed

'Processing' is described earlier in this chapter and readers may want to refresh their memories before responding to this element of a data subject access request. What is crucial is to describe not merely what the data is, but how it is being utilised and processed.

40. An online photo developing company allows anyone to store digital images and other files on their servers. Revenue to support this flows from advertising and printing. Its research suggests that men tend to use the storage facilities to store pornographic material. They therefore target 'relevant' advertising at those of its members who are male with many image files stored. To comply with a subject access by a male, the company must therefore include details of this processing and not merely report the member's sex and number of files held.

(iv) Data controller to describe to subject recipients or classes of recipients of personal data

A recipient is defined as being any person, even an employee of the data controller, to whom data is disclosed in the course of processing the data. Data controllers do not need to disclose those recipients of data who receive it pursuant to a legal power, such as a police enquiry. Data controllers should be aware, therefore, that the suggested recipients of data in a fair collection notice or, privacy policy and notification can be confirmed by a data subject. Data controllers cannot hide their true processing of data.

41. TCI collects data from its membership and, for financial reasons, exports it for processing in Russia. A Russian company will therefore be a recipient of the data. This can consequently be discovered by any data subject. TCI will not be able to covertly send the data to Russia (potentially in breach of the eighth principle), without risk of it being discovered by any subject.

(v) Data controller to communicate to data subject in intelligible form the information constituting the personal data

The key aspect of this obligation is 'intelligible' form. Sending the data subject a series of zeros and ones may well provide the *data* to the subject; it does not provide the *information* underlying or surrounding the data. Data controllers must be prepared to disclose 'what the data means to them' not merely the data that has been recorded.

42. A business user of an online travel agency makes a valid subject access request. The agency provides a response detailing the user's name and address, the flights he has booked and a reference to 'cookie data' being 'AC8924EA29BBE'. To comply with the subject access request, the site should have resolved this cookie data into information making it clear what it means to the site.

(vi) Data controller to communicate to the data subject any available information on the sources of the data

Unlike under the 1984 Act, sources of data do not need to be specified to the Commissioner in the data controller's notification (then registration). The information to be provided as to the sources of the data is only that which is available to the data controller. Clearly, a 'scorched earth' policy of destroying all source information would leave the controller unable to provide any information to the data subject.

Data controllers must be warned, however, that with no information about the source of personal data they may find it more difficult to defend an action brought under the first principle. Similarly, unless the source's information is retained, it will be difficult for the data controller to prove that they took reasonable steps to confirm the accuracy of the data, under the fourth principle.

(vii) Data controller to inform data subject as to any logic involved in automated significant decision-taking, subject to the information being a trade secret

This applies only where the decision being automatically taken is the sole basis of something which may significantly affect the data subject. It is therefore safe to opine that, automatic processing of a cookie to determine which adverts to show or which books to recommend, will not fall within the remit of this section. Conversely, decisions taken relating to a person's creditworthiness are more likely to be deemed to be significant.

43. A car manufacturer establishes a site at which prospective customers may enter their name, telephone number and postcode to receive a telephone call from their nearest dealer. In truth, they also utilise the postcode to decide the potential affluence of the customer and prioritise their enquiry appropriately. This automated decision-taking is unlikely to be significant enough to justify needing to inform the data subject.

Preventing direct marketing, including emails

In the context of the Internet, a significant right is to prevent processing for direct marketing, at any time. Even where the relevant 'tick' boxes have been 'ticked' (or 'unticked') an individual may change their mind and prevent further direct marketing at any time. Databases must be constructed to allow such processing to be stopped at any time.

Direct marketing is widely defined as:

> 'the communication (by whatever means) of advertising or marketing material which is directed to particular individuals.'[90]

This definition certainly will encompass emails and instant messages whether sent automatically or processed individually by a human. This author believes that the definition also encompasses marketing included on a website which is 'directed' at a particular individual.

> **44. Forex4X.com uses cookies to enable its site to show particular information based on previous uses by the particular member. It does not send out emails or faxes to its members. Nevertheless, its members are entitled to prevent Forex4X from processing their data for the purposes of customising the site they view.**

Ceasing processing, not merely sending direct marketing

The subject's right is framed in terms of ceasing processing for the purposes of direct marketing. It is therefore a substantially wider right than one which merely prevents direct mail being sent subject to certain requirements. The right, once activated will prevent all data manipulation and mining activities, even where this processing does not result in material being sent.

Unlike many other provisions in the Act, data controllers cannot rely upon any exemptions. If they do not comply with a written request within a reasonable period[91], the subject may request that the court orders that the notice is complied with[92]. Data-intensive companies must ensure that the architecture of their databases is sophisticated enough to block this type of processing.

> **45. E-masp is an Application Service Provider which facilitates companies in targeting and sending relevant emails to their customers. In the usual course of events, any individual who indicates that they do not consent to receive mailings is simply not included in the final, compiled, list. Their details are, in contrast, still analysed and processed. E-masp must refine its database to ensure it is able to exclude blocked individuals from even the first batch processing well prior to any mailing itself.**

90 Data Protection Act 1998, s 11(3).
91 Data Protection Act 1998, s 11(1).
92 Data Protection Act 1998, s 11(2).

Preventing automated processing

There can be little doubt that computers are incredibly valuable when used to process personal data. Indeed, a whole sector of the IT industry, Customer Relationship Management, is fundamentally concerned with capturing, processing and better utilising personal data. These sophisticated 'back office' systems are increasingly utilised to process data on visitors to websites. They allow regulars to be greeted appropriately, allows orders to be tracked and requests pre-empted. In the broadest terms, they make automated decisions relating to personal data. Controllers of data need to consider whether this processing is 'solely' used to make decisions which 'significantly affect' an individual. If their systems do make such decisions, while no doubt very efficient, they are prone to subjects exercising their right under s 12 of the Act to prevent decisions being taken in that manner.

Significant effects

The Act and Directive provide a non-exhaustive list of significant issues. These include 'performance at work', 'creditworthiness', 'reliability' and 'conduct'.

Sole basis for decision

This aspect of the Act[93] and art 15 of the Directive is aimed at preventing computers making important decisions without humans being involved. Consequently, any human input into the decision, even where supported by volumes of automatically processed quantitative data, will bring the processing outside the ambit of s 12.

46. A busy recruitment department in a management consultancy builds a new online recruitment section to the firm's website. It requires that each candidate wanting to attend an open day enters their answers to a series of questions to create their VCV (Virtual Curriculum Vitae). To save reviewing certain applications by hand, the system automatically sends (a few hours later) a polite rejecting email to any candidate acknowledging less than a 2:2 in their first degree. Any candidate will be entitled to prevent the firm from taking such decisions in this way.

Exemptions

Automated decisions are exempt from the application of s 12 where they fall into one of a number of categories. These are where the effect of the decision is to grant the data subject a request relating to:

(a) considering whether to enter a contract with the subject;
(b) with a view to entering such a contract;
(c) in the course of performing such a contract.

93 Data Protection Act 1998, s 12(1).

Alternately, as long as the legitimate interests of the data subject are safeguarded, for example, permitted representations like an 'appeal', automated decisions can also be taken in relation to (1), (2) and (3) above[94].

47. RideLiketheWind is a 'name your price' website for businesspeople who would prefer to travel by private jet rather than traditional airlines. Financing deals are available to allow one to travel today and pay off the cost over a subsequent number of months. An individual becomes convinced that his requests to obtain credit are automatically refused because of his home postcode. Even if such an automated decision is significant enough, the decision is exempt because the individual is making the request of the website with the view to entering into the contract to buy a seat on credit.

Procedure to prevent

A subject must write to a data controller asking them not to take such an automated decision[95]. As soon as reasonably practical, the controller must reply confirming (or not) that the decision was so taken[96]. Within 21 days, the individual may then demand that a new, non-solely automated decision is taken[97]. A further 21 days may lapse before the controller must explain how they now intend to re-consider the decision[98]. The court can force the data controller to comply with the individual's request[99].

48. A data subject requests from a data user relevant information under the seventh principle and s 7. The data controller duly retrieves the pertinent data from the various relational databases and then realises that more data are held than has been notified or consented to by the data subject. If the data controller supplies all the data to the subject they are admitting processing data illegally. If the data user supplies the data only mentioned in the notification, they can be forced to comply with s 7(1)(a) which demands that all the data held by the controller must be supplied to the subject. The data controller must immediately contact the Commissioner and the data subject to rectify the data held and widen the notification if necessary for further processing.

7. Kept secure

> 'Appropriate technical and organisational measures shall be taken against unauthorised or processing of personal data and against accidental loss or destruction of or damage to personal data.'

This seventh data protection principle applies both to data controllers and data processors. It is part of the Data Protection Act 1998 that demands lawyers understand, at the least, the basics of computer security. Complying with this

94 Data Protection Act 1998, s 12(6) and (7).
95 Data Protection Act 1998, s 12(1).
96 Data Protection Act 1998, s 12(2)(a).
97 Data Protection Act 1998, s 12(2)(b).
98 Data Protection Act 1998, s 12(3).
99 Data Protection Act 1998, s 12(8).

part of the Act can be expensive. It is, however, essential that these controllers of personal data employ appropriate technological and supervisory methods to secure their subjects' data.

Security under the seventh principle

This principle tackles one of the most obvious tensions between the Internet and data protection. In the Data Protection Registrar's 1995 annual report it is stated that:

> '[i]n connecting to the Internet [data users and computer bureau operators] are entering an open environment which exists to facilitate the exchange of and the publication of information. It is inherently insecure.'

In contrast, data protection legislation attempts to ensure that personal data are not left in open environments but are stored in controlled, private environments. The seventh principle takes the idea of a controlled environment to its logical extreme by demanding that data are not simply secure from unauthorised or unlawful processing but also from alteration, destruction, damage and loss.

Appropriate

In the abstract it is difficult for a lawyer or security consultant to advise on the appropriate level of security for personal data. The Act's interpretation of this seventh principle highlights that one must have regard to 'state of technological development and cost of implementing the measures' appropriate to ensure a level of security taking into account the possible 'harm' and 'nature of data to be protected'[100]. The level of the security should be in proportion to the nature of the data and the harm which would ensue should there be a breach in security. For example, the Commissioner is likely to distinguish between personal data compiled from readily available sources, such as a list of names and addresses, and data which are sensitive[101] or are acquired in confidence[102]. On 18 January 2002, Eli Lilly, the pharmaceutical manufacturer of Prozac, settled a claim with the US FTC relating to sensitive data held on Prozac takers. It had established in March 2000 an email reminder service for those recovering from depression using Prozac. On 27 July 2001 it sought to tell all its subscribers by email that it was cancelling the service. Instead of sending each an individual email, or using the BCC field, an employee sent a group email to all the subscribers. Each was therefore able to see who else took Prozac. Not surprisingly, there were complaints about this disclosure of sensitive data and an investigation began in July 2001. The lesson for those needing to observe the seventh principle is simple. Even the greatest security systems can be useless if those using them are inappropriately qualified and trained.

100 Data Protection Act 1998, Sch 1, Pt II, para 9(a), (b).
101 Personal data that may be seen as sensitive are defined in s 2(3). These include: racial origins; political opinions, or religious or other beliefs; membership of a trade union; physical or mental health or sexual life; and criminal convictions or alleged offences.
102 1984 Data Protection Guideline 4, para 8.3.1.

Data controllers and data processors must make their own decisions as to the adequacy of their data security, but they should consider their obligation to the data subjects and the possibility of a compensation claim by a data subject.

Appropriate outsourcing and ASPs

Data controllers do not shirk their responsibilities under this principle by shunting off their data to a third party processor such as an outsourcing company or Application Service Provider. In fact, the data controller must not only carry out due diligence to check the processor provides sufficient guarantees as to security but also take reasonable steps to ensure compliance with the technical and organisational measures[103]. Further, data controllers are obliged to enter into a written contract with the processor under which the processor will only act under instructions from the data controller and under which the data processor will comply with equivalent obligations to those of the data controller[104].

49. ByteSyze is an office delivery fast-food outlet, well-utilised by London's IT community. Orders placed on their website are delivered within 64 minutes and the full range of 'geek food' (pizzas, high caffeine drinks etc) is offered. After a successful initial quarter, ByteSyze outsources their delivery to a squadron of motorcycle couriers. ByteSyze will be passing personal data to the courier companies and therefore must enquire and ensure that they take appropriate steps to protect the personal data.

Unauthorised

The seventh data protection principle stresses that security measures must be in place preventing unauthorised and unlawful processing of personal data. This does not refer solely to outsiders such as hackers; it is referring also to insiders who are acting outside the scope of their authority, potentially unlawfully. Controllers and processors should consider this authority from two angles: technical authority and social authority.

Technical authority

All equipment which stores, processes, transmits or discloses personal data must have passwords which only authorised people know. These passwords must not be the same for all aspects of data security within the organisation. Data controllers and data processors must treat distinctly those aspects of their equipment which they will use for activities relating to personal data.

To stop as early as is possible any security compromise it is advisable that each person granted the authority to access the personal data has an individual password. This, combined with an audit trail of all personal data, can permit a data

103 Data Protection Act 1998, Sch 1, Pt II, para 11(a), 11(b).
104 Data Protection Act 1998, Sch 1, Pt II, para 12(a), 12(b).

controller or data processor to 'trace' the human source of compromised data, and so prevent its reoccurrence. It is essential that this technical authority is granted by providing individuals each with a unique password, not by allocating one password for 'all personal data activities'. This latter method does not allow a data user to trace the source of a security leak as easily and results in one password being known by more people.

Social authority

Establishing a strict regime with passwords is not adequate unless there is also a strict regime over who has these passwords and how they are used. Data controllers and processors must give proper weight to the discretion and integrity of members of staff who are to have these passwords. They should be given adequate technical and data protection training; they should be made aware of the seriousness of their responsibilities. They should not process data outside of the appropriate consents and obligations of the data controller. If the unfortunate event occurs where a member of staff leaves the department, or is found to be unreliable, the data users must immediately 'lock out' that member from the system. There should be no 'old' or 'general' password for accessing personal data.

Processing

The obligation to take appropriate measures to prevent unauthorised and unlawful processing is obviously a wide obligation because of the all-encompassing definition of 'processing'. Some aspects of 'processing' are described below.

Organisation, adaptation or alteration

Certain data should be 'read-only': that is, the data cannot be altered or even deleted without appropriate authority. This authority is generally in the form of a password that allows the password-user to alter the 'read-write' properties of the data.

50. An Internet Service Provider allows its members to sign up to various services using an online form. As well as address and surname, one field of this form is the forename of the member. Unless it is clearly appropriate this particular field should retain a 'read-only' status. If it is freely able to be overwritten, it is feasible an accidental alteration will result in another member of the same family, at the same address, being treated as the data subject.

As is stated below, the safest solution is to have 'read-only' status both for data and the database structure along with regular, archival backups. If the backup is archival it will highlight any changes in data since the previous backup, so alerting a data user to a potential alteration. It will also allow the data user to regenerate an unaltered copy of the data, if necessary, from the previous backup. It is also recommended that only a limited set of reports and processes are available over a series of data.

Entitled deletion and backups

The fourth data protection principle entitles a data subject to delete data which it is inappropriate for a data user to continue holding. This required deletion will include both the personal data on the usual storage system and any backup copies of the data on whatever medium. Data users must therefore ensure that their archival backup system is sufficiently sophisticated to allow them to remove data fields without compromising the security of the remaining data which may breach the seventh data protection principle.

Destruction

The same security considerations apply to avoiding destruction, accidental or not, of data and avoiding alteration of data. Data users should classify as much data as possible as 'read-only' and maintain regular and frequent backups of the data. In this way, if data are destroyed on the main system, it is an easy task to regenerate those data. As above, data users should ensure that their backup facilities, while secure, do not prevent the deletion of personal data where this will be necessary to comply with a data subject's request.

Internet security issues

Connecting a computer to the Internet is easy and commonplace. But, with present levels of standard Internet security, going onto the Internet will result in the personal data held on the computer online becoming less secure. Data controllers and data processors must not rely on the inherent security on the Internet if they wish to avoid possible breaches of the seventh data protection principle. Some of the various ways that a data controller or data processors may tighten security are considered below[105].

Automatic-answer modems

A modem connected to the Internet that is set to accept incoming calls will weaken security. The mere fact that an outsider can access a computer which is holding personal data reduces the security of that data. Data controller or data processors should take expert advice from the manufacturers of their automatic-answer software on how to partition securely certain aspects of their storage system from third parties. They should also investigate how to encrypt the personal data left on the connected system[106].

105 Data controllers and data processors should take specialist advice; the comments on data security within this chapter are intended only to illustrate possible methods of improving security. The comments should not be implemented before checking with a security adviser that they are appropriate for the equipment and data in question.

106 The key to de-encrypt the data must not be stored on the computer storing the encrypted data.

Remote access

One of the advantages of the Internet and related networks is that it has made it possible for individuals easily to access computers from remote locations. This may be through a simple website, a Virtual Private Network (VPN), a bulletin board, an ftp site, a Telnet connection, or even a standard dial-up connection. All these methods, without tight security measures, can as easily allow an individual to leave data on the remote computer as to copy data from the computer.

Security should therefore be in place which, unless it can be justified otherwise, does not permit remote users to access all the personal data on the system: a firewall. The passwords and logins used by remote users should be 'rolled' on a frequent basis. Remote users should not use an automated login procedure that stores the login details and password on their computer. With this set-up, if someone steals the computer the entire security of the personal data is at risk.

Email transactions

If a data controller or data processor uses the email system to send personal data he should be aware that a standard email system is not completely secure. He must not rely on the security of the Internet itself. Again, a good policy is to use encryption on all emails which contain personal data. It must also be remembered that any email is both a transferral and a disclosure of personal data or information. Data controllers should appropriately notify for such an activity.

Web servers

By definition a web server is connected to the Internet. As much as is possible, these computers should not be used for storing data collected from the World Wide Web. The use of an online form on a home page to collect personal data from, for example, customers, should generate data which is either encrypted on the server or is transmitted automatically to a further computer beyond a firewall. Users of the web to collect personal data must also enlist expert advice to ensure that while such an online form is being transmitted to the server from the customer-client, the most stringent safety measures are in place. The transferral of personal data between the subject and the data user is the most insecure time for the subject's personal data. Subjects must be informed of this risk before they transmit the data particularly to web sites not utilising standard encryption methodology. Some sites 'pop up' a window allowing the subject to choose to transmit the data or to disconnect from the website.

Viruses

The Internet allows its users to 'view' documents on their screen, but it is also used to download material into the client computer. Sometimes this is with the knowledge of the user: he requests a file to download. At other times, the user may be unaware that the site on the Internet is accessing the user's computer and may be storing files and running programs on his computer. There is a real risk that with any file downloaded there will have been a computer virus in tow.

Viruses generally attach to programs, but have been found incubating in word processing documents and even innocent looking pictures. There have also been growing concerns that there is an increased risk of viruses being spread over the Internet owing to the more sophisticated, 'client-side' methods of presenting information on the World Wide Web such as Sun Microsystem's Java, Macromedia's Shockwave and Microsoft's Active X[107].

To take appropriate security measures, data processors and controllers must install virus scanning software set to screen regularly for viruses.

Network or intranet

All the above security issues are equally, if not more, relevant where an internal network or intranet is connected to the Internet. This may be through one computer connected to one modem or an established gateway, available to all users. The two scenarios pose risks to any personal data held on the network or intranet.

One computer to Internet

The ease with which one may connect a computer on an internal network to the Internet is almost inversely proportional to the risk involved with such a connection. That the connected computer does not hold or process personal data does not greatly reduce the threat to the personal data stored on the network. Because the computer is connected both to the Internet and the internal network it can act as a conduit for hacking attempts and the promulgation of viruses, network-wide. Data controllers and processors should therefore periodically check that no computer on an internal network is connected to the Internet without their knowledge. If one computer is to be connected, an appropriate technical and social security regime must exist.

Technically, the single computer should be appropriately firewalled from the main network; if it is not, it can form a very weak link in the data security of the network. The social security measures relate to the responsibility of those persons who will use the connected computer. Employers should give employees clear guidelines about whether they are permitted to download software; it is safer not to download. Employees should have clear instructions never to divulge any internal passwords to any other individual using email or any other means.

Network hacking

Hacking into the internal network from the Internet is always a great threat where any computer on the network is connected to the Internet. In this situation, a hacker can attach directly into the connected computer and, from there, may be able to penetrate the internal security of the network. Clearly this poses a substantial risk to any personal data on the network, previously treated as

107 '[Digital signatures] are clearly of great importance for executable code on the web': Tim Berners-Lee, W3C Director, viewed as the creator of the World Wide Web; 'Industry embraces Microsoft's Internet digital signature', Microsoft Press Release, PR1382/14 March 1996.

being secure. The risk from hacking is currently not as significant, however, as the threat from viruses and other rogue programs.

Network viruses

Every user who has access to the Internet will be tempted to download a file. In doing so, as described above[108] the user risks introducing a virus to the client computer. But where this computer is connected to an internal network, the virus can spread throughout the network threatening the destruction and alteration of any personal data held within the network. Operators at a data controller and processor should install and update anti-virus programs throughout the network, and where possible utilise virus antidote software to screen for viruses as software and emails are being downloaded from the Internet.

8. Prohibition against data transfers

> 'Personal data shall not be transferred to a country or territory outside the European Economic Area, unless that country or territory ensures an adequate level of protection for the rights and freedoms of data subjects in relation to the processing of personal data.'

The harmonisation of data protection rules in the EU aims to ensure the free movement of information including personal data between Member States whilst at the same time ensuring a high level of protection for any person concerned. In the case of non-EEA countries, the Directive 95/46/EC therefore requires Member States permit transfers of personal data only where there is 'adequate protection' in a particular country for such data, unless one of a limited number of specific exemptions applies. There are accordingly a number of ways available in order to facilitate transfers of personal data avoiding the prohibition of the eighth principle.

EU publication of a country's adequacy

The European Commission has the authority to publish findings that a regime in a particular State ensures an adequate level of protection for the rights and freedoms of data subjects. Transfers to such states will therefore be treated in the same way as transfers to an EEA State. At the time of writing, Switzerland, Hungary and Canada (although not in the case of the latter in relation to all types of personal data) have been approved in this manner.

US Safe Harbour Scheme

Under this self-regulatory scheme, US companies signed up to the scheme and complying with the rules issued by the US Department of Commerce are

108 See 'Viruses', at p 388.

recognised[109] as offering adequate protection. Businesses have been markedly slow in signing up to the US Safe Harbour, however[110]. Most are evidently preferring to take a 'wait and see' approach, before investing the effort and resources required in order to join.

51. A UK-based advertising company is considering using a third party company to manage its personnel databases. It is choosing between companies based in Norway, Holland, Canada, the US and New Zealand. The transfer to the US will contravene the eighth principle unless the company has signed up to the Safe Harbour Scheme or one of the other exemptions applies. Another exemption must apply with respect to New Zealand, but an automatic assumption of adequacy exists in relation to the other jurisdictions.

Own assessment of adequacy

Data controllers are open to make their own findings as to whether the level of protection afforded by all the circumstances of a particular case is adequate when weighed against the potential risks to the rights and freedoms of data subjects which may arise.

Although this may sound an easy option it carries grave risks and will demand that each transfer is considered carefully on a case-by-case basis. Unsurprisingly, the Information Commissioner warns in her official guidance on the subject[111] that a data controller is likely to consider the other options instead since self-assessment it is a time-intensive exemption with no guarantee of being correct and significant sanctions if the conclusion is incorrect.

For businesses with branches in several different European jurisdictions, the key problem is that national data protection authorities apply their own interpretations of the concept of 'adequacy'. This makes it extremely problematic to establish a suitable and practical transfer procedure which can be used again and again from several countries within the EU.

Standard contractual clauses

EU data protection authorities are obliged[112] to recognise that transfers have adequate protection where the model clauses approved by the EU Commission are used.

There are two different sets of model clauses:

(1) *Controller to Processor*, for the transfer of personal data from data controllers in the EU to processors (subcontractor) established in non-EU

109 European Parliament resolution of July 2000.

110 As at 14 November 2002, only 259 US organisations had signed up.

111 'The Commissioner's legal analysis and suggested good practice approach to assessing adequacy including consideration of the issue of contractual solutions' first issued in July 1999.

112 Except in exceptional circumstances eg where a competent authority has established that the data importer has not respected the contractual clauses or there is a substantial likelihood that the standard contractual clauses are not being or will not be complied with and the continuing transfer would create an imminent risk of grave harm to the data subjects.

countries[113] under which the data exporter instructs its subcontractor to treat the data with full respect of the EU data protection requirements and guaranteeing that suitable technical and security measures are in place in the country to which they are sent.

(2) *Controller to Controller* for the transfer of data from a data controller in the EU to another data controller outside the EC[114].

Use of the model clauses offers an attractive pan-European approach to businesses but does not offer room for flexibility. Parties are free to agree to *add* other clauses where they do not contradict, directly or indirectly the standard contractual clauses. The model contracts may not however be changed in other ways. Essentially, data controllers are required therefore to follow the clauses word-for-word 'filling in the blanks'. Where businesses may seek to amend the clauses to suit their own business needs (even where this does not alter the meaning or effect of any clause), the Information Commissioner has stated that this will not amount to use authorised by her under[115] the Act. In such a situation, it would then be up to the data controller to take its own view that either the transfer gives data subjects sufficient safeguards with the resulting risks that this brings. Alternatively, it should seek individual approval for that contract.

At the time of writing, a more business-friendly version of the Model Contract, redrafted by a consortium of business and trade associations, is currently awaiting approval from the EU Commission.

Approval on a case-by-case basis

Under art 26(2), Directive 95/46/EC, national authorities may authorise on a case-by-case basis specific transfers to a country outside the EEA where the data exporter in the EU is able to demonstrate that adequate safeguards are in place to protect the personal data protection rights of the data subjects. This is usually through a contractual arrangement made between the exporter and the importer which are then submitted to the national authority for approval.

This is a lengthy and difficult process which is not suitable for organisations which will be regularly sending data abroad. This option is particularly cumbersome since each EU data protection authority has a different procedure for granting such approval, different time scales, formalities and grounds for assessment.

At the time of writing, the UK Information Commissioner has not yet granted an individual approval in this way.

Other derogations

Under art 26(1), Directive 95/46/EC, data may be transferred to a country outside of the EEA where:

113 The European Commission adopted a Decision on 29 December 2001 effective from 3 April 2002.

114 As contained in the European Commission Decision on Standard Contractual Clauses for the transfer of personal data to third countries under Directive 95/46/EC.

115 Sch 4, para 9.

(1) the data subject has given his consent unambiguously to the proposed transfer; or
(2) the transfers necessary for the performance of a contract between the data subject and the controller or the implementation of pre-contractual measures taken in response to the data subjects request; or
(3) the transfer is necessary for the conclusion or performance of a contract concluded in the interests of the data subject between the controller and a third party; or
(4) the transfer is necessary or legally required on important public interest grounds, or for the establishment, exercise or defence of legal claims; or
(5) the transfer is necessary in order to protect the vital interests of the data subject; or
(6) the transfer is made from a register which according to laws or regulations is intended to provide information to the public and which is open to consultation either by the public in general or by any person who can demonstrate a legitimate interest, to the extent that the conditions laid down by the law for consultation are fulfilled in the particular case.

In practice, the first two of these will be the most attractive to data controllers. It will be relatively straightforward for a data controller to incorporate consent provisions at the point of data capture and at the time that other consents are being obtained (eg for direct marketing). Careful attention will have to be had to properly informing individuals what they are consenting to, however, in order to ensure that their consent is 'unambiguous'. Data controllers must also remember that consent can always be revoked at any time and that a clear audit trail evidencing such consent will be needed.

Data controllers relying on derogation (b) must also remember that the threshold for demonstrating that processing is 'necessary' for the performance of a contract is a high one. In illustration, this may not always be an attractive option for multinational companies transferring employees' personal data to other branches.

52. Mexican Bliss is an online travel agent. It specialises in honeymoons and arranges everything for the happy couple from transfers to and from the airports to champagne on arrival. It is obviously necessary that Mexican Bliss transfers the names of the honeymoon couple to the hotel in Mexico.

There is a clear message in this discussion. There is no obvious or automatic method for transferring personal data outside the EEA. Transfers are not impossible but the needs of a data controller, the purpose and scope of the transfer and therefore the exemptions to the eighth principle must be considered on a case-by-case basis.

DIRECT MARKETING – REQUIREMENTS UNDER ADDITIONAL LEGISLATION

In addition to a data subject's underlying right to prevent the sending to them of direct marketing messages and the principle of fair collection under the Act, those wanting to send such mailshots must also comply with the consent and information requirements of certain other legislation. This includes the

Telecoms Regulations, the Electronic Commerce Regulations 2002 and the Electronic Communications Directive.

Consent to send marketing emails

The sending of unsolicited marketing messages by email is not specifically covered by the current in-force legislation. The Telecoms Directive refers only to 'calls' and 'called lines'. Some countries have interpreted the Directive in their national legislation to require prior positive (or 'opt-in') consent for unsolicited marketing emails[116]. Others have not imposed this higher standard and the online industry has been busy setting up opt-out registries in accordance with the Electronic Commerce Directive[117].

There are apparent contradictions between these various European directives. There is also an un-harmonised approach across Europe and lack of uniformity of trade practices. It is not therefore surprising that most businesses are still unclear as to the obligations imposed upon them. Many have taken the risk of ignoring the issue altogether. In the UK, businesses should be wary of assuming that a loophole exists in this confusion that is open for exploitation. Indiscriminate sending of marketing emails without consideration for the recipient's rights is contrary to the Act. Also, the Information Commissioner has stated that under the Telecoms Regulations, unsolicited marketing emails may not be sent in the UK where recipients have previously indicated that they do not wish to receive such 'calls'. Although actions against offenders are rare in comparison to the US, the negative publicity generated by those that have been taken up is a clear warning to all.

In an attempt to finalise the position the Electronic Communications Directive also addresses email consent requirements. Article 13 gives Member States no option. Unsolicted emails shall not be allowed 'without the consent of the subscribers concerned'; this is basically an opt-in option. This author is of the opinion that the legislation is unlikely to have any practical effect. EU measures cannot stem the EU-bound flow of junk email from outside the EU, and in any event, 'spammers' are, by definition, no respectors of legal niceties.

A word on opt-in and opt-out consent

Reference is constantly made to the distinction between the need for 'opt-in' or 'opt-out' consent and therefore it is useful to consider the meaning behind these concepts. Complicating matters further, the European Parliament uses the term 'soft opt-in' in its justifications for its proposed changes to the Electronic Communications Directive[118]. These terms are not in fact used in the legislation. In some respects, the simple terms opt-in and opt-out do help make the legislative requirements easier to understand in practical terms and have become entrenched in the language used by members of industry and the law profession alike.

116 Presently Austria, Denmark, Finland, Germany and Italy.

117 This aspect of the Directive is not implemented in the UK under the Electronic Commerce (EC Directive) Regulations 2002. It obliges businesses to consult a general-purpose opt-out list (national, European or transnational) which may prevent them from sending commercial communications to potential customers which have notified their desire not to be contacted.

118 22 April 2002, FINAL, A5-01301/2002.

As a guide, opt-in requires that a positive act is needed before processing in order to signify the intention and therefore consent of the data subject. The data subject has given 'prior consent' or 'previously notified' the data controller of their consent. This may be achieved, for example, through use of a tick box, or signature of a contract containing such a term. Opt-out refers to the requirement only that the individual has not yet indicated[119] before or at the time that processing commences that they object to such processing. Thus use may be made of a statement informing a data subject that if they do not wish their data to be processed for this purpose then they should contact this address/number etc or tick a given box.

53. Tunz4U sells games for mobile phones from its website. It cold-calls previous phone customers who have not expressed any objection to receiving such calls and intends to follow this up with a demo sent to them by email attachment. Tunz4U will need also to ensure that the customers have not objected to being contacted directly by email and that residents of countries with an opt-in requirement are asked directly whether they can be contacted in this way.

Information requirements

The Telecoms Regulations require that senders of unsolicited direct marketing emails identify themselves and if requested by the recipient, provide an address or a freephone number on which they can be reached. Similarly, the Electronic Commerce (EC Directive) Regulations 2002 require that marketing communications are subject to transparency requirements and must be easily identifiable as such. And, as if not to be outdone, the Electronic Communications Directive, art 13(4) also prohibits 'disguising or concealing' the sender's identity.

JURISDICTION OF DATA PROTECTION

The global reach of the Internet makes it vital that its users are aware of the English law that may impinge on them.

Territorial reach of the Act

Section 5 contains details of those to whom the Act applies. It applies to both data controllers established and not established in the UK under different circumstances. First, therefore, one must determine whether or not a data controller is established in the UK. Depending on the place of establishment, one must then determine details relating to the processing taking place. These complex issues need to be examined in detail.

119 For the time being, since as mentioned, in accordance with the sixth principle, this can be revoked at any time.

Jurisdiction over data controllers

There is a two-stage test to assess whether the Act applies in situations with a foreign element. First, where is the data controller established; second, what is the nature of the processing.

Place of establishment

There are four specific situations where a data controller will be deemed established in the UK. In addition, it is submitted there is a general test of establishment which is wider in interpretation than the four specific situations amalgamated.

The four specific situations are[120] an individual who is ordinarily resident in the UK; a body incorporated under the law of, or of any part, of the UK; and, any person who does not fall within the previous three situations but maintains in the UK a regular practice or office, branch, agency through which he carries out any activity.

While the first three concepts of 'residence', 'incorporation' and 'unincorporated association' are relatively straightforward legal constructs, the final concept needs investigation. For example, if a US company has no employees in the UK, and no equipment in the UK, but has a group of UK-established individuals who work on the company's behalf, is the US company under the jurisdiction of the Act?

It is submitted that to answer such a question one must refer to both art 4 and recital 19 of the Directive. These clarify that the concept of 'establishment' is not determined by legal 'personalities' but by 'effective and real exercise of activity through stable relationships'. It follows that the US company mentioned above is likely to be seen as being 'established' (for the purposes of this but maybe no other Act) in the UK.

Finally, it is possible for one data controller to be deemed established in more than one member state. In such a situation (likely for multinationals) the controller must ensure that such establishment complies with the local national law[121].

Established in the UK

If the previous test determines that the data controller is established in the UK, one further test is applied to determine whether the controller is fully within the jurisdiction of the Act. This second test is whether or not the data are processed in the context of that establishment[122].

The word 'context' is not defined by the Act, nor by the Directive. Taking the ordinary meaning of 'context', it is difficult to conceive of processing being carried out by a UK establishment that would not be in the 'context' of that establishment. It seems likely, therefore, that any data controller established, per the Act, in the UK will process personal data under the jurisdiction of the Act.

120 Data Protection Act 1998, s 5(3)(a), (b), (c) and (d).
121 Directive 95/46/EC, art 4(a).
122 Data Protection Act 1998, s 5(1)(a).

Established outside UK and other EEA states

Where a data controller is deemed to be established outside the UK and other EEA states, they may still fall within the jurisdiction of the Act. These data controllers fall within the jurisdiction of the Act where they also meet a second 'equipment' test. This 'equipment' test is that the foreign controller must use equipment in the UK for processing data otherwise than for the purposes of transit through the UK[123]. The first issue to address is that this 'equipment' may be automated and that would be enough to bring the foreign controller within the ambit of the Act. The second issue is that only 'transmission' equipment (such as routers and switches) will not bring the controller under the auspices of the Act.

54. A US corporation houses all its servers, bar one, in the United States. This one non-US server sits in Telehouse in London, England and processes the credit card transactions for the corporation. Its work is generated from the US and no UK company or individual has the right to access the data stored on the server. The US company is established in a non-EEA state but uses equipment in the UK to process its data. It must comply with the Data Protection Act 1998.

55. A US Internet Service Provider prides itself on allowing its members to access their accounts from anywhere in the world, on any computer they choose. The Provider has a server in every major jurisdiction of the world, each with a complete set of data. One of the features of the system is that its members do not store their address book of email addresses on their computer, but on the Provider's servers. This has the result that its members can process personal data using the Provider's equipment. If one of the servers is in the UK, the Provider will be resident here and will be governed by the Data Protection Act 1998.

JURISDICTION UNDER THE MODEL CONTRACT CLAUSES

Jurisdiction and applicable law

The model clauses are governed by the law of the Member State in which the data exporter is established and both parties agree to:

> 'accept the decision of the data subject:
> (a) to refer [a dispute] to mediation by an independent person or, where applicable by the supervisory authority;
> (b) to refer the dispute to the courts in the Member State in which the data exported is established.[123]
> This is therefore without prejudice to the data subjects' rights to seek remedies in accordance with other provisions of national or international law.'

123 Data Protection Act 1998, s 5(1)(b).

Liability

Certain clauses protecting the rights of data subjects[124] require that the parties accept joint and several liability where it is necessary to compensate individuals as a result of the violation of the contract. Data subjects are therefore entitled in such circumstances to seek compensation from either the exporter, importer or both. This is intended to prevent any difficulty in establishing exactly who is responsible for the violation from preventing the pursuit of a claim. An EU company required to pay compensation to an individual as a result of a violation committed by the data importer can seek compensation from the importer under the indemnity clause which arguably imposes a heavy burden on the exporter.

56. A French Internet solutions business consultancy sends to a software company in Japan details of individuals who have expressed an interest in purchasing a solution using their software. The companies have entered into a contract for the transfer of this data diligently following the model contract clauses approved by the European Commission. As a result of a security negligence breach by the Japanese company, a reputable Dutch client has their database hacked into causing extensive damage. The Dutch client can seek compensation from the French company and if successful in his claim, the French company can seek financial redress from the Japanese company under the indemnity clause.

124 Clause 7.
125 See clause 3 on third party beneficiaries.

Chapter Seven

Taxation

Retail and wholesale commercial activities on the Internet include those that equate to traditional mail order, the sale and transfer of digital material, advertising and the provision of services. Moreover, as retail methodologies and the relevant technologies develop it can be assumed that more new and innovative business unknown in the non-virtual world will be created. This flurry of new activity poses a range of taxation questions. This chapter addresses the following.

1. What are the tax considerations of starting an Internet business?
2. What is the tax treatment of digital cash/payments?
3. Because the Internet is transnational, what are the issues of international taxation and tax planning?
4. How does Value Added Tax (VAT) apply to supplies made over the Internet?

In examining these topics it is important to bear in mind that tax policy can have an important impact upon the creation of online and ecommerce businesses and this can equally have a reciprocal effect on tax policy. Thus, for example, in recent years there has been an explosion in offshore gambling sites intended to circumvent the imposition of UK betting duty. The direct effect of this development was the abolition of general betting duty in the March 2001 budget and its replacement with a tax on bookmakers' gross profits.

Liability to tax in the UK is, in the main, imposed by a series of Finance Acts following the Budget each year (in recent years there have normally been two). Periodically the Finance Acts and other taxing statutes are consolidated: the most recent consolidating legislation is the Income and Corporation Taxes Act 1988 (ICTA 1988), commonly called the Taxes Act 1988; also the Taxation of Chargeable Gains Act 1992 (TCGA 1992) and the Capital Allowances Act 2001 (CAA 2001). All of this legislation is amended frequently[1].

Other than VAT, tax is administered by the Inland Revenue under the Taxes Management Act 1970. The basic system is that a taxpayer (or his accountant) completes a tax return and the Inland Revenue then produces an assessment. Tax is payable in accordance with the assessment unless the taxpayer appeals against it. Since 1996 a system of self-assessment has been introduced, whereby the taxpayer is permitted to calculate his own tax liability. Similarly companies are now subject to a self-assessment system.

1 For the legislation currently in force, see Butterworths' Yellow Tax Handbook published annually.

For most taxpayers the guidance issued by the Inland Revenue is sufficient to enable the correct amount of tax to be paid, and so there is no need to resort to the underlying law. It is certain that the novelty of the Internet is giving rise to fresh questions of tax law; accordingly it is perhaps worth discussing the appeal procedure in a little detail. An appeal against an assessment or a decision of a tax inspector may be on any grounds. The appeal is heard by one of two tribunals: the General Commissioners or the Special Commissioners. A hearing before either body of Commissioners is similar to other legal proceedings in the UK, except that the strict rules of evidence do not apply, and usually each side bears its own costs. Decisions of the Commissioners are subject to a right of appeal to the High Court, and thereafter to the Court of Appeal and the House of Lords. It is sometimes possible to leapfrog so as to omit either the High Court stage or the Court of Appeal stage.

Tax appeals tend to be on pure questions of law, usually questions of statutory construction. Due to the general public interest it is not uncommon for tax appeals to proceed all the way to the House of Lords, and thus besides the statutes mentioned above there is a strong body of judge-made law. The well-known Hansard case *Pepper v Hart*[2] is one such example; another example is *Furniss v Dawson*[3], a very important case which sometimes enables the courts to disregard artificial transactions done purely for tax avoidance purposes.

The tax year runs from 6 April to 5 April in the following year. Individuals pay income tax on their year's income at the basic rate; above a certain threshold higher rates of income tax apply.

Sole traders are, of course, individuals and so are liable to income tax, although their trading income is computed from profit and loss accounts drawn up in the same manner[4] as those of a company. Partners in a partnership are also taxed as individuals, although a few special rules apply. In addition to income tax, individuals must pay capital gains tax on capital profits.

Where an individual derives income from being an employee, then under the PAYE scheme income tax is deducted from each payment of salary; it is normally mandatory for the employer to operate this scheme, even if there is only a single employee and the employer is a private individual.

Companies pay corporation tax on both income and capital profits. Corporation tax is calculated in respect of each accounting period of a company; accounting periods normally last one year, but do not have to coincide with the tax year. Advanced corporation tax (ACT) was abolished in April 1999[5].

STARTING UP AN INTERNET BUSINESS

Clearly, tax planning is a essential element of any new business start-up. Persons setting up a new business from scratch are well advised to consider what type of business structure to use.

A limited company is perhaps the most common vehicle for such businesses. It may, however, not be the most appropriate. The protection offered by limited liability may be illusory where shareholders or directors are in practice required

2 [1993] 1 All ER 42, HL.
3 [1984] 1 All ER 530, HL.
4 Trading income is computed under the 'Schedule D' rules, found in ICTA 1988, ss 18 and 53.
5 Finance Act 1998, s 31.

to guarantee its debts. Further, from a tax perspective, a limited company is not necessarily the most sensible idea: for a small but successful business sometimes a partnership provides the best solution. The reason is that if a company is used the shareholders and the company together pay tax on distributed income at an effective rate of approximately 50% (this assumes the shareholders are subject to higher rate income tax at 40%), whereas the partners in a partnership pay tax at a maximum of 40%. However, the advantage of a company is that retained profits are subject only to corporation tax which is normally set at a lower level in an attempt to encourage growth. A further factor which advisers should bear in mind is that it is relatively easy to incorporate a business which has previously been conducted by a sole trader or a small partnership[6]; it is harder to do this in reverse[7].

1. Alex and Bill decide to set up an ecommerce company to develop and sell their online debugging package Nitscope. They decide to form a company, Nitscope Ltd (having been unsuccessful at attracting external investment they persuade their parents to take out second mortgages in order to secure its bank overdraft). In its first year, before taking into account the salaries of Alex and Bill, Nitscope makes a profit of £25,000: it makes little difference to the overall tax and National Insurance contribution bill whether that is paid as salary or as dividends; nor would it make much difference if Nitscope were a partnership. In the second year the business does much better since, even though it is essentially a two-man band, Nitscope is able to generate large sales through its website. Before taking into account Alex and Bill's salaries, the company makes a profit of £1,000,000. In this case a significant amount of tax and National Insurance contributions could be saved if Nitscope were a partnership rather than a company. Furthermore on the sale of the business the capital gains tax position could be improved.

Expenditure relating to the Internet – is it deductible?

A taxation question commonly of concern to businesses is whether items of expenditure are deductible in computing the amount of taxable profits. The relevant legislation is simple: s 74(1) of the Taxes Act 1988 provides that in computing the amount of the profits to be charged with tax

> 'no sum shall be deducted in respect of –
> (a) any disbursements or expenses, not being money wholly and exclusively laid out or expended for the purposes of the trade, profession or vocation . . .'

In general, expenditure on establishing a website will be an expense incurred wholly and exclusively for the purposes of the trade, and thus it will be a deductible business expenditure. This should even be the case where the material

6 Capital gains are rolled over into the company – see TCGA 1992, s 162.
7 Fuller considerations may be found in the chapter 'Choice of business medium' in *Revenue Law – Principles and Practice* by Chris Whitehouse (Butterworths, republished annually).

provided online is free of charge to users, since even then any expenditure incurred in making the material available has presumably been incurred in order to market products or otherwise to provide publicity for the business.

Capital allowances

Expenditure on capital items used in the business is treated in a different way: capital expenses are not deductible in computing trading profits. However, the system of capital allowances does permit some kinds of capital expenditure to be taken into account over a period of years. The most important kind is expenditure on 'plant and machinery'. These words are not defined in the legislation, but 'plant' has been held[8] to include whatever apparatus is used by a businessman for carrying on his business. An important exclusion is expenditure on the premises from which business is conducted: this does not qualify for allowances as plant and machinery (but note that there is a parallel system[9] of industrial buildings allowances that applies to factories and the like, and which can also extend to office buildings)[10]. Computers, servers, telecommunications equipment and other electronic apparatus will qualify for capital allowances under the heading 'plant' (despite the common usage of the word 'machine' as a synonym for computer, in a capital allowances context 'machinery' means apparatus having moving parts and thus would not normally apply to electronic apparatus). Normal domestic mains electricity services do not qualify as plant, being part of the premises, but special electrical installations 'provided mainly' for computers and other equipment do qualify[11]. Wiring and other links between equipment also qualify as plant, even if forming part of the structure of an office building[12].

Expenditure on computer software (if it is not revenue expenditure) always qualifies for capital allowances: s 71 of the Capital Allowances Act 2001 provides:

> '(1) For the purposes of this Part computer software is treated as plant (whether or not it would constitute plant apart from this section).
> (2) If a person carrying on a qualifying activity incurs capital expenditure in acquiring, for the purposes of the qualifying activity, a right to use or otherwise deal with computer software, this Part applies as if –
> (a) the right and the software to which it relates were plant,
> (b) the plant were provided for the purposes of the qualifying activity, and
> (c) so long as the person is entitled to the right, the person owned the plant as a result of incurring the capital expenditure.'

This applies to all software, whether an off-the-shelf package (even if nothing is purchased but a licence to use the software), or software that is bundled with

8 *Yarmouth v France* (1887) 19 QBD 647, 4 TLR 1.
9 CAA 2001, Pt 3 (ss 271–360).
10 CAA 2001, ss 271(1) and 277(1).
11 *Cole Bros Ltd v Phillips* [1982] 2 All ER 247, HL; provisions recently enacted confirm the decision in that case – see CAA 2001, s 23, List C, Item 2.
12 CAA 2001, s 23, List C, Item 8.

hardware, or bespoke software. Similarly, capital allowances are available in respect of the cost of developing software in-house, assuming that is a capital expense.

By virtue of the CAA 2001 special provisions also exist for the promotion of UK ebusiness[13].

Taxation of video and audio downloads

Certain payments in respect of foreign-owned copyright material are subject to deduction of income tax at source, otherwise known as withholding tax. The rule applies if the 'usual place of abode' of the owner of the copyright is not within the UK, and catches any payment of, or on account of, royalties or sums paid periodically for or in respect of that copyright[14].
Royalty payments can be defined as payments of:

> 'any kind received as a consideration for the use of or the right to use, any copyright or any literary, artistic or scientific work, including cinematograph films, any patent, trademark, design or plan, secret formula or process, or for information concerning industrial, commercial or scientific experience.'[15]

Despite the above definition, video recordings and films are specifically excluded from the rule, as are their soundtracks if not separately exploited: thus 'video on demand' services provided over the web are likely not to be caught, so long as it can be established that the copyright exploited is a copyright in a video recording or cinematograph film.

Payments for 'audio on demand' and software licences are potentially caught however. The downloading and subsequent licensing of such material for use by a single user for a one-off payment would not be subject to withholding tax, since the payment in that case would not be a royalty nor would any sum be paid periodically: but the commercial arrangements adopted by large users, for example UK-based content providers, may well be subject to this rule. Note that by virtue of the double taxation treaties between the UK and many countries, the application of this rule may differ depending on the country of residence of the copyright owner[16].

Electronic Money

'Electronic Money' is used here as a broad term applying to a range of transaction payment media. At one end of the spectrum it includes payment methods similar to traditional debit cards and based on the transfer of funds between bank accounts. At the other, it embraces new forms of currency based on software systems that operate independently of the banking system. Certain

13 See for example s 45.
14 ICTA 1988, s 536.
15 OECD Model Treaty.
16 See 'International taxation', below.

commentators have suggested that the anonymous nature of payments made using software-based systems will make the task of tax collection impossible for national authorities. The consideration of such difficulties is beyond the scope of the present work. However, insofar as digital cash transactions do remain identifiable, it is suggested that its use will not substantially alter the tax treatment of any person in the UK.

Taxing legislation is concerned with the bottom line: the profits of a company or the annual income of an individual. It is not concerned with the details of individual transactions nor the form that a company's assets may take from time to time. The precise method used to calculate profits is largely a matter of accountancy practice, given that almost all businesses are subject to tax on an accruals basis. For example, the acquisition of a right to receive payment may add to the taxable profits even though payment has not yet been received, and the incurring of future liabilities may similarly be taken into account to reduce profits; sometimes even contingent liabilities may be taken into account. The details of the system used do not matter: it is immaterial whether digital tokens are prepaid, or whether Internet transactions give rise to electronic money debits after the event. So long as a reasonably reliable system of exchanging digital cash is in use then a person's accrued rights and liabilities in respect of that system should properly have exactly the same effect upon taxable profits as do accrued rights and liabilities in respect of a bank account.

Residence and the source of profits

The use of the Internet will not change the residence of a company since this depends upon where it is incorporated and where it is managed and controlled[17]. However, the use of the Internet may have an effect on the country in which profits are considered to arise. For a UK-incorporated company there will be no practical consequences, since such a company is required to pay tax in the UK on its profits wherever arising[18]; the same applies to an individual resident in the UK. A foreign resident, on the other hand, whether a company or an individual, is only assessable in respect of profits from a trade exercised in the UK[19]. Trading in the UK is to be distinguished from trading with the UK[20]: is the trade conducted in the UK, or is the only connection with the UK that orders are obtained in this country? A common test is whether the contracts are concluded in the UK, although where the circumstances render other factors more important then these other factors may be taken into account[21].

Even if it is trading in the UK and thus taxable in the UK on the profits arising, a foreign resident company only becomes liable to pay corporation tax if it is trading through a branch or agency in the UK. If this is not the case it merely pays income tax at the basic rate[22]. Unless there are special trading arrangements in force it seems very likely that a foreign-resident company trading in the

17 See 'International taxation' below.
18 Schedule D (a)(ii) – see ICTA 1988, s 8(1).
19 Schedule D (a)(iii) – see ICTA 1988, s 18(1).
20 *Grainger & Son v Gough* [1896] AC 325, 3 TC 462, HL.
21 See *Firestone Tyre and Rubber Co Ltd v Lewellin* [1957] 1 All ER 561, 37 TC 111, HL.
22 ICTA 1988, s 1(2)(a).

UK via the Internet will not be doing so through a branch or agency, since the various UK routers and Internet Service Providers cannot be considered to be agents of the foreign company: their machinery is simply automatic machinery transmitting packets.

Those owning the infrastructure of the Internet may have cables or other links extending into many countries, and may thus make profits in many countries: however, an early Privy Council case[23–24] concerning the transmission of telegrams would appear to indicate that, in the case of a hub-star network, the source of profits is located in the country where the hub is situated.

INTERNATIONAL TAXATION

UK taxation is based on the relevant party's place of residence. For a individual, 'residence' means 'to dwell permanently or for a considerable time, to have one's settled or usual abode, to live in or at a particular place'[25]. Most countries tax their residents on their worldwide income, but tax non-residents only on income actually earned in that country. This applies both to individuals and to businesses. It is thus possible for income to be taxable in two countries simultaneously, but this situation is mitigated by Double Taxation Treaties which have the effect that tax is only charged in one or other of the two countries, or sometimes that a part of the tax is chargeable in each country. Not every pair of countries has a Double Taxation Treaty. The UK, which has treaties with approximately one hundred countries, has the most extensive network.

Treaties are almost always bilateral and are often based upon a model treaty created by the Organisation for Economic Co-operation and Development. Treaties on the OECD model tax a business on the basis of the location of its 'permanent establishment' (PE)[26]. If there are permanent establishments in both countries, then such of the income as can be attributed to each establishment should be taxed in each respective country. There is also a UN model treaty which is often used by developing countries; this tends to tax business income in the territory in which it has its source, irrespective of whether there is a permanent establishment there or not. The US and the Netherlands have their own model tax treaties. In certain cases treaties depart from the models substantially; in particular, in modern treaties the more obvious methods of offshore tax planning are specifically excluded from treaty benefit.

The term 'permanent establishment' means a branch, an office or other similar entity; in general, it covers any fixed place of business. The Internet was, of course, not in contemplation when the model treaties were originally drawn up, as a result of which the issue of whether any presence which a business may have in another country by virtue of the Internet amounts to permanent establishment

23–24 *New Zealand Taxes Comr v Eastern Extension Australasia and China Telegraph Co Ltd* [1906] AC 526, PC.

25 *Levene v IRC* [1928] AC 217, HL.

26 OECD Model Convention, art 5 (new). For a detailed discussion of the OECD's position on the attribution of profits see the discussion paper 'Attribution of Profit to a Permanent Establishment involved on Electronic Commerce Transactions' (February 2001).

is one that may have to be decided on a case-by-case basis[27]. However, the UK's view, like that of the Electronic Commerce Directive, as set out on 11 April 2002, is that a website of itself is not a permanent establishment, and that a server is insufficient of itself to constitute a permanent establishment of a business that is conducting ecommerce through a website on the server.

2. A UK-incorporated and resident company owns a website providing an information service to subscribers from all over the world, but in particular from the US. The company has just one office, in the UK, and all information is collated there; and the web pages are stored on the company's own server in the UK. Even though in 2002 the company's accounts show profits of £1,000,000 from its subscribers in the US, these profits are not subject to tax in the US but are only taxed in the UK. This is because it does not have a permanent establishment in the US.

In the above scenario both the company and its web server are in the UK: interesting questions may arise where the company (the author of the web pages) and the web server are in different taxing jurisdictions. Most third party web servers are simply passive repositories for information, but the situation can be imagined where the server carries out a certain amount of processing: it could, for example, be the server which authorises credit card transactions. It could be that the web server will be treated as a branch of the company.

Withholding taxes

Some foreign countries impose a tax on licence fees paid abroad: payments made to download material from the Internet may well constitute licence fees. This is similar to the UK's deduction of tax at source on royalty payments paid abroad[28].

Under double taxation treaties which the UK is party to, this type of tax (a 'withholding tax') is generally reduced to 10% or 15%. The UK may thus be a sensible base from which to conduct a worldwide operation deriving its revenues from licence fees. The procedure for claiming withholding tax reductions varies from country to country; but it would seem sensible for operations of this nature to maintain records of the countries from which payments are received.

27 For a discussion of this matter see the OECD document, 'Clarification on the Application of the Permanent Establishment Definition in E-Commerce: Changes to the Commentary on the Model Tax Convention on Article 52' (22 December 2000). The OECDs have suggested that: (a) a website cannot, of itself, constitute a permanent establishment; (b) a website-hosting arrangement does not normally result in a permanent establishment for the enterprise that carries on business through that website; (c) an Internet Service Provider will not (save in very unusual circumstances) constitute a dependent agent of another enterprise so as to constitute a permanent establishment of that enterprise; and (d) while a place where computer equipment, such as a server, is located may in certain circumstances constitute a permanent establishment, this requires that the functions performed at that place be significant as well as an essential or core part of the business activity of the enterprise. The UK's view, in contrast, is that, 'With regard to the fourth point above, the UK continues to hold the view that in no circumstances do servers, of themselves or together with websites, constitute permanent establishments of e-tailers' (http://www.inlandrevenue.gov.uk/e-commerce/ecom15.htm).

28 ICTA 1988, s 536.

It is anticipated that where software sales are web-based and automated there may be practical problems in maintaining such records.

Corporate residence and taxation

The UK and most Commonwealth countries tend to treat a company as resident in the territory where it is 'managed and controlled'; the UK additionally regards all UK incorporated companies as being UK-resident[29] no matter where they are managed and controlled. In *De Beers Consolidated Mines Ltd v Howe*[30], the leading English case on the residence of companies, it was held that a South African-incorporated company was resident in the UK because a majority of the directors lived in London and the board meetings, by which the operations of the company worldwide were controlled and managed, were held in London – even though shareholders' meetings were held in South Africa, and the registered office and head office were in South Africa.

The civil law countries, on the other hand, usually regard a company as taxable in the country of its domicile, that is where it is incorporated. The territory from which it is managed and controlled becomes irrelevant. The US adopts a similar approach.

Certain countries, notably in South East Asia, tax on a purely territorial basis: that is, while all businesses pay tax on income which has its source in the country in question, no business pays tax there on income sourced outside the country in question.

And then of course there are the offshore tax havens, amongst which the best known are perhaps the Bahamas, Bermuda, Panama, and the Channel Islands; in some of these jurisdictions there is simply no tax at all; in others, if certain conditions are fulfilled (these usually being that the company must be 100% foreign-owned and must not do business with residents of the jurisdiction) then a company may be both incorporated and resident in one of these territories without having to pay any tax there other than an annual licence fee.

Tax planning

It is beyond the scope of this chapter to do more than provide an outline of the type of tax planning techniques that may be considered. In general, tax planning is not recommended except for the very determined: it is expensive and always carries a degree of uncertainty due both to the prospect of future legislative change and to the risk of the Revenue authorities successfully arguing that it does not work.

The use of offshore structures cannot usually assist companies which are both owned and doing business in the UK to escape taxation in the UK. The same is also true of the other 'strong' taxing jurisdictions, notably the US, the Netherlands, France, Germany, Canada, Australia and New Zealand. The reason is that these jurisdictions have extensive anti-avoidance legislation

29 Finance Act 1988, s 66.
30 [1906] AC 455, 5 TC 198, HL.

designed to prevent the use of offshore structures. For example, the UK's 'controlled foreign companies' provisions[31] apply where a company is non-resident and, by virtue of that, is subject to a lower level of taxation, but nevertheless is controlled by UK-resident persons.

For a company with business of a traditional type, then, at best the use of an offshore structure does nothing to improve the UK tax situation, and at worst there are large registration fees and taxes to pay in the offshore jurisdiction or, worse still, the company loses business or demoralises its employees because it is perceived as being shady.

Companies trading over the Internet, in contrast to traditional kinds of companies, may find that an offshore structure does have its advantages. This is partly because an Internet-based business is considerably more mobile than a traditional business, and so centres of activity can more easily be relocated to any convenient jurisdiction; and partly because the customers in relation to business done over the Internet may be from any country in the world, whereas a traditional business would normally require a branch in each country in which it has customers.

For a company resident in a tax haven jurisdiction to escape taxation in the UK, not only must it be managed and controlled outside the UK, but because of the controlled foreign company rules referred to above, it must not be controlled by persons resident in the UK. Control is defined in s 416 of ICTA 1988 and the test for control is wide, applicable to shareholders, directors or others[32]. In practice, it is necessary for a majority of the persons actually able to exercise control over the company to be non-UK residents.

Besides avoiding UK tax liability on its non-UK source income, an advantage of non-resident status for a company doing business over the Internet is that even profits arising in respect of trading in the UK are only taxed at the basic rate. This is because a company whose only presence in the UK is through the Internet does not carry on a trade through a UK branch or agency[33]; accordingly the company falls outside the corporation tax net and instead pays income tax[34] like an individual, but not being an individual it never becomes liable to pay tax at the higher rate.

An alternative approach, where a company is essentially owned and controlled by UK residents, is not to seek to pay no tax, but simply to site the company in a jurisdiction where there is tax but at a lower rate than in the UK. If the amount of tax paid in that other territory is at least 75% of the amount of tax that would be paid in the UK then the controlled foreign company provisions do not bite[35]. Various territories have taxation structures specifically designed to allow companies to take advantage of this rule[36].

Whether it is best to site a business in a tax haven, in the UK or another taxing jurisdiction with a good tax treaty network very much depends on the nature of the business. In addition, in determining the most appropriate location

31 ICTA 1988, s 747.
32 For further details, see Simon's Direct Tax Service.
33 Defined in ICTA 1988, s 834(1), to mean 'any factorship, agency, receivership, branch or management'.
34 ICTA 1988, s 11.
35 ICTA 1988, s 750.
36 For a list of such territories see Offshore Red, Vol 1 no 6, p 110 (Campden Publishing Ltd, 1996).

from which to conduct an Internet business, the effect on VAT payments should also be considered. This is discussed below.

Finally, it should be noted that various jurisdictions offer special tax incentives to those setting up in high technology industries; these can amount to complete tax exemptions for five years or more. The following countries offer some form of incentive for high-technology start-ups, although incentives may only be available to businesses employing a minimum number of persons or setting up in particular areas of the country: Canada; China; Denmark; Malaysia; Saudi Arabia; Singapore; Spain (Canary Islands); Taiwan; and Vietnam. Those contemplating setting up their own communications links should bear in mind that many of the smaller island jurisdictions are prepared to negotiate very generous terms to attract businesses which will provide them with a modern communications infrastructure.

Filing tax returns over the Internet

The Inland Revenue's Internet service for self assessment allows a taxpayer to use compatible software to complete tax returns and submit that information over the Internet. The site can be found at http://www.ir-portal.gov.uk.

VAT

Introduction

Value added tax is an indirect tax on consumers imposed by all Member States of the European Union. The primary EU legislation is EC Council Directive 77/388 of 17 May 1977, universally referred to by practitioners as the Sixth Directive[37]. Member States are required to enact domestic legislation giving effect to the Sixth Directive. In a few areas Member States have some freedom in the precise rules they adopt: an example is the standard rate of VAT itself, which is at the discretion of each Member State so long as it is at least 15%.

VAT is only imposed on supplies of goods and services carried out for a consideration (money or something of value exchanged for the goods or services)[38]. Therefore, no VAT would be chargeable on items supplied for free (such as free downloads or genuinely free Internet access). However, VAT is still chargeable if there is some form of indirect payment for the goods or services: there could be payment in advance, perhaps in the form of a periodic subscription, there could be a fee per use, or there could be some other method for payment after the event. Shareware, for example, involves the gratuitous transmission of software but the imposition on the user of an obligation later to pay a fee in certain

37 Official Journal of the European Communities [1977] Vol L145, p 1, as from time to time amended. The current text is set out in Butterworths' Orange Tax Handbook, published annually.

38 Article 2 of the Sixth Directive.

circumstances, for example if the software is used commercially or if the user wishes to register it. Similarly, an ISP will have to account for VAT on gifts or prizes (costing more than £50) which are used to attract subscribers to its service[38a]. So long as there is a direct link[39] between the supply over the Internet and the payment received then such payment will constitute consideration for the supply. VAT is charged at a percentage rate on the consideration for the supply, which is normally the selling price.

The VAT system basically taxes the end consumers of goods and services. The producers of those goods and services merely collect the tax on behalf of the national tax authorities and account for it to the authorities. They do not bear the burden of the tax as they are able to deduct any VAT which they have themselves been charged on any goods or services they have used to make their own supplies[40]. For an example, an ecommerce company charging VAT on services it provides to its customers would be able to reclaim any VAT incurred on buying computers necessary to run the business and on any telecommunications services used. It would only have to account to the national tax authorities for the difference between the tax which it had charged to other businesses or end consumers (its 'output tax') and the VAT which it had itself been charged on the goods and services it had used to operate its business and make supplies (its 'input tax'). Similarly, a traditional non-Internet business may be able to deduct any VAT charged to it on the cost of setting up a website against VAT it itself has charged to its customers on sales[41]. Thus each supplier in the supply chain accounts to the national tax authorities for the value which it has added at its stage of the supply chain. The only person who cannot reclaim VAT is the end consumer, who bears the burden of the whole of the VAT on the goods or services in question.

Although the end consumer bears the burden of paying VAT on taxable goods and services, it is the supplier of goods or services who is legally responsible to account for the VAT charged[42]. Thus if a supplier omits to charge his customers VAT he is nonetheless liable himself to pay the VAT. Furthermore, in order to make supervision of the system of deducting input tax possible, a business can only reclaim VAT on its inputs if it holds an invoice from its supplier to show that VAT has been paid[43].

There are two special categories of supplies:

(1) *Exempt supplies*: The supplier of an exempt supply is not required to charge VAT on those goods or services[44]. However, he cannot recover as input tax any VAT charged to him on supplies which have been used as components of the exempt supply. Thus, he is effectively treated as the final consumer of those components. For example, insurance transactions are exempt.

38a VAT Tribunal Decision 17682 *Supanet Limited* of 31 May 2002 (unreported).

39 See *Apple and Pear Development Council v Customs and Excise* [1988] STC 221, ECJ.

40 Pursuant to art 17 of the Sixth Directive.

41 VAT Tribunal Decision 16883 of 20 September 2000 (unreported), *Scottish Tourist Board.*

42 Pursuant to art 21 of the Sixth Directive.

43 See arts 18(1)(a) and 22(3) of the Sixth Directive. From 1 January 2004, Member States will be required to implement common arrangements for electronic invoicing and the electronic storage of invoices, see Council Directive 2002/115/EC, OJ 2002 L 15/24. See also Directive 1999/93 establishing a Community framework for electronic signatures; OJ 1999 L13/12.

44 Article 13 of the Sixth Directive.

Therefore, an insurance broker would not charge VAT for his services, but equally could not reclaim any VAT incurred on the setting up of a website to market those services.

(2) *Zero-rated supplies*: The supplier of a zero-rated supply is required to charge VAT, but at a reduced rate[45]; in fact the reduced rate is 0% in the UK[46]. Reduced rates of VAT are applied differently in different member states, but in the UK the most important categories for zero-rating are foodstuffs, passenger transport services, and books and newspapers[47].

Although for the purchaser of a zero-rated supply there is no practical difference to an exempt supply because no tax is in fact charged, zero-rating is advantageous to the supplier as he is able to deduct input VAT incurred in respect of the components of the supply. For example a publisher will often have no output tax to pay, due to all his supplies being zero-rated, but will nevertheless have incurred input tax due to purchases of paper, inks, binding materials, office equipment, etc. Equally, he may incur input tax on the setting up of a website to advertise his business. Accordingly, every VAT period the publisher will actually receive money from Customs & Excise.

The VAT system in the UK

The rate of VAT in the UK is currently 17.5%[48].

In the UK, VAT is imposed by the Value Added Tax Act 1994 (VATA 1994) as amended by the annual Finance Acts following the Budget[49]. Secondary legislation often contains important provisions; for example, the Value Added Tax Regulations 1995[50] contain much of the law relating to administration and collection of VAT in the UK.

Collection of VAT is the responsibility of HM Customs & Excise. All persons making taxable supplies (basically, all businesses) whose turnover exceeds a certain threshold (currently £55,000) must register for VAT. In respect of each period (usually three months, but exceptionally one month or twelve months) the taxable person is obliged to complete a VAT return and to pay any VAT due[51]. Businesses are also required to maintain proper records[52] and to supply customers who are themselves registered or required to be registered with a VAT invoice[53] in respect of every taxable supply[54].

45 Pursuant to art 12(3) of the Sixth Directive.
46 VATA 1994, s 30.
47 VATA 1994, Sch 8.
48 VATA 1994, s 2(1).
49 Again, an up-to-date version may be found in Butterworths' Orange Tax Handbook, published annually.
50 SI 1995/2518.
51 Value Added Tax Regulations 1995, reg 25(1). Since 1 March 2000, taxpayers have been able to submit VAT returns via the Internet and pay the tax due electronically; see the Value Added Tax (Amendment) Regulations 2000, SI 2000/258.
52 Value Added Tax Regulations 1995, reg 31.
53 Value Added Tax Regulations 1995, reg 13(1).
54 Other than a retailer – Value Added Tax Regulations 1995, reg 16.

There is a right of appeal from any decision of HM Customs & Excise to a judicial body known as the VAT Tribunal. Further appeals from decisions of the Tribunal on questions of law may be made to the High Court, Court of Appeal and ultimately the House of Lords. Since VAT is a European tax, points of European law often arise: it is not uncommon for questions to be raised as to whether the UK legislation, or the way in which Customs & Excise seek to implement it, exceed what is permitted under the European legislation and are thus *ultra vires*. Both the VAT Tribunal and the higher courts hearing VAT appeals are able to refer questions for decision by the European Court of Justice in Luxembourg.

Purchase of goods over the Internet

Often the Internet is simply used as a form of mail order. In such circumstances, the normal VAT rules applicable to such transactions continue to apply even though the method of ordering is different.

To be liable to UK VAT, a supply of goods or services must be made in the UK[55]. Where goods are ordered over the Internet by a UK purchaser from a UK VAT-registered business, VAT will be charged in the normal way at 17.5% by the business on standard rated goods (for example, a CD). Similarly, no VAT will be charged on zero-rated goods such as books[56] or food[57].

Supplies of goods made by UK businesses to customers outside of the EU are zero-rated[58]. Therefore, no VAT should be charged on the supply of a CD ordered by a Venezuelan customer from a UK website. However, the UK supplier would be able to recover the VAT on any component costs of the supply from Customs.

Supplies of goods made by UK VAT-registered businesses to customers within the EU are zero-rated if they are supplied to a person registered for VAT in another Member State, the supplier obtains his customer's VAT registration number and shows this on his VAT invoice and if he holds commercial documentary evidence that the goods have been removed from the UK[59]. If the customer is not registered for VAT, the UK registered supplier must charge VAT at the UK rate. However, where supplies made by the UK registered supplier to any particular EU country exceeds an annual threshold set by that country for distance selling (set at between about £25,000 and £70,000), the supplier must register for VAT in that country and then charge VAT at the rate applicable in the country of destination.

Where a UK customer buys goods over the Internet from outside the EU VAT

55 VATA 1994, s 4.

56 Where in hardcopy format; for digital books, see fn 70 below.

57 In *Emphasis Ltd v Customs and Excise* Decision 13759, 20 November 1995, the VAT Tribunal confirmed that the use of the Internet to order goods within the UK made no difference to the normal VAT treatment. It held that a business which accepted orders for sandwiches and other food via computer was held to be making a zero-rated supply of foodstuffs, and was not, by virtue of the use of the computer, making a standard-rated supply of services as Customs & Excise contended.

58 VATA 1994, s 30(6).

59 VATA 1994, s 30(8); Value Added Tax Regulations 1995, reg 134; and Notice No 725 (May 1998), para 2.2.

is payable by the purchaser on the entry of those goods into the UK[60]. For example, where goods are ordered by a UK private customer over the Internet from a non-EU website and sent by mail, the Post Office will require payment of the VAT due from the purchaser before delivery will be made[61].

Acquisitions of goods from other EU member states are also subject to VAT at the UK rate if the customer is VAT-registered here[62]. Thus, a VAT registered UK customer could buy books over the Internet at the zero-rate. However, private customers would be charged VAT at the rate applicable in the other Member State, save where the supplier is also registered for VAT in the UK under the distance selling rules referred to above, in which case UK rates of VAT would be charged. EU suppliers must register for VAT in the UK if the annual value of supplies made to the UK exceeds £70,000[63].

The Commission is not proposing any change to the above rules at this time, although, because of the increase in volume of such sales, it is asking Member States to consider simplification of the customs clearance procedures for imports of small consignments and the updating of their distance selling rules[64].

Purchase of services over the Internet

For most common types of services (known as 'Schedule 5 services'[65]) (eg legal, accountancy, advertising, banking and insurance services) supplies made by UK registered businesses are not subject to VAT in the UK if (i) the customer is outside the EU, or (ii) the customer is a business customer in another EU member state[66].

On the other hand, supplies of services made by UK registered suppliers of services to private customers in other member states are always subject to VAT in the UK. There is no equivalent for supplies of services of the distance selling rules in place for goods. Services which are not Schedule 5 services made by UK registered suppliers are also subject to UK VAT, regardless of whether the customer is registered or unregistered[67].

In contrast with the position for imported goods, private customers in the UK receiving supplies of services from outside the EU do not have to pay any VAT. On supplies within the EU, they pay VAT at the rate applicable in the supplying country. However, UK VAT-registered persons receiving services from abroad must themselves account for VAT in the UK under the 'reverse charge' procedure on all services[68]. In general VAT registered persons paying VAT under this rule may then deduct such VAT again as input tax.

The only exception under the current law is telecommunications services, including provision of basic access to email and the Internet (without any content), where private customers who are not registered do have to pay VAT on

60 Under s 1(4) of VATA 1994, VAT is due on imports as if it were a customs duty.
61 See the Postal Packets (Customs and Excise) Regulations 1986, SI 1986/260.
62 VATA 1994, s 10(1).
63 VATA 1994, Sch 2, para 1.
64 Explanatory Memorandum to the Commission Proposal of 7 June 2000 for a Regulation amending Regulation 218/92 and a Directive amending Directive 77/388, COM (2000) 349 final, p 3.
65 Those listed in VATA 1994, Sch 5, paras 1–8.
66 VAT (Place of Supply of Services) Order 1992, SI 1992/3121.
67 VATA 1994, s 7(10).
68 VATA 1994, s 8 and Sch 5.

services supplied by non-EU suppliers[69]. The UK does not regard Internet service packages as telecommunications services and non-UK ISPs making supplies of such services to UK non-business customers are not required to charge VAT[69a].

> **3. Whoopee, a US corporation, has a popular website stored on a US-owned server. It reserves spaces on its home page for other people's advertisements. One such advertising space is made available for a substantial charge to XYZ Ltd, a UK company which is VAT registered.**
>
> **This is, for VAT purposes, a supply of advertising services by Whoopee to the UK company. Because XYZ Ltd has its only business establishment in the UK, and because the supply is made for business purposes, the supply of services is treated as made by the recipient in the UK and accordingly XYZ Ltd must account for VAT on that supply under the reverse charge rules (VATA 1994, s 8). But unless its own supplies are exempt supplies XYZ Ltd will be entitled to a full credit for this VAT as input tax.**

Specific problems with VAT treatment of the purchase of digitally delivered services over the Internet

Problems arise with the current regime with electronically delivered services supplied for a payment or other consideration, such as software for downloading, information and news services, database and search services such as LexisNexis, website design and hosting, online books and newspapers[70] and also subscription TV, pay-per-view TV and video or audio packages for downloading. All such supplies are in law clearly supplies of services[71]. Therefore, under the rules for supplies of international services explained above, non-VAT-registered private customers within the EU can at the moment obtain all of these services from suppliers outside the EU without paying VAT. They would pay VAT at the rate applicable in the supplier's country if they bought the services from an EU based provider (or at their own national rate if they purchased them from a non-EU provider in a hard-copy format). Meanwhile, EU-based suppliers providing such services to non-EU based customers are required to charge VAT. If the current rules remained in force, the VAT taxbase could be eroded and the EU's own ecommerce industry would be damaged, largely to the benefit of that in the US. The EU Commission regarded this situation as clearly untenable[72].

69 See art 9(4) of the Sixth Directive, as inserted by Council Directive 99/59/EC of 17 June 1999; OJ 1999 L162/64 and VATA 1994, Sch 5, para 7A.

69a See HM Customs and Excise Business Briefs 22/1997 and 06/2002. Freeserve has recently been granted permission to bring judical review against Customs and Excise regarding the non-taxability of non-UK ISPs providing Internet service packages to UK non-business customers (see *R v Commissioners of Customs and Excise, ex parte Freeserve.com plc* Moses J, 25 September 2002.

70 Although hardcopy books and newspapers would be zero-rated in the UK, the relief does not extend to digitized publications; see VAT Information Sheet 3/01 of April 2001.

71 See art 6 of the Sixth Directive and pp 4 and 12 of the Explanatory Memorandum to the Commission's proposal, fn 64 above. This reflects agreement reached at the 1998 OECD Ottawa Conference that electronically delivered products should be characterised as services.

72 See the Explanatory Memorandum to the Commission's proposals, fn 64 above.

4. A computer game is created by a corporation whose office is in California and which has no offices in the EU. The game is made available for downloading on this corporation's website, in return for credit card payments. Four UK residents purchase a copy of the game.

Penelope, who wishes to play the game, downloads it from the website, and as she is not a VAT-registered person there is currently no VAT to pay. When the new Directive 2002/38/EC comes into force on 1 July 2003, Penelope will be charged VAT.

Quentin, a journalist who wishes to write a review of the game, also downloads it from the website, but because he is a VAT-registered person and the service is supplied to him for the purposes of a business carried on by him, there is VAT to pay: under the self-supply rules he must account for VAT on the supply of the game to him as if it were his own output tax, but in the same VAT period he is able to deduct an equivalent amount as input tax.

Roger uses the website to order a copy of the game on a disk, and this is subsequently sent to him by post. When the disk comes into the UK there is a charge to VAT, and the Post Office on delivery of the postal packet will require Roger to pay the VAT due.

Samantha imports 100 copies of the game on disk in order to sell them in her shop. She too has to pay VAT on these imports, but at this stage VAT is only chargeable on the wholesale price that she pays. If she is VAT-registered then she may obtain an input tax credit for the VAT paid on importation, but on the other hand she has to pay VAT on any sales she makes. Accordingly her customers will have to pay a VAT-inclusive price.

The EU Council finally took action on this problem on 7 May 2002 when it adopted Directive 2002/38/EC[73] which modifies the Sixth VAT Directive for a period of three years from 1 July 2003 by exempting supplies of electronically supplied services[74] by EU sellers to non-EU customers and introducing a special scheme for the taxation of such supplies made by non-EU based suppliers to non-business EU customers.

Under the special scheme, suppliers of electronically supplied services based outside the EU will have to register with a Member State of their choice under a special simplified registration scheme which can be completed online. The Directive does not specify a turnover threshold for registration[75]. Non-EU suppliers will also be able to check electronically whether an EU resident claiming to be VAT-registered is indeed a taxable person[76]. Therefore, a US software

73 OJ 2002 L128/41.

74 Which the Directive defines in Annex L as including website supply, web hosting, distance maintenance of programmes and equipment, supply of software and updating, supply of images, text and information and making databases available, supply of music, text, films and games, including games of chance and gambling games, and of political, cultural, artistic, sporting, scientific and entertainment broadcasts and events and supply of distance teaching.

75 The EU Commission had earlier proposed a threshold of 100,000 euros.

76 Over the VIES (VAT Information Exchange System) at http://www.europa.eu.int/comm/taxation_customs/vies/en/vieshome.htm.

company will have to ascertain whether its EU customers are VAT registered or not. If they are, the US company will not be required to charge them VAT, as the customers will be required themselves to account for VAT at their national rate under the 'reverse charge' procedure. However, if they are not registered, the US company will be required to charge and account for VAT.

Non-EU suppliers will have to levy VAT at the rate applicable in the Member State where the customer is established, has his permanent address or usually resides. It is not yet clear how the supplier will be able to verify the location of its customers. Currently, the best substitute is for the supplier to require the customer to provide a verifiable credit card billing address[77]. The country of registration will reallocate the VAT revenue to the authorities in the customer's country under a procedure set out in Regulation 792/2002[78], which was also adopted on 7 May 2002. The original proposal was that non-EU based suppliers would levy VAT at the rate set by the Member State in which they were registered, but this was obviously unpopular with EU countries with high VAT rates (such as Denmark whose rate is 25%) who were concerned that non-EU sellers would choose to register in low VAT member states, benefiting those countries but undermining the revenue base and ebusinesses of member states with higher rates of VAT.

There are a number of problems with the Directive. First, because of the extra-territorial nature of the requirement on non-EU businesses to charge VAT and account for it to EU member states, there may be problems of enforcement against non-EU businesses with no presence in Europe unless agreement can be reached through the OECD with non-EU governments. Other options would be to deny intellectual property protection to non-compliant non-EU sellers or to threaten to arrest executives of non-compliant companies when visiting Europe. The Directive may also lead to retaliation by other countries, such as the US, imposing sales taxes on EU-based suppliers. Second, the scheme is likely to lead to compliance problems. The 6th recital to the preamble to the Directive requires non-EU suppliers to comply, not only with the Directive, but also 'with any relevant existing provision in the Member State where the services are consumed' – ie to comply with the VAT rules of all 15 separate EU Member States. Furthermore, the new art 26c(B)(9) of the Sixth VAT Directive inserted by art 1(6) of the Directive requires non-EU suppliers to 'keep records of the transactions covered by this special scheme in sufficient detail to enable the tax administration of the Member State of consumption to determine that the [supplier's] value added tax return . . . is correct'. Again, the non-EU supplier would appear to be subject to audit by all 15 Member States.

77 Explanatory Memorandum to the Commission Proposal, fn 64 above, p 8.
78 OJ 2002 L128/1.

Chapter Eight

Competition Law and the Internet

Whether you want car parts, foreign currency or an original 7" of 'Material Girl' the Internet can offer a range of options for you find what you want. Potentially it provides a level of choice and transparency that has not previously been available to customers. To compare prices of goods in the shops a consumer would have to travel to various retailers or make a series of phone calls. Where companies sell via the Internet, however, the consumer has the opportunity to browse the wares and compare prices with all the effort of a series of mouse clicks. Indeed they may be able to get electronic agents to do their searching for them.

The result of the development of the Internet appears to be enormously pro-competitive. It is highly innovative and constantly changing. And it is against this background that the application of competition law to Internet-related business must be considered.

However, whilst we can accept that the development of the Internet and its use for business is, in general terms, pro-competitive, ordinary competition law still applies. As with any industry, there are ways in which Internet businesses develop or operate which may raise competition concerns. Anyone involved in the business of the Internet needs to know how competition law can affect them. And how it can be used to their own advantage. This chapter examines the following issues:

1. Are business-to-business exchanges contrary to Competition Law?
2. For an Internet competition law complaint, how should one determine the 'relevant market'?
3. How does the European Commission distinguish Internet services from interactive television services?
4. For the purposes of the vertical agreement Block Exemption, does website advertising amount to 'passive selling'?
5. How is 'dominance' determined in the Internet sector?
6. Is it predatory pricing for a dominant company to make beta software available to download free-of-charge?
7. What can English lawyers learn from the Microsoft US anti-trust litigation?

Relevant Legal Provisions

Domestic provision	European provision	Focus
Chapter I prohibition	Article 81	Anti-competitive agreements
Chapter II prohibition	Article 82	Abuse of dominance
Fair Trading Act (ss 57–77)	EC Merger Regulation	Merger control
Fair Trading Act (ss 47–56)		Investigation of whole industries

INTRODUCTION TO COMPETITION LAW

Competition law can be seen as a sophisticated form of consumer protection. Whilst unfair contract terms legislation tries to prevent consumers from being bound by unjust conditions, competition law tries to ensure that markets operate competitively so that consumers benefit from lower prices, better service and wider choice. It assumes that the natural state of markets is not necessarily to move towards increasing competition. As Thurman Arnold, the one time head of the US Department of Justice Anti-Trust Division[1], explained '[t]he maintenance of a free market is as much a matter of constant policing as the flow of traffic on a busy intersection. It does not stay orderly by trusting to the good intentions of the drivers or by preaching to them'.

But just because competition law controls certain types of behaviour, does not mean that it tries to make markets cosy places. On the contrary, a key aim of competition law is to prevent cosiness between competitors. Another important role of competition law is to ensure that companies that have market power do not use it to suppress competition. However, it should not be assumed automatically that 'big is bad' in competition law terms. It is not. Although, being big can give companies the power to be bullies, it can also be a sign of simple success. Companies grow big when they do things well.

Just as big is not necessarily bad, small is not necessarily good. Whilst we might feel sympathy for small businesses who try hard and do not succeed against larger competitors, competition law has no such sentiment. If larger organisations can deliver products and services more efficiently, then competition law will offer no protection to the small guys who suffer as a result. Competition law, as its name suggests, protects competition not competitors.

THE LAW

Competition Act 1998 and articles 81 and 82

Since 1 March 2000 the UK has been subject to a new competition law regime. Gone is the old Restrictive Trade Practices Act 1976 and in has come the

1 1939–43.

Competition Act 1998. This marks a huge change in the operation of competition law in the UK. At the time of writing, the proposed Enterprise Bill will, if enacted, make further radical changes to competition. As well as modifying the structure of the OFT and amending the domestic merger control regime, it will introduce a criminal offence of participating in cartel activity. In addition, it will enable the disqualification of directors whose companies infringe Ch I or II or art 81 or 82. It is expected these changes will come into force in early 2003.

Under the RTPA there operated a form-based system of control. When an agreement had a particular form it fell within the scope of the RTPA and had to be notified to and scrutinised by the Office of Fair Trading[2] whether it had anti-competitive effects or not. This meant that many innocuous agreements churned through the Restrictive Trade Practices Act process whilst other agreements which did, in fact, have anti-competitive effects, but fell outside the scope of the Restrictive Trade Practices Act, were left untouched. In addition, the investigation and enforcement powers available to the Director General of Fair Trading[3] were weak and meant he often struggled to prevent anti-competitive activity.

The new system of competition law introduced under the Competition Act is effects-based: it targets arrangements and activities which have anti-competitive effects. The prohibitions in the Act are based upon the competition law provisions in the EC Treaty: Arts 81 and 82[4].

Competition Act 1998 – s 60

One of the principal goals of the Competition Act is to bring domestic competition law into line with European law in order that companies will only be faced with what is effectively the same set of rules whether the problem arises at a domestic or European level. In fact, European law dictates the way in which domestic courts will interpret the Competition Act. Section 60 of the Act requires that courts must act with a view to securing that there is no inconsistency between domestic decision and '*the principles laid down by the Treaty and the European Court, and any relevant decision of that Court . . .*'[5]. In addition to ensuring compliance with European Court of Justice rulings, the domestic court must '*have regard to any relevant decision or statement of the [European Commission]*'[6]. In other words, the new Act comes with a ready made jurisprudence in the form of European competition law.

Since it is intended that the domestic and European competition law systems should be congruent, they will be discussed alongside one another. Only where there are specific differences between the regimes will they be dealt with separately.

Sector specific legislation

Although there is no Internet specific competition law, there are specific regimes both at domestic and European level governing telecommunications and broad-

2 The OFT.
3 The DGFT – the head of the Office of Fair Trading.
4 Prior to May 1999 and the coming into force of the Amsterdam Treaty, these were numbered arts 85 and 86 respectively. This renumbering makes reading (and searching for) relevant European cases a rather frustrating experience.
5 CA 98, s 60(2).
6 CA 98, s 60(3).

casting. It is beyond the scope of this chapter to explore these regimes but it is notable that in the telecommunications field, the Office of the Telecommunications Regulator (OFTEL) has the power to control prices, set minimum quality and service standards and impose 'interconnection' obligations requiring infrastructure owners to allow third party access to their system. Therefore if any Internet-related agreement, merger or potentially anti-competitive behaviour involves issues of line pricing or access, it is important to consider the effects of the relevant telecommunications legislation and the possible reactions of the sectoral regulator. It is proposed that in the face of digital convergence a single regulator for communications and media in the UK should be created entitled 'Ofcom' and that unified regulator will focus on the use of general competition law, rather than sector specific regulation. At the time of writing those proposals are not law and are not discussed further in this chapter[7].

It is important to note that the Competition Act confers upon the sectoral regulators and, in particular, OFTEL, the power to apply the Act's prohibitions to the relevant sectors concurrently with the Director General of Fair Trading[8]. Therefore, even when considering the specific legislation governing the telecommunications industry to bear in mind the overarching operation of the Competition Act.

CHAPTER I[9] AND ARTICLE 81

The most important operative part of Ch I (s 2(1)) provides:

> '. . . *agreements between undertakings, decisions by associations of undertakings or concerted practices which –*
> *(a) may affect trade within the United Kingdom, and*
> *(b) have as their object or effect the prevention, restriction or distortion of competition within the UK,*
> *are prohibited unless they are exempt in accordance with the provisions of this Part . . .*'

A prohibited agreement is void[10] unless it is exempted. Article 81 is in almost identical terms, the key difference between it and Ch I is that in order to be contrary to art 81, an agreement or concerted practice must have a European dimension: it must have an actual or potential effect on trade between member states the EU[11].

7 See the Communications White Paper *A New future for Communications* and the Communications Bill 2002.
8 CA 98, s 54 and Sch 10. See also OFT *Guidance note 405 on current application to regulated industries* for further details of the OFT's views on the manner of the concurrent implementation by the DGFT and the sectoral regulators.
9 See OFT Guideline 401 'The Chapter I Prohibition'.
10 Section 2(4). The nature of voidness is currently a matter of some discussion, in *Passmore v Morland* [1999] 3 All ER 1005 the Court of Appeal held that whether an agreement was void or not depended upon the economic context including the appreciability of the agreement. It was possible for an agreement to be void at one moment and to become 'unvoid' the next if market circumstances changed.
11 Save for this difference between the Ch I prohibition and Art 81, the interpretation of the two provisions is the same (in the light of s 60 of the Competition Act). Throughout the remainder of the chapter, references to the Ch I prohibition should be read as references to both it and art 81 unless otherwise specified.

Undertakings

Any entity capable of carrying on commercial or economic activities in relation to goods or services will be considered an 'undertaking' for the purposes of the Competition Act. This means that either natural or legal persons, be they companies, partnerships, sole traders, co-operatives or even charities, are undertakings.

It should be noted that although there is a wide range of entities which are undertakings, where two undertakings form part of a single economic unit, for example, parent and subsidiary companies, agreements between them are not relevant for the purposes of Ch I. This means that arrangements between subsidiaries and parents can include provisions which, if they formed part of an agreement between independent companies would fall foul of Ch I[12].

Agreements and concerted practices

Just as the definition of 'undertaking' is widely drawn, so is the definition of 'agreement'. In fact it is hard to distinguish from the European case law what is an agreement and what is a concerted practice. Since nothing hinges on identifying arrangements as one or the other, trying to draw a clear distinction is a sterile exercise.

It is clear that for the purposes of Ch I 'agreement' includes far more than just enforceable contracts as defined by English law; gentlemen's agreements are also covered. More informal co-operation or understandings between undertakings also fall within the scope of the Ch I prohibition although they are usually referred to as a concerted practices. The breadth of the definitions of these terms reflect the fact that anti-competitive behaviour may be arranged by a nod and a wink rather than through laboriously drafted contracts. As Adam Smith observed in his oft-quoted comment 'people of the same trade seldom meet together, even for merriment and diversion, but the conversation ends in a conspiracy against the public, or in some contrivance to raise prices'[13].

When the Director General is considering whether there is a concerted practice between undertakings, he will consider whether there have been contacts between the parties; regular gatherings of competitors in obscure hotels and frequent emails marked 'Private and Confidential' tend to raise suspicions rapidly. He will also consider whether the behaviour of the parties has affected the market in which they are operating in ways might not be dictated by market forces. Deciding whether this is the case will tend to depend on a relatively complex analysis of the nature of the market, the type and number of competitors, their cost structures and their overall pricing behaviour.

Decisions of associations of undertakings[14]

Both 'association of undertakings' and 'decision' are broadly defined and the scope of the provision is not limited to any particular form of membership

12 See Case 22/71 *Beguelin Import v GL Import Export* [1972] CMLR 81.
13 Adam Smith, *The Wealth of Nations*, Book 1, Ch X.
14 See also OFT *Guideline 408 Trade Associations, Professions and Self-Regulating Bodies*.

structure or to any particular type of resolution by the members. This element of the prohibition covers trade associations and other standard setting bodies who have trade members. The decisions in question may be parts of the constitutions of these associations or may be mere recommendations which, although not enforced, are generally applied. The key issue is whether the decision in question limits the freedom of the members in relation to some commercial matter.

In industries, such as those associated with the Internet, where standard setting may be important and may be achieved by associations of companies who are otherwise direct competitors, it is important to note that competition law applies just as it would to bilateral agreements between the individual companies. Of course, agreements to create truly open standards are generally highly pro-competitive. Therefore, even if they fell within the scope of the Ch I prohibition, they might well be exempted.

May affect trade

This requirement is often a key threshold over which small agreements do not pass in the context of European law. It is necessary to show that trade between member states is affected and that the repercussions were not simply domestic[15]. An arrangement which only affects competition in the UK will often not affect trade between member states and so will not be considered under Art 81.

With the introduction of the Competition Act 1998, however, agreements or concerted practices which only affect the UK market, or part of it[16], may be held to be anti-competitive.

It should be noted that the test for affect on trade is whether the flow of trade is *changed*. It is not a question of whether or not trade has been *reduced*. Some anti-competitive arrangements may be intended simply to shift custom from one undertaking to another by illegitimate means; overall there may be no change in the total volume of sales, but the arrangement still affects trade.

Jurisdiction

Although the Ch I prohibition is a domestic law provision, it applies to any agreement or arrangement which 'is, or is intended to be, implemented in the

15 See *Vereening van Cementhandelaren v EC Commission* Case 8/72 [1972] ECR 977; *AEG-Telefunken v Commission* Case 107/82 [1983] ECR 3151.

16 What constitutes a 'part' of the UK for these purposes remains unclear. 'Section 64 of the Fair Trading Act 1973 refers to a substantial part of the UK. Lord Mustill described it as a part 'of such size, character and importance as to make it worth consideration for the purposes of the Act', and the House of Lords held that a part of South Yorkshire and Derbyshire amounting to 1500 square miles and with a population of 1.8 million was not too small to comprise a substantial part of the UK in relation to the provision of a bus service. See *R v Monopolies and Mergers Commission, ex p South Yorkshire Transport* [1993] 1 WLR 23. It will be interesting to see how the relevant Tribunals tackle this question with reference to a 'part' only (Chapter I and Chapter II) rather than a 'substantial part' (the Fair Trading Act) of the UK and whether they prefer Lord Mustill's somewhat homely approach to the European Commission's more challenging 5-10% rule.' Skilbeck, *Solicitors Journal*, 21 January 2000.

United Kingdom'[17] (or part of it). This means that even if the parties to the arrangement are not situated within the UK, they can still fall foul of the Ch I prohibition.

If companies are based outside the UK but the anti-competitive arrangement relates to supplies of goods or services made in the UK, such an arrangement will be prohibited. In the context of the global Internet industry, the nature of the UK courts' jurisdiction is important. Even if you are based in California and you enter into an agreement with a company in Moscow which is implemented in the UK, your agreement may be caught. A similar approach to jurisdiction is adopted at European level – if the agreement in question affects trade within the EC, it can be caught by art 81. This extended jurisdiction reflects the judgment of the ECJ in the *Woodpulp* case[18].

Object or effect

Arrangements which have as their object the prevention, restriction or distortion of competition are invariably within the scope of Ch I. However, the intention of the parties in entering into the arrangements at issue will not be crucial in deciding whether they fall within Ch I. The key question is what the effect of the arrangements is upon the effective functioning of the market. This means that arrangements which have an effect upon actual or *potential* competition may come within the scope of Ch I[19].

Prevention, restriction or distortion of competition

What constitutes an illegitimate constraint on competition is a question at the heart of all anti-trust systems. As *Bellamy & Child* puts it:

> 'In one sense almost every commercial contract can be said to 'restrict' competition, since once A has sold goods to B, A cannot sell those goods to anyone else and B is no longer interested in obtaining them from elsewhere.'[20]

But competition law does not impinge on every contract entered into. Most contracts are pro-competitive in that they facilitate economic activity. Without a contract (in whatever form) it is unlikely that people would commit to participating in transactions which are efficient and beneficial in improving welfare. Indeed, it is arguable that it is in order to satisfy the need for certainty and efficiency in transactions that contract law systems have grown up the world over.

The Ch I prohibition and art 81 provide identical lists of examples of behaviour which may caught:

Directly or indirectly fixing purchasing or selling prices is almost certain to infringe the prohibition. Formation of a price cartel is a serious infringement

17 CA 98, s 2(3).

18 See Cases 114, 125-129/85 *Ahlstrom v EC Commission (Woodpulp)* [1988] ECR 5193.

19 The intentions of the parties may be relevant to the level of any fines imposed (see page 448 below).

20 *Common Market Law of Competition* Bellamy & Child (4th edn) at 2–057.

under this head but prices can also be fixed by, for example, agreement to adhere to published price lists or to forewarn competitors of intended price rises. Similarly, prices may be indirectly affected by agreeing to limit discounts or credit terms or charges for transportation.

Where companies exchange price information (or other relevant data such as their strategies) so that uncertainties in the market are removed, such arrangements may be contrary to the prohibition. Whether such information-sharing has an anti-competitive effect will depend upon the nature of the market in question and the information exchanged – where there are a small number of competitors in a market for relatively undifferentiated products and sensitive sales information is exchanged, the authorities are likely to consider it unacceptable.

It has been suggested by some that Internet business-to-business ('B2B') marketplaces may be the smoked filled rooms of the future – the places where competing undertakings get together, share information and collude, in particular, on pricing. In principle, the regulatory authorities will treat the possibility of cartel-like behaviour in B2Bs in the same way as in any other industry. They will consider the structure of the arrangement, the levels and types of information passing between the members and, in the context of price fixing, the levels of prices being charged and the basis upon which changes occur.

In none of the cases that have come before the EC Commission in relation B2Bs (whether under art 81 or the Merger Regulation) has there been any finding of collusion between parties. That, of course, is not surprising since the EC Commission was scrutinising the arrangements at their outset before they had been put into practice[21]. Nonetheless, in the *Volbroker*[22] case the EC Commission required that conditions be complied with to prevent unnecessary risk of collusion or information sharing before an agreement between major banks to establish a foreign exchange B2B could be approved.

Volbroker.com was created through an agreement between subsidiaries of six major banks who were market makers in the market for foreign currency options. It provided the first brokerage service to bring automated trading in foreign currency options for banks. The parent banks sought clearance under art 81 from the EC Commission. They secured a comfort letter (informal clearance) for the arrangements on the basis of the following assurances:

None of Volbroker.com's staff of management to have any contractual or other obligations towards any of the parent banks (and vice versa);

Volbroker.com's staff and management to be in a geographically distinct location;

The representatives of the parent banks who sat on Volbroker.com's Board of Directors would not have access to commercially sensitive information relating to each other or to third parties;

21 See, for example, Case No COMP/M 1969 – *UTC/Honeywell/i2/myaircraft.com* decision of 4 August 2000.

22 See Commission Press Release 31 July 2000, IP/00/896.

The parents would not have access to the information technology and communication systems of Volbroker.com; and

The parent banks would ensure that staff and management understood the importance of keeping commercially sensitive information confidential and that sanctions for breach were spelled out.

Limiting or controlling production, markets, technical development or investment: in economic terms limiting output has a similar detrimental effect to raising prices. Output restrictions are, therefore, treated with a similar severity to price fixing arrangements. In the context of high technology Internet-related business, agreements to restrict the development of new products and innovations could clearly inhibit competition and retard the development of the market. Although in many circumstances agreements between undertakings to set standards may reduce waste and consumers' search costs, such agreements can restrict competition by reducing the scope for innovation.

Sharing markets or sources of supply: competitors dividing up markets whether into geographical sectors or by types of customer means that there is a loss of competition. A customer in a particular area (or particular group) has less choice and the incumbent supplier is insulated from competitive pressures which would drive down prices, increase levels of service or increase choice of products.

In the US, a challenge was brought (under US anti-trust law) against the 'Baby Bell' telecoms companies[23] for their alleged formation of a cartel to dominate the Internet yellow pages market[24]. The key allegations were (a) that the various telecoms companies had agreed amongst themselves to share geographical markets across the US and control essential points of access to the Internet and (b) that major ISPs had made agreements with the telecoms companies to exclude competitors including GTE New Media by giving prominence to their own yellow pages on the ISPs' guides. The matter was settled before it came to court but it illustrates how market sharing arrangements may be challenged in the context of Internet-related activity.

Discriminating between customers whether on the basis of price or the conditions of sale may place certain customers at a competitive disadvantage and thereby distort the operation of the market. In particular where a trade association or other association of undertakings sets prices or conditions for sales between its members different from those on which the members set to non-members, the arrangement may infringe the prohibition.

Attaching supplementary obligations unconnected to the subject of the agreement may also infringe the Ch I prohibition. In other words, burdening companies with obligations which are irrelevant to the subject-matter of the principal transaction is anti-competitive.

23 The regional companies which resulted from the break-up of certain parts of AT&T ordered in 1984.

24 *GTE New Media Services Inc v Ameritech Corpn* (DDC complaint filed 6 October 1997).

Appreciability

The arrangements in question must not just effect competition in the relevant market, they must effect competition to an appreciable extent[25].

In the UK

The DGFT has indicated that unless the parties' combined market share exceeds 25%, he will generally take the view that any agreement or concerted practice between the parties does *not* have an appreciable effect on competition.

There are three exceptions to this important rule of thumb:

agreements fixing prices;
sharing markets; or
imposing minimum resale prices

may be considered to have an appreciable effect on competition even where the combined market share of the parties is less than 25%.

In addition, where an agreement is part of a network of similar agreements which have a cumulative effect on the market in question, the appreciability threshold will not apply. This last exception is included because some agreements do not have anti-competitive effects when only one or two competing companies enter into them but where they are part of a series of similar agreements governing a whole market, they may prevent new competitors entering. Of course, in order to assess whether an agreement is part of a 'network' of similar agreements it is necessary to consider the behaviour of other players in the market, not just the agreement in question.

In the EC

In relation to European law, the rule-of-thumb threshold is much lower (although, as described above, it is necessary to show an effect on inter-state trade in order to fall within the scope of the prohibition in the first place). The Commission notice on agreements of minor importance[26] indicates that where the agreement is made between undertakings operating at the same level of production or marketing ('horizontal agreements'), then the market share threshold is 10%. However, for 'vertical agreements' (those between undertakings at different levels in the value-chain), the threshold is 15%. This distinction is made because in general policy terms vertical arrangements are considered to have greater pro-competitive (or fewer anti-competitive) effects than horizontal arrangements. In practice, however, this higher threshold for vertical arrangements may be effectively irrelevant due to the possibility of exemption discussed below.

In any event, the difficult question in applying these tests is deciding what is the 'relevant market'.

25 See, for example, *Volk v Vervaecke* case 5/69 [1969] ECR 295.
26 Notice on agreements of minor importance which do not appreciably restrict competition under art 81(1) of the Treaty establishing the European Community OJ [2001] C 368/13.

Market definition

Market definition is a vexed question which has bedevilled the application of anti-trust law throughout the world. There is, however, a general consensus between US, European and UK competition authorities as to how the analysis should generally be carried out[27].

A market has two key dimensions: product and geography. It is necessary to identify the group of products with which the products at issue compete and the geographical area within which they compete. Formally, these dimensions are identified by applying what is known as the 'hypothetical monopolist' test. This works as follows: you define the smallest group of products (and geographical area) which, if it was controlled by a single (hypothetical) company, would allow that company to raise prices by a small but significant amount (5–10%) for the foreseeable future[28].

If the hypothetical monopolist can raise prices by 10% for the foreseeable future that means that (a) consumers do not consider other products to be substitutes for the products over which there is a monopoly (demand-side substitution), and (b) new suppliers would not enter the market to produce the products which the monopolist controls (supply-side substitution). If consumers could switch to other products then the hypothetical monopolist could not sustain higher prices (and maintain his profits) similarly, if new suppliers could enter the market, the new suppliers could charge lower prices and again, the hypothetical monopolist could not impose prices 10% above competitive levels.

In order to run the test it is necessary to consider whether there are any substitutes for the product or service at issue in the eyes of customers and whether a rival supplier of similar products or services could enter the market if prices were raised so that the hypothetical monopolist was making excessive profits. This is where the nice neat test becomes rather difficult to apply for two reasons: first, it is often difficult to gather evidence to support a particular result of the thought-experiment; second, if the company at issue is already charging monopoly prices then when you run the experiment you might consider that people are switching to substitute products when in fact they are just giving up on that product and turning to different activities. From the subject matter of the American case in which this latter problem first arose, it is known as the 'cellophane fallacy'[29].

The EC Commission has considered the nature of the relevant market in a number of cases involving the Internet, a number of them mergers. Although the relevant market in which a company is operating is dependent upon factors specific to that company and the behaviour or arrangement at issue in a particular case, the following examples are useful illustrations of how Internet-related markets have been defined.

The *Worldcom/MCI* merger[30] was only approved on the undertaking that MCI divest itself of its Internet business. Initially the parties argued that other

27 See OFT *Guideline 403 market definition, Commission Notice on the definition of the market for the purposes of Community competition law* [1997] OJ C 372/5; and the Department of Justice and Federal Trade Commission Horizontal Merger Guidelines 1992.

28 This test is sometimes referred to as the 'SSNIP' test – Small but Significant, Non-transitory Increase in Price.

29 *United States v Dupont (cellophane)* (351 US 377 (1956)).

30 Case IV/M 1069 *Re Concentration between Worldcom Inc and MCI Communications Corpn* [1999] 5 CMLR 876.

forms of data transmission were a substitute in the eyes of consumers for Internet services. The Commission quickly rejected this suggestion because customers purchasing an Internet access service do so in the expectation that they will be able to access the full range of services available on the Internet and make contact with all other users. Whilst one-to-one data transmission systems might enable customers to perform certain tasks outside the Internet, it would not provide 'the permanent, unfettered access to the community of Internet users which is the main purpose of buying the service'[31]. So, on the demand-side there was no substitute for the Internet.

The Commission then went on to consider whether these two large telecoms companies who had substantial fibre networks carrying Internet traffic were in a narrower market than that for Internet access services. The Commission held that the structure of the market was in fact hierarchical: there was a tier of top-level ISPs; a group of ISPs with smaller networks; and then ISPs who simply resell access to other ISPs' networks. If top-level ISPs raised the prices of their Internet connection services by 5%, resellers would have to keep using their systems and so would pay the increase and, in due course, pass it on to consumers. Smaller ISPs would also have to continue to deal with the top-level ISPs if a price rise was imposed and so would not act as a competitive constraint on the top-level ISPs.

In terms of geography, the Commission found that for top-level ISPs the market was global because, although they were based in the US, operated at an international level providing services throughout the world.

The Commission has recognised that different Internet-related services can, clearly, constitute different product markets. In the *Telia/Telenor/Schibsted* case[32] it distinguished the market for Internet access from those for paid-content eg games, special news services and for Internet advertising. It also recognised the weight of the parties' argument that website production services may be a sufficiently technical and specialised activity to constitute a separate market.

In addition to distinguishing between different Internet-related services, the Commission has also distinguished the Internet provision of services from other channels. The *Bertelsmann/Mondadori*[33] case concerned two major publishing enterprises wishing to create a joint venture to combine their respective book club activities. Although the Commission did not have to reach a final conclusion on market definition, it considered that it might be possible to distinguish between 'distant selling' of books (including book club sales, mail order and Internet sales) from the retail sale of books. This reasoning follows the earlier decision in *Advent/EMI/WH Smith*[34] where a similar distinction between the distant selling and retail selling of books was drawn. Were such a distinction to be sustained by the Commission as ecommerce develops, it could have a profound impact upon the competitive analysis of Internet retailers: if the Internet is a separate market from retail, Internet retailers will be considered to have far larger market shares than would otherwise be the case. However, it is suggested

31 Case IV/M 1069 *Re Concentration between Worldcom Inc and MCI Communications Corpn* [1999] 5 CMLR 876 at 894.

32 Case No IV/JV 1 – *Telia/Telenor/Schibsted* (27 May 1998, unreported). See also Case No IV/JV 5 *Cegetel/Canal+/AOL/Bertelsmann* (4 August 1998, unreported); Case No IV/JV 11 *@Home Benelux* (15 September 1998, unreported); and *DeTeOnline/Axel Springer/Holtzbrink/Internet Corpn* (12 October 1998, unreported).

33 Case No IV/M 1407 *Bertelsman/Mondadori* OJ C 145 26/05/1999.

34 Case No IV/M 1112 *Advent International/EMI/WH Smith* OJ C 172 06/06/1998. See also, in the context of catalogue sales Case No IV/M 0070 *Otto/Grattan* OJ C 093 11/04/1991.

that as consumers become more used to Internet shopping and the dynamics of retailing change, such distinctions will need to be reconsidered[35].

In the *myaircraft.com* case[36–39] which concerned the creation of a B2B market place for aircraft parts and attendant services, the parties argued that the provision of aircraft parts and services over the Internet was part of the general market for aircraft parts and services. The submission was that '*. . . e-commerce should be considered as one segment among the many modalities by which companies transact business*'. Whilst the Commission did not find it necessary to make a definitive finding upon the relevant market in question the competitive assessment of the arrangements takes into account the position of the participants in the general market for aircraft parts and services, not just Internet-based sales.

Convergence

A particular manifestation of the way in which the Internet changes the competitive structure of other industries is seen in what is referred to in the jargon as 'convergence'. Television, computers and telephony are all beginning to be able to perform similar functions as digital technology develops. We can, for example, access the Internet through our televisions and mobile phones (without the need for a computer) and, equally access television and make phone calls through our computers. The technology to do this is available now. It remains to be seen how quickly systems will be adopted, which systems will prove popular and what technological developments will appear.

From the competition law point of view, the key issue is that those people wanting to provide television programming, telecommunications links or online shopping will have a variety of routes by which they can reach the consumer. The result is that different infrastructure systems (or 'platforms') may be competing against one another for business.

When considering whether the activities of Internet businesses are anti-competitive it may be necessary not just to consider the market for Internet provision of the relevant services or products but also to look at other distribution mechanisms. Equally, it means that agreements or mergers between businesses which have little or no overlap in their existing activities require close scrutiny because each set of activities reinforces the other in the convergent world[40].

Perhaps most notably in the *British Interactive Broadcasting* joint venture, the Commission found that there was a separate market for the supply of interactive services via the television as distinct from via computers or indeed through high street retailers. It is not necessarily surprising that the supply of

35 In relation to the geographical extent of the market, emphasis was placed on language barriers and the market limited to Italy. See also Case No IV/M 1459 *Bertelsmann/Havas/BOL* (6 May 1999, unreported).

36–39 Op cit.

40 The *Time Warner/AOL* merger is the most poignant example of this phenomenon. Time Warner had relatively limited Internet interests but was a major broadcaster with access to substantial valuable content. AOL had large numbers of people to whom they were ISP and to whom they wished to provide content. By merging Time Warner was able to provide content which AOL lacked to AOL's subscribers using Internet technology. See below and Commission Press Release IP/00/1145 of 11 October 2000 *Commission gives conditional approval to AOL/Time Warner merger*.

services (and goods) from high street retailers was not considered a substitute for interactive services accessible from the comfort of your own home using the television (although it should be noted that the companies with virtual shops on the Open system were, in many cases, high street retailers).

Rather more surprising is the distinction between interactive services accessed through a computer and those accessed through the television. The Commission concluded that a small but significant increase in the prices of interactive television services could be sustained. The possibility of accessing such services through a computer would not constrain prices for two reasons: first, only 25% of households in the UK had computers; and secondly, the cost of switching between television and computer is high because a whole PC system had to be bought. A further reason adduced was that TVs are traditionally found in the living room and are a focal point of family life whereas computers are tucked away elsewhere. The characteristics of the use of the television therefore meant that people would not start using computers as a substitute.

As convergence continues this may be found to be an untenable distinction in future cases. The traditionally defined roles of the television and computers could rapidly erode (the 'tradition' can, after all, have been in place for no more than about 10 years). People might use computers more for receiving films and other entertainment. Substitutability might substantially increase and the relevant market would, therefore, widen.

A more sustainable distinction might be that which the Commission drew between interactive television services, pay television and free to air television[41]. The idea that free to air television does not constrain the pricing of pay television is widely accepted (although not uncontroversial) – it is easy to argue that if free to air TV was a substitute for pay TV everyone would watch free TV because everyone prefers not to pay. The distinction drawn between pay TV services, which are principally entertainment services, and interactive TV services, which are largely transactional or information providing, is, perhaps, more interesting. The Commission considered that interactive TV was a complement to pay TV, not a substitute.

It is also notable in the context of the pay television market that the Commission distinguished between the wholesale supply of films and sports channels and other pay TV content. Films and sports channels are often referred to as 'premium' channels due to their higher pricing as compared with basic channels. This higher pricing itself tends to indicate a separate market for such services[42]. It also vindicates the hackneyed new media saying that 'content is king'.

Finally, the Commission considered the infrastructure market within which Open was to operate. Commentators have suggested that cable networks have had a significant technological advantage over satellite broadcasting systems since satellite systems lack a simple 'return path' – a route by which the viewer can easily communicate with the broadcaster. By linking BskyB's satellite broad-

41 Free to air: programming that customers do not have to pay a subscription for such as ITV1 and BBC1.

42 A similar distinction was drawn by the Monopolies and Mergers Commission in its report on the proposed merger between *BskyB and ManchesterUnited* [1999] Cm 4305, in particular, paragraphs 2.25–2.51.

casting system to the narrowband telephone network Open was able to compete against the UK cable system by providing a return path which enabled interactivity between consumers and the service providers. The Commission concluded that Open was, therefore, competing in an infrastructure market which included the BT copper wire network and the fibre cable network. Notably, mobile networks were excluded from the market definition.

Exemption and exclusion[43]

Article 81(3) provides that certain agreements which fall within the scope of art 81(1) ie they prevent, restrict or distort competition, can be exempted from the adverse consequences of falling foul of the prohibition. There are two types of exemption available under European law: individual exemptions; and block exemptions.

The Ch I prohibition[44] also makes provision for the exemption of agreements. Under domestic law a system of individual exemptions and block exemptions similar to that available under European law has been provided for. In addition, any agreement which benefits from a European individual or block exemption (or would have done if the arrangement had a European dimension) will also be exempt for the purposes of domestic law. Such exemptions are referred to in the domestic context as 'parallel exemptions'.

In addition, under domestic law certain types of agreement are entirely excluded from the ambit of the Ch I prohibition.

Individual exemptions

An agreement which contributes to:

(i) the improvement of production or distribution; or
(ii) promotes technical or economic progress

may be exempted if it provides consumers with what is referred to as 'fair share' of these benefits and does not impose on the parties restrictions which are not indispensable to the attainment of the objectives specified[45]. In addition, the arrangements in question must not give either of the parties the ability to eliminate competition in respect of a substantial part of the products in question.

Although this test is stringent, it is essentially carrying out the balancing exercise discussed above. In other words, is the agreement pro-competitive and are all the restrictions included in the agreement necessary to achieve the pro-competitive ends?

43 These exemptions and exclusions are subject to a 'clawback' provisions which enable the relevant authorities to remove their protection in certain circumstances.
44 CA 98, ss 4–11.
45 Under domestic law the exemption is granted by the DGFT, in European law it is granted by the Commission.

An example of a case in which an individual exemption has been granted to an agreement relating to Internet access or services at the European level is the *British Interactive Broadcasting* ('BiB') joint venture[46] referred to above. BiB, which traded as 'Open', was a joint venture company whose parents were BSkyB, British Telecom, HSBC and Matsushita. It was established to provide digital interactive television services to consumers in the UK. Using BskyB's digital satellite broadcasting system and BT's telecommunications network, consumers were able to access a range of interactive services including home banking, home shopping and a limited 'walled garden' of websites. The arrangement was notified to the European Commission seeking individual exemption pursuant to art 81(3).

As described above, difficult questions as to the competitive effect of the joint venture arose, in particular in relation to market definition. The EC Commission was concerned that the arrangement would appreciably restrict competition between BT and BskyB. Conditions were, therefore, imposed upon the parties to ensure that competition could come from cable networks, that third parties had sufficient access to Open's subsidised set-top-boxes (and BskyB's film and sports channels) and that it was possible set-top-boxes other than Open's own could be developed. The arrangement was granted an individual exemption once undertakings to comply with the conditions had been given.

Applying for individual exemption

An undertaking can request the DGFT to give a decision as to whether the agreement notified falls within the Ch I prohibition or is exempt whether under a block or parallel exemption or should be granted an individual exemption[47].

Instead of requesting a final decision on an agreement, parties can ask the DGFT for confidential guidance as to whether their agreement is likely to fall foul of the Ch I prohibition and, if so, whether it would be likely to be exempted. Favourable guidance gives the parties protection from further action by the DGFT and if, at a later stage, the DGFT wishes to take further action, he must communicate with the parties. However, favourable guidance can be more easily disturbed than a decision should, for example, a third party make a complaint about the arrangements.

If an agreement has a European dimension[48] and it is believed that it is necessary to secure individual exemption for it (in other words it falls within the scope of art 81(1) but is not block exempt) then it is necessary to notify the Commission and seek individual exemption. It should be noted, however, that *vertical agreements* no longer require prior notification in order to secure individual exemption[49]. In addition, the Commission has published proposals for

46 Case No IV 36 539 *British Interactive Broadcasting/Open* [1999] OJ L312/1. See also comment upon the decision by Andres Font Galarza in the *Competition Policy Newsletter* [1999] No 3 October.

47 CA 98, s 14.

48 In other words, it has an appreciable effect on interstate trade. See above.

49 Amendment was made to Regulation 17/62 (adopted 29/04/99) see Press Release IP/99/286.

the end of the notification system generally although at the time of writing these proposals remain only at the consultative stage[50].

Apart from formal exemption, informal contact with the relevant EC Commission personnel to discuss any proposed arrangements is a very important step to take prior to any notification.

UK block exemptions and exclusions

Block exemptions are exemptions covering a particular type of agreement rather than specifying a particular agreement. In addition, various exclusions are provided for under the Competition Act 1998 and accompanying secondary legislation. Most notably merger agreements[51], ie agreements falling within the scope of the Fair Trading Act 1973 merger control regime, are excluded. Also excluded are agreements relating to land[52], professional rules[53], and agreements already covered by specific competition regimes such as financial services[54].

In addition, an exclusion covering all vertical agreements has been enacted[55]. This vertical restraints exclusion excludes from the scope of the prohibition any agreement between two or more undertakings, each operating at different stages in the economic process for the purposes of that agreement. The only type of vertical agreements not covered are those which involve the fixing of prices whether directly or indirectly.

This is an extremely broad exclusion and could cover sales and distribution agreements and may also cover software licensing agreements. The exclusion enormously increases legal certainty in competition law and reflects economic thinking which sees vertical agreements as generally harmless or pro-competitive unless the parties have significant market power.

The DGFT retains the ability to withdraw the protection of the exclusion from particular agreements where he believes it is protecting harmful arrangements.

European block exemptions (domestic 'parallel exemptions')

There are a range of block exemptions covering, amongst other things, exclusive distribution, exclusive purchasing and franchising (all vertical agreements)[56],

50 Commission White Paper on Modernisation of the Rules Implementing Articles 81 and 82 of the EC Treaty [1999].

51 CA 98, Sch 1.

52 Competition Act 1998 (Land and Vertical Agreements exclusion) Order 2000 SI 2000/310; *OFT Guideline 420.*

53 CA 98, Sch 4.

54 CA 98, Sch 2, Pt I.

55 Competition Act 1998 (Land and Vertical Agreements Exclusion) Order 2000 SI 2000/310; *OFT Guideline 419.*

56 *Commission Regulation on the application of Article 81(3) of the EC Treaty to categories of vertical agreements and concerted practices* [1999] OJ L336/21. This vertical restraints block exemption replaces Regulations 1983/83, 1984/83 and 4087/88 the block exemptions relating to exclusive distribution, exclusive purchasing and franchising all of which expired on 31 May 2000.

57 Regulation 417/85.

58 Regulation 418/85.

research and development[57], specialisation[58] and know-how and patent licensing agreements[59]. These block exemptions specify certain clauses within the different types of agreement which are permitted and those which are not ('black-listed' clauses).

It is notable that the EC vertical agreements block exemption is not as broad as the domestic vertical restraints exclusion although it, nonetheless, covers a wide range of agreements between parties at different levels in the production and distribution chain. Agreements containing restrictions on resale prices or 'passive sales' (sales where the customer approaches the supplier rather than where the supplier has touted for the customer's business) are not covered by the block exemption. Furthermore, where the supplier (or, in certain circumstances, the buyer) has 30% of the relevant market for the products at issue it cannot benefit from block exemption protection.

The guidelines accompanying the block exemption indicate that the use of the Internet to advertise or sell products is, in general, considered a form of passive sales insofar as the website is not directed towards a territory or customer group exclusively allocated to another distributor[60]. This implies that exclusive distribution or purchasing agreements which prevented any use of websites would not benefit from the protection of the vertical restraints block exemption. It might, however, be permissible to restrict the use of links or on-site advertising which specifically targeted customers allocated to other distributors.

In addition, the vertical restraints block exemption does not apply where a supplier has established a 'selective distribution' system. That is to say where the supplier has selected his distributors on the basis of objective criteria such as service quality or nature of premises. Where such arrangements have been put in place no restriction can be placed on either active or passive selling. However, it appears arguable that a ban on Internet sales altogether might be justified if it could be argued that face to face contact with a retailer was the optimal way of selling particular goods or services[61].

CHAPTER II AND ARTICLE 82

Subject to the exclusion of mergers and specific exclusions, the Ch II prohibition provides:

> '. . . any conduct on the part of one or more undertakings which amounts to the abuse of a dominant position in a market is prohibited if it may affect trade within the United Kingdom.'

The only significant difference between this provision and art 82 is that art 82 refers to a dominant position '. . . within the common market or in a substantial

60 Commission Notice: *Guidelines on vertical restraints* [2000] OJ C 291/1 para 51.

61 An analogous argument was accepted by the Commission in Case IV/33 242 *Yves Saint Laurent* [1992] OJ L12 p 24. In that case the Commission considered that the optimum conditions for supplying luxury cosmetics were where there was direct contact between customers and sales staff. A ban on mail order sales was, therefore, permissible. See Gahnstrom and Vajda 'EC Competition Law and the Internet' [2000] ECLR.

part of it' requires an affect on trade between Member States. Under domestic law, a dominant position means a dominant position within the UK or part of it[62].

Dominance

The definition of a dominant position which has been applied in European case law and will, in virtue of s 60, be applied under the Competition Act 1998, was given in the *United Brands* case[63] where the ECJ stated that a dominant position is:

> 'a position of economic strength enjoyed by an undertaking which enables it to prevent effective competition being maintained on the relevant market by affording it the power to behave to an appreciable extent independently of its competitors, customers and ultimately of its consumers'.

Where an entity is able to act without normal competitive pressures, ie independent of them, then it is likely to be considered dominant. When we talk of 'dominance' we refer to it as being in the context of a particular market and so the question of what the relevant market is for particular goods or services raises its ugly head again. The considerations and difficulties which were set out above in relation to market definition become important once more.

Market share

It is a broad rule of thumb that an undertaking holding a market share of over 40% may be considered dominant. Much will depend upon the structure of the market in question. If the undertaking in question is the only large player in the market and competition comes from far smaller players, it is more likely that a finding of dominance will be made. On the other hand if the market is oligopolistic, so that there are a small number of large players, it is less likely that an undertaking with 40% of the market would be found to be dominant since it is unlikely to be able to effectively ignore its competitors in setting terms or prices.

In addition to considering market shares it is important to look at the nature of the market for the products in question. If there are low barriers to entry for new competitors and there is a great deal of innovation in the market, a company with a large market share at any particular moment, might quickly see it diminished. Although brought in the context of different legislation, this was one of Microsoft's key arguments in the case brought against it by the Department of Justice in the US. Microsoft argued that in the market for operating systems, although it had a substantial market share, there was competition emerging from Java systems and from web browsers which could provide platform-neutral operating systems and thereby undermine Microsoft's

62 Section 18(3).
63 Case 27/76 *United Brands v EC Commission* [1978] ECR 207 at 277.

position[64]. The Court did not accept the argument although it recognised the importance of innovation in relation to competition on the Internet[65].

Growth and innovation

Almost all sectors of Internet-related activity are highly innovative. The hardware which enables people to use the Internet has changed beyond recognition in the past decade. Processor speeds have increased rapidly whilst prices have fallen. Routers and switching systems manage greater and greater volumes of traffic. Applications software from accountancy packages to browsers is constantly changing and improving. And ecommerce is growing. Forecasts for the scale of ecommerce in the UK alone in the next decade run into many billions of pounds. The whole manner in which people trade and do business is being reshaped by the Internet.

This rapid change and rapid growth has significant implications for the application of any competition law system. Where products and services are constantly evolving it tends to be more difficult for any one company to secure the sort of market power which will enable them to distort the proper functioning of the market. Although a product may be very popular at a particular time, the possibility of a new, more advanced, product coming in and replacing it in the near future are higher in dynamic high-technology markets. The result is that whilst there may be certain concerns about the manner in which the market operates from time to time, authorities should be slow to intervene because the market is more likely to rectify its own problems within a short time.

In addition, there are major practical problems with intervention in dynamic markets. First, it is often hard to gather sufficient quantities of useful data to enable a regulator to get an accurate picture of how the market is operating. Secondly, any regulatory intervention tends to take time for consideration and implementation. By the time a conclusion that intervention is necessary is reached, the market may have moved on and, whilst the proposed solution might have been appropriate six months ago, it is now too late to be useful.

In trying to identify dominance, a court will consider whether, on the evidence, (a) features of the market mean that it will be easier or more difficult for parties to gain and sustain market power; and (b) the behaviour of the undertaking is consistent with that which would be expected if it held market power. It was a crucial finding by Judge Penfield Jackson in *Microsoft* that the company had priced its products without any regard to its supposed competitors. It had market power such that it was able to price its products (in particular Windows 95 in the run-up to the release of Windows 98) entirely independent of competitive pressures[66].

64 See *United States of America v Microsoft Corpn* Civil Action No 98-1232 ('*Microsoft*') Transcript of Proceedings 21 September 1999, closing submissions of Microsoft.

65 See *Microsoft* Findings of Fact 5 November 1999, in particular at paras 408 and 409.

66 See *Microsoft* Findings of Fact 5 November 1999, in particular at para 62.

Network effects

There are certain features of Internet-related industries which might incline authorities to intervene. The Internet is a network of networks which is dependent upon common language, protocols and applications in order to confer benefits on individuals. As more people adopt a particular standard the more value it has to all those using it as a network grows. Each new potential user will have a greater incentive to adopt the standard. The phenomenon is referred to as Metcalfe's Law: the value of a network to its users grows exponentially with the addition of each new user. It is known by competition lawyers as a 'positive network effect'. In practice it means that if you can be the first to get an application into the market so that you build up a base of users, it is more likely that your application rather than a competing application will become the industry standard. In other words, by getting a good start in the market you can have significant advantages in securing a powerful market position.

Any competition regulator would prefer to stop competition problems before they start. Early intervention to prevent any individual or group of individuals getting undue power in the market place is better than waiting until they have market power and actually use it to distort competition. By that time, many potential competitors may have already suffered and potential entrants will have been deterred. It tends to require government with a very heavy hand to unravel monopolies. There is, therefore, a temptation for regulators to step in earlier on in the development of a market which exhibits network effects in order to prevent those effects maintaining a monster (in competition terms).

Marginal Costs

Network effects in an Internet-related market may be reinforced where the market is in knowledge-based products or services. In such markets marginal costs may be zero. For example, once you have made the effort to produce some software, the cost of producing an additional copy is negligible. Developing the knowledge may have been expensive and the initial investment in exploitation may have been high, but once those investments have been made, further exploitation is cheap. It is, therefore, extremely easy to scale-up your operations quickly.

Once a company in a market with network effects has a small advantage it is able to able attract new customers more easily than its nearest rival. The company's attractiveness to customers rapidly increases and so its advantage over its rivals extends. And it can bring in new customers easily without incurring significant cost.

One particular matter which is important to the competition law analysis of so-called knowledge based industries is the role played by intellectual property rights. Intellectual property law would appear to enable companies to develop significant market power by ensuring that nobody else uses their unique hardware, software, ideas or branding.

Whilst intellectual property law confers exclusive rights on owners, it is dangerous to think of intellectual property as property in the same way as a pioneer might have thought of his claim to a patch of land in frontier country: something which was his and with which he could do as he wished. Although the possession or use of an intellectual property right is not in and of itself anti-competitive, intellectual property rights can, in certain circumstances, be used to anti-competitive effect, for example, to control supply or raise prices excessively.

The relationship between intellectual property rights and competition law is vexed. A patent, for example may be seen as a sanctioned monopoly in relation to particular works, products or processes. It is justified on the basis that the prospect of winning such a monopoly encourages innovation and endeavour, if there were no such monopolies, writers and inventors would be unable to reap any benefit from their work since it would be copied as soon as it became public. The extent of these mini-monopolies is limited by competition law. There is therefore a tension between what intellectual property rights can legitimately be used to achieve and what is anti-competitive. A substantial body of European case law on the relationship between intellectual property rights and competition has developed without resolving this tension in a way that provides companies or practitioners any great certainty when they are deciding how to behave[67].

Joint dominance

Both art 82 and the Ch II prohibition explicitly refer to '. . . one or more undertakings . . .' being dominant. This provision admits the possibility that, in certain situations, more than one company, when they are considered together, are able to effectively act independently of competitive pressures[68]. In the *Almelo* case[69] the ECJ held that '*[i]n order for . . . a collective dominant position to exist the undertakings must be linked in such a way that they adopt the same conduct on the market*'. It is clear that contractual links may be sufficient to give rise to a position of joint dominance. But other economic links between the parties to a tight oligopoly within may be sufficient to result in collective dominance in a market with the appropriate characteristics, in particular in terms of market concentration, transparency and product homogeneity. Where parties are in a position to anticipate one another's behaviour and are therefore strongly encouraged to align their conduct in the market so as to maximise their joint profits by restricting production with a view to increasing prices then collective dominance may exist. In such a context, each trader is party to a 'game' where it is aware that highly competitive action on its part designed to increase its market share (for example a price cut) would provoke identical action by the others, so that it would derive no benefit from its initiative. All the traders would thus be affected by the reduction in price levels[70].

However, whilst the possibility of collective dominance existing in markets is recognised it will often be difficult to prove in practice[71].

67 A detailed discussion of the relationship between intellectual property and competition is beyond the scope of the present chapter.
68 See, in particular, Case T-68/89 *Societa Italiano Vetro v EC Commission* [1992] ECR II-1403.
69 Case C-393/92 [1994] ECR I-1477.
70 See, in particular, Case T-102/96 *Gencor Ltd v Commission* [1999] ECR II–753 where it was suggested that in certain circumstances companies in oligopolistic markets may have a jointly dominant position even without contractual links.
71 See Case T–342/99 *Airtours v EC Commssion* [2002] 5 CMLR 317.

Abuse

The concept of abuse of a dominant position covers a range of behaviour. As with art 81/Ch I, art 82/Ch II includes a list of examples of the types of behaviour which may fall foul of the prohibition[72].

Pricing

In terms of general principle, excessive pricing is the most obvious form of abuse of a dominant position. Prices are excessively high where they are above the prices which would be charged by undertakings if the market was competitive.

In *Napp Pharmaceuticals v Director General of Fair Trading*[72a] the Competition Commission Appeals Tribunal held that the following methods could be used in assessing whether prices were excessive:

(i) A comparison of prices against costs;
(ii) A comparison of prices against the costs of the next most profitable competitor;
(iii) A comparison of prices against the prices of competitors;
(iv) A comparison of prices against the undertaking's own prices in other markets.

But precisely how much higher prices would need to be above costs to indicate excess is not clear.

In fact, excessive pricing is one of the hardest forms of abuse to prove. Indeed, referring to profitability in assessing excessive pricing can be highly unreliable. In the OFT Economic Discussion Paper 377 'Innovation and Competition policy' Charles River Associates state:

> 'Measuring profitability is a poor way of conducting competition policy in standard industries. It is likely to be even worse in high technology industries. The very high ex ante risks of failure mean that the returns to 'winners' in high technology markets should be very high.'

As the OFT have stated in their guidelines '[t]o be an abuse, prices would have to be *persistently* excessive without stimulating new entry or innovation'[73].

Predation

An alternative strategy that a dominant firm might adopt, rather than trying to secure higher profits in the short run by pricing excessively high, is to drop prices to drive competitors out of the market. The intention of this strategy is that once the competitors are driven out the incumbent will be free to increase

72 There is no system of exemption for breaches of art 82/Ch II. Limited exclusions are provided for in s 19 of the CA 98, the key area excluded is mergers and concentrations.
72a [2002] Comp AR 13.
73 OFT Guideline 402 p 9.

prices and recover the losses it incurred in dropping the prices and go on to make greater profits overall.

Again, predatory pricing is an abuse which is often difficult to prove. After all, where markets are competitive it would be expected that competitors would drop prices in order to increase market share. Lower prices may simply be a reflection of increased efficiency.

The general rule adopted by the EC Commission in European cases is that where a company price below its average variable cost of production, ie the average of those costs which vary according to the amount of the product produced, predation is to be presumed.

However, in high technology markets standard price tests are likely to be unhelpful if fixed costs are high and marginal costs are close to zero. As OFT Discussion Paper No 377 points out:

> 'In one sense, such tests are likely to be far too permissive: they would allow pricing in response to a new entrant that could not possibly be the rational response except for the anti-competitive benefits of exclusion. In another sense such tests are not permissive enough: when competition is for the market, very low penetration pricing may be a perfectly rational and pro-competitive form of competition.'[74]

This 'rational' explanation is often the true state of affairs on the Internet. On the Internet much content and software is available at no apparent cost to the end-user.

What amounts to predation in such markets may, therefore, be more difficult to identify. It has been suggested that the relevant test should focus upon whether the alleged infringer only took the action because of the anti-competitive (often exclusionary) benefits[75].

Discrimination

Price discrimination essentially comes in two forms. The most easily identifiable is where undertakings charge different prices to different categories of customer without a justification for the distinction. Customers might be divided into regional price categories or by type of activity. In the *Microsoft* case the US Court found that the company was charging different OEMs different prices simply depending upon their level of co-operation with Microsoft[76]. It would be unsurprising were a UK or European court to consider this unjustifiable price discrimination on the basis of such facts.

It should be noted, however, that the prohibition on discriminatory pricing does not mean that discounting structures are prohibited. Discounts are a form of price competition and so are to be encouraged. It is only where a discount structure is not justified by the economies of bulk buying, but is based on a formula which has the effect of rewarding exclusivity that it is likely to be found to be abusive. Where a discount structure is put in place which is conditional upon customers buying all or a very large proportion of their needs from a dominant undertaking (what are known as 'fidelity discounts') they will be prohibited

74 Paragraph 1.11.
75 OFT Economics Discussion Paper No 377 at para 1.13.
76 See *Microsoft* Findings of Fact 5 November 1999, in particular at paras 64–66.

because they foreclose the market for other sellers competing with the dominant undertaking.

In addition to discrimination on the basis of price, discriminatory terms of sale including access to new developments or updates may constitute an abuse.

Vertical restraints

As described above, in the context of the art 81/Ch I prohibition the authorities are adopting a progressively more beneficent approach to vertical restrictions. However, arrangements which might otherwise be exempted by a block exemption can still constitute an abuse of a dominant position. The market power of a dominant player can, for example, render exclusive purchasing and distribution arrangements anti-competitive. Where a dominant undertaking enters into such arrangements they can foreclose the market to other manufacturers because only a limited number of available retail outlets exist.

Tying and bundling

Tying sales of one product or service to another may also constitute an abuse particularly if the tie is intended to ensure that the retailer takes the full range of the manufacturers goods when, in fact, the retailer would prefer to be more selective. The tying together of products is often referred to as 'bundling'.

In the *Microsoft* case one of the key issues was whether Microsoft had, effectively, abused its dominant position by bundling its Internet Explorer browser product with Windows. The District Court found that it had abused its market power in relation to operating systems to force OEMs to take Explorer rather than competing browsers such as Netscape's Navigator[77]. However, the Appeals Court was unconvinced, recognising that consumers benefited from the bundling of additional products.

Refusal to supply

Although it might be thought that anyone is free to do business, or not do business, with whomsoever they choose, dominance can limit this freedom. If a dominant undertaking wants to refuse to supply a customer there must be an objective justification for the refusal to supply. Examples of justifications for refusal to supply include a lack of capacity to make the supply, the cost of dealing making the supply unprofitable or the creditworthiness of the customer being extremely dubious. It is generally far harder to justify the termination of supply to an existing customer than it is to justify the refusal of supply to an entirely new one (save in the case of essential facilities, discussed below).

77 *Microsoft* Findings of Fact 5 November 1999 at para 216.

***Jobserve v NMTV*[77a]**

Jobserve operated a website, Jobserve.com, on which IT recruitment agencies advertised placements. It was very successful and large numbers of adverts were placed on the site and places were often quickly and efficiently filled by people who saw the placements advertised on Jobserve.com. It was arguably dominant. A new IT recruitment web site, named 'ATSCOjobs.com' was created. Jobserve told ATSCO members advertising vacancies on Jobserve.com that they would not be allowed to do so if they advertised vacancies on ATSCOjobs.com.

Jobserve.com was the most widely used online IT job board by both agencies and IT job seekers. Refusing to supply agencies with the advertising services could 'strangle a potential competitor at birth'.

The court found that there was an arguable case that Jobserve breached the Ch II. It held that Jobserve should allow ATSCO members to continue to use its services.

In general a refusal to licence an intellectual property right is not an abuse of a dominant position. However, the OFT guidelines[78] refer to the situation which arose in the *Magill*[79] case in relation to a refusal to licence copyright of television schedules. In that case the television stations transmitting in Ireland and Northern Ireland sued Magill who had begun to publish a comprehensive listings guide on the basis that the listings were the copyright of the respective TV stations. Although the ECJ confirmed that mere ownership of an intellectual property right does not confer a dominant position in the particular circumstances of the case the stations were the only source of the information and were, therefore, dominant.

The *Magill* decision has generally been interpreted as being a fairly exceptional circumstance. The refusal to grant the copyright licence prevented the production of a new product, there was no justification for the refusal and, by their refusal, the broadcasters were essentially reserving the secondary market for listings magazines for themselves. However, given the importance of trade marks and copyright to the development of many Internet businesses, this doctrine is likely to be further explored in future.

Essential facilities

It has been suggested that in certain circumstances access to facilities controlled by an undertaking are *essential* if someone is to compete in a particular market. It is argued that such access is indispensable where it is not possible (or extremely difficult) to duplicate the facility due to physical, geographic or legal constraints. Proving that a facility is essential tends to be a difficult task[80].

Where an undertaking controls an essential facility, it is likely to be found to be in a dominant position and that refusal to allow access to the facility on fair

77a [2001] UKCLR 814.
78 OFT Guideline 402 p 18.
79 Cases C 241 and 242/91 *Radio Telefis Eireann v EC Commission (Magill)* [1995] ECR I-743.
80 See, in particular, Case C-7/97 *Oscar Bronner v Mediaprint* [1998] ECR I-7791.

terms is likely to constitute an abuse. In the context of the Internet it may be possible to argue (in certain circumstances) that telecommunications networks are essential facilities. In the *Worldcom/MCI* merger case, although the term 'essential facility' was not used, the reasoning of the Commission decision would tend to suggest that the provision of top-level Internet connectivity by ISPs could arguably be an essential facility.

In contrast, in the US, Cyber Promotions, who were sending millions of email advertisements to AOL subscribers, claimed that AOL monopolised the essential facility to advertise to AOL's subscribers using electronic mail[81]. The argument was given short shrift by the court: Cyber could send electronic adverts to AOL subscribers by other means and, in any event, Cyber was not even completely barred from the AOL network. There were no grounds whatsoever for suggesting that the facility was essential.

Microsoft

The most famous case relating to abuse of a dominant position in Internet related activities was that brought by the US Department of Justice (and several states) against Microsoft. Although the legal conclusions may be of less relevance to UK and European lawyers, the analysis of the market and the identification of problems in Judge Jackson's findings of fact and the Appeals Court's decision are extremely useful.

The Judge found that the relevant market in which Microsoft operated was the market for Intel-compatible PCs since it would be difficult and expensive for users to switch to other systems. Microsoft provided operating systems to 90% of all the world's Intel-compatible PCs. He found that 'Microsoft enjoys so much power in the market for Intel-compatible PC operating systems that if it wished to exercise this power solely in terms of price, it could charge a price for Windows substantially above that which could be charged in a competitive market. Moreover, it could do so for significant period of time without losing and unacceptable amount of business to competitors'[82]. In other words, Microsoft could be considered dominant in UK and European terms.

The Judge then considered Microsoft's behaviour in relation to various competitors and, in particular, the way in which it tried to increase the market share of its Internet browser, Internet Explorer. He made a key finding that it was extremely difficult for rivals to launch a competing operating systems because there were so many applications available for Windows that it would be difficult for a potential competitor to accumulate a similar range of applications to offer to consumers. He cited IBM's heavy investment in OS2/Warp and its subsequent failure as evidence that there was a high 'applications barrier to entry' to the operating system market.

He also found that developing 'middleware' technologies – software that sits between operating systems and application software such as Java and Netscape Navigator – would not offer a sufficient range of applications in the foreseeable future to truly compete with Windows.

81 *Cyber Promotions Inc v America Online Inc* 948 F Supp 456 (ED Pa 1996).
82 Paragraph 33.

Further evidence for Microsoft's market power (and its potential to abuse) was the manner in which Microsoft priced windows. The Judge noted that '. . . Microsoft raised the price that it charged OEMs for Windows 95, with trivial exceptions, to the same level as the price it charged for Windows 98 just prior to releasing the new product. In a competitive market, one would expect the price of an older operating system to stay the same or decrease upon the release of a newer, more attractive version'[83].

The Judge went on to find that Microsoft tried to protect the applications barrier to entry in its dealings with OEMs and other software manufactures. The maintenance of this barrier and the reduction in competition harmed consumers. Its behaviour retarded the development of middleware technologies so that Internet Explorer would gain a stronger position through its bundling with Windows[84].

The Judge's approach illustrates the types of issues which would be considered by a domestic or European court dealing with such questions under the relevant legislation. It further highlights the general problems of the relationship between the Internet and competition law. First, the Judge had to make findings about the likely developments in fast moving, innovative technological markets. Secondly, as in the Worldcom/MCI merger, having sufficiently up-to-date and comprehensive market information was difficult. Thirdly, the Judge identified what he referred to as 'the intractable chicken and egg problem'[85] : since consumers want operating systems which give access to a wide range of high quality applications, developers will concentrate on developing applications for the operating system which has the most users. Once you have an advantage in terms of the number of users of your operating system more applications will be developed for it and so more consumers will want to use it. In other words, there is a positive network effect in the market for operating systems (and potentially other Internet related markets).

On the issues of substance, the Appeals Court upheld in large part the finding that Microsoft had illegally monopolised the PC operating systems market. However, it rejected the finding that Microsoft had illegally attempted to extend its monopoly power into the Internet browser market. The third finding that the tying of Internet Explorer to Windows was anti-competitive was remitted for reconsideration; the issue whether tying and bundling is anti-competitive remains an important and controversial question.

The Appeals Court also recognised the broad problems with anti-trust litigation in fast moving industries such as IT, saying the six years since the anti-competitive activity had begun 'seems like an eternity in the computer industry'. The judgment highlighted the difficult arguments about how one might analyse innovative markets where wave upon wave of creative destruction enables market shares to be built up quickly and then blown away with equal speed.

However, apart from the detailed substantive analysis, the Appeals Court judgment will also be remembered for its consideration of issues of due process. The Appeals court found that the Judge had failed to conduct a full exploration of the facts relating to remedies and that the conduct of the Judge himself 'seriously tainted the proceedings before the District Court and called into question the integrity of the judicial process'.

83 Paragraph 62.

84 See Section VII *The Effect on consumers of Microsoft's efforts to protect the applications barrier to entry* (paras 408–412).

85 Paragraph 30.

Whilst proceedings were still pending, the Judge carried out a series of secret interviews with *The New Yorker*. During these he characterised Microsoft's crime as 'hubris' – a refusal to acknowledge that the nation's anti-trust laws applied to them.

Indeed he said that if he were able to propose a remedy of his own devising it would be to require Bill Gates to write a book report on a recent biography of Napoleon 'because I think he has a Napoleonic concept of himself and his company, an arrogance that derives from power and unalloyed success'.

At one point he even compared the Microsoft executives' declarations of innocence to the protestations of gangland killers.

When it came to remedies, the Judge Jackson initially intimated to reporters that he was not minded to order break up. But as the months of remedies negotiations wore on, he became tired of what he perceived to be Microsoft's intransigence. He moved to favouring break up and, in support of his change of heart, told one reporter a parable about a North Carolina mule trainer who had taught his mule to do all sorts of tricks. When an astonished passer-by asked how he managed to teach the mule, the trainer pulled out a piece of 2-by-4 and 'whopped it upside its head'. As the mule fell to his knees the trainer gave the moral of the story: 'you just have to get his attention'.

GUIDANCE IN CHAPTER II PROHIBITION CASES

There is no scope for exempting an abuse of a dominant position so no exemption/clearance decisions can be made. However, guidance can be sought from the OFT as to whether a particular course of conduct could amount to an abuse of dominance. As with guidance given in relation to the application of the Ch I prohibition to particular arrangements, favourable guidance in relation to the Ch II prohibition can be disturbed if complaints are subsequently made about it.

ENFORCEMENT PROCEDURE

Complaints

An interested party can make a complaint to the DGFT in relation to the Ch I and II prohibitions or to the EC Commission in relation behaviour which is alleged to be contrary to art 81 or art 82. No particular form is required to make a complaint, it can simply be by letter. A complaint should include details of the following:

- The nature of the complainant's interest;
- The facts alleged;
- The reasons why, on the facts alleged, it is concluded that there is a *prima facie* case of infringement;
- A request that the relevant authority act; and
- Details of any interim measures sought.

Investigation

Whether matters come to the DGFT or Commission's notice through notification, complaint or press report, both authorities have wide powers to pursue alleged anti-competitive activity. They can both request information from undertakings and conduct direct investigations.

The general purpose of investigation is to check the 'actual existence and scope of a given factual and legal situation'[86].

Where an investigation is made under a decision without prior notice to the relevant undertaking, it is known as a 'dawn raid'.

Three principles may act as a bulwark against the authorities' investigatory powers: confidentiality of sensitive information; legal professional privilege; and the privilege against self-incrimination. However, it should be noted that it is for the officials conducting the investigation to determine what the relevant documents to be examined are. They are not only entitled to examine but also to take copies of the books and other business records – undertakings will be reimbursed for reasonable photocopying costs.

In particular, it should be noted that the investigating authorities have the power to interrogate computer databases and copy computer files, disks and drives as well as simply removing computers for further examination[87].

An undertaking may consult a legal adviser during an investigation but the presence of a lawyer is not a requirement for the validity of the investigation. Any delay pending a lawyer's arrival must be kept to the minimum and will only be allowed where an undertaking has been given not to disturb any business records. In-house lawyers will be considered to be legal advisers for these purposes and the investigation will not be delayed whilst an external legal adviser is sought. It is extremely important, therefore, for companies' lawyers to be well prepared to deal with the competition authorities.

Interim measures

Regulation 17 which sets out the Commission's powers of investigation does not expressly provide for the Commission to take interim measures, however it is clear that it is able to do so and may do so on its own initiative. The Commission may order positive measures (such as resumption of supply) as well as prohibitory orders. Section 35 of the Competition Act 1998 gives the DGFT powers to make similar interim orders.

In *La Cinq v EC Commission*[88] the CFI set out the criteria to be applied by the Commission when considering adopting interim measures. It is necessary to show a prima facie infringement of Arts 81 or 82, urgency and serious and irreparable damage to the party seeking the interim measures or, alternatively, serious injury to the public interest. The Competition Act 1998 introduces less stringent criteria for the DGFT's making of interim directions under s 35: there is only a requirement to show harm to the public interest not serious harm or irreparable damage[89].

86 Case 136/79 *National Panasonic v EC Commission* [1980] ECR 2033.
87 Se reg 17; CA 98, s 27.
88 [1992] ECR II-1.
89 See also OFT Guideline 407 *Enforcement*.

Clearance

As set out above, the Commission and the DGFT can give formal decisions that an arrangement or some behaviour either does not fall within the scope of the relevant prohibitions or (in the case of Ch I and art 81) is exempted. In addition the DGFT can give guidance as to the status of particular arrangements in relation to the Ch I prohibition, where guidance indicating that the arrangements are unlikely to be of concern to him, an immunity from fines is conferred and the DGFT cannot take further action without informing the parties concerned.

Rather than going through the often time-consuming process of making a final assessment whether an agreement notified to it pursuant to art 81, the Commission will often simply close the file on a case and issue a 'comfort letter' to the notifying parties. This letter is not a legally binding exemption but is an indication of the Commission's view of the arrangements on the basis of the information with which it has been provided.

Orders to terminate infringements

Under art 3 of reg 17 the Commission may, by a decision, require an undertaking or an association of undertakings to terminate infringements. The Commission must make it clear what is the infringement to be terminated but need not set out detailed requirements as to what specifically should be done by the undertakings to whom the decision is addressed. The Commission may additionally order that the undertakings refrain from any similar conduct in future[90].

FINES

The DGFT and the Commission can impose fines where undertakings or associations of undertakings 'intentionally or negligently' infringe Chs I or II or Arts 81 or 82 respectively. Fines are intended to secure implementation of competition policy by suppressing illegal activity and preventing recurrence. They are also used as a general deterrent. European penalties may range from €100 to a maximum of whichever is the greater of €20 million or 10% of worldwide turnover in the preceding business year. UK penalties are capped at 10% of UK turnover for each year of infringement[91] but this is not limited to the turnover relating to the goods or services which are the subject of the legal restriction.

Calculating the fine

In setting fines the DGFT and the Commission will take into account both the gravity and the duration of the infringement. In January 1998 the Commission published its Guidelines on the Method of Setting Fines[92]. The DGFT's guideline 423 provides domestic guidance.

90 The DGFT has similar powers under ss 32–33 of the CA 98.
91 Up to a maximum of three years.
92 OJ [1998] C 9/3.

Although the two sets of guidelines are structured slightly differently, the basic principles to be applied are the same. The authorities will start by assessing the gravity of the infringement. There are three broad categories of seriousness:

Minor infringements – trade restrictions with a limited impact on the market and affecting only a limited part of the Community UK market.
Serious infringements – horizontal or more severe vertical restrictions with wider market impact. There may also be abuse of a dominant position.
Very serious infringements – the most anti-competitive horizontal restrictions including major price fixing cartels and market sharing arrangements – practices which jeopardise the proper functioning of the market.

The duration of the infringement will affect the amount determined for the seriousness of the infringement. Where the infringement has occurred for more than one year, an increase in the fine of an appropriate percentage will be made.

The sum set for the seriousness and duration of the infringement is known as the 'basic amount' in Community law. This basic amount can be increased or reduced depending on whether there are aggravating or attenuating circumstances.

Aggravating circumstances:

- Repeated infringements of the same type by the same undertakings;
- Instigating or leading the infringement;
- Retaliating against other undertakings in order to enforce the infringement;
- Need to increase the penalty in order to exceed gains improperly made by the infringing undertaking.

Attenuating circumstances:

- A passive or 'follow-my-leader' role;
- Non-implementation of the infringement in practice;
- Termination of the infringement as soon as the Commission intervenes;
- Reasonable doubt as to whether the practice constitutes an infringement;
- Infringements committed as a result of negligence or unintentionally;
- Co-operation with the Commission outside the scope of the Notice of 18 July 1996 (see below).

Whistleblowing

The Commission has published a notice on the non-imposition and reduction of fines[93] which is intended to give incentives to participants to blow the whistle on cartels and cooperate with the Commission in its investigation. Those who co-operate will have their fines reduced. The key point to bear in mind is that if you are the first undertaking to approach the commission and you co-operate fully you can secure a 100% reduction in any subsequent fine. The domestic guidelines are to similar effect[94].

93 OJ [2002] C 4/3.

94 Draft OFT Guideline 423. The immunity is only available where the DGFT does not have sufficient evidence of a cartel already; the whistleblower was not a ringleader or instigator; and it co-operates fully with the remainder of the investigation.

These guidelines are likely to be a significant consideration for companies who have been involved in anti-competitive activity and want to end it but are concerned about possible penalties.

In the case of *Arriva/FirstGroup*[95] the DGFT found that the two companies had engaged in market sharing by swapping bus routes. Each was fined substantial amounts. However, FirstGroup had gone quickly to the OFT and offered to co-operate with its investigation when it found out about it. FirstGroup received a 100% reduction in its fine. Arriva subsequently approached the OFT seeking leniency and only received a 36% reduction. The case illustrates the importance of approaching the OFT or the commission as quickly as possible if you are involved in anti-competitive activity and are thinking about coming clean (the 'grass first' premium).

MERGER CONTROL

Whilst the Competition Act 1998 and arts 81 and 82 principally operate to prevent anti-competitive behaviour once it has started, merger control effectively gives regulatory authorities the chance to stop such behaviour before it starts. Essentially, the merger control regimes of the UK and EC provide the authorities with the opportunity to prevent the creation of such market power as would jeopardise the proper functioning of the market. Small mergers are not generally of interest to the OFT or Commission unless the merger gives the new entity significant power in a narrow market. For this reason both the domestic and European regimes contain 'threshold' tests for when a merger qualifies for scrutiny.

When considering whether a merger should be allowed the factors taken into account will be similar to those considered when assessing whether an arrangement or certain behaviour is anti-competitive under the provisions referred to above. A number of illustrative examples given above in relation to the Chs I and II prohibitions refer to merger decisions[96]. Indeed at the present time, with Internet industries developing and substantial consolidation activity occurring, it is unsurprising that much of the most interesting analysis of competition on and around the Internet relates to merger inquiries.

It is beyond the scope of this chapter to give a detailed account of merger control in the UK and EC. The following sections indicate the basic tests which should be applied in deciding whether a merger will qualify for investigation and what broad principles will be applied in assessing the merger.

EC Merger Regulation

The EC Merger Regulation[97–98] is intended to be a one-stop-shop for European merger control. If an arrangement falls within the scope of the Regulation it will

95 This and other OFT decisions under the CA 98 can be found at www.oft.gov.uk/Business/Competition+Act/Decisions/index.htm.
96 See, for example: *MCI/Worldcom; Telia/Telenor/Schibsted*; *Bertelsmann/Mondadori*.
97–98 Council Regulation (EEC) 4064/89 OJ [1989] L 395, reprinted with corrections OJ [1990] L 257.

not be scrutinised by member states' national merger control authorities nor will the merger itself be separately scrutinised under arts 81 and 82.

The Merger Regulation requires the prior notification to the European Commission of 'concentrations having a Community dimension'.

A 'concentration' is defined by the Merger Regulation as being a situation where two or more independent undertakings merge, or where one or more undertakings acquire the ability to exercise 'decisive influence' over another undertaking. Generally, acquisition of under 25% of the voting rights of a company will not give rise to decisive influence[99].

Whether or not a merger has a Community dimension is determined by a series of complex turnover thresholds which relate to aggregate worldwide, EC and domestic turnover respectively. These thresholds are set out in art 1(2) and (3). If:

1. the aggregate world-wide group turnover of all the undertakings concerned amounts to more than Euro 5bn; and
2. the overall EC turnover of each of at least two of the undertakings is more than Euro 250m;

then the concentration will have a Community dimension unless:

3. each of the parties achieves more than two-thirds of its turnover in one and the same member state[100].

Alternatively, if:

1. the aggregate world-wide group turnover of all the undertakings concerned amounts to more than Euro 2.5bn; and
2. the aggregate turnover of the undertakings concerned is more than Euro 100m in each of at least three member states; and
3. in each of the same three member states, the aggregate turnover of at least two undertakings concerned is each more than Euro 25m; and
4. the EC turnover of each of at least two of the undertakings is more than Euro 100m;
5. then the concentration will have a Community dimension unless:
6. each of the parties achieves more than two-thirds of its turnover in one and the same member state.

So, if the worldwide turnover of the undertakings concerned is less than Euro 2.5bn or each of the parties achieves more than two-thirds of its turnover in one and the same member state then there is no Community dimension to the concentration under either set of threshold tests. The Merger Regulation gives detailed guidance on the manner in which the relevant turnover is to be

99 The position in relation to joint ventures is more complex. Amendments to the Merger Regulation made in 1997 mean that where a joint venture is created which can perform, on a lasting basis, all the functions of an autonomous economic entity, it shall constitute a concentration. Council Regulation (EEC) 4064/89, art 3(2), as amended by Council Regulation (EC) 1310/97, art 1(3)(b).

100 This provision is intended to exclude mergers which primarily concern a single member state.

calculated. See also Commission Notice of the calculation of turnover under Council Regulation (EEC) 4064/89 on the control of concentrations between undertakings OJ [1995] C66/4.

If a merger does constitute a concentration with a Community dimension, the merger must be notified to the European Commission in the manner prescribed by Form CO[101]. The Commission will appraise the merger's compatibility with the Common Market on the basis of the following principle: a concentration which 'creates or strengthens a dominant position as a result of which effective competition would be significantly impeded in the Common Market of in a substantial part of it shall be declared incompatible with the Common Market'[102].

UK

The Fair Trading Act 1973 gives the Secretary of State for Trade and Industry the power to refer to the Competition Commission for investigation situations where:

1. two enterprises cease to be distinct[103];
2. at least one of the enterprises is carried on in the UK or by or under the control of a company incorporated in the UK[104];
3. the situation arose with the preceding four months[105]; and
4. either (a) the merging parties have more than 25% of the UK market for the good or services concerned (the market share test)[106]; or
5. (b) the gross value of the assets taken over exceeds £70m (the assets test)[107].

Initially the OFT considers whether or not a qualifying merger situation has occurred and decides whether or not to recommend to the Secretary of State that the matter should be referred to the Competition Commission for investigation. If an investigation is ordered, the Competition Commission will carry out a wide ranging inquiry into the circumstances and likely effects of the merger in order to decide whether or not it is in the public interest. In its final report the

101 Commission Regulation (EC) 447/98 OJ [1998] L61/1. For the timing of notification see Commission Regulation (EEC) 4064/89, art 4(1).

102 Council Regulation (EEC) 4064/89, art 2(1).

103 Fair Trading Act 1973, s 64(1). See ss 65 and 66 for definitions of when enterprises 'cease to be distinct' and the time at which that occurs. It should be noted that enterprises can be considered as having ceased to be distinct where one party has material influence over the policy of another and this can occur where the acquisition in question is of a stake as small as 10% of a company.

104 Fair Trading Act 1973, s 64(1).

105 Fair Trading Act 1973, s 64(4)(a), as amended by Deregulation (Fair Trading Act 1973)(Amendment)(Merger Reference Time Limits) Order 1996, SI 1996/345.

106 The cumulative market share of the parties must be increased by the merger. If one party already has 25% of the relevant market and the other has 0%, a merger between the two would not fulfill the market share test.

107 Fair Trading Act 1973, s 64(1)(b). The manner in which the valuation of assets taken should be made is described in s 67. Under the proposals in the Enterprise Bill this will be amended to refer to *turnover of £70 million*.

Competition Commission can either recommend to the Secretary of State that the merger is in the public interest in which case it is cleared or that it is contrary to the public interest. If the Secretary of State agrees that the merger is contrary to the public interest, behavioural remedies (such as price monitoring) or structural remedies (such as divestment of all or part of the business) can be ordered.

It is extremely common for merging enterprises to seek prior clearance from the OFT. The OFT has the power to seek undertakings from the companies instead of recommending a reference to the Competition Commission with all the delay and expense that an investigation can cause. In addition it is possible to seek confidential guidance from the OFT and Secretary of State as to whether or not they would consider a merger as qualifying for investigation and whether the Secretary of State would be likely to refer the matter to the Competition Commission for investigation.

Where an agreement or arrangement results in two enterprises ceasing to be distinct, the Ch I and II prohibitions will not apply to that agreement[108].

MONOPOLY INVESTIGATIONS

In addition to the powers conferred on the OFT and Secretary of State in relation to mergers, the Fair Trading Act 1973 also gives the power to UK authorities to remedy the adverse effects of a monopoly. For the purposes of the Fair Trading Act 1973, a monopoly exists when[109]:

1. one person supplies 25% of all goods or services (of a particular description) in the UK or a specific part of it (a 'scale monopoly situation'); or
2. 25% of all goods or services (of a particular description) in the UK or a specific part of it are supplied by or to a single group who act so as to prevent, restrict or distort competition in the market for those goods or services (a 'complex monopoly situation' sometimes referred to as a 'behavioural monopoly situation')[110].

This power continues to exist even though the Ch II prohibition has been introduced and gives the authorities the opportunity to impose structural remedies such as divestiture of parts of a business.

108 Competition Act 1998, Sch 1, Pt I.
109 Fair Trading Act 1973, ss 6 and 7.
110 There need not be any agreement between the members of the group in question for a complex monopoly situation to exist.

Glossary

Definitions are reproduced with kind permission from The Economist Pocket Information Technology *by John Browning (published by Profile Books).*

Active X

A set of standards created by Microsoft for downloading small programs over the World Wide Web that will extend the capabilities of a web browser. An Active X control might, for example, create an animation or do specialised tax calculations. Active X controls can be written in almost any programming language. But this flexibility has not headed off a running battle between backers of Java and proponents of Active X over security.

Java runs in a protected environment called a 'sandbox', which limits the damage a malicious Java program might do. Java programs, for example, cannot delete files that they themselves have not created. Active X, by contrast, has no such limitations. A malicious Active X program could quite merrily wipe out the entire contents of your hard disk, or worse. To demonstrate just how tricky a rogue Active X application could be, hackers from Germany's Chaos computer club built and publicised a game which also surreptitiously checks to see if the user of the computer it landed on used any of the more popular programs to pay bills electronically. If so, it adds a new entry to the list of bills to be paid – an account controlled by the hackers in Switzerland.

Java proponents argue that this is exactly why Active X should be avoided. Microsoft argues that its security can be guaranteed by a digital signature system. By placing an electronic signature on Active X programs, trustworthy companies (like Microsoft) vouch for their safety. Java backers reply that knowing who to sue after you have been robbed or vandalised is poor consolation, particularly when it is easy to avoid the damage in the first place. Perhaps the best compromise, for those who worry about security but still want the capabilities Active X can offer, is simply to use only Active X controls written in Java.

ADSL

Short for Asynchronous Digital Subscriber Loop, a proposed technology for sending video and other high-bandwidth data over existing copper wires running to homes and businesses, without investing billions in upgrading basic infrastructure to fibre optic. ADSL assumes that most homes and businesses will consume far more data than they produce. So although it manages to send over 6m bits of information per second into the home, it does so by restricting the amount that can be sent in the other direction. This makes ADSL suitable for showing films, but not for video-conferencing.

Agent

A much-ballyhooed piece of software that will do its master's bidding without direct supervision, even remotely, over a network. For example, an agent will find travel information without requiring its owner to know anything about electronic airline reservations systems. In practice this is easier marketed than done.

Anti-viral
A program that can detect, and sometimes eliminate, computer viruses.

Applet
Either an extremely simple, small application or, more usually, a software program written in Java for distribution over the World Wide Web.

Arpanet
Grandfather of many of today's large-scale computer networks, particularly the Internet. The Arpanet began in 1969 as a research project led by the Defence Advanced Research Projects Agency, from whose acronym, DARPA, the network derived its name. The goal was to create a computer network capable of supporting the USA's defence through a nuclear war. This meant that the network could not have a central switch or authority which could be pre-emptively destroyed. Taken together with the decision to encourage the researchers building the network to use it to share information, this lack of central structure meant that the Arpanet could, and did, evolve into more or less whatever size and shape its denizens desired; in this case, the Internet.

Back-up
To save a copy of data stored on a disk on to another medium, usually tape or optical disk. Back-up is meant to provide a reserve copy of data lest something terrible should happen to the disk.

Bandwidth
Loosely, the amount of information or data communicated: a high-bandwidth communication is, or should be, more informative than a low-bandwidth one. Strictly, bandwidth refers to the difference between the highest frequency that a given communications channel can carry and the lowest. Channels in which this difference is large can carry more data than those in which it is small. Indeed, given a strict mathematical definition of information, Harold Nyquist, a theoretician from the US's Bell Labs, proved in 1924 that the maximum number of bits a channel could carry was equal to twice the bandwidth.

Baud
A measure of the speed of digital communications equipment which is closely related to the maximum number of bits that can be sent in a second.

Beta
The final stage of software quality testing. Before general release, selected people are typically given beta copies of software to use as if it were finished in order to see what, if anything, breaks.

Binary
Loosely used to describe anything without shades of grey; that is, which can be either black or white, true or false, on or off. Strictly, it refers to a number system based on the number two. Instead of powers of ten, as in the decimal system, numbers are expressed in terms of powers of two. The only allowable digits are zero and one. Thus 27 in decimal ($2 \times 10^1 + 7 \times 10^0$) is 11011 in binary ($1 \times 2^4 + 1 \times 2^3 + 0 \times 2^2 + 1 \times 2^1 + 1 \times 2^0$). This number system is convenient for describing electronic circuits, which are either on (with current) or off (without).

Bit map
A grid of dots which contains the information needed to display a picture on a computer screen or printer. Typically each dot corresponds to the colour of a particular point, or pixel, on the screen. Display the dots in the appropriate rows and columns and, lo and behold, a picture appears. (The colour of dots, in turn, is coded as bits, hence the name).

This correspondence between dots in the bit map and points on the screen makes bit maps easy to use on any given screen. But it also makes them extremely hard to move from one screen to another, because different screens lay out rows and columns in different proportions.

Bridge
Equipment used to connect two local area networks. Bridges can connect networks using different communication protocols (for example, TCP/IP and AppleTalk), as well as different transmission mechanisms (for example, Ethernet and Token Ring). A router, by contrast, is used to connect networks with the same protocol.

Broadband
Loosely used to describe signals of high bandwidth. It is specifically used to describe the use of (high-bandwidth) coaxial cable to transmit radio, television or other analogue signals that would typically be sent over the airwaves. Also used as a generic term for high-speed telecommunications circuits and services.

Broadcast
Describes a signal sent indiscriminately to all receivers with range, such as television, in contrast to point-to-point communication (such as a telephone), or person-to-person communication (such as conversation). With computer networks researchers are developing new forms of communications, between broadcast and point-to-point, called multicast.

Bug
An error or problem with computer hardware or software. It is named after a moth, discovered by a computing pioneer, Grace Hopper, which immolated itself in the circuitry of an early computer. The computer was repaired by replacing a damaged vacuum tube. The moth is preserved in the Computer Museum in Cambridge, Massachusetts.

Bulletin board
A computer system used for posting electronic messages. Messages are organised into files on the bulletin board's hard disk, usually by topic. People can dial up the bulletin board and read what has been said on a given topic and, if they like, add their own comments. Little more is required to run a bulletin board than a PC and modem.

Byte
Eight bits, the most commonly used measure of data-storage capacity. Large hard-disk drives, for example, store gigabytes (that is, billions of bytes) of information. A nibble is half a byte, or four bits.

Cable modem
A modem built to take advantage of the high bandwidth available on the coaxial cable laid to distribute television signals. Cable modems can achieve data-transmission speeds equal to that of Ethernet, or around 10m bits per second.

Cache
A small area of very fast memory, typically on a microprocessor, which is used to store (what the machine hopes will be) the next instructions used in the computation, and thus to eliminate delays by making them available more rapidly than if they had to be fetched from the main DRAM. Caching is when a server with vast storage capacity holds copies of the most popular pages on the world's wide web. If this web cache is located on the local area network users are saved the delay of gaining access to overburdened websites.

CD-ROM
Short for Compact Disk, Read-Only Memory, the medium of choice for the first generation of multi-media publishers. Compact disks, the same kind as are used for sound recording, can store a lot of data – about 640 megabytes, 600 or so times more than a floppy disk. That is enough to store the text from several hundred books, two hours of high-quality sound, an hour of television-quality video, or some combination of the above.

CGI
Short for Common Gateway Interface, a protocol used to enable programs to work together over the World Wide Web. CGI links executable programs to Web pages. So, instead of just sending text in response to each click of the mouse on a hypertext link, some links can run programs to make calculations or make new pages on the fly, perhaps by running a query on a database to find up-to-the-second information.

Checksum
A way of detecting errors in computer data. The binary values of the data are added together to form a checksum. The checksum is transmitted with the data. If the sum of the binary values of the received data differs from the received checksum, then something has gone wrong.

Client server
Describes computer systems which divide labour among machines linked by

networks. Rather like Adam Smith's pin factory, each machine does what it is suited for. So a file server is equipped with lots of disk space to store data; a name server holds the information necessary to serve as the network's telephone directory. Not only does specialisation avoid duplication of effort, but it also makes client-server systems easier to improve. If, say, all heavy-duty number-crunching is done by a calculation server, then simply replacing that one machine with a more powerful one can improve the performance of the whole network.

Compression
Techniques for reducing the amount of data needed to convey some amount of information.

Cookie
A common but somewhat convoluted way of gathering and storing information about World Wide Web users. It is disk-space-consuming and complicated for a Web site to store on its own computers all the information it might want about its users. So it uses cookies, which store and retrieve the same information on users' computers.

Say a Web site wants to track which of its pages a particular user visits most. It sends the user a message called a cookie, which contains both the usage information to be stored and some indexing information. The web browser stores the information in a file name suggested by the cookie. Next time the user visits the site, the site asks for the cookie back, and so gets back up to speed with what the user has been doing.

CPU
Short for central processing unit. The brains of a computer; the chip or chips that execute programs.

Crash
A verb or noun describing what happens when a computer ceases to function. It derives from disk crash, which describes what happens when the magnetic heads designed to read information from a disk drive instead bury themselves into it.

Cyberspace
The virtual geography created by computers and networks.

Daemon
A program which sits unobtrusively in the background waiting for some event to happen, which it then deals with. In the UNIX operating system, for example, daemons handle the delivery of email and other network requests.

Data warehouse
A database which brings together in one place information from different systems working in different parts of a company. Often that data is further supplemented with additional information from outside the company. Data warehouses typically serve two purposes. One is to provide a wide range of data for analysis. Retailers, for example, use data warehouses to devise marketing strategy – to understand the statistical patterns in customer purchases and so to present the right product to the right customer at the right time. Another is to help create more flexible companies by making it easier for different departments to share information. This not only improves co-operation; it also makes it easier to shift work and responsibility between departments, as changing circumstances require.

Debug
To correct errors in a computer program.

Digital signature
A cryptographic technique which ensures that an electronic document really does come from the person whose name is at the top. Strictly, a digital signature has two functions: it serves as proof of identity, like a regular signature, and as proof that the document has not been tampered with.

Implemented with public-key cryptography, the workings of the signature parts are straightforward. All or part of the document is encrypted with an individual's private key, which is (or should be) known only to him. That text can only be decrypted with the corresponding public key.

Ensuring that a document has not been tampered with relies on a hash function, which condenses the text into a short but unique series of numbers. When the document is received, it is checked to ensure that the hash function returns the same numbers.

Crucial in making this scheme work is ensuring that public keys really do come from who they purport to. Some governments propose to license a network of trusted third parties to do this job.

Domain name
A network address. To save the trouble of typing gibberish numbers like 207.46.138.20, the Internet is organised as a collection of named domains. Each domain name serves as a mnemonic way of referring to a specific set of network numbers.

Domain names, like domains, are typically arranged in a hierarchy. At the most general level of the hierarchy are country names, like .uk, or sectoral names, like .gov for government. Next come names referring to a specific institution within that general sector, then names referring to parts of the company and lastly a name referring to a specific machine.

Download
To transfer data from a remote (usually large) computer to a local (usually small) one. (Contrast with upload.)

Extranet
Another word that has lost much of its meaning since its appropriation by the marketing department of major software and computer manufacturers. Strictly, an extranet is a network, built using the Internet's technical standards, which links two or more different companies but is not open to the general public. Contrast to the wholly private intranet and the wholly public Internet.

Firewall
Hardware, but more usually software, designed to protect networked systems from damage by outsiders, while maintaining connectivity. The firewall sits between a local network and the big, wide world (usually the Internet). To protect the local network from unwelcome intruders, the firewall may admit only designated users, or allow only designated commands to be issued from outside. Balancing flexibility with security is a perennial headache in designing firewalls.

FTP
Short for File Transfer Protocol. This refers to both the program which transfers files from one computer to another across the Internet, and the technical standards it uses. Bulk transfers of data with FTP make up about one-third of Internet traffic.

Gateway
A device that connects different computer systems or networks, particularly those using different technical standards or communications protocols.

Header
Data about data. Typically included at the beginning of a file, a document or a data packet sent over a communications network, the header typically contains information to identify the attached data, to state how much data is attached, what sort of data it is, how long it is and to help detect and/or correct errors.

HTML
Short for HyperText Mark-up Language, the programming language which creates the documents and links used by the World Wide Web. The language contains commands for laying out text and graphics on a page, as well as commands to link one document to another, or to link a document to an interactive computer program.

HTTP
Short for HyperText Transfer Protocol, the protocol used to move Web pages across the Internet.

Hypertext
Text that need not be read from beginning to end, but can instead be browsed in any number of different orders, at the reader's whim, by following internal route-marks called links. A typical application of hypertext is in reference works, like this one. In an electronic version of this book, cross-references would not only be distinguished by special type, but they could also be 'live'. Click on them with a mouse and, whoosh, the computer

brings up the appropriate entry on the screen.

Internet protocol
The IP in TCP/IP, these are the technical standards which specify how packets on the Internet are routed from one machine to another. Each packet travels independently, and packets may follow very different routes.

Internetworking
A generic term used to describe the process of linking together different networks – as is done, for example, in the Internet (and from which the Internet took its name).

Internet service provider
A company that provides connections to the Internet.

Intranet
A NETWORK using the same TCP/IP technology as the global Internet, but designed primarily for use within a single organisation.

Java
A programming language designed for use on the Internet. Created by Sun Microsystems, Java is the first popular language to take it for granted that the computers it runs on will be seamlessly linked over networks. So Java was built to new design criteria.

Link
A connection between two items of hypertext. In some hypertext systems links can be labelled to make explicit the relationship they denote. So one link might be labelled 'supporting argument' and another 'contrary argument'. In theory, labels make it easier to solve the perennial problem of hypertext links, which is maintaining a sense of direction in the sea of information. In practice, adding more information (on the labels) to all that is already there can easily be mishandled to create more confusion.

Log on
To begin using a computer, a process which usually requires entering your name and password at the keyboard. Hence 'log-on prompt', which is what appears on the computer display after you have successfully logged on. Log in is of course the same thing with different words.

Modem
Acronym for Modulator-Demodulator, a device that translates a stream of digital data into a staccato series of bleeps and bloops that can be sent over a telephone line, or some other analogue communications channel. More specifically, it is a device that does, and undoes, modulation.

MPEG
Short for Moving Pictures Experts Group, standards which compress video and other moving pictures into a size that can be more easily stored on a CD-ROM or transmitted across a network. The grail of MPEG is so-called full-screen, full-motion video – which, as the name implies, would include every frame of motion at a size to cover a full screen.

Name server
A computer on a network which translates mnemonic machine names and addresses, (used for example, to address email) into the sequences of numbers machines use to talk to other machines.

News group
An electronic forum for the discussion of a given topic. Tens of thousands of news groups now make up the Usenet, a part of the Internet devoted to debate on topics ranging from sex to high-energy physics. News groups are open to all, and are organised as an exchange of email messages.

Online
The opposite of offline; that is, enjoying a network connection to another computer.

Packet
A way of organising data for communication. Instead of a steady stream of bits and bytes, most computer communications split data into discrete packets. As well as data, each packet typically contains the address to which the packet is being sent, a number which denotes that packet's place in the sequence, and

information which helps to detect and correct errors. Some packets also contain information about what type of data is being sent. Others serve administrative functions in setting up routes and managing the flow of data.

The advantage of packets is their flexibility and efficiency. Packets from different communications can easily be intermixed to maximise use of a line. Packets from the same communication can travel by different routes to speed passage over a crowded network. Given the speed of today's computers, packets can easily carry time-sensitive data, like interactive video, or voice conversations. But the drawback to packet data is, nonetheless, the extra overhead of splitting data into packets at one end and recombining them at the other.

Packet-switched

Describes a network that sends data one packet at a time, and so does not keep open a connection between two machines when no data is flowing between them. For many applications, particularly with computer data, the extra overheads of addressing each packet separately are well worth the savings in efficiency gained from not holding open temporarily unused connections.

PGP

Short for Pretty Good Privacy. PGP began as a freely distributed implementation of the RSA Algorithm for public-key encryption, created by Phil Zimmerman. PGP is controversial for several reasons. It has been distributed internationally in defiance of a US export ban on software containing technology for public-key cryptography. It was also distributed without the permission of the holders of the patent on the RSA algorithm. Yet it works and, for those concerned with privacy, PGP is the most secure way of keeping computer data from prying eyes. In late 1996 Zimmerman founded a company, also called PGP, to commercialise and further improve the technology he created.

Pixel

Acronym for picture element, or the dots which make up an image on the typical computer screen. Black and white images need only one bit per pixel, but colour images require that each pixel be represented by a binary number. With a byte, or eight bits, for each pixel, a screen can contain up to 256 different colours. With 24 bits for each pixel, it can contain 16,777,216 different colours – the biggest number 24 bits can express.

PPP

Point to Point Protocol, technical standards that enable the use of the Internet's communication protocols, TCP/IP, over a dial-up telephone line. (An alternative to SLIP.)

Search engine

Software that finds things on the World Wide Web. Type in a few of the words that the Web pages you are looking for will contain and others will not and – hey presto – back comes a list of material.

Shareware

Software that is freely distributed, so as many people as possible can try it out at no cost. Satisfied users are asked to pay a (usually small) fee to the author, and many do. One of the nice things about the online world is that it is still possible to make money by trusting in the goodness of your fellow human beings, at least so far.

SMTP

Simple Mail Transfer Protocol, a set of technical standards for the transfer of email from one machine to another. This is the mail protocol most commonly used on the Internet.

Spam

Unsolicited junk email; mass-mailings which typically offer products you could never imagine buying or opportunities to get rich quick (usually by selling products you could never imagine anybody else buying either).

TCP/IP

The network protocols used on the Internet. It stands for Transmission Control Protocol and Internet Protocol.

Telnet

The process which enables someone to log-in to a remote computer and use its services via the Internet. Contrast to FTP, which enables a person to get data from a remote computer, or remote procedure call, which enables a program to access the services of a remote computer.

Upload

To send data 'up' from a small computer to a larger one. (Contrast with download).

URL

Short for Universal Resource Locator, an address describing the location of a document, computer program or other resource used by the World Wide Web. URLs are the Web's way of finding things. The strength of the Web is the way it unifies the different communications protocols used on the Internet, and the URL is where that unification occurs. The first half of the URL specifies the protocol which determines how communication is to take place: HTTP or FTP or mailto (to send email) or whatever. The second half specifies what is to be communicated: the Web page or file to be downloaded or the e-mail address a message is to be sent to.

Virus

A self-replicating and often malicious computer program. A virus typically stitches its code into that of another program. Each time that program is executed in a new machine, the virus looks for a way of infecting that computer as well.

Web browser

Software used to navigate the vast network of hyperlinks that makes up the World Wide Web.

World wide web

The technology that made the Internet usable by mere humans, the World Wide Web (WWW) is a system of hypermedia linking text, graphics, sound and video on computers spread across the globe. By making the Internet both a more expressive and easier to use medium, the Web should take most of the credit for that network's explosive growth.
The basic technology of the Web was originally created by Tim Berners-Lee at CERN, Europe's atom-smasher sited near Geneva, to help physicists keep track of all the data generated by their experiments. At the heart of the technology is a programming language HTML, which allows a phrase or graphic in one document to be linked to another document anywhere on the global Internet. When a person clicks a mouse on that highlighted phrase, the linked document is fetched and brought to the screen automatically.

Worm

A program that propagates itself across a network, automatically transferring itself to distant machines and running itself there (from whence it transfers itself to more machines). In contrast to a virus, which secretes itself inside another program – and thus is only spread when the program carrying it is spread – worms take charge of their own reproduction. Perhaps the most famous worm was created by a computer science student called Robert Morris in 1988. In what seems to have been a misguided attempt to map the global Internet, Morris created a worm which replicated itself so rapidly that it brought thousands of computers to a standstill.

Index